IMPERIAL
CHINA

The Terracotta Army
Around 7,000 life-size warriors, 150 cavalry horses, 130 chariots, and 520 chariot horses guard the tomb of China's First Emperor, Qin Shi Huangdi. He had planned to continue ruling from his tomb for all eternity.

IMPERIAL
CHINA

THE DEFINITIVE VISUAL HISTORY

中国大百科全书出版社
Encyclopedia of China Publishing House

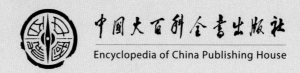

Encyclopedia of China Publishing House

DK LONDON

Senior Editor Abigail Mitchell
Senior Art Editor Jane Ewart
Editors Elizabeth Blakemore, Penny Warren
US Editor Jennette ElNaggar
Managing Art Editor Anna Hall
Managing Editor Christine Stroyan
Production Editor Rob Dunn
Senior Production Controller Jude Crozier
Creative Technical Support Sonia Charbonnier
Picture Researchers Liz Moore, Sarah Smithies
Senior Jacket Designer Surabhi Wadhwa-Gandhi
Jacket Design Development Manager Sophia M.T.T.
Associate Publishing Director Liz Wheeler
Art Director Karen Self
Publishing Director Jonathan Metcalf

DK INDIA

Editor Devangana Ojha
Senior Art Editor Vikas Sachdeva
Designer and DTP Designer Anita Yadav
Managing Editor Soma B. Chowdhury
Senior Managing Art Editor Arunesh Talapatra
Assistant Picture Researcher Geetika Bhandari
Picture Research Manager Taiyaba Khatoon
DTP Designer Vikram Singh
Production Manager Pankaj Sharma
Pre-production Manager Balwant Singh
Senior Jacket Designer Suhita Dharamjit

COBALT ID

Designers Paul Reid, Darren Bland, Rebecca Johns
Editors Marek Walisiewicz, Diana Loxley,
Kirsty Seymour-Ure, Johnny Murray

Founded in 1978, Encyclopedia of China Publishing House is a leading Chinese publisher of encyclopedias and reference books, along with academic and popular titles. It is known for publishing the *Encyclopedia of China* and the Chinese edition of *Encyclopedia Britannica*, plus approximately 500 titles a year on various subjects.

Encyclopedia of China Publishing House
Editors Wang Jiangshan, Tian Yi
Art Director Wu Dan
Publishing Director Yang Zhen

First American Edition, 2020
Published in the United States by DK Publishing
1450 Broadway, Suite 801, New York, NY 10018

A catalog record for this book
is available from the Library of Congress.
ISBN 978-0-7440-2047-2

DK books are available at special discounts when purchased in bulk for sales promotions, premiums, fund-raising, or educational use. For details, contact: DK Publishing Special Markets, 1450 Broadway, Suite 801, New York, NY 10018
SpecialSales@dk.com

Printed and bound in China

For the curious
www.dk.com

contents

1 From Legend to History
Before 2000 BCE

2 The First Dynasties
C. 2070 BCE to 221 BCE

3 China United and Divided
221 BCE to 581 CE

4 The Sui and Tang Dynasties
581 to 960 CE

5 Chinese and Foreign Dynasties
960 to 1368

6 Stability and Wealth
1368 to 1644

CONSULTANTS

Professor Edward Shaughnessy

Professor Shaughnessy is the Herrlee G. and Lorraine J. Creel Distinguished Service Professor of Early China in the Department of East Asian Languages and Civilizations of the University of Chicago. He received a BA (Theology, 1974) degree from the University of Notre Dame, and MA and PhD (Asian Languages, 1980 and 1983) degrees from Stanford University. Most of his career has been devoted to the cultural and literary history of China's Zhou dynasty (c. 1045–249 BCE), the period that has served all subsequent Chinese intellectuals as the golden age of Chinese civilization. The author or editor of over 20 books and well over 100 scholarly articles, he has focused in his work on archaeologically recovered textual materials from this period, especially inscriptions on ritual bronze vessels from the beginning of the first millennium BCE and manuscripts written on bamboo and silk from the last centuries of the millennium, though he also remains fascinated by the classic literary tradition of the period.

Professor Zhao Dongmei

An explorer and presenter of historical knowledge, Professor Zhao Dongmei received her PhD in history from Peking University and studied further at St. Antony's College, Oxford. She is now a professor in the history department at Peking University. As a visiting professor, she has taught at Julius-Maximilians-Universität Würzburg in Germany and at the École des hautes études en sciences sociales in Paris, France. Her publications include *Between Civil Officials and Military Officers: A Study of the Military Officials in Northern Song China*; *A History of Martial Examination and Military Academies in Pre-modern China*; *Sima Guang and His Contemporaries, 1019–1045*; and *A Biography of Early Song Politician Kou Zhun (962–1023)*. She also translated *China Turning Inward, Intellectual-Political Changes in the Early Twelfth Century* and *Branches of Heaven: A History of Imperial Clans of Sung China*. She is a guest speaker on China Central Television (CCTV)'s *Lecture Room* and has her own audio course, "Dongmei Teaches Chinese History," on Himalaya FM.

7 The Last Dynasty
1644 to 1912

AUTHORS

Tony Allan
Tony Allan studied history at Oxford University and journalism at the University of Indiana and went on to a career as an editor with Time Life Books. He has published more than 20 books in his own name, including *The Long March and the Rise of Modern China* (Heinemann Library) and *Ancient China* (Cultural Atlas for Young People, Chelsea House, US).

Kay Celtel
Kay Celtel is a writer, researcher, and editor. She has written extensively on history, biography, and culture, including numerous articles on East Asian history. She graduated from Oxford University with a doctorate in history before working in reference publishing for several years.

Jacob F. Field
Jacob F. Field is a historian and writer who received his undergraduate degree at the University of Oxford and his doctorate at Newcastle. He has taught world history at the University of Waikato and has written several books on a range of subjects, including military history, economics, and the Great Fire of London.

R. G. Grant
R. G. Grant is a historian who has published some 20 books for adults, as well as writing numerous children's history titles and contributing to many multiauthored works. He has contributed to several wide-ranging global histories, including *History* (2007) and *History of the World in 1,000 Objects* (2014). His most recent publication as sole author was *Sentinels of the Sea* (Thames & Hudson, 2018), a history of lighthouses.

Philip Parker
Philip Parker is a medieval history specialist, whose books include the *Sunday Times* bestselling *The Northmen's Fury: A History of the Viking World*. He is the author of the *DK Companion Guide to World History* and has contributed to the Chinese and East Asian sections of a number of DK titles, including *Battle*, *History of the World in 1,000 Objects*, and *History of the World Map by Map*.

Sally Regan
Sally Regan has contributed to more than 20 DK titles, including *History*, *World War II*, and *The History Book*. She is an award-winning history documentary filmmaker for Channel 4 and the BBC in the UK.

Imperial ceremony
This 19th-century painting shows the presentation of gifts for the empress at the wedding of the Guangxu Emperor in 1889. The ceremony was held in front of the Hall of Supreme Harmony in the Forbidden City, Beijing.

Forewords

Imperial China is the result of a unique collaboration between two leading global publishers—
DK and Encyclopedia of China Publishing House—to present a balanced account of China's
history. Providing a unique insight into Chinese culture and society, this book presents a stunning
visual chronicle of China's magnificent past, from the mythical sovereigns who ruled 5,000 years
ago to the last Qing emperor, Puyi.

One of the world's most ancient and important civilizations, China leaves a legacy of technology, philosophy, and art that is of abiding importance to us all. DK—the world leader in illustrated reference books—is honored to work with the prestigious Encyclopedia of China Publishing House in this unique collaboration. We have combined scholarship, design expertise, and publishing vision to bring this beautiful celebration of imperial China to a worldwide audience.

Authenticated by both Chinese and Western scholars, *Imperial China* tells the epic story of China's past, which reaches back more than 5,000 years to the mythic sovereigns of prehistory. It answers questions such as how the Tang and Song dynasties managed to control their vast empires, when writing and money were first invented, and why the Great Wall was built. It explores key Chinese concepts such as Heaven, and charts the broad sweep of history over millennia, describing hundreds of key conflicts. It also highlights the stories of extraordinary individuals, such as Admiral Zheng He, who sailed to Africa in the 15th century with ships the size of which the world had never seen.

Imperial China is a visual treasure trove of portraits, paintings, photographs, and artifacts. Every page has unique wonders, such as the First Emperor's terracotta army, architecture from the Forbidden City, and exquisite objects, including ceramics, gold jewelry, silks, and porcelain tableware. Woven into the narrative, you can also find stories of legendary technical prowess, including Chinese innovations ranging from silk making and printing to the invention of iron, compasses, and gunpowder.

Imperial China's history and culture were, in a word, extraordinary, and at DK, we are extremely proud to be associated with this book and to work with the Encyclopedia of China Publishing House to bring a deeper understanding of China's past to people around the globe.

Stretching back more than 5,000 years, China was one of the earliest civilizations in the world. The emperors Yandi and Huangdi, widely respected as the progenitors of Chinese humanity, lived around 2700 BCE near the Yellow River in China's central plains. Since then, China has been the source of many iconic innovations, including silk making, rice cultivation, and the invention of jade, bronze, and ceramics. These are all integral to world civilization. And thanks to the invention of characters and writing—as early as 1500 BCE—the world has a unique account of the government, laws, religion, and culture of ancient China.

As China's leading publisher, Encyclopedia of China Publishing House is honored to cooperate with Dorling Kindersley, the prestigious global publisher of illustrated reference titles, to create *Imperial China*. We first had the intention of jointly publishing a book about ancient China in 2017. At that time, we agreed that the book would be for a worldwide audience and would take a unique global perspective, exploring how China's politics, economy, culture, art, and technology had evolved through the ages.

Imperial China is the result. It is an illustrated reference book that combines stunning images of some of China's most important artifacts with text authorized by leading historians. With a unique perspective endorsed by both Chinese and Western scholars, it offers so much more than a narrative of key events. It tells the story of important figures from China's history and explains the invention of basic necessities, from rice and ceramics to weapons and literature. It offers readers a glimpse into people's lives and invites them to share their sorrows and happiness. In enabling readers to understand China's past, it helps them to connect our history with our nation today.

We sincerely hope this book will give readers a greater understanding of our extraordinary civilization and will be both an enlightening and an enjoyable read.

Jonathan Metcalf, *Publishing Director, Knowledge, DK*

Liu Guohui, *President, Encyclopedia of China Publishing House*

△ **Moon-Embracing Pavilion**
This Ming-style pavilion stands by the scenic Black
Dragon Pool in Yunnan Province. Yulong (Jade
Dragon) Snow Mountain can be seen behind it.

Introduction

China is one of the cradles of world civilization. Its early settlements on the Yellow River gave rise to kingdoms and dynasties that ruled for centuries, until the country was finally unified under the Qin dynasty in 221 BCE. So began China's long imperial era, which saw the rise and fall of several powerful ruling houses, and would last until the establishment of the Republic in 1912.

China's written history dates back to bone inscriptions made in the 2nd millennium BCE. Detailed records of ancient China and its later rise as an imperial power in East Asia are captured in a rich tradition of history writing that includes works of astonishing depth, such as Sima Qian's *Historical Records* (c. 100 BCE). No nation can boast a longer, more closely connected historical narrative, nor one affecting a greater share of the world's population. Yet China remains an enigma to most people in the West. This can be traced in part to China's relative self-containment through the centuries. The nation has had its periods of expansion—such as the early 15th century, when Admiral Zheng He made his maritime expeditions—but for most of its history, China's rulers focused attention on their own immediate territories.

Geography, culture, and cohesion

The continuity of Chinese culture is striking. In the first half of the 1st millennium CE, both the Western Roman Empire and China's Han dynasty collapsed under pressure from "barbarian" invaders and internal weaknesses. Yet while Roman culture disappeared into the history books, Chinese civilization rebounded to enjoy golden ages under the Tang and the Song dynasties. Over the centuries, many features have contributed to the constancy of China's narrative. One of these is China's relative geographical isolation: it is protected by the sea to the east and deserts and mountains to the west (territory through which the Silk Road would later run). The main threat to the nation traditionally came from the north, where the Great Wall was built to serve as a barrier, only to be penetrated time and again by the nomadic peoples of the plains: the Xiongnu, Jurchen, Tuoba, and Mongols.

Just as important as a thread binding China through the ages was the nation's cultural continuity, and particularly its most distinctive element—the Confucian tradition of good government, responsibility, and civic obligation. In time, Confucius's name would become tarnished as a symbol of elitism, yet for many centuries the tradition of an educated bureaucracy selected by competitive examination established in his name served the nation extremely well. So, too, did the associated concern for culture, which gave rise to a fascinating heritage of literature, history, painting, calligraphy, and porcelain manufacture stretching back over two and a half millennia.

> Today, more than one billion Han Chinese trace their ethnic identity to a dynasty founded in the 3rd century BCE.

In some ways, imperial China's technological innovations were even more startling than its cultural achievements. The British sinologist and historian of science Joseph Needham (1900–1995) once drew up a list of Chinese inventions, noting by how long they preceded "discovery" in the West: porcelain and the crossbow, 13 centuries; cast iron, 12 centuries; draught-animal harnesses, eight centuries; and mechanical clocks, six centuries. In addition, gunpowder, the magnetic compass, and movable-type printing all appeared in China long before they were known in the wider world.

Yet for all its triumphs, China's history has also charted deep lows: times of foreign domination, eras of disunity, and periods when the nation split apart into a cacophony of warring states. Perhaps China's most remarkable feature is the resilience it has shown in recovering from these episodes, to move forward repeatedly from disorder and chaos into cohesion and prosperity.

Chronology of Dynasties

Chinese history is the story of the rise and fall of dynasties. Each dynasty passed from optimistic beginnings through stagnation to decline and replacement by a new claimant to the "Mandate of Heaven." Some dynasties lasted hundreds of years, others only a few, but each can be taken as defining a historical period.

Xia dynasty
C. 2070–C. 1600 BCE

According to traditional Chinese history, the founding father of China was the Yellow Emperor, Huangdi, the first of the "pre-dynastic" Five Emperors. The first dynasty was set up around 2070 BCE by Yu, who established the hereditary principle by passing on the throne to his son. Yu's dynasty was named Xia for the clan to which he belonged. There were 14 Xia rulers. Some historians believe the story of the Xia dynasty to be mythical.

Shang dynasty
C. 1600–1046 BCE

The Shang is the first Chinese dynasty whose existence is supported by solid archaeological evidence. It is said to have been founded when King Tang, the ruler of Shang, defeated the Xia tyrant King Jie in battle. Tang's successors fought many wars, employing horse-drawn chariots, bronze weapons, and bows. The surviving relics of the dynasty include royal tombs, bronze vessels, and oracle bones inscribed with ancient writing. The dynasty came to an end when the brutal Shang ruler Di Xin was defeated by King Wu of Zhou.

Zhou dynasty
C. 1046–221 BCE

Founded after the victory of King Wu over the Shang at the Battle of Muye, the Zhou dynasty lasted for 790 years. However, for much of that time, its rule over other supposedly subordinate Chinese states was nominal, with the lords of those states acting independently. Historians divide the dynasty into two periods, Western Zhou (1046–771 BCE) and Eastern Zhou (770–221 BCE). The Eastern Zhou is further divided into the Spring and Autumn period (770–476 BCE) and the Warring States period (475–221 BCE). It was in the Zhou era that sages such as Confucius and Laozi established the principles that would shape Chinese society.

Qin dynasty
221–206 BCE

The ruler of Qin, King Zheng, emerged victorious from the inter-state warfare that followed the fall of the Zhou. Adopting the title Shi Huangdi, which means "first emperor," he unified China under his absolute rule. Imposing forced labor on the mass of the population, he improved frontier defenses with the Great Wall

and built himself a vast burial complex guarded by thousands of terracotta warriors. After the First Emperor's death in 210 BCE, his heirs were swept from power by popular uprisings.

Han dynasty
206 BCE–220 CE

Contemporary with the Roman Empire, the Han dynasty ruled China for four centuries. It was founded by a low-born rebel, Liu Bang, who took the throne as Emperor Gaozu. In later times, the Chinese came to idealize the Han era as a golden age of unity and cultural achievement. From their capital at Chang'an, the Han rulers directed a centralized state based on Confucian principles. They expanded China's borders, spread its influence into Central Asia, and promoted a flourishing trade with the West along the Silk Road. The first period of Han rule, known as the Western (or Former) Han, ended when usurper Wang Mang established the short-lived Xin dynasty in 9 CE. The Han dynasty was restored in 25 CE, as the Eastern (or Later) Han, with its capital at Luoyang. From 184 CE, the empire was fatally weakened by the Yellow Turban peasant revolt and broke apart in warfare between rival warlords.

Time of division
220–581 CE

The forced abdication of the last Han emperor in 220 CE was followed by a period in which power was contested between three states, Wei, Han, and Wu. The Western Jin dynasty briefly reunited the country in 280 CE, but in the 4th century, invaders occupied northern China, beginning a succession of short-lived regimes. Meanwhile, the south was ruled by a series of more stable dynasties that held their capital at Nanjing.

Sui dynasty
581–618 CE

The Sui dynasty restored unity after centuries of division. The Sui emerged from the Northern Zhou dynasty, which supplanted the Wei as the major power in northern China in 557 CE. In 581 CE, General Yang Jian overthrew the Northern Zhou ruler, declared himself emperor, and conquered the south of China. He and his successor, Yang, launched huge building projects and embarked on wars in Vietnam and Korea. The demands they placed upon their people ultimately led to rebellion and the Sui dynasty's downfall.

Tang dynasty

618–907 CE

The Tang dynasty was founded by Li Yuan, who took power as Emperor Gaozu. His ruthless son Taizong built on the foundations laid by the Sui, building a strong centralized state and conducting military campaigns in Central Asia. From 690 CE, Empress Wu ruled as head of her Zhou dynasty, but the Tang dynasty resumed in 705 CE. Under Emperor Xuanzong (712–756 CE) China reached a peak of wealth and culture. In 755 CE, General An Lushan launched a rebellion that devastated the empire. Tang rule survived, but from the mid-9th century, the dynasty fell into terminal decline.

Five Dynasties and Ten Kingdoms

907–960 CE

After the fall of the Tang, China experienced civil conflict as strongmen declared independent states. The Ten Kingdoms ruled in fragmented southern China while the Five Dynasties succeeded one another further north, ending with the Later Zhou dynasty. None established effective leadership of China. Meanwhile, in the far north, the nomadic Khitan people established the Liao dynasty (916–1125), which ruled over present-day northeastern China, Mongolia, and North Korea.

Song dynasty

960–1279

The Song dynasty was founded by Zhao Kuangyin, who seized power from the Later Zhou. Known as Emperor Taizu, he unified China, but within smaller borders than his Tang predecessors. The Song empire was well governed through a bureaucracy of scholar-officials, and the economy flourished. Major innovations included gunpowder, paper currency, and the compass. But the Song remained vulnerable to attacks by steppe warriors. In 1115, the Jurchen people proclaimed the Jin dynasty, destroyed the Khitan Liao state, and in 1127 captured the Song capital, Kaifeng. The Song survived this disaster, withdrawing to southern China. Referred to after this time as the Southern Song, they presided over expanding cities and maritime trade. But fresh invaders from the north, the Mongols, overran the Jurchen Jin in 1234 and in 1279 conquered the Southern Song.

Yuan dynasty

1279–1368

Led by Kublai Khan, the Mongols were the first non-Chinese warriors to conquer the whole of China. Kublai ruled from his capital at Beijing, employing native Chinese officials and advisers while keeping real power concentrated in Mongol hands. He pursued military expansion, mounting two failed invasions of Japan and campaigns in Southeast Asia. International trade burgeoned across the wider Mongol empire, which linked China to western Asia and Europe along the Silk Road. After Kublai's death in 1295, the Yuan dynasty declined. Plague, floods, and excessive taxation stimulated peasant rebellions and stoked resentment at foreign rule. Most of China had fallen out of Yuan control before the Mongols were forced to flee Beijing in 1368.

Ming dynasty

1368–1644

Founded by peasant rebel Zhu Yuanzhang, leader of the Red Turban movement, the Ming dynasty reasserted Chinese traditions, including the Confucian examination system for selecting officials. In the early 15th century, the energetic Yongle Emperor built a great new capital at Beijing and sent a powerful fleet on voyages into the Indian Ocean. But after Yongle's reign, the dynasty adopted a defensive posture, extending the Great Wall and emphasizing self-sufficiency. Seaborne European traders arriving in the 16th century were met with suspicion and hostility.

Under Ming rule, China enjoyed a vibrant urban culture, with vigorous commerce and manufacturing, but the quality of government was often poor, plagued by conflict between court eunuchs and Confucian scholar-officials. Battered by natural disasters and widespread lawlessness, the dynasty was overthrown by rebels in 1644, allowing Manchu invaders from the north to seize Beijing.

Qing dynasty

1644–1912

China's final imperial dynasty was established by the Manchu, a people native to Manchuria. They proclaimed the Qing dynasty north of the Great Wall in 1636 and in 1644 penetrated the wall to seize Beijing and claim rulership of China. They suppressed Ming loyalists and imposed Qing rule on the entire country. Although a culturally distinct group, the Manchu adopted many Chinese Confucian traditions of government. The country prospered and military campaigns expanded its borders deep into Central Asia.

From the early 19th century, however, economic setbacks provoked revolts, one of which, the Taiping Rebellion, almost overthrew the empire. Taking advantage of Chinese weakness, the European powers and Japan defeated China in a series of wars, imposing harsh peace terms. The Qing failure to modernize China undermined support for the imperial system. The last emperor, Puyi, was forced to abdicate in 1912 when China became a republic.

NAMING CONVENTIONS

Rendering the names of Chinese people and places in the Western alphabet ("romanization") is a challenging task. The current recommended system of romanization is Hanyu Pinyin, devised by Chinese linguists in the 1950s, but many names are still familiar in older versions, such as those produced by the British-devised Wade-Giles system in the 19th century, or casually invented and adopted at an even earlier time. Thus, the area now referred to in the Pinyin version of its name as "Guangdong" appeared as "Kwangtung" in the Wade-Giles system but was traditionally called "Canton." A few names are so well established in conventional if inaccurate forms that these are commonly retained, "Confucius" being a notable example.

The naming of emperors poses special issues. Each emperor has a family and a given name, which is used until they ascend the throne: the family name comes first, followed by the given name. As emperors, they may be referred to by their "temple name," "posthumous name," or "era name." For example, the fifth emperor of the Qing dynasty, who ruled from 1735 to 1796, is usually known by his era name, "the Qianlong Emperor," but can also be identified by his posthumous name, "Chun," or his temple name, "Gaozong." The era name is the one most commonly used in this book, unless clarity or common sense dictate otherwise.

1

From Legend to History

Before 2000 BCE

Introduction

In prehistoric times, the course of events in China largely paralleled that in other parts of the world. In common with the rest of the Eurasian landmass, China was settled by waves of human ancestors migrating out of Africa—first *Homo erectus* around 1.5 million years ago and then *Homo sapiens*, modern humans, around 100,000 years ago. These prehistoric peoples left traces—mainly tools and burial remains—that have been subject to extensive archaeological study, but the real story of culture in China began, as it did elsewhere in the world, with the end of the last ice age, around 11,000 BCE. The warming of the climate was followed in about 7500 BCE by the emergence of agriculture in China—rice growing in the south and millet cultivation in the north—as well as the domestication of pigs, sheep, and cattle.

The earliest cultures

Geography (see pp. 18–19) played a huge role in China's development. Its historic boundaries were defined in part by formidable obstacles, such as mountains, deserts, and jungles; and China's comparatively flat interior was crisscrossed by great river systems (see pp. 20–21). Just as in Egypt and Mesopotamia, where agriculture developed along the banks of the Nile and the Euphrates, the earliest Chinese farmers built their settlements close to the Yellow and Yangzi rivers (in central China), whose waters they harnessed for irrigation—and much later for transportation.

Regional cultures gradually began to emerge during the Neolithic period (before the invention of metallurgy). Among the first of these was the Yangshao culture (which

> China's Neolithic period began around 10,000 BCE and lasted to the introduction of metallurgy some 8,000 years later.

appeared around 5000 BCE), centered on the Yellow River in Henan and Shaanxi provinces. The Yangshao were millet farmers who created fine white and red pottery and also produced silk. They were one of the first cultures to create bowls and other utensils using the technique of lacquering. The Yangshou appeared at about the same time as the

1.5 MILLION YEARS AGO *Homo erectus*, an early human ancestor, arrives in China

c. 8000 BCE–3000 BCE The Neolithic Dingsishan culture flourishes in southern China

c. 5500 BCE–3300 BCE The Hemudu culture flourishes in the lower Yangzi valley

c. 5000 BCE Cultures such as the Yangshao appear along the Yellow and Yangzi rivers

c. 8000 BCE Millet cultivation begins in villages along the Yellow River

c. 7500 BCE Earliest evidence of rice cultivation in southern China

c. 5400 BCE–2900 BCE The Zhaobaogou Hongshan culture flourishes in northern China

Hemudu culture of the lower Yangzi, who were known to cultivate rice; their distinctive pottery employs rich visual symbolism, portraying fish, flowers, and motifs of shamans.

Similar Neolithic cultures appeared elsewhere in the world, such as the Ubaid in Mesopotamia and the Badarian and Naqada in Egypt. In Egypt, these developed into a few large kingdoms and then a unified state by 3000 BCE; and in Mesopotamia a network of city-states emerged in the 4th millennium BCE. In China, however, the evolution of chiefdoms into larger cultures was more prolonged. In part, this was a consequence of the country's vastness, which made anything approaching a unified state impossible before the development of more sophisticated government structures.

Growing organization

By 4000 BCE, there were clear signs of increasing cultural complexity in China. The Yangshao village of Banpo, near Xi'an (in central China), had a population of around 600 people, and soon this and other large villages began to grow into towns. By about 3000 BCE, the Longshan people were building defenses made of stamped earth walls around their settlements. Burials from this period show increased social differentiation, with elite figures sent to their resting places accompanied by rich grave goods, such as jade pendants.

The increasing wealth of some villages invited the hostile attention of outsiders and called for organized physical defenses and armies. Later traditions spoke of the early 2nd millennium BCE as the period of *wan guo* (10,000 states), a time of warfare, partly confirmed by archaeological evidence. Chinese scholars would see in this period the creation of the essential components of Chinese culture and the imperial system. The Three August Ones and Five Emperors (see pp. 28–29), who were believed to have invented writing, agriculture, pottery, and the calendar, are almost certainly mythical. Yet figures such as Shun, the last of the Five Emperors, said to have reigned around 2200 BCE and to have dealt with great floods, represent the real struggles of the rulers of the first Chinese statelets. Shun preceded the Xia, traditionally the first Chinese dynasty, whose existence may be represented by the sites of the Erlitou culture in the Yellow River valley, and who were succeeded in around 1600 BCE by the Shang.

c. 3000 BCE Appearance of the Longshan, China's most advanced Neolithic culture

2255 BCE Traditional date for the accession of Shun, the last of the Five Emperors

c. 4000 BCE–3500 BCE The Keqiutou culture flourishes in what is now Fujian province

2900 BCE Traditional date for the accession of Fuxi, China's first named ruler

c. 2100–1800 BCE Period of the Erlitou culture, which may represent the Xia dynasty

Land and People

Topography that shaped one of the world's great cultures

The vast expanse of China covers an astonishing diversity of landscapes. Its rugged mountains and spectacular waterways, its arid deserts and varying climates have all shaped the country's political and cultural history.

At around 3,400 miles (5,500 km) from north to south and 3,100 miles (5,000 km) from west to east, China's expanse provided an immense area that was regarded by its ancient rulers as *tianxia* ("all under Heaven")—in essence, everything that mattered.

The isolation—and autonomy—of China from other early centers of civilization was aided by the fact that it contains several formidable geographical barriers. To the west, the barren Plateau of Tibet, ringed with vast mountain ranges soaring to over 26,000 ft (8,000 m), presents a daunting obstacle, as do the dry sands of the Taklamakan Desert and the gravel wastelands of the Gobi. The grasslands of the steppe to the northwest and north of China once provided pasture for nomadic tribes who made frequent raids south but gave little opportunity for a settled culture to take root. In the south of the country, jungle uplands presented a significant, though permeable, barrier to communication with Southeast Asia. Indian influences reached China intermittently over the mountains, but more regular contacts were maintained by means of the Silk Road and the Hexi corridor—a string of oases, such as Dunhuang, on the edge of the Tibetan Plateau.

Climate and crops

Geography and climate split China's heartland into two zones. In the north, above the 33rd parallel (a circle of latitude 33 degrees north of the equator) and the Huai River, the climate—from the beginnings of Chinese agriculture around 7500 BCE—was cold and dry, with rainfall below 20 in (50 cm) a year. Here, the growing season lasted less than six months a year

▽ **Dragon's backbone**
The magnificent Longji (or "dragon's backbone") rice terraces in Longsheng, southern China, are so called because when saturated with water they resemble the backbone of a dragon.

▽ **Glorious coexistence**
Lying south of Dunhuang city in northwestern China is Crescent Lake Oasis, a small, half-moon-shaped lake cradled by the massive sand dunes of the Gobi, which tower above it up to a height of 820 ft (250 m).

▷ **Records of life**
This Han dynasty brick decorated the tomb of a noble. It is engraved with scenes of cultivation, celebration, and ritual, as well as depictions of human figures, animals, and deities.

and crops that thrived in relatively dry climates, such as wheat and millet, predominated. The land was covered by a layer of fine wind-blown silt (loess), originally from the Mongolian desert, which required water for fertility. The need for irrigation fostered the community cohesion that gave rise, around 5000 BCE, to northern China's first agricultural settlements along the banks of the Yellow River.

To the south, the climate was wetter, having a summer rainfall of more than 60 in (150 cm). Rice thrived in such conditions, with two or even three harvests possible each year. Whereas the Yellow River was largely unnavigable, the south's major river, the Yangzi, was passable for much of its length. Its many tributaries provided the south with a network of waterways that made transportation far easier than in

Demons being driven away

Dancing and celebration

A tiger swallowing a goddess

A farmer plowing the soil

the north. This, together with the labor-intensive operations needed to tend to the rice paddies throughout the year, helped the Yangzi valley become one of the principal cradles of Chinese civilization.

The very different nature of these regions provided a fault line along which China's unity shattered in times of political turmoil or under pressure from outside invasion. Yet the generally flat and accommodating terrain—enclosed within frontier mountains, steppe, desert, and jungle—meant that when it did unify under effective administration, the vast area within which Chinese dynasties could operate offered immense opportunities and the potential to flourish.

CHINA'S PEOPLES

The Han Chinese were the dominant ethnic group in China as the country expanded; today, they continue to form the majority of the population. Even so, they were divided by language, with variants of Chinese such as Cantonese and Hakka predominating in the south and the group of dialects that evolved into Mandarin in the north. Peoples whose homelands in premodern times lay beyond China's frontier regions, such as the Tibetans, Manchurians, and Uighurs, and indigenous peoples of the south, such as the Miao and Lolo, make up most of the rest of modern China's population.

▽ **Roof of the world**
An aerial view of the spectacular mountain ranges of the Muztagh Ata in Xinjiang, northwestern China, which form the northern edge of the Tibetan Plateau.

Two Great Rivers

A civilization shaped by the histories of two waterways

△ **China's Sorrow**
The Yellow River is so called because it takes on the color of the yellow soil blown into it. The river's nickname—China's Sorrow—derives from the terrible flooding that frequently took place.

Of China's many large waterways, two in particular—the Yellow River (or Huang He) and the Yangzi—played a critical role in the formation of China's earliest cultures and the development of its imperial dynasties.

At around 3,400 miles (5,460 km) in length, the Yellow River is the world's sixth longest, winding through northern China from its source high in the Bayan Har Mountains on the edge of the Tibetan Plateau to the Bohai Gulf southeast of Tianjin. From its source, the river takes a series of sharp turns through the northern deserts before reaching China's central plain. From here, it flows more or less straight, widening to almost a mile (1.5 km), down to the sea.

The plain is an area of low rainfall, so irrigation of its windblown yellow soil, or loess (see p. 19), was essential to sustain agriculture. This fertile soil made the Yellow River valley one of the cradles of Chinese civilization, with the Yangshao—one of the first developed Neolithic cultures—appearing there c. 5000 BCE. Since then, most dynasties have based their capitals near its banks: for example, the Shang at Anyang, and the Zhou, Han, and Tang at Chang'an.

"History was like an immensely long river: sometimes it twisted and turned, sometimes it gathered new tributaries to it."

CAO JINQING, *CHINA ALONG THE YELLOW RIVER: REFLECTIONS ON RURAL SOCIETY*, 2004

▷ **Mesmerizing and dangerous**
This view is of Xiling Gorge in Hubei province, the largest and easternmost of the famous Three Gorges on the Yangzi River. Xiling is known for its fearsome whirlpools and rapids.

The fertile loess, in the form of silt, clogged up the river and caused regular, destructive flooding. People built dykes to contain it, but when these burst, the floods were more devastating still. As late as 1887, one such incident killed 900,000 people. The buildup of silt also caused the waterway to change its course. This happened at least twice in the Neolithic period: once around 2600 BCE, when it moved southeast, and 600 years later when it reverted to its previous course.

The Yangzi

If the Yellow River was China's curse, the Yangzi was its blessing. At 3,900 miles (6,300 km), it is the third longest river in the world and was known first as the Jiang ("river"); its lower section is now named Chang Jiang ("long river"). The Yangzi rises in the Tibetan Plateau and then rushes down into Yunnan province, flowing through mountains and gorges before emerging into well-watered plains and finally reaching the sea just north of Shanghai. Unlike that of the Yellow River, the floodplain of the Yangzi receives a substantial amount of rainfall. The large number of tributaries that join the river's main course make it the hub of a water world in which communication by boat is easier and cheaper than by land, and in which rice, rather than the millet of the north, is the main crop. The Yangzi is a source of wealth to southern China. It has flooded less often than the Yellow River, though occasionally with equally devastating results—as in 1931, when it burst its banks, killing up to four million people. It has also been more consistent in its course than its northern cousin.

Southern wealth

Early peoples clustered around the Yangzi, attracted by the fertility of the land, but they never attained the political might of the kingdoms and imperial dynasties in the north. Instead, the river marked the division between north and south at times of disunity. Nanjing acted as capital for a variety of southern dynasties, including the Eastern Jin from 317 to 420 CE, while Hangzhou was the seat of the Southern Song from 1127 to 1276. As an alternative center of wealth, and sometimes of power, the Yangzi ensured that the China that eventually developed was an alliance of north and south rather than a country dominated by the imperial cities of the wayward Yellow River.

▽ **Inspection tour**
This scroll painting of 1770 shows the confluence of the Yellow and the Huai rivers during one of the Qianlong Emperor's six "Southern Inspection Tours," which took place between 1751 and 1784.

Zhangjiajie National Forest Park
The towering sandstone-quartzite pillars of Zhangjiajie in Hunan province are among the most dramatic of China's landscapes. Shaped by millennia of water erosion and weathering by ice and plant life, the columns rise up to 660 ft (200 m). The park's cliffs and deep gullies—and the exceptionally high rainfall in the area—have created a mosaic of habitats that support more than 500 tree species, including the dawn redwood, which was once thought to be extinct. Biologists have recorded 116 species of vertebrates in the park; these include rhesus and macaque monkeys and giant salamanders. The park was recognized as a UNESCO World Heritage Site in 1992.

△ **Cradle of civilization**
The vast loess plateau of Shaanxi in north-central China, shown here, was once one of the Earth's most fertile plateaus. Scholars believe that *Homo sapiens* lived in this area at least 200,000 years ago.

Chinese Prehistory

Early humans and the beginnings of agriculture

❖

Human ancestors arrived in China more than one million years ago. Over millennia, they developed from primitive stone-tool users to agriculturalists, living in a string of villages along the Yellow and Yangzi rivers.

❖

The first hominins (human ancestors) to arrive in China were almost certainly *Homo erectus*, a species that developed in East Africa around two million years ago. Scavengers and hunters who cooked their meat, they stood on average about 5 ft 3 in (1.6 m) tall and had a brain size of around 76 cubic in (1,250 cubic cm)—some 10 percent smaller than modern humans. There were once suggestions that they evolved separately in China, but scholars now believe it is more probable that they migrated slowly eastward from Africa and may have crossed into East Asia around 1.3–1.6 million years ago, which is the date of crudely flaked stone tools that were unearthed at the Nihewan Basin, some 93 miles (150 km) west of Beijing. The first *Homo erectus* skeletons were found in the Zhoukoudian caves, southwest of Beijing, in

1921. The oldest skeletons are believed to be those from Gongwangling in Shaanxi province; they date to around 800,000 years ago.

Chinese *Homo erectus* developed a distinctive culture. They used sharp-edged tools made by striking off flakes from a stone core but notably did not produce

◁ **Buffalo pendant**
Water buffalo were one of the first large animals to be domesticated in southern China. They were used for plowing and other forms of labor as well as for their milk, meat, leather, and horns. The Chinese jade water buffalo pictured here dates to c. 1100 BCE.

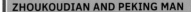

> *Homo erectus* stood upright, shaped stone tools, and may have used fire to cook food.

the hand axes that are a feature of African hominins from the same period. Their main prey was deer, but smaller quantities of the bones of leopard, bear, tiger, hyena, camel, and boar have also been found at their sites, and evidence from human skull cases suggest they may have practiced cannibalism—the manner in which the skulls were broken is a possible indicator that the brains were eaten.

By around 200,000 BCE, early *Homo sapiens*, with a slightly larger brain size and a wider repertoire of tools, had entered China and settled in sites around the Yellow River valley, on the loess plateau of Shaanxi, and on the western fringes of the North China plain. Their way of life remained essentially unaltered for tens of thousands of years, constrained by the bitterly cold phases of successive ice ages.

Agriculture spreads

The end of the ice age in 11,000 BCE brought enormous change to human societies. Small villages appeared and people began to cultivate crops. Studies at sites in the Xiachuan basin in Shaanxi, east of the Yellow River, show that foxtail millet (the ancestor of modern millet) was collected from around 7500 BCE using an early form of sickle. Evidence of the domestication of pigs and the manufacture of pottery from around 8000 BCE have been found at sites such as Mengjiaquan, 125 miles (200 km) east of Beijing.

Some 2,000 years later, larger agricultural villages developed in the region of the Yellow River, around the Wei and Huai rivers, and on the Hebei plain. Evidence suggests that by around 5500 BCE, people in the Wei valley were building semisubterranean houses and storing the crops they collected—millet and rapeseed—in pits. The inhabitants of these early Neolithic (New Stone Age) settlements in the north had certainly domesticated dogs and pigs by 5000 BCE and, by 3000 BCE, had added sheep and cattle to their herds. The villages of the north grew larger: Banpo, near Xi'an, for example, had a population of some 600 people by 4000 BCE, their houses clustered together in a way that suggests social or kinship units.

▽ **Ancient pottery**
This red pot with two handles is thought to have been produced by the Neolithic Peiligang culture. Active in the Yi-Luo river basin in north-central Henan from around 6500 to 5200 BCE, they were among the first Chinese peoples to produce pottery.

ZHOUKOUDIAN AND PEKING MAN

The caves at Zhoukoudian, 25 miles (40 km) southwest of Beijing, were occupied by human ancestors around 500,000 years ago and remained in more or less constant use for 200,000 years. In 1921, archaeologists there discovered teeth that they first identified as belonging to a new species, *Sinanthropus pekinensis* (or Peking Man): this was later incorporated into the species *Homo erectus*. The remains of about 40 further *Homo erectus* individuals, including the fossilized skull shown below, were later discovered at the site. Fossils of many animal species and thousands of pieces of stone tools were also discovered in the caves, along with evidence that Peking Man had made extensive use of fire.

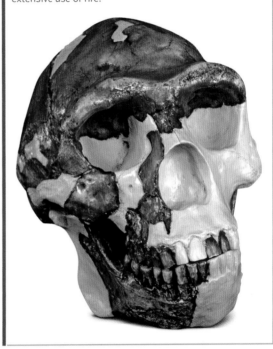

Settlements in southern China

In the wetter southern regions of China, the domestication of wild rice, which requires a high annual rainfall to thrive (see pp. 18–19), was considerably more successful than that of millet. Its cultivation probably began in the Yangzi valley between 8000 and 6000 BCE. Gradually, agricultural villages with groups of houses, storage pits, and cemeteries were founded along the middle stretch of the Yangzi. One of the largest villages was Bashidang in Hunan, which was also among the first of the settlements to be protected by a defensive wall and ditch system and to use wooden shovels in the cultivation of an early form of rice.

The development of agriculture and stock breeding was central to the emergence of a new series of more complex Neolithic cultures, which were differentiated by their levels of social complexity, architecture, and burial customs, and also by their varied artifacts, particularly pottery and jade.

Neolithic pottery

The earliest Chinese artifacts

Once agriculture had become established in China around 6000 BCE, a variety of local Neolithic cultures emerged (see pp. 24–25), differentiated by their artifacts and levels of social complexity. Among the earliest was the Painted Pottery culture, or Yangshao, named after a village in Mianchi County, Henan province, which was the first excavated site related to the culture. The Yangshao flourished at more than 1,000 sites in the Central Plain around the Yellow River. Millet-growing village dwellers who kept pigs, dogs, and sheep, the Yangshao people produced reddish-brown ceramics decorated with geometric patterns. At the best-known Yangshao site at Banpo (near modern Xi'an), archaeologists discovered semisubterranean houses, ringed by a defensive ditch, suggesting that the relative wealth of such settlements was already attracting raiders.

Later cultures

One of the next cultures to arise was the Hongshan, centered on Liaoning in the northeast, which developed from around 4700 BCE. Its skilled craftsmen fashioned jade into turtles, birds, and curious "coiled pig"-shaped dragons, and made flat-bottomed red-striped pottery. It is likely that the culture was organized centrally because the people built one of the earliest known sacrificial temples in East Asia, at Niuheliang. The "spirit temple" there consisted of

an underground temple complex with painted walls in which was found a clay figure of a female goddess with inlaid jade eyes.

In eastern China around 3300 BCE, the rice-growing Liangzhu culture developed from earlier Neolithic peoples. They sited villages near waterways and had knowledge of boats and oars, and their craftsmen wove silk and made lacquerware. They also created beautiful objects from jade, which is extremely hard and requires skill to shape. Objects included ritual items such as the *cong* (hollow cylinder) that would be produced into Shang times and beyond.

Longshan culture

The most advanced Neolithic Chinese culture was the Longshan. Developing around 3000 BCE near the middle and lower Yellow River, this culture may have had links to the Yangshao. The Longshan produced thin-walled polished black ceramics made on the potter's wheel, and the increasing wealth and social differentiation of their society may be seen in the ritual pottery vessels found in their tombs. The Longshan stood at the threshold of Chinese dynastic history—a time when local communities were beginning to coalesce into larger groups that were the forerunners of the Xia and Shang dynasties.

▷ **Yangshao ware**
This urn lid comes from the Yangshao site at Banshan. Painted with reddish-brown paint, it is thought to depict a shaman. It is one of the oldest known representations of a human being.

Lid painted
with geometric
patterns

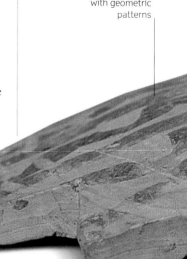

Markings suggest that Neolithic shamans wore face paint

Base of neck painted with snake pattern

△ **Bird bowl**
This Yangshao *ding* (a vessel for food) is shaped like an owl. This tripod shape remained popular for vessels throughout China's dynastic history.

Hand-painted geometric pattern

△ **Funerary jar**
This Yangshao jar would have been produced on a slow-turning wheel and then painted with its bold designs. It probably held food or liquid buried with the dead.

China's Heroes

The legendary founders of Chinese culture

The time spanning the Neolithic period and the rise of the first dynasties—the Xia and the Shang—is filled with semilegendary figures who were said to have laid down the foundations of much of Chinese culture.

China's earliest figures are best viewed as archetypes and semilegendary beings rather than as actual historical personalities. Nevertheless, their stories are a powerful document of how the ancient Chinese people perceived the establishment of their society. Many of these tales are based on information that was contained in the *Roots of the Generations* (*Shiben*), which was known to Han historians in the 1st century CE but subsequently lost in its complete form.

According to tradition, the earliest recorded ruler in China was Fuxi, the first of the August Ones, or the Three Sovereigns. He is believed to have come to power some time around 2900 BCE. Fuxi and his sister (or wife) Nüwa fashioned the first human beings. Fuxi taught these beings skills such as fishing and hunting; Nüwa saved the world from a terrible flood that occurred when a great rift was torn in the sky. She melted rocks of five different colors together to form a poultice with which she repaired the break.

Fuxi's successor, Suiren, was known for introducing fire and cooking to his people, while the last of the August Ones, Shennong, Lord of the Earth, brought agriculture to China and taught people to plow and harvest. The father of Chinese herbal medicine, he is said to have died when his intestines burst after he sampled the yellow flower of a weed.

The Five Emperors

Shennong was followed by Huangdi (a name that means "Yellow Emperor"), who ruled from around 2737 BCE. The Yellow Emperor began the line of the so-called Five Emperors, a type of proto-dynasty in which the basic principles of government were established. The subject of a cult during the early Han dynasty, he is said to have invented the calendar, the imperial crown, and wooden houses; his officials devised the first Chinese writing system. The next of the Five Emperors, Zhuanxu, instructed the gods to separate Heaven and Earth so that it became harder to communicate with the spirit world, while the third emperor, Ku, invented several musical instruments and traveled around his realm on a dragon.

The next in line, Yao, developed a solar and lunar calendar that had 366 days in a year and a leap month. He also introduced religious rituals at court and established a hierarchical system of central government. Yao saved the nation when he ordered the legendary archer Hou Yi to shoot down nine of 10 suns that were scorching the Earth (perhaps a folk memory of a serious drought). His reign was also troubled by a great flood. However, he did not contain the flood but instead passed on the problem to his successor, Shun, the last of the Five Emperors,

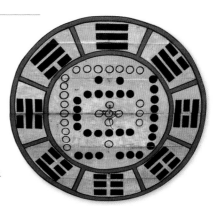

△ **Fuxi's trigrams**
According to legend, Fuxi invented the eight trigrams, which were later used in divination. The trigrams here are from the Ming dynasty Temple of Fuxi in Tianshui.

△ **Contributions to Chinese culture**
In this painting, Shennong, Lord of the Earth (center), is flanked by Fuxi (right) and Huangdi (left). All three of these rulers made major contributions to Chinese culture.

◁ **The tools of creation**
The creators of the world, Nüwa and Fuxi, are shown entwined on this painted silk banner from Astana Cemetery, Turfan. They are holding a compass and a square, symbolizing measurement of the world.

who reigned until about 2205 BCE. Shun was a humble farmer who had been born into an impoverished peasant family. According to tradition, he was selected by Yao as a successor for his patience, his loyalty, and his devotion to his harsh, unjust parents—a possible indication that the royal title was, at this stage, awarded on the basis of merit rather than by virtue of family connections.

Organizing the empire

Shun organized the empire, dividing it into 12 separate provinces. He entrusted the onerous task of dealing with the great flood to Gun, a prince of the royal house, who built a series of dykes to hold the waters in check. However, these defenses were soon overwhelmed and, in frustration, Shun turned to Gun's son, Yu—the man who would ultimately succeed him as emperor (see pp. 30–31).

△ **Transmitting knowledge**
Flanked by officials, Huangdi, the Yellow Emperor, is shown in a 16th-century painting beneath a canopy, passing on medical books to Lei Gong, god of thunder (center, kneeling).

"[Shun] **delimited** the **twelve provinces** and **raised altars** on **twelve mountains**, and he **deepened** the **rivers**."

THE *BOOK OF DOCUMENTS (SHUJING)*

Yu and the Xia Dynasty

The beginnings of recorded history in China

The reign of Emperor Yu—who succeeded in ending a great flood that plagued China—marks the boundary between China's legends and its first dynasty, the Xia, who may have ruled from the late 3rd to the mid-2nd millennium BCE.

Emperor Yu the Great, reputed founder of the Xia dynasty, is said to have lived around 2100 BCE, but some scholars believe him to be legendary. Much of what is known about Yu comes from a considerably later source, the *Book of Documents* (see box, below). According to traditional accounts, he was appointed by Emperor Shun to solve the long-standing problem of flooding along the Yellow River—a task at which Yu's father had failed (see p. 29). To address the problem, Yu consulted a renowned agricultural expert, Hou Ji, who advised him to dig irrigation canals to drain away the floodwaters rather than trying to contain them with more dykes and embankments. Thereafter, Yu committed himself to this task, eating, sleeping, and digging with common laborers, and even neglecting his family until the job was finally complete.

His plan succeeded. The ruler, Shun, was so impressed with Yu that he resolved to abdicate and pass on his throne to his protégé—an act that he carried out in the 42nd year of his reign, citing in the ceremony the great moral virtues of his new successor. Yu was 53 years old when he ascended to the throne, but his energy was undimmed. He taught his people how to plant rice and methods of goose and duck husbandry. He melted down all the bronze he received in tribute from the different parts of his kingdom and had it recast into nine bronze tripods, symbolizing the nine provinces into which he reorganized his territory. After a reign of 45 years, Yu died while on a hunting expedition on Mount Kuaiji, south of Shaoxing. He became renowned as a sage and a model emperor and, among Daoists, was revered as a water deity.

The birth of the Xia dynasty

Yu had originally intended to pass the throne to his chief minister, Gao Yao, continuing the meritocratic tradition of his predecessors. However, Gao died before Yu, so the emperor gave way to pressure from his subjects to appoint his own son, Qi, as his successor. The passage of power from Yu to Qi marks the beginning of the tradition of hereditary succession in China and the establishment of the Xia dynasty.

The traditional account of the Xia ends with its final ruler, Jie. Reportedly dissolute and too fond of wine, he faced internal rebellion and invasions from barbarian hordes. Astrological portents showed

△ **Ancient wine cup**
Chinese *jue* vessels—as in this example from Erlitou in Henan province, excavated in the early 1970s—often have high, thin sides, a distinctive U-shaped body, and three splayed legs. They were used as ceremonial wine cups in ancient China.

YU AND THE XIA IN THE *BOOK OF DOCUMENTS*

The *Book of Documents* (*Shujing*), one of the Five Classics of the Confucian canon (see pp. 54–55), is among China's earliest historical texts. Shown here is a 7th-century copy. Two chapters in the book cover the reign of Yu the Great and the Xia dynasty. The chapter on Yu describes his role as the tamer of floods and tells how he divided China into provinces, grading each province for its various attributes, such as quality of soil and local produce. The chapter on the Xia focuses in particular on speeches by various kings and ministers.

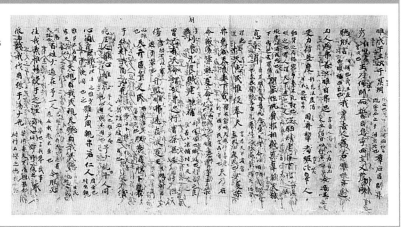

that Heaven was also displeased with his reign—the planets, for example, changed their natural course, and two suns were said to have appeared. Many of Jie's people turned for help to Tang, ruler of the kingdom of Shang. Tang led an uprising against Jie, defeated him around 1600 BCE at the Battle of Mingtiao, and established his own Shang dynasty.

The evidence of Erlitou

There are no contemporary written records of the Xia dynasty. This led scholars in the 1920s to question the dynasty's existence. However, in 1959, archaeologists discovered a site at Erlitou in Henan province that provided some factual basis for the Xia.

The Erlitou site dates to around 1900–1500 BCE, and the excavations there—including magnificent bronze artifacts and two palaces—suggest that it was a large, well-laid-out city with a high level of culture and organization. Claims by some scholars that Erlitou was the Xia capital have not been confirmed; indeed, the suggestion that the three first Chinese dynasties (Xia, Shang, and Zhou) succeeded one another are based largely on much later accounts. It is possible that they were among hundreds of states that coexisted in northern China at the same time.

△ **Tamer of the flood**
This painting by Qing dynasty artist Xie Sui shows Yu the Great (center, wearing a red robe) heading efforts to control the floods. He is assisted by the gods (on the left of the painting) and a force of men wielding picks.

△ **Erlitou creature**
This bronze ornamental plaque (1700–1500 BCE), inlaid with turquoise, was one of many artifacts found at the Erlitou site in Henan. Scholars are uncertain what the stylized creature, with its bulging eyes, represents.

2

The First Dynasties

C. 2070 BCE to 221 BCE

Introduction

China's first hereditary dynasties—the Xia, Shang, and Zhou—emerged from 2000 BCE to 221 BCE, a time of profound change, during which China made the transition from Bronze Age to Iron Age technology. Traditional sources state that the first ruling house, the Xia dynasty, was established by Yu the Great, who won acclaim after controlling the disastrous flooding of the Yellow River. Yu was succeeded by his son, Qi, setting a precedent for hereditary rule. The Xia dynasty continued until around 1600 BCE, when it was overthrown by Tang, ruler of the small kingdom of Shang, at the Battle of Mingtao. At around this time, the Mycenaean Civilization was emerging in mainland Greece, and the New Kingdom was being established in Egypt.

Shang rise and fall
Although the Shang dynasty expanded the area under its control, they ruled just a small part of modern-day China, largely centered around Henan province. They changed their capital several times, notably establishing themselves in Yin (see pp. 42–43), near modern-day Anyang, around 1300 BCE. It was there that archaeologists unearthed the earliest evidence of Chinese writing, on oracle bones (see pp. 44–45), which the Shang kings used to divine the future. The power of the Shang was sapped by the dynasty's conflicts with its neighbors, among whom were the Zhou. Claiming that the Shang king, Di Xin, had lost his divine right to rule—the so-called Mandate of Heaven (see pp. 49)—through his corrupt actions, Wu of Zhou defeated the Shang in 1046 BCE. The Zhou kings would rule even less of modern-day China than their Shang predecessors.

The Zhou dynasty
Wu of Zhou died just three years after becoming king of China, having founded the Zhou dynasty. The mantle of ruler was taken up by a regent—the Duke of Zhou— who ruled wisely, defeating rebels and conquering much of the North China Plain. This heralded a period of stability under the Zhou (later called the Western Zhou because their capital, Haojing, was in the west). However, the Zhou rulers granted land and titles to their allies and relatives, a policy that eventually led to the creation of dozens of semi-independent states that fought among themselves. In 771 BCE, after years of

c. 2070 BCE Beginning of the Xia dynasty, founded by Yu the Great

c. 1300 BCE Shang dynasty moves its capital to Yin, near present-day Anyang

1050 BCE King Wen of Zhou dies and is succeeded by his son Wu

1043 BCE Cheng becomes king; his uncle, the Duke of Zhou, acts as regent for eight years

c. 1600 BCE Tang of Shang wins the Battle of Mingtao, overthrowing the Xia dynasty

c. 1250 BCE Wu Ding becomes the first Shang king

1046 BCE Wu overthrows the Shang, so beginning the Western Zhou period

957 BCE Zhao of Zhou dies in battle in Hubei province

infighting, a powerful feudal lord sacked the Western Zhou capital, killing the king. The king's successor moved the royal capital to Luoyang, beginning the Eastern Zhou dynasty, under which the local lords became ever more powerful.

The Eastern Zhou dynasty is often divided into two parts: first, the Spring and Autumn period (see pp. 56–59), then the Warring States period (see pp. 42–43). The so-called Spring and Autumn period saw China divide into rival states. From

> More than 100 states existed in China over the course of the Spring and Autumn period.

the 7th to the 6th centuries BCE, the most prominent local rulers were acknowledged as "hegemons"; their role was to protect the states—and the Eastern Zhou kings, who ruled in name only—from foreign invaders. By the 5th century BCE, this form of organization had broken down, and China entered the Warring States period. Larger, more successful

states conquered weaker, smaller ones (or forced them into submission) until there were just seven major states left: Qin, in the southwest; Chu, in the southeast; Yan to the north; and the states of Zhao, Wei, and Han in central China.

Despite these periods of conflict and disorder, the Zhou dynasty was a time of technological and intellectual development. The Iron Age, which began around 500 BCE, enabled the mass production of weapons made from iron; and the Five Classics (the key texts of ancient China) were first compiled in this period. Scholars also debated the most effective way to rule states and organize society, leading to the creation of many schools of philosophy. The most prominent thinker of the time was Confucius (551–479 BCE), whose ideas became a major influence on Chinese thought and society. At the same time, the foundations of Western philosophy were being laid by the Athenians Socrates, Plato, and Aristotle, and Siddhartha Gautama was establishing Buddhism in India. The Zhou dynasty ended in 221 BCE, when Qin (one of the Warring States) defeated all the others, leading to the creation of the first unified Chinese empire, and the first imperial ruling house—the Qin dynasty.

771 BCE You of Zhou is killed when one of his lords revolts

770 BCE Beginning of the Spring and Autumn period

643 BCE Death of Duke Huan of Qi, the first "hegemon"

551 BCE Birth of Confucius; he dies in 479 BCE

475 BCE Beginning of the Warring States period

C. 300 BCE Only seven major states remain: Qi, Chu, Yan, Han, Zhao, Wei, and Qin

770 BCE The Zhou dynasty moves its capital to Luoyang, beginning the Eastern Zhou period

632 BCE The state of Chu is defeated at the Battle of Chengpu

476 BCE End of the Spring and Autumn period

221 BCE Qin defeats the other states

The Bronze Age

A giant leap in China's material culture

The ability to cast and work bronze is a landmark achievement in a society's development. In ancient China, the metal was shaped into practical objects, such as tools and weapons, but also into magnificent items used in sacred rituals.

The earliest known Chinese bronze items are knives dating to around 3000 BCE, which were found in Gansu province in the northwest. However, bronze took some time to displace stone as a widely used material, so historians place the start of the Chinese Bronze Age a millennium later, coinciding with the advent of the Xia dynasty. Bronze craftsmanship reached the peak of its sophistication in the Shang and Zhou Dynasties but was supplanted in the Warring States period by iron, which was a more suitable material from which to mass-produce weapons.

▽ **The Houmuwu *ding***
This giant bronze vessel was commissioned by the Shang king Zu Geng to honor his mother, Fu Jing.

Bronze is made by adding tin or lead to molten copper. The resulting alloy is harder than its constituents, which means that it can be made into sharp, durable items. In the Xia and Shang periods, craftsmen produced bronze objects by pouring the molten alloy into ceramic molds carved into the desired shape. When making more complex items, such as vessels with handles or legs, they cast the components in different molds and then joined them to the main body of the piece. By the middle Zhou era, bronze workers had developed a new technique, now called the lost-wax process. They first made a model of the object in beeswax and enclosed it in clay. They baked the clay in a fire, a process that melted the wax, and then poured molten bronze into the cavity. This process was more precise and allowed for the creation of more complex shapes.

Ceremonial objects

At first, bronze was highly valued, so objects fashioned from the alloy were usually items of high significance. Intricate vessels were made for ceremonial events, such as sacrifices, banquets, and funerals, and the number and quality of such bronzes possessed by a family was a sign of its social rank and status. One type of vessel, the *ding*, was a square or round cauldron with legs and handles and was used

△ **Ordos belt plaque**
The Ordos culture produced small bronze artifacts, which often depicted animals. This gilt bronze belt plaque shows a horse attacked by a tiger.

Weighing 1,836 lb (833 kg), the Houmuwu *ding* is the largest piece of surviving bronzework from the ancient world.

to cook and store food offered to gods and ancestors. *Ding* were often decorated with images of animals or *taotie* motifs (see below). Another important type of vessel was the bowl-shaped *gui*, used to hold offerings of grain. Bronze was also used to make instruments for playing ritual music; these ranged from small bells to large percussion instruments that were hung on racks and struck with clubs.

Regional styles and decorations

By the Zhou dynasty, abstract designs and inscriptions (see pp. 52–53) became more popular than animal decorations. There were distinct regional styles: objects from the Sanxingdui site (dating from c. 1700 to 1150 BCE) in Sichuan province feature sculptures of trees and life-size human figures with exaggerated facial features. In comparison, bronzes excavated from the Dayangzhou site (from c. 1200 BCE) in Xingan County, Jiangxi province, depict tigers and patterns. The ancient bronzes uncovered from sites in Ordos in Inner Mongolia are far simpler and often incorporate animal forms in jewelry, adornments, and harnesses for animals.

▷ **Shang dynasty totem**
This highly stylized bronze head is believed to have been the totem of a Shang king. The bronze is gilded, emphasizing the value of the head as a ritual object.

THE *TAOTIE*

The *taotie* (the "glutton," so called because it represents a voracious beast) is a prominent decorative motif in ancient Chinese bronzeware, as seen in the mask below, which dates from the Western Zhou dynasty. The *taotie* is an animal face, often with eyes, ears, mouth, horns, and claws, but usually has no body. The design—symmetrical, and often surrounded by ornate decoration—was used on a wide variety of objects. Its precise meaning is unclear, although it is thought by many to represent the all-consuming forces of nature.

Gilding on bronze head

Ancient Bronze

Crafts from the early dynasties

Bronze was an important metal during the early dynasties, when it was used to make weapons and ritual objects. Inlaid with precious metals, gilded, or carved with auspicious patterns and inscriptions, many of these ancient objects have retained their fine details thousands of years later.

◁ **Shang *ding***
This ritual tripod vessel (*ding*) dates from the Shang dynasty. The triangular patterns below the band of whorls and shapes may represent mountains.

▷ **Hanging hook**
This hook, inlaid with decorative gold, would have been attached to an official's belt during the Warring States period to hang things from.

△ **Dagger-axe**
The blade of this dagger-axe (*ge*) dates from the Warring States period. Inlaid with gold decoration, it is 9 in (22 cm) long.

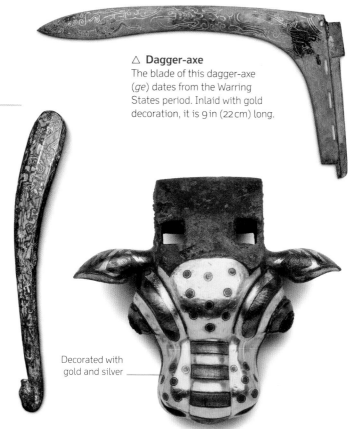

Decorated with gold and silver

△ **Bronze bull**
This decorative chariot fitting from the Zhou dynasty is shaped like a bull's head.

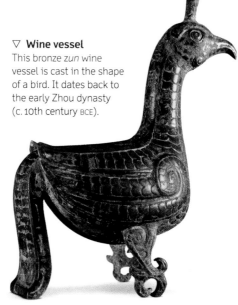

▽ **Wine vessel**
This bronze *zun* wine vessel is cast in the shape of a bird. It dates back to the early Zhou dynasty (c. 10th century BCE).

▷ **Ceremonial bell**
This 15 in (38 cm) tall ritual bell (*zhong*) is part of a set dating to the 5th century BCE. These bells have no clapper so would have been rung using a mallet.

Hands raised to hold reins

△ **Frontier man**
This bronze figure depicts a charioteer from the northern frontier during the Warring States period.

Crane symbolizes longevity

Decoration mimics open lotus leaves

△ Knife money
Shaped like a knife, this bronze currency from the Xin dynasty contains holes to allow pieces to be strung together.

△ Official headwear
Decorated with gilt bronze patterns and inlaid gemstones, this plaque would have adorned the hat of an Eastern Jin official.

◁ Heavenly being
This Han figure represents a "celestial horse," a fabled horse based on the fine specimens Han envoys had seen on their trips to Central Asia.

Remaining traces of original paint

▷ Bronze bird
This gilded phoenix is one of a set of 26 Eastern Han plaques from Sichuan province. Made from thin sheets of bronze, it probably decorated a tomb.

△ Ornate vase
One of two matching vessels, this pot comes from the state of Zheng during the Spring and Autumn period. It features a crane standing on the top and dragons and beasts climbing its sides.

▷ Cart and ox
This bronze representation of a farmer with an ox and cart is a rare example from the Han dynasty. It would have been placed in a noble's tomb to ensure a bountiful harvest in the afterlife.

The Shang Dynasty

China's first historical dynasty

The conquerors of the semi-mythical Xia dynasty, the Shang kings left behind archaeological remains that proved their existence. However, after more than five centuries of rule in China, the Shang were themselves vanquished.

The Shang originated from—and held their earliest territories in—modern-day western Anhui, eastern Henan, and northern Shandong. The beginnings of the dynasty are described in legends reported by the great historian Sima Qian (see pp. 106–107), according to which Jiandi, wife of the mythical Emperor Diku, became pregnant after swallowing a bird's egg. She miraculously gave birth to Xie, who aided Yu the Great (see pp. 30–31) in his efforts to control China's floods and was rewarded with a territory called Shang, which became the name of his dynasty.

Tang of Shang

Historians believe that the Shang existed at first under the control of the Xia dynasty. The ruler who transformed them from a local principality into the kings of China was named Tang. He annexed neighboring states and gained the support of numerous small kingdoms, before conquering the Xia dynasty (which was then under the harsh rule of King Jie) at the Battle of Mingtiao in around 1600 BCE. Tang, assisted by his chief adviser (and former chef) Yi Yin, soon established the Shang as the new rulers of China. Some sources suggest Yi Yin had been a slave; others claim he had been found in a hole in a mulberry tree by a member of Tang's mother's

clan. With Yi Yin's counsel, Tang ruled wisely, extending Shang control; after his death, Yi Yin advised his successors and served for a while as regent.

Tang was known as a generous ruler, even offering himself as a sacrifice at the altar of the Mulberry Grove during a ritual ceremony to end a drought. According to the *Announcement of Tang (Tang gao)*, a great rain came before he could complete the ceremony, and the Lord of Heaven spared the king.

An expanding empire

From the 16th to the 14th centuries BCE, the Shang expanded their area of influence, relocating their capital at least five times. The probable site of one of their capitals was Erligang, a settlement on the outskirts of the modern city of Zhengzhou, in Henan province. Archaeological studies at the site began in 1952, and excavations show that the city flourished from about 1600 to 1400 BCE, supporting a population of around 100,000 people. Excavations have also revealed that the city was protected by massive walls; and the sheer size and diversity of the bronzes unearthed at Erligang attests to the wealth of the Shang population. The further spread of Shang influence across China is evidenced by the presence of Erligang-style bronzes across a wide area extending as far south as Panlongcheng (see below).

> ▷ **Bronze weapon**
> Shang weapons included bows and arrows, as well as bronze swords and daggers, and bronze-tipped axes and spears.

THE SHANG SITE OF PANLONGCHENG

Discovered in 1954 and excavated during the 1970s, the Panlongcheng archaeological site, in Hubei province, is 300 miles (480 km) to the south of Erligang. The two sites share many features, such as the presence of Erligang-style bronzes. Panlongcheng is thought to have been conquered by the Shang as they expanded southward during the 15th century BCE. They were attracted to Panlongcheng because the region was rich in copper deposits; under their rule, it grew into a walled city with an area of 0.8 sq. miles (3 sq. km). However, by 1300 BCE, the Shang had abandoned Panlongcheng as the center of gravity of their realm shifted northward.

△ **The first king**
Tang rose up against the Xia after a prophecy made using oracle bones (see pp. 44–45) predicted his victory. This depiction of the king is on a silk scroll from the 13th century CE.

"Our king of Shang **brilliantly displayed** his sagely prowess; for oppression he substituted his **generous gentleness**."

BOOK OF DOCUMENTS (SHUJING), 11TH–3RD CENTURIES BCE

Around 1300 BCE, King Pan Geng of Shang established a new city, Yin, near the modern city of Anyang (see pp. 42–43). From there, the Shang sent out armies of thousands of men to campaign against their enemies. The booty they plundered boosted the Shang treasury, and the captives they took were often enslaved. Many prisoners were sacrificed, usually by beheading, as offerings to the gods or ancestors, to gain divine favor, and to forestall disasters such as invasion or drought. In addition, it was common for the servants and slaves of Shang royalty to volunteer to be put to death or die by suicide after their master or mistress died. Such practices declined under the Zhou dynasty.

Decline and fall of the dynasty

Wu Ding acceded to the Shang throne around 1250 BCE and is the first of the Shang kings for whom contemporary historical records—in the form of oracle bone inscriptions found at Anyang—exist. They reveal that he had 64 wives and was a highly active and successful ruler. After his death around 1189 BCE, Shang power declined and their territories were eroded both by frequent wars with their neighbors and by the increasing encroachment of nomadic tribes from the north.

To make matters worse, around 1100 BCE, temperatures and rainfall decreased markedly throughout Central Asia and northern China. This climatic change reduced soil fertility, causing northern nomads to range further south into areas populated by settled farmers, forcing them off their land. The resulting famine and instability culminated in the overthrow of Di Xin, the final Shang king, in around 1045 BCE, ending his dynasty's rule of China. His conquerors were the Zhou, rulers of a state that lay to the west.

▷ **Ritual bronze**
The Shang dynasty was known for its detailed bronzework, which often featured birds, dragons, and bovine heads, alongside complex geometric patterns. This bronze ritual *you*, a jar for wine storage, dates from when Erligang was the Shang capital and is shaped like a tigress carrying other creatures.

The Shang City of Yin

An ancient capital of royal palaces and tombs

Near modern Anyang in Henan province is an archaeological site that has transformed the understanding of ancient China. It contains the remains of the ancient city of Yin, the capital of the Shang dynasty for more than 250 years.

Around 1300 BCE, King Pan Geng of the Shang dynasty moved his capital and ritual center to a site on the Huan River, toward the northern border of his domain. This new city was located near present-day Anyang. Pan Geng decided to make this move after 15 years of careful consideration, and only after he had received approval from his oracles.

His new capital was named Yin, a name sometimes given to the Shang dynasty itself from this point on. Before its founding, the Shang had changed their capital several times, but the dynasty would now rule China from Yin until its overthrow by the Zhou in 1046 BCE. Soon after this date, the city was abandoned and fell into decay, becoming known as Yinxu, meaning "Ruins of Yin."

Rediscovery of the city

The city of Yin was rediscovered after some oracle bones (see pp. 44–45) were traced back to their origins close to Anyang. Analysis of the inscriptions on these bones, completed in 1917, confirmed that Yin was an important Shang site. Initial archaeological work began along the banks of the Huan River in 1928 and soon uncovered an organized cluster of settlements, workshops, and burial grounds set around a political and ritual center comprised of temples, palaces, and a royal cemetery. Most of the buildings were elevated, built on rammed-earth platforms, and the ruins suggest that the city may have had more than 100,000 inhabitants at its height.

At the end of 1933, archaeologists finally examined the largest royal tombs at the site. Their excavations revealed that each tomb was a pit, sometimes cross-shaped, with a ramp to allow access. At the center of each pit were wooden chambers that housed the

◁ **Shang ceremonial sickle**
This ornate sickle found at Anyang is made of bronze inlaid with turquoise. The ritual weapon's blade is crafted from a piece of carved jade.

coffins of members of the Shang royal family. Human sacrifices and offerings were placed around the chambers, and the pits were filled in with earth.

Close to the royal tombs at Yin, archaeologists also discovered about 1,200 smaller graves—some of which were for individuals, and some containing multiple remains—arranged in rows. The careful ordering of the graves suggests that they were connected to the royal burial and may have contained bodies of royal servants who were interred with their king. Other graves probably held the remains of foreign prisoners sacrificed to please the ancestors. At least 10,000 human sacrifices were made in Yin under Shang rule. Also buried on the site were animals, including horses, dogs, and even elephants.

Fu Hao's journey to the afterlife

Perhaps the most spectacular of all the Yin tombs is that of Fu Hao, the first wife of the Shang king Wu Ding, who died around 1200 BCE. She was a powerful woman, who led an

> "**Heaven** will perpetuate its decree in **our favor** in this new city."

KING PAN GENG AT THE FOUNDING OF YIN,
BOOK OF DOCUMENTS (SHUJING), 11TH–3RD CENTURIES BCE

▷ **Tomb of Fu Hao**
Fu Hao's tomb escaped the attention of looters over the centuries and so contained a rich abundance of Shang burial goods.

THE DISCOVERY OF SHANG CITY HUANBEI

In 1999, archaeologists discovered another ancient Shang city, named Huanbei, which was established about 50 years before Yin. Huanbei was a walled city covering more than 1.9 sq. miles (5 sq. km), with a palace-temple complex that included 60 buildings. The city was abandoned around 1300 BCE. Analysis of the site suggests that it was destroyed in a fire that may have been started deliberately (as indicated by the small number of relics at the site).

army of 13,000 against nomadic warrior tribes from the north. Her tomb, which fortunately escaped the attentions of looters over the years, was discovered in 1975. Excavations revealed that Fu Hao had been accompanied in death by six sacrificed dogs, as well as 16 humans, one of whom had been cut in half at the waist in accordance with Shang sacrificial practices. These also included live burial, burning, beheading, and dismembering.

Fu Hao's tomb contained 468 bronze objects (including more than 130 weapons, 23 bells, and 27 knives); 755 jade items; and around 7,000 cowrie shells intended to be used as currency in the afterlife. Many of the engravings found on bronzes in the tomb include Fu Hao's name, providing scholars with the first solid historical connection between a Shang archaeological site and a named individual.

Modern discoveries

A further program of excavation at the Anyang site in 1936 revealed a huge trove of 16,000 oracle bones, and thousands more were discovered in subsequent digs. Engravings on the bones and on ritual bronze vessels carry some of the earliest examples of Chinese writing, as well as other historically important information. They record, for example, how many people were offered as sacrifices, the state of the king's health, and the foundation of schools where young people are thought to have been trained in reading, in writing, and in the art of divination. In 1939, archaeologists at Yin discovered the Houmuwu

(formerly Simuwu) *ding*—a four-legged cooking vessel that is the largest and heaviest bronze artifact ever excavated (see p. 36).

Archaeologists continue to search the site at Yin for new discoveries and have unearthed the remains of Shang settlements beyond Yin. In 1999, they discovered another Shang capital—an earlier city known as Huanbei (see above). In 2010, researchers found the remains of human sacrifices at the temple complex there.

▽ **Bronze *gui***
This ornate food container is one of more than 200 ritual vessels unearthed at the tomb of Fu Hao at Anyang.

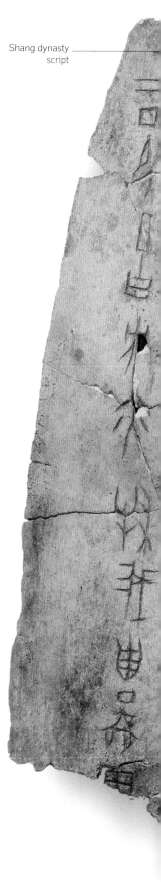

Shang dynasty script

Oracle Bones

Royal divination in ancient China

The Chinese practiced divination using "oracle bones" from the 3rd millennium BCE. During the Shang dynasty, from the 16th to 11th centuries BCE, divination developed into a ritual that officials performed to answer questions posed by their kings. The ritual involved heating specially prepared animal bones and interpreting the pattern of cracks that appeared on their surface. It was believed that deities and dead royal ancestors—who had the power to influence the present—could communicate through the bones.

Reading the patterns of cracks

The materials used in divination were the scapulae (shoulder bones) of cattle and the plastrons (lower shells) of turtles. The diviner stripped the bones or shells of any remaining flesh, cut them into the desired shape, and polished them to a high sheen (so that the cracks could be seen more clearly). He then chiseled a series of hollows into the bones or shells, which made them thinner and more able to crack. Finally, he washed the bones with blood, imbuing them with spiritual powers.

When a king wished to seek the advice of his ancestors, the diviner would heat the bones, usually with a hot metal poker, allowing cracks to form. He then carefully examined the resulting patterns of cracks and interpreted them to determine the ancestors' responses to the king's questions.

The diviner recorded the king's questions on the bones in the script of the Shang dynasty—the oldest known form of Chinese writing. The text was inscribed into the bones using a knife or, later, painted on the bones with a brush and ink. It usually consisted of a "preface," which recorded when the divination was made, by whom, and where, and the "charge"—the questions posed by the king.

Many of the questions asked related to the nature and timing of religious sacrifices, although kings also sought advice about many other issues, including the wisdom of planned military campaigns or hunting expeditions, the weather, the best timing for the harvest, and the interpretation of the king's dreams. The answers to the questions posed by the diviner were also inscribed on to the bones, which were then usually buried.

Qing rediscovery

The use of oracle bones declined in the Zhou dynasty, which followed the Shang. The significance of the bones was forgotten—indeed when unearthed, they were sometimes ground up for use in medicine. Their importance as records of the concerns of the Shang kings was rediscovered as late as the 19th century by Wang Yirong, director of the Imperial Academy in Beijing. Scholars have since continued his work to reveal the rich history inscribed on the bones.

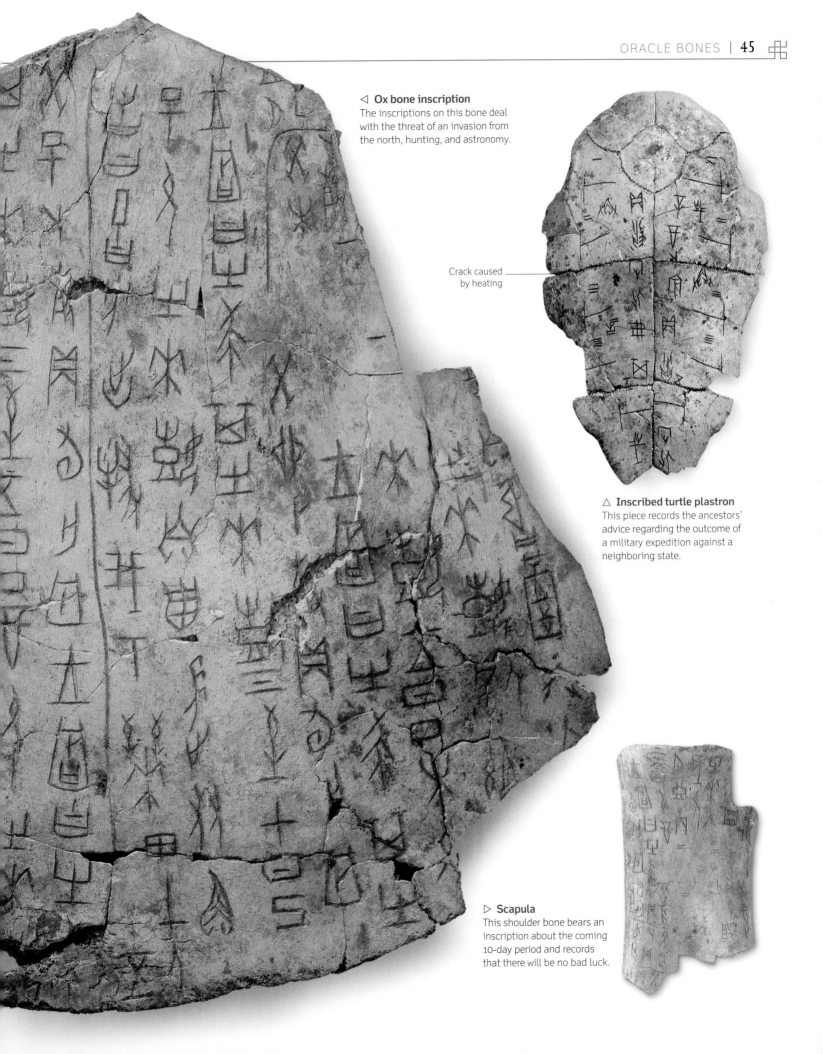

◁ **Ox bone inscription**
The inscriptions on this bone deal with the threat of an invasion from the north, hunting, and astronomy.

Crack caused by heating

△ **Inscribed turtle plastron**
This piece records the ancestors' advice regarding the outcome of a military expedition against a neighboring state.

▷ **Scapula**
This shoulder bone bears an inscription about the coming 10-day period and records that there will be no bad luck.

The rise of the Zhou

The dynasty that ruled China for eight centuries

Rising from a small frontier state in the highlands to the west of the Shang heartland, the Zhou founded a dynasty that ruled China from c. 1046 BCE to 256 BCE, a period that extended from the Bronze Age into the Iron Age.

The early history of the Zhou is uncertain, but they are thought to have originated from the northwestern margins of the Shang dynasty's territory. The Zhou traditionally considered themselves the descendants of a woman named Jiang Yuan (meaning "source"), one of the five wives of the mythical Emperor Diku, who was believed to be a great-grandson of the Yellow Emperor (see pp. 28–29). Jiang Yuan became pregnant after stepping into the giant footprint of the deity Di, the high power of the Zhou pantheon, and gave birth to a son, whom she attempted to abandon several times. This earned him the nickname Qi (literally "the abandoned"). A heroic figure, Qi is said to have fed his people by introducing millet to China. He was rewarded with land by the Xia dynasty (see pp. 30–31), and his descendants would become rulers of the Zhou.

The Zhou and the Shang

In the middle of the 2nd millennium BCE, the Zhou may have adopted an agricultural existence in Bin, which is thought to have been in Shaanxi province. In the 12th century BCE, their ruler, Gugong Danfu (who became known posthumously as King Tai), led them to a new settlement at the foot of Mount Qi in the Wei valley of western Shaanxi province.

By this time, the Zhou had made contact with the Shang dynasty and had developed an uncertain relationship with their neighbors. Sometimes they

◁ **The Shi Qiang pan**
This bronze ritual vessel was excavated from a storage pit in Shaanxi province in 1976. Its inscription, which was probably cast around 900 BCE, records the virtues and highlights of the reigns of the earliest Zhou kings.

fought one another, but on other occasions, they were allies—for example, the Zhou once welcomed a Shang king on a hunting expedition in their lands and made sacrifices to the Shang's ancestors. Gugong Danfu died in the middle of the 12th century BCE and was succeeded by his youngest son, Ji Jili, who fought

▷ **Zhou learning**
The lengthy Zhou period produced some of China's greatest thinkers and most famous texts. These pages from a Ming edition of the Zhou dynasty's *Sundial of Astronomy and Calculation* show the Gougu Rule (Pythagoras's Theorem).

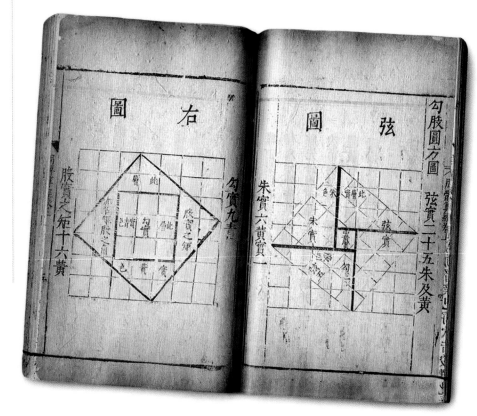

受天眷命　繼志前人
邁迹悅脈　偃武修文
惟賢是寶　法度彰明
建用皇極　愛叙彝倫

武王

▷ **King Wu of Zhou**
In the mid-11th century BCE, King Wu defeated the forces of the Shang and became the founder and first ruler of the Zhou dynasty. Wu was judged by later scholars to have been a wise ruler, though he died soon after his conquest of the Shang.

successful campaigns against nomadic tribes in the west. He visited the Shang court in Yin, wisely submitting to its authority. Ji Jili was rewarded by being raised to the rank of prince. However, his growing status soon began to trouble the Shang king, Wen Ding, who saw the Zhou as a potential threat and ordered the capture and execution of Ji Jili.

Ji Jili's son Ji Chang succeeded to power, but he too was taken captive by the Shang and was released after only seven years, in 1067, following the payment of a ransom. The Shang king Di Xin attempted to secure Chang's loyalty by giving him the title "Chief of the West." Chang himself had other plans. After returning home, he began to gather his forces together and make alliances against the Shang with other states. He assumed a new royal title, Wen Wang (meaning "the cultured king"), which signaled his challenge to the Shang.

King Wen of Zhou died in 1050 BCE, and the task of overthrowing the Shang dynasty fell to Fa, his eldest son and successor. Fa took the regnal name Wu (meaning "martial") and began campaigning in earnest against the Shang, first launching attacks against states on their periphery and then establishing bases from which to launch assaults on the core Shang territories.

A war of ideas

In order to gain support for their cause from China's civilian population, the Zhou painted the Shang king Di Xin as an immoral ruler who placed his own needs above those of his people. Zhou histories record that Di Xin levied punitively high taxes and treated his subjects cruelly, torturing those who had wronged him. They also describe the lengths to which Di Xin would go to please his beautiful but corrupt concubine Daji (see box, p. 49). The excesses in the Shang court apparently included heavy drinking, orgies, and even the building of a pool filled with wine. »

"They shall be **illustrious** from **age to age**, zealously and reverently **pursuing** their **plans**."

"THE DECADE OF WEN OF ZHOU", FROM THE *BOOK OF SONGS (SHIJING)*, 11TH–7TH CENTURIES BCE

"The **iniquity** of **Shang** is full. **Heaven** gives **command** to destroy it."

KING WU OF ZHOU BEFORE THE BATTLE OF MUYE, ACCORDING TO THE *BOOK OF DOCUMENTS* (*SHUJING*), 11TH–3RD CENTURIES BCE

Around 1046 BCE, King Wu, supported by eight allied states, led a force of some 45,000 soldiers and 300 war chariots across the Yellow River. After a march of five days, he met the Shang armies, led by King Di Xin, at an area called Muye (meaning "shepherd's wild") in Henan province.

▽ **Zhou bronze dragon**
By the time of the Zhou dynasty, the dragon had become associated with wisdom and rule—and specifically with the guardianship of the Mandate of Heaven. Dragons often appear in imperial art, as in this (late) Eastern Zhou stand.

The Battle of Muye

Although the Shang armies greatly outnumbered Wu's forces, their loyalty to Di Xin was questionable; many of Di Xin's lords and soldiers held him in very low esteem. In contrast, the morale of Wu's men was high; they were also better trained and equipped than their enemies, carrying pole-mounted daggers and protected by bronze armor. Most feared of all were the Zhou's well-drilled charioteers, who were capable of quickly flanking and disorienting an enemy.

As the battle commenced and the Zhou advanced, thousands of Di Xin's men deserted or defected, after which the disciplined Zhou quickly broke through the Shang lines after a massed chariot charge. Realizing that defeat was certain, Di Xin retreated, leaving his men to be slaughtered.

△ **The Duke of Zhou**
This portrait of the Duke of Zhou is from the *Sancai tuhui*, an illustrated Chinese encyclopedia compiled by Wang Qi during the Ming dynasty.

He fled to one of his pavilions in Yin, where he died by suicide. When Zhou forces arrived in Yin, Wu ordered Di Xin's head to be placed on a stake outside the city for all to see. The Zhou army remained in the field for two further months, putting down the remaining pockets of Shang resistance and gaining the loyalty of local lords. Wu then returned west with his army to his capital at Haojing (near present-day Xi'an), leaving his younger brothers to oversee his new conquests.

Expansion under the Duke of Zhou

Wu died around 1043 BCE, not long after his victory at Muye. His son, Cheng, was too young to ascend to the throne, so control passed to the Duke of Zhou, a son of King Wen, who became regent. The duke soon faced a rebellion led by his elder brothers Guanshu and Caishu, and by Wugeng, son of the last Shang king. He succeeded in defeating his challengers and expanded Zhou control all the way to the sea, bringing the entire Yellow River plain under his influence. The duke founded a stronghold,

Chengzhou, at a strategic site on the Yellow River, which eventually became the eastern capital of the Zhou dynasty.

The Mandate of Heaven

The Zhou formulated a concept known as the Mandate of Heaven—a divine justification for earthly authority. This gave kings the right to rule but could be lost if those rulers were unjust. If a king violated the cosmic order, Heaven was seen to call for a new dynasty. Invented at the start of the Zhou, the mandate was used to justify the overthrow of the Shang: the alleged evil actions of the Shang king, Di Xin, gave the Zhou a right to found a new dynasty, and Wu's victory at Muye was seen as Heaven transferring its mandate from the Shang to the Zhou. The mandate was used to legitimize the rule of emperors and the transfer of power right up to the 19th century.

The duke controlled the Zhou domains by setting up a feudal system in which trusted officials, many of whom were family members, oversaw local administration. He was an accomplished poet and scholar—a number of his pronouncements were included in the *Book of Documents* (*Shujing*); he was also said to be the author of the *Rituals of Zhou* (*Zhou li*), which sets out the principles of governance and justice; and some scholars claim he wrote part of the *Book of Changes* (*Yijing*). Confucius (see p. 62) declared the duke the archetype of the selfless servant of the state and urged all officials to follow his example.

When Wu's son, Cheng, came of age, the duke dutifully relinquished his position as regent and became a loyal subject. Cheng proved himself an able ruler, as did his son and successor, Kang. They both fought wars of conquest against states on their borders, extending their empire outward.

DAJI

One of the most infamous figures at Di Xin's court was Daji, who some sources held to be responsible for the moral decline of the Shang dynasty. Daji was from a noble family that Di Xin had defeated and became his concubine. He was entranced by her beauty. She encouraged his dissolute and spendthrift behavior and was permitted to carry out acts of torture, which apparently gave her immense pleasure. After the Battle of Muye, Daji was put to death.

Bird-shaped handle

Body of bowl holds inscription

Square pedestal with *taotie* motif

◁ **Li** *gui*
Excavated from Lintong in Shaanxi province, the Li *gui* is the earliest known Zhou bronze vessel. Cast by an official named Li, it is inscribed with 32 characters that commemorate the overthrow of the Shang dynasty at the Battle of Muye.

The Western Zhou

From harmony to disarray

The first half of the Zhou dynasty's rule saw a rapid expansion of their dominion through their efficient implementation of a feudal system of governance. However, loosening loyalties to the king caused a descent into civil strife.

The early Zhou period, from c. 1046 to 771 BCE, was a time of peace and order. The dynasty ruled from its power base in the west, Haojing (near present-day Xi'an), leading historians to refer to this period as the Western Zhou. This differentiates it from the Eastern Zhou, which prevailed from 770 BCE to 256 BCE, after the dynasty moved its capital east to Luoyang.

The Western Zhou ruled through a system called *fengjian*, a form of feudalism based on kinship. They granted close relatives and trusted officials lands from their conquests in the east and recognized some existing local rulers, giving them hereditary titles. These feudal lords founded garrison cities (cities with military bases), from which they controlled the local population; they were, in exchange, expected to show deference and provide tribute and military service to the Zhou rulers. This allowed the Zhou to rapidly expand their area of influence, but it also meant that they lacked direct control over their kingdom. Rather, they were rulers of a patchwork of independent states that were joined through their acceptance of Zhou authority.

The weaknesses of the *fengjian* system became apparent over time. The Zhou kings had decreasing amounts of new land available to grant to supporters, and the lords began to identify more closely with local territorial issues than with the overall authority of the Zhou king. Rivalries and disputes between different states began to preoccupy the lords, who

> "The **virtue** of the **house of Zhou** may be said to have reached the **highest point**."
>
> CONFUCIUS, *ANALECTS*, 450–350 BCE

◁ **Bronze altar set**
This altar set, unearthed in the tomb of a Western Zhou aristocrat in Shaanxi province, demonstrates the sophistication of Zhou metal workers in the 11th century BCE.

◁ **Mu's journey**
A 17th-century silk painting depicts King Mu in a chariot drawn by his eight favorite chargers. The king's travels, notably his visit to the mythical Queen Mother of the West, became a popular subject for later poets and artists.

△ **Zhou armor**
Zhou soldiers wore coats made of thick, stiff hide and bronze helmets. The helmet shown here has a raised holder at the top, to which a colored plume could be attached.

ignored their obligations to the Zhou court in favor of focusing on regional disputes. The situation led to disarray and political fragmentation.

Losing control

A turning point came in 957 BCE, when the king of the Zhou, Zhao, was killed leading a disastrous campaign against the state of Chu in the valley of the Yangzi River. Zhao's defeat and the loss of his armies curtailed Zhou expansion and forced his son and successor, Mu, to focus on regaining domestic control. Mu attempted to replace the weakening *fengjian* system with a more bureaucratic state, recruiting and promoting officials based on talent and performance. However, these moves toward more efficient government could not mask the wider problems that the Zhou faced. Invasions by nomadic groups (known as the Rong, and generally referred to as "barbarian" nomads) tested Zhou forces that were already overstretched trying to maintain their authority over the disaffected lords in the east. By the 8th century

BCE, some of the 200 or so feudal lords who were theoretically under Zhou control thought themselves to be strong enough to challenge royal authority. Their revolt eventually came in 771 BCE under the Zhou king You; it was heralded by earthquakes and eclipses, which were taken as Heaven's displeasure at You's rule and a reason to transfer the Mandate of Heaven (see p. 49).

The trigger for the revolt was the question of succession. King You exiled his wife, the queen, and passed over their son, Prince Yijiu, as his successor. Instead, he chose as his heir the child he had with his concubine, Bao Si. These actions angered the queen's father, the Marquess of Shen, a powerful lord. In 771 BCE, Shen, allied with Quanrong nomads, launched an attack against Haojing. The city was sacked, You was killed, and Bao Si was captured. In 770 BCE, Yijiu inherited the throne as King Ping, and established his capital to the east, in Luoyang. This marked the end of the Western Zhou and the start of a new dynasty, the Eastern Zhou (see pp. 56–59).

"Inscriptions are the words of **achievements**, merits, and reputations of ancestors recorded … to **commemorate** them."

RECORD OF RITES (LI JI)

Handles depict highly stylized horned beasts swallowing birds; the birds' beaks are protruding from the animal's jaws

△ **Suppressing rebellion**
The inscription in the Kang Hou *gui* describes the Rebellion of the Three Guards—a revolt by the Shang—which was quashed by the Zhou.

△ **Kang Hou *gui***
The vessel is named after the brother of the Zhou king Wu—Kang Hou—who is cited in the inscription inside the vessel.

Bronze Inscriptions

Lasting records of ancient Chinese history

Bronze is a highly durable material. Inscriptions on ritual bronze objects—usually vessels or bells used on ceremonial occasions—are among the oldest surviving examples of Chinese writing. They provide invaluable records of history and evidence for the development of Chinese script. The earliest date back to the Shang dynasty, with the best examples found on bronzework in the tomb of Fu Hao in Anyang (see pp. 42–43).

Early Shang inscriptions were simple, made up of just two or three characters that gave the name of the clan or the ancestors of the owner; however, by the late Shang, inscriptions of tens of characters were common. The characters were written from top to bottom in vertical columns and were almost always on the inner, rather than outer, surface of a vessel. The inscriptions were incised into a clay block using a stylus; an impression was then taken into another piece of clay, which was then used in the casting. The resulting characters were therefore raised above the surface of the bronze.

Zhou developments

Under the Zhou dynasty, inscriptions became ever more intricate, reflecting the needs of a more complex society. The earliest known vessel from the Zhou dynasty is the Li *gui* (a *gui* is a bronze ritual vessel), which was unearthed by archaeologists in Shaanxi province in 1976. It carries a 32-character inscription that describes the Zhou overthrow of the Shang in 1046 BCE (see pp. 46–49). However, Zhou bronze inscriptions were not reserved solely for such epochal events. The nobility also used them to record their deeds, as well as the past achievements of their own clan—military campaigns, expeditions, honors, appointments of landlords, and imperial decrees. Some inscriptions were records of the political relationships between different Zhou noble houses: in this context, they served both as contracts and as celebrations of the wealth and status of their owners.

The inscriptions were made on vessels used to hold offerings in religious ceremonies that honored the ancestors. In this way, the writings were seen as a form of communication with past generations; they also provided a link to the future because they would survive to be read by the family's descendants.

Kang Hou *gui*

The historical value of bronze inscriptions is evident in items such as the Kang Hou *gui*, a magnificent ritual food vessel (left). The Kang Hou was cast in the 11th century BCE and measures about 16½ in (42 cm) across. The inscription inside the vessel outlines the suppression of a Shang rebellion by the Zhou—it is by means of this, and other inscriptions, that scholars have a clear sense of the conflicts that took place between the two during the 11th century BCE.

Bird wings, bodies, and tails adorn the base of the handles

The Chinese Classics

A history of China's classical texts

For centuries, the five texts known as the Chinese Classics have been studied for their literary value and the insights they provide into society and politics. Few collections of writing can match their impact and influence. The texts—the *Yijing* (*Book of Changes*, or *I Ching* in the West), *Shujing* (*Book of Documents*), *Shijing* (*Book of Songs*), *Li Ji* (*Record of Rites*), and *Chunqiu* (*Spring and Autumn Annals*)—have long been linked to Confucius as an author or editor, but some parts of them were probably evolving in oral or written form long before he lived. They were among the books that the First Emperor (see pp. 78–81) tried to destroy but were reconstructed by scholars in the Han dynasty.

The oldest of the Classics, the *Yijing*, was originally a guide to divination. Sometimes attributed to King Wen of Zhou and his son the Duke of Zhou, it was probably written later, in the 8th century BCE. The *Yijing* assumes that the universe is in a state of constant (albeit orderly) change, which can be understood by carrying out divinations that reveal the correct actions to take. The text includes 64 hexagrams, each of which is made up of two trigrams—combinations of three broken and solid lines. Each hexagram has a name and an explanatory text. One of them would be chosen by chance and used to guide future decisions.

The *Shujing* is a compilation of works, the earliest of which were written in the Western Zhou dynasty (c. 1046–771 BCE); they are dated to this time because they match the type of language used in bronze inscriptions of the period. The book's 58 chapters contain edicts and narratives dating back to the 10th century BCE, forming one of the oldest written histories of ancient China, detailing events that took place during the Xia, Shang, and Zhou dynasties.

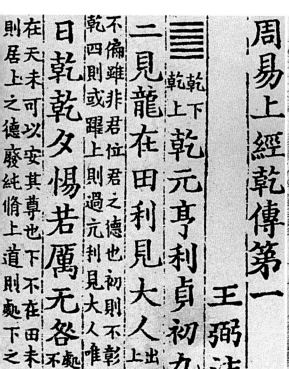

△ **Divination and the *Yijing***
This page is from a Song dynasty copy of the *Yijing*. The book presents 64 hexagrams (six stacked horizontal lines) along with a commentary on each one. Interpretation of the hexagrams was said to provide profound insights on past, present, and future events.

△ **Underpinnings of the *Yijing***
This illustration from a copy of the *Yijing* shows patterns of dots on the flank of a dragon-horse (*Hetu*) and on the shell of a turtle (*Luoshu*). These patterns are cosmological diagrams used by both Daoists and Confucians to explain the correlation of the hexagrams of the *Yijing* with the universe and human life.

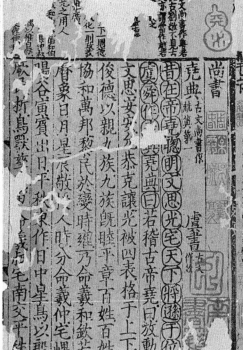

△ **The *Shujing***
There are many different commentaries on the *Shujing*. This Song dynasty copy was compiled by the great Confucian scholar Jin Luxiang in the 13th century. The book is organized into four sections covering periods of history from the reign of Yu the Great to the Zhou dynasty.

"Learning begins with chanting the Classics out loud."

XUN KUANG, THE *XUNZI*, A PHILOSOPHICAL TEXT, 3RD CENTURY BCE

The *Shijing* is a collection of 305 poems dating back to 600 BCE, though it was not fixed in its present form until the 3rd century BCE. Many of the poems were originally liturgical hymns, sung in ancestral temples during sacrificial ceremonies, while others dealt with earthly concerns, such as love, nature, and war, and may have had their origins in folk songs.

The *Li Ji* deals with ceremony and ritual at the royal court. It is composed of around 3,000 rules and descriptions, which together describe the structure of an ideal government.

The *Chunqiu* (see pp. 56–59) is an official chronicle of the State of Lu (located in Shandong province), between 722 and 481 BCE. Although traditionally regarded as the work of Confucius, it was probably a collection of works written by several different historians. A further "Sixth Classic," the *Yuejing* (Book of Music), may also have existed but was a casualty of the Qin book burning. Scholars speculate that it detailed the ritual music played at the Zhou court.

Classical curriculum

For much of the period from 136 BCE to 1905 CE, knowledge of the Five Classics formed the core of imperial China's rigorous civil service examinations. Candidates were expected to write essays in which they explained ideas from the Classics and how they could be applied to solve problems in government. Passing these exams gave candidates access to the best jobs in the state bureaucracy; not surprisingly, the Classics occupied a central role in school curricula for centuries, not only in China but also in neighboring countries such as Japan, Korea, and Vietnam, where Chinese culture, education, and ideas were adopted.

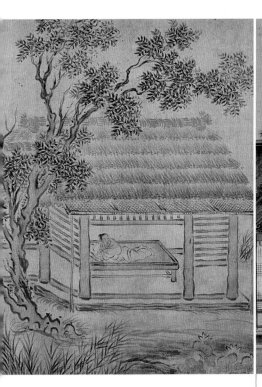

△ **Illustrating the *Shijing***
This scroll painting was commissioned by the Southern Song emperor Gaozong in the 12th century as part of a project to illustrate all 305 poems in the *Shijing*. This enterprise was designed to revive Song spirits after their defeat by the Jurchen (see p. 171).

△ **Studying the Classics**
This 19th-century painting, produced in the style of the Song and Yuan dynasty masters, shows a scholar studying the Chinese Classics. These texts were required reading for Chinese officials and the literary elite; the knowledge they contained was central to Chinese cultural identity.

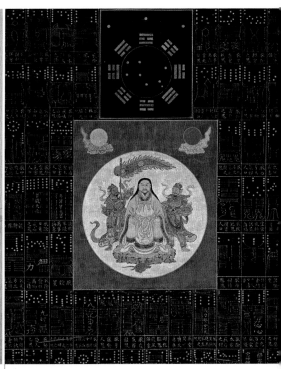

△ **Eight trigrams**
The trigrams (*bagua*), pictured at the top center of this Qing chart, are all of the possible ways to stack three broken or unbroken lines. Each trigram stands for an element: Heaven, Earth, Water, Fire, Wind, Thunder, Mountain, and Lake. Two trigrams combine to make a hexagram.

The Spring and Autumn Period

The power of the Zhou dynasty fragments

After the Zhou moved their capital east from Haojing to Luoyang, their kingdom divided into many states. From 770 to 476 BCE, these states fought one another in a struggle for survival and supremacy.

The Spring and Autumn period gets its name from the *Spring and Autumn Annals* (Chunqiu), a written history of Lu—one of the many states struggling for power at the time. The text was so titled because the phrase "spring and autumn" was used to represent the passage of one year. According to tradition, the account was compiled by Confucius himself (see pp. 54–55).

The Spring and Autumn period is known as a time of bitter conflict, but despite the violence of the era, China managed to maintain its cultural integrity throughout. Diplomats moved between the courts of the competing states, and marriages between members of courts helped forge alliances. Intellectual life thrived, fueling the emergence of the "Hundred Schools of Thought" (see pp. 64–65), and economies grew as state rulers supported commerce in order to finance their armies.

The rise of the lords

At the beginning of the period, around 770 BCE, the Zhou dynasty moved its power base from Haojing in the west to Luoyang in Henan province, leading historians to refer to the dynasty as the Eastern Zhou from this point. Their first king, Ping (r. 770–720 BCE), and his successors claimed the Mandate of Heaven and the right to perform important rituals, but they had no effective control over powerful regional lords, who commanded stronger forces than the Zhou and began referring to themselves as kings. Unable to defend themselves from foreign invaders, the Zhou at first

relied for protection on the powerful state of Zheng, which was ruled from 743 to 701 BCE by Duke Zhuang. The relationship between Zhuang and the Zhou king Huan (who succeeded Ping in 720 BCE) deteriorated into rivalry and culminated in Huan attacking Zheng in 707 BCE. Zhuang counterattacked and inflicted a humiliating defeat on Huan at the Battle of Xuge (in Henan province), which further undermined the authority of the Eastern Zhou.

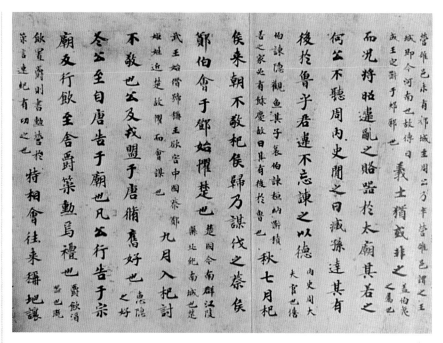

△ **Written history**
This is a 19th-century copy of the *Spring and Autumn Annals* as annotated by the 3rd-century scholar Du Yu. The *Annals* recorded significant events in the state of Lu.

◁ **Jade belt ornament**
These four jade disks, which date back to the Eastern Zhou period, probably decorated a belt. Jade was valuable because it was hard and difficult to work.

With little central control, the lords fought among themselves: strong rulers subjugated weaker ones, conquering their territories or forcing them into vassalage. States poured huge resources into their armies and into building earthen walls to protect their capitals from attack. At the start of the Spring and Autumn period, more than 140 states existed; by its end (see pp. 68–69), only a handful remained.

Age of the hegemons

The chaos of conflict between the states in the Spring and Autumn period left China's central plains vulnerable to invasions by northern nomads as well as the rising force of the state of Chu (see box, below).

To combat these threats, a system was introduced in which the most powerful of the lords was appointed hegemon or *ba* (meaning "the senior one") by the Eastern Zhou and took responsibility for coordinating defenses against foreign invaders.

The first man widely recognized as a hegemon was Duke Huan of Qi in the 7th century BCE. Qi was a wealthy state in what is now Shandong province. Huan was appointed hegemon by King Hui of Zhou in 667 BCE. For 24 years, he provided strong central leadership and commanded the respect of the other lords; he resisted the rise of the Chu, even forcing them to sign a peace treaty and pay tribute to the Eastern Zhou. After Huan died in 643 BCE, Duke Xiang of Song, the ruler of a state in eastern Henan province, became hegemon. He campaigned aggressively against the Chu, but his forces were defeated at the Battle of Hongshui, where Xiang himself was mortally wounded. After their victory at Hongshui, the Chu, led by King Cheng, saw a new opportunity to expand northward. One of the few powers in the central plains able to resist them was Jin—a state that traced its history back to the Xia dynasty (see pp. 30–31).

The Jin leader was Chong'er, a prince who had been forced to flee his home state in his youth owing to civil war, and spent almost two decades in exile before returning in 636 BCE to claim his throne. He transformed Jin into a powerful state and »

Delicate open cast work

◁ **Eastern Zhou dagger hilt**
This gold dagger hilt dates from around 500 BCE. Too fragile to be of practical use, it is thought to have been a funerary item owned by a Zhou aristocrat.

THE STATE OF CHU

According to tradition, the state of Chu (in the area of modern-day Hubei and Hunan provinces) was founded by the direct descendants of the Yellow Emperor (see pp. 28–29). Some scholars suggest that Chu may have been established in the mid-11th century BCE as a state under the control of the Western Zhou dynasty. Its rulers initially held the rank of viscount, but they soon established a high degree of autonomy from the Zhou, building up their power base in the fertile Yangzi basin. Chu lay to the south of the Chinese heartland in the central plains and, for this reason, was regarded as a "barbarian state," even though it initially shared many cultural features with its northern neighbors (a Chu carving of a phoenix is shown, right). However, over time, Chu culture diverged as it became more influenced by peoples on its southern and eastern borders. During the 8th century BCE, Chu took advantage of the weakness of the Zhou dynasty to expand north and east. To symbolize their power and military strength, the Chu ruler Xiong Che (r. 740–690 BCE), posthumously known as Wu, adopted the title of king (*wang*).

became known as Duke Wen (the "cultured duke"). In the winter of 633 BCE, the Chu attacked the state of Song—an ally of the Jin: Duke Wen responded by launching offensives against two Chu satellite states, Wei and Cao. With a clash between Jin and Chu inevitable, both sides began to build up their armies and set about forging alliances.

Rivalry between states

In April 632 BCE, the Jin army met Chu forces, led by Cheng's prime minister, Ziyu, at the Battle of Chengpu (thought by scholars to be in Henan province). The Jin charioteers led the assault against the Chu lines. After attacking, they feigned retreat, tempting the Chu into a pursuit. Screened by a dust cloud created by dragging branches along the ground, the Jin regrouped and encircled their enemy: the Chu were defeated and Ziyu died by suicide as a result of his failure. One year after the battle, Duke Wen presided over a conference at Jiantu attended by the leading lords as well as King Xiang of Zhou. Having proved his strength at Chengpu, Duke Wen was confirmed as the hegemon.

After Wen's death in 628 BCE, the desire of the regional lords to act in unity to protect the Eastern Zhou gave way to their personal ambitions for power.

The result was that by 550 BCE China was dominated by four great states—Jin at the center, Qin in the west, Chu in the south, and Qi in the east. Worn down by the relentless fighting, the larger states tried to negotiate peace in the 540s, but the attempts broke down owing to mutual mistrust. To compound the existing conflicts, new warlike states, such as Wu, emerged to challenge the status quo.

The war between Wu (located at the mouth of the Yangzi River) and Yue, a "barbarian" state to its south, was to be one of the last conflicts of the Spring

JIN WEAPONS

Soldiers who fought in the Jin infantry were equipped with pole arms—blades mounted on wooden shafts. Such weapons were commonplace across the ancient and medieval world. The first such weapon developed in China was the *ge*, a dagger (first made of stone but later bronze) mounted on a pole, which could be swung like an axe (a Zhou dynasty example is shown here). Later, this was modified by adding a spearhead that also allowed for a thrusting strike; this weapon was known as the *ji* (halberd). During the Warring States period, the blades of these weapons were increasingly made from iron.

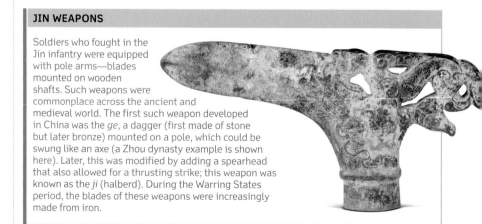

△ **Duke Wen**
This painting, attributed to the Song dynasty artist Li Tang, shows Duke Wen of Jin—the leader of a powerful state in central China in the Spring and Autumn period.

▷ **Sword of Goujian**
This well-preserved tin-bronze sword was discovered in the ruins of Jinan, capital of the ancient Chu state. It was cast in 510 BCE for Goujian, king of the Yue state.

perfected their metallurgical skills to produce some of the finest weapons of the imperial era. Two such weapons, the Sword of Goujian and the Spear of Fuchai (pictured) were closely tied to the conflict and are acknowledged as being among China's most valuable treasures.

The end of the Spring and Autumn period came not through peace or unification but further fragmentation. Internal power struggles between noble families began to undermine the stability of some of the larger states, and the fall of the Jin state and its partition among its aristocracy marked the start of a new and even more bloody phase of history, the Warring States period (see pp. 68–69).

▷ **Spear of Fuchai**
According to its inscription, this bronze spearhead was made for Fuchai, king of the state of Wu. It is decorated with a delicate pattern of black flowers.

and Autumn period. A feud between the two powers developed when a Yue princess, who was married to a Wu noble, left her husband to return home. King Helü of Wu attacked Yue but was defeated—and mortally wounded—at the Battle of Zuili in 496 BCE by the forces of Wu's King Goujian. Helü's son Fuchai continued the feud, capturing Goujian and forcing him to work as his servant for three years. On his release, Goujian returned to Yue, determined to take revenge: he transformed Yue society, creating a fearsome army that he led against Wu in 473 BCE. He besieged and took the Wu capital, slaughtered the Wu court, and forced Fuchai to die by suicide.

The war between the two states has taken on near-legendary status in Chinese history, inspiring works of literature, art, and film. The Wu and Yue states were famous for their craftsmen, who had

"Wen of Jin was crafty and not upright … Huan of Qi was upright and not crafty."

CONFUCIUS, *ANALECTS*, 450–350 BCE

The Iron Age

The material that revolutionized warfare and agriculture

One of the greatest technological achievements of the Zhou dynasty was the mastery of smelting iron ore to extract the base metal, which was used to make ever sharper and stronger tools and weapons.

△ **Iron-bladed weapon**
This magnificent axe from the Western Zhou dynasty has an iron blade and a bronze handle decorated with dragons and masks. It originates from China's Henan province.

Historians usually consider China's Iron Age to have begun in the Spring and Autumn period (see pp. 56–59) and to have lasted well into the era of imperial rule. Iron ores—rocks and minerals that contain compounds of iron—are far more abundant in the earth than deposits of copper and tin, the components of bronze. However, extracting iron with useful properties from its ores is a complex process that requires extremely high temperatures. Bronze therefore prevailed in the Shang and Zhou dynasties until metal workers developed techniques for iron production.

To extract iron from its ores, it must be smelted in a furnace. Ancient furnaces were not capable of reaching high enough temperatures to remove all the impurities from iron. They were able to produce a form of iron that could be hammered or "wrought" into shape, but this was a skilled, laborious process.

A tremendous breakthrough in China took place around 500 BCE, when metal workers developed a new kind of furnace in which air was forced through a mixture of charcoal and iron ore. It reached temperatures of more than 2,640°F (1,450°C)—hot enough to liquefy the iron. The molten metal could then be poured into molds, enabling the large-scale production of implements of almost any shape and size. This smelting technique rapidly spread across the country from Wu, on the banks of the Yangtze, where it had first been developed.

Iron under the Warring States

Metal workers preferred bronze over iron when making ritual vessels and utensils because bronze is more durable and decorative. Mass-produced iron, however, was ideal for warfare. Innovations in ironworking were driven by the near-constant conflict

> "Such is **the divinity** of the **iron weapons**."

ON SWORDS MADE FOR THE KING OF CHU, *END OF THE KINGDOM OF YUE (YUEJUESHU)*, 1ST CENTURY CE

of the Spring and Autumn and Warring States periods, as competing states sought to increase the production of iron for weapons and decrease the costs of processing the ore into metal. States such as Chu and Jin, both major powers during this era, flourished partly as a result of their ability to produce iron to make weapons for their armies.

Falling costs

Iron manufacture was initially so cost-intensive that it was administered by the various regional states, which employed bureaucrats specifically to oversee and supervise its production and distribution. The process also required large numbers of workers—an inscription on an iron bell made in the state of Qi

METEORIC IRON

Archaeological finds in Beijing, Hebei, and Shanxi provinces show that iron was used in the 14th century BCE in China, well before the development of smelting technology. The source of this metal was not ore but recovered meteorites. The meteoric iron shown at right was very rare and typically made by Shang craftsmen into prestige items, such as blades for ornate bronze-handled weapons used by the aristocracy.

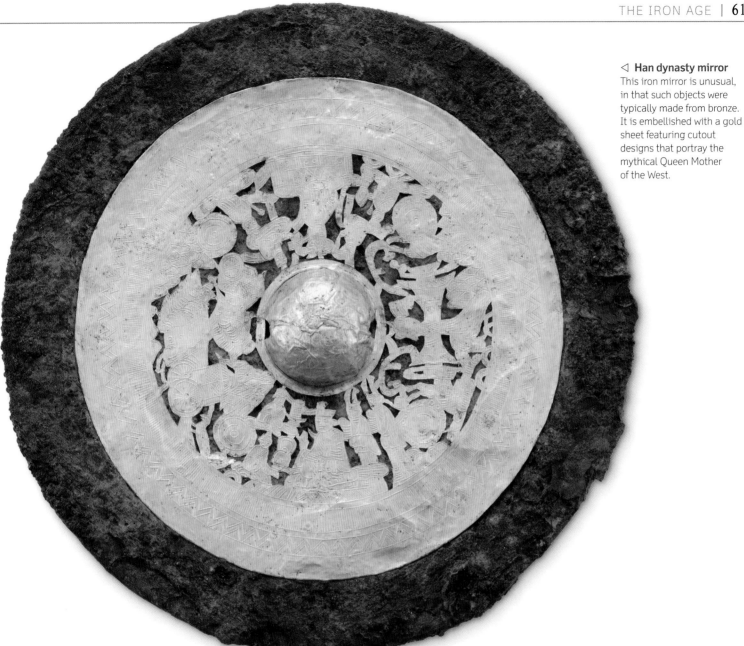

◁ **Han dynasty mirror**
This iron mirror is unusual, in that such objects were typically made from bronze. It is embellished with a gold sheet featuring cutout designs that portray the mythical Queen Mother of the West.

noted there were 4,000 people employed in the foundry where it was produced. Indeed, iron was so valuable that, according to an inscription on a *ding* vessel that was made in the state of Jin in 513 BCE, it was collected as a form of military tax.

At this time, iron was rarely used to make farming implements: cheaper, easily available materials such as stone, bone, shell, and wood were preferred. But over time, as the costs of production fell, cast-iron tools, including plowshares, sickles, and hoes (as well as everyday items such as axes, knives, hammers, anvils, and coins), were made. Iron plows, capable of cutting through heavy soils, brought new areas of land into cultivation, allowing states to support ever larger armies. After the Warring States period, the Qin dynasty (221–206 BCE) promoted the iron industry.

As the Qin First Emperor embarked on his efforts to unify China (see pp. 78–81), he appointed officials in iron-producing areas to support the industry and to gather income from its activities.

By the early Han dynasty (206 BCE–220 CE), new smelting technologies, such as waterwheel-powered bellows that blew air into furnaces, made iron production cheaper and created greater demand for new products for military and industrial uses. For example, leather armor was largely supplanted by chain mail; and iron drill bits are known to have been used by Han miners to extract valuable brine from deep wells. Under the Han dynasty, iron production reached a scale and sophistication that was not achieved in the West until the 18th century.

△ **Metal currency**
By the Qin dynasty, coins such as this Ban Liang were being struck from iron and bronze.

Confucianism

A history of the philosophy of Confucius

The Chinese sage Kongzi (551–479 BCE), known to Westerners as Confucius, was one of the most influential teachers in history. He advocated social order and a humane morality at a time of conflict and widespread misrule. The teachings of Confucius became the foundations of a philosophy that would endure throughout the rest of Chinese history.

Zhou scholar

Confucius was born in 551 BCE in Lu, a state in northeast China ruled by the Duke of Lu, a feudal lord who officially owed allegiance to the Zhou kingdom. Confucius's family belonged to the lowest rank of nobility. His father, Kong He, a military officer, died when he was three years old, so he was brought up by his mother, Yan Zhengzai. Confucius lived at a time in which families competed for power, when greed and

corruption held sway, and armed conflict was common. In response to this imperfect world, he developed a desire to instill virtue into society. He became a teacher and opened a school, taking on pupils regardless of their status or wealth, paying attention only to their intellectual and moral qualities. He attracted young people from far and wide and is believed to have taught more than 3,000 students.

Confucius believed that good government depended on the strong central authority of a wise ruler inspired by humane principles. Around the age of 50, he achieved public office, rising to be minister of justice and a senior adviser to the Duke of Lu. Although he had some success in improving the running of the state, his policies were opposed by the great families, determined to uphold their independent power. Frustrated in Lu, Confucius went into self-imposed

△ **Confucius**
Confucius's own humble upbringing could explain his advocacy for education to be accessible to anyone who wished to learn—regardless of their social or economic status. He encouraged continuous self-improvement and interaction with the outside world.

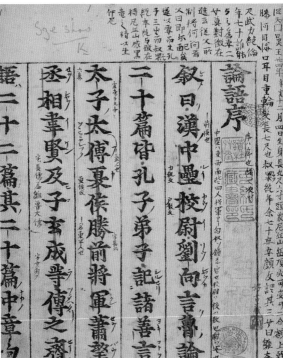

△ **The Analects**
Confucius and his teachings live on through the Analects (Lunyu), a collection of his thoughts and teachings recorded by his students. Grouped into themes, the now-sacred scriptures allow the reader to enter a philosophical "conversation" with Confucius. They became the foundation of Chinese education.

△ **Confucian disciples**
Confucius devoted his life to educating others in line with his moral beliefs. According to the historian Sima Qian, he had 72 followers (known as his disciples) who were able to master his teachings. Many of these followers are mentioned in the Analects.

"Learning without reflection is a waste; reflecting without learning is dangerous."

CONFUCIUS, *ANALECTS*, 450–350 BCE

exile in 497 BCE, spending 13 years wandering northern China with a band of dedicated followers. He traveled from state to state, trying in vain to find a ruler who would adopt his principles of government.

Around 483 BCE, Confucius returned to Lu and settled to the life of a teacher and scholar, editing and commenting on the classic texts. He had 72 pupils who mastered his philosophies sufficiently to be known as his disciples. After he died, these disciples preserved and elaborated his teachings for future generations.

Tradition and respect

Based on the principles of harmony, tolerance, and excellence, Confucianism offers guidelines for creating successful individuals, families, and societies. Confucius wanted people to love and respect others (especially elders and superiors), to do good, and to honor tradition. He recommended two ways of achieving these things—the principles of *ren* (humane behavior) and li (manners, ceremony, and ritual). The *Analects*—sayings and teachings of Confucius collected by his pupils—established a philosophy of morality in which the superior man, or *junzi* (literally "gentleman"), devotes himself to the acquisition of *ren* for its own sake—he learns for the sake of learning and is good for the sake of goodness. Confucius believed that by honoring ties of loyalty, ritual, and tradition, society would be bound together in a positive way. By revering the ancestors and performing the correct rites in their honor, humans could maintain a state of harmony between this world and Heaven. At the family level, such rites were an echo of the sacrifices that emperors made to their ancestors to confirm the Mandate of Heaven.

△ **European interest**
This engraving presents a European vision of Confucius. His philosophies first reached Europe in the 16th century, carried by Jesuit missionaries returning from China. Confucianism went on to have a greater influence and readership in Europe throughout the 17th century.

△ **Influence across Asia**
This 19th-century Japanese print shows Confucius in conversation with a boy. Confucianism became embedded in the practices of many East Asian countries. The Korean Joseon dynasty (1392–1910) was by far the most influenced by Confucian belief, both in terms of court politics and cultural values.

△ **Confucian temple, Nanjing**
Although it is not an organized religion, Confucianism has a strong influence on the spirituality and way of life of people throughout East Asia. To this day, adherents follow its ethos of working as part of a harmonious community rather than as individuals.

The Hundred Schools of Thought
The growth of Chinese philosophy

The deeply troubled times of the Warring States period sparked an upsurge in philosophical inquiry, making the era a crucible for the exchange of new and vibrant ideas on morality and government.

Amid the uncertainties of the later Zhou period (see pp. 56–59), the rulers of China's states struggled to hold on to power when faced with external aggression and internal unrest. These tensions sparked a remarkable outburst of intellectual and philosophical inquiry over three centuries that is referred to as the Hundred Schools of Thought. This name reflects the Confucians, Daoists, Mohists, Legalists, and numerous other philosophies and schools of thought that flourished during this period and their attempts to develop and theorize a more effective social and political order. The innovators came mostly from the *shi* (scholar-gentleman) class of the lesser nobility, the cleverest of whom attracted disciples and traveled from court to court to promote their ideas.

The development of philosophical thought
Confucius himself was the model for these wandering *shi* scholars, and the *Analects* (see pp. 64–65)—pieced together by his followers after his death—became a key document. The Confucian message evolved hugely in the 4th and 3rd centuries BCE through the works of Zisi, Confucius's grandson, and Mencius, who is sometimes known as the "second sage." Mencius stressed the essential goodness of human nature and the importance of nourishing qi—moral vitality—to fight the risk of corruption brought on by negative social or environmental factors. Politically, he taught rulers to concentrate on promoting their subjects' well-being. He argued that the surest way to retain power was to maintain the goodwill of the ruled.

◁ **Representing sacred stories**
Relief carvings from the Wu family funerary shrines (the Wu Liang shrine) in Jiaxiang, c. 151 CE, depict scenes from Confucian and Daoist tales.

Mencius's thinking was contradicted by a later, 3rd-century BCE Confucian philosopher, Xunzi, who saw human nature as at best neutral, if not actually evil. For him, education, moral training, and strict social rules were essential if people were to be successfully taught to live together in harmony.

The philosophy of Daoism (see pp. 114–115) was also spread around this time, by Zhuangzi, whose work bearing his own name was to find a lasting place among the masterpieces of Chinese literature. Another key school of thought was centered on the teachings

▽ **Essential reading**
This fragment from a Tang dynasty manuscript of the Confucian *Analects*—which was required reading in schools—was unearthed in 1967 at Turfan, Xinjiang.

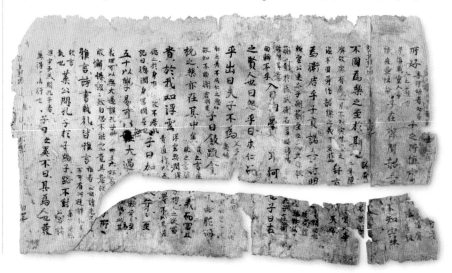

▷ Principles of existence
According to Daoist theory, all energy and matter is made up of *yin* and *yang*, the two complementary but opposing forces of the universe (see pp. 98–99). The circular, black and white *yin–yang* symbol is the central focus of this 17th- or 18th-century painting, which also includes symbols of long life and immortality— a tree, a deer, and a peach.

of Mozi (c. 470–391 BCE). Known as Mohism, this form of philosophy advocated universal love (*jian ai*) and the well-being of all classes as the basis of good government. Mozi was a bitter opponent of aggressive military action and extravagant rites, and his thought was proscribed by the First Emperor; his humanistic doctrines failed to survive the book burnings of the Qin ruler's reign (see pp. 78–81).

In marked contrast was the school that helped prepare the way for the First Emperor's triumph. This was the doctrine of Legalism, which had been developed by the scholar Shang Yang (c. 390–338 BCE) during the Warring States period. Legalists held a pessimistic view of human nature, insisting that people's natural inclinations and weaknesses could be held in check only by strict laws and savage penalties. Politically, Legalists favored a rigid authoritarianism, enforcing absolute obedience to the will of the ruler. A prosperous state needed a flourishing agricultural base but at the same time an invincible army that could keep the population under control and bring hostile neighbors to heel.

Changing times

The Legalist message was clearly conveyed when the Qin triumphed decisively over all the other warring states; nonetheless, its brutality also ensured that the Qin would be short-lived. In Han dynasty times, Legalism would cede the field to a state-sponsored version of Confucianism and to the ever-popular Daoist undercurrent. A significant survivor in this respect was the Daoist theory of *yin* and *yang*—the passive and active principles of existence—whose complementary interchange of forces would be used throughout much of the rest of Chinese history to provide a compelling explanation of the cycles of human life and of the universe at large.

> **"Nothing** is better for **nourishing the mind** than lessening **desire.**"
>
> MENCIUS, c. 300 BCE

Daoist Philosophy

A history of the *Daodejing*

The *Daodejing* (*Classic of the Way and Its Power*) is a poetic masterpiece that sets out the Daoist way of life, a philosophy focused on spontaneity and quietism. Amid the outpouring of philosophical debate inspired by the discord of the Warring States period (see pp. 68–69), one voice stood out as advocating a retreat from the world of statecraft and political action. The *Daodejing* put forward the idea that human influence and ambition disturb the natural order of the world. It advocates withdrawing into an inner life and favors spontaneity over planned action and direct experience over rational thought.

The *Daodejing* takes the form of a collection of aphorisms, or short poems, written by someone with a taste for paradox. The text is traditionally ascribed to the philosopher Laozi, also sometimes called Lao Dan, who is said to have lived in the 6th century BCE as a contemporary of Confucius. Scholars today, however, mostly hold that the work had more than one author and date it to the late 4th or early 3rd century BCE.

Man and myth

Evidence for Laozi's life comes primarily from Sima Qian's *Historical Record* (see pp. 106–107), written a couple of hundred years later. In the historian's telling, the "Old Master" or "Old Child" (the meaning of "Laozi") was born in what is now Henan province. He earned his living as a record keeper in the Zhou dynasty imperial household. According to Sima Qian, Laozi met Confucius one day and upbraided him for his pride and ambition. Eventually, weary of the corruption and political machinations at court, he left Zhou and headed for the western frontier riding a

△ **Miraculous birth**
According to ancient Chinese tradition, Laozi was born from the armpit of a virgin mother who carried him for 81 years. He later became the founder of Daoism. Some modern scholars believe Laozi to be a wholly legendary figure rather than even a partly historical one.

△ **Silk manuscript**
This section from a partially damaged 2nd-century BCE silk book was unearthed from Mawangdui in Changsha, Hunan. It was one of several Chinese philosophical and medical works discovered at the archaeological site in 1973 and is said to be the earliest complete hand-copied version of the *Daodejing*.

△ **Supreme purity**
Daoism's highest gods are said to be the Three Pure Ones: Yuanshi Tianzun (the Jade Pure One), Daode Tianzun (the Grand Pure One), and Liangboa Tianzun (the Supreme Pure One), shown here. They were the personification of spirit (*shen*), energy (*qi*), and essence (*jing*).

"The **Master's power** is like this. He lets all things **come and go effortlessly...."**

DAODEJING, 4TH–3RD CENTURY BCE

water buffalo. An official at the frontier, seeing that Laozi was leaving, asked him to put his thoughts into writing. The account ends: "So Laozi wrote a book in two parts, explaining the Way and its Power in something over 5,000 words. Then he went away. No one knows where he died."

Following the way of nature

The *Daodejing* recognizes no god in the mold of the Abrahamic religions (though Daoists do have gods, many borrowed from other cultures). Instead it offers up the *dao*, the "way of nature" or life force, which exceeds human comprehension but to which people must nonetheless seek to attune their lives. Doing so involves going with the grain of the physical world rather than seeking to impose a pattern upon it. A key concept is *ziran* (self-so), or more colloquially "going

with the flow." In political terms, the book promotes small government, suggesting that the best ruler is one not seen to be governing at all. Unusually, the work removes humankind from the center of the cosmos, seeing people as only one manifestation of the *dao*, the wellspring of all being, and not even the most important one.

In China, the mystical sense of a larger sphere of existence expounded in the *Daodejing* acted as a counterbalance to the rationalism of the Confucian world view, with its emphasis on social interaction and moral obligation. Together with another key text, the *Zhuangzi*—attributed to the 4th-century BCE philosopher of the same name—it provided the philosophical basis for later Daoism and as such has had a profound influence on the course of Chinese culture over the past 2,000 years.

△ Zhuangzi's butterfly dream
A 16th-century ink painting on silk illustrates a famous story in the *Zhuangzi*. In it, Zhuangzi is confused about whether he has dreamed he is a man transformed into a butterfly, or vice versa. The tale points to Daoist ideas about the nature of reality and illusion.

△ The Daoist pantheon
This detail from an anonymous 17th-century, Ming dynasty handscroll depicts the inauguration of a local god into the Daoist pantheon. The section here shows haloed deities, attendants, and officials involved in the ceremonial procession. The dragons on the scroll's border are chasing flaming pearls.

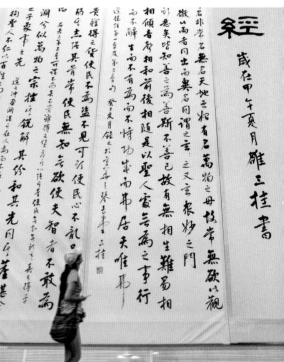

△ Modern-day representation
A visitor contemplates the world's largest work of calligraphy, entitled *The Daodejing*, by Chinese calligrapher Luo Sangui, during the Grand Art Exhibition in Nanjing in 2014. There has been a resurgence of interest in Daoism in China in recent decades.

The Warring States

Seven states struggle for supremacy

During the second part of the Eastern Zhou era, from around 475 to 221 BCE, China's regional states fought among themselves. Eventually, just seven major states would survive, with Qin rising to be the most powerful.

The *Strategies of the Warring States* (Zhan Guo Ce) is a record of political events in China from the 5th to the 3rd century BCE. Compiled two centuries afterward, it gave its name to a period in Chinese history that lasted from around 475 BCE to 211 BCE. During this time, the kings of the Eastern Zhou ruled over China in name only—the real power was held by feuding states that fought one other in a quest for supremacy.

By the end of the Spring and Autumn period around 475 BCE (see pp. 56–57), the state of Jin had become one of the most powerful in China. Its decline and partition set the stage for the Warring States period. Jin's ruling dukes gradually lost influence as the state's nobles grew in power.

By the end of the 5th century BCE, the three most powerful families had partitioned Jin among themselves, wiping it from the map and establishing three new states—Han, Zhao, and Wei. These states became bitter rivals, and the conflict between them spread throughout the rest of China.

Militant states

Over time, weaker states were conquered or forced to become vassals to their powerful neighbors, and by 300 BCE, only seven major states remained: Qi, Chu, Yan, Han, Zhao, Wei, and Qin. Sometimes known as the "ten-thousand chariot" states (named for the sizes of the forces they could muster) or *qixiong* ("Seven Strong Men"), they dominated China and, from the middle of the 4th century BCE, the rulers of these states began to claim royal status and adopt

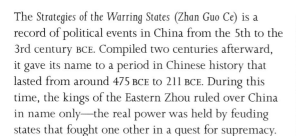

◁ **Weapon of war**
This bronze short sword (3rd century BCE) is typical of swords from the Warring States period. It has two ridges on the handle and is decorated with silvery spots on the blade.

> **BURIAL RITES IN THE WARRING STATES**
>
> By the Shang era, burial mounds (*tudunmu*) were more common in the Lower Yangzi, while the use of pits for burial prevailed in the Central Plains. In *tudunmu*, bodies of the deceased and burial goods were placed on stone mounds that were then covered with earth. This became commonplace in Chu by the Warring States period. In other states, pit burials remained widespread, although increasingly they were topped with a high mound of earth. The more esteemed the person being buried, the larger was their mound, symbolizing their status.

the title of king (*wang*), in defiance of the Eastern Zhou. The seven great states fought against each other in an ever-shifting shifting pattern of alliances: sometimes these coalitions were "vertical" (meaning that states from the north were allied with states from the south), and sometimes "horizontal" (meaning that states from the west formed alliances with states from the east).

Rise of mass armies

The states conscripted people into large standing armies to wage their wars. They were made up mainly of infantry, although cavalry became more

△ **Tomb treasures**
A slender, antlered bronze crane was buried near Duke Yi of Zeng at Suizhou. It was one of some 15,000 objects unearthed from the 5th-century BCE tomb.

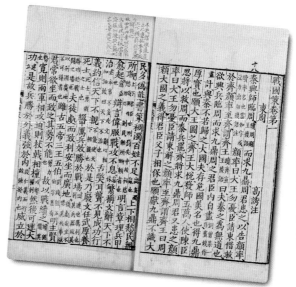

◁ **The *Zhan Guo Ce***
These pages are taken from an 1869 edition of the *Strategies of the Warring States* (*Zhan Guo Ce*), a text that chronicles military and ideological strategies as well as political events and opinions throughout the Warring States period.

▷ **Conference of states**
This Qing dynasty painting shows a conference of six Chinese states during the Warring States era, a period characterized by conflict and the struggle for power.

important as the use of the war chariot declined. Iron swords and crossbows—which could be produced very quickly and in large quantities—gradually came to replace bronze weapons, making warfare considerably more deadly than it had been in previous eras. New defensive fortifications were built throughout the land and the scale of battle increased dramatically—the states sent out armies of at least 100,000 men, compared to the more usual 10,000 during the Western Zhou dynasty.

War and taxation
Militarization was financed by means of taxes, which were drawn primarily from agricultural land. Private landowners were expected to give a share of their crops to the state as a form of taxation, which meant that the most powerful and successful states were always those that had an efficient administration, the most productive lands, and the most advanced agricultural practices.

The Legalist transformation
Philosophy flourished during the Warring States period as scholars sought to find the best way out of chaos and disorder. One of the most successful schools of philosophy was Legalism (see pp. 64–65), which focused on identifying efficient and practical ways of strengthening the state.

The Legalist philosophers argued that government should be run through a centralized meritocratic bureaucracy that would keep order by means of strong and consistent enforcement of the law. Among the most influential of the Legalist thinkers was the 4th-century BCE scholar Shang Yang, whose policies—particularly the expansion of the army by giving land to peasants who enlisted—were instrumental in transforming the western state of Qin into China's greatest power.

Shang Yang was executed after insulting the Qin aristocracy and attempting to create his own territory, but his reforms ensured Qin dominance by the 3rd century BCE. The dynasty eventually grew strong enough to defeat all its rivals and establish imperial rule in China (see pp. 78–81), ending the Warring States period.

"If the **people are stronger** than the government, the **state is weak**; if the **government is stronger** than the people, the **army is strong**."

LEGALIST SCHOLAR SHANG YANG, *THE BOOK OF LORD SHANG*, 3RD CENTURY BCE

Sacred mountain

In ancient China, mountains were seen as the closest points on Earth to the realm of the gods and held immense sacred power; in Daoist belief, they are where immortals reside. The mountain shown here—Mount Hua in Shaanxi province—is one of China's Five Great Mountains. According to myth, they were formed from different parts of the body of Pangu, the mythical first being. Their ritual significance stemmed from a belief that they linked Heaven and Earth: the emperor, who held the Mandate of Heaven (see p.49), was the intermediary between the two. A key step in proving his mandate was to climb the peaks to perform sacred rituals that strengthened the bond between Heaven and Earth.

The Art of War

A history of Sunzi's famous work

The Art of War, a treatise on military strategy written more than two millennia ago, is still consulted to this day—not just by scholars and historians but also by army commanders, guerrilla leaders, businesspeople, lawyers, and even sports players. According to tradition, the author of *The Art of War* was Sunzi, a contemporary of Confucius, born late in the Spring and Autumn period (see pp. 56–59). He won employment with Helu, king of the state of Wu, rising in royal favor to become a commander at the Battle of Boju in 506 BCE, a decisive victory over neighboring Chu. This practical experience of generalship fed through into the work for which Sunzi is remembered.

The traditional account of Sunzi's life, drawn from the *Spring and Autumn Annals* (see pp. 54–55) and Sima Qian's *Historical Record* (see pp. 106–107), has been challenged by modern scholars, who have noted that earlier accounts of Boju make no mention of Sunzi's name and have pointed to perceived anachronisms in the text; for example, the author of the treatise mentions crossbows, which were not widely used in warfare until a century after Boju. However, a descendant of Sunzi, Sun Bin, also wrote on military strategy, so it is possible that the earlier work, kept in the family for generations, was added to or amended in the Warring States period (see pp. 68–69).

Sunzi's theories

What is certain is that the work takes a highly original approach to its subject. While direct conflict remains at its center, it also focuses on alternatives to battle, including diplomacy, alliances, and, when necessary, temporary submission in the face of a more powerful foe. It emphasizes the importance of deceit to mislead

△ **Sunzi**
According to traditional histories, Sunzi was born in the state of either Qi or Wu. He was employed by Helu, king of the state of Wu, only after passing a test in which he was tasked with training Helu's concubines as soldiers—a feat Sunzi accomplished using logic and punishment.

△ **Preserved on bamboo**
The Art of War was required reading for officers of China's imperial army. Before the widespread use of paper, the text was inked on to bamboo slips (see pp. 108–109), which were bound into a book, as shown in this modern reproduction. The earliest surviving copy of the work dates to around 140 BCE.

△ **Zhang Liang**
One of China's Seven Military Classics, *Three Strategies of Huang Shigong* is associated with the Han dynasty statesman Zhang Liang (pictured in this Japanese woodcut). According to tradition, Zhang Liang was presented with the book by an old sage named Huang Shigong.

"Know the **enemy**, know **yourself**; your **victory** will **never be endangered**."

SUNZI, *THE ART OF WAR*, 5TH CENTURY BCE

the enemy and devotes a whole chapter to the use of spies. Discipline is also crucial. Sunzi recounts approvingly the story of a Chu officer who, before a battle, succeeded on his own initiative in taking the heads of a couple of Qin opponents, only to be beheaded himself at the behest of his general for acting without orders. An important element in Sunzi's vision is his concept of the ideal military commander, who should be "serene and inscrutable," in keeping with Daoist notions of emotional noninvolvement (see pp. 66–67).

Lasting influence

The work has had an enduring influence, both in China and abroad. Qin Shi Huangdi, the First Emperor, admired it; and the Three Kingdoms warlord Cao Cao wrote the earliest known commentary on the text.

In 1080, during the Song dynasty, it became the centerpiece of the Seven Military Classics, a collection of ancient texts that was required reading for candidates in the examinations for would-be army officers. Other texts included the Warring States era's *Wei Liaozi*, named for its author, and Zhang Liang's *Three Strategies of Huang Shigong*, from the Han period.

In recent times, both Chinese leader Mao Zedong and the Vietnamese independence leader Ho Chi Minh held it in high regard, while in the West it still features on the US Marine Corps Professional Reading Program list. Its influence is not limited to military circles. Popular works have adapted its precepts to the fields of business and law, and sportspeople too have been affected—Brazilian soccer coach Luiz Felipe Scolari is said to have used *The Art of War* in training the squad that won the 2002 FIFA World Cup.

△ **Interpreting *The Art of War***
Cao Cao (pictured in this Japanese print) was a Han general who gained control over much of northern China in the turbulent years before the collapse of the Han dynasty. He was a keen student of *The Art of War* and compiled extensive commentaries on Sunzi's famous text.

△ **Napoleon Bonaparte**
The Art of War made its way to Europe after its translation into French by Jesuit missionaries in Qing China. Some of the military strategies employed by the great French leader Napoleon Bonaparte are similar to those described in the book, suggesting that he may have been aware of Sunzi's writings.

△ **Sunzi in the modern era**
The Art of War has influenced many politicians and generals in the last century. General Douglas MacArthur (pictured), the architect of some of the most famous US campaigns in World War II, stated that he always kept a copy of the book on his desk.

◁ **Seated Buddha**
This polychrome statue
of the Buddha was made
under the Northern Wei
dynasty, which ruled northern
China from 386 to 534 CE.
The Northern Wei were great
patrons of Buddhism.

3

China United
and Divided

221 BCE to 581 CE

Introduction

In the eight centuries from 221 BCE to 581 CE, China grew into a great empire. Much of the groundwork for its future was laid down by Qin Shi Huangdi, the First Emperor of Qin. The Han historian Sima Qian (see pp. 106–107) would later describe the emperor as a tyrant: "if the King of Qin should ever get his way with the world, then the whole world will end up his prisoner."

From Qin to Han

After the First Emperor subdued the last of the Warring States (see pp. 68–69), he and his minister Li Si took control of China, ruling through the strict philosophy of Legalism. Their uncompromising, and often punitive, approach produced results quickly: the First Emperor's reign included the subjugation of the feudal aristocracy, the launch of monumental canal- and road-building projects, and the creation of the first Great Wall, which was erected to shield China from the nomadic peoples to the north. The First Emperor also imposed a standardized form of the language across the entire nation, so that to this day all Chinese can understand each other's written communications.

The First Emperor ruled for just 11 years. When he died in 210 BCE, the brutality of the system he had created helped ensure that his dynasty, the Qin, did not long survive him. Infighting among his heirs quickly broadened into civil war. The victor was a commoner, Liu Bang, who went on to establish the Han dynasty, which would govern the nation (with one interruption) for the next four centuries. Its first period of rule, from 206 CE to 9 CE, is now known as the Western Han dynasty.

The Han years would see a benign form of Confucianism replace the Legalism of the First Emperor's reign as the state's governing ideology. The emphasis was now on correct behavior and respect for authority rather than fear of draconian punishment. Yet in other respects, the dynasty's rulers maintained the foundations that their Qin predecessor had put in place, while also extending their dominions. Under Emperor Wu, whose long reign stretched from 140–87 BCE, China extended the Great Wall westward to protect itself from the Xiongnu (the Mongol empire of the time) and consolidate its frontiers. The Han ruled over a larger empire than their Qin predecessors—they enlarged

221 BCE The First Emperor, unifies China under his Qin dynasty

209 BCE Civil war breaks out after the First Emperor's death

202 BCE Liu Bang establishes the Han dynasty, taking the imperial name Gaozu

138 BCE Zhang Qian journeys west, opening a way for the future Silk Road

140 BCE Wu becomes emperor, reigning for the next 53 years

23 CE Han rule is restored following Wang Mang's overthrow

9 CE Regent Wang Mang takes power in his own name, founding the short-lived Xin dynasty

their territories northward into what is now Korea and south to Vietnam. A groundbreaking journey of exploration, setting out in 138 BCE, also made contact with Central Asia, paving the way for the Silk Road that would one day open a lucrative path from China to the West.

The empire splits

Dynastic strife among the ruling classes caused a temporary break in Han rule in the year 9 CE, when a regent acting for a child emperor took power in his own name to declare the short-lived Xin dynasty. This perished with its founder 14 years later, and the Han (now known as the Eastern or Later Han) was restored for a further two centuries. In this period, Chinese power initially revived, only to finally collapse amid an upsurge of feudal power and palace intrigue.

Eventually, the unified empire that had been created by the First Emperor of Qin split apart. For the next 60 years, three states struggled for dominance. This time, which is known as the Three Kingdoms period, ended in 280 CE when Sima Yan briefly reunited the realm under his Jin dynasty. Yet this regime, too, barely survived its founder, and its demise left

China split for centuries along a north–south divide. The north fell under the control of foreign rulers, ushering in an age known to classical Chinese historians as the Sixteen Kingdoms of the Five Barbarian Peoples.

Meanwhile, China south of the Yangzi River became the base of a regime that clung tightly to tradition, stressing continuity with the past even in its name—the Eastern Jin. However, it too succumbed, ushering in a time of short-lived dynasties (known as the Six Dynasties period) set up by a series of victorious generals or governors. This time of division came to an end when north and south were finally reunited by another warlord late in the 6th century, paving the way for a period of renewed imperial greatness under the Sui and then Tang dynasties.

China emerged from its time of troubles restored but altered. The focus of the nation had shifted southward, from the wheat-growing lands of the north to the rice paddies below the Yangzi divide. Foreign influences had also been absorbed into the culture, notably in the form of the Buddhist religion. The imperial tradition, however, survived, moving from the ruins of one great age into the dawn of another.

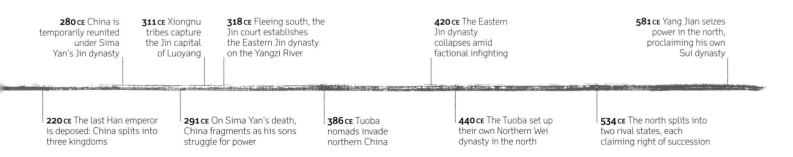

280 CE China is temporarily reunited under Sima Yan's Jin dynasty

311 CE Xiongnu tribes capture the Jin capital of Luoyang

318 CE Fleeing south, the Jin court establishes the Eastern Jin dynasty on the Yangzi River

420 CE The Eastern Jin dynasty collapses amid factional infighting

581 CE Yang Jian seizes power in the north, proclaiming his own Sui dynasty

220 CE The last Han emperor is deposed: China splits into three kingdoms

291 CE On Sima Yan's death, China fragments as his sons struggle for power

386 CE Tuoba nomads invade northern China

440 CE The Tuoba set up their own Northern Wei dynasty in the north

534 CE The north splits into two rival states, each claiming right of succession

The Qin Dynasty

The First Emperor unites China

The Qin dynasty lasted just 15 years, yet it altered the course of Chinese history forever. Its creator, the First Emperor, laid the foundations of the centralized bureaucratic state that has survived into modern times.

The state of Qin had been a vassal of the Zhou dynasty since the 9th century BCE. Located at the northwest edge of Chinese civilization in Gansu province, its primary role had been to keep the nomadic barbarians beyond its borders in check. Yet this frontier province emerged as a unifying power from the chaos of the Warring States period (see pp. 68–69), when seven kingdoms fought for supremacy in east-central China.

The Qin were favored by geography, protected by their relative isolation and by the mountains on their borders, and had a reputation for ruthlessness in battle and skill with the crossbow and chariot. However, the underpinnings of their ascent lay as much in strict governance as in military efficiency. From the 4th century BCE, the Qin governed according to the philosophy of Legalism (see pp. 64–65), which argues that people are motivated primarily by self-interest, so human actions must be highly regulated by a totalitarian state. In line with the Legalist view that put state before family, anyone held to be working against the common good could expect to be severely punished. In extreme cases, offenders suffered castration, mutilation, or death in a variety of painful forms, which included being cut in two or torn apart by horse-drawn chariots.

◁ **Qin records**
This rubbing is taken from a Qin dynasty stele in Shandong province that commemorates the achievements of the First Emperor.

Enemies vanquished

The disciplined Qin waged successful campaigns against the other Warring States, defeating the Chu—the single greatest power in China at the time, with more than a million men—in 316 BCE. According to Wu Qi, author of the classic military text the *Wuzi*, Qin soldiers were brave and high in morale, and the Qin's military decrees were strict and impartial, spelling out the rewards and punishments for meritorious or disruptive actions, so establishing a direct and clear chain of command.

The conquest and subjugation of the other states continued when Ying Zheng came to the Qin throne in 247 BCE at the age of 13. Aided in his youth by his regent, Lü Buwei, and later by his chancellor Li Si, he saw the Qin victorious over, respectively, its Han, Zhao, Yan, and Wei rivals. When the troops of Qi, the last remaining independent state, surrendered without resistance in 221 BCE, Zheng found himself ruler of a unified nation. He styled himself Qin Shi Huangdi ("First Emperor of Qin"), introducing the title Huangdi ("August Lord") that would be used by China's rulers for the next two millennia.

A new nation

The political unification of China proved to be just the first step in a hugely ambitious program of nation building undertaken by the First Emperor and Li Si. Installed in absolute power, the two set about imposing unity on the newly enlarged realm. The first step was to do away with the existing power structures of the conquered states. To achieve this, they summoned all the leading families to the imperial capital at Xianyang, where they could be kept under close watch; Han historians would put the number summoned at 120,000. Meanwhile, the lands these families had controlled were handed over to state appointees answering directly to the emperor. The territories of the former Warring States were combined with that of the Qin and split into 36

◁ **Body armor**
This ceremonial armor suit from the First Emperor's tomb is comprised of rows of scales that articulate at the shoulders to allow for movement.

▽ **Tomb finds**
Excavations of the First Emperor's tomb (see pp. 82–83) revealed limestone replicas of Qin armor and helmets, which would have been made of iron.

separate prefectures, each in turn subdivided into counties, townships, and subdistricts. Each unit was given a governor, inspector, and army commander reporting back to the emperor to manage its affairs.

Building infrastructure

The empire's reforms extended beyond matters of government and administration to affect the structure of society as a whole. The First Emperor abolished feudalism and gave peasants the right to own their own land. However, the peasants were also made liable for service to the emperor and were drafted into a vast imperial building program. This saw the construction of a network of roads and canals, huge new palace complexes, and the Great Wall (see pp. 84–85). According to one estimate, China's road-building project exceeded that of the Roman Empire, with around 4,300 miles (6,800 km) of thoroughfares created in comparison with Rome's 3,700 miles (6,000 km). To make the empire's new roads more navigable, the administration established a fixed gauge for vehicle axles, ensuring that wheeled vehicles could move down muddy roads along a single set of tamped-down ruts. »

The name "China" is thought to be derived from the Qin (or Ch'in) dynasty.

△ **The purge of old ideas**
This 18th-century painting shows the First Emperor (top)
ordering the burning of books and the execution of scholars.
The clothing worn by the figures reflects Qing style.

Setting the standards

Among the most profound and enduring of the emperor's reforms were those that directly impinged on the everyday lives of his subjects. Separate currencies were abolished, and the economy was standardized by the introduction of a single coin, the Qin Ban Liang (a coin with a square hole in the middle), which became the accepted coinage of the empire. Uniform weights and measures were introduced, facilitating trade. One innovation that the emperor pioneered was a standard vessel for measuring grain and wine, defined not only by size and shape but also by pitch—when struck, only vessels of the proper dimensions gave off the correct note.

Perhaps the most significant of all the empire's new measures was the enforced adoption of Qin written characters across the entire kingdom, thereby introducing a single Chinese script, which has survived as the basis of the written language to this day. Chancellor Li Si ordered a wordbook to be drawn up that contained around 3,300 characters for common use by all the emperor's subjects. Known as "small seal," the script would be much altered over the years in order to adapt it to innovations—such as the use of the writing brush with the introduction of paper under the Han dynasty and the spread of printing in the latter half of the 1st millennium CE. The adoption of a common written language meant that Chinese people from across the kingdom, who spoke different dialects or languages, could all communicate through the written word—a measure that did much to cement a heterogenous nation.

Rule with an iron fist

The First Emperor's methods for enforcing the reforms across China were brutal and aroused considerable hostility in some quarters. He became the target of several assassination attempts, leading him to become preoccupied with death and the search for immortality (see box, left). He tolerated no criticism of his policies and supposedly burned texts hostile to the Legalist creed promoted by Li Si. According to historian Sima Qian (see pp. 106–107), only works on practical subjects such as agriculture and medicine were spared. Chroniclers in the years after the Qin's fall would portray the emperor as a brutal tyrant, spreading the story—which has since been disputed—that he had 460 Confucian scholars buried alive because of their opposition.

Death and decline

The First Emperor died in 210 BCE, and the dynasty that he had hoped would last for 10,000 generations rapidly came to an end. Li Si and the emperor's chief eunuch plotted the death of the heir to the throne, hoping to rule through a more pliant second son. But the two conspirators soon quarreled, and the eunuch Zhao Gao engineered Li Si's arrest and execution. Meanwhile, revolts against the new ruler broke out among a people who were exhausted by the First Emperor's backbreaking public-work programs. Zhao himself died soon after, when another ruler whom he placed on the throne turned against him and had him killed. Within four years of the First Emperor's death, his capital of Xianyang had been sacked and his final successor was dead. Even so, his legacy survived under the ensuing Han regime, and the imperial tradition he had started would continue for more than 2,000 years.

△ **Ban Liang coin**
This bronze coin was struck in the 3rd century BCE as part of the standardization of Qin trade. Before the Qin dynasty, a variety of coins were used across China.

▽ **Bronze chariot**
This half-size chariot was excavated from the First Emperor's burial site. It was intended to be used by the emperor for tours of his domain in the afterlife.

The Tomb of the First Emperor

A hidden burial site guarded by a terracotta army

Work on the tomb of Qin Shi Huang began soon after he came to the throne of Qin at the age of just 13, but the project escalated after 221 BCE, when he declared himself First Emperor. Obsessed by immortality (see p. 81), he spared no expense in providing for his afterlife and conscripted thousands of laborers to build a suitable resting place. The result was a huge complex covering 38 sq. miles (98 sq. km), of which his mausoleum—located within a mound 165 ft (50 m) high—is just a small part.

Excavation of the Terracotta Army

The scale of the project became clear in 1974, when farmworkers near Xi'an, Shaanxi province, accidentally unearthed fragments of statues. Subsequent archaeological excavations revealed a rectangular pit, 750 ft (230 m) long by 195 ft (60 m) wide, containing the broken pieces

◁ **Kneeling archer**
One pit at the burial site contained a battle formation of kneeling archers surrounded by ranks of standing archers.

of thousands of life-size clay figures. Once they were painstakingly reconstructed, the figures found in this and other smaller pits at the site constituted an army of some 8,000 foot soldiers, 130 chariots, and 150 horses, which guarded one side of the tomb complex. Each terracotta figurine was made of molded parts, hand-finished so that no two were exactly alike. The heads, for instance, consist of front and rear sections formed in any one of at least eight molds. Other molds were pressed into the clay to create hair, and pointed tools were used to shape individual portraits.

The mausoleum

Archaeologists have not yet excavated the emperor's mausoleum but have delayed work until they can be sure not to cause unnecessary damage. The only existing account of its contents is found in the *Historical Records* (*Shiji*), compiled by the great historian Sima Qian (see pp. 106–107). He describes the tomb as "filled with models of palaces, pavilions and offices, as well as fine vessels, precious stones, and rarities." Some reports also suggest that the tomb's builders booby-trapped it with loaded crossbows. However, they failed to protect the tomb. Two or three years after the emperor's death in 210 BCE, rebel soldiers invaded the necropolis, subjecting it to 30 days of plundering. The site was then abandoned, awaiting its modern rediscovery.

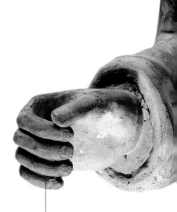

Once held real weapons, long since lost to looters

▷ **Clay figures**
An officer (right) of the Terracotta Army stands guard next to a general (far right) wearing chest armor.

Prefabricated ears, noses, lips, and eyebrows fixed to faces with a thin paste of clay and water

Originally painted, but lost color over time

The Great Wall

A history of the defensive bulwark

China had a tradition of defensive walls long before the first Great Wall along the northern border was constructed. From the very earliest times, towns had been enclosed within earthen fortifications—the same Chinese character denoted both "city" and "wall." As the land broke up into competing polities in the late Spring and Autumn period, individual states built defensive walls along their borders. The earliest surviving example, the Great Wall of Qi, was started in 685 BCE and stretched for some 373 miles (600 km).

Northern states also put up frontier defenses to protect their lands from the nomadic raiders across their borders. The threat from the north increased with the growing power of the Xiongnu people. In 215 BCE, the First Emperor dispatched his general Meng Tian with a huge force to drive the raiders northward, subsequently settling 30,000 families in the newly conquered lands. Once victory had been secured, Meng Tian began to defend the frontier by linking the various existing fortifications into a single bulwark stretching from what is now Gansu province to the Yellow Sea.

Labor and resources

There are no written records of the construction of Meng Tian's wall, but it would have involved a huge labor force—possibly a million strong—made up of soldiers, convicts, and conscripted peasants from all parts of the nation. They used local resources, so the main building material on the plains was rammed earth, sometimes faced with brick, while in mountain regions stone was used. Towers were erected at intervals, both for defensive purposes and to aid communication, using smoke and fires. Estimates

△ **An ancient relic**
The Great Wall of the state of Qi, built during the late Spring and Autumn period, wound its way, west to east, from the Yellow River to the Bay of Bohai. The ancient wall passed through 19 counties of Shandong province, often by way of mountain peaks.

△ **Layered construction**
This section of the Han dynasty Great Wall is at Dunhuang in Gansu province. Although badly eroded, the original construction materials are clearly visible; instead of using stone and brick, the Han used layers of local sand, gravel, rose willow, and reeds, which gave the wall great strength and resilience.

△ **Buddhist inscriptions**
Juyongguan Pass, just outside Beijing, is one of the three most famous mountain passes of the Great Wall. Buddhist texts in six different languages and scripts adorn the interior walls of Cloud Platform gate at Juyongguan (built c. 1345); a detail of the script is shown here.

"I built walls and dug moats for over 10,000 li ... I broke the earth's veins on the way...."

MENG TIAN, 210 BCE

of the total length vary. Meng Tian himself claimed he had "built walls or dug moats for over 10,000 li," or more than 2,485 miles (4,000 km), but that figure would undoubtedly have also included the vast network of supplementary defenses and supply roads providing support for the work. Yet, remarkably, the task was completed in just seven years.

China and the outside world

Very little of Meng Tian's wall has survived, but its long-term historical significance is impossible to overestimate. The fortifications forced any hostile mounted nomads to concentrate their attacks in one location, at which point the defenders would use smoke or fire signals to summon reinforcements. Not all incursions could be prevented, but without the wall, China would have suffered far greater losses.

Later rulers extended the wall; as Han forces drove westward under Emperor Wu (see pp. 86–89), the wall was extended by 298 miles (480 km) to provide protection for the new conquests. Early in the 5th century CE, the Tuoba rulers of the Northern Wei undertook major works to the north of the original Qin line. And 100 years after that, Yang, the second ruler of the short-lived Sui dynasty (see pp. 134–135), sent more than a million men to rebuild and extend the fortifications.

The wall that tourists visit today dates mostly from the 15th and 16th centuries and runs to the south of Meng Tian's line. Yet the role it played for the Ming emperors who built it (see pp. 224–225) was similar to the function of the Qin wall—not simply to provide a barrier against northern raiders but to help define the extent of the Chinese homeland.

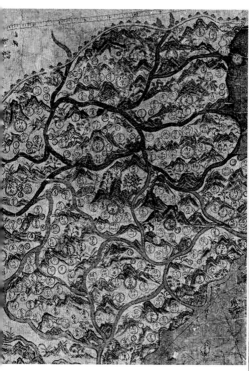

△ **Ming dynasty representation**
The Selden Map of China, shown here, is a navigational map produced during the Ming dynasty. The Ming built 5,500 miles (8,850 km) of the Great Wall, its most extensive section. The wall is visible running across the top of the map, defining China's northern frontier.

△ **Enduring attraction**
One of the world's most popular tourist sites, the Great Wall attracts more than 10 million visitors each year. In recent times, however, the government has taken steps to restrict numbers in the most popular sections owing to overcrowding and safety concerns. This view of the wall was taken around 1950.

△ **Old Dragon's Head**
The Great Wall meets the sea around 190 miles (305 km) east of Beijing at Laolongtou (Old Dragon's Head), so named because the wall here resembles a dragon drinking from the water. This section of the wall was built under the Ming dynasty in 1381.

The Western Han Dynasty

A golden age of stable government

For more than 400 years (206 BCE–220 CE), with one brief interruption, the Han dynasty ruled a realm larger than the Roman Empire. The first half of that period, known as the Western Han, was a time of immense achievement and prosperity.

As the Qin dynasty collapsed into chaos, rebel factions coalesced behind two leaders—Xiang Yu, an aristocrat of the Chu state (who was widely expected to become the next emperor), and Liu Bang, a commoner who promoted himself as a man of the people. The two were initially allied against the Qin armies but later turned against one another in a bitter struggle for power that culminated in the Battle of Gaixia in 202 BCE. Liu Bang's forces won the day, and Xiang Yu chose to die by suicide rather than be captured by the enemy. Following his victory at Gaixia, Liu Bang assumed the title of Gaozu, emperor of the Han dynasty.

The rise of the Han

Historians divide the lengthy Han era into two sections: the Former or Western Han (206 BCE–9 CE) and the Later or Eastern Han (25 CE–220 CE). These two periods were separated by the short-lived Xin dynasty (see pp. 110–111).

After ascending the throne, Emperor Gaozu founded his capital at Chang'an in Shaanxi province (see box, right), which rose to become a city of international importance thanks to its position at the eastern end of the Silk Road (see pp. 104–105). Much of Gaozu's energy was absorbed in dealing with foreign threats to the empire's borders, the most serious of which was

◁ **A rocky start**
Gaozu ruled China for seven years. Initially, he reacted against Qin centralization by awarding fiefdoms to his relatives, but the policy weakened his control over the empire.

posed by the Xiongnu—a confederation of nomadic peoples living to the north of Han China—who had recently unified under a new leader (or *chanyu*) named Modu. A gifted strategist, Modu took advantage of the chaos following the collapse of the Qin to expand Xiongnu control and made incursions into Han China. In 200 BCE, Gaozu sent an army to subjugate the Xiongnu, but the mission ended in failure. The Han were surrounded at Baideng, and the emperor narrowly escaped capture. After this defeat, Gaozu aimed to placate the nomads instead of trying to overcome them. He sent the *chanyu* a Han princess in marriage and thereafter paid the Xiongnu an annual tribute in silk, liquor, and rice. The Great Wall (see pp. 84–85) was accepted by both sides as the border. This arrangement lasted for around 60 years, during which the treaty was broken

▷ **Guardians of the soul**
Armed personnel and wild geese stand guard inside this three-tiered Han dynasty watchtower. Made from pottery with a green lead glaze, it was created to furnish a tomb.

"Where will I find **brave men to guard** the **four corners** of **my land**?"

FROM A SONG COMPOSED BY EMPEROR GAOZU, 195 BCE

△ **Strategic marriage**
Wang Zhaojun, one of the Four Great Beauties of ancient
China, attended the court of Emperor Yuan (see p.89). Like a
princess before her, she was gifted in marriage to the Xiongnu.

A NEW CAPITAL FOR THE HAN

After the destruction of the Qin capital of Xianyang, the
victorious Emperor Gaozu established a new city for his
administration at Chang'an, on the opposite bank of the
River Wei. Noble families and their retainers were ordered
to move there, and by the time of its official foundation in
195 BCE, it already had a population of 146,000. Chang'an
remained the center of imperial power throughout
Western Han times (206 BCE–9 CE) until it was replaced by
Luoyang at the start of the Eastern Han era (25 CE–220 CE).

and renewed several times, each time with an increase
in the tribute that was paid by the Han. However,
conflict with the Xiongnu continued on and off for
many years, both during the Han and after its fall.

A new era

After Gaozu's death in 195 BCE, Han power passed
through a series of weak rulers until the accession of
Wen in 180 BCE. He restored imperial authority and
set the scene for the ascent of the Han under his
grandson, Wu, who became emperor in 141 BCE.

Wu's rule—which lasted 54 years—was a time of
stability and prosperity, and he is generally considered
by scholars to have been one of China's greatest and
most politically astute leaders. Wu ignored the
traditions of court seniority, choosing instead to
surround himself with young, dynamic officials,
whose advice he heeded—though they were subject
to harsh punishment if they betrayed his trust.

Some historians have criticized Wu for over-
concentration of power at the center at the expense
of the provinces and for the tremendous harshness of
his rule; he had many of his adversaries executed and
made liberal use of brutal punishments, such as
castration (a fate that was suffered by the historian
Sima Qian; see pp. 106–107). Nonetheless, Wu
expanded the extent of the empire, established central
control and an effective bureaucracy, launched
military campaigns that crippled the Xiongnu and
shifted the regional balance of power in the Han's
favour, and embarked on a series of bold initiatives
that significantly altered the course of Chinese history.

Prior to Wu's reign, the empire that Gaozu inherited
from the Qin had an extreme, autocratic, and unduly
harsh government that was founded on the principles
of Legalism (see pp. 64–65, 78–81). In an attempt
to temper this authoritarianism, Wu gradually
introduced Confucian ideals, based on education,
learning, a sense of duty toward subjects, and loyalty
to the emperor. He encouraged scholarship and began
drawing Confucian scholars into government. These
enlightened policies were continued and expanded by
his Han successors as well as by later dynasties. »

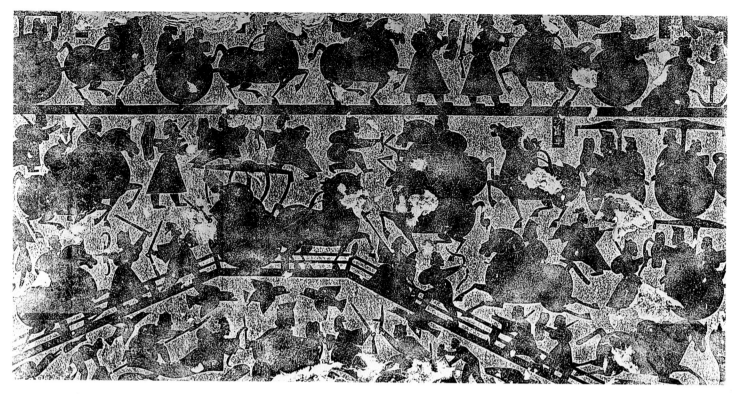

As a result of these policies, bureaucrats were selected on the basis of merit rather than inheritance and social standing, and the Han court thrived.

Division and rebellion

The early Han government attempted to weaken the centralization of Qin rule by placing Gaozu's former comrades in positions of power, governing large territories as vassal states. However, this dispersal of power made it difficult to control such a large empire

▽ **A jade enclosure**
Han rulers were encased in jade in the belief that it repelled bad spirits and prevented the body from rotting. This magnificent jade burial suit is thought to have belonged to the second king of Chu, who died around 175 BCE.

and significantly weakened the Han's ability to rule effectively. By 157 BCE, all the semiautonomous kingdoms in the eastern part of the country were therefore placed in the hands of relatives of the imperial family. Despite this, several rebellions broke out against the government—the most serious of which was the Revolt of the Seven Kingdoms in 154 BCE, which was an attempt by the regional kings to resist Han centralization. The central government acted swiftly to suppress the challenge.

When Wu became emperor, he set out to dilute the power of the kings and reduce their threat to his rule. He decreed that all their offspring (rather than just the first-born children) had the right to inherit land. This measure effectively split their kingdoms into ever-smaller units, which he then assimilated into

△ **Battle on the Bridge**
This rubbing of an engraved Han dynasty tomb slab is from the Wu Liang shrine in Shandong province. The scene, known as the "Battle on the Bridge," depicts war chariots and horsemen in armed combat.

Made up of more than 4,200 jade plaques

Gold wire threaded through holes to link the plaques

provinces that were brought under the control of governors who were loyal to him. He established a system of oversight, whereby 13 inspectors reviewed the work of the governors, reporting back to the emperor himself.

Han achievements: economy and society

The Han dynasty was one of China's longest ruling dynasties and—despite numerous wars, internal conflicts, and persistent threats to its frontier regions—it is notable for several remarkable achievements. These ranged from important cultural and artistic developments to the substantial reorganization of the economy and society. Farming formed the basis of Han society, and the taxes that were paid by the nation's peasant landowners provided the bulk of the imperial revenue.

Wu fostered a cash economy: in 118 BCE, he introduced a new coin, the *wuzhu*, which remained the standard currency for much of the following millennium.

According to the 1st-century CE historian Ban Gu, the Han reordered China's already existing four-tiered society to give scholars the highest status; they were followed by farmers, then craftsmen, and finally merchants at the bottom. The merchants were often accused of ruthless profiteering—under Wu, they were therefore taxed heavily and banned from holding government posts, and merchant families were prohibited from owning land. To reduce the risk of speculation by unscrupulous businessmen, the Han nationalized the salt, iron, and liquor industries and established state-run granaries, buying in supplies when prices were low and selling cheaply when times were especially hard. The period also saw the opening of thriving trade networks with the West via what was to become China's most famous ancient thoroughfare, the Silk Road (see pp. 102–103).

The Han era is also particularly notable for the establishment, in 124 BCE, of an Imperial Academy for the training of future officials, the promotion of Confucianism as the official ideology at court, and the creation of civil service examinations to test potential government officials on their knowledge of the Confucian Classics (see pp. 54–55). When the academy opened, there were approximately 50 students; by the end of the

Eastern Han dynasty, enrollment had risen to around 3,000. The Han's Confucian-based bureaucracy was to continue for some 2,000 years.

Cultural developments

The Han made tremendous advances in the arts, notably in jade carving, pottery, calligraphy, painting, lacquerwork, and silk work, as well as in bronze, ceramic, and terracotta sculpture—all of which flourished during the period.

Several exceptional individuals were active during the Western Han period. Among them, from the 2nd century BCE, was the philosopher and political theorist Dong Zhongshu, who was a major influence on Emperor Wu's decision to promote Confucianism as the state ideology. In the same century, the poet Sina Xiangru was prominent in the development of the literary genre of *fu* (rhapsodies): lengthy, highly descriptive prose poems on a range of topics—including plants and gardens—which were meant to be recited aloud. But arguably one of the most important and influential individuals of the Western Han period was the eminent historian—and chronicler of Emperor Wu—Sima Qian (see pp. 106–107).

Under Wu, the Western Han came to govern a vast area, whose stability was dependent on regional and tribal loyalties. The country had almost doubled in size during his rule to become the largest empire in the world, overshadowing even the Western world's mighty Roman Empire.

Troubled times

Emperor Wu died in 87 BCE. Toward the end of his life, he chose his youngest son, Liu Fuling (later known as Emperor Zhao), as his heir. Liu ascended the throne at the age of just eight years old, and Huo Guang, a high-ranking official, was appointed as regent. This began a period of turmoil for the dynasty that was blighted by a series of inept rulers. Among them was Emperor Yuan, whose failure to oversee his secretaries and those closest to him contributed to the ruin of the dynasty. Weak leadership and palace intrigues led to the founding of the Xin dynasty in 9 CE (see pp. 110–111), which lasted for 14 years, until the restoration of the Han in 25 CE.

△ **Female archer**
Women's leisure activities during the Han included ball games and archery. For this, they often wore loose, long-sleeved garments—as depicted by this tomb figure, whose arms are outstretched, as if poised to pull a bow.

◁ **Symbols of wealth and prosperity**
Han *wuzhu* coins, with their distinctive central square, are shown on this bronze money tree. The trees were placed in tombs to bring prosperity in the afterlife.

The Tomb of Lady Dai

Revealing discoveries from Mawangdui

Cover illustrating two
tigers fighting
two dragons

In 1972, the authorities in Changsha, the capital of Hunan province, decided to build a military hospital on a saddle-shaped mound outside the city. The location had long been known as Mawangdui, or "Prince Ma's Mound." However, ground works were halted when the escape of gas suggested the presence of an undiscovered tomb. Archaeologists could not find any trace of Prince Ma, a local ruler from the 10th century CE, but instead discovered something much older and more exciting. The tumulus was in fact the burial place of a family of Han aristocrats, dating back to the 2nd century BCE.

Preserved burial site

The site contained three separate shaft tombs. One was that of Li Cang, Marquis of Dai, Chancellor of Changsha when it was a principal fiefdom of the early Han rulers. Another held the remains of a man in his 30s who had died in 168 BCE and was thought to be the marquis's son. By far the best preserved was the tomb of a woman of about 50, her skin still soft and her hair and eyelashes intact. The luxury of the grave goods surrounding her indicated that she had been Li Cang's wife, Xin Bi—the Marchioness of Dai.

The extraordinary state of preservation of Lady Dai's body was largely due to the care with which she had been buried. The remains lay in the innermost of three coffins at the bottom of a shaft 52 ft (16 m) deep, surrounded by 5.5 tons (5 metric tons) of moisture-absorbing charcoal and topped by a 3 ft (1 m) thick layer of clay. Clinicians were able to carry out a full autopsy, revealing a history of illnesses that included tuberculosis, gallstones, and a deformed spine. Most seriously, the marchioness had been suffering from advanced atherosclerosis, a condition associated with obesity and a sedentary lifestyle; her restricted arteries probably caused her death.

Prepared for the afterlife

The opulence of the treasures surrounding the dead marchioness was as remarkable as the state of her body. Thirty bamboo baskets held prepared meats and fruits, and 51 pots contained other foods; small bamboo slips suggested recipes for the afterlife. Although there was no gold, silver, or bronze— forbidden by Emperor Wen of Han—the tomb was rich in beautifully decorated lacquerware objects and an entire wardrobe of fine silk garments, from underwear and socks to robes and coats. To ensure that she was as well served after death as before, there were 162 wooden statuettes of servants, among them musicians and dancers to provide entertainment, as well as a 25-string zither and a bamboo mouth organ with 22 tubes. Lady Dai had obviously been used to luxury in life, and she took all possible steps to ensure that state continued beyond the grave.

▷ **Screen for the soul**
This lacquer screen, found in one of the tombs, is a piece made specifically for tomb burial. It was found standing behind a seat placed there for the departed's spirit.

Border with a vermilion diamond pattern

◁ **Eternal servitude**
In the tomb, 162 wooden figurines depicting servants attended to Lady Dai's spirit in the afterlife.

Ornamental artwork was said to bring good fortune

A red lacquer finish preserved the wooden coffins and Lady Dai for over two millennia

△ **Afterlife of luxury**
The preserved remains of Lady Dai were found enveloped in 20 layers of silk, encased within the innermost of three coffins. The luxurious material and intricate decoration reflect Lady Dai's privileged status.

The Chinese Zodiac

The history of the *shengxiao*

From the earliest times, prophecy played a significant part in Chinese life. Rulers of the Shang dynasty turned to diviners to interpret the cracks in heated oracle bones (see pp. 44–45), seeking to answer questions about the future. Another marked trait of the early cultures was a concern with the magical potency of numbers. Five had a special significance, as exemplified in the Five Directions (including the center as well as north, south, east, and west), the Five Blessings (piety, uprightness, good manners, knowledge, and trust), and the Five Sacrificial Beasts (ox, sheep, fowl, pig, and dog).

The number 12 also carried philosophical weight, expressed from early times in the 12 Ornaments—auspicious symbols used to decorate official robes of state—as well as the 12 meridians of traditional medicine. In Han China, days were divided into 12 units, known as the *dizhi*. The first of these periods was called *zi*, followed by *chou, yin, mao, chen, si, wu, wei, shen, you, xu,* and *hai*. The *dizhi* were believed to correspond with animals, according to their temperament—they aligned with the rat, ox, tiger, rabbit, dragon, snake, horse, sheep, monkey, rooster, dog, and pig, respectively.

Zodiac animals

Astronomers also identified the 12 new moons of the lunar year, which determined the Chinese calendar year. The years were then counted in 12-year cycles, forming the basis of the Chinese zodiac, the *sheng xiao*. The earliest record of years being associated with animals dates from the Han dynasty, in Wang Chong's *Balanced Discourses (Lunheng)*. As they were in the *dizhi*, the 12 zodiac animals became associated with specific

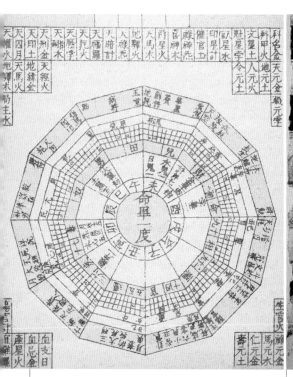

△ **Astrology chart**
Dating from the 14th century, this Chinese astrological chart records how the Five Elements corresponded to the recorded positions of the moon. Astrology was a science with meticulous mathematical calculations, and these were recorded in manuals for future generations.

△ **Ming mural**
This is one of 12 zodiac wall paintings from a temple in northern China, created in the 17th century. The tiger is the third animal in the zodiac and is associated with bravery and authority. According to the Chinese zodiac, all individuals born in a given year are believed to share some characteristics.

△ **The Five Elements**
This 19th-century wheel depicts the elements that the zodiac animals are aligned with. The snake and horse are associated with fire; the ox, dragon, goat, and dog with earth; the tiger and rabbit with wood; the monkey and rooster with metal; and the pig and rat with water.

character traits assigned to individuals at the time of their birth. In this way, the Chinese system closely resembles the Western zodiac which also has 12 signs. The Western version, however, linked each sign to a particular month. Some scholars have also linked the *shengxiao* to aspects of Hindu astrology, which came to China from India in the 3rd century CE, via Buddhist texts.

The animals of the *shengxiao* were ranked in strict order, and this ranking was explained by various legends. A popular version claimed that the Jade Emperor—the Daoist ruler of Heaven—invited the animals to a celebration, and they raced to get there first. On the way, they had to cross a river. The best swimmer was the ox, so the cat and the rat decided to help their chances by jumping onto its back. Halfway over, however, the rat pushed the cat into the water,

and then scuttled in as the winner. The other 11 arrived in the order still celebrated in the annual cycle—the same order used for the *dizhi*—but the cat was excluded from the final 12 animals of the zodiac. As part of the Daoist tradition, the zodiac animals are each associated with one of the five elements, and with either *yin* or *yang*. In Buddhist versions of the legend, the Buddha himself invited the 13 animals to the Great Race.

Lasting significance

From the Zhou dynasty onward, the zodiac animals were depicted in ceramics, art, and architectural features. The zodiac is still in use today and is celebrated in Chinese culture during the Spring Festival (Chinese New Year) around the first new moon of the Chinese year.

△ **Divine symbols**
This Daoist divination wheel is part of a chart showing good and bad days for bloodletting. Within the circle are the 12 zodiac animals, the eight trigrams, and nine figures symbolizing the elements of geomancy. All of these played important roles in divination.

△ **Asian zodiac**
While it is known as the Chinese zodiac, some scholars believe it might have been brought to China from Central Asia. Today, many Asian nations have a zodiac similar to China's, but they might differ by one animal. Japan, for example, has a boar rather than a pig. This painting of a zodiac goat was created in Korea.

△ **Spring celebration**
The Spring Festival, or Chinese New Year, is celebrated at the time of the first new moon—between January 21 and February 20. This photograph shows a giant dog lantern at the Shanghai Yu Garden Lantern Show in 2018, celebrating the advent of the Year of the Dog.

Auspicious Beasts

Animal art through the ages

China has a long tradition of recognizing auspicious beasts. From the Western Han period especially, these animals were depicted on ritual and everyday objects. As well as portraying mythical beasts such as dragons and phoenixes, crafts depicted real creatures that were revered and respected within Chinese culture.

Hinged beak opens to pour liquid

△ Ritual wine vessel
This ram-shaped vessel is decorated with dragons and *taotie*. The ram was associated with good fortune in ancient China.

△ Faithful bird
This ritual vessel from the Zhou dynasty is shaped like a goose. Geese and swans were associated with marriage and fidelity.

△ Lost species
This Eastern Zhou bronze depicts what looks like a tapir. The giant tapir lived in China about 4,000 years ago.

Gold and silver inlaid patterns

△ Tortoise
Symbolizing longevity, the tortoise is one of the four most auspicious animals of ancient China. This lamp from the 4th–5th century CE is shaped like a tortoise holding a cup.

△ Leaping protector
This Eastern Zhou bronze depicts a creature somewhat resembling a tiger. This fierce animal was associated with protection.

Decorative cloud patterns

Side carved to look like an owl's wing

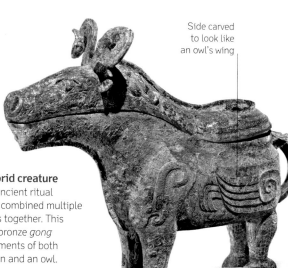

▷ Bronze beast
This wine vessel dates from the Western Han. The Sumatran rhino was hunted by the Han for its tough skin and for its horn, which was thought to ward off evil.

▷ Hybrid creature
Some ancient ritual vessels combined multiple animals together. This Shang bronze *gong* has elements of both a dragon and an owl.

Decorative
antlers

Gold
animal
head

△ Animal protection
This *buyao* (headdress) dates from the
Sixteen Kingdoms period (see pp. 126–
127). The Xianbei people wore animal-
shaped ornaments to exorcize evil spirits.

▷ Peacock censer
Made in the Qing dynasty
during the rule of the Qianlong
Emperor, this cloisonné
standing peacock
functioned as an incense
burner (censer).

Peacock feathers
symbolized rank

▷ Cloisonné deer
This ornament from the Qianlong
period of the Qing dynasty is
made from gilt-copper studded
with semi-precious stones.
Deer were a symbol of longevity
and richness.

△ Prowling tigers
This container shows the
importance of the buffalo to
the prosperity of the Dian
people and the threat that
herds faced from tigers.

Cloisonné vase
decoration

Deer inlaid with
lapis lazuli
and turquoise

"Cloth" made
from enamel

△ Phoenix vessel
This 18th-century wine vessel depicts a phoenix
in cloisonné. The phoenix was seen as the king
of birds and represented harmony and grace.

▽ **Sacrificial scene**
This Dian cowrie container from the Western Han dynasty was found at Shizhaishan with more than 300 cowrie shells still inside. The lid depicts at least 127 people, including the king, at a sacrificial ceremony—a common event in the Dian kingdom that is also recorded in ancient texts.

Roof of building housing the sacrificial ceremony

The king of Dian sits on his throne

Objects on a sacrificial altar

Tiger prowling at the edge of the scene

Container stands 21 in (53 cm) tall

Feet shaped like tiger paws

Ancient Currency

Cowrie shells and containers

For centuries, the shells of the cowrie—a type of sea snail—were used as money across the trade networks of Africa, South Asia, and East Asia. The Yellow Emperor (see pp. 28–29) is said to have introduced cowrie money to China in the 3rd millennium BCE; the currency reached its height under the Shang and Zhou dynasties. According to some theories, emperors were able to control the currency's value by managing the supply of cowrie shells, which were found only on the southern coast of China. However, as the population grew, there were not enough real cowries to satisfy demand, so the Chinese also began to use artificial cowries carved from stone, bone, ivory, and jade, or cast in bronze.

Other currencies also circulated in pre-Qin China, including bronze tokens shaped like knives, spades, keys, and other domestic and agricultural items. However, the use of both these forms of money and cowrie shells faded out after

▷ **Royal tribute**
The scene on this Western Han-era cowrie shell container represents people from seven different tribes paying tribute to the King of Dian.

the First Emperor, Shi Huangdi, founded the Qin dynasty (see pp. 78–81) and introduced a standardized coinage of Ban Liang (half-ounce) coins in 221 BCE.

Bronze money pots

In 1956, archaeologists discovered tombs belonging to elite members of the Dian culture at Shizhaishan in Jinning County, Yunnan. The Dian people inhabited the Dian Lake plateau from the Spring and Autumn period (c. 771–476 BCE) to the Eastern Han dynasty (25–220 CE). Among the discoveries at the tombs were several cast-bronze cowrie containers, each of which could hold hundreds of shells. The quality of the workmanship of these containers shows that the Dian were sophisticated metalworkers. Wealthy members of Dian society commissioned elaborate lids for the containers in order to reflect their high status. The lids show people training horses, weaving, tending livestock, offering tribute, in battle, and hunting. The containers provide a unique insight into an ancient culture about which little was written and show the importance of the cowrie shell as a currency.

△ **Snail money**
The cowrie was so closely associated with money that the Chinese ideogram *bei* meant both money and cowrie shell.

Health and Medicine

A history of the Chinese tradition of healing

An interest in illness, health, and well-being extends deep into China's history. Among China's earliest writings are inscriptions on oracle bones dating from the 2nd millennium BCE that address the maladies that affected the Shang royal family. And the *Compendium of Materia Medica (Bencao gangmu)*—a huge compilation of all medical knowledge written in the Ming dynasty (see pp. 232–233)—includes works from as early as 1100 BCE. Centuries later, Qin Shi Huangdi, the First Emperor, became obsessed by the quest for an elixir for everlasting life (see p. 81), and even though he is remembered for burning books that contradicted his beliefs, he notably spared medical and other practical texts from destruction.

By the First Emperor's day, a rational approach to healing was already in development. The chronicler Sima Qian tells the story of Bian Que, a physician from the 4th century BCE, who developed a simple diagnostic formula: look (at the patient's physical appearance); listen (to breathing and voice); ask (about symptoms); and take (the pulse). Bian Que was reportedly so skilled that he was able to detect illness in people who were unaware that they had a problem.

Health, nature, and balance

The approach to medicine that developed in China was holistic, inextricably connected to all aspects of the Chinese world view. The condition of the individual body itself was seen as intimately linked to that of the surrounding environment—indeed, to the entire cosmos. According to this perspective, good health reflected a balance of the forces of *yin* (female and submissive) and *yang* (male and assertive), as well as of the influence of the Five Elements (water, fire,

△ **Yin and yang**
In traditional Chinese thought, *yin* and *yang* are seen as the opposing and complementary principles of the body and the universe. They are represented by a dragon (symbol of authority, strength, and vigor) and a tortoise (symbol of stability) in this 8th-century CE wall hanging.

△ **Mawangdui chart of physical exercises**
A series of therapeutic movements is shown in this reconstruction of a 2nd-century BCE colored silk manuscript excavated from the archaeological site of Mawangdui in Changsha. It depicts men and women, old and young, in various postures. The complete chart shows 44 figures engaged in the exercises.

△ **Han acupuncture**
One of the key techniques of traditional Chinese medicine is acupuncture—the insertion of needles into the body to stimulate the flow of *qi* (vital energy). This painting shows Han dynasty physician Hua Tuo using acupuncture to anesthetize a patient prior to an operation.

"[T]he occurrence of any **disease is** … **due to** the … **imbalance of yin and yang**."

INNER CANON OF THE YELLOW EMPEROR (HUANGDI NEIJING), HAN DYNASTY

metal, wood, and earth). This equilibrium expressed itself in the flow of qi, or vital energy, through the body. Illness was caused when the flow of qi was disrupted. Medicine or therapeutic treatment could be prescribed to counter the disruption.

Han dynasty innovation

Medical practice evolved significantly—and became more sophisticated—during the Han dynasty. The best-known medical text of the period, the *Inner Canon of the Yellow Emperor (Huangdi Neijing)*, focuses on the cosmic element in medicine. It also devotes one of its sections to acupuncture, the insertion of needles into the skin to promote the flow of qi through the body. This, along with moxibustion (the burning of herbs on specific points of the body), remains a staple of traditional medicine to the present day.

Other Han texts, such as those found at the Mawangdui burial site (see pp. 90–91), describe treatments such as bloodletting (releasing blood from the body to prevent illness) and cauterization, and cover more than 250 ailments, ranging from warts and hemorrhoids to snake bites.

In the last years of the Han dynasty, the scholar-physician Zhang Zhongjing, in works such as his *Treatment on Febrile Diseases*, wrote about the use of medicinal herbs to treat fevers. Another notable Han physician, Hua Tuo, is said to have developed an early form of anaesthetic for use in performing operations. Hua Tuo built such a strong reputation for his healing abilities that one of the warlords competing for power at the time summoned him to serve as his personal physician; when Hua Tuo proved unwilling, the ruler had him executed.

△ **Bodily tracts**
This 18th-century Chinese medical illustration depicts two male figures labeled to show the distribution of some of the acupuncture points of the body's 14 meridians. Such documentation shows tremendous knowledge of how the inner body responds to external stimulation.

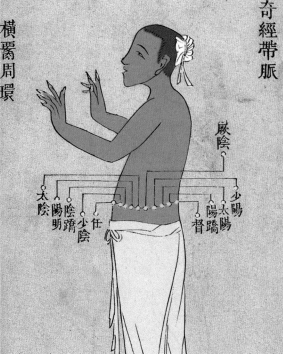

△ **Qi and horizontal balance**
According to Chinese medicine, the "belt vessel" (*daimai*) regulates strength around the waist and the qi's horizontal balance. The 19th-century illustration shown here charts the route of the belt vessel around the waist and also indicates the points at which it intersects with other channels in the human body.

△ **Acupuncture-moxibustion chart**
The text on this page from an acupuncture and moxibustion (or acu-moxa) book of 1869 states: "The *zhiyin* point is located on the outer side of the little toe…. This point is moxibusted with three moxa cones, the size of a grain of wheat. It can cure severe complications of childbirth."

Confucian Governance

An ideology for the new imperial age

Under the Han dynasty, the philosophy of Confucianism became established as a central pillar of government. It remained at the heart of Chinese intellectual life for the next 2,000 years.

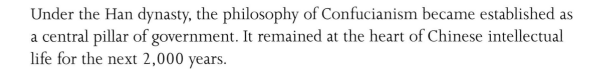

The First Emperor and founder of the Qin dynasty sought to impose his will over a newly unified China (see pp. 78–81). One method of doing this was to silence his critics, especially the Confucian scholars who compared his reign unfavorably with past dynasties of a "golden age." The First Emperor ordered the burning of all books that could possibly act as a challenge to his authority, including the works of Confucius (see p. 81).

Attitudes changed with the coming of the Han dynasty in 202 BCE, and particularly with the accession of Emperor Wu in 141 BCE. Eager to boost his status and to win the support of Confucian academics, he promoted scholarship and encouraged followers of Confucius in their reassembly of the sage's classic texts. They drew on the memory of disciples who had learned the texts by heart, as well as hidden copies that had escaped the Qin conflagration.

Official endorsement

By the time the Han emperor Wen came to power in 180 BCE, the humane influence of Confucian thought had filtered into legislation. Despite his own Daoist inclinations, Wen appointed followers of Confucian thought to high offices of state. At their prompting, he supported measures to abolish the very harshest elements of the Qin legal code, to provide assistance for people in need, and to promote officials on the basis of merit rather than birth.

Under Emperor Wu, whose reign lasted 54 years, Confucianism became the ruling orthodoxy in China. It would hold this position for the next 2,000 years. Wu was attracted by the ethical basis that the philosophy provided to the relationship between ruler and ruled. In particular, he supported the idea that in a harmonious society people should accept their

THE BUREAU OF MUSIC

Confucius believed that music had the power to elevate or degrade the spirit. Former Han rulers set up a bureau to support musicians (pictured) and to organize performances for official ceremonies and banquets. Yet suspicion of intellectual pursuits remained and the Bureau of Music was dissolved by the emperor in 7 BCE as part of a drive to reduce government costs. At the time, it had some 829 employees.

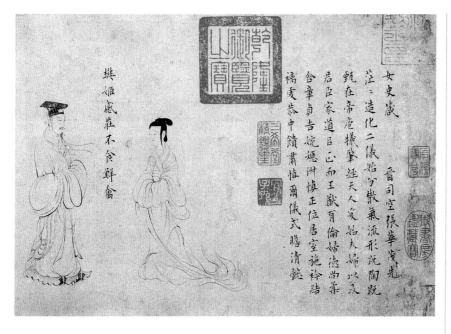

△ **A warning to women**
This Han painting on silk, *Admonitions of the Court Instructress*, illustrates a poem by Zhang Hua (292 CE). The poem is a parody of Confucian beliefs. It reprimands Empress Jia—a court instructress who advised imperial wives on correct behavior—for improper conduct.

allotted role, as Confucius himself had advocated—be it, for example, as a prince, a minister, a father, or a son. In adopting these ideas, Wu was able to provide a moral basis for kingly authority. He cemented the status of Confucianism by cutting support for teachers of competing doctrines. He also set up the Imperial Academy to train future officials; its curriculum was focused on the study of the Confucian classics (see pp. 54–55).

The scholar Dong Zhongshu was influential in shaping Wu's views. Dong Zhongshu's writings did much to reconcile Confucius's works with the cycles of *yin* and *yang* and the Five Elements that were also central to the Chinese world view. Wu took advantage of this synthesis to institute a round of rituals and sacrifices that helped both highlight and justify the authority of kingship, complementing the rationalism of its Confucian underpinning (see pp. 62–63).

△ **Filial piety**
In Confucianism, filial piety—the respect of a child for its parents—is believed to underpin the moral fabric of society and ensure order and stability. This Han dynasty lacquer basket shows the "Paragons of Filial Piety."

The scholar class

Wu's innovations rapidly took root in society, particularly as exams based on Confucian teachings provided the main path to jobs in government. Scholar-gentlemen (see pp. 174–175) came to form the top tier of the social hierarchy, above farmers and artisans, with the despised merchant class officially at the bottom. The prestige associated with learning also gave scholars leeway in criticizing government policy: in Wu's reign, for example, scholars spoke out against the establishment of government monopolies on salt, iron, and alcohol on the grounds that they represented an overextension of state power.

In Later or Eastern Han times, the influence of Confucianism grew even greater. Under Guangwu, sacrifices were offered to the sage just as they were to the gods. His successor, Ming Di, went on pilgrimage to the philosopher's birthplace and personally enjoyed debating with scholars. Meanwhile, the standing of the Imperial Academy continued to increase—by the mid-2nd century CE, it boasted over 30,000 students.

> "An **oppressive government** is more to be **feared** than a **tiger**."
>
> CONFUCIUS, *ANALECTS*, 450–350 BCE

The Silk Road

A history of China's trade route to the West

In the year 138 BCE, a military officer named Zhang Qian received an extraordinary commission. It was a time of tension between the Han empire and the Xiongnu nomads to the north, whom the First Emperor had attempted to pin back behind the Great Wall (see pp. 84–85). Subsequent Han rulers had sought to buy off the steppe warriors with tribute, but that policy proved costly and ultimately unsuccessful.

The energetic new Han ruler, Emperor Wu, planned to confront the Xiongnu militarily, but to do so he needed help. Zhang Qian's task was to travel westward into territory far beyond China's borders to establish relations with a possible ally—the Yuezhi people, who had fought against, and been defeated by, the Xiongnu some 40 years earlier. The mission almost failed at the start. Zhang was captured by the Xiongnu and held captive for 10 years, during which time he married

a local woman and fathered a son. He escaped and continued westward, reaching the Yuezhi in what is now Tajikistan and northern Afghanistan, only to find them settled and with no wish to resume their struggle. Zhang set off on his return journey, this time choosing a southerly route in the hope of evading capture. But he again fell into Xiongnu hands, and another two years passed before he was able to return to the Han capital of Chang'an, accompanied by his guide, his wife, and his son.

Trade with the West

Although Zhang failed to recruit allies, he brought back with him something of great value—reports of previously unknown lands, of distant cities, of people who grew rice and wheat and cultivated grapes, and of powerful horses that he described as sweating blood

△ **Hazardous terrain**
Traveling along the Silk Road was arduous and dangerous. Holdups were frequent; in one raid in the 2nd century BCE, bandits are said to have seized more than 1,000 cartloads of goods. This 8th-century painting from the Mogao Caves in Dunhuang shows bandits holding up travelers.

△ **Cultural interaction**
The Silk Road was dotted with caravanserais, inns where travelers could eat, rest, and interact with people from other cultures. They were particularly prevalent along the Persian Empire's Royal Road, a highway that stretched from Susa to Sardis. This caravanserai was photographed, c. 1898, in Persia.

△ **Ships of the desert**
With their padded feet and their ability to carry immense weight, store fat, eat thorns and desert grasses, and exist on very little water, camels were the ideal pack animals for the arduous trek along the Silk Road. This camel driver poses with his camel loaded with packs, c. 1910.

"The inhabitants **ride elephants** when they go into **battle**."

ZHANG QIAN'S TALES OF INDIA, AS RECORDED BY SIMA QIAN (c. 145–c. 91 BCE)

(perhaps from parasitic infestation). Intrigued, Wu sent Zhang back 10 years later to the horse-breeding Wusun people of the Ili valley (now on the Chinese–Kazakh border). Zhang forged an alliance with this group then returned to an honored position at court.

Luxury goods

The results of Zhang's discoveries were rapid and dramatic. Caravans carrying silk, gold, cinnamon, and animal skins were soon moving west from northern China to Central Asia, and returning with wine, spices, and linen, as well as exotic foods such as sesame and pomegranates. Most importantly, they brought Zhang's "blood-sweating" horses, which were bigger and stronger than the ponies ridden by the Xiongnu. In the closing years of the 2nd century BCE, Emperor Wu conquered the territory of Dayuan in Central Asia,

opening the way for a route that would later link China to the Mediterranean world. In the Han era itself, contact was limited by the Parthians of northern Persia, who acted as middlemen in the east–west trade. Even so, word of the Roman Empire, known in China as *Da Qin*, filtered through to court circles, and Chinese silk found its way westward, creating a craze for the new material among wealthy Romans.

In 166 CE, contact between the two imperial courts was established when a Roman embassy dispatched by Marcus Aurelius Antoninus (known in China as Andun) reached Luoyang. By then, goods were also flowing west via sea routes to India. In centuries to come, in spite of periodic closures of the route in times of unrest, traffic between China and the West would grow, cementing the importance of what became known as the Silk Road.

△ City ruins
This view is of the ruins of the 2nd-century BCE Silk Road city of Jiaohe, just west of Turpan, in Xinjiang Uygur Autonomous Region. A natural fortress built on a steep cliff, Jiaohe was abandoned following its destruction during an invasion by Genghis Khan in the 13th century.

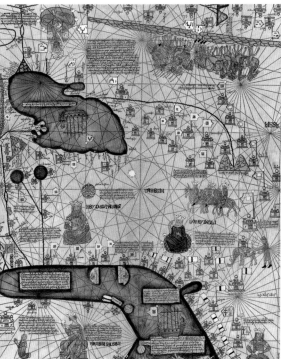

△ Mapping the Silk Road
The magnificent *Catalan Atlas*, commissioned by Charles V of France, is said to have been created by Majorcan cartographer Abraham Cresques in 1375. The Silk Road is shown top right, with Marco Polo's camel train (see p. 199) appearing on it upside down (the map was designed to be viewed from all directions).

△ Ancient trade route
Passing through mountains, deserts, and inhospitable terrain, the Silk Road had been used by traders carrying goods between China and Europe for millennia. The route became known as the Silk Road in the 19th century. This view is of the road at Kizil in Xinjiang in 1988.

Along the Silk Road
This photograph, taken in 2012, shows Kazakh nomads crossing a plain in Altay, in China's Xinjiang region—an arid and mountainous area crossed by the Silk Road. The nomads are part of a tradition that goes back hundreds of years to when caravans traversed the deserts of Xinjiang, carrying goods between China and cities to the west, such as Baghdad, Constantinople, and Rome. The Silk Road split into two—a northern and a southern branch—in the Xinjiang desert, connecting a constellation of oasis towns such as Kashgar and Khotan, where traders carrying spices, ivory, and slaves stopped to rest and restock.

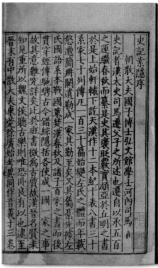

Sima Qian and the Writing of History

Chronicling the annals of the nation's past

△ **The *Shiji***
The *Historical Records* (*Shiji*) contains more than 500,000 characters. Shown above are pages from early editions of the work. The first complete printed copy dates from the Southern Song dynasty.

Sima Qian, an official in the court of the Han emperor Wu, undertook the monumental task of documenting all of China's history. In doing so, he created a model of scholarship for future generations to follow.

Sima Qian was born in about 145 BCE and raised in a scholarly environment. His father held the position of Grand Astrologer (or Grand Historian), and his duties included regulating the calendar, taking astronomical observations, and keeping a daily record of court ceremonies and state occasions. Sima Qian himself was a bright student and, around the age of 20, set off on a grand tour of the Chinese provinces, continuing his education by visiting sites of historical interest.

On his return, he gained a place at court. While accompanying a military expedition against western tribes in 110 BCE, he received the news that his father was gravely ill. He came back home in time to receive a request from the dying man to complete a task he had barely begun—to put together a record of all of China's history from the earliest times. Sima Qian took the commission to heart, and over the next two decades, it became his life's goal. He managed

to write this colossal work while fulfilling his other duties at court. He took over his father's position in 107 BCE and played a prominent part in the reformation of the Chinese calendar a couple of years later.

Sima Qian's work was interrupted in 99 BCE, when he fell out of favor with Emperor Wu for defending a disgraced general and was sentenced to death. His sentence was commuted to castration and imprisonment, but he never outlived his terrible shame, describing castration as "the worst of all punishments." Even in the face of this

▷ **Sima Qian**
Sima Qian was among the first to write about history in a systematic, analytical, and even-handed manner.

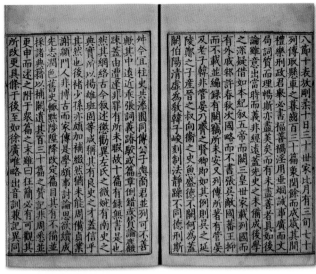

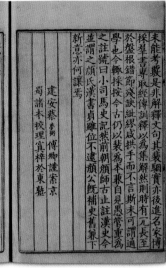

▷ **Emperor Wu of Han**
Sima Qian served Emperor Wu (r. 141–87 BCE), a keen patron of the arts. In this 17th-century painting, the emperor is shown welcoming a man of letters; the clothing of the figures reflects Qing dynasty styles.

"I have **gathered up** and **brought together** the **old traditions** of the **world** that were **scattered** and **lost**."

FROM A LETTER BY SIMA QIAN, c. 98 BCE

adversity, he persevered with his task, seeing it as a way to preserve his name for future generations. He was released from confinement after a couple of years and returned as a court eunuch to a position as an archivist, which gave him the security he needed to finish his work. The date of his death is uncertain; the last record he left was a letter written in 91 BCE.

The result of Sima Qian's efforts was a monumental work of 130 chapters. The manuscript was divided into several sections. One was a straightforward narrative of historical events, starting from the reign of the mythical Yellow Emperor and continuing to Sima Qian's own day. These annals were complemented by chronological tables that linked the timelines of the various kingdoms of feudal China into a coherent whole. Eight treatises followed on different matters of government interest, including state ritual and the provision of waterways; 30 chapters were devoted to the history of the ruling houses since the Zhou era. The book ends with a lengthy compilation of biographies of significant figures from China's past—not just rulers and statesmen but also philosophers, businessmen, poets, and rebels— along with accounts of foreign peoples beyond the nation's borders, a topical subject in Wu's reign.

A pioneering approach
The *Shiji*, or *Historical Records*, as the work became known, exercised an enduring influence on the way future generations would view the nation's past. Sima Qian's multiform approach, blending straightforward narrative with chronologies and memoirs, set a pattern that was followed in the state-sponsored annals compiled by subsequent dynasties. Yet none of those works has anything like the comprehensive sweep and vividness of Sima Qian's approach, which combined a telling eye for detail with a clear moral perspective and a critical approach to his sources. Many other historians followed in his footsteps, but none measured up to his achievement.

From Bamboo to Paper

A history of the revolutionary medium

Before paper was developed, people inscribed texts on bone, bronze, or stone. By the late Shang period (c. 1250 BCE), they began to write in vertical columns on strips of bamboo (slips) or, more rarely, on silk, using animal-hair brushes and ink made from pine soot. Silk was costly and favored for images, maps, or charts, while bamboo slips were preferred for text. By the Han era, these slips were the normal medium for writing, and they were superseded by paper only from around the 2nd century CE. Han writing covered a diverse array of subjects, from myth and divination to medicine and law, as well as the earliest known versions of the *Daodejing* (see pp. 66–67).

Bamboo slips provide invaluable evidence for the standardization of written Chinese under the Qin First Emperor, which forms the foundation of the nation's language to this day. So many of the slips survived the centuries because they were often interred in the tombs of rulers and high officials, sometimes accompanied by decorated knives—marks of status that symbolized their owners' power to scrape away and amend the texts of public documents, even after their death. By Han times, it had become common to bind slips together before writing on them, beginning at the right-hand edge. Such bundles of slips were heavy, so collections of texts were measured by the cartload, hence the traditional description of a highly educated individual as "having five cartloads of learning."

Paper production

The oldest recognizable piece of paper from China—thought to be part of a map produced during the Western Han dynasty—dates back to 179–141 BCE,

△ **Bamboo records**
Bamboo slips, such as these carrying legal text, were the main medium for documents from the late Shang period into the Han dynasty (206 BCE–220 CE). Each slip was inscribed with one column of brush-written text, making whole documents heavy and unwieldy.

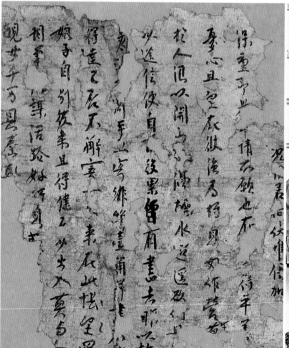

△ **Tang paper**
This fragment of paper with inked Chinese characters dates from the Tang dynasty (618–907 CE) and originally lined a silk painting. It was discovered in the Caves of the Thousand Buddhas in Gansu province. The widespread availability of paper in the Tang era allowed literacy and calligraphy to flourish.

△ **Ancient papermaking craft**
This Chinese woodcut from the 17th century shows workers taking freshly made sheets of wet paper and placing them on a wall near a fire to dry. The papermaking process was standardized by court official Cai Lun in the 2nd century CE and was used for centuries to follow..

> ## "Being **unable to afford** a **copy of silk**,
> ## I provide only a **paper copy**."

CUI YUAN, HAN OFFICIAL, C. 120 CE

and fragments have been found in tombs from the reign of the Han emperor Wu (141–87 BCE). However, the widespread use of paper followed later, after innovations in its manufacture made around 105 CE by Cai Lun, a court official.

Paper had many advantages over bamboo and silk— it was cheap, strong, and lightweight. Its development coincided with a time when the Han emperors were encouraging literary scholarship and expanding a bureaucracy that produced ever-increasing numbers of documents. Cai Lun devised a way to produce paper with relative ease. His raw materials are thought to have included bamboo, hemp, tree bark, and rags, which he probably pounded with water using a mallet. Pouring the resulting slurry on to a piece of cloth, he allowed the water to pass through, leaving a thin sheet of fiber (paper), which was then air-dried.

The spread to Europe

Paper was widely used across China from the 3rd century CE onward, and its uses proliferated. Toilet paper was introduced from the late 6th century, and tea bags made from paper emerged in Tang dynasty times (618–907 CE). Printed paper money followed in the 10th century under the Song dynasty.

By the 600s, the use of paper had spread to Korea, Vietnam, and Japan. In the 8th century, Chinese papermakers captured in battle by Arab warriors at the Battle of Talas (see p. 151) took the skill to the Middle East, and knowledge of the process percolated from there to Western Europe in the 12th century as a result of the Crusades. The basic principles of papermaking in today's mechanized mills, which produce hundreds of tons of paper per day, are much the same as those pioneered by Cai Lun.

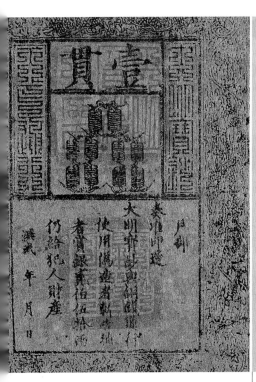

△ **Ming paper money**
In 1374, the Ming introduced printed notes in a variety of denominations. Each had a distinctive design with dragons and clouds and carried a warning that counterfeiting was punishable by death. Initially, the dynasty issued too much paper money, resulting in hyperinflation.

△ **Carp woodblock print**
The invention of color woodblock printing in the Tang dynasty made it possible to create sophisticated images, such as this blue carp leaping from the water toward a willow tree. It was printed in Suzhou around 1644 and is thought to symbolize a young man hoping to pass his civil service exams.

△ **Traditional paper industry**
A worker in Guizhou stirs and pounds plant material in water, in a process that has remained much the same since Cai Lun's day. Originally invented as a writing medium, paper was used in imperial China in items such as screens, armor, tea bags, hats, and packaging.

The Xin Dynasty

An imperial regent briefly seizes power

Known to Han historians as "the Usurper," Wang Mang took power at a time of chaos and sought to create order. His reforms failed, and his Xin dynasty lasted only 14 years before it fell to the resurgent Han.

Under Emperor Wu of Han, China emerged as one of the most powerful nations in the world, governed by a centralized Confucian bureaucracy. However, after Wu's death in 87 BCE, China entered a period of turmoil marked by weak rulers and palace intrigue (see pp. 88–89). From this disorder, the regent Wang Mang emerged. Nephew of the influential Empress Dowager Wang, he first served as regent to Emperor Ping and, when the child emperor died in 6 CE, after fewer than six years in power, had an even younger contender crowned in his place. In 9 CE, Wang Mang claimed power for himself as the first emperor of the Xin ("new") dynasty. Wang Mang was a traditionalist with a deep respect for the Confucian world view and a conviction that China needed structural renewal. Decades of poor governance had seen growing inequality as peasant farmers were forced into destitution, obliged to sell their land to wealthy landowners in times of famine.

A champion of the peasantry

Wang Mang introduced sweeping reforms aimed at restoring the harmony of the early Zhou period (see pp. 46–49). Slavery was abolished, and the sale of private land prohibited. Owners of large estates were ordered to divide them up, and loans were provided to peasant farmers. To pay for his policies, Wang Mang set up state monopolies on salt, iron, and alcohol. He also tried to nationalize gold, demanding that all holders of the metal exchange it for bronze. The property-owning classes bitterly opposed his reforms, most of which were repealed within three years.

◁ *The Yellow River Breaches Its Course*
This 12th-century work by landscape painter Ma Yuan depicts the turbulent Yellow River. The river has changed its course several times in its history, including in the Xin and Song dynasties.

△ Grain measure
This vessel is a rare surviving grain measure from the Xin dynasty. Its sides are decorated with reliefs of the five auspicious crops.

Wang's downfall, however, was caused less by his political opponents than by the forces of nature. After heavy rains, the Yellow River changed course, triggering floods that left millions dead or homeless. Opportunistically, the Xiongnu (see pp. 86–89) renewed their incursions across the Great Wall and succeeded in overrunning the northwestern lands. Soon, bands of displaced peasants were roaming eastern China, forming rebel groups such as the Red Eyebrow movement (after the pigment daubed on their faces). By 18 CE, full-scale rebellion had broken out, and was strengthened when members of the Liu—the ruling family of the Western Han years—lent their support.

The Eastern Han

Wang held out for a further five years, but in 23 CE, opposition forces broke into his capital of Chang'an, killing him in his palace and so ending the Xin dynasty. The Han dynasty was subsequently restored, although it would take 13 years for its rulers to regain control over all its former territories. A new capital was established further east at Luoyang, and for this reason the dynasty's last two centuries became known as the Eastern or Later Han period, in contrast to the Western or Former Han years, before the Xin interregnum. Yet Wang Mang's reforms were not entirely abandoned. The new Eastern Han rulers followed his example in upholding the nation's peasant farmers as the basis of their

rule, and China returned briefly to prosperity. However, continued Xiongnu incursions and the search for fresh agricultural land led to a southward migration; between 2 CE and 140 CE, as many as 10 million people left the north for the Yangzi valley and the lands beyond. By the later date, problems at the center of imperial power had caused instability in China. In 124 CE, court eunuchs (see pp. 116–117) staged a coup, placing a child emperor, whom they could control, on the throne.

For the last century of Eastern Han rule, the court was mostly at odds with the Confucian officials beyond. Eventually, military warlords moved in, and in 220 CE, the state finally broke up, splitting into three competing kingdoms (see pp. 118–119). The long Han era of stability stuttered to an end.

▷ Xin mirror
A bronze mirror from the Xin dynasty is richly decorated with depictions of animals, Daoist immortals, and the Guardians of the Four Directions.

Cults and Beliefs

A patchwork of diverse traditions in early China

China's earliest religious beliefs drew on the legends and traditions of the many different parts of the country. The result was a rich mosaic of faiths that eventually fed into the Daoist, Confucian, and Buddhist canons.

For more than 2,000 years, the three major faith systems of Confucianism, Daoism, and Buddhism (known as the Three Ways) have shaped how people in China think about the cosmos. These faiths have been variously combined and developed in Chinese popular religion and are the means by which people seek the aid of the gods—who may be based on Daoist immortals, bodhisattvas, or deified figures such as Confucius—to help solve their problems.

Before the rise of the Three Ways, the ruling class used oracle-bone diviners to make contact with gods and deified ancestors (see pp. 44–45), while the bulk of the population took their spiritual guidance from local traditions and wu (shamans), who claimed to have access to supernatural powers. The word wu dates back at to Shang times in the 2nd millennium BCE, but by the late Zhou in the 4th century BCE, it came to denote female sorcerer-priests. The wu were not an organized caste but self-appointed individuals who claimed an ability to bridge the gap between human and spirit realms. The entities the wu sought to contact ranged from deified ancestors to supernatural beings who governed the forces of nature, such as Leigong, the dragon-bodied thunder god.

The wu did not follow formal rituals, although some performed dances, whirling themselves into an altered state of consciousness. In this ecstatic state, they might speak in tongues—seen as the language of their unseen interlocutors—or cut themselves with knives. A few claimed to be able to make themselves invisible. There was an element of sympathetic magic about their performances—a belief that they could produce an effect through imitating the desired outcome; for example, one account describes wu dancing within a ring of fire during a time of drought in the hope that the drops of sweat that fell from their bodies would bring rain.

A huge pantheon

By the end of the Shang dynasty, many hundreds of gods were recognized across China's pantheon. Some of these entities had only local significance—they

A PROPITIOUS BEAST

China had its own version of the unicorn in stories of the *qilin* (depicted in the court rank badge below). Sightings of this beast were said to coincide with the presence of great men in the land. In legend, a *qilin* graced the garden of the Yellow Emperor; and two appeared in Confucius's lifetime, one signaling his birth, the other his death. When the first giraffe reached China in 1414 as a gift to the emperor from the Sultan of Malindi in East Africa, courtiers and court historians diplomatically called the exotic animal a *qilin*.

△ **Han shaman**
This pottery figure from the Han dynasty depicts a shaman grasping an axe and a serpent. Such figures were often left in the tombs of the deceased to serve as guides in the afterlife.

"[A] robe of **yellow brocade** … **flowers in her coiffure** … with **a face matchless** in the world."

ON THE QUEEN MOTHER OF THE WEST, *TAIPING GUANGJI*, SONG DYNASTY

◁ **The Queen Mother of the West**
This painted silk screen from around 1800 shows the goddess seated with the Daoist immortals at a banquet to celebrate the ripening of the fruit of peach trees.

were, for example, the founders of lineages or spirits associated with landmarks or features of the landscape, such as mountains (which themselves were considered especially sacred). Other gods became venerated more widely. Of these, several were purely mythical beings. The Queen Mother of the West, for example, was a prominent female deity said to live in a golden palace on the legendary Mount Kunlun, the ladder between Heaven and Earth. Described in Zhou texts as "timeless and deathless," she became the focus of a cult of immortality, which in the 1st century BCE drew thousands of ecstatic enthusiasts to the Han capital, seeking her help. Over time, the Queen Mother of the West was integrated into the Daoist canon, along with many aspects of the early beliefs surrounding her. These beliefs helped inspire the Yellow Turbans—peasant rebels whose long-running resistance would later play a significant part in the Han dynasty's collapse (see pp. 88–89).

Confucians held up quasi-historical figures as models of good government, often revering them as gods. They include the Yellow Emperor, who is said to have introduced law and order to humankind and invented the arts and music; and the Three Sage Kings, who introduced the use of fire and agriculture. Another of the legendary rulers was Yu the Great, who is traditionally regarded as the founder of the Xia dynasty (see pp. 30–31). Deified, these culture heroes had a prominent place in the pantheon and were worshipped as role models, from whom all wise rulers should learn.

△ **Mount Huashan**
In Chinese belief, mountains are holy places, invested with immense spiritual power. This pagoda sits on Mount Huashan, one of China's five great sacred mountains (see p. 70).

The Rise of Daoism

A history of the way of peace in China

Although it took its inspiration from the *Daodejing* (see pp. 66–67), a sacred text that advocated retreat from the world, the Daoist religion developed into a messianic movement foretelling a coming Great Peace for its believers. The *Daodejing* itself recognized no central god. Instead, it presented the *Dao* or Way—a life force to which people were invited to attune their lives. However, over the centuries, Daoism acquired many deities and a host of rituals and beliefs that turned it into a popular cult. Some of these beliefs and practices came from the folk traditions of shamans (see pp. 112–113), others from the quest for immortality that had long attracted nobles and emperors.

Daoism was already a force at the imperial court in the early Han years. Dou, consort of Emperor Wen (r. 180–157 BCE), was a follower who supported the Huang-Lao ("Celestial Masters") school, which linked Laozi, the *Daodejing*'s supposed author, with Huangdi, the Yellow Emperor, treating both as gods. In the Han dynasty's troubled later years, Daoism emerged as a popular movement with a revolutionary message. In 142 CE, a magistrate-turned-hermit named Zhang Ling had a vision of the deified Laozi, who charged him to recruit followers who would lead pure lives in order to achieve salvation in a time of destruction that was soon to be unleashed on man. The movement became known as the Way of the Five Pecks of Rice (or the Way of the Celestial Master) because that amount of rice (about 66 lb, or 30 kg) was the price of admission.

According to legend, Zhang Ling died 14 years later, disappearing from view after mastering the secret of immortality. The movement continued to spread under his heirs: in 191, his grandson Zhang Lu allied

△ **Laozi in the Han dynasty**
This fresco, discovered on the wall of a tomb in Dongping County, southwestern Shandong province, dates back to the Han dynasty. Painted with blue, green, black, and red pigment, it depicts an imagined meeting between Laozi and the great sage Confucius.

△ **Daoist stele**
This stele dates from the Northern Zhou dynasty, which briefly ruled over northern China in the 6th century CE. Eager to unify China, the Zhou emperor Wu commissioned a report to choose between Daoism and Buddhism as a suitable religion for the empire. The emperor supported the adoption of Daoism.

△ **Zhang Ling**
The founder of the Daoist sect known as the Way of the Five Pecks of Rice, Zhang Ling, also called the "First Master of Heaven," is depicted here in a 20th-century painting. He rides a tiger and carries a sword, which gives him the power to battle demons.

"A journey of a **thousand miles** must **begin** with a **single step**."

DAODEJING, 4TH–3RD CENTURY BCE

with a local warlord to rebel against the Han court, conquering the Hanzhong valley on the borders of present-day Shaanxi and Sichuan. This theocratic state was later incorporated into the Wei kingdom of the warlord Cao Cao (see pp. 118–119), who accepted Celestial Masters Daoism as the ruling ideology.

The Yellow Turbans

In other parts of China, rebel groups gathered under the banner of a similar sect led by Zhang Jue. Like Zhang Ling, he preached that a time of profound change was coming (and was expected in 184 CE). At that time, he claimed, the sky would turn yellow and the dynasty would fall, ushering in a new age of peace and prosperity. As drought and famine swept the land, the call had widespread appeal, its followers wearing yellow turbans as a mark of allegiance. The rising was

eventually put down, but Yellow Turban groups prevailed for years afterward, contributing to the spreading anarchy that accompanied the Han's end.

An evolving faith

Daoism continued to consolidate its position. A first version of the Daoist canon, the *Daozang*, appeared in the 4th century, at which time the Shangqing or "Supreme Clarity"—which would become the accepted form of the religion under the Tang—was taking shape. This emphasized breathing exercises and meditation over the magical paraphernalia of earlier days. At the same time, the Lingbao school emerged with a different vision, accentuating collective rituals. The separate traditions would eventually coalesce to provide the foundation of Daoism as it survives to this day as one of China's official religions.

△ **The Eight Immortals**
These eight beings—endowed with supernatural powers—are a common theme in Chinese art. According to tradition, they were born in the Tang or Song dynasties; they were incorporated into Daoist belief, symbolizing the ability to transcend ordinary human life.

△ **Robe of a Daoist priest**
This robe, woven in the 17th century from silk and metallic thread, would have been worn by a Daoist priest when conducting ceremonies. The back of the garment, shown here, depicts dragons hovering above a primordial landscape of stylized mountains and a frothy sea.

△ **Daoist temple**
This temple, the Purple Heaven Palace, is part of a complex of places of Daoist worship in the Wudang mountains in Hubei province, central China. The mountains have been a center of Daoism since the Tang dynasty and continue to attract many pilgrims.

Imperial Court Eunuchs

A history of power behind the throne

Eunuchs worked in the Chinese court from at least the 6th century BCE. At first, they served as attendants in the women's apartments, but over the years, they gained influence, forming factions that—in times of weak government—could take a grip on the levers of power. Many of the eunuchs had been castrated as a punishment for crimes; some had been condemned to their fate as prisoners of war; but others had been willingly emasculated by their parents in the hope that they would gain employment in the palace. As well as serving women, eunuchs also had other roles as watchmen, chair carriers, cooks, gardeners, and cleaners. Offering no dynastic challenge, some rose to become trusted confidants of their employers. For example, Cai Lun, the inventor of papermaking (see pp. 108–109), attained wealth and a title of nobility under Emperor He.

In the secretive environment of the imperial court, eunuchs had unique access to the heart of power. Some became closely involved in the affairs of state, gaining personal influence that they used for their own benefit. One of the most disruptive eunuchs was Zhao Gao (c. 240–207 BCE), who served the First Emperor. On the emperor's death, Zhao Gao engineered the death of the First Emperor's chosen heir, installing a more pliable candidate, Hu Hai, on the throne instead. However, Hu Hai's regime was not popular, and as discontent spiraled, rebels marched on the capital. Fearing that he would be blamed, Zhao Gao tried to save his own skin by arranging the death of his imperial protégé. The move failed to rescue him; the next (and final) Qin ruler had him assassinated. Three centuries later, under the Han dynasty, the power of the eunuchs rose again. A significant factor was the

△ **Cai Lun in the Han court**
This image from a postage stamp depicts Cai Lun, who is regarded as the inventor of the papermaking process. Cai Lun served the Han court as a eunuch from around 75 CE and, after several years, was promoted to a role in charge of manufacturing instruments and weapons.

△ **Tang eunuchs**
This Tang dynasty mural is among the earliest depictions of court eunuchs. It is one of many murals that adorns the walls of the Qianling Mausoleum in Qian County, Shaanxi province. The tomb complex was built in the late 7th century to house the remains of various members of the royal Li family.

△ **Courtly games**
One of the tasks of eunuchs was to entertain members of the court. Here, a group of eunuchs plays *chuiwan*, a game similar to golf, with the Ming emperor Xuande (r. 1425–1435). Xuande set up a palace school for eunuchs and appointed them to senior positions at court.

"Among defilements, none is as great as castration."

HISTORIAN SIMA QIAN, COMMENTING ON HIS OWN CASTRATION, 93 BCE

accession of a series of child emperors: in the power vacuums around these youthful rulers, struggles broke out between eunuchs and the clans of nobles who wished to enthrone their own chosen candidates. In these conflicts, eunuchs sometimes worked to protect the interests of the emperor: the eunuch Zheng Zhong, for example, defended 12-year-old Emperor He from the influence of a corrupt empress dowager. At other times, however, the eunuchs seized power for themselves by installing puppet rulers.

The influence of the eunuchs reached its height in the Han dynasty in the 21-year reign of Emperor Ling (168–189 CE). Top government jobs were openly sold to the highest bidders to the benefit of the principal court eunuchs, known as the "Ten Attendants," who built themselves grand palaces with the proceeds. The dominance of the court eunuchs finally came to an end on the death of Ling, when their faction faced the might of the military in a confrontation over the succession. Armed troops stormed the imperial palaces in Luoyang, and in the ensuing slaughter, more than 2,000 eunuchs were killed.

Decline in influence

Eunuchs continued to play an important role in court life, and by the mid-17th century, there were at least 70,000 working at the palace. The Qing dynasty (1644–1912), fearing their potentially hostile influence, reduced their number to less than 3,000 and divided the eunuch-staffed administration into 48 departments, each with its own particular set of duties, in order to dilute its power. The eunuch system was finally abolished on November 5, 1924, when the last emperor, Puyi, was driven out of the Forbidden City.

△ **Yonghe Temple**
In 1694, Emperor Kangxi built this palace in Beijing for his fourth son, the future Emperor Yongzheng. The site of the palace once accommodated the eunuch organizations of the Ming dynasty. From 1722, part of the building was converted into a Tibetan Buddhist monastery.

△ **Eunuchs in the Qing court**
This photograph shows Tong Dazhen, a eunuch in the Qing court, with his adopted son. Tong Dazhen served Empress Dowager Cixi (see pp. 286–287). Under the Qing, the influence of eunuchs declined. Many of the administrative roles they once fulfilled were taken over by the Imperial Household Department.

△ **Qing eunuch's robe**
Eunuchs in the Forbidden City typically wore a *paozi*, a long gray garment, under a *guazi*, a short, dark blue coat. For ceremonial occasions they wore more elaborate clothing, such as this ornately embroidered robe, which belonged to a eunuch of the Qing court.

The Three Kingdoms

The demise of the Han heralds a new age of division

As Han authority collapsed and rival warlords vied for power, China split three ways into the competing kingdoms of Wei, Shu, and Wu. The breakup of the empire was accompanied by steep economic decline and population collapse.

By the 2nd century CE, central authority had declined and a series of floods, famines, and plagues convinced the Chinese people that the Han emperors had lost the Mandate of Heaven (see p. 49). Popular discontent was expressed in a series of revolts that culminated in the Yellow Turban rebellion (named for the color of the scarves worn by the rebels) of 184 CE. The rebellion was quashed but at the cost of many lives and the destruction of trust in the Han. Rival warlords confronted each other for control of the emperor and

mastery over the nation. Foremost among them was soldier-poet Cao Cao (see pp. 194–95), chancellor of the Eastern Han dynasty, who won control over much of northern China. Opposition to Cao Cao came from warlords in the south, notably Liu Bei and Sun Quan.

In the winter of 208 CE, Cao Cao's forces met those of the southern warlords at the Battle of the Red Cliffs—a naval battle fought on the Yangzi River, probably at a location southwest of present-day Wuhan. Cao Cao was defeated, stifling his ambitions

▽ **Seven sages**
This scroll depicts the Seven Sages of the Bamboo Grove, a group of scholars who escaped the intrigue of the Wei court to enjoy a simpler life of contemplation, writing, and drinking.

△ **Ready for battle**
This ceramic statue of a knight astride his horse was created during the turbulent Three Kingdoms period.

to control the south; meanwhile Liu Bei and Sun Quan were able to consolidate their power, setting the scene for the tripartite division of China.

The Wei kingdom

Cao Cao died in 220 and was succeeded by his son Cao Pei, who forced the abdication of the last Han puppet emperor and proclaimed his own Wei dynasty. The dynasty controlled most of the Yellow River region and was centered on the former Han capital of Luoyang. The Wei made a number of administrative changes, including strengthening the army and introducing a fairer system for recruiting civil servants, and claimed to have inherited the legitimacy of the Han. However, in practice, they were embroiled in near-constant warfare with their rivals to the south. This conflict made the Three Kingdoms period one of the bloodiest in Chinese history, but also one of the most romanticized, most famously through the Ming novel *Romance of the Three Kingdoms* (see pp. 226–227).

The Shu kingdom

In Sichuan, to the southwest, Liu Bei had set up a kingdom that would become known as Shu. He refused to recognize the authority of the Wei and used his pedigree as a distant Han relative to proclaim himself emperor. During his reign—and that of his son Liu Shan—the real power behind the throne was chief minister Zhuge Liang, a brilliant strategist who managed to maintain Shu's position against its more powerful rivals to the north and east. On his death in 234, the state declined, finally falling to the forces of Wei in 263.

The Wu kingdom

Wu, the third of the Three Kingdoms, occupied the largest territory, stretching from the Yangzi River into what is now northern Vietnam. This

◁ **Crouching Dragon**
This 13th-century painting depicts Zhuge Liang, chief minister and strategist of the Shu kingdom, who was given the nickname "Crouching Dragon."

region was relatively sparsely populated and incorporated many ethnic groups. It had been a vassal kingdom of the Wei until 229, when Sun Quan proclaimed himself emperor. His rule lasted for more than 30 years, but his death in 252 unleashed a period of infighting among his heirs.

Temporary unification

The Three Kingdoms period was effectively ended by the rise of the Jin (see pp. 126–127) in 279, which temporarily reunified China once again. By this time, however, years of conflict had taken their toll. Once-great cities had fallen; barter had largely replaced the money economy; and the population had fallen to 16 million, compared to its height of 50 million under the Han.

> "Though **fierce as tigers** soldiers be, **battles are won** by **strategy**."

LUO GUANZHONG, *ROMANCE OF THE THREE KINGDOMS*, 1522

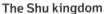

▷ **Tomb guardian**
Around 10 in (25 cm) high, this earthenware beast, dating from c. 265 CE, was a guardian animal designed to serve as a tomb ornament.

The Calligrapher's Art

A history of the art of written characters

The origins of Chinese writing stretch back to the late Neolithic period, when people inscribed symbols on to earthenware pots. By the Shang dynasty, full sentences were being written on oracle bones used to communicate with divine spirits and royal ancestors (see pp. 44–45). In the Zhou dynasty, writing was cast into bronze vessels (see pp. 52–53) and began to be used in administrative records: a number of written forms emerged, each with its own local flavor.

Written characters were standardized in the 3rd century BCE, when the First Emperor, guided by his chancellor, Li Si (see pp. 78–79), imposed the so-called "small seal" script—initially used in his own state of Qin—on the entire nation. This act played a decisive role in unifying China and in shaping its development.

Even as the First Emperor's neat, balanced, and symmetrical "small seal" script came into widespread use, Cheng Miao, a Qin official, developed another style, called "clerical" script. This used short, straight brushstrokes, suitable for quick annotations on documents; less evenly spaced than seal script, it allowed for less individuality in its execution. By Han times, calligraphers had created a new style known as "regular" script; from the Tang onward, this became the standard script used in the imperial examinations.

The mark of a good person

Over the centuries, Chinese artists and intellectuals saw beauty in the abstract forms of the logograms of their written language and turned calligraphy—the pursuit of writing for its own sake—into one of the

△ **Wild cursive script**
Zhang Xu is credited with inventing "wild cursive" script—an unconventional, abbreviated form of clerical script (see above)—in the Tang dynasty. Emperor Wenzong is said to have considered this script to be one of the "exquisite talents" of the Tang.

△ **Letter from Cai Xiang**
This exquisite brushwork was produced by the 11th-century calligrapher, scholar-official, and poet Cai Xiang. Revered as the greatest calligrapher of the Song, he did much to aid the development of the art. Calligraphy was often considered to be an expression of the writer's personality and moral code.

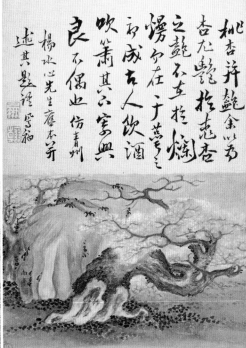

△ **Paintings with calligraphy**
Using brush and ink to shape the symbols that make up China's written language developed into an art that was as revered as painting. This work from 1736 by Gao Fenghan combines both art forms. In 1737, aged 54, the artist lost his right arm but learned to work with his left hand.

"I've always had my full reward / **On paper**, my **snakes and dragons** fall **in rows**."

MI FU, SONG DYNASTY CALLIGRAPHER AND POET, c. 1095

fine arts. Calligraphy was a form of expression in which the strokes made by the brush could convey not only mood and emotion but also the character and moral standing of the writer—so much so that in the Tang dynasty, quality of calligraphy was used to assess a candidate's suitability for civil service posts.

Tools and techniques

The tools of calligraphy were simple enough. All that was needed were the so-called Four Treasures of the Study: a fine-haired brush, typically made of goat or rabbit hair; ink, which in early times was derived from minerals, including graphite and vermilion; an inkstone, in which powdered pigment could be mixed with water; and a writing surface. At this time, the writing material would have been bamboo or silk (see pp. 108–109), but from c. 100 CE, it was most likely paper. Students of calligraphy practiced the main types of script—from the clear and formal small seal to the more fluid cursive script (in which characters would flow into one another)—exploring their expressive possibilities. They honed their skills by copying the works of past masters, which were often transcribed on to stone, from which ink rubbings could be made. Building their knowledge of composition and aesthetics, and their aptitude in brush control, they slowly developed their own unique styles.

The art of calligraphy reached a zenith in the 4th century CE, with the career of the eminent calligrapher Wang Xizhi (see p. 129), often regarded as the greatest master of the craft. Calligraphy remains a living and vibrant art form to this day and has become part of the school curriculum as a way of ensuring literacy in the use of the Chinese language.

△ **Cai Wenji**
Later generations venerated the skills of earlier calligraphers. This portrait depicts Cai Wenji, a Han dynasty artist, musician, and poet. She is shown here at work, with her books and calligraphy in the foreground. Cai Wenji's father, Cai Yong, was also a prominent calligrapher.

△ **Street calligrapher**
Private calligraphy galleries, street stalls, and vendors—as well as shops selling calligraphy-related items such as brushes, papers, and inks—have been popular in China for decades. This photograph shows a calligraphy artist working in a street in Hong Kong in the mid-20th century.

△ **Modern calligraphy**
Calligraphy remains a flourishing art form, which has developed unique styles that appear quite different from the earliest forms of script. Moreover, while during the Qin dynasty 3,300 small seal characters were recognized, a recent dictionary lists more than 70,000.

Spirited Carvings

Jade through the ages

Jade, a term for the gemstones jadeite and nephrite, has a spiritual significance in China, where it is believed to offer protection against evil spirits. Ritual objects have been carved from jade since the Stone Age, becoming increasingly intricate and detailed throughout Chinese history.

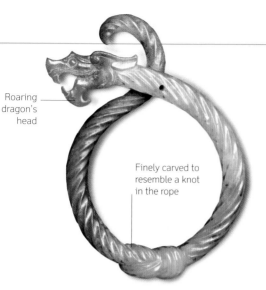

Roaring dragon's head

Finely carved to resemble a knot in the rope

Flat jade disk represents the realm of heaven

◁ **Western Han *bi***
The *bi* disk is one of the earliest known objects the Chinese made from jade. Along with the *cong*, these finely carved disks were placed in tombs in large numbers, but their function is unknown.

▷ **Ritual *cong***
Decorated jade towers, known as *cong*, originated in the Neolithic cultures of southeast China.

▷ **Ancient ornament**
This bird plaque, made from a thin sheet of nephrite, probably adorned clothing during the Warring States period.

△ **Dragon pendant**
Dating from the 3rd century BCE, this dragon pendant is made from nephrite, expertly carved to look like a twisted rope.

△ **Qing elephant**
Depictions of elephants were common during the Qing dynasty. This nephrite figure wears a saddle cloth patterned with birds and clouds.

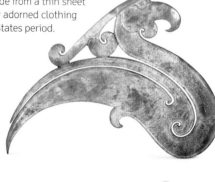

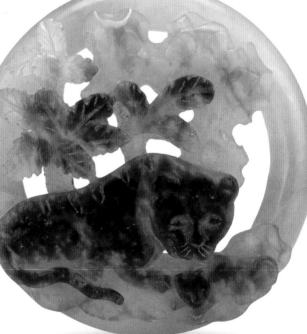

A katydid, an insect that symbolizes fecundity

△ **Tang ox**
This small carving from the Tang dynasty depicts a resting animal—probably an ox.

△ **Jin tiger pendant**
This pendant from the Western Jin dynasty uses white and brown jade together to depict a tiger in repose.

▷ **Jadeite cabbage**
This 19th-century sculpture is thought to have been made for the Forbidden City. It was intricately carved from a single piece of half white, half green jadeite.

Phoenix symbolizing
the union of male
and female

Chrysanthemum,
symbolizing fall
in China

◁ **Pink Buddha**
While much traditional Chinese jadeite is
white or green, this Qing Buddha statue is
carved from a naturally lavender-pink jade.

Wang Xizhi's
prose carved
on the front

△ **Jade mountain**
The Qianlong Emperor commissioned this jade
boulder, which depicts scholars at the Orchid Pavilion
from Wang Xizhi's famous poems (see p. 129).

Leaves made
from coral

◁ **Qing splendor**
Depicting several
birds and flowers,
this garden scene is
typical of the detailed
jade carving of the
Qing dynasty.

Natural color
variation at the
base of the jade

△ **Potted bonsai**
During the Qing dynasty, jade was
combined with other precious materials
to create treasures such as this potted
garden—a bonsai tree with begonias,
made from jade, glass, and bronze.

The Rise of Buddhism

A religion that took root after the fall of the Han

Buddhism reached China from its birthplace in the basin of India's Ganges River in the 1st century CE. During the century that followed, it became a refuge for those who were seeking salvation in an insecure world.

△ **Artistic masterpieces**
The immense rock-carved Buddha statues at the Yungang Grottoes in Datong city, Shanxi province, are considered masterpieces of Chinese Buddhist art. They were carved during the 5th and 6th centuries CE.

Buddhism originated in the 6th century BCE in the north of India, when Siddhartha Gautama, or the Buddha, began to spread his spiritual teachings. By the 1st century CE, traders and missionaries traveling along the Silk Road (see pp. 102–103) had carried its central ideas and practices—of suffering and impermanence, meditation and reincarnation—into China, where the faith's otherworldliness at first seemed alien to traditional beliefs. When Buddhism initially made inroads into China, it was seen largely as an offshoot of Daoism, because its advocates used Daoist terminology to explain its unfamiliar concepts.

The civil strife that accompanied the decline of the Han dynasty in the late 2nd century increased the appeal of Buddhism. Confucian notions of duty and respect for authority lost support and people turned

"No **district** was **without** a **monastery**."

THE SCHOLAR YANG XUANZHI ON THE CITY OF LUOYANG, 6TH CENTURY CE

△ **Early representations**
A heavenly palace, ringed by auspicious animals, sits at the top of this 3rd-century CE Chinese funerary urn. Below the animals are meditating Buddhas—these are thought to be among the earliest Chinese Buddhist images.

instead to a belief system that offered them a path to individual salvation. That need grew with the fall of the Jin dynasty (see pp. 126–127), which briefly united China after the Three Kingdoms period. Following its demise, northern China became a battleground for foreign warlords for almost three centuries.

Imperial approval

While northern China was torn apart by competing kingdoms, the south enjoyed relative stability under the Eastern Jin (see pp. 128–129). This native dynasty was dominated by great landowning families, many of whom had fled south to escape the invaders. They brought the new faith of Buddhism with them as an aristocratic creed, which, in time spread out to other social classes. Growing numbers of individuals opted to become monks, choosing a life of celibacy that also freed them from the usual civic responsibilities of taxation and labor service. The austerity of monastic life was eased by the presence of temple servants to perform menial tasks; criminals were sometimes sentenced to take on this role, many of them subsequently embracing the faith.

One barrier to Buddhism's acceptance was the lack in China of the religion's essential texts. This need was filled by monks such as Faxian (see box, below) who brought Buddhist wisdom from India to China, and others such as the 4th-century scholar Kumarajiva, who gained fame as translators of Buddhist texts.

China's Buddhist community was unwilling to yield to secular authority—a stance that ran counter to Chinese tradition. In 403, the Eastern Jin ruler sought the views of the Buddhist teacher Huiyuan

△ **Buddhist pagoda**
Songyue Pagoda on Mount Song in Henan province was built in 523 CE and is the earliest brick Buddhist pagoda in China. Chambers within were used to store Buddhist texts and relics.

on this matter. While personally reassuring the emperor that Buddhism was not subversive, Huiyuan made the Buddhists' position clear in a celebrated tract entitled *Why Monks Do Not Bow Down Before Kings.*

By the end of the age of division that gripped China from the late 2nd to the late 6th century, Buddhism was deeply embedded in the nation's culture. Nobody better personified its hold than Wu, the 6th-century emperor of the Liang dynasty, who not only wrote commentaries on Buddhist scriptures but also— from time to time—raised money by having himself held "hostage". The money wealthy families paid for his "ransom" went to fill the coffers of Buddhist monasteries. By this time, there were more than 10,000 monasteries across the nation, entrenching Buddhism along with Confucianism and Daoism as an essential part of the nation's religious underpinning.

FAXIAN'S JOURNEY

Buddhist pilgrims from China traveled to India by way of the Silk Road (see pp. 102–103). The route was long and hazardous, yet at least 60 pilgrims are known to have followed it in the 5th century CE alone. In 402, a group of Chinese monks led by the elderly Faxian (pictured right in this painting from the Mogao Caves, Dunhuang) embarked on a journey through what is now Afghanistan to India, where they spent a decade gathering scriptures before returning home by ship. Storms disrupted their passage, and a further year passed before they finally arrived, still guarding the precious manuscripts that Faxian would spend his remaining years translating from their original Sanskrit into Chinese. Over the following years, many hundreds of Buddhist monks followed in Faxian's footsteps.

The Northern Dynasties

Northern China falls to a succession of foreign rulers

In the 4th century CE, northern China came under the control of nomadic peoples from beyond its borders. The invaders largely became assimilated into Chinese culture, which survived until the empire was reunited under the Sui dynasty.

After the chaos and conflict of the Three Kingdoms (see pp. 118–119) China enjoyed a brief period of stability under the Jin dynasty (later called the Western Jin). This was founded by Sima Yan, a nobleman who had built up enough power in the Wei court to topple its emperor, Cao Huan, in 265 CE. Fourteen years later, Sima Yan's armies conquered the Wu—the last of the powerful Three Kingdoms—reuniting China for the first time since the Han. Sima Yan ruled until 290 CE, but his successors proved less able, and their control began to crumble.

States from the north, whose rulers were heirs to the old Xiongnu empire (see pp. 86–89), took advantage of Jin weakness. One of these states, Han Zhao, took the capital of Luoyang in 311 CE and, in 316 CE, captured the emperor, putting an end to Han Chinese control of northern China. The Jin court fled south to Jiankang (Nanjing), establishing a new dynasty that became known as the Eastern Jin (see pp. 128–129).

Power struggles in the north

Northern China again became a battleground as warlords from five distinct ethnic groups competed for control, setting up a succession of temporary regimes known as the Sixteen Kingdoms. Three of these ethnic groups (Xiongnu, Xianbei, and Jie) were from the northern steppes of what is now Mongolia; the other two (the Qiang and Di) originated from the Tibetan region to the northwest.

The most successful of the 16 kingdoms was established by the warlord Fu Jian, who by 376 CE had extended his rule across all northern China. An attempt to invade the Eastern Jin lands in the south proved his undoing, when his huge army was defeated at the Battle of the Fei River in 383 CE.

 First Emperor of the Jin
Sima Yan, or Emperor Wu, was the founder of the Jin dynasty; under the Jin, China was briefly united following the collapse of the Han empire. Emperor Wu was responsible for introducing one of China's earliest legal codes.

Two years later, Fu Jian was assassinated by a turncoat follower, and the region once again collapsed into turmoil and chaos.

The Northern Wei

A degree of unity was next restored by the Tuoba clan of the Xianbei, a Turkic people who had crossed the border from southeast Mongolia in the 3rd century. By 440 CE, the Tuoba had swept away all opposition, setting up the Northern Wei dynasty in order to rule all the lands north of the Yangzi River. Vastly outnumbered by their ethnic Chinese subjects, they adapted to their new realm, using the Chinese language at court, adopting Chinese dress and surnames, encouraging intermarriage, and

THE LONGMEN CAVES

Buddhism became firmly entrenched in northern China under the Tuoba rulers of the Northern Wei dynasty. The faith found expression in the magnificent rock-cut statuary of the Yungang Grottoes, near their headquarters at Pingcheng (modern-day Datong). When the capital was moved to Luoyang, Buddhist adherents felt the need for some similar focus for their faith in the new location—another cave complex therefore grew up at Longmen, 7½ miles (12 km) outside the city. Today, the site houses as many as 100,000 carved images, a group of which is shown here.

△ **A major battle**
This painted silk screen depicts the Battle of the Fei River of 383 CE, in which ethnic Di forces led by Fu Jian were defeated by a smaller Eastern Jin army.

governing with the help of Chinese advisers. To help the assimilation of the Northern Wei, the Tuoba made a symbolic decision to move their headquarters from the northern border area to the former Eastern Han and Jin dynasty capital of Luoyang, which by now had been rebuilt after its earlier destruction. Under their rule, Buddhism became virtually a state religion.

The court's adoption of Chinese ways aroused considerable resentment away from the capital;

> "If I told you all **the details** of how **China fared**, it would be a **tale of debts** and **woe**."

A MERCHANT DESCRIBING THE STATE OF 4TH-CENTURY CE NORTHERN CHINA IN A LETTER TO HIS EMPLOYER

in 524 CE, rebellion broke out among the soldiers manning the border regions. Ten years later, the Northern Wei split into two rival states, each claiming to be the true guardians of their Tuoba heritage. One of these states—Northern Zhou—prevailed and briefly unified northern China in 577 CE. However, the dynasty proved unstable and in a battle for succession, a noble named Yang Jian seized power, proclaiming his own Sui dynasty in 581 CE. Yang Jian led his army south, subduing the lands beyond the Yangzi River (see pp. 134–135) and bringing the whole of China under his rule as Emperor Wen of Sui. After almost three centuries, China's age of division was finally over.

◁ **Beast of burden**
Camels were introduced into China by northern peoples. This statue, which dates from the Northern Wei dynasty, was designed as a tomb ornament.

The Shift to the South

New horizons south of the Yangzi River

As foreign rulers fought for control of the north, the Han (ethnic) Chinese moved in their millions south of the Yangzi River in search of security and stability. There they were ruled by a series of dynastic powers.

The civilization of China's early dynasties was based in the north of the country, centered on the Yellow River and its tributaries. However, the collapse of the Han dynasty (see pp. 86–89) and a changing political environment led to large-scale migration to the lush, semitropical lands south of the Yangzi River. The region's indigenous peoples were forced to accept ethnic Chinese domination, often at the cost of exploitation and in many cases enslavement.

The pace of the southerly movement of Han people increased dramatically with the breakup of the Jin dynasty, which had briefly reunited China in the last decades of the 3rd century CE. Following its disintegration, nomadic tribesmen seized control of China's northern heartlands, ushering in the era that historians would later call the Sixteen Kingdoms period (see pp. 126–127). The sacking of the former imperial capitals of Luoyang in 311 CE and Chang'an five years later, and the destruction and massacres that followed, drove a fresh wave of scholars and officials south.

A new dynasty

In 318 CE, a Jin prince, Sima Rui, established himself as emperor of a new dynasty to rule over the southern lands, naming it the Eastern Jin to emphasize continuity with its predecessor. With its capital at Jiankang (Nanjing), the dynasty held power for a century, preserving an unbroken tradition of Chinese culture south of the Yangzi in the nation's time of trial. Eastern Jin culture was deeply conservative, dominated by the large landowning families who had first occupied what had once been a frontier region.

△ **Terracotta figurine**
This patinated terracotta female figurine dates from the Eastern Jin dynasty. The figure is 13 in (33 cm) high; the woman has folded arms and wears a long dress and a head garment.

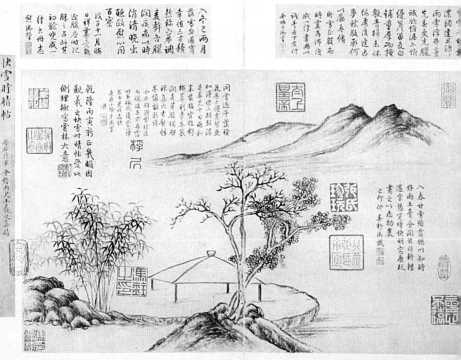

▷ **River nymph**
Gu Kaizhi was an artist of the Eastern Jin dynasty who also wrote three books on art theory. This painting, *Nymph of the Luo River* (a tributary of the Yellow River), is a Song dynasty copy of a work by Gu Kaizhi.

At first, they were heavily outnumbered by the indigenous peoples, but that balance changed with the continued influx of newcomers from the north. More than a million ethnic Chinese are thought to have arrived in the south during the first quarter of the 4th century. The landowning aristocracy kept a tight grip on the higher offices of state, making and unmaking a series of weak emperors; only four of the 11 Eastern Jin emperors were able to hold on to power for more than six years.

▽ **Jin masterpiece**
These extracts are from the painting and calligraphy book *Clear Day After Brief Snow*, attributed to Wang Xizhi (c. 303–c. 361 CE). The work became a favorite of the Qianlong Emperor in the Qing dynasty.

Under the Eastern Jin, the economy expanded rapidly, and Jiankang became a hub of a huge international trade network, its treasury filled with sales taxes and tolls. The leisured lifestyle of the wealthy noble families encouraged a flowering of culture, which was expressed in the new art of landscape painting, as well as in poetry and calligraphy: particularly notable in this respect was the highly revered poet, calligrapher, and artist Wang Xizhi.

Decline of the Eastern Jin
The Eastern Jin relied heavily on their generals to repel invasions from the north, which was a battleground for competing warlords (see pp. 126–127). However, this dependence came at a steep price. The generals grew in power and installed a series of puppet emperors on the throne. They orchestrated coups that ushered in four short-lived dynasties—the Liu Song (420–479 CE), the Qi (479–502 CE), the Liang (502–557 CE), and the Chen (557–589 CE)—that ruled over southern China for 170 years, each one unable to establish a firm grip on power.

Nonetheless, despite significant political instability, economic development continued and the population of the region continued to grow. The distribution of people was shifting markedly—and within a few centuries, the south would overtake the north as the most populous and prosperous part of China.

> "Let us **sing** our **rain-making dances**, So that the **different ages flow in unison**."
>
> WANG XIZHI, POET AND CALLIGRAPHER, *THE ORCHARD PAVILION*, 353 CE

4

The Sui and Tang Dynasties

581 to 960 CE

Introduction

The period from the foundation of the Sui dynasty in 581 CE to the collapse of the Tang in 907 CE saw a cultural, economic, and government renaissance in China. Many aspects of the imperial system that would endure for the next millennium were established during this time.

The accession of Wen, the first Sui emperor, was followed by the reunification of China as northern armies overcame the southern states by 589 CE. However, the high ambitions of the new dynasty almost shattered the country once again: grand building works commissioned by the Sui strained resources, and their foreign campaigns sapped morale. In spite of these troubles, the short-lived Sui dynasty bequeathed China a precious legacy in the Grand Canal, a waterway that allowed grain to be carried from the agricultural regions of the lower Yangzi River to the eastern capital, Luoyang.

Rise of the Tang

The Sui were replaced by the Tang dynasty in 618 CE. The rapid replacement of the Sui by the Tang was achieved without any further period of political fragmentation. Under Emperor Gaozu (see pp. 138–139), the Tang moved quickly to reinforce a strong central administration that was able to gather taxes efficiently and boost the stability of China's social and political structures. This achievement stood in contrast to other Eurasian empires that had collapsed in late antiquity. In Western Europe, too, empires were contracting: the successor states to Rome operated in diminished spheres, such as Visigothic Spain or Frankish Gaul, and the reconstruction of centralized governments was a prolonged process. In India, the Gupta empire, which had dissolved in the 6th century, would not be replaced by anything like a unified state until the Mughals, around a thousand years later.

The firm hand of the early Tang emperors made China into a self-confident realm that was open to outside influences, notably Buddhism. Originally an Indian import, Buddhism established itself at the center of court life in the early Tang period and was in turn exported to neighboring countries. Chang'an, the Tang capital, became the largest city in the world, with more than a million people—the meeting place of ideas and merchants from many lands. The contrast with Europe was stark. Although continent-wide trade had started

581 CE Wen declares himself first emperor of the Sui dynasty

617 CE The expense of a campaign against Korea leads to a revolt that topples the Sui

649 CE Tang armies occupy Khuqa, establishing a firm foothold in Central Asia

680 CE Knowledge of poetry is introduced into China's civil service examinations

610 CE First section of the Grand Canal opened to navigation

629 CE Xuanzang travels to India, returning with Buddhist scriptures

657 CE The Big Wild Goose Pagoda is constructed in Chang'an

690 CE Wu Zetian declares herself empress

to revive in Europe by the 8th century, the efforts were on nothing like the scale achieved in China. Tang success owed much to their reopening of the Silk Road—the trading routes that ran from China through Central Asia and down into Persia and to the shores of the Mediterranean. From the 620s, Tang armies surged through the Hexi Corridor—the most important route from northern China to Central Asia—reoccupying ancient oasis trading towns that had been lost under the Han dynasty, such as Dunhuang, and establishing a series of western prefectures that protected Chinese merchants and projected Tang power into Central Asia.

Rebellion and collapse

The early Tang success proved its eventual undoing. Muslim armies sweeping out of Arabia in the 630s rapidly overcame the Sassanian Persian empire and pushed ever closer to Chinese territory. An uneasy coexistence was ended in 751 CE when an Islamic army defeated a Chinese force at the Battle of Talas (in the valley of the Talas River in modern Kyrgyzstan), putting an end to Chinese ambitions for further westward expansion and destabilizing a state that had grown too dependent on military strongmen. One of them, General An Lushan, revolted, took the capital, and plunged Tang China into a devastating civil war (see pp. 150–153).

Although the Tang recovered, healing was brittle. The military governors on the borders became virtual lords in their fiefdoms, which they defended from nomadic groups such as the Khitan. In the Tang court, eunuchs battled with bureaucrats for power, sapping the authority of the state. Another serious revolt in the 880s left the Tang gravely wounded until one of its generals, Taizu, delivered the final coup de grace in 907 CE. After these events, China again fell apart into a series of warring states (see pp. 162–163), and Chang'an's role as the world's leading city was taken by Baghdad—the center of a golden age for Islamic innovation.

However, the foundations the Tang had laid were deep and provided a strong platform for China's future. While the Islamic empire would eventually fall apart, India would remain divided, and Europe still—centuries after the fall of the Roman Empire—remained a cultural backwater, China reemerged just 50 years after the fall of the Tang as a strong, unified state.

751 CE A force sent by the Abbasid caliph defeats a Tang army at the Talas River

792 CE The Tang lose their last strongholds in the western regions

827 CE Emperor Jingzong is murdered by eunuchs, who have become powerful at court

907 CE Taizu, a Tang general, overthrows Ai, the last Tang emperor, to establish the Later Liang dynasty

755–760 CE The An Lushan Rebellion threatens China's unity

875–884 CE The Huang Zhao revolt briefly captures Chang'an and overthrows the Tang

907–960 CE Period of the Five Dynasties and Ten Kingdoms, in which China is once again disunited

The Sui Dynasty

The reunification of China after 370 years

In the late 6th century CE, China was united again under the Sui. Legal and economic reforms promised an era of prosperity, but ambitious building projects and foreign wars led to raised taxes and revolts that caused the dynasty's downfall.

North China emerged uncertainly from the chaos of the Sixteen Kingdoms (see pp. 126–127) and in 535 CE eventually divided into two rival states, the Northern Qi and the Northern Zhou. Through conflict and diplomacy, the Northern Zhou prevailed and unified northern China in 577.

After the death of the Northern Zhou emperor Wu in 578 CE, the throne passed to his son, who ruled as Emperor Xuan. However, the young Xuan succeeded

▽ Emperor Wen of Sui
The emperor is pictured with his attendants in this detail from *Portraits of Thirteen Emperors*, a 7th-century work attributed to Yan Li-pen, a master figure painter of the Tang dynasty.

in little other than alienating his officials and creating dissent in his kingdom and—perhaps fortunately for the dynasty—died at the age of 20 in 580 CE. Xuan's father-in-law, Yang Jian, the Duke of Sui, stepped in as regent, and before long he took to wearing the imperial regalia himself. In 581 CE, he declared himself emperor and first ruler of the Sui dynasty.

An experienced administrator and general, Yang Jian (posthumously named Wendi, "Emperor Wen") was a devout Buddhist, though reputedly given to violent fits of rage. He streamlined government and established a Board of Civil Office to centralize the appointment of officials. He extended the "equal field" system (a policy devised in the 6th century CE, under which land was redistributed in equal plots to peasants) and so doubled the tax base to nine million families by 606 CE. Wendi also took close control of the military, abolishing private armies and introducing militias made up of volunteers.

Conquest of the south
Wendi planned to unify China by capturing the south from the weak Chen dynasty, which at the time was led by the ineffectual Emperor Hou Zhu. He first wrote to Hou Zhu, accusing him of 20 crimes for which he should be deposed. He then sent an army, reputedly of 500,000 men, and a naval flotilla, which included massive ramming ships, southward. In 589 CE, the Sui took the Chen capital of Nanjing; the hapless Hou Zhu was caught hiding in a well. After the capture of Hou Zhu, the Chen governors along the Yangzi River surrendered to Wendi, and Chen forces

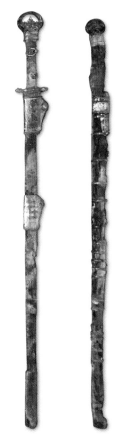

△ **Sui swords**
These swords, recovered from a tomb at Mang Shan, north of Luoyang, date from c. 600 in the Sui dynasty. They are of a type known as *zhirendao*, having a straight back and a single cutting edge.

In order to establish himself as the first Sui emperor, Yang Jian had more than 50 of his own relatives put to death.

△ Emperor Yang
This silk painting of the Sui ruler Yangdi riding in his gardens accompanied by his wives was made in the mid-17th century.

on the coast were soon overcome by the Sui navy. Wendi wisely moved the vanquished Chen officials to his own capital at Chang'an, effectively neutralizing any future threat from the south. With China united for the first time in 370 years, he continued his reforms, issuing a harsh code of law (the *Kaihuang*), which included severe punishments, particularly for the "Ten Abominations" that could not be pardoned, even by the emperor himself.

Murder and succession

Wendi died in 604 CE, with some accounts suggesting that he was murdered by his son Yang Guang (posthumously known as Yangdi, "Emperor Yang"). Soon after Yangdi took the throne, he committed himself to a number of grandiose building projects; he ordered, for example, the construction of a new eastern capital at Luoyang, the rebuilding of sections of the Great Wall, and the establishment of the Grand Canal (see pp. 136–137), which would unite his empire.

It was in foreign policy that Yangdi overreached himself. Wendi had previously attacked Champa (in present-day Vietnam) in 594 CE, with mixed results:

its king, Cambhuvarman, submitted, but the Sui army was decimated by an epidemic. Yangdi had bigger plans and turned his attention to Korea. Supported by a special war tax, he raised a huge force and in 612 CE launched an invasion, which progressed no further than unsuccessful sieges of Korean border cities. The Sui force was recalled. Another attack in 613 CE also foundered, but Yangdi ordered a further expedition in 614 CE. This reached the outskirts of the Korean capital, Pyongyang, but the cost of supporting the army was too great, so it, too, returned to China.

The high taxes collected to support Yangdi's foreign adventures and the resources and labor required for his building projects left the country in turmoil. In 615 CE, during a tour of China's northern provinces, Yangdi was almost captured by Turkic forces led by Shibi Khagan, who was stirring up rebellion in the region; shaken by these events, Yangdi fled south to Jiangdu (Yangzhou). In his absence from the capital, he was deposed and his grandson was enthroned by rebels. In 618 CE, Yangdi was murdered in his bedroom, but by then the Sui were already powerless and being supplanted by the Tang.

The Grand Canal

A history of the world's longest canal

The early Chinese dynasties had a logistics problem. Many resources, particularly food, were concentrated in the south, while the centers of political power were located in the central plains and the north. China's major navigable rivers run from west to east. Attempts to link these waterways into a useful transportation network began as early as the 5th century BCE, when King Fuchai of Wu dug canals linking the Yellow, Ji, and Huai rivers. Work continued under King Hui of Wei in the 4th century BCE and intensified under the Han, but the network was still very restricted.

Unity and prosperity

After their reunification of China (see pp. 134–135) the Sui identified the importance of linking the centers of rice cultivation in the south with the imperial capital of Chang'an. They made a start in 584 CE when the first Sui emperor, Wendi, restored an old Han-era canal parallel to the Wei River to permit faster transportation from the Yellow River plain to Chang'an. His successor, Yangdi, continued the process, ordering old waterways to be dredged and a new canal to be dug to link Luoyang with the Hui River and then on to Yangzhou. New sections also ran from the Yangzi near Jingkou (Zhenjiang) to the coast at Hangzhou and connected the Yellow River to Beijing.

Around three million workers were needed to build the 1,250-mile- (2,000-km-) long waterway, known as the Grand Canal. When it was completed in 610, it offered huge benefits: communication became faster and commerce was boosted, grain could be moved rapidly from south to north, and enormous granaries were built as stores against times of famine. A store at Xingluo could hold more than 600 tons (540 metric

△ **Emperor Yang's fleet**
A fleet of luxurious vessels transports the second Sui emperor, Yang (r. 604–618 CE), along the Grand Canal. The emperor can be seen here in a dragon boat, while the empress's phoenix boat sails in the background. This 17th-century depiction was painted on silk.

△ **Mapping the waterway**
The course of the Grand Canal changed over its history, as new parts were added and rivers burst their banks. A huge flood in 1855 even severed the course of the canal in Shandong. This detail comes from an 18th-century scroll map that shows the canal's entire route and the towns, rivers, and landscape around it.

△ **Hub of activity**
This British depiction shows the Grand Canal in 1783 at its height, crowded with sailing craft. The British sent an embassy led by Lord Macartney to petition for a better trade deal with China, and spectators lined the banks to watch the procession pass through a sluice.

"If **water transportation** is **cut off**, then it might not be **possible to survive**...."

HU SANXING, SONG HISTORIAN AND OFFICIAL, c.1270

tons) of grain. There were also military advantages, as soldiers guarding China's northern borders could be resupplied more quickly. However, Yang's requisitioning of workers—as well as the sight of his "dragon fleet" of luxurious vessels along the canal—caused resentment that contributed to the fall of the Sui dynasty.

The system of waterways was extended by the Tang, who built 30 new canals. Such was the importance of the Grand Canal that, when transportation was disrupted in 786 CE under Emperor Dezong, the Tang court nearly starved. Hugely expensive to maintain, the canal system periodically fell into disrepair.

Growth and developments

Later dynasties, such as the Song, Yuan, and Ming, engaged in large-scale programs to bring the canal back into use. For example, the world's first pound lock system (one that uses a pair of gates to enclose water around a boat and allows it negotiate gradients) was created by a Song administrator, Qiao Weiyue. The Yuan emperors built the Huitong Canal, a section that linked the Yellow River with the Wei River at Linqing but did not use the canal to its full advantage. The Grand Canal was then extensively rebuilt under the Ming and was regularly dredged for maintenance by the Qing rulers until around 1855.

The entire Grand Canal was navigable in the 19th century, when junks were still a regular sight on the water. However, disastrous floods in 1855 and the advent of rail curtailed use of the canal in the late 19th century. Its restoration in the mid-20th century revived traffic on a section extending 500 miles (800 km), and in 2014 the Grand Canal was named a UNESCO World Heritage Site.

△ **The modern canal**
At the beginning of the 20th century, the Grand Canal was still used by local people, as this image taken in 1900 at Wumen Bridge in Suzhou shows. However, parts of the canal were falling into disrepair as the newly built railroads took over the transportation of goods.

△ **Canal junks**
Characterized by their large, wide sails, junk boats have been used to transport cargo on the Grand Canal since the Song dynasty (960–1279). They vary in size, and their flat underside makes them suitable for shallow waterways. In the 13th–15th centuries, they were the largest and most advanced ships in the world.

△ **Scenic Suzhou**
The 1,250-mile (2,000 km) Grand Canal passes through cities as well as tranquil scenery, and the waterside has become popular with tourists from China and beyond. The active section of the waterway, the Beijing–Hangzhou Canal, passes directly through Suzhou.

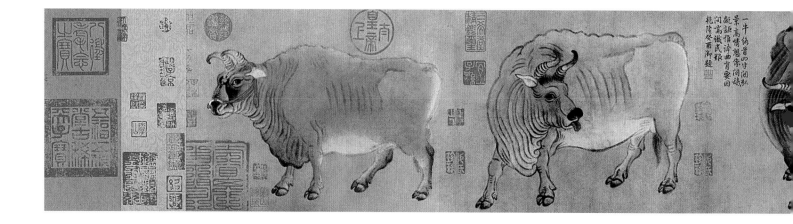

The Rise of the Tang

Laying the foundations of a golden age

Founded in 618 CE, the Tang dynasty ruled a unified China that extended its influence deep into Central Asia. Through strong administration and blossoming trade, the early Tang rulers oversaw a period of prosperity and stability.

In 618 CE, amid the power struggle triggered by the fall of the Sui dynasty, Li Yuan—Governor of Shanxi and a relative of the Sui imperial family—proclaimed himself emperor of a new dynasty, taking the regnal name Gaozu of Tang. The prime mover behind this bid for power was Gaozu's son, Li Shimin. Largely through his efforts, Gaozu's domestic rivals were defeated, and invasions by Turkic tribes on the northern frontier were repulsed through a mixture of military action and the payment of subsidies to the tribes.

Gaozu increased the stability of his empire by restoring a system of administrative prefectures and by minting copper coins—an act that helped resolve the currency shortages that had plagued the Sui and made tax collection difficult. However, Gaozu's reign was cut short in 626 CE by his son. Li Shimin assassinated his own two brothers, murdered their 10 sons, and forced his father to abdicate, taking the imperial throne as Emperor Taizong.

Triumphs of Taizong

Taizong mounted a series of triumphant campaigns in Central Asia against the Khitan tribes. A sequence of events—the split of the Göktürk Khanate (which had been founded in the 6th century CE in Mongolia) and a series of rebellions—allowed him first to subdue the eastern Turks and then, in 642 CE, to gain the submission of the Western Khan. Chinese suzerainty (control over tributary states who kept their own internal autonomy) extended deep into Central Asia and as far as Persia. Trade blossomed—the Silk Road (as it was later known) was secured, and the Tang capital, Chang'an, became a cosmopolitan center.

Despite his violent path to power, Taizong proved an effective ruler. He consolidated the unifying achievements of the Sui dynasty, promoting peace and prosperity under a strong central

> ## "I have **organized** a **righteous army** ... to try to **calm the earth**."
>
> LI YUAN, FOUNDER OF THE TANG DYNASTY, C. 617 CE

▽ **Tang official**
This Tang burial figure depicts a court official prostrating himself, showing his respect to the emperor.

◁ **Age of innovation**
Tang art and sculpture have been celebrated for their innovation. As well as experimenting with color and new techniques, artists blended together existing art forms like calligraphy and painting, as seen here in Han Huang's famous *Five Oxen*.

administration. He lowered taxes, eased the burden of military service, and improved social mobility. A noted scholar himself, he later earned the reputation of being the ideal of a Confucian ruler.

The rise of Empress Wu

The Tang period is often considered a golden age for China, and this was true for women as well as men. While Confucian philosophy saw the woman's place as in the home and made her subordinate to her male relatives, many women in Tang China enjoyed freedoms and influence unparalleled in most other contemporary societies. A widowed woman, for example, had rights to the property of her deceased husband, although in practice this could depend on the cooperation of his brothers. Many women were educated and some went on to find fame as scholars and poets, such as the 7th-century Shangguan Wan'er,

who would serve as an adviser to Empress Wu (see pp. 144–145). Wu herself was an example of the power that could be wielded by a Tang woman.

Central authority weakened in the latter part of Taizong's reign, and the Tang made two disastrous attempts to conquer the northern Korean state of Koguryo. Taizong's successor, Gaozong, came to the throne in 649 CE but failed to regain control over China. Gaozong was a weak ruler, increasingly influenced by Wu Zetian, the concubine who rose to become his second empress. After Gaozong suffered a stroke in 660 CE, Wu took full control, exercising real power in China. Ruthless in suppressing opposition, Wu formally declared herself reigning empress in 690 CE, founding her own dynasty. The only woman ever officially recognized as a ruler of imperial China, Empress Wu reigned until 705 CE when, aged 81, she was overthrown in a palace coup.

△ **Reigning legacy**
Emperor Taizong continues to be remembered as one of the greatest emperors in Chinese history.

◁ **Court visitors**
The Tang court welcomed a number of ambassadors from Japan, who came seeking knowledge of Chinese civilization and cultural practices. Their visits led to a blossoming trading relationship.

Tang Hand Mirrors

The golden age of mirror making

From as early as 1300 BCE, China had a well-developed bronze industry, but mirrors began to be made only during the Qin and Han dynasties. The manufacture of these luxury items was formalized and regulated by imperial officers, who published reports outlining each step of production. The Directorate for Imperial Manufactories oversaw production in all workshops, where, according to imperial regulations, a meticulously measured mixture—71 percent copper, 26 percent tin, and 3 percent lead, designed to minimize imperfections as the bronze cooled—was poured into a clay mold. When cool, one surface was polished to a mirrored finish. The reverse sides of the mirrors were decorated with intricate patterns and designs of birds, dragons, and serpents. Over the centuries, the designs became more sophisticated and began to include mythological figures, deities, Chinese zodiac animals, patterns, textures, gilding, and enamelwork, as well as inlaid jade, turquoise, and mother-of-pearl.

> "Mornings **in her mirror** she sees her hair-cloud **changing**."

POET LI SHANGYIN, *TO ONE UNNAMED III*, c. 813–858 CE

The quality of bronze mirrors declined after the end of the Han, but the Tang dynasty reinvigorated and innovated production in the 7th century CE, and many beautiful examples survive from the period. The Tang produced square, oblong, and octagonal mirrors in addition to the traditional round versions, and both male and female poets of the period used mirror imagery or referenced the objects in their works. Tang mirrors were often decorated with *ruishou* (auspicious animals) and floral, grapevine, or lotus motifs.

Beautiful gifts

Mirrors had both practical and symbolic value in Tang China. While used for cosmetic purposes, they were also frequently given cosmological, spiritual, and even magical meanings and functions. They were believed to ward off evil and were often buried with their owners to protect them in the afterlife. Mirrors were also used as love tokens and given as part of dowries because their round shape represented perfection, union, fortune, and marital bliss. Many of the inscriptions found on Tang mirrors expressed marital happiness, and broken halves of mirrors have been found in the tombs of spouses. Mirrors were often given as gifts, by all ranks of Chinese society. Chinese bronze mirrors found in Japan, Vietnam, Afghanistan, and Iran also suggest that mirrors were given as gifts to representatives of foreign states.

Mother-of-pearl lotus decoration

"Cloud" of hair
worn in a bun

△ **Self-reflection**
This Tang burial figurine shows
a woman admiring herself in a
small hand mirror—a popular
motif of the time.

Pronounced
lobed edge

Bronze rim

△ **Duck pond mirror**
Produced some time in the 8th century CE,
this hand mirror back is decorated with
mother-of-pearl and agate, depicting ducks
on a lotus pond.

▷ **Floral treasure**
This lobed Tang mirror is made from
bronze with a sheet of gold affixed to the
back. The decoration contains symmetrical,
ring-punched birds and floral patterns.

The Growth of Chang'an

The political, cultural, and commercial center of the Tang

After a period of instability, Xuanzong's reign saw China grow and thrive once more. The Tang capital of Chang'an blossomed into a cosmopolitan hub teeming with foreign merchants, artists, and religious figures.

The overthrow of Empress Wu (see pp. 144–145) in 705 CE was followed by seven chaotic years in which one of her sons, Zhongzong, presided over a corrupt court, and another son, Ruizong, abdicated after just two years of ineffective rule. Despite the inauspicious circumstances under which Ruizong's son, Xuanzong, ascended to the throne, he proved an able ruler. During his reign from 712 to 756 CE, China reached a peak of prosperity and cultural growth. Xuanzong patronized poets, painters, and musicians, founding an Imperial Literary Academy and a Palace Music School that attracted artists to the imperial court. The Tang capital, Chang'an, grew to be the largest city in the world, and the ports and waterways of southern China teemed with ships.

Chang'an was a strategically important city, located at the eastern end of the Silk Road (see pp. 102–103), and had been a capital of several ancient dynasties, including the Western Zhou and the Han. In 582 CE, it was refounded by Yang Jian—the first Sui emperor—

as a grand gesture to signal his determination to reunify China (see pp. 134–135). Taking the advice of geomancers (experts in auspicious building planning), he ordered the construction of a rectangular city, laid out in a grid and bounded by earthen walls. Despite the huge effort devoted to its building, many of the 108 walled wards into which the city was divided still lay empty when the Sui were replaced by the Tang in 618 CE. Under the Tang, the city reached its height; it had a population of over a million people; its bustling streets were a riot of market sellers, entertainers, and festivals; and its palatial mansions and offices were the bases of a powerful nobility and bureaucracy.

Commerce and culture

The Imperial Palace of Long-Lived Benevolence sat against the northern edge of the city. Beyond its 36 ft (11 m) high wall lay government offices and training establishments for the civil service. Arrayed around these in a crescent were the residential

△ **Crossing cultures**
The Greek-inspired shape of this Tang amphora shows the influence of foreign contact on Chinese culture.

◁ **The Silk Road**
This depiction of the Silk Road from the Ming dynasty shows people of many nationalities carrying goods along the trade route.

△ **Floral finery**
Tang artists were known for their skills in producing beautiful silk wares. This 8th-century silk fragment depicts a floral medallion.

△ **Tang water jug**
This wide-mouthed glazed earthenware ewer was molded and decorated to resemble a phoenix.

wards—more fashionable in the east, where one of the city's two markets sold rarer commodities, and less prosperous in the west, where the Western Market offered more everyday goods. The securing of the Silk Road meant that traders and merchants traveled into China from Central Asia, bringing their wares to Chang'an and practicing trades there. Tang ceramics celebrated this newfound diversity, portraying foreign merchants, traders, and musicians riding on horses and camels.

The early Tang had ushered in a cultural golden age. Art and crafts flourished, with the development of a school of black ink and brush painting (exemplified by masters such as Wu Daozi), and the emergence of landscape painting that evoked mood as much as place. The Tang dynasty produced some of China's most celebrated poets, including Li Bai and Du Fu (see pp. 154–155). Meanwhile, Tang kilns produced high-quality ceramics, many of which were decorated in a bright three-color (*sancai*) glaze.

Religious diversity
A tolerant atmosphere prevailed in the early Tang empire, encouraging the growth of foreign communities in the city—up to 500,000 non-Chinese lived there—and the acceptance of their beliefs. Several Zoroastrian temples

were built in Chang'an in the 7th century; Manichaeism, a dualist religion from Persia, and Nestorianism, a Christian sect, also flourished in the Tang capital. The city's major Daoist sites included the Ancestral Temple, where imperial rituals were carried out, and the Big Wild Goose Pagoda, a structure erected in 657 CE at the suggestion of the Buddhist pilgrim Xuanzang (see pp. 146–147) to house the religious texts he had brought back from India.

Buddhism and Daoism reasserted themselves under Wuzong, who in 845 CE banned foreign religions, leading to an exodus of foreigners. By then, however, the city was already in decline; any remaining nobles had fled after it fell to An Lushan in 756 CE (see pp. 150–153); and the capture of Chang'an by the late Tang rebel Huang Chao in 880 CE saw large-scale looting of the city. Huang Chao briefly declared himself the "emperor of Qi" before being defeated by Tang forces. Ultimately, Chang'an was abandoned: some of its great wooden buildings were dismantled and moved elsewhere; others were simply left to decay.

▽ **A symbol of commerce**
This earthenware Bactrian camel, mounted by a sleepy cameleer, was made for the tomb of a wealthy Tang merchant. The figure of a camel was significant because these animals were used to carry goods across the arid parts of the Tang empire.

Buddhist empress
Wu Zetian rose to power at a time when Buddhism prevailed in China. The Buddhist faith was more accepting of women than traditional Confucianism.

Empress Wu

China's first and only empress regnant

Rising from her status as a concubine, Wu Zetian was able to manipulate weak emperors to become China's first ruling empress. An effective political force, she used religious propaganda to burnish her public image and cement her rule.

There are various accounts of the early life of Wu Zetian. It is thought that she came from a merchant family in Shanxi province and entered the court as a concubine. On the death of Emperor Taizong in 649 CE, Wu attracted the attention of his successor, Gaozong. She eliminated all rivals for his affection, including Consort Xiao (with whom Gaozong had a son) and Empress Wang, whom she had executed on charges of witchcraft. Gaozong was sickly, and Wu's strong personality made her the de facto ruler of China by 660 CE. She was challenged upon Gaozong's death in 683 CE, when their third son, Zhongzong, briefly reigned and his supporters tried to remove her. Wu responded by executing members of the imperial family and replacing officials with men loyal to her. She reigned at first through her fourth son, Ruizong, but in 690 CE she deposed him and declared herself empress of the Zhou dynasty. She took the title *huangdi*, which was only used by emperors.

At first, her position was precarious. Advances by the Khitan, Tibetans, and Turks threatened to push into Tang

△ **Buddha Maitreya**
Wu Zetian identified with Maitreya, an incarnation of the Buddha, and used the association to further her political agenda.

heartlands, but Wu's generals repelled them, and by 697 CE, peace was restored. The empress used religion to legitimize her rule and counter dissent from the traditional Confucian establishment. She patronized Buddhist and Daoist temples, even taking the Daoist title of "Sage Mother". Her consort, the Buddhist abbot Xue Huaiyi, also uncovered a new text (almost certainly a forgery) that proclaimed the imminent incarnation of Maitreya, a female manifestation of Buddha. Wu claimed this mantle for herself.

The fall of Wu Zetian

Wu's grip on power weakened, and in 698 CE she was forced to recall Zhongzong and make him crown prince. Rather than reasserting her authority, the empress began to spend ever more time with her young lovers, the Zhang brothers, leading to a scandal. Court officials ordered the arrest and execution of the Zhang brothers, and the empress was forced to abdicate in favor of her son.

△ **Tang beauty standards**
Wu fitted the mold of the great Tang beauties, who were plump, round-faced women. This ideal was depicted in Tang tomb figurines.

"A Sage Mother shall come to **Rule Mankind**; and her Imperium shall bring **Eternal prosperity**."

TANG DYNASTY INSCRIPTION, 688 CE

638 Aged 14, becomes a junior concubine in the court of Emperor Taizong

673 Has a gigantic statue of the female Buddha Maitreya built at Longmen

690 Declares herself Empress Wu of the Zhou dynasty and moves her capital to Luoyang

624 Born into a prominent Tang merchant family

655 Becomes empress and has Gaozong's wife, Wang, executed

683 Survives an overthrow attempt and has seven temples built to honor her ancestors

705 Deposed following a court scandal and dies in the same year

The Spread of Buddhism

A history of the rise and fall of Buddhist influence

Buddhism was slow to reach China from its Indian homeland. A document from 65 CE mentions Buddhist monks, but it was not until the 4th century CE that the religion began to make inroads into the country. Buddhism was carried by merchants along the Silk Road (see pp. 102–103), and was assisted in its spread by imperial patronage in the early 6th century. Even so, adherents of the Daoist and Confucian faiths showed hostility toward Buddhism, accusing its followers of not respecting traditional values. In response, Chinese Buddhists adapted their practices, for example, by incorporating ancestor worship into their beliefs.

Buddhism flourished under the Sui, with Emperor Wen ordering the distribution of relics of the Buddha throughout China in 601 CE. The patronage of Tang emperors Taizong and Gaozong and Empress Wu (see pp. 144–145) cemented the position of Buddhism, and great monasteries were founded in the Tang capital, Chang'an. Several distinct Chinese traditions of Buddhism emerged, including the Tiantai (Heavenly Terrace) founded by Zhi Yi at the start of the Sui dynasty; the Huayan (Flower Garland); and the Jingtu (Pure Land).

A thirst for Buddhist texts

The lack of Buddhist texts in Chinese meant that the emerging faith lacked a scriptural base. To remedy this deficit, foreign monks were invited to China; for example, Kumarajiva (343–413 CE), a scholar from the Kucha (near present-day Kashmir), came to the Chinese court armed with 300 texts whose translation into Chinese he then supervised. Chinese pilgrims also brought back Buddhist wisdom and writing from their travels. The most famous of these travelers was

△ **Xuanzang's odyssey**
The monk Xuanzang (c. 602–664) traveled to India, returning with around 700 texts and descriptions of wonders such as the stone Buddhas of Bamiyan. He was the inspiration for the central character in the 16th-century novel *Journey to the West* (see pp. 226–227).

△ **Buddhist grotto art**
Early Buddhist art found expression in murals within caves. In places such as Longmen and Dunhuang, networks of caves were hollowed out and decorated to serve as spaces for reflection. Their elaborate murals depict Buddhist beliefs and stories to aid meditation but may also illustrate contemporary events.

△ **Mogao Caves, Dunhuang**
The Mogao Caves in Gansu province are often called the Caves of the Thousand Buddhas and contain murals and statues from several periods of Chinese history. They were dug out from the cliff face in the 4th century CE, when a Buddhist community grew up in the vicinity of Dunhuang.

"It is **indispensable** to have the **right names**, in order that there be **no mistakes**."

XUANZANG, ON INTERPRETING THE BUDDHA'S WORDS, *RECORD OF THE WESTERN REGIONS*, 646 CE

Xuanzang, who spent 16 years on a pilgrimage that included five years at the Buddhist monastery in Nalanda, India, and translated 73 of the many texts that he brought back with him.

Chinese Buddhists making a spiritual journey to India faced a new obstacle when Arab expansion blocked the western arm of the Buddhist pilgrim route. Travelers to India were forced to take a far more dangerous and lengthy route by sea. One of the most notable of these pilgrims was the Buddhist monk Yijing (635–713), who brought more than 400 Buddhist texts back to China after 25 years abroad.

From privilege to persecution

At home, Chinese attitudes toward Buddhism were hardening. The wealth of Buddhist institutions, which by the 840s housed 260,000 monks and nuns, aroused the jealousy of the traditional Confucian bureaucracy. Following the An Lushan rebellion in the 750s (see pp. 150–153), the Tang emperors became less open toward outside influences, including Buddhism. The Japanese monk Ennin, whose nine-year visit to China began in 838 CE, documented these changes, recording that in 841 CE, Emperor Wuzong distributed purple robes on his birthday to Daoist priests but denied them to the Buddhists. Wuzong's later persecution closed many imperial monasteries.

Although Chinese Buddhism survived, its power was broken. By 956 CE, most large Buddha statues had been melted down and their bronze used to mint coins. The great age of expansion was over. While some adherents of Buddhism remained, Confucianism became the dominant force at the imperial court and in Chinese religious life for the next millennium.

△ **Leshan's giant Buddha**
A Buddhist monk, Hai Tong, was concerned about tempestuous rivers close to Leshan in Sichuan and raised money to carve a statue of Maitreya (a future incarnation of Buddha) to calm the waters. Work began in 713 on the 233 ft (71 m) statue and took 90 years to complete.

△ **Tibetan wheel of life**
The hillsides in Dazu, near Chongqing, have more than 50,000 rock carvings from the 9th to the 13th centuries, including this Tibetan Buddhist wheel of life, depicting the cycle of birth, death, and rebirth. A form of Tibetan Buddhism was practiced by China's Mongol rulers during the Yuan dynasty.

△ **Modern monks**
Buddhist monks, such as these working in a monastery garden in Yunnan, are part of a revival that has been taking place in China since the 1970s. They adhere to teachings that have shaped Chinese culture, philosophy, and art over millennia.

凡欲讀經先念淨口業真言三遍

補唎　補唎

摩訶補唎

婆婆訶

補補唎

奉請青除災金剛

奉請辟毒金剛

奉請黃隨求金剛

奉請白淨水金剛

奉請赤聲金剛

奉請定除尼金剛

奉請紫賢金剛

奉請大神金剛

金剛般若波羅蜜經

如是我聞一時佛在舍衛國祇樹給孤獨園與大
比丘眾千二百五十人俱爾時世尊食時著衣持
鉢入舍衛大城乞食於其城中次第乞已還至本處
飯食訖收衣鉢洗足已敷座而坐時長老須菩提在大

祇樹給孤獨園圖
長老須菩提

Frontispiece of the *Diamond Sutra*

Produced in 868 CE, during the Tang dynasty, *The Diamond That Cuts Through Illusion* is the world's oldest surviving printed book. The sacred text, known for brevity as the *Diamond Sutra*, is made up of around 6,000 words; Buddhists believe it is a transcribed conversation between the Buddha and his elderly pupil Subhati. The *Diamond Sutra*, complete with its illustrated frontispiece, was printed using wooden blocks onto a 17½ ft (5.3 m) scroll. It was discovered by a monk in 1907 at the Dunhuang, or Mogao, Caves. The illustration shows the Buddha addressing his disciple Subhati beneath a grove of trees.

The Decline of the Tang

The Battle of Talas and the An Lushan Rebellion

The success of the early Tang emperors caught the attention of other empires, which pushed back against Tang expansion. The external and internal conflicts of Emperor Xuanzong's reign signaled the beginning of the end for the dynasty.

The Tang emperor Xuanzong, who came to power in 712 CE, streamlined the government, cutting away at the bloated bureaucracy that had grown up under his predecessors. While earlier Tang emperors had standardized the empire's currency—delegitimizing the coinage of previous dynasties and creating a new bronze-cast coin—Xuanzong wanted to provide more financial stability for his people. Xuanzong's reform of the *zuyongdiao* tax system—which originally comprised three taxes, to be paid in grain, cloth, and labor—simplified the structure even further, removing the labor tax. The government also ensured that coins and silk were used as currency in equal measure, to avoid potential circulation issues.

Despite the economic growth and stability that came with these changes, unrest was brewing within the Tang government. A divide grew between court officials and those in the provinces, including military governors whom the emperor had appointed to command border regions. It was the frontier that was to prove Xuanzong's undoing.

Pressure on the borders

The early Tang emperors greatly expanded China's Central Asian lands—securing territories lost since the height of the Han empire—and by 642 CE had annexed the eastern and western Turkish khanates (see pp. 138–139). As Chinese armies moved westward, ever closer to the ancient trading cities of Samarkand and Bukhara, they were confronted with a new adversary—the Tibetan

empire. In 665 CE, the Tibetans attacked Khotan, cutting off the southern arm of the Silk Road. By 670 CE, they had captured Kuqa. The Tang reinforced the Western Regions in response, but their hold on the area was precarious. This was partly because the Tang court exercised weak control over its provincial governors, who were highly likely to defect if the opportunity arose, but also because it was under military pressure from other quarters when its resources were already being depleted. The successful reclaiming of territories came at a price to the Tang. The cost of the strengthened garrisons (some 50,000 men by Xuanzong's reign) came at a time when other forces were rising. A revived western Turkish khanate was raiding across the Gobi into China, and a revolt in 696 CE by the Khitan—a Northeast Asian people—almost overwhelmed its northwestern frontier.

The advance of the Arab caliphate's armies from Persia proved yet another challenge to China's military. First capturing Khorasan in 651 CE, the Arabs went on to successfully take Bukhara and Samarkand in 708 CE and threatened to push into Chinese-controlled territory. The Chinese army's ability to head off the Arab expansion was hindered by renewed attacks from Tibet: in 736 CE, the Tibetans invaded Gilgit, cutting off the main route from Kashgar to Kashmir. It was not until 750 CE that the Tang reclaimed the

△ **Emperor Xuanzong**
Despite constant threats to his empire, Xuanzong ruled for 43 years, the longest reign of the Tang dynasty.

▷ **Ornate weaponry**
Shaped to look like a dragon fish holding a pearl in its mouth, this silver gilt axe head—which dates back to the 8th century CE—was probably a weapon reserved for ceremonial purposes.

"The **state** is **destroyed**, the mountains and rivers **remain**."

DU FU, *THE VIEW IN SPRING*, 757 CE

△ **Loyal imperialists**
This wall painting, found in the Mogao Caves, portrays Zhang Yichao, a Tang loyalist, and his men attacking the Tibetans.

town. Barely had they done so when the Tang general Gao Xianzhi met an army sent by the Arab Abbasid caliph (ruler) as-Saffah, who had just overthrown the preceding Umayyad dynasty and wished to secure his position in Central Asia.

In July 751 CE, Tang forces clashed with as-Saffah's army at the Talas River in the Ili valley, north of the Tarim Basin. Over the course of five days, Gao Xianzhi's army fought against the Abbasids. Bolstered by Tibetan allies and defecting Turks, as-Saffah's men crushed the Chinese. Of the 20,000 Tang soldiers, only a tenth—including Gao Xianzhi—escaped. The rest were cut down as they fled. The defeat at the Talas River would have a great impact on religion in central China. Until this point, Buddhism had been an integral part of Chinese life. However, as the Arabs made further inroads into the Tang territories and the dynasty's financial situation became more unstable, Buddhism's influence began to weaken. In Xinjiang and the regions to the south and west, Uighurs and other ethnic groups converted to Islam. Cut off from distant Buddhist areas, Buddhism in China began to decline and lost its philosophical prosperity.

Li Linfu and Yang Guifei

In addition to the threats posed to Xuanzong's empire by the Tibetans, Turks, and Arabs, Nanzhao—a new, united Tai kingdom—ate away at Chinese territory in the southwest. To face these various threats, in 742 CE, the emperor's chief minister, Li Linfu, ordered the reorganization of the north and west frontier armies into 10 frontier commands, each headed by a military governor. In 747 CE, he decreed that these governors were all to be non-Chinese to prevent his competitors from rising up to ministerial positions. »

▷ **New money**
The new Tang coinage was inscribed with the phrase *Kaiyuan tongbao* (literally "Circulating treasure of the new beginning").

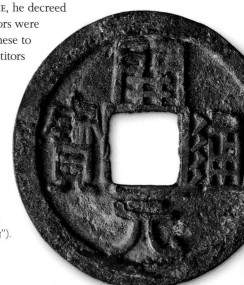

The decision proved disastrous. Although Li Linfu ruthlessly eliminated rivals at court, his position came under threat after Xuanzong began a relationship with Yang Guifei, the beautiful wife of one of his sons. She promoted the interests of her cousin, Yang Guozhong, along with a half-Turkish, half-Sogdian army officer named An Lushan—even, it was said, adopting him as her son. Her new protégé built up a formidable power base as the military governor of three frontier provinces, commanding 200,000 troops.

However, relations between Yang Guozhong and An Lushan soured, and when Yang Guozhong became chief minister following Li's death in 754 CE, he had An Lushan's supporters arrested. The outraged general vowed to get his revenge, and late the following year he advanced southward, capturing first the eastern capital, Luoyang, and then approaching Chang'an.

Panicked by his approach, Xuanzong fled toward the safety of Sichuan, but on his way the imperial guard mutinied, killing both Yang Guozhong and Yang Guifei. In 756 CE, Xuanzong had no choice but to abdicate after his heir declared himself China's new emperor: Emperor Suzong.

The triumphant An Lushan also declared himself the first ruler of the Yan dynasty. His self-proclaimed reign was short; he was nearly blind and his fits of temper led his own son, An Qingxu, to have him assassinated. As the Yan dynasty dissolved into chaos, Tang loyalist forces under Suzong retook Luoyang and Chang'an. Even then, the rebellion reignited under An Lushan's former general, Shi Siming, who killed An Qingxu, declared himself emperor, and succeeded in recapturing Luoyang. It was not until 763 CE that the eastern capital was secured by the Tang and the final

▽ **Historical record**
Artists recorded significant events of the Tang dynasty on a large silk scroll painting. The section displayed below depicts Emperor Xuanzong's escape from Chang'an to Sichuan during the An Lushan Rebellion. This version is a Ming copy of a painting by the celebrated Ming artist Qiu Ying.

"The **regret** of our **parting** will last forever and **never end**."

BAI JUYI, *SONG OF EVERLASTING SORROW*, 806 CE

◁ **Under siege**
This 18th-century painting by Japanese artist Toyoharu Utagawa depicts An Lushan and his troops attacking the emperor in his palace.

Yan forces were defeated. By then, the empire was devastated. Luoyang had been pillaged in 762 CE by the Uighur mercenaries who had been called in to help secure it, and the recorded population of China fell from 53 million at the census of 754 CE to just 17 million in 764 CE. The recall of foreign troops from Central Asia caused the Tang position there to collapse, and the resurgent Tibetans sacked Chang'an in 763 CE.

Tang decline

The repercussions of the An Lushan Rebellion fatally weakened the dynasty. Central Asia was left open for continued infiltration by Arabs, who radiated out from Samarkand, and by Tibetans, who in 792 CE took Turfan—the last major Tang stronghold in the Western Regions. Military governors who had become semi-independent during the rebellion could not be brought back to obedience. In the northeast, generals formerly loyal to An Lushan ruled Hebei, and the cost of subsidies to the Uighur allies who propped up the dynasty grew unsustainable. Following the defeat at

THE HUANG CHAO REVOLT

The increasing power of eunuchs within the Tang court—especially during the reigns of the emperors Yizong and Xizong—aggravated grievances against the Tang, causing banditry to become rife. In 875 CE, a revolt broke out after a drought in Henan, and this soon engulfed eastern and western China. In 880 CE, its leader, Huang Chao, entered Chang'an in a golden carriage while the Tang court fled to Sichuan. Although he declared the establishment of the Qi dynasty, his harsh rule was unpopular—he had all poets in the capital executed after an unflattering poem was found pinned to a city gate. This allowed the Tang to regroup, retake Chang'an, and finally put down the revolt in 884 CE.

Talas, the Tang sought stability by establishing state monopolies on salt and iron. In 780 CE, they reformed the tax system by creating a new tax that was to be paid twice a year and exclusively with the dynasty's coinage—no longer permitting the exchange of silk as currency. Despite these attempts to stabilize the empire, the new taxes became oppressive, leading to a series of agrarian revolts in the 820s.

The rebellions overshadowed a series of successful campaigns led by Emperor Xianzong against rebel provinces, which resulted in all but three being back under central control by 820 CE. The social unrest, combined with a succession of weak emperors dominated by eunuch factions, undermined the Tang once more. An army mutiny in 868 CE nearly brought down the dynasty, while a serious revolt in 880 CE ended in the sacking of Chang'an. By the time the Tang finally fell in 907 CE, it had long since lost any real grip on power. The loss at Talas proved a turning point, after which Chinese armies would not operate in the region for another thousand years.

▷ **Muse for the poets**
Yang Guifei's tragic love affair with Emperor Xuanzong became the subject of a poem by the Tang poet Bai Juyi in 806 CE titled *Chang hen ge*, or *The Song of Everlasting Sorrow*.

Poetry

The history of the literary form in China

China has long regarded poetry as an elevated form of expression. The earliest anthology of Chinese poetry, the *Shijing*, features poems that could date as far back as 1000 BCE. It wasn't until the Tang dynasty, however, that classical Chinese poetry reached its height.

The great Tang poets

Tang poetry is among China's most notable contributions to world literature. With its roots in classical tradition, the poetic form diversified in the Tang dynasty to appeal to a wide audience and become the foundation stone of China's literary golden age. Tang poetry reached its peak in the middle years of the dynasty. Wang Wei (701–761 CE), a career civil servant who rejected the bureaucratic path for a life of austere simplicity, crafted exquisite poems celebrating the Chinese landscape. Li Bai (701–762 CE)—who had

Central Asian ancestry—espoused Daoism and eclectic philosophy, and his poetry encapsulates a profound feeling for nature's grandeur. He was called to Chang'an in 742, where he received a court position, but his unconventional morals made his tenure in the capital awkward. Li Bai was one of the "Eight Immortals of the Wine Cup." Gaining their name from a satirical poem, this was a group of Tang scholars and writers known for their love of wine and the inspiration they apparently took from drinking. Their images were a popular motif on Chinese drinking vessels and paintings.

The most revered of all the Tang poets was Du Fu (712–770). Having failed the civil service examination, he set out on a series of travels, which inspired his early works. Like Li Bai, he became caught up in the turmoil of the An Lushan Rebellion (see pp. 150–153);

△ **Ancient poetry**
Although the *Shijing* features poetry dating back to the Zhou dynasty, one pre-Tang poet particularly fascinates readers today. Su Hui, a 4th-century CE poet, wrote *"Xuanji Tu,"* a poem with a palindrome effect that means it can be read in almost 8,000 different ways.

△ **Li Bai**
Li Bai sought an official post when he first came to Chang'an in 742, but he was instead welcomed into a group of esteemed court poets. The romantic style of his poetry complemented his works exploring themes such as friendship, time, solitude, and nature. He also had a reputation for celebrating the joys of wine.

△ **Du Fu**
Many literary critics cite Du Fu as being the greatest Chinese poet of all time. The Confucian poet's work is celebrated for its complexity and respect for classic traditions. His most famous works are written in *lüshi*, a form consisting of eight lines of five or seven characters each.

"... the **sword** is a **cursed thing**, Which the **wise man** uses only if he **must**."

"FIGHTING SOUTH OF THE RAMPARTS," LI BAI, 751

the conflict and suffering that he witnessed—and experienced himself—inspired darker works that lamented the loss of stability and hope.

Poetry continued to flourish under the later Tang emperors, even though the dynasty itself was in decline. The idea of pursuing the poetic vocation for its own sake emerged, and poets such as Bai Juyi (772–846) were held in great esteem; when Bai Juyi was visited by fellow poet Yuan Zhen, huge crowds are said to have lined the streets of Hangzhou just to gain a glimpse of the two literati. Yet later Tang poetry was tinged with regret, and works such as those by Du Mu (803–852) are characterized by a clear, incisive style and a nostalgia for better times. A desire to capture this past led to the creation of anthologies, and by the time Wei Zhuang created one in 900, Du Fu, Li Bai, and Wang Wei were firmly established as China's premier poets. It is a position they have retained ever since, with their works making up more than a third of those included in Sun Zhu's *Three Hundred Tang Poems* in 1763, a collection that Chinese schoolchildren had to learn by heart for centuries.

Beyond the golden age

Poets who lived during the Song dynasty attempted to maintain and imitate the literary excellence of their Tang predecessors. Yet the territorial losses inherited from the Tang meant that the Song dynasty became more introspective in its poetry, resulting in a more contemplative and philosophical poetic style.

After the end of imperial China, some poets attempted to change the style of Chinese poetry. Despite these moves to reject the past, China's classical poetry remains emblematic of the nation's values.

△ **Wang Wei**
Wang Wei's legacy is built on both his poetic and his artistic majesty. A government official for most of his life, he witnessed the political turmoil within Chang'an, including the An Lushan Rebellion. His best poetry came after he abandoned the capital and studied Buddhism.

△ **Bai Juyi**
Although remembered for his poem about Emperor Xuanzong and Yang Guifei, *Song of Everlasting Sorrow*, most of Bai Juyi's poetry criticized the corruption and the decadent lifestyles of court officials. He advocated poetry that had a moral compass, and his poetry is noted for its elegant simplicity.

△ **Modern poetry**
To this day, literary critics and readers revere Tang poetry. But from the 20th century onward, some poets have attempted to break away from tradition, exploring Western styles. Written in free verse and vernacular language, modern poetry was born, though to fierce criticism.

Tang Tomb Figures

Earthenware from the Tang dynasty

Many of the clay figures buried in Tang tombs have survived the test of time. Excavations have revealed a cast of characters intended to attend the souls of the wealthy and powerful in the afterlife—from guardians and terrifying beasts to the more everyday figures of farmers, dancers, and polo players.

◁ **Tomb guardian**
This terracotta sculpture, which has been painted and glazed, depicts a *lokapāla* (or *tianwang*)—one of the protective spirits from Buddhist mythology who were placed as tomb guardians.

Cap covering rider's hair indicates her female gender

Twisted strands of clay creating fur-like texture

△ **Equestrienne**
Ceramic burial figures often depicted the favorite pastimes of the deceased. This figure captures the tranquillity of a woman riding her horse.

◁ **Man with a hoe**
This 7th-century CE figure portrays a man with a farming hoe. Other figures have been found holding similar agricultural tools.

▷ **Female attendant**
Colorful tomb figures were commonly found positioned outside the burial chamber. This terracotta figurine would have been left there to care for the deceased in the afterlife.

Bright pigment

△ **Tang polo player**
A love of horses led to polo becoming a popular sport within the Tang court. Both men and women could play, as reflected in this ceramic of a female polo player.

Snake
headdress

▽ **Tang horse**
A symbol of wealth and power, horses
were a popular subject in Chinese art
and sculpture. The mane and saddle of
this 8th-century CE horse appear to
have been restored at a later time.

Pigment
retouched on
horse's mane

△ **Figure of a dancer**
Dancers, like this terracotta
figurine, were often left in
tombs with the hope that they
would entertain the dead.

Pendants
hang from
the horse's
harness

△ **Male official**
This figure was discovered in
the tomb of Li Zhen, the son
of Emperor Taizong, who
tried to provoke an uprising
against Wu Zetian.

Brightly
colored
pigment
remains on
the wings

▷ **Warrior guardian**
Grave guardian figures from the
Tang dynasty often portrayed the
tomb keeper overcoming an evil
creature, reflecting their ability
to protect the deceased.

The cart would
have been used to
transport a person

▽ **Ox and cart**
Ceramic sculptures of oxen
and their carts were common
tomb ornaments; they were
left for the deceased's future
travels in the afterlife.

△ **Two-headed creature**
This early Tang sculpture depicts
a two-headed mythical beast with
humanlike facial features.

Afterlife Entertainers

Lively Tang music and dance

Painted earthenware figurines (see pp. 156–157) were commonly found in the tombs of important people from Tang China. Historians believe that these figurines had a spiritual significance and served different functions in the afterlife: some were representations of warriors and guardian beasts, intended to protect the souls of the dead from evil spirits. The female figures shown here, dancing and playing instruments, were likely put into tombs to provide entertainment for the deceased in death. Each figure stands about 8 in (20 cm) high and is around 5 in (13 cm) wide at the base.

Music was an important accompaniment to life in the Tang dynasty, in part because people believed that a musical education was essential to the promotion of social harmony in Confucian society. A court orchestra performed for the emperor at the royal palace, and ceremonial music also accompanied religious rituals. The burial figures of the Tang tombs tell us a lot about the performance of music, providing depictions of the instruments and dress of musicians, as well as the movements of the dancers.

Court music

By the beginning of the Tang dynasty, in the early 7th century CE, 10 different musical bodies had been established in the imperial court. These included the Office of Grand Music and the Office of Drum and Wind Music. The Tang had elaborate musical rituals for occasions such as military exercises and religious sacrifices. They also had specific banquet music (*yanyue*) and entertained guests with extended suites (*daqu*) and even longer instrumental suites for the revered Chinese zither, the *qin*. Diverse musical traditions also flourished outside the court, and court music was often influenced by folk traditions. In fact, many instruments used in Tang court music still feature in folk music today.

Tang dances

Dating back to the Zhou dynasty (see pp. 46–49), female dancers often wore long sleeves, like those of the tomb figures, to highlight their movements. There were many dances performed in the Tang era whose names are known to us thanks to court records. These include energetic movements, as in the "Whirling Dance" (also called the "Hu Spinning Dance") and an exuberant "Sabre Dance"; in contrast, slower and sedate dances included numbers such as the "Echo Dance." These dances were divided into two categories: civil dance, which was softer, and martial dance, which mimicked the explosive vigor of warfare. Under the late Tang emperor Xuanzong, even horses were taught to dance and made to perform in "horse plays" at palace feasts, dressed in fine robes and mane ornaments.

▷ **Clay artistry**
These clay burial figures are depicted midperformance. Their appearances reflect the fashions of the Tang period, with high-waisted pleated dresses, cherry-red lips, and thin black eyebrows.

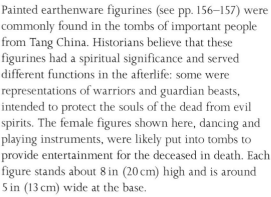

Hair worn in a double bun in the Tang fashion

Chinese wind instrument, *sheng*

Chinese harp, *konghou*, played solo or as accompaniment

Long sleeves billowing

A *pipa*, a four-stringed lute with a flat back

Tea

A history of the drink that conquered the world

Tea, *Camellia sinensis*, originated in Southeast Asia. Its cultivation spread northward into China through Sichuan, where it was mentioned in a Han document of 59 BCE that names a town near Chengdu as a market for its purchase. In the Sui dynasty, tea was drunk mainly as a medicinal tonic and an aid to digestion. Its transformation into a popular drink owes much to the spread of Buddhism throughout China.

At this time, people sought alternatives to alcohol, which was incompatible with Buddhist doctrines; also, Buddhist monks were not allowed to eat solid foods after midday, so they drank tea to remain alert during their meditational practices.

Travelers staying in monasteries spread the drink into society, where it was celebrated for its mind-enhancing qualities. Imperial patronage made tea desirable and by the middle of the Tang dynasty, tea plantations were a common sight on hillsides as far north as the Yangzi valley. By the end of the dynasty, tea was grown in more than 40 prefectures in the south, with many people employed in its production.

By 779 CE, under Daizong, 30,000 laborers worked in the imperial tea garden on Guzhu Mountain near Yixing. Tea boosted the imperial finances; in 782 CE, a 10 percent tax was imposed on its sale; by the 820s, it raised around 60 million bronze coins in revenue per year. Tea sales became an imperial monopoly; anyone engaging in large-scale trading of tea outside approved government markets risked execution.

A fashionable commodity

Scholars, literati, and bureaucrats led the fashion for tea, and competitions were held to determine who could prepare it best, taking care to retain a froth that

△ **Lu Yu**
Born in Hubei province, Lu Yu, pictured here, was raised in a Buddhist monastery, where he learned the art of tea making. His *Classic of Tea* helped ignite the Tang craze for the drink. In it, he discusses the shape of the leaves, how to pick them, and the care to be taken in the preparation and drinking of tea.

△ **Liao dynasty tea ceremony**
In this detail from a 12th-century Liao dynasty fresco in the tomb of Zhang Shiqing in Hebei province, servants are shown getting ready for a ceremony. Their activities include the careful preparation of tea, evident in the left of the image. By the time of the Liao, the drinking of tea was thought to aid concentration.

△ *Sipping Tea under a* Paulownia *Tree*
One of 12 Qing dynasty portraits of women of the imperial court, this screen painting was commissioned by the Yongzheng Emperor for his rooms at the Summer Palace near Beijing. It shows an elegant woman sipping tea beneath the shade of an ornamental *Paulownia* tree.

"The first cup should have a **haunting flavor, strange and lasting**."

LU YU, *THE CLASSIC OF TEA (CHA JING)*, c. 775 CE

stuck to the sides of the cup. Lu Yu's *The Classic of Tea* (*Cha jing*), published around 775 CE, became the manual for its cultivation, production, and consumption. In the early Tang, tea leaves were dried and formed into cakes, which were then grated to a powder. This was steeped in boiling water to make the drink. Later in the Tang, a different processing method—roasting and baking individual leaves—produced the leaf tea still popular today. Tea was drunk black. The addition of milk gained acceptance under the Qing, a nod to their nomadic Manchu heritage.

A valuable export

Buddhism took tea to Japan; in 1191, the monk Myoan Eisai planted tea seeds at the Senkoji Temple on Hirado Island, initiating Japan's tea culture, which culminated, in the late 16th century, in the elaborate Japanese tea ceremony. Tea reached the Islamic world in the 17th century via Central Asia and became an alternative to coffee in cities from Bukhara to Baghdad. The first shipments were carried to Europe in 1609 by Dutch merchants from Hirado. By 1851, some 100 million lb (45 million kg) were being exported annually from Guangzhou (Canton) to Europe. The trade exacted a heavy political price on China. The Europeans imported so much tea that it drained their coffers of silver; in an attempt to redress the balance of trade, the British East India Company flooded China with opium. The damage wrought on Qing society by the drug caused two disastrous wars with Britain (see pp. 274–275; 280–281).Today, tea is the world's second most popular drink (after water), with annual consumption at around 5.5 million tons (around two-fifths of it in China alone).

△ **Tea plantation**
Tea came to occupy a major role in the Chinese economy. Easy to dry, store, and transport, it became a valuable commodity. Tea plantation laborers are shown here working on the banks of a river, with boxes of tea—packed and ready to transport—visible in the left of the painting.

△ **Serving tea**
Although originally grown solely for its medicinal properties, from the 8th century CE, tea drinking was associated with pleasure and was adopted as a daily ritual in the households of some of China's most cultured individuals. Here, it is shown being prepared in an affluent home in Peking (Beijing) in 1901.

△ **Shanghai teahouse**
Since the 8th or 9th century CE, teahouses have been an integral part of Chinese culture and social interaction. As evident in this view of a teahouse in 20th-century Shanghai, they remain popular haunts where people of all ages meet to exchange news and ideas.

△ **Night entertainment**
A detail from a 10th-century scroll painting, *The Night Entertainments of Han Xizai*, illustrates Han Xizai, a minister of the Southern Tang, listening to musicians.

The Five Dynasties and Ten Kingdoms

A time of political turmoil

Between 907 and 960 CE, China dissolved into a mosaic of competing states in which a succession of dynasties of largely Turkic origin struggled for dominance in the north and a proliferation of more stable regional kingdoms ruled the south.

Although most often remembered as a time of strife and misery, the Five Dynasties and Ten Kingdoms was also a period of significant cultural achievement. The first full printed edition of the Confucian classics was completed in 953 CE by a scholar named Feng Dao, after 21 years of labor under four successive dynasties and eight emperors. Even in times of division, a passion for learning united the Chinese.

This period of Chinese history is known for its many "dynasties" and "kingdoms"—most of which were in fact short-lived political entities run by warlords. The rulers gave their states grand names—often borrowing from past dynasties—in order to stress continuity and boost their own standing.

The division of China into the Five Dynasties (in the north) and the Ten Kingdoms (in the south, apart from the Northern Han) had its roots in the Tang dynasty, as powerful military governors came to command strong regional armies. In the north, the first to take control was Zhu Wen, a former general in the rebel army of Huang Chao (see p. 153). He deposed the Tang emperor, Ai, in 907 CE and installed himself as first emperor of the Later Liang dynasty.

Zhu Wen made himself unpopular through his attempts to reduce the powers of the other governors and by imposing harsh discipline. In 912 CE, he was murdered by Modi, his son. Modi then struggled for a decade to hold off the advances of Li Cunxu, the son

(see p. 153)

CHRONOLOGY

The years that the Five Dynasties and Ten Kingdoms spanned brought chaos, conflict, and change to the whole of China.

The Five Dynasties
Later Liang: 907–923
Later Tang: 923–936
Later Jin: 936–947
Later Han: 947–951
Later Zhou: 951–959

The Ten Kingdoms
Yang Wu: 902–937
Southern Tang: 937–975
Former Shu: 907–925
Later Shu: 934–965
Southern Han: 917–971
Chu: 927–951
Wuyue: 907–978
Min: 909–945
Nanping: 924–963
Northern Han: 951–979

of a Shatuo general. The Shatuo were a Turkic tribe who had helped suppress the Huang Chao revolt. In 923 CE, Li Cunxu finally overcame the Later Liang and formed the Later Tang dynasty—using this name as a means of attracting Tang loyalists.

Short-lived dynasties

Li Cunxu (Emperor Zhuangzong) moved his capital to Kaifeng from Luoyang, accentuating an eastward shift in the empire's center of gravity, but his successors were too weak to hold off another Shatuo warlord, Shi Jingtang, who founded the Later Jin dynasty in 936 CE.

Shi Jingtang had been helped into power by Khitan mercenaries (see p. 150), but their help came at a price. Shi was forced to gift the Khitan the Sixteen Prefectures (a region in the north around Hebei and Beijing), but even then the Khitan attacked their former allies, occupying Kaifeng in 946 CE. The damage to the Later Jin was fatal, but the Later Han who succeeded them lasted barely three years before Guo Wei, one of their generals, usurped the throne in 951 CE. The Later Zhou dynasty, which he founded, consolidated its control in the north, even retaking two prefectures from the Khitan.

Guo Wei died in 954 CE and was succeeded by his adopted son Shizong, who proved to be an effective leader. He reformed and strengthened the military and expanded the Zhou territories in the north and

▷ **Entrance guardian**
This brass door knocker showing the head of a beast was found at the tomb of Wang Jian, an emperor of the Former Shu.

south. When Shizong died young, leaving the empire to his seven-year-old son, one of the Zhou's military governors, Zhao Kuangyin, stepped in and declared himself emperor. There was every reason to think that his dynasty, the Song (see pp. 168–171), would be another short-lived power, yet they were to rule China for the next 300 years.

Kingdoms of the south

While the succession of Five Dynasties reigned in the north, southern China was ruled by a shifting—but more generally stable—constellation of regional states known as the Ten Kingdoms. Notable among them were the Shu, in Sichuan, which became a haven for many former Tang officials and scholars who fled south after the collapse of their dynasty, and the Southern Tang, which in the 940s came close to unifying large parts of the south.

For six decades, the Ten Kingdoms held off repeated attempts at invasion by the northern dynasties but were eventually absorbed back into a united China under the Song dynasty. During this lengthy period of transition, however, southern China retained both its cultural distinctiveness and its economic power.

▽ **Buddhist discourse**
This detail from a Five Dynasties period scroll from the Mogao Caves complex, Dunhuang, depicts the judgment of the Ten Kings of Hell. The scroll illustrates the *Ksitigarbha Sutra*—a series of Buddhist discourses on concepts such as karma and reincarnation.

5

Chinese and Foreign Dynasties

960 to 1368

Introduction

The Song era (960–1279) stands out as period of humane rule, prosperity, and significant scientific and cultural achievement. Thanks in large part to the dynasty's founder, Taizu, and his successor, Taizong, internal divisions were healed and the overpowerful military brought under control. For the next century and a half, China would for the most part know peace, albeit at the cost of paying annual tributes to maintain a fragile accord with its troublesome northern neighbors, the Western Xia and the Khitan Liao.

Under the Song emperors, China was smaller in extent than it had been under earlier dynasties. Yet trade flourished as never before and its cities grew in size and sophistication. Even though the vast majority of Chinese continued to live in the countryside, the capital, Kaifeng—strategically located on the Grand Canal—grew to host almost 1.5 million people and became one of the most cosmopolitan cities in the world. Overall, the nation's population increased from 60 million to more than 100 million, thanks in part to improved agricultural production; in particular, new strains of rice were imported from Champa (in what is now southern Vietnam) that could produce more than one crop a year.

With the army under tight control, power passed increasingly into the hands of civil servants chosen through a rigid system of examinations. The prevailing ideology was a neo-Confucianism (see pp. 178–179) that stressed the importance of good governance and social responsibility. While the upper classes continued to dominate the higher ranks of government, steps were taken to encourage talent among the less privileged by opening new educational opportunities. The arts flourished: literature, history, painting, and porcelain manufacture all enjoyed a golden age.

Northern warfare

In time, a greater threat came from the north, specifically from the Khitan people, who had established their own Liao dynasty (see pp. 180–181). Seeking to regain the glory of the Tang empire, a Song emperor in the 12th century made the error of siding with another, more aggressive force, the Jurchen, against the Liao. The Jurchen duly crushed the Liao, but then turned their attention to their former ally. They took Kaifeng in 1127, capturing the Song emperor and installing their own Jin dynasty in his place.

960 Taizu becomes first emperor of the Song

979 Taizong completes the reunification of China

976 Taizu dies, to be succeeded by his brother Taizong

1004 Peace is signed with the Khitan Liao kingdom on China's northern border

1069 Minister Wang Anshi launches a reform program

1116 Jurchen forces crush the Khitan Liao

1124 The Jurchen found the Jin dynasty in the conquered Khitan lands

1127 The Jin take the Song capital of Kaifeng, forcing a move south to Hangzhou

1132 The Southern Song establish China's first permanent navy

The Song survived. Even though they lost the northern third of their territory, they succeeded in holding on to the south, where they established a new capital at Hangzhou. There, the Southern Song—as they would become known—held sway for another century and a half, maintaining within their domains much of the prosperity of former times. The sea now took on additional importance; Song engineers built multi-decked junks that could hold as many as 1,000 men, and in 1132 the emperor created the nation's first standing navy. Trade flourished, encouraging the introduction of banking drafts and bills of exchange that in time developed into a fully fledged paper currency.

Mongol conquest

The Southern Song held their own against the Jin, but they failed to cope with a much more lethal adversary that rose on the horizon of the 13th century. Genghis Khan became sole ruler of the nomads of the Mongolian plains in 1206 and soon unleashed his Mongol forces on the Jin. Repeating their earlier mistake, the Southern Song initially viewed the new power as an ally, only to once again realize their error after

the Jin were overwhelmed. One of Genghis's successors, Kublai, quickly set his sights on the Southern Song realm, finally succeeding in taking Hangzhou in 1279.

By 1279, Kublai Khan had followed Chinese precedent by proclaiming his own Yuan dynasty, and this foreign line would govern the nation for the better part of a century. Under Mongol rule, ethnic Chinese people became second-class citizens in their own country, ceding status not just to the Mongols but also to the foreigners they brought in to help them govern. However, Chinese culture and civilization survived these challenges.

After Kublai's death, Mongol rule deteriorated in the hands of his weak or incompetent successors. National resentment rose in the face of exorbitant tax demands and forced military and labor service and was also stirred up by a series of natural disasters that between them wiped out many millions of people. Peasant uprisings broke out across the land, and in 1356, the leader of one of them, Zhu Yuanzhang, succeeded in taking control of Nanjing. From there, the rebel commander drove out the last Yuan ruler, declaring himself first emperor of the new Ming dynasty 12 years later.

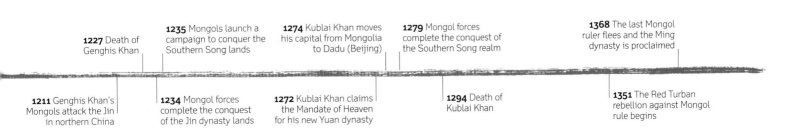

1227 Death of Genghis Khan

1235 Mongols launch a campaign to conquer the Southern Song lands

1274 Kublai Khan moves his capital from Mongolia to Dadu (Beijing)

1279 Mongol forces complete the conquest of the Southern Song realm

1368 The last Mongol ruler flees and the Ming dynasty is proclaimed

1211 Genghis Khan's Mongols attack the Jin in northern China

1234 Mongol forces complete the conquest of the Jin dynasty lands

1272 Kublai Khan claims the Mandate of Heaven for his new Yuan dynasty

1294 Death of Kublai Khan

1351 The Red Turban rebellion against Mongol rule begins

The Northern Song

Unity and prosperity return to a long-divided empire

After the chaotic Five Dynasties and Ten Kingdoms period, the Song reunified northern and southern China, ushering in a time of growth, prosperity, and unprecedented innovation in art, science, and technology.

The Song dynasty is conventionally divided into two parts: the Northern Song (960–1127), which ruled most of China, and the Southern Song (1127–1279), which controlled only the south following the Jin dynasty's conquest of the north.

The Song dynasty was founded in 960 CE by Zhao Kuangyin (later named Emperor Taizu), a general under one of the Five Dynasties that ruled northern China after the Tang. Taizu reunited the empire, bringing north and south under Song control and ending the turmoil caused by warlords during the Five Dynasties and Ten Kingdoms period (see pp. 162–163). Taizu appealed to a war-weary people by emphasizing reunification under a just imperial bureaucracy.

A CULTURED EMPEROR

Huizong, the penultimate emperor of the Northern Song, was a highly cultured man. An excellent calligrapher and painter (his *Peach Blossom and Dove* is shown below), he also wrote poetry and collected art and antiquities on a large scale. Huizong promoted Daoism and involved himself in the layout of the imperial gardens, and in music and medicine. However, his neglect of the army weakened China. He died in captivity, in miserable circumstances, after being taken captive by the Jurchens.

He consolidated power by weakening the military establishment and persuading potential rivals—including generals and provincial governors—to renounce their offices in exchange for generous pensions. Taizu promoted loyal junior officers in their place and reformed the civil service examinations to favor talented, rather than high-born, candidates. His reforms ensured that no one person could challenge his power. The resulting political stability not only enabled the Song to prosper economically (the Song dynasty saw the use of the first Chinese banknotes) but also encouraged greater freedom of thought, fueling advances in science, philosophy, and the arts.

Threats from the north

When he died in 976 CE, Taizu was succeeded by his brother, who reigned until 997 CE as Emperor Taizong. Unconfirmed stories of the time suggest that Taizong murdered his brother to take power. In any event, Taizong ruled sagely, continuing the drive to Chinese unification and reform, and the dynasty endured until the reigns of Huizong and his son Qinzong in the 12th century. The Song empire faced a continual military threat from its northern frontier regions, which were occupied by two kingdoms—the Western Xia and the powerful Khitan Liao. To defend themselves against these kingdoms, the Song spent heavily on equipping their army and also attempted to appease their neighbors by paying them annual tributes in the form of silver and silk.

International relations

Despite international tensions, the Song benefitted greatly from trade with the north, setting up supervised markets along the border. Chinese goods that flowed north in large quantities included tea, silk, paper and printed books, rice, and spices.

Under the Song, China retreated into a defensive mindset—unsurprising given its recent emergence from the turmoil of the Five Dynasties and Ten

△ **Emperor Taizu**
Taizu oversaw the expansion of China's examination system and set up academies that promoted scientific thought and allowed for unprecedented freedom of discussion.

▷ **Song silk**
The Song were known for creating beautiful and elaborate silks, like this red dragon piece from the imperial workshop. The blue border was added in the Ming period.

▽ **Jun ware**
The Song dynasty had five "Great Kilns" producing its best pottery. This ewer is an example of Jun ware, from Junzhou, in Henan province.

Kingdoms period. The notion of Chinese superiority over other nations resurfaced and "foreign" doctrines were shunned, while Confucianism and Daoism, both native to China, were championed. The philosophy of Neo-Confucianism (see pp. 178–179) was seen as the best way to strengthen and stabilize Chinese society, and an ideal of benevolent paternalism emerged, in which the state was likened to a large family and the authority of the ruler was that of a kind father. However, these doctrines also led to a decline, from the Song period onward, of the rights of women, whose subservience they emphasized.

Growth under the Song

Under the Northern Song, China became the most populous country in the world, with some 100 million inhabitants, and the most technologically advanced. Cities all over China flourished, none more so than the capital, Kaifeng, which developed into a dense metropolis crisscrossed by commercial streets. The city's population grew to more than 400,000, and its economy became increasingly diverse and sophisticated, with structured businesses such as guilds, partnerships, and stock companies developing into large enterprises. New opportunities opened up as—for the first time—an urban class began to emerge in China.

China's extensive river and canal systems (see pp. 136–137) contributed greatly to the growth of trade within China and abroad, as did sea ports such as Quanzhou on the southeast coast. Quanzhou became a major hub for goods to and from Japan, India, and the east coast of Africa. »

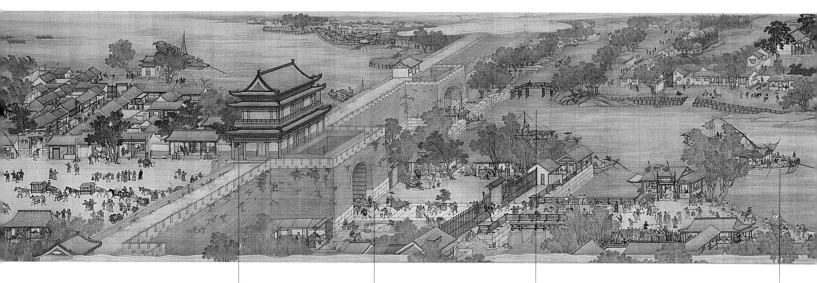

△ **Kaifeng under the Song**
A section of the famous scroll painting *Along the River During the Qingming Festival* shows people at work and play during the festival at Kaifeng. The original was painted in the Northern Song dynasty; shown here is a Qing copy.

A towering gate building marks the entrance to the city; within are hotels, temples, offices, and homes

Traders carry their wares into the city during the Qingming Festival, which was held in April, 100 days after the winter solstice

The Bian River was the lifeline of the city; it joined numerous canals along which goods were carried

The river is busy with fishing boats and ferries carrying passengers

Economic growth coincided with a long and productive period of scientific inquiry and technical innovation. The Song emperors invested heavily in military technology, developing the tools and methods needed to build huge naval ships capable of carrying 1,000 men and making vessels powered by paddle wheels rather than oars or sails. Song engineers also designed floating pontoon bridges that could help move troops and supplies.

The first surviving formula for gunpowder dates from the Song, and they also developed weapons such as the fire lance, which could shoot flames and projectiles at an enemy, and gunpowder-propelled arrows. These and other weapons were produced in great quantities: records show that more than 40,000 workers were employed in Song munitions workshops, many centered around Kaifeng.

Other industries thrived under the Song, too, as new enterprises produced textiles, lacquerwork, and ceramics of the highest quality. Song dynasty silks, for example, were woven on sophisticated looms with up to 1,800 moving parts.

By 1078, China's iron production had grown to 125,000 tons (113,400 metric tons) per year, six times the output in 800. This metal was used to manufacture a range of products—from ships' anchors to bridges and pagodas to agricultural equipment that boosted food production.

▽ **Early compass**
In the first Song compasses, a magnetized needle was fixed to a float and placed in a water-filled bowl so that it could turn freely.

Science and scholarship

The scholars of the Song period made significant scientific advances in astronomy, producing detailed star maps and designing instruments for astronomical measurement and timekeeping. These included water clocks and giant armillary spheres made of copper, which could model the movements of celestial objects. One of the greatest innovations of the Song dynasty was the magnetic compass; lodestone, a naturally magnetic iron ore, was used to magnetize a fixed needle so that it would point to the north or the south. The device was a revolution in navigation technology and was soon put to use in maritime expeditions along the coast and beyond—to the East China Sea, Arabian Sea, Red Sea, Pacific Ocean, and Indian Ocean.

Song advances in the sciences also exerted their influence on culture. Many artists sought to reveal the patterns and principles that they believed (according to the prevailing Neo-Confucian ideas) lay beneath the natural world, leading to the flourishing of landscape painting. Meanwhile, a revived interest in China's past created new fields of study in archaeology and antiquarianism.

Looking backward

Some Song scholar-officials, such as Sima Guang and Fan Zuyu, turned their attention to writing histories of past dynasties. These works were in a style called *shilun*, which mixed the telling of history with

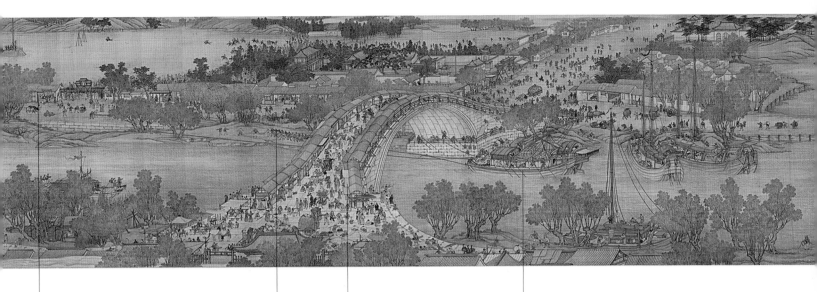

Businesses selling all sorts of goods, including wine, grain, cookware, lanterns, and musical instruments, line the river banks

Workers struggle to pull a boat safely upstream and clear of the bridge, as observers on the banks shout instructions

The steeply arched wooden Rainbow Bridge spans the river without piers; it is crowded with people and lined with food stands

A boat approaching Kaifeng lowers its mast to clear the underside of the bridge

political and Confucian commentary. Sima Guang became known for his *Comprehensive Mirror for Aid in Government* (*Zizhi tongjian*), in which he analyzed history from 403 BCE up to 959 CE, searching the past for models of clean government and criticizing the nepotism and favoritism that characterized some historical Chinese courts. He wrote that those who gained power through such methods were either incompetent or corrupt. Sima Guang used his knowledge of history to advise modern emperors, cautioning against extravagance and indulging women, who, he argued, were capable of dividing loyalties.

As well as creating a wealth of knowledge, the Song pioneered its dissemination. Combining a knowledge of printing and paper manufacture, they were able to produce documents inexpensively, so promoting widespread literacy and participation in cultural activity. Art and literature expanded their reach through the printed medium, as did pursuits such as gardening and cooking, which gained popularity in the Song period. The first movable type, made from ceramic pieces, was invented by Bi Sheng in the 11th century, some 400 years before Gutenberg's printing press was unveiled in the West.

The Song disaster
Song China's age of prosperity and tranquility did not last. A famine ravaged the north of China in 1074–1076, and continuing clashes with foreign enemies in the north sapped the strength of the imperial army

"On the **checkerboard streets** … there are **thousands of shops**."

ACCOUNT OF THE CITY OF KAIFENG BY SONG OFFICIAL AND WRITER MENG YUANLAO, 1147

and drained the Song economy. In the 12th century, the Song emperors made an alliance with the Jurchens, a tribal group to the northeast of China. Assisted by the Song, the Jurchens crushed the Khitan Liao in 1114–1116 and founded their own dynasty—the Jin. However, they soon came to envy the material wealth of their former Song allies and moved southward, sacking the Song capital, Kaifeng, in 1126, and occupying all of northern China. The Song court was taken to the far northeast, where the former emperor Huizong died in captivity in 1135. Huizong's younger son fled south and was declared the next Song emperor, ruling over a southern territory with its capital at Hangzhou (see pp. 184–185).

▽ **Gold dish**
The design of this Song gold vessel was inspired by the shapes of popular foodstuffs, namely okra and bitter melon.

Silk Production

The history of China's most famous fabric

The Chinese silk industry has prehistoric origins. Archaeological evidence from Neolithic sites indicates that sericulture (silkworm cultivation) was already established by the start of the 2nd millennium BCE. Tombs from the Eastern Zhou dynasty (see pp. 56–57) have also yielded fabrics elaborately decorated with dragons, phoenixes, and abstract patterns. By that time, silk was not just being used to make clothes and items but had also become an important commodity. Bolts (measured units) of silk served to pay off debts and functioned as a medium of exchange long before metal coinage was introduced. Silk would continue to play this role through much of Chinese history; when the Southern Song rulers agreed to a temporary peace with their Jurchen Jin enemies in 1142 (see pp. 184–185), part of the annual tribute they agreed to pay took the form of 250,000 bolts of silk.

Silk has always been a luxury item, since its production is time-consuming and labor-intensive. The moths that lay the eggs from which silkworms hatch have to be selected and mated, and the eggs must be stored in buildings where warmth, humidity, and light are carefully controlled. Once the larvae hatch, the worms need to be fed mulberry leaves at regular intervals throughout the day and night. After several molts, they create a fiber intended to serve as a protective cocoon—a process that can take several days. At this point, the cocoons are dipped in boiling water, killing the silkworms inside, and the protective filament surrounding them can be unwound onto reels, each containing almost a half mile (kilometer) of usable raw silk. Some four dozen strands have to be twisted together to make usable threads before the process of weaving and dyeing can begin.

△ **Silk painting**
This silk painting fragment dates from before the 10th century CE and is thought to depict a woman swimming. Painting on silk probably began as early as the Zhou dynasty but reached new heights under the Western Han, when artists began to paint humans and animals.

△ **The mulberry tree**
Collecting mulberry leaves is an important part of the silk production process. This led mulberry trees themselves to take on a symbolic significance in China. In ancient times, people planted mulberry trees around their houses, and in poetry, the tree became a symbol of home.

△ **Women's work**
This Yuan dynasty scroll painting by Wang Zhenpeng, itself painted on silk, depicts many steps of silk production. The artist depicts only women, because silkworm raising and silk production were mainly undertaken by women—at first in the home, and later in factories.

"In a **single meter of silk**, the **infinite** universe exists...."

LU JI (261–303 CE), *THE ART OF WRITING (WEN FU)*

The end product is treasured, not just for the trouble that went into its manufacture but also for its aesthetic uses. From early times, silk provided a canvas for Chinese artists. The painted silk banner found on the coffin of Lady Dai (see pp. 90–91) dates from the early 2nd century BCE, while in Song times, landscape artists such as Ma Yuan continued to use silk scrolls as the preferred medium for their works. Before the introduction of paper in the Later Han period, silk was also used as a writing material (see pp. 108–09).

New markets for silk

The delicacy and softness of Chinese silk gained it a reputation far beyond the nation's borders. When the Han dynasty explorer Zhang Qian (164–113 BCE) made his epic journeys—which would in time open a path to Central Asia and beyond—he was amazed to find that Chinese silk had reached the bazaars of northern Afghanistan ahead of him, apparently imported via a sea route connecting Sichuan to India. As the route that he pioneered opened up to trade, silk was the main commodity moving westward along it. Because of this, it gained the name "Silk Road."

By the time of Julius Caesar, in the 1st century BCE, silk was already highly prized in Rome. Even after the secrets of sericulture had spread beyond China's borders—to Japan by the 4th century CE, then eventually to the Arab nations and the Byzantine world—China remained central to the trade. Today, China still produces almost 75 per cent of global raw silk, and the material has found a variety of new uses, from the manufacture of parachutes to the preparation of surgical sutures.

△ **Ming weaving**
Created between 1650 and 1726, this silk painting depicts a person weaving silk on a wooden loom. Under the Ming, the demand for silk was so great that some official orders were filled by workers with privately owned looms, as well as by official looms in the palace.

△ **Qing embroidery**
This Qing dragon robe dates from the 19th century. Dragon robes were symbols of imperial power, and the five-clawed dragon, shown here, was only worn by the emperor himself. This robe is embroidered with colored silk, gold, and silver threads. Scrolling cloud patterns, as here in blue, often appeared on the robes.

△ **Modern workshop**
This 21st-century photograph shows a woman unspooling silk from cocoons (in the large bowl) at a modern silk workshop. Hanging behind her are large bundles of white raw silk, harvested from the pods. In some places, the production process remains unchanged from ancient times.

Confucian Bureaucracy

Scholar-gentlemen emerge as a new elite

During the Song dynasty, China transitioned from an aristocratic society to a bureaucratic one, with the recognition of the "scholar-gentleman" as a new elite class with political status and social prestige.

From the late 10th century CE, the Song bureaucracy was dominated by a cadre of officials known as *shi*, or *shidafu*, meaning "scholar-gentleman." Highly literate and educated in Confucian philosophy, they were recruited into the government through a stringent examination system. The state facilitated their presence in the various levels of national and regional government in order to prevent the dominance of the military in Chinese administration. This helped give the government a new basis for legitimacy—one founded on learning and talent rather than rank.

The rapid rise of examination-recruited officials was made possible—in large part—by advances in printing technology, which led to the wider availability and lower cost of books. Increases in the funding of schools and academies also played a significant role in improving literacy and education across China.

Civil service examinations

The examination system had been established centuries before the Song under the Han dynasty; the Song overhauled the system and made it more consistent. It became the main path into government office and remained so up to the early 20th century. The teachings of Confucius were central to the knowledge tested in the exams; candidates had, for example, to learn the Five Classics (see pp. 54–55) by rote. Reformers, such as the Song minister Fan Zhongyan, only partly succeeded in their attempts to update the examinations so that they would also test knowledge of economics and administration.

Examinations were rigorous and impartial. The government took steps to prevent favoritism; for example, candidates' names were replaced by numbers so that examiners had no way of knowing whose scripts they were assessing. As a result, men from central and southern China gained positions in government for the very first time, addressing the previous predominance of northern bureaucrats.

Once qualified, Song scholar-officials joined the 20,000 mandarins responsible for governing an empire of more than 100 million people. Most took low-level positions in the provinces. There, with the help of the local gentry, they were responsible for tax collection, water conservation, agricultural development, and management of their own offices (called *yamen*), often with a low salary and little support from central government. The coveted policy-making posts at court were reserved for the most outstanding students.

Magistrates and Song justice

The Song justice system was maintained by sheriffs and county magistrates, who were typically scholar-gentlemen. These magistrates were expected to apply practical knowledge as well as the written law in making judicial decisions, while promoting ethical and moral values in the Confucian tradition. One of the most famous magistrates in Chinese history was Bao Zheng. He loathed corruption, championed the poor, and gained a reputation in the mid-11th century as being unflinchingly upright and honest, famously convicting even his own uncle. His court cases became popular with storytellers and were later widely adapted into novels and plays.

△ **Zhou Dunyi**
The scholar-gentleman class produced some of China's most respected philosophers, including Zhou Dunyi (1017–1073), pictured with his attendant on this Ming dynasty dish. Zhou Dunyi drew on metaphysics and Confucian ethics in his attempt to explain creation.

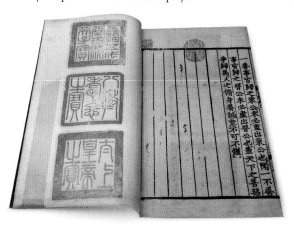

◁ **Preserving wisdom**
Song scholars sought to preserve the Confucian tradition even in times of adversity. This collection of Confucian texts was made by Master Kong, the 47th descendant of Confucius, after the Song were forced to move south (see pp. 128–129).

△ **Imperial examination**
This silk painting shows an examination in the reign of the
Song emperor Renzong (r. 1022–63). Figures wear the clothes
of the 17th century, when the painting was made.

Poetic journey
This 16th-century screen illustrates a poem written by Su Shi. The poem describes a journey made by Su Shi (shown here wearing a green robe), with his servant, to meet the young poet Li Bi.

Su Shi

An outstanding Song "scholar-gentleman"

A well-known figure in Song China, Su Shi was a poet, essayist, and calligrapher. Though he followed Confucian ideas, his inquisitive mind also led him to other philosophies and put him in conflict with orthodox beliefs.

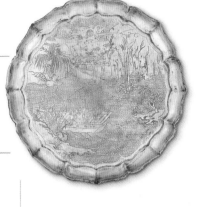

△ **Red Cliff scene**
This 13th-century silver plate is decorated with a scene inspired by *Ode to the Red Cliff*. It shows its author, Su Shi, with two companions boating below the cliff, an ancient battle site on the Yangzi River.

Born into a literary family in 1037, Su Shi passed the highest-level civil service examinations at the age of 20 and was marked out as a rising star in government. He was a brilliant thinker whose essays were admired by Emperor Renzong (r. 1022–1063), and by the time Emperor Shenzong came to the throne in 1067, Su Shi was a respected scholar-gentleman (see pp. 174–175).

However, Su Shi repeatedly fell foul of the rivalries that existed between factions at court. He was an outspoken critic of new reform measures and in particular of the leading reformer, prime minister Wang Anshi. As a result, he was demoted and exiled from the capital, Kaifeng, and took a magistrate's post in the provinces. This was a turning point in his life. For almost a decade, he held a variety of positions in prefectures, including Mizhou, Xuzhou, and Huzhou, where he broadened and deepened his thinking and entered into a period of creativity.

His poetic essays, including *Ode to the Red Cliff*, *Cherishing the Past*, and *Prelude to Water Melody*, have entered the canon of Chinese literature, loved for their warmth, humanity, and humor. Su Shi was also a superb painter of bamboo and popularized "landscape poems," which he inscribed on his paintings. Su Shi's belief that a painting should be an expression of the internal feelings of the artist (much like a poem) was revolutionary for the time.

The Master of the Eastern Slope

In 1079, Su Shi was jailed for writing a verse that satirized the reformists at court. Exiled to Huangzhou in provincial Hubei, he built a farm in the foothills of what became known as the Eastern Slope (Dongpo) and began to call himself Su Dongpo, "Master of the Eastern Slope." For all the hardships he experienced in exile, it was during this period that he produced some of his best poetry. He was recalled to the capital in 1086 but again fell foul of authority and was banished in 1094 to become prefect of Danzhou in the island province of Hainan. Although Su Shi survived the malaria that plagued Danzhou, he died in 1101, just a year after returning to his home in Changzhou.

▽ *The Cold Food Observance*, 1079
Inspired by the changing seasons and his own shifting fortunes, Su Shi wrote this manuscript while he was exiled in Huangzhou.

1061 Takes up his first government post

1079 Jailed for a satirical poem criticizing the government's reforms

1086 Serves in the elite Imperial Hanlin Academy

1037 Born in Meishan (now in Sichuan province)

1071–1079 Banished from court, he takes a series of provincial posts

1080–1083 Exiled to Huangzhou, he writes some of his best poetry

1101 Dies in Changzhou (now in Jiangsu province)

Neo-Confucianism

Developing new truths from old rhetoric

Confucian philosophy reached new levels of social and intellectual creativity in the 11th century. Neo-Confucianism revitalized almost all facets of life under the Song dynasty, producing reformers, dedicated teachers, and philosophers.

Following the collapse of the Han dynasty in the early 3rd century CE, China's official philosophy of Confucianism (which was closely associated with government, duty, and convention) became eclipsed by the more esoteric belief systems of Daoism and, especially, Buddhism, which reached the peak of its influence in China under the Tang dynasty (618–907 CE). However, by the late Tang, a reaction to the "foreign" religion of Buddhism promoted the revitalization of the "lost" Confucian tradition.

Officials in the Tang court—most notably, the prominent scholar and poet Han Yu—argued that the Tang state would benefit from a revival of Confucian ideals. Han Yu led an initiative to clarify these ideals through a literary movement called *guwen* ("ancient prose movement"), which aimed to do away with needlessly complex interpretations of the philosophy. Han Yu was also a prominent critic of Buddhism, which he labeled a "barbarian cult" in his *Memorial on Bone-relics of the Buddha*, a document that he presented to Emperor Xianzong. His opinions greatly offended the emperor, who condemned Han Yu to death. Only the intervention of his friends at court saved the philosopher's life.

"[We should] **burn** the **books** of **Buddhism** and **Daoism**."

HAN YU, *STUDY OF THE WAY*, c. 810

The revival of Confucian thought that had taken root among thinkers such as Han Yu developed further in the 11th century. At that time, factional disputes raged among scholars in the Song court. Reformers, such as the chancellor Wang Anshi, sought changes in China's society and economy, favoring, for example, the development of government monopolies on trade. They were bitterly opposed by the traditionalists, who included the historian Sima Guang.

Order from chaos

Disillusioned by the level of vindictiveness at court, a small group of men withdrew from the arena of political partisanship to live as semi-hermits near the city of Luoyang. This group—which included Shao Yong, Zhou Dunyi, Zhang Zai, and the brothers Cheng Yi and Cheng Hao—came to be known as the Northern Song Masters. They elaborated an idea that would become central to Neo-Confucian thought—that existence is a dynamic, integrated system and that the principle behind the unity of the universe can be understood by the human mind.

The intellectual and political confusion brought on by the loss of northern China to Jurchen invaders in 1127 (see pp. 170–171) created a climate in which the teachings of the Northern Song Masters came to the fore. Philosophers tried to redefine man's position in the universe and reignite the debate over what constituted a better society, giving Confucian teachings new relevance. There was a drive to start again from the bottom up, reforming communities, founding schools and academies, and spreading the Neo-Confucian message.

ZHU XI (1130–1200)

Zhu Xi was born in Nanping (Youxi), Fujian, and passed the imperial examinations for the state bureaucracy at the age of 19. He served several terms as an official but dedicated much of his life to writing and educating his disciples. His criticism of corruption led to political disgrace, as a result of which his doctrines were regarded as heretical. His ideas were accepted officially only after his death, when he was seen as an intellectual colossus of Confucianism.

▷ **Contemplating nature**
This fan-shaped painting on silk by Qing artist Xu Hao shows the 11th-century Neo-Confucian scholar Zhou Dunyi admiring a lotus. Among Zhou's various philosophical works was the essay "On the Love of the Lotus" (*Ailian shuo*).

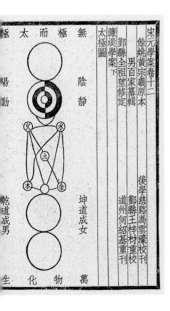

◁ **Supreme polarity**
The *Taijitu* or Diagram of Supreme Polarity, shown here, is Zhou Dunyi's most famous contribution to Neo-Confucian philosophy. The diagram explains the relationship between the cosmos and human behavior.

One 12th-century scholar, Zhu Xi (see box, left), devoted himself to mastering the ideas of the Northern Song philosophers—not only reconciling all their contradictions but also editing their works into a coherent synthesis that finally came to form the basic structure of Neo-Confucian philosophy. Zhu Xi's philosophical doctrine explained the world using the concepts of qi (or vital energy)—from which all things are made—and li (a universal principle).

According to Zhu Xi, human beings were essentially good, but impure qi accounted for their persistent selfishness and waywardness. It was essential that qi was constantly worked on in order to achieve purity and an ordered family, good government, and peace under Heaven. Zhu Xi's interpretation and elaboration of Confucianism wedded metaphysical speculation (concern with matters that transcend the senses) to Confucian practicality. In creating this synthesis, Neo-Confucianism offered an alternative to the otherworldliness of Daoism and Buddhism.

Zhu Xi pared down the Confucian classics, creating a canon of texts that became known as the Four Books—*Analects, Mencius, Great Learning,* and *Doctrine of the Mean*—which stressed the humane and socially responsible aspects of Confucianism. These works gradually took priority over all other classics and, by the 14th century, formed the basis of the civil service examinations. Neo-Confucianism guided followers in all aspects of life—from leisure and the arts to political and social reform.

The Liao and the Jin

New empires of the north threaten Song China

The founding of the Liao dynasty in the 10th century and the Jin dynasty in the 12th century saw a period of extensive foreign dominance in China. Never before had China suffered such a degree of political and military control by foreigners.

As the Tang dynasty disintegrated under pressure from internal revolts (see pp. 150–153), powerful new states began to emerge north of the Chinese plain, notably the Xi Xia (Tangut) in the northwest and the Khitan kingdom in the northeast. In 907 CE, Abaoji from the nomadic Yelü clan (one of the principal groups of the Khitan) became the unchallenged leader of the Khitan and in 916 established himself as emperor of the Liao dynasty. He named his son as heir apparent, imposing a hereditary rather than a tribal or elective system of succession.

The Liao dynasty

Abaoji (posthumously known as Emperor Taizu) created a "north-facing" government ruling the nomadic Khitan tribes by tribal laws and a "south-facing" government modeled on the administration of the Tang dynasty. This ruled over the three million Chinese (principally Han) settled in his territory. The Khitan recognized the need for a written language for their proto-Mongol spoken language and developed a script to help preserve Khitan identity (see box, right).

In 936, Abaoji's successor Yelü Deguang gained control over the Sixteen Prefectures (border areas of north China). In 946, his troops ventured as far south as the Yellow River, briefly occupying Kaifeng city. With this occupation of Chinese territory, Yelü renamed his dynasty the Great Liao.

The formidable Khitan forces continued their incursions into Song China until agreeing to peace with Emperor Zhenzong at Chanyuan in 1005. Over the next century, the Jurchen—a confederation of tribes from the mountainous area of far northeastern Manchuria—emerged as a growing influence in the region. The Jurchen were vassals of the Great Liao,

◁ **Exquisite metalwork**
This exquisitely crafted elaborate gilded crown is from the Liao dynasty. Liao metalwork drew great inspiration from the preceding Tang dynasty.

and traded both with them and with Song China. However, in the early 12th century, they began to develop their own territorial ambitions and started to pose a threat to their neighbors.

The Jin dynasty

In the early 12th century, Aguda, a warrior of the Wanyan clan, formed a confederation of Jurchen tribes and proclaimed the Jin dynasty. In 1119, he joined forces with the Song, who offered help in the war against the Liao in exchange for the return of the Sixteen Prefectures that had been ceded to the Liao. They attacked the Liao and by 1122 had taken its southern capital (now Beijing). Aguda established a system of mobilizing and organizing subject peoples by grouping them into units, headed by trusted kinsmen, each of whom was responsible for raising

KHITAN SCRIPT

The Khitan script was written using two different language systems: a Khitan large script and a Khitan small script. The Khitan large script was derived from Chinese characters. Each word was depicted with a special character, of which there were more than 1,000. The Khitan small script (shown here inscribed on a Liao dynasty mirror) was a mixed writing system that mostly comprised phonetic elements (ones that represent sounds). Khitan script continued to be used by the Jurchen decades after the fall of the Liao.

△ Dragon textile
The Jin dynasty is renowned for its textiles brocaded in gold. This striking example shows a coiled dragon with a flaming jewel—a design that was often used on Tang princes' robes.

1,000 fighting men. By the time he died in 1123, Aguda's empire covered most of what is now northeastern China.

The fall of the Song

In 1125, the Jin turned on the Song, twice besieging their capital, Kaifeng, which fell in 1127. The Jin army captured the Song emperor Qinzong and members of the imperial family. The Song court was pushed out of northern China and made a humiliating retreat across the Yangzi. The surviving Song were forced to pay an annual tribute to the Jin and, in the treaty oath, made to refer to Jin as "your superior state."

The Jin moved their capital from central Mongolia to Beijing in 1153 and then to Kaifeng in 1161 and put its administration into the hands of a Han-style bureaucracy partly recruited through examinations, which started to be offered in the Jurchen language. The imperial examination system helped spread Confucianism. Although the Jin attempted to maintain

▽ In pursuit
A detail from a Jin dynasty painting, c. 1120, attributed to Huang Zongdao, captures the power and potential violence of the hunt as horse and rider pursue their prey.

> "The **dusty horde** did **roar**, as their **arms swept** even to the Han shore."
>
> KOREAN POET HYONJONG ON THE KHITAN INVASIONS, 11TH CENTURY

their Jurchen traditions (including promoting Jurchen as a written language), their assimilation was rapid. By the end of the century, most Jurchens spoke Chinese.

The Jin dynasty prevailed in northern China until the 13th century, when nomadic Mongol tribes assembled under the mighty Genghis Khan (see pp. 186–187) repeatedly attacked and plundered the Jin state. The Jin refused to submit as vassals to Genghis, who launched major attacks in 1205 and 1209, followed in 1211 by a full-scale invasion. The Jin dynasty offered fierce resistance, but in 1233, Kaifeng fell to the enemy.

A Liao Funerary Mask

Beauty immortalized

The funerary customs of the Liao dynasty (916–1125) were unique to the Khitan people and unlike other Chinese burial practices. Low-ranking people were likely to have been cremated, and around a third of the Liao tombs discovered contain people's ashes. Members of the Khitan nobility, however, met a different fate. Excavations of Liao tombs have revealed that the bodies of the deceased nobles were wrapped in shrouds made of copper wire, while the faces of the deceased were covered by metal masks made out of a thin sheet of bronze, silver, or gold. Many Liao tombs fell victim to looters, so relatively few of these masks have survived, but from those that have been recovered, scholars have theorized that the size of the mask and type of metal used represented the individual's social rank. Gold and silver were precious metals to the Liao and appear to have been reserved for the imperial elite. There have been only two gold masks recorded, found in the shared tomb of Princess Chen and her husband, Xiao Shaoju—immediate members of the imperial family. One text from the Yuan dynasty suggests that a Liao princess would have been gifted with her burial mask on her wedding day.

Few texts exist that explain the reasoning behind the use of funerary masks. A record from around 1138 written by Wen Weijian, a Southern Song scholar, refers to the use of masks made from silver or gold in the Liao's funerary practices. His work gives little detail about these masks but does go on to describe the Liao practice of embalming their dead by removing the deceased's blood, fat, and organs from the abdomen, then replacing them with fragrant herbs and preserving minerals, such as salt and alum. Wen's account, however, may not be strictly reliable—it is seen by some historians as an attempt to degrade the Khitans and their nomadic ancestry. The iconographic nature of the masks has also led some historians to compare the masks to the faces of Buddhist statues. Given the Khitans' reverence of their ancestors, some have suggested that the funerary masks were used to present the deceased as sacred figures.

Eternal peace

The mask pictured right was found in the tomb of a young woman about whom very little is known. Though made of gilded bronze rather than gold or silver, the mask is striking in its definition and finish. True to life in size, the pronounced features and roundedness of the face offer a portrait that could have closely resembled the deceased woman. Unlike the jade masks that covered the dead during earlier Chinese dynasties, the funerary masks crafted by the Liao were individual to each departed figure, representing their facial features. Here, the closed eyes, relaxed eyebrows, and little tension in the mouth suggest the deceased's serenity in death.

Well-defined facial features

▷ **Funerary features**
Crafted from a thin sheet of metal, Liao funerary masks were hammered into shape. Prominent eyebrows like this young woman's were typical of Liao funerary masks, though some masks found show the deceased with their eyes open.

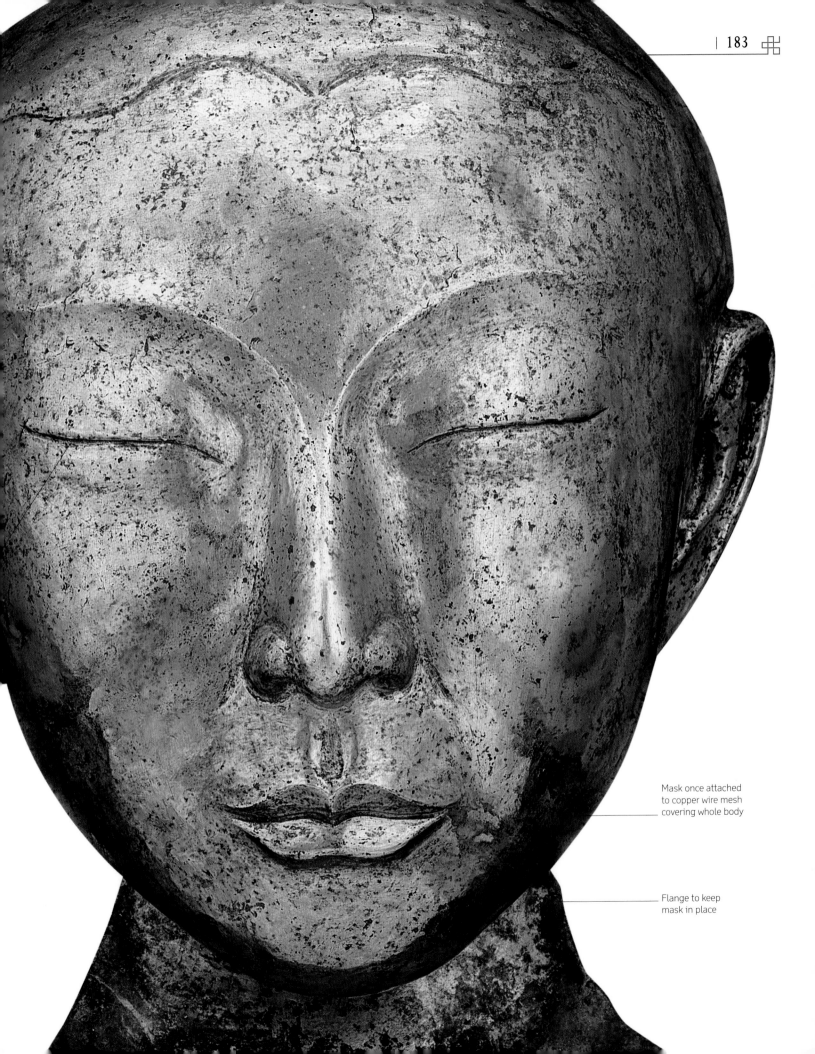

Mask once attached
to copper wire mesh
covering whole body

Flange to keep
mask in place

The Southern Song
The dynasty survives military defeat to rise again

After the invasion of China by the Jurchen Jin—a seminomadic people from northeastern Asia—the Song court fled south and established a new capital at Hangzhou. Here, the Southern Song dynasty rose to new heights of prosperity.

After capturing the Song capital of Kaifeng in 1127 (see p. 171), the Jurchens—who became the Jin dynasty at the time of the conquest—went on to take control of the rest of northern China. The Song court retreated to the south, taking up temporary residence at Nanjing, where a surviving son of Emperor Huizong (who had been captured by the Jurchen) was proclaimed Emperor Gaozong.

◁ **Black lacquerware plaque**
The art of carving into very thick lacquer first appeared in the Southern Song. Black and red lacquerware was typical of the period.

The rise of the Southern Song

Gaozong's new Southern Song dynasty settled south of the Huai and Yangzi rivers, establishing a capital in the maritime port of Hangzhou in 1132. Although they signed a treaty with the Jin in 1141, which set out their respective territorial boundaries, they continued renewing their defenses against their enemy. At the same time, the Southern Song set about rebuilding their administration following the Han model greatly admired by Emperor Gaozong.

The Southern Song grew and prospered around their new capital. Under their rule, China became the first country in the world to issue paper money on a national scale. This development meant that traders in far-flung parts of the empire were able to buy and sell goods at established prices. Private business was permitted in industries that were not already government-operated monopolies, and merchants formed guilds in order to regulate the conditions of commerce, including setting standard workers' wages and the prices of goods.

Maritime trade

The Southern Song encouraged trade and contact with the outside world. The government sponsored harbor improvement projects and the construction of beacons and warehouses, while shipbuilding flourished. New designs of junks with multiple masts, stronger hulls, and stern-mounted rudders meant that traders could travel further and faster, while the development of the magnetic compass and the compilation of detailed star charts aided navigation at

△ **Ingenious inventions**
This illustration from a military manual shows a Song dynasty naval ship. The top deck of the ship is equipped with a traction catapult for launching projectiles.

△ **The first ruler**
After having fled to the south of China following attacks from the Jurchens, Gaozong reestablished the Song dynasty as the Southern Song in 1127. He was the dynasty's first emperor and ruled for 35 years.

The Southern Song capital of Hangzhou had a population of well over a million by the dynasty's end.

sea. Merchant ships carried a great range of Chinese goods, including ceramics, silks, and fine lacquerware, on the East China Sea and Yellow Sea to Korea and Japan and traveled as far west as India and Arabia. Ships returned to China laden with products such as perfumes, medicine, pearls, cotton, and spices.

To protect its growing merchant fleet, the Song established China's first permanent navy in 1132. Headquartered at Dinghai, the navy was initially 3,000 strong but within a century had expanded to 52,000. The Song deployed huge paddle-wheeled warships armed with deck-mounted trebuchets that fired both smoke bombs and incendiary shells. Such weapons were used in their ongoing struggles with the Jin, such as at the naval battles of Tangdao and Caishi on the Yangzi River in 1161.

Adaptation and innovation

From their southern capital, the Song continued to innovate in science and technology. The survival to this day of structures such as the 197 ft (60 m) Liuhe Pagoda in Hangzhou (completed in 1165) testifies to the great strides they made in architectural engineering. The Song were also great innovators in agriculture. Having moved from the wheat- and millet-growing areas of the north to the south, where rice was the primary crop, they sought to maximize the yield of their staple food. They traveled to the area of modern Vietnam to seek out fast-ripening and resilient varieties of rice, which allowed them to harvest multiple crops a year to feed their burgeoning population; they also developed dams, dikes, and water pumps to optimize their use of land.

Despite their achievements, the dynasty was militarily weak. When the Mongols arrived in the north, the Song helped the newcomers destroy the Jin dynasty in 1233–1234 in exchange for a share of territories that lay to the south of the Yellow River. However, in 1235, war broke out between the former allies over the allocation of these territories. Although the Southern Song survived for more than 40 years after the war, this engagement ultimately led to the destruction of the dynasty (see pp. 186–187).

SHEN KUO (1031–1095)

One of China's greatest scientists, Shen Kuo was an astronomer, engineer, and mathematician who invented spherical trigonometry. He was the first to describe magnetic declination in his *Brush Talks from Dream Brook*, transforming navigation. His astronomical observation project—which involved measuring planets' positions three times a night for five years—was on a vast scale. He established the exact position of the pole star and discovered true north. *In Dream Pool Essays* (1088), he described the principles of erosion and sedimentation.

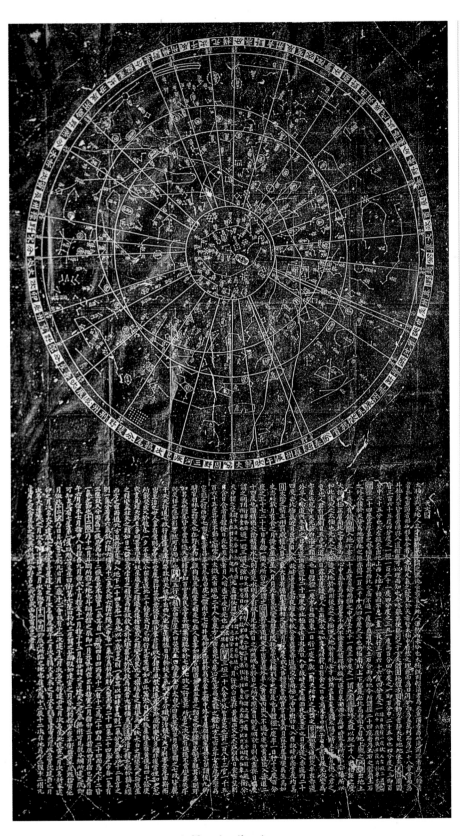

△ **Mapping the stars**
This Southern Song astronomical chart shows 1,434 stars grouped into 280 asterisms, or star groups; the accompanying text is a key to the chart and lists 1,565 stars in 283 asterisms.

The Yuan Dynasty
The Mongols create the largest land empire in history

In the 13th century, warriors originating from the Mongolian steppe swept first over Asia and then across Europe. In just 70 years, they grew from an obscure nomadic group to the greatest land empire in world history.

The Mongols were a combination of Mongolian and Turkic nomadic tribes from the mountainous borderlands between Mongolia and Manchuria. They rose to power after they were united under the rule of a great leader who was born the second son of a chieftain. By making strategic alliances with other clans, and defeating others in battle, he gained control over much of Mongolia by 1206 and took the title Genghis Khan). He established a military state with himself as its head and built a large, resolute, and well-organized army, which developed novel tactics for defeating its enemies. Genghis was a ruthless

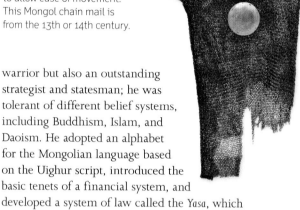

> ▷ **Dressed for war**
> Mongol armor was made from lightweight, flexible chain mail or leather plates to allow ease of movement. This Mongol chain mail is from the 13th or 14th century.

warrior but also an outstanding strategist and statesman; he was tolerant of different belief systems, including Buddhism, Islam, and Daoism. He adopted an alphabet for the Mongolian language based on the Uighur script, introduced the basic tenets of a financial system, and developed a system of law called the *Yasa*, which helped establish a tribal empire that would long outlive him.

"At **military exercises** I am always **in the front**, and in time of battle am **never behind**."

ATTRIBUTED TO GENGHIS KHAN BY A DAOIST MONK, c. 1222

Mongol expansion

Genghis began raiding farther afield, attacking the Xi Xia (in the northwestern provinces of China) in 1209. The Mongols secured the Xia's submission (and a bride for Genghis) before launching a full-scale invasion of the Jurchen Jin (see pp. 180–181). The weakened Jin dynasty finally collapsed in 1234.

The Mongols were a formidable foe (see box, right). Mounted on sturdy horses, they would descend swiftly on their enemies, destroying property and massacring entire populations. Their conquest of Eurasia was rapid. Genghis first turned west, defeating the Kara Khitai empire (Western Liao dynasty) in Central Asia in 1218 after besieging the capital, Balasaghun. He then turned to the Islamic world,

◁ **Mongol warriors**
In this detail from a miniature painting, c. 1430, Genghis Khan and his troops are shown in armed combat. The Mongol warriors were daunting opponents on the battlefield.

overwhelming the lands of the Khwarezm Shah (roughly Uzbekistan) and sacking the major cities of Bukhara and Samarkand.

By the time of Genghis's death in 1227, the Mongol empire extended from Iran and Kazakhstan in the west, across Central Asia and northern China to the Pacific Ocean. Yet this was just the start. Genghis's third son, Ögedei, organized a Mongol campaign in Europe, capturing major towns, including Vladimir and Moscow. In 1241, the Mongol army overwhelmed Poland, Hungary, and Bulgaria. Seventeen years later, in 1258, Hulagu Khan, a grandson of Genghis Khan, led an attack on, and brutally destroyed, Baghdad, following a 12-day siege. Palaces, mosques, churches, hospitals, and the city's 36 public libraries were either smashed to pieces or burned to the ground. The House of Wisdom—with perhaps the largest collection of books in the world at that time—was also destroyed. The books were ripped apart and thrown into the Tigris River, which was said to have run black from the ink.

Conquest of the Song

Another grandson of Genghis Khan, Kublai Khan (see pp. 192–193), set his sights firmly on China's Southern Song. He studied, mastered, and adopted almost every Song development in military technology. In 1267, Kublai set off with his troops to attack Xiangyang, a city that was surrounded by reportedly impenetrable walls that overlooked the Han River, a tributary of the Yangzi. The siege went on for five long years, despite countless strenuous attempts to break in and out.

In 1271, while the Song still reigned in the south, Kublai formally claimed the Mandate of Heaven and declared the first year of the "Great Yuan" dynasty. Xiangyang finally fell in 1273 and, despite further resistance, the Southern Song dynasty was finished by 1279. With the incorporation of the south into Yuan China, centuries of division came to an end. Historians consider the conquest of the Southern Song to be Kublai's greatest achievement.

△ **The fall of Baghdad**
This painting depicts the conquest of Baghdad by the Mongols in 1258. The image appears in the lavishly illustrated world history *Jami' al-Tawarikh* (c. 1314), by the Persian historian Rashid al-Din.

THE MONGOL FIGHTING FORCE

Mongols spent their lives on horseback, herding and hunting. These skills easily transferred to warfare. Every soldier had four to six horses, ensuring that no one horse was ridden to exhaustion. Diminutive, sturdy, and tough, Mongol horses were revered. The Mongol warriors could travel great distances, covering 100 miles (160 km) in a day. Soldiers trained every day, making them the most mobile and best-disciplined fighting force in the world.

Sheep and Goat

This ink painting was made by Zhao Mengfu (1254–1322), one of the most accomplished artists and calligraphers of the early Yuan dynasty. The artist wrote of his effort to capture his animal subjects: "Though I cannot get close to the ancient masters, I have managed somewhat to capture their essential spirit." The painting is embellished with the seals of Ming and Qing dynasty collectors who once owned the scroll. Among them was the Qianlong Emperor himself (r. 1735–1795), who provided the title frontispiece, which reads: "Divine likeness [of sheep] in motion and repose."

子昂常畫馬仰

信奇來羊三百

羣衆富一隻性

Sacred Sculptures

Buddhism through the ages

Since Buddhism arrived in China in the 1st century CE, it has risen and fallen in popularity as one of the country's religions. Thanks to the influence of Silk Road travelers, as well as foreign rulers, multiple branches of the Buddhist traditions have flourished in China over the last two millennia.

Incense burner in the shape of the Buddha

◁ **Stele fragment**
This stele depicts the Buddha with two bodhisattvas and two dragons. It dates from the Eastern Wei period, when Buddhism was the official state religion.

△ **Guanyin at ease**
The compassionate bodhisattva Guanyin was usually portrayed as female in China, though was seen as male elsewhere. This Jin-era figure shows Guanyin in the relaxed "royal ease" pose.

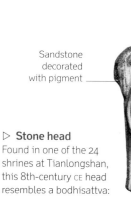

Sandstone decorated with pigment

▷ **Stone head**
Found in one of the 24 shrines at Tianlongshan, this 8th-century CE head resembles a bodhisattva: a once-mortal individual seeking to become a buddha, who achieved nirvana but chose instead to continue helping others.

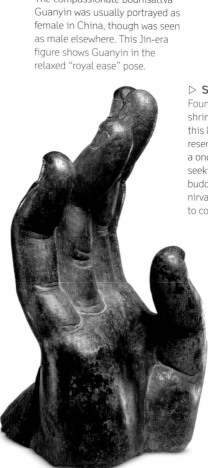

◁ **Right hand of the Buddha**
This lifelike hand once belonged to a cave statue of the Buddha sculpted between 550 and 560 CE, during the Northern Qi dynasty.

▷ **Sutra stele**
Made between 533 and 543 CE, this stele shows a debate from a Buddhist sutra. The limestone's dark appearance is due to its being touched countless times over the centuries, to the extent that some of the stele had to be reengraved.

△ Guanyin head
At the center of this sculpture's elaborate crown is the Tibetan character for Buddha.

△ Lion mount
In the Ming period, Guanyin was commonly depicted astride a lion. She was believed to have the power to relieve suffering.

△ Tibetan dagger
The *phurba* or *kila* is a Tibetan Buddhist dagger that symbolizes the Vajrakila Buddha and his ability to overcome all evils, including greed, delusion, and ignorance.

◁ Ming ritual staff
Dating from the Yongle era, this Buddhist staff, or *khatvanga*, reflects the obstacles an individual must face and overcome on their spiritual journey.

Iron inlaid with gold and silver

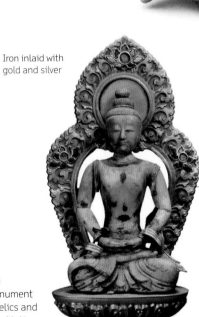

△ Ivory staff head
These three heads—one aging and another only a skull—represent change and death, parts of life that Buddhists are taught to accept.

△ Golden gods
This Qing ornament depicts three wrathful Tibetan Buddhist deities, with Yamantaka, lord of death, at its center. These deities are said to wage war on enemies of Buddhism.

◁ Offering
This Qing gold talisman is one of a set of altar offerings used in Tibetan Buddhism. Each offering would represent an auspicious symbol.

Guardian beast engraved in gold for protection

◁ Ming stupa
A stupa is a monument used to house relics and is a focus for meditation. This spectacular gold example dates from the Ming dynasty.

Gilt bronze throne inlaid with turquoise and other gemstones

◁ Qing jade Buddha
This blue jade Buddha retains the serenity of Buddha statues from earlier periods but sits on an ornate throne typical of Qing crafts.

Kublai Khan
The great Mongol leader and founder of the mighty Yuan dynasty is shown here in an ink portrait on silk made soon after his death in 1294. Kublai brought great wealth and power to China but never forgot his Mongol origins.

Kublai Khan

The Mongol warrior who ruled over all China

The first emperor of the Yuan dynasty, Kublai Khan subjugated the Song in southern China to rule over a vast empire. Respectful of Chinese culture, he presided over a period of prosperity and cultural achievement.

A favored grandson of the Mongol emperor Genghis Khan ("khan" meaning "ruler"), Kublai was born in 1215 in the heart of Mongolia. As a young man, he gained a reputation as a courageous warrior, and when his brother Möngke became khagan ("great khan") of the Mongol empire in 1251, Kublai was given control of territories in the east and placed in charge of the ongoing conquest of China. Kublai admired China's wealth and technological accomplishments. He employed Chinese advisers to introduce reforms in his territories, and in 1252 he commissioned architect Liu Bingzhong to build an impressive Chinese-style summer capital at Kaiping, later renamed Shangdu (Xanadu), in Inner Mongolia.

When Möngke died in 1259 with no named successor, a war of succession broke out between Kublai and his brother Arik Böke. In 1260, Kublai named himself khagan of the new Yuan dynasty (and, in the Chinese tradition, Son of Heaven), even though he did not defeat his brother until 1264. He shifted his headquarters to Khanbalik, or Dadu (Beijing), where he ordered a building program that reflected his grand tastes and gave rise to the Imperial City. By 1279, Kublai had defeated the Song dynasty and placed all of China under Mongol rule (see pp. 186–187).

Expanding empire

Kublai extended his authority overseas: in 1277, he launched campaigns against Burma and Vietnam and in 1274 and 1281 tried to subjugate Japan with naval expeditions. The second attempt ended in disaster when his forces were met with Japanese resistance and his ships were battered by a fierce typhoon. The Japanese believed that they had been saved by "divine winds" (*kamikaze*).

Kublai welcomed non-Chinese advisers, including Marco Polo (see pp. 198–199), to his empire. Many aspects of Chinese life flourished under his rule. He reopened the Silk Road, rebuilt and extended the Grand Canal, and sponsored poets and writers, painters, and calligraphers. Kublai died in 1294, having created the largest empire since the fall of Rome, with a unified China at its heart.

△ **Trophy of war**
This Yuan helmet was seized by the Japanese following their victory against a Yuan invasion of either 1274 or 1281.

▽ **Diplomatic missive**
This is a section of a letter in Mongolian script sent to Philip IV of France from Kublai Khan in 1289. The document proposes a military alliance against the Arab world.

1215 Born on September 23, the fourth son of Tolui, who was the second son of Genghis Khan

1260 Declares himself great khan of the Yuan dynasty

1279 Becomes the first non-Chinese ruler of a unified China

1281 Attempts to invade Japan, with disastrous consequences

1259 Kublai and his brother Arik Böke begin a war of succession

1266 Orders the reconstruction of Zhongdu and renames it Khanbalik (Beijing)

1294 Dies and is buried at a secret site in Mongolia reserved for Mongol leaders

Chinese Warfare

A history of changing tactics to control an empire

For more than two millennia, China's imperial armies were tasked with enlarging the empire and defending it from foreign and domestic foes. The empire tended to prosper when its armed forces came under a strong and unified command, but its borders to the north and the west were vulnerable to invaders, particularly when the empire's central administration was weak.

Military technology

Developments in weaponry were central to the evolution of Chinese warfare. At the beginning of the 1st millennium BCE, armies were relatively small, composed of thousands of serf or peasant infantrymen supporting charioteers of noble birth, who were protected by metal helmets and armed with spears and halberds made from expensive bronze. Battles tended to be short and were governed by strict codes of honor and ethical conduct. This pattern changed in the Spring and Autumn period (see pp. 58–59) when the number of conflicts between states escalated and battles became bigger, longer, and more brutal.

Iron-smelting technology effectively brought the age of the aristocratic warrior to an end. During the Warring States period (see pp. 68–69), iron swords and armor started to be mass-produced. These replaced expensive wrought weapons that had been the preserve of the nobility. The introduction of crossbows around the 2nd century BCE was also significant. With a lethal range of some 650 ft (200 m), these weapons were effective against charioteers and their horses in a way that earlier bows had not been. With the new weapons came new armies that are thought to have been composed of hundreds of thousands of men, led by a professional

△ **Formidable assembly**
The Terracotta Army (see pp. 82–83) comprises more than 7,000 lifelike warriors belonging to the First Emperor. The figures were unearthed in 1974 by local farmers near the emperor's tomb at Lintong in present-day Xi'an. They are thought to have been buried there c. 210 BCE.

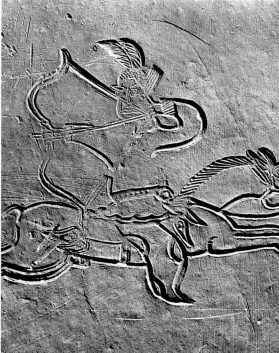

△ **Military strategies**
A brick from a tomb structure shows an image of a warrior taking a "Parthian shot" from his horse. According to this tactic, the warrior turns his upper body while in full gallop to shoot the pursuing enemy. This Han-period illustration (206 BCE–220 CE) is the earliest known depiction of this form of fighting.

△ **Battle on the Bridge**
These tomb rubbings from 2nd-century CE relief carvings on clay brick depict a series of Eastern Han dynasty combatants, war chariots, and battle scenes in silhouette. The animated carvings are from the west wall of the Wu Liang shrine at Jiaxiang, in Shandong province.

"There is **no instance** of a country having **benefitted** from **prolonged warfare.**"

SUNZI, *THE ART OF WAR*, 5TH CENTURY BCE

officer class. The nature of warfare also changed: cities and states built defenses from mounds of earth for protection, and sieges became a regular part of military confrontations. Under the Han dynasty (see pp. 86–89), cavalry grew in importance as commanders in border areas learned new skills from the horse-borne nomads with whom their forces clashed. The introduction of stirrups (probably by nomads) from the 4th century CE gave warriors far greater control over their mounts.

The troubled times of the northern and southern dynasties period (see pp. 126–127) saw the introduction of the *fubing* system, under which detachments of reservists were assigned tracts of land and could be called up for military service, mobilizing rapidly in times of war. By the 570s, there were said to be 200,000 men serving in these forces.

Gunpowder weapons appeared in late Tang times—four centuries before their use in the West. At first, these were flaming rockets, described at the time as "arrows of flying fire," and cast-iron grenades, but by the Song dynasty, the first recognizable cannons had been produced. The Southern Song also achieved a world's first with the introduction of a standing navy.

The early Ming emperors relied on a modified version of the *fubing* system for their armies, but from the 1430s, these hereditary soldiers were replaced by conscripts and mercenaries. Yet despite the crucial role played by armed forces in Chinese history, from the Ming dynasty onward, the military never gained the esteem of the Confucian bureaucrats who set the tone of culture. A popular saying captured their distaste: "A good man is not made from a soldier, nor fine furniture from rotten wood."

△ **Subterranean soldiers**
These murals depicting soldiers on horseback date from the Tang dynasty. They decorate the walls of Qianling Mausoleum, Shaanxi province, which holds the remains of members of the Tang imperial family, including Emperor Gaozong (r. 649–683) and his wife, Wu Zetian.

△ **Early firearms**
One of the first known depictions of firearms—namely, a grenade and a fire lance (a spearlike weapon containing gunpowder)—is shown in this detail from a 10th-century mural illustrating the temptation of the Buddha. The mural is from Dunhuang's famous Mogao Caves, which contain masterpieces of Buddhist art.

△ **Ming crackdown on pirates**
This battle between *wokou* (Japanese pirates) and Ming forces is from a late 16th- or early 17th-century scroll painting. Since the end of the Yuan, Japanese piracy in coastal regions had proved a major problem. The Ming took various steps to eradicate it, particularly in the 1540s.

Tools of War

Weapons through the ages

The warring kingdoms of ancient China commonly used swords, daggers, and bows in battle. Even in the Qing period, the bannerman shooting arrows on horseback remained an enduring image of Chinese warfare. Yet the Chinese invention of gunpowder in the 9th century CE revolutionized warfare and its tools.

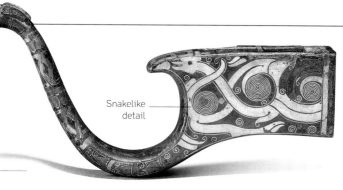

Snakelike detail

△ Crossbow fitting
This bronze crossbow fitting, inlaid with silver, dates from the late Warring States period. Often found in pairs, such fittings may have been used to attach a crossbow to a chariot or to support the bow itself.

Cork grip with iron hinge

△ Repeating crossbow
In this 18th-century weapon, the bow is flexible bamboo while the body is made from dark wood. The horizontal position of the stock meant that soldiers could use their hips as support when firing.

△ Qing bow
This 19th-century bow was hinged, allowing it to fold with its tips overlapping. Decorating the tips are human figures, their flowing robes painted on to the ends of the bow.

◁ Spearhead
This 17th–18th-century steel spearhead is embellished with golden illustrations showing flaming pearls, waves, and mountains.

△ Dragon blade
Decorating the handle of this double-edged bronze dagger is a column of dragon heads. It dates from the 7th–6th century BCE.

△ Ming glaive
The blade and haft (handle) of this *yanyue dao* knife are from different periods. While the scalloped, single-edge blade dates to the early 16th century, the haft was added at least a century later.

Gunpowder is loaded here, at the muzzle

▷ Artillery weapon
Mounted on a Russian base, this 18-pound Chinese cannon dates from 1830. It could hit a target 1.1 miles (1.8 km) away.

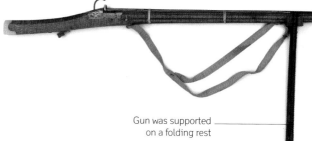

△ Metal gun
While matchlock guns, such as this Qing example, were used in China in the 19th century, European firearms of the time were more advanced.

Gun was supported on a folding rest

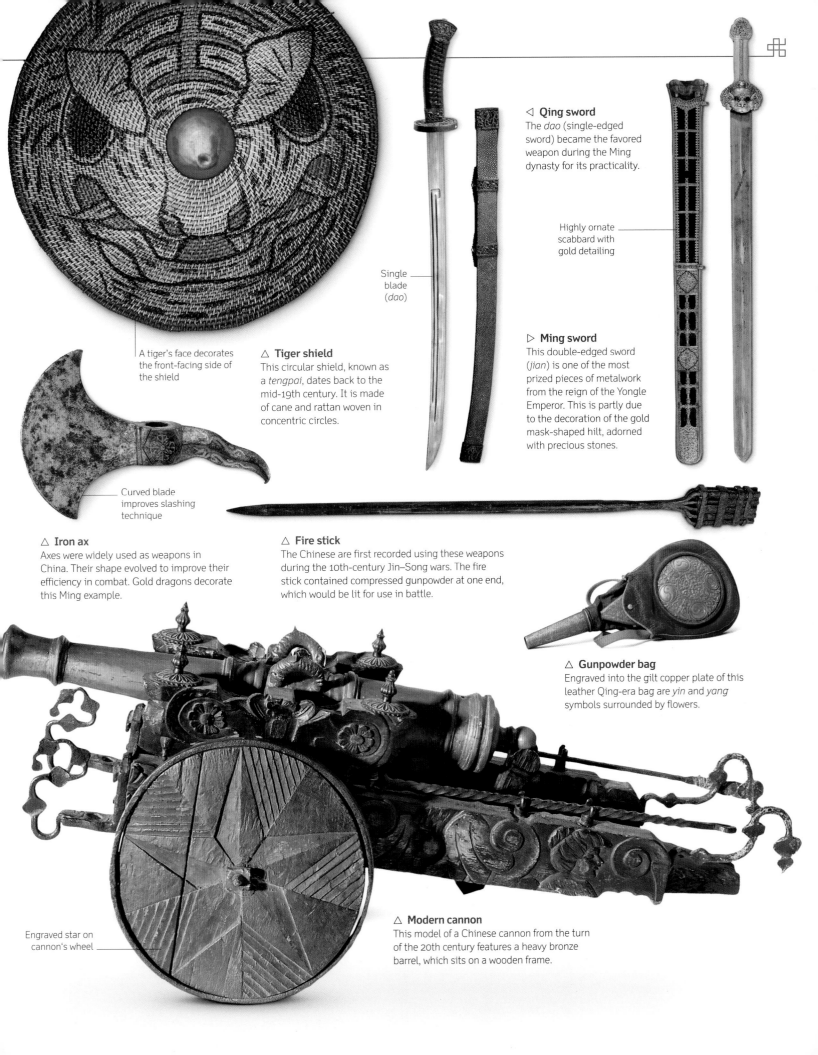

◁ **Qing sword**
The *dao* (single-edged sword) became the favored weapon during the Ming dynasty for its practicality.

Highly ornate scabbard with gold detailing

Single blade (*dao*)

▷ **Ming sword**
This double-edged sword (*jian*) is one of the most prized pieces of metalwork from the reign of the Yongle Emperor. This is partly due to the decoration of the gold mask-shaped hilt, adorned with precious stones.

A tiger's face decorates the front-facing side of the shield

△ **Tiger shield**
This circular shield, known as a *tengpai*, dates back to the mid-19th century. It is made of cane and rattan woven in concentric circles.

Curved blade improves slashing technique

△ **Iron ax**
Axes were widely used as weapons in China. Their shape evolved to improve their efficiency in combat. Gold dragons decorate this Ming example.

△ **Fire stick**
The Chinese are first recorded using these weapons during the 10th-century Jin–Song wars. The fire stick contained compressed gunpowder at one end, which would be lit for use in battle.

△ **Gunpowder bag**
Engraved into the gilt copper plate of this leather Qing-era bag are *yin* and *yang* symbols surrounded by flowers.

Engraved star on cannon's wheel

△ **Modern cannon**
This model of a Chinese cannon from the turn of the 20th century features a heavy bronze barrel, which sits on a wooden frame.

The Travels of Marco Polo

An early traveler to China who chronicled the Mongol court

The Venetian merchant Marco Polo was one of the first Europeans to visit China. He was welcomed into the court of Kublai Khan and traveled widely through the empire as part of a 24-year odyssey recorded in his *Travels of Marco Polo* (Il Milione).

◁ Leaving Venice
A 15th-century illustration shows Marco Polo setting out from Venice in 1271, with his father and uncle, for the court of Kublai Khan. They arrived four years later.

Marco Polo was born around 1254 into a prosperous merchant family in the Italian city-state of Venice. When he was six years old, his father, Niccolò, and his uncle, Maffeo, left Venice on a trading mission, passing through the Black Sea region and Central Asia and eventually joining a diplomatic trip to meet the Mongol ruler Kublai Khan (see pp. 192–193) at Dadu, present-day Beijing.

Setting out

Kublai was intensely curious about the European legal, political, and administrative systems and wanted to learn more about Europe's religious beliefs. Accordingly, he sent Niccolò and Maffeo Polo on a goodwill mission to meet the pope in Rome. They returned to Italy in 1269. Two years later, they set out again—this time with the 17-year-old Marco Polo—bearing gifts from the

pope for Kublai Khan. They sailed first to Acre (in present-day Israel) and continued, possibly by camel train, to the Persian port city of Hormuz. From there, they followed the Silk Road (see pp. 102–105). Mongol control over much of Eurasia had ushered in a period of peace known as the *Pax Mongolica* in which travel and trade along the Silk Road had increased greatly.

In the court of Kublai Khan

Finally, around 1274–1275, after trekking across the great Gobi Desert and skirting the northern frontier of China, the family arrived at Kublai Khan's opulent summer palace at Shangdu (Xanadu), north of Beijing. Kublai took Marco Polo into his court and he became a great favorite of the emperor's. Polo was educated in the court, where he learned Mongolian and Chinese customs. He attained such a position of trust that he was sent on official business to the port city of Hangzhou, which, like Venice, was built around a series of canals. The young Polo was overawed by its huge population, its bustling commerce, its market squares, and its traders, who brought food on carts and in boats. Polo also traveled across inland China into present-day Myanmar. The Polo family finally returned home in 1295—the year after Kublai's death sent

△ Paper money
In his account of his travels, Marco Polo describes how Kublai Khan produced paper currency from the bark of a mulberry tree. This banknote was printed on the orders of Kublai Khan in around 1269.

◁ Intrepid explorer
This striking depiction of the celebrated Marco Polo is by the 19th-century Italian painter Annibale Strata.

△ **Polo's travels**
The Polo family and their party are shown in this detail from an illustration in the *Catalan Atlas* of 1375, traveling on horseback and on foot. A train of camels leads the group.

the Mongol Empire into decline. Shortly afterward, Marco Polo was captured in battle by Venice's archrival Genoa. During his time in prison, Polo met a fellow captive, the Italian adventure writer Rustichello of Pisa, to whom Polo dictated a 298-page manuscript that was entitled "Description of the World."

Remarkable adventures

First published around 1300, the "Description of the World" has become better known as *The Travels of Marco Polo*. In it, Polo chronicles his encounters with people from diverse religions and cultures and with unfamiliar animals and birds. He describes his extraordinary adventures in some of the world's harshest and most inhospitable regions, including high mountain passes, arid deserts, and treacherous seas. He also paints a vivid picture of Kublai Khan and life in his imperial palaces, paper money, coal, gunpowder, printing, and many other innovations that had not yet appeared in Europe.

The book became a bestseller and awakened Europe to the potential benefits of international trade and expansion. Although early commentators disputed the credibility of Polo's work, most modern scholars accept that his text is based on authentic experience, in part thanks to his incidental descriptions, such as his discussion of currency, salt production, and revenues from the salt monopoly. Although prone to embellishment and some self-aggrandizing tales, the narrative has an immediacy that is difficult to dismiss.

"I did not tell **half** of what **I saw**, for I knew I would not be **believed**."

REPORTED DEATHBED STATEMENT OF MARCO POLO, 1324

The Late Mongol Dynasty

The Han react to the rule of an alien minority

Political cohesion disintegrated in the Yuan dynasty. Intrigues at court, corruption, discrimination against the Han Chinese, and a series of natural calamities led to resentment, rebellion, and the collapse of the Yuan Mongol empire.

Following Kublai Khan's death in 1294, Kublai's grandson Temür Khan became emperor, reigning until 1307. After defeating various rebellions and challenges to the throne, he was the last Mongol ruler to maintain truly effective control over China. The following 25 years saw a series of short-reigned emperors, the longest ruling for just eight years and several for just one or two years. Some of these rulers were very young and lacked experience in governing a volatile and hugely complex empire. In 1315, the Yuan reintroduced the Confucian examination system (see pp. 174–175) but changed its parameters so as to favor Mongol candidates. Discrimination against the Han population led to resentment and revolts.

Opposing views on government

In 1333, a factional struggle at court resulted in the ascendancy of Toghon Temür, who would go on to rule for 35 years, until the end of the Yuan dynasty. His long reign was controlled by two chancellors: Bayan, from 1335 to 1340, and Toghoto, from 1340 to 1344 and again from 1349 to 1354. These two chancellors adopted very different policies. Bayan purged non-Mongols at court (see below), imposed ethnic separatism, and forbade Chinese people from owning weapons; one rumor suggested that he also proposed killing all Chinese people who bore the five most common surnames. Toghoto reversed many of these policies and decentralized government authority.

DRAMA OF DISSENT

Discriminated against and excluded from government, many of the Chinese elite withdrew from public life to pursue their own artistic goals, often with the support of Buddhist or Daoist religion: in this way, Han culture flourished under Yuan rule. Some turned their hand to drama (a mural of a play from 1324 is shown here), producing a number of notable works, many of which criticized the alien rulers. For example, Guan Hanqing's play *Injustice to Dou E* (also known as *Snow in Midsummer*) was a courtroom drama that subtly reflected the perceived injustice of Mongolian rule.

△ **Bathing Horses**
Zhao Mengfu was one of the Yuan dynasty's most revered artists. His silk handscroll *Bathing Horses* is shown here.

▽ **Mongol figure**
This 14th-century burnished earthenware figurine depicts a Yuan dynasty man—his head is covered and he is wearing simple robes.

However, from the late 1340s, the state was beset by numerous environmental catastrophes—including harsh winters, floods, epidemics, and famines—which led to the depopulation of northern China. These cataclysmic events were interpreted by the Chinese as divine signs that the Yuan had lost the Mandate of Heaven (see p. 49). In an attempt to pay for relief measures, the government printed paper money, which soon led to rampant inflation. Despite this—and alongside weak government, ruinous taxation, and corruption—parts of the Yuan economy prospered: cotton production increased, and sorghum was introduced on a large scale. The Grand Canal was restored and extended to reach the Yuan capital in Beijing, but this was a costly enterprise. It resulted in destructive flooding and caused more resentment from peasants who were coerced into working without pay on the huge engineering project.

The Red Turban Rebellion

Kublai Khan had divided China into 12 provinces for administrative and military purposes. However, by the 1340s, much of southern China had begun to act more or less independently; by 1355, this had led to a breakdown of central control.

Han discontent began to coalesce around groups that identified themselves as the Red Turbans (after the color of their headbands). They advocated armed rebellion and called for a social order that excluded

△ **Final ruler of the Yuan**
Toghon Temür, shown here to the left of his brother, ascended the throne at the age of just 13. Later in life, he withdrew from politics and engaged in debauchery. He died in 1370.

Mongol rule. Their principal ideas were drawn from the White Lotus (a Buddhist sect from the Southern Song), Confucianism, and Daoism. In 1356, the Red Turbans, under Zhu Yuanzhang, took the city of Nanjing. The Yuan gave way to the Ming dynasty in 1368, after rebels surrounded Dadu (Beijing) and expelled the Mongol rulers—Toghon Temür fled with his empress and concubines to Mongolia.

"Although you inherited [China] on **horseback,** you **cannot rule** it from **that position.**"

ADVISER YELÜ CHUCAI (1190-1244) TO ÖGEDEI KHAN (r. 1229–1241)

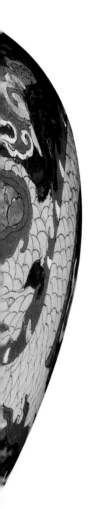

6

Stability and Wealth

1368 to 1644

Introduction

For almost three centuries, from 1368 to 1644, China was ruled by the Ming dynasty. The Ming presided over a period of flourishing culture and expanding population but failed to provide consistent good government or to guarantee the empire's security against external threats. Founded by a peasant rebel, Zhu Yuanzhang, the Ming dynasty reasserted native Han Chinese traditions and modes of government. The dynasty reacted against the era of foreign dominance under the Mongol Yuan dynasty by harking back to the practices of the Tang and the Song. Confucianism was restored as the empire's official ideology, and the Confucian examination system revived as the main means of selecting bureaucrats. But despite this conservatism, the new dynasty at first seemed set to release dynamic forces for growth and change.

In the early 15th century, the Yongle Emperor had an imposing new capital built at Beijing, centered around the Forbidden City, which functioned as an imperial residence and seat of government. The Grand Canal was renovated and extended to create a major artery of internal trade and supply the capital with grain. The southwestern provinces of Yunnan and Guizhou were fully integrated into the Chinese empire for the first time, although attempts to conquer Vietnam failed. In a spectacular gesture that linked imperial power and maritime commerce, the Yongle Emperor sent an intimidating "treasure fleet" (see pp. 222–223) on official voyages into the Indian Ocean as far as the Red Sea and East Africa, obliging local rulers to acknowledge the supremacy of the Chinese emperor. At this time, European explorers were also opening new routes for trade and colonization. Portuguese ships sailed down the west coast of Africa, although they would not reach China for another century.

Looking inward

In principle, Ming ships could have rounded Africa and reached the Americas in the 1420s. This did not happen, mainly because the Yongle Emperor's successors curtailed the period of oceanic exploration, putting a new emphasis on the Confucian notion of Chinese self-sufficiency. In the 16th century, Ming emperors would go so far as to attempt a ban on all maritime trade. The defensive posture and inward-looking policies adopted by the Ming emperors from the 1430s onward were partly triggered by the weakness of the

1368 Zhu Yuanzhang founds the Ming dynasty as the Hongwu Emperor

1405 The Ming treasure fleet embarks on its first ocean voyage

1420 The construction of the Forbidden City in Beijing is completed

1433 The treasure fleet completes its final voyage

1402 The Yongle Emperor initiates the "Second Founding" of the dynasty

1407 Chinese forces invade and occupy Vietnam

1428 The Ming abandon their attempt to conquer Vietnam

1449 The defeat of a Chinese army by the Oirats destabilizes the empire

empire's strategic position. The Mongols had been driven out of China in the overthrow of the Yuan dynasty, but the tribes beyond the empire's northern borders remained a threat.

The northerly location of Beijing made the capital especially vulnerable to incursions by steppe warriors (see pp. 224–225). Efforts to impose dominance on the steppe through military force failed when an army led by the Yingzong Emperor was defeated by the Oirats in 1449. Major resources were then devoted to rebuilding and extending the Great Wall along China's land border to keep the steppe horsemen at bay, but this fortification was never more than partially successful. At the same time, China's coasts were being raided by pirates, both Japanese and native Chinese. The security of China's population was not supported by the faltering central government, as officials and court eunuchs vied for power and emperors often proved cruel, wanton, and irresponsible.

Western influence

Ming China still remained the most populous country in the world, with cities that surpassed all foreign rivals in prosperity and sophistication. The lure of Chinese luxury goods, such as ceramics and silks, drew European sailors, who began to arrive in the 16th century. The Europeans, even at this early stage, had a significant impact on China, introducing new food crops from the Americas and unbalancing the country's finances through the large quantities of silver with which they paid for their purchases.

Ming achievements were impressive, from the exquisite products of craftsmen to the vibrancy of popular culture expressed through novels and plays. However, the sense of Chinese superiority could not completely obscure a global shift that was taking place. Whereas at the time of the Song dynasty, China could realistically claim to lead the world in science and technology, by the 17th century, Europeans were on the verge of their Scientific Revolution.

In the early decades of the 17th century, the Ming dynasty entered a terminal decline, natural disasters exposing and compounding the failings of a government that had become ineffectual and corrupt. Internal revolts brought down the dynasty, allowing the Manchu, another people from north of the Great Wall, to impose their rule on China. Their new Qing dynasty would endure into the 20th century.

1513 The Portuguese are the first European sailors to reach China

1550 Mongol raiders under Altan Khan burn the suburbs of Beijing

1572 The Wanli Emperor begins his 48-year reign

1601 Jesuit priest Matteo Ricci is invited to reside in the Forbidden City

1644 The Chongzhen Emperor dies by suicide; the Manchu seize Beijing

1522 The first printed edition of the *Romance of the Three Kingdoms*

1557 Portuguese traders are permitted to settle in Macau

1592 Chinese forces intervene to defeat Japanese invaders in Korea (to 1598)

1616 The Manchu leader Nurhaci challenges waning Ming power

1627 Zhu Youjian accedes to the throne as the Chongzhen Emperor

The Rise of the Ming

Restoring Han Chinese rule and national unity

The Ming dynasty was proclaimed in 1368 by the peasant rebel Zhu Yuanzhang, who laid the foundations of a strong centralized state. He set out to restore Chinese traditions after the foreign rule of the Mongol Yuan.

Zhu Yuanzhang, who took the title of the Hongwu Emperor in 1368, was born a poor peasant and lived his early life as an itinerant Buddhist monk. Amid the chaos of the declining years of the Yuan dynasty (see pp. 200–201), he joined the Red Turban rebels and, rising through a mixture of competence and cunning, made himself leader of a guerrilla army. By 1356, he had seized control of the city of Nanjing. There he established the basis of his future dynasty, winning the support of the educated elite by promising to restore Han Chinese rule and Confucian values. In a series of lengthy campaigns, he extended his control over southern China before striking northward to capture the Yuan capital at Beijing.

Hongwu's administration

It was not until he had put the Mongols to flight that he officially declared himself emperor, asserting a convincing claim to the Mandate of Heaven (see p. 49). The new emperor was brutal and ruthless but also

▷ **Ming paper currency**
The Ming tried to regulate the economy by replacing metal coins with notes printed on paper. However, by the 1420s, inflation had severely undermined the value of notes.

proved himself to be shrewd and effective. Keeping his capital at Nanjing, he created a court modeled on that of his Song dynasty predecessors—one staffed by scholar-officials recruited through a restored Confucian examination system—and tried to curb the power of palace eunuchs. Having come to power through force, he focused on military matters, building China's navy into the world's largest and creating an army of more than one million men. It was strictly organized into units composed of five battalions and 10 companies. Soldiers were allocated land to farm, and their jobs were made hereditary.

A strengthening empire

These reforms helped sustain the forces needed to secure and maintain the country's borders. Still fearing a Mongol invasion, Hongwu made his 25 sons princes in the border areas, allowing him to closely monitor the foreign threat. Through a major military effort completed in 1381, he brought the southwestern provinces of Yunnan and Guizhou fully under imperial control for the first time.

Hongwu maintained many of the attitudes of his peasant origins. He was instinctively hostile to the wealthy

△ **The Hongwu Emperor**
The first emperor of the Ming dynasty ruled for 30 years. When he died at the age of 70, his physicians and concubines were put to death on his instructions.

"In the morning I **punish a few**; by the evening **others commit** the **same crime**."

PROCLAMATION OF THE HONGWU EMPEROR, c. 1382

▷ *Jinyiwei* **badge**
This badge identified the bearer as a member of the *Jinyiwei*, Hongwu's private guard, which the emperor used to spy on and punish his rivals.

merchants of southern China as he was to the educated elite, despite depending on them to administer his empire. He shifted the main burden of taxation from the peasantry to merchants and officials and broke up large estates to provide land for peasants. The efficiency of food production, grain distribution, and tax collection improved, but the population was strictly controlled, with many peasants forced to relocate to farm virgin soil. A new legal code based on Confucian principles was enforced by brutal punishments.

Paranoia and punishment

Hongwu's cruelty and paranoia made him a dangerous master; any suspicion of disloyalty could lead to torture and execution. In 1380, convinced that his chancellor Hu Weiyong was plotting to usurp power, the emperor launched a purge that eliminated not only the chancellor's entire clan but numerous other officials and their extended families, considered guilty by association. By the time this bloodbath had subsided, some 30,000 people had been put to death. The emperor henceforth dispensed with a chancellor, ruling directly through his ministries with the aid of a group of officials called the Grand Secretariat. He established the *Jinyiwei*, or Embroidered Uniform Guard, as a secret police force with special powers to crush dissent.

In 1392, the aging Hongwu Emperor's plans for the succession were thrown into disarray by the death of his eldest son, crown prince Zhu Biao, at the age of 36. The emperor designated his young grandson Zhu Yunwen (the son of Zhu Biao) as his successor. In doing so, however, he aroused the jealousy of his other sons, who had their own imperial ambitions.

The Hongwu Emperor died in 1398, and Zhu Yunwen briefly took the throne. Four years later, however, Hongwu's son Prince Zhu Di seized the throne as the Yongle Emperor (see pp. 208–209), beginning what is known as the "second founding" of the Ming.

△ **Guandi, god of war**
The Ming adopted Guandi as a patron and embodiment of their values. Much like Hongwu himself, Guandi had arisen from humble origins— he was a Han warrior who had been deified.

The Second Founding

Ming China under the Yongle Emperor

Historians refer to the reign of Zhu Di, the Yongle Emperor, as the "Second Founding" of the Ming dynasty. Under Yongle's rule, a resurgent China—with a new capital at Beijing—set out to assert its power abroad.

Zhu Di, the Prince of Yan, was one of the many sons of Hongwu, the first emperor of the Ming dynasty. Sharing his father's bullish characteristics, and benefitting from military experience on the northern frontier, he became one of Hongwu's favorites. Hongwu, however, had nominated his grandson Zhu Yunwen as his successor (see p. 207), and on Hongwu's death, the young man took the throne as the Jianwen Emperor. Hongwu's other sons, who coveted their father's inheritance, challenged the new emperor, and Zhu Di launched an uprising in 1399, declaring his intention to free the emperor from the influence of his "evil" advisers. After a prolonged civil war, Zhu Di's forces captured the imperial capital of Nanjing in 1402. The Jianwen Emperor disappeared, probably burned to death in the fire that destroyed his palace.

Establishing authority

Zhu Di relied on the court eunuchs for support (see pp. 116–117). They had helped bring him to power and had control of the secret police. Once proclaimed emperor, Zhu Di began to impose his authority with absolute ruthlessness. He persecuted and put to death supporters of the Jianwen Emperor throughout the country and exterminated Confucian officials along with their extended families. One famous Confucian scholar, Fang Xiaoru, who disobeyed an order to write the proclamation of Yongle's enthronement, was killed by dismemberment.

Throughout his reign, Yongle built a reputation for unbridled cruelty. One particular example was his mass execution of 2,800 concubines and harem staff in 1421, which he ordered to extinguish a minor palace scandal. The method of execution favored by the emperor was *lingchi* ("slow slicing," or death by a thousand cuts). The emperor's brutality was offset by the effectiveness and energy he brought to the task of ruling China. He shifted the capital northward to his own power base at Beijing, where he had the magnificent Forbidden City built as a new seat of government for the empire (see pp. 214–217). Partly in order to keep his new capital supplied with grain, he carried out a large-scale refurbishment of the dilapidated Grand Canal (see pp. 136–137), which

△ **Ritual blade**
Decorated with cloud and serpent motifs, this ritual flaying knife was a gift from the Yongle Emperor to a high-ranking Tibetan monk, who visited his court in 1407.

◁ **The Yongle Emperor**
The third Ming emperor was one of China's most effective rulers. His ruthlessness and ambition were only somewhat tempered by his devout adherence to Buddhism.

◁ **The Porcelain Tower**
The Yongle Emperor ordered the building in Nanjing of an octagonal pagoda made from porcelain brick. It was destroyed in the 19th century in the Taiping Rebellion (see pp. 278–279).

△ **Lacquer disc**
This carved lacquer disc from the Yongle period depicts figures in a tranquil garden scene. Its inscription suggests it may have been used as a platter in the imperial court's kitchens.

linked Beijing to Hangzhou south of Nanjing on the Yangzi delta, a distance of more than 1,000 miles (1,600 km). Around 165,000 laborers were employed on dredging work between 1411 and 1415. The restored waterway transformed internal trade and the distribution of imported goods.

Foreign ambitions

The Yongle Emperor pursued an aggressive policy toward the other eastern powers, reasserting the imperial tradition that regarded all foreign countries as owing China homage and tribute. He sponsored the seven voyages of the eunuch Admiral Zheng He (see pp. 222–223)—expeditions that were intended to radiate Chinese power over distant states in Southeast Asia and the Indian Ocean.

However, Yongle's foreign ambitions ran up against the limits of China's military strength. An attempt to assert control over neighboring Vietnam proved an embarrassing failure. Invading forces sent by Yongle in 1406 succeeded in taking control of the country, but the Chinese occupiers were soon comprehensively defeated in an independence struggle led by the Vietnamese leader Le Loi between 1418 and 1427. Yongle's efforts to defeat the nomadic tribes on China's open steppe frontier also failed. Between 1410 and 1424, the emperor personally led five campaigns across the Gobi against the Mongol Oirats and the

Tatars. He was unable to decisively defeat them and subdue the threat they represented, largely owing to the speed and mobility of the enemy forces.

Death and succession

Yongle died while campaigning against the Oirats in the Gobi Desert in 1424. He was interred in an imperial burial ground outside Beijing, which would eventually hold the tombs of 13 Ming emperors. His successors, the Hongxi and Xuande emperors, inherited a relatively stable empire. Less militaristic than Yongle, they concentrated on issues such as fairer taxation and reduced spending on state projects. Ocean voyages were canceled and troops withdrawn from Vietnam. The Ming dynasty entered a less assertive, more defensive, inward-looking phase.

THE YONGLE ENCYCLOPEDIA

In 1403, Yongle ordered his scholars to create the *Yongle dadian* ("vast document of Yongle"), a compendium of Chinese texts covering all areas of knowledge, from history, philosophy, and religion to astrology, medicine, and farming. More than 3,000 scholars worked on the project for five years, compiling an encyclopedia of 11,095 volumes. The world's largest encyclopedia before the internet age, it was never printed. The original manuscript was destroyed and only around 3 percent of an early copy survives today.

Ming Crafts

Highlights from the great dynasty

Under the Ming dynasty, Chinese crafts flourished. The development of different art forms led to the production of intricately decorated wares that showcased craftsmen's skills in lacquerware, cloisonné (enamel), and wood carving. The Ming period produced some of China's most celebrated objects and furniture.

△ **Incense burner**
This enamel vessel is made of a variety of materials, including gilt metal handles, a wooden cover, and a jade knob.

△ **Lacquer plate**
Carved into this dish, which dates back to the Jiajing Emperor's reign, is a scene featuring various figures alongside dragons.

△ **Lacquer tray**
Garden scenes featuring Chinese scholars were a popular subject of late Ming art and can be seen here on this elaborately decorated dish.

◁ **Cloisonné plate**
This 15th-century dish is one of the earliest known examples of cloisonné, a decorative art where wire cells were fixed to an object, then filled with colored enamel.

△ **Sutra box**
This gold-inlaid chest from the Yongle period would hold a sutra (Sanskrit literature) used at court.

△ **Cloisonné creature**
Mythological creatures were a popular subject among artists. This incense burner depicts Luduan, a detector of truth.

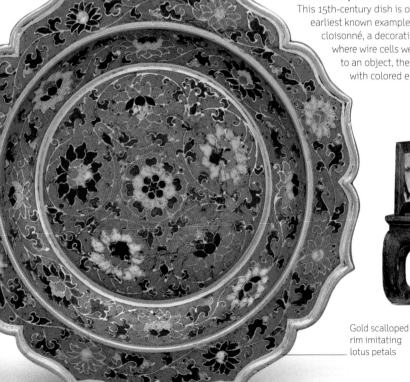

Decorative panel screens

Gold scalloped rim imitating lotus petals

△ **Bed with screens**
Hardwood furniture became popular during the Ming dynasty, and *luohanchuang*, or couch beds, like this one would be found in studies, women's bedrooms, or the main hall.

△ **Cloisonné chair**
The rare enamel finish on this wooden chair makes for a striking piece of furniture.

Carved flower decoration

△ **Lacquer incense stand**
The use of lacquer was not limited to ornaments—it was also used to decorate elaborate pieces of furniture.

▷ *Pipa* **(front and back)**
This stringed instrument gets its name from the way it is played: using a plectrum, the musician strums the strings *pi* (forward) and *pa* (backward).

Silk strings

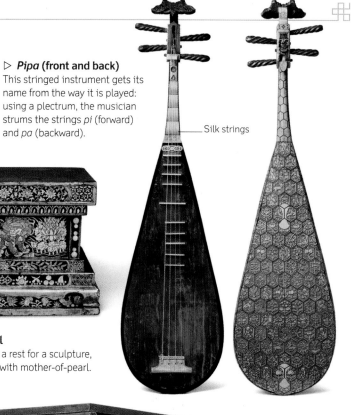

◁ *Dungchen* **trumpets**
Decorated with a cloisonné finish, these long, collapsible trumpets were sent as gifts to foreign dignitaries to impress them.

△ **Lacquer pedestal**
Thought to have been a rest for a sculpture, this pedestal is inlaid with mother-of-pearl.

◁ **Canopy bed**
Few Ming beds of this quality still exist today. They not only were used for sleeping but also provided a space in which to entertain guests and relax during the day.

Geometric
pattern on
border

◁ **Floral charger**
This plant-patterned dish was produced in Jingdezhen in the late 14th century. It is a large piece, about 19 in (47.5 cm) in diameter.

"The **earth is so refined** that dishes made of it are of **an azure tint**...."

MARCO POLO, THEORIZING ON CHINESE PORCELAIN, 13TH CENTURY

Blue-and-White Wares

World-famous Ming china

The Ming dynasty is famous for the blue-and-white porcelain mass-produced in its imperial workshops. Popular not only in China, these wares were exported to customers in the West on such a large scale that porcelain itself came to be called "china" in English. Cobalt ores imported from Persia by the Silk Road, albeit in small quantities, were used to make the three-color glaze found on Tang dynasty ceramics (see pp. 156–157). The Yuan dynasty produced special blue-and-white pieces with cobalt ore that can be seen as a precursor to the Ming designs. They used Samarra blue and Sumatra blue cobalt, iron-rich types that created darker spots in the paint. The colors represented the Mongols' legendary ancestors: a blue wolf and a white doe. Perhaps the most famous examples of Yuan porcelain are the "David Vases" (see pp. 266–267), named for the 19th-century art collector Sir Percival David. These two altar vases are among the world's oldest examples of blue-and-white pottery.

Ming wares

During the Ming dynasty, the fleets of explorer Zheng He (see pp. 222–223) brought smalt cobalt back to China. This, along with the locally mined cobalt that became more prominent in the mid-15th century, was used to create the elaborate and subtly toned porcelain that categorized the Ming period. At some point between 1369 and 1402, the Ming rulers reestablished the Song imperial porcelain factories in Jingdezhen, Jiangxi province. During the 15th century, blue-and-white porcelain used the "heaped and piled effect," where texture and shading were created by the cobalt concentrating in particular areas. Common motifs included flowers, gardens, dragons, and phoenixes. The pottery using this technique reached its high point during the reign of Xuande (1425–1435). By the 18th century, the patterns on porcelain had a more uniform blue tone.

Foreign demand

The demand in Europe for Ming blue-and-white porcelain was insatiable. It came to be known as Kraak ware (after "carrack," the name for Portuguese merchant vessels). In the early 17th century, the Dutch capture of two Portuguese carracks carrying more than 200,000 pieces of porcelain helped fuel the craze in Europe for Chinese wares, which in turn influenced the design of Dutch Delftware. Much of the Kraak ware was produced at Jingdezhen—in the late Ming period, factories there began to produce ceramics made for the export market, such as bowls with Latin inscriptions and flasks with European crests.

▽ **Dragon jar**
Fifteenth-century jars often depicted dragons. The number of claws signified the owner's rank, with five-clawed dragons reserved for the emperor.

The Ming Capital

Building Beijing and the Forbidden City

The decision of the Yongle Emperor to move the Ming capital to Beijing led to the construction of the spectacular Forbidden City, which was to remain at the heart of Chinese government for almost 500 years.

The Yongle Emperor's decision in 1403 to move his government to Beijing from Nanjing was dictated by personal interest: he was an insecure usurper and Beijing was his power base. Nanjing remained a major administrative center, where China's financial business was handled, while in Beijing, scholars, geomancers (experts in auspicious building), and architects had the formidable task of creating a city from scratch. The remains of the Yuan capital in Beijing (known by the Yuan as Khanbaliq or Dadu) were plundered for building materials.

△ **Symbolic dragon**
Green and yellow ceramic works decorated the red walls of the Forbidden City. This one depicts a dragon—a symbol of imperial power.

Designing the capital

The new capital had to provide a secure imperial residence and a functioning center of bureaucracy. It also needed to symbolize the emperor's sacred role as the link between Earth and Heaven. Fourteen years were spent on ensuring that the detail of the layout was auspicious and accorded with ancient custom before construction began.

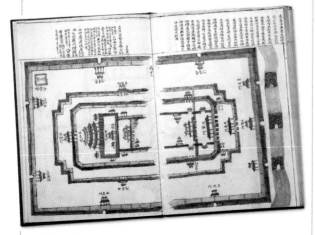

△ **City plan**
This 18th-century map was drawn during a Vietnamese embassy to China. It depicts the layout of the Forbidden City, with its symmetrical enclosed courts and nine gates.

SITING THE IMPERIAL TOMBS

In 1407, the Yongle Emperor ordered his geomancers to identify a suitable place for an imperial burial ground near Beijing. An auspicious location was found in a mountain valley north of the city. Approached by a sacred way lined with statues, each burial mound lay within its own walled enclosure, with its own dedicated hall for ritual offerings. The necropolis eventually covered an area of 15 sq miles (40 sq km), providing a final resting place for 13 Ming emperors up to 1644.

The city was built symmetrically along a north–south axis, with the principal buildings and gates all facing south—an auspicious alignment. The urban layout resembled a nest of boxes centered around the emperor's palace, the Forbidden City—so called because access to it was strictly limited. This rectangular enclosure, measuring 3,150 ft by 2,470 ft (961 m by 753 m), nestled within the Imperial City, a larger walled area that housed offices, military barracks, warehouses, and workshops. The Imperial City was in turn surrounded by streets of the walled Inner City—where ordinary residents lived.

Located outside Beijing, but an essential part of its symbolic conception, were the imperial burial grounds to the north; the various temple complexes—notably the temples of the sun and moon—to the east and west of the city, respectively; and the temples of agriculture and Heaven to the south. At fixed times of the year, the emperor and his entourage would go from the Forbidden City through the Meridian Gate (the southern and largest city gate), processing along the Imperial Way to the temples south of the city.

Imperial enclosure

Construction of the Forbidden City was completed between 1417 and 1420, using a workforce of 100,000 skilled artisans and countless laborers. Precious woods were brought from the forests of southwestern China and more than 100 million tiles and bricks »

△ **Yongle's triumph**
A Ming official—possibly the chief architect—stands
larger than life at the front gate of the Forbidden City
in this Ming dynasty painting.

△ **From left to right**
Statuettes of auspicious animals were placed prominently on the ridge lines of official buildings.

This intricately carved marble slope, decorated with dragons and clouds, adorns the steps to the Hall of Supreme Harmony.

This detail depicts one of the dragons on the Nine Dragon Screen, a screen wall built by the Qing in 1773.

The altar of the Palace of Heavenly Purity is framed by red pillars, enamel censers, and lavish roof tiles.

in the imperial color, yellow, were specially manufactured at Suzhou in eastern China. Giant blocks of marble were quarried 45 miles (70 km) outside of Beijing and then dragged to the city by teams of 40 or 50 men. These laborers mostly worked in the depths of winter, when the blocks could be slid on ice to move them more easily.

A city divided

The Forbidden City was enclosed by a broad moat and high walls of rammed earth lined with brick. The four corners of the walls were marked by towers with elaborate roofs, and impressive gates pierced the enclosure at each point of the compass. Inside, the Forbidden City was formally divided into two halves, the Outer Court and the Inner Court. Deliberately designed to inspire awe, the Outer Court was entered through the monumental Meridian Gate in the south wall. Crossing a square bisected by a meandering stream, privileged visitors passed through a second

MING ARCHITECTURE

The principles of Ming architecture reflected traditional Chinese beliefs about numerology (the sacred meaning of numbers) and geomancy (the spiritual significance of place and positioning). The numbers three and nine were sacred in numerology and dictated design in various aspects, such as the number of figures on a roof (see top left) or temples in a temple complex. Geomancy decided the orientation of buildings toward points of the compass, as well as their relation to natural features such as rivers and hills. Shapes also had symbolic significance; a square was believed to represent the Earth, while a circle represented Heaven.

gate into an extensive courtyard where a trio of large halls stood atop a three-tiered marble terrace. One of these buildings, the Hall of Supreme Harmony, was the largest wood-built structure in China, measuring roughly 213 ft by 115 ft (65 m by 35 m).

The Outer Court was mostly reserved for ceremonial use and for formal meetings between the emperor and his ministers or secretaries. No woman was ever allowed to set foot there. The Inner Court, entered by the north gate—effectively the back door of the palace—was a more intimate space with smaller halls and pavilions where the emperor and his wife, concubines, and eunuchs lived their heavily ritualized, enclosed lives. Most of the inhabitants of the Forbidden City rarely ventured outside its walls.

Building Beijing

The buildings of the Forbidden City were generally simple in basic plan, either rectangular or square structures that were enlivened by decorative detail in color and carving. However, Ming architecture was certainly capable of being more inventive and flamboyant. One example that is contemporary with the Forbidden City is the Porcelain Tower at the Great Bao'en Temple in Nanjing. An octagonal structure 270 ft (79 m) tall and made of glazed porcelain bricks, this spectacular building stands as evidence that the old capital was far from being neglected during Yongle's reign.

In Beijing, the Hall of Prayer for Good Harvests (see pp. 218–219), a part of the Temple of Heaven complex completed in 1530, provides one example

of architectural innovation. It was built with three concentric circles of columns, symbolizing the four seasons, the 12 months, and the 12 hour spans of the day. In a striking feat of engineering, the columns support three levels of roofs, with the inner cupola decorated with golden dragons and clouds.

Although many building designs were innovative, the design of the new city closely embodied Ming architectural principles (see box, left) and practices, many of which were based on traditional ideas. Much-studied manuals such as the Song-era *Yingzao fashi* ("Building Standards") set out rules for the construction and decoration that were appropriate for different types of buildings. These were ranked according to a hierarchy of importance. Enclosures and courtyards were also fundamental to Ming architecture at every level, with buildings generally encircled by walls penetrated by narrow gates.

From Ming to Qing

As the administrative center of the empire, Beijing expanded rapidly. By the 1440s, the city and its surroundings may have had as many as 960,000 residents, making it the world's largest urban center at that time. Renovated and extended by the Ming rulers, the Grand Canal served as the route by which this massive concentration of population was kept supplied with grain, a task that occupied some 160,000 soldiers and 15,000 barges.

The capital continued to grow throughout the 16th century. The suburbs sprawling to the south of the walls of the Inner City were eventually enclosed

> ## "The **whole city** is **arranged in squares** just like a **chessboard.**"
>
> MARCO POLO ON BEIJING, *THE TRAVELS OF MARCO POLO*, c. 1300

with a new wall, forming the Outer City. Beijing was captured by rebel leader Li Zicheng (see pp. 238–239) in 1644. After they supplanted the Ming dynasty in the 17th century (see pp. 244–245), China's Qing rulers kept Beijing as their capital, and it retained this status for the duration of China's imperial history. The Forbidden City is still in use today as the home of China's National Palace Museum.

▽ **Temple of Heaven**
The architecture of the Temple of Heaven, built under the Ming rulers, was intended to reflect the relationship between the Earth and Heaven.

Hall of Blessings

The Hall of Blessings is a remarkable circular wooden building within the huge Temple of Heaven complex (see p.217) in Beijing. Originally constructed in the reign of the Yongle Emperor, this complex was where emperors hosted ceremonies each spring to solicit good weather and prosperity. Supporting the roof are concentric circles of columns symbolizing the four seasons, the 12 months, and the 12 hours of the day. The ceiling and columns are decorated with bright designs. When viewed from above, all of the halls within the temple complex are round, but their bases are actually square, following the ancient cosmological idea that "Heaven is round; Earth is square."

Classic Chinese Gardens

A history of imperial garden design

China has a long and rich history of garden design in the imperial era. There are, for example, early accounts of vast parks designed for China's kings and emperors dating back to the Shang period in the 2nd millennium BCE; and the First Emperor of the Qin dynasty created a palace garden that included a lake with an island representing the legendary home of the Eight Immortals.

Nature, harmony, and the garden in art

By the time of the Eastern Han dynasty, around the 2nd century CE, a tradition had been established of representing all elements of the natural world in a garden by means of a harmonious layout of lakes, streams, miniature mountains, and forests. Although a celebration of nature—and envisioned to both imitate and work in close harmony with

it—Chinese gardens were skillfully designed, highly regulated environments, whose development was closely linked to the artifice of painting and poetry.

A whole genre of poetry dedicated to the celebration of gardens arose in works such as the *Poems Composed at the Orchid Pavilion* by the celebrated 4th-century CE calligrapher and writer Wang Xizhi. By the Tang era, gardens were being created with pavilions, which functioned as resting places and viewing areas. From these vantage points, visitors could admire different aspects of the garden, in much the same way as they might appreciate a landscape scroll painting.

Large rocks with contorted shapes became essential elements in well-designed gardens from the Tang period onward. Symbols of stability and virtue, rocks were sometimes used in imitation of hills and mountains, which are revered in China as sacred

△ **Scholars in a garden**
Chinese artists and scholars saw gardens as a retreat from the mundane reality of the outside world—intimate, idyllic, harmonious natural spaces where they could meet, reflect, and meditate, as depicted in this atmospheric Qing dynasty hanging scroll.

△ **Gardens and animals in art**
Painting has always inspired garden design, and vice versa. Chinese gardens often strive to represent aspects of the natural landscape and have even included birds and animals, such as peacocks and rabbits. This hanging scroll, *Twin Rabbits under an Osmanthus Tree*, is by Qing dynasty painter Leng Mei.

△ **The garden pavilion**
Pavilions have been prominent features in Chinese garden design since the Tang dynasty. They are intended as places where people can rest, enjoy the views, and take shelter from the sun or rain, as in this scene from an 18th-century painting on silk by Leng Mei.

"To the east of Bamboo Torrent are a hundred flowering plum trees...."

WEN ZHENGMING, *RECORD OF THE HUMBLE ADMINISTRATOR'S GARDEN*, 1535

places invested with special power. Rocks of the required size and form—preferably eroded limestone from Lake Tai—were expensive and difficult to obtain. In the 12th century, the Song emperor Huizong reportedly had all the low bridges on the Grand Canal dismantled so that huge rocks could be brought by barge to embellish his imperial garden.

Private gardens

By the time of the Ming dynasty, sophisticated gardens had long ceased to be the preserve of the country's rulers and were within reach of private individuals, who created them to display their wealth and taste, as well as provide a private retreat from the hubbub of urban life. The city of Suzhou in Jiangsu province—a flourishing center of trade and manufacture—was especially notable for its refined

gardens, mostly commissioned by scholars or retired bureaucrats. The most famous of these, the Humble Administrator's Garden, was created between 1513 and 1526 by the retired official Wang Xiancheng, aided by his friend, the landscape painter and poet Wen Zhengming. Its maze of artificial streams and ponds, pavilions and bridges, towers and gazebos, rocks, and fruit trees was intended to be viewed from specific points to make visual sense. In 1535, Wen Zhengming painted a celebrated album of 31 views of the garden, accompanied by poetry, which sealed the fame of the garden.

Similar Chinese gardens were made through to the end of the imperial era; the gardens of the Qing dynasty Summer Palace were designed in accordance with ancient traditions, including a lake with islands representing the home of the Immortals.

△ **Musicians in a Chinese tea garden**
This photograph from the late 19th century shows musicians in a tea garden. The Chinese have a long tradition of drinking tea outside— in gardens and on terraces and balconies— surrounded by nature. Music is a popular entertainment in Chinese tea gardens.

△ **Water features**
Water—a *yin*, or feminine, element—is one of the most important features in Chinese garden design. It is traditionally introduced in the form of lakes, streams, and ponds, as in this example of Kunming Lake at the Summer Palace in Beijing. The reflective qualities of water are especially revered.

△ **Modern appreciation**
Appreciation of classic Chinese garden design persists to the present day, confirmed by the millions of visitors from around the world who visit the country's most glorious examples. This view is of the stunning Humble Administrator's Garden in Suzhou, designed in the 16th century.

Voyages of Exploration

Ming China sends a great fleet on oceanic journeys

Long before European explorers made their renowned voyages of discovery, a mighty Chinese naval fleet, commanded by the eunuch Zheng He, sailed across the Indian Ocean as far as the coast of Africa.

In 1403, the Yongle Emperor ordered the construction of an oceangoing fleet of ships, known as the "treasure fleet." China already had a powerful navy, but the scale of the shipbuilding undertaken by the Ming ruler was unprecedented. Almost 3,000 vessels were built on imperial orders between 1403 and 1419, including about 150 huge "treasure ships" (see right) constructed in vast dry docks at Nanjing.

Projecting power

The emperor's purpose in creating the treasure fleet was to assert Chinese authority over the wide area of Southeast Asia and the Indian Ocean, to which the country was linked by maritime trade routes. The fleet would display the might and wealth of China, inducing foreign states to pay tribute and formal homage to the emperor. The man tasked with building and commanding the fleet was a trusted

"We have **set eyes** on barbarian regions far away **hidden** ..."

INSCRIPTION BY ZHENG HE, 1431

palace eunuch, Zheng He (1371–1433). Although commonly referred to as an "admiral," he had never been to sea before making the treasure fleet voyages. Zheng He was a Muslim by birth, hailing from Yunnan in the remote southwest. He had previously served the emperor well, commanding forces that helped Yongle seize power and had been rewarded with high rank.

Seven voyages

Zheng He led the fleet on the first of its seven epic voyages in 1405. He commanded 63 treasure ships and a host of support vessels, with around 28,000 varied personnel on board—from soldiers and scholars to accountants and astrologers. This armada passed down the coast of Vietnam, then via Java and the Strait of Malacca into the Indian Ocean, finally stopping at the great spice center of Calicut (Kozhikode) before turning back for home. The voyage lasted two years. Further expeditions followed in 1407–1409, 1409–1411, 1413–1415, 1417–1419, and 1421–1422, pressing beyond India to the Persian Gulf and the Red Sea and cruising the east coast of Africa as far south as modern-day Kenya and possibly Mozambique. On landing, Zheng He always met with the local kings and leaders, offering messages of peace and goodwill from China. The voyages were a success: a series of ambassadors from countries around the Indian Ocean made their way to Beijing bearing tribute to the emperor, symbolizing their

△ **Admiral Zheng He**
Zheng He was a favorite of the Yongle Emperor and had served as commander of the southern capital, Nanjing.

◁ **Charts of exploration**
The charts used by Zheng He, such as this map showing routes to India, Ceylon, and Africa, were published in the 17th century.

◁ **Living tributes**
This painting from the Ming dynasty depicts a giraffe brought to the Yongle Emperor's court from East Africa by the treasure fleet of Admiral Zheng He.

acknowledgment of Chinese overlordship. Although Zheng He's fleet was packed with soldiers and weapons, he rarely used force in his encounters. The few exceptions included his suppression of pirates in Sumatra and an armed intervention in the internal politics of Ceylon (Sri Lanka).

Return to China

Curiosity about foreign countries was not the prime motivation for the voyages, but it certainly played a part. Ma Huan, a young Chinese Muslim translator, kept notes on social customs of the countries visited during the expeditions and later published a book of his observations. Exotic animals such as giraffes, ostriches, and zebras delivered as part of a state's tribute were met with wonder in China and kept in the imperial menagerie in Beijing.

In 1422, the Yongle Emperor suspended Zheng He's voyages. They were too expensive and resources were needed for campaigns against the Mongols. Yongle died in 1424 and was succeeded first by Honxi, and in 1426 by the Xuande Emperor, who ordered one last voyage of the treasure fleet from 1431 to 1433. Xuande was dismissive of the tribute it brought back, asserting: "We have no desire for goods from distant regions." Zheng He himself never returned to China, dying on the final voyage.

THE TREASURE SHIPS

Constructed between 1403 and 1419, the Ming treasure ships were around 400 ft (120 m) long and 150 ft (45 m) wide—dimensions that would make them the largest wooden sailing ships ever built. Wood from 18,000 trees was needed to make a single ship. Each ship had nine masts with 12 square sails. Like other Chinese junks, their hulls were divided into watertight compartments. There is no record of any treasure ship being lost on the seven voyages.

The Ming Turn Inward

China under the successors of the Yongle Emperor

From the mid-15th century, China's imperial rulers sought stability and self-sufficiency behind the defensive barrier of the Great Wall. In practice, engagement with the wider world and foreign trade could not be permanently suppressed.

In 1449, Ming China experienced a crisis that shocked the dynasty to its roots. Zhu Qizhen, who had inherited the imperial throne as the Zhengtong Emperor in 1435, faced a threat from Mongol Oirat tribes on China's northern border, united under the leadership of Esen Tayisi. In response to an Oirat incursion, the emperor assembled a large army to strike deep into Oirat territory but unwisely decided to accompany his forces in person. The imperial army ran into difficulties and was destroyed at Tumu, where the emperor was taken prisoner.

Imperial instability

Zhu Qizhen's half brother Zhu Qiyu assumed the throne as the Jingtai Emperor in 1449. Oirat horsemen raided the suburbs of Beijing, but they were eventually repulsed and Zhu Qizhen was freed. Returning to the Forbidden City, he was placed under house arrest by his half brother, who retained his hold on the throne. In 1457, when the Jingtai Emperor became seriously ill, Zhu Qizhen seized back power, adopting a new regnal name, the Tianshun Emperor. In the midst of this instability, a disgraced general, Cao Qin, supported by Mongol soldiers serving in the Ming army, narrowly failed to overthrow the emperor in an attempted coup.

Controlling the borders

These traumas fed a growing Ming preoccupation with security, which was expressed in the repressive policies of the Chenghua Emperor (r. 1464–1487) and a defensive attitude that prompted the rebuilding and extension of the Great Wall. The new fortifications, largely completed in the 16th and 17th centuries, extended over 5,500 miles (8,850 km) from Gansu province in the west to the North Korean border.

▽ **Wall works**
The Jinshanling section of the Great Wall (pictured) was built in the 16th century, during the Ming dynasty.

▷ **Portuguese base**
This painting from the late 18th century shows the region of Macau, with European ships in the harbor. The Portuguese settled in Macau in 1557.

Nevertheless, the horsemen of the steppe warrior Altan Khan were still able to invade Chinese territory and burn the suburbs of Beijing in 1550.

Controlling China's coast posed its own problems. Ming rulers held that the only legitimate form of maritime commerce was tribute and imposed tight restrictions on trade—for example, allowing Japanese traders limited access to just a single port. Such overregulation stimulated smuggling and piracy, and the Chinese navy, which had been allowed to decay, proved unable to defend the coast or enforce trade regulations. Under the Jiajing Emperor, who ruled from 1521 to 1567, all maritime activity along China's coasts was declared illegal—a draconian ban that was not lifted until the emperor's death.

Portuguese sailors had first reached China in 1513 during the reign of the Zhengde Emperor, who was known for being more open to foreigners. A Portuguese embassy was welcomed in 1517, but relations soon soured and the Europeans were banned from Chinese soil. However, by 1557, the persistent Portuguese had set up a permanent base at Macau, on the Chinese coast.

The paradox of Ming China was that, despite the negative attitude of imperial officials, foreign trade flourished, with merchants operating all around the South China Sea. While officials reflected the ideal of a static, self-sufficient rural society, by the second half of the 16th century, urban growth was rapid and business was booming.

The Four Classic Novels

A history of Chinese vernacular fiction

By the late 16th century, advances in printing technology had made books cheap and widely available in China. Literacy rose fast, and reading was no longer exclusively associated with study or administrative tasks. The most striking development during the later Ming period was the vernacular novel. Traditional literature was written in classical Chinese, which was difficult to understand. Vernacular novels, in contrast, were written in the regional languages and dialects of the common people. Mass-produced fiction known as "plot books" (huaben) flooded the market. These included retellings of legends but also tales from contemporary life, including stories of palace intrigue, as well as romantic and erotic adventures. Full-length novels also grew in popularity; many of these were clever adaptations of stories that had been part of oral tradition for centuries.

Two of the classic novels of the period had their origins in earlier storytelling. The *Romance of the Three Kingdoms* (*Sanguo yanyi*) was based on historical accounts of the power struggles of generals and statesmen between 169 and 280 CE, previously told by oral storytellers. It contains a variety of stories, with vivid descriptions of heroes and villains. The original written version was probably the work of Luo Guanzhong, about whom little is known. It was first printed in 1522, in 24 volumes, but the version known today is a shortened, revised edition produced in 1679.

The Water Margin (*Shuihu zhuan*) had its roots in folk tales of events that occurred under the Song dynasty. A group of outlaws who have taken refuge in the marshes, resisting corrupt officials and standing up for the poor, eventually fight in defense of the empire, defeating the rebels at the cost of most of their lives.

△ **Printing novels**
From the Song dynasty, novels were printed from carved woodblocks. This practice continued even into the Ming, when movable type was available. The block would be brushed with ink; a sheet of paper placed over the block would be pressed down to produce the final print.

△ *Romance of the Three Kingdoms*
A detail from a magnificent Chinese imperial vase from the Qing dynasty illustrates an episode from the classic novel *Romance of the Three Kingdoms*. This book tells the story of Guan Yu, a Chinese folk hero—and later the popular god Guandi—who was revered for his immense courage and loyalty.

△ **Knowledgeable Star**
This portrait, c. 1827–1830, is of *The Water Margin*'s fictional astronomer, Wu Yong (nicknamed Knowledgeable Star), with a celestial globe and quadrant. The painting is by Utagawa Kuniyoshi, a towering figure in Japanese woodblock printing and painting.

"The **empire**, long divided, must **unite**; long united, must **divide**. Thus it has **ever been**."

LUO GUANZHONG, *ROMANCE OF THE THREE KINGDOMS* (OPENING LINE), 1522

The first manuscript appeared in the early Ming period and the earliest known printed version dates from 1589. Its influence on Chinese popular culture has lasted into the present day.

The late Ming period

The *Journey to the West* (*Xiyou ji*) was written in the late Ming era. Published anonymously in 1592, it is thought to be by Wu Cheng'en, a poet and minor official who did not want his name publicly associated with what was considered a lowly genre. Loosely based on the story of the Tang-era Buddhist monk Xuanzang (see pp. 146–147), the novel tells of an incident-packed journey to India in search of sacred scriptures. The most prominent character is not the monk-hero but his companion, the Monkey King— a mischievous character with supernatural powers.

Another famous late Ming novel, *The Plum in the Golden Vase* (*Jinping mei*) was first printed anonymously in 1610. It tells the story of ambitious merchant Ximen Qing, who appears as a minor character in *The Water Margin*. The novel focuses on his erotic relations with his six concubines, as well as with other partners, painting an explicit portrait of a society driven by desire and vanity. For long periods, the novel was banned as pornographic, but it is now widely admired for its characterizations and its details of social life.

The tradition of the novel continued in the Qing era, notably with Cao Xueqin's *Dream of the Red Chamber* (see pp. 262–263), which is considered to be the masterpiece of classic Chinese fiction. The *Romance of the Three Kingdoms*, *The Water Margin*, *Journey to the West*, and *Dream of the Red Chamber* are often referred to in China as the Four Classic Novels.

△ *Journey to the West*
This Qing dynasty mural decorates the wall of the 12th-century Dafo (Great Buddha) Temple in Zhangye, Gansu province. The painting tells the story of *Journey to the West*, depicting the monk Xuanzang and his followers, including the Monkey King, Sun Wukong.

△ **A controversial classic**
According to some scholars, *The Plum in the Golden Vase*, c. 1618, whose author is unknown, should be recognized as China's fifth classic novel. The text was tremendously popular but was censored because of its explicit sexual realism. The painting here shows a scene from the late Ming dynasty novel.

△ *Dream of the Red Chamber*
A 19th-century painting by Sun Wen depicts a scene from Cao Xueqin's saga, which tells the story of a family's fall from grace. As well as being considered one of the finest works of world literature, it is also among the largest— twice the length of Tolstoy's *War and Peace*.

Late Ming China

Imperial government under strain

The Ming Empire reached its peak in the 1570s but within 50 years had entered terminal decline. The imperial regime failed to cope with the multiple challenges of governing a dynamic, fast-changing society.

The Wanli Emperor came to the throne in 1572, and the early years of his 48-year reign were recorded as a time of prosperity and good governance across China. The emperor was only eight years old at his accession, so Zhang Juzheng, his chief minister, initially held the reins of power. Zhang embarked on an ambitious program of reform. He strengthened the central authority of the state, improved flood control and irrigation, reformed the tax system, and attempted to balance the government's finances. Grain tax and forced labor were replaced by monetary taxation (which was paid in silver), while numerous tax exemptions for the privileged were ended.

The economy prospered as looser restrictions on foreign trade allowed Chinese manufacturers of silk, porcelain, and other luxury products to sell their goods abroad. The imperial coffers filled with silver.

However, Zhang's economic and administrative reforms were not maintained after his death in 1582. At first, the Wanli Emperor took personal control of government and carried out his duties diligently. He waged successful campaigns against the Mongols on the northern frontier and against the Japanese, who had invaded Korea as the first step toward an intended conquest of China. But in the 1590s, Wanli entered into conflict with officials at court over his favorite concubine, Lady Zheng. He was forced to accept that his eldest son be nominated as successor to the throne—rather than his son by Lady Zheng—and reacted to this by effectively going on strike. For the last 20 years of his reign, Wanli performed no official business, instead living as a recluse inside the walls of the Forbidden City.

Turmoil in the Ming court

In the void created by Wanli's withdrawal, court eunuchs (see pp.116–117) took control and began issuing their own orders. From 1604, their influence was contested by Confucian traditionalists from Donglin Academy in Wuxi, who challenged the increasing moral laxity and abuse of power in government. The protests of the Donglin movement became a focus for political dissidence.

The struggle came to a head after the succession of the 15-year-old Tianqi Emperor in 1620. The new ruler was more interested in carpentry than in running an empire. Effective power fell into the unscrupulous hands of the eunuch Wei Zhongxian, who elevated his relatives to important positions and had numerous temples built in his own honor. When Confucian officials challenged Wei's policies, he had hundreds of Donglin adherents executed.

△ **Silver sycee**
This waisted silver ingot dates from the late Ming dynasty. Sycees were a form of currency made by individual silversmiths for local exchange.

◁ **The absent emperor**
Wanli turned his back on his official duties for the last 20 years of his reign. In this depiction, the artist has rotated the emperor's hat so that his face is visible.

△ **Pouring vessel**
Trade with the West and the Middle East grew in the late Ming dynasty: the blue-and-white porcelain known as Kraak ware was first exported to Europe in the 30th year of Wanli's reign. Kraak gained its name from the Portuguese ships, or carracks, that transported it.

Tianqi died in 1627 and was succeeded by his brother, who became the Chongzhen Emperor. Soon after this, Wei Zhongxian fell from power but died by suicide before he could be arrested. It was then the turn of Wei's followers to face mass arrests and executions.

A climate of discontent
This chaos in government occurred during a period in which a number of major problems urgently required addressing. Fluctuations in the supply of silver were disrupting the monetized economy. Furthermore, the unusually cold global weather of the early 17th century had an adverse effect on food crops. Between 1615 and 1618, China was racked by a terrible famine that reduced much of the country

△ **Japanese landing at Busan**
In 1592, Japanese forces landed at Busan in the Korean peninsula. Wanli sent forces to help repel the invasion, forcing the Japanese into a stalemate and eventual withdrawal.

to starvation. As bureaucracy grew less efficient and more corrupt, government revenues fell dramatically. In response to this, the government raised taxes, provoking protests both in rural areas and among silk weavers and porcelain makers in the towns. The Ming emperor could not afford to pay his soldiers, so the empire's frontiers were poorly defended and deserters roamed the countryside. The dynasty was close to collapse and on the verge of losing the Mandate of Heaven.

Matteo Ricci

A missionary who bridged cultural divides

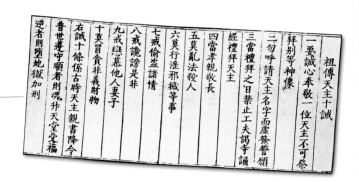

On a mission to convert the people of China to Christianity, Ricci won the respect of the court and transformed the way the cultures of Europe and China viewed one another.

Born in central Italy in 1552, Matteo Ricci joined the Jesuit order in Rome in 1571, following a course of humanistic and scientific studies. He requested a posting to the Jesuit mission of India and in 1580 arrived in Cochin, where he was ordained a priest. Two years later, he was sent to Portuguese-controlled Macau, off the south coast of China. His intention was to convert the Ming emperor, Wanli, to Catholicism, in the hope that his subjects would follow. While in Macau, Ricci immersed himself in Chinese culture and language, cowriting a Chinese–Portuguese dictionary with Michele Ruggieri.

In September 1583, Ricci moved to Zhaoqing in Guangdong province, where his learning, knowledge of Chinese customs, and respectful manner soon made him popular among local scholars. Traveling next to Shaozhou in 1589, he collaborated with the eminent Chinese scholar Qu Taisu, before relocating to Nanjing in 1599. In 1601, Ricci went to Beijing as an adviser to the imperial court; he was the first European to be invited into the Forbidden City. He introduced the court to Western science, astronomy, mathematics, and art and fascinated them with his collections of clocks and astronomical and musical instruments. With his friend the statesman and scientist Xu Guangqi, he translated the ancient Greek mathematician Euclid's *Elements of Geometry* into Chinese. He also published several editions of the first world map known in China; completed his major work, *The True Sense of the Lord of Heaven* (*Tianzhu shiyi*); and wrote an exposition of Christian doctrine, *The Doctrine of the Lord of Heaven* (*Tianzhu jiaoyi*).

Ricci sought to build a Christian community in China. He allowed converts to continue to practice ancestor worship. This won many followers, and some Confucian scholars even adopted Christianity; by Ricci's death in 1610, the religion had more than 2,000 Chinese adherents. Christianity was welcome in China for another 100 years until the Vatican banned ancestor worship for converts, and the emperor closed the door to Western missionaries. During the last decade of his life, Ricci focused on the emerging Catholic community of Beijing, where he died in 1610.

△ **The Ten Commandments**
This image shows a translation of the Ten Commandments into the Chinese language made by Ricci and his fellow Jesuit Michele Ruggieri.

▽ **Charting the land**
Ricci was a meticulous scholar and cartographer. He compiled this Chinese-language map of the Far East in 1602.

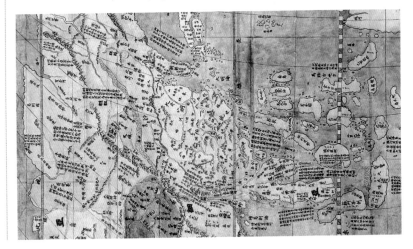

Progress in Medicine

A history of the evolving tradition of healing

For centuries, the theory and practice of Chinese medicine was conservative in its outlook, adhering unswervingly to the classical medical tradition established in the Han dynasty (see pp. 98–99). In the Ming era, this vast body of traditional knowledge was collected together in the *Compendium of Materia Medica* (*Bencao gangmu*), an immense tome, revered as the great therapeutic text of the period.

The great work of Chinese medicine

The encyclopedic *Bencao gangmu* was compiled by Li Shizhen, who was born in 1518 at Qizhou, Hubei province, to a medical family (both his father and his grandfather had been physicians). When he was a young man, Li aspired to join the civil service, but after failing the entrance examination three times, he found his true vocation in medicine.

In 1556, Li successfully treated a son of the Prince of Chu, winning an official post as a reward. A few years later, he was appointed assistant president of the Imperial Medical Institute in Beijing but soon left the job to devote himself to his life's work— summarizing the entire corpus of Chinese medical writing. Li completed a first draft of his text in 1578 but continued to expand the book until his death 15 years later. In the course of his research, he consulted more than 800 earlier works and also traveled widely to further his understanding.

Seeking to systematize all previous studies, he itemized almost 2,000 plants, animals, minerals, and other objects said to have medicinal properties. Some eccentricities found their way into his account—for example, he recounted an Arab tradition by which the dead bodies of men, preserved in honey, could

△ **Mural at Wutaishan**
A mural in the Hall of the Medicine Buddha (Bhaisajyaguru) at Wutaishan (Five Terrace Mountain) in Shanxi province depicts a traditional Chinese pharmacy. The grasses and spring water around Wutaishan are renowned for their healing properties.

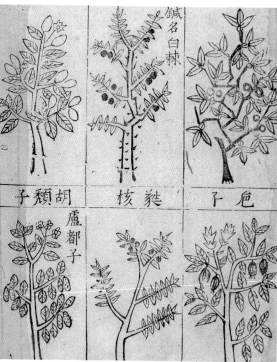

△ *Bencao gangmu*, **first edition**
Li Shizhen's *Bencao gangmu* is a richly illustrated, painstakingly researched encyclopedia of hundreds of plants and minerals that draws on a wide range of disciplines, including zoology, medicine, and pharmacology. It remains a valuable resource for modern practitioners of traditional Chinese medicine.

△ **Herbal dispensary**
A painting from the 1930s shows a Chinese dispensary, with its neat wooden cabinets and jars of prepared medications. Chinese herbal medicine has been increasingly used in the West to treat numerous ailments, from heart and gynecological issues to stress and anxiety.

"The Chinese **do not draw** any **distinction** between **food** and **medicine**."

LIN YUTANG, *THE IMPORTANCE OF LIVING*, 1938

be used to treat wounds and fractures. The bulk of the text, though, was devoted to herbal medicine and detailed descriptions of the nature and medicinal uses of more than 1,000 different plants. The result was a classic reference work that is still consulted to this day.

Ming and Qing advances

Major medical advances were made in Ming China. The first documented use of vaccination comes from 15th-century China. It took the form of variolation— deliberate infection with smallpox. Scabs taken from smallpox patients with a mild form of the disease were left to dry and crushed to powder. Physicians used a silver pipe to blow this substance up the nostril of people not yet affected by the condition. Variolated patients were kept in isolation for a week or so to avoid any risk of passing on the infection.

Ming practitioners pioneered new approaches to diagnosis. They analyzed individual case histories and viewed each patient's ailment as a combination of personal and environmental factors. One physician who exemplified this approach was Chen Congzhou, from Yangzhou in eastern China, who published an account of 93 specific cases in 1644.

The epidemics sweeping through China in the 1640s inspired physicians to search for the causes of infection. In a work published in 1642, Wu Youxing argued that diseases were spread—directly or indirectly—by the entry into the body (especially via the nose and mouth) of *liqi* (literally, "excessive influences") as opposed to the traditional belief that they were carried by wind, heat, cold, and damp. His findings advanced research into the pathogens responsible for infectious diseases.

△ **Traditional Chinese pharmacy**
Chinese medicine today adheres to many of the principles of traditional theory and practice that were developed more than 2,000 years ago. Pharmacy interiors have remained relatively unchanged over the centuries; this view of a pharmacy was taken in the early 20th century.

△ **Workers processing medicines**
The workers pictured here in 1977 are preparing herbs for medicinal use. Doctors are able to draw on more than 8,000 traditional medicines, which can be processed in different ways: some are made into teas, decoctions, powders, capsules, or tablets; others are processed into rubs, ointments, or salves.

△ **Herbal remedies**
In Chinese herbal medicine, the term "herbs" refers not to a small group of food flavorings but to a vast range of medicinal plants and minerals. Among those most widely used are star anise, mushrooms, ginkgo nuts, nutmeg, ginseng, cinnamon, and ginger.

Golden Treasures

The work of Chinese goldsmiths through the ages

Today, China is the world's largest gold producer. The precious metal has a long history in China, where gold mining took off during the Zhou dynasty (c. 1050–256 BCE). Over time, Chinese craftsmen developed methods to fashion ornate decorations out of gold, from the jewelry that adorned court women to ritual vessels and even cooking tools.

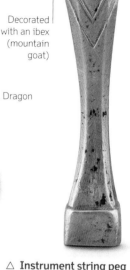

Decorated with an ibex (mountain goat)

Dragon

△ **Gold earrings**
Dragon–fish hybrid earrings were a popular design during the Liao dynasty and usually had a flower bud below the creature's mouth.

△ **Decorative buckle**
Mysterious creatures adorn this gold buckle from the Western Jin period.

△ **Flower-shaped ornament**
This gold ornament from the Jin–Yuan period depicts dragons and other creatures.

△ **Instrument string peg**
This decorative peg from the Han period would have been attached to a musical instrument.

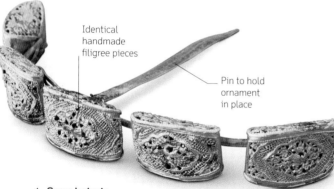

Identical handmade filigree pieces

Pin to hold ornament in place

△ **Song hairpin**
This bridge-style Song dynasty hair decoration contains five ornate gold pieces on a single gold band.

△ **Woodpecker ornaments**
Highly decorated birds, such as these golden woodpecker ornaments, were common in Chinese goldwork.

Dish for cooking food over a brazier

△ *Jiao dou* **vessel**
This gold cooking vessel with a crane's head and dragon's feet dates from 220–589 CE.

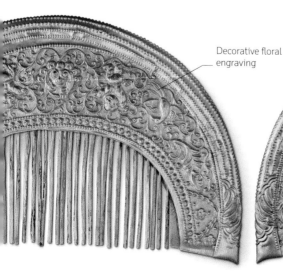

Decorative floral engraving

◁ **Comb ornaments**
Made during the Song dynasty, these comb-shaped hairpins are decorated with intricate floral patterns.

△ **Yuan dynasty earrings**
These earrings with a gemstone inlay date from the Mongol Yuan dynasty. Yuan jewelry was influenced by the delicate designs of Song China.

Ruby

Saltwater pearl

▷ **Qing emperor's cup**
One of four wine cups made for the Qianlong Emperor, this vessel contains many precious gems. It bears characters meaning "Eternal Territorial Integrity."

Dragon face

Ruby

Hairpins could also be made from jade, metal, wood, or bone.

Filigree pattern

Jade surface

Elephant trunk and tusks form the legs

Ruby

Sapphire

△ **Ming hairpins**
This pair of gold hairpins combines gold filigree work and precious stones to create a decorative dragon hairpiece.

◁ **Qing bowl stand**
The lid and stand for this 19th-century jade bowl are made from intricately patterned gold.

▷ **Lady Mei's treasures**
Many gold treasures—including this decorative hairpin and bracelets—were found in the tomb of a Ming dowager duchess named Lady Mei. Her son ruled the province of Yunnan.

◁ ***Jue* cups**
Made during the Ming dynasty, these vessels would have been used to hold warm wine for ceremonial purposes.

Turquoise

The Manchu Qing
The founding of the Qing dynasty

In the early 1600s, the Jurchen leader Nurhaci united tribespeople living north of China into a formidable military force. These people, who took the name "Manchu," established the Qing dynasty, which was later to overthrow the Ming.

Nurhaci was born into a leading clan of the Jurchen, a people who had once ruled northern China as the Jin dynasty (see pp. 180–181). Living as farmers, hunters, and traders in areas to the northeast of the Ming empire's borders, the Jurchen acknowledged Chinese suzerainty and served the Ming as soldiers.

▷ **A skillful strategist**
Nurhaci, shown here enthroned and dressed in yellow, was the founder of the Later Jin dynasty. He rose to power in the late 16th century and ruled for 10 years from 1616.

In some areas, notably the Liaodong peninsula, Jurchen and Chinese farmers and townspeople lived together side by side.

The rise of Nurhaci
In 1582, Nurhaci's father and grandfather were murdered by a rival Jurchen, whom Nurhaci pursued and eventually killed in 1587. Thereafter, Nurhaci's authority over his tribespeople steadily grew. He first emerged as a dominant figure during a period of infighting for tribal leadership, which culminated in the battle of Gure in 1593. He was adept at using a combination of brute force and skillful marriage diplomacy (for example, he married several of his children into powerful and prominent Mongol families) to unite the Jurchen and a number of Mongol tribes under his rule. Nurhaci organized his subjects into "banners" (see pp. 244–245), which acted both as military formations and as social groupings, identified by a distinctive flag.

Banner armies
Nurhaci introduced a script for writing the Jurchen language and instituted an administration that borrowed heavily from Ming bureaucratic and legal practices. Chinese craftsmen were put to work manufacturing arms and armor for the banner armies. By 1616, as head of a well-armed and efficiently organized state, Nurhaci was ready to renounce his allegiance to the Ming and declare himself head of a revived Jin dynasty. Two years later, he issued a document known as the "Seven Grievances," which was in effect a declaration of war against Ming China.

"Even if you **fight**, you **certainly** will not **win**...."

NURHACI, MESSAGE TO MING FORCES IN LIAODONG, 1618

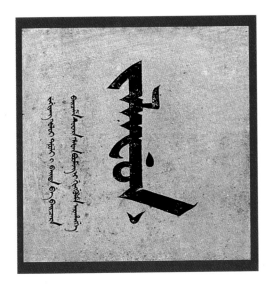

△ **Manchu script**
The Manchu language derives mainly from the Jurchen language, but with many words drawn from Mongolian and Chinese. In this example of Qing dynasty Manchu calligraphic script, the word in the center means "longevity."

Nurhaci's banner armies took the offensive in Liaodong, northeast China, scoring a series of victories against the Ming, aided by the defection of many Ming officers into their ranks: the defectors were well rewarded with lands and titles. Nurhaci moved his palace to newly conquered Mukden (modern-day Shenyang) in 1625, and, when the Chinese population of Liaodong revolted against the Jurchen, he brutally suppressed their opposition.

The Ming mustered a few loyal generals—notably Yuan Chonghuan, who was a master of using the cannon on the battlefield—to counter Nurhaci's armies. At the battle of Ningyuan in 1626, Yuan's forces, using Portuguese-made cannons, inflicted a rare defeat on the bannermen. Nurhaci died of wounds sustained in the battle and Yuan was appointed governor of Liaodong as a reward.

Beginnings of the Qing dynasty

Nurhaci's successor, Hong Taiji, adopted the name "Manchu" in place of "Jurchen." He followed a far more conciliatory policy toward the ethnic Han Chinese, drawing many of them into his service. Chinese banners were added to his army, alongside the Manchu and Mongol banners. But Hong Taiji continued to aggressively challenge the Ming. In 1636, he proclaimed the Qing dynasty ("qing" meaning "pure" or

"clear") in a gesture that was clearly intended to associate him with the earlier Jin dynasty. His army invaded Korea, forcing the Korean Joseon king to renounce his loyalty to the Ming and pledge allegiance to the Qing. As the Ming empire was plunged into terminal chaos through social breakdown and widespread revolts, Manchu raiding parties crossed the Great Wall of China and plundered the countryside to the north of Beijing.

Succession and preparation

The sudden death of Hong Taiji in 1643 threatened to precipitate a damaging succession struggle for leadership of the Manchu. However, a compromise was soon found. At five years old, one of Hong Taiji's sons took the throne in Mukden as the Shunzhi Emperor, while Hong's brother Dorgon acted as regent. With the succession resolved, the Manchu were in an ideal position to benefit from the internal strife that was soon to affect the Ming in the south of the country (see pp. 238–239).

▷ **Military banner**
This imperial military silk banner with a red border depicts a ferocious five-clawed dragon chasing a pearl. In Chinese belief, the pearl is traditionally associated with immortality, wisdom, prosperity, and power.

The Fall of the Ming

China comes under the rule of the Manchu

Natural disasters, administrative inefficiency, and popular revolt led to the collapse of the Ming dynasty in 1644. In the wake of this turmoil, China was vulnerable to attack by Manchu invaders, who took control of the empire.

In the reign of the Chongzhen Emperor, who took power in 1627, the Ming dynasty faced adversity: the Manchu, who would later declare their Qing dynasty (see pp. 236–237) posed a potent military threat; cold weather brought severe famine to China in the 1630s; and epidemics raged across the land, killing thousands. The flow of taxes to central government broke down and soldiers went unpaid. As social organization collapsed, desperate people formed armed bands that roamed the countryside in search of plunder. Leaders emerged who attracted disaffected peasants to form larger rebel forces. The armies of Li Zicheng and Zhang Xianzhong, both former soldiers, swept through inland China, ravaging the districts in their path, from Shaanxi to Sichuan. Riddled by inner conflicts between court factions, the Ming government was unable to reassert control.

Rebel armies take Beijing

Li Zicheng won peasant support with promises of equal land distribution and an end to the grain tax. In February 1644, he captured the old imperial capital of Xi'an in Shaanxi province and proclaimed himself ruler of a new dynasty, the Dashun. In April, Li's forces attacked Beijing. A traitor within the city opened the gates, and the rebels entered unopposed. The Chongzhen Emperor, finding that there were no ministers in the palace to obey his commands, walked into the imperial garden and died by suicide.

Despite capturing Beijing, Li could not command the obedience of Ming generals and officials. The leader of the Ming forces defending China's northeast border against the Manchu, General Wu Sangui, decided that the prospect of orderly government by the non-Chinese Qing dynasty was preferable to chaos under Li's bandits. Wu joined forces with the Manchu,

allowing them to sweep through the Shanhaiguan Pass and descend upon Beijing. Li's army fled the city, laden with plundered goods, and the Qing Shunzhi Emperor, aged six, mounted the throne.

Qing supremacy

These dramatic events did not immediately settle the fate of the Ming dynasty. There were plenty of Ming princes at liberty across China, providing a pool of contenders for the throne. The Prince of Fu, a grandson of the Wanli Emperor, was declared Ming emperor in Nanjing. But the momentum of the

◁ **Military successes**
The Manchu prince Dorgon, depicted here in ceremonial dress, directed the invasion of Ming China as regent of the early Qing dynasty.

▽ **Lethal sabre**
This massive 17th-century sabre—with two narrow grooves on each side—is an early, rare example of the *yanmaodao* sabre. Blades like this would have been used by the Manchu.

△ **Escape from turmoil**
The artist Fan Qi created this tranquil painting in 1646 as an antidote to the turmoil in China in the aftermath of the Manchu invasion of 1644. The work depicts the countryside around Beijing. During the chaos, Fan fled to a Buddhist monastery in the hills to the north of the city.

Manchu invasion was unstoppable. Directed by the regent, Dorgon, in 1645, Qing armies advanced down the Grand Canal to capture Nanjing. Ming loyalists who resisted were treated with utter ruthlessness. Hundreds of thousands of Chinese were massacred at the sieges of cities such as Yangzhou, Jiading, and Nanchang. Nanjing surrendered without a fight. The Prince of Fu was taken prisoner and died in captivity. At the same time, the Qing destroyed the rebel forces of Li Zicheng and Zhang Xianzhong.

▷ **Rebel coin**
In the period between the fall of the Ming dynasty and the rise of the Qing, rebels issued coins in their own names.

As the conquest proceeded, most Chinese chose to submit to the Qing rather than face the brutal consequences of disobedience, but armed opposition persisted in areas of southern China such as Fujian and Guangdong. In quick succession, three more Ming princes were proclaimed emperor. Only the Prince of Gui, declared the Yongli Emperor, proved resistant. It was not until 1661 that, driven back through Yunnan province into Burma, he was captured by General Wu Sangui. At least in name the last Ming emperor, the Prince of Gui was executed in 1662. Although revolts against Manchu rule continued into the 1680s, the Ming era was over.

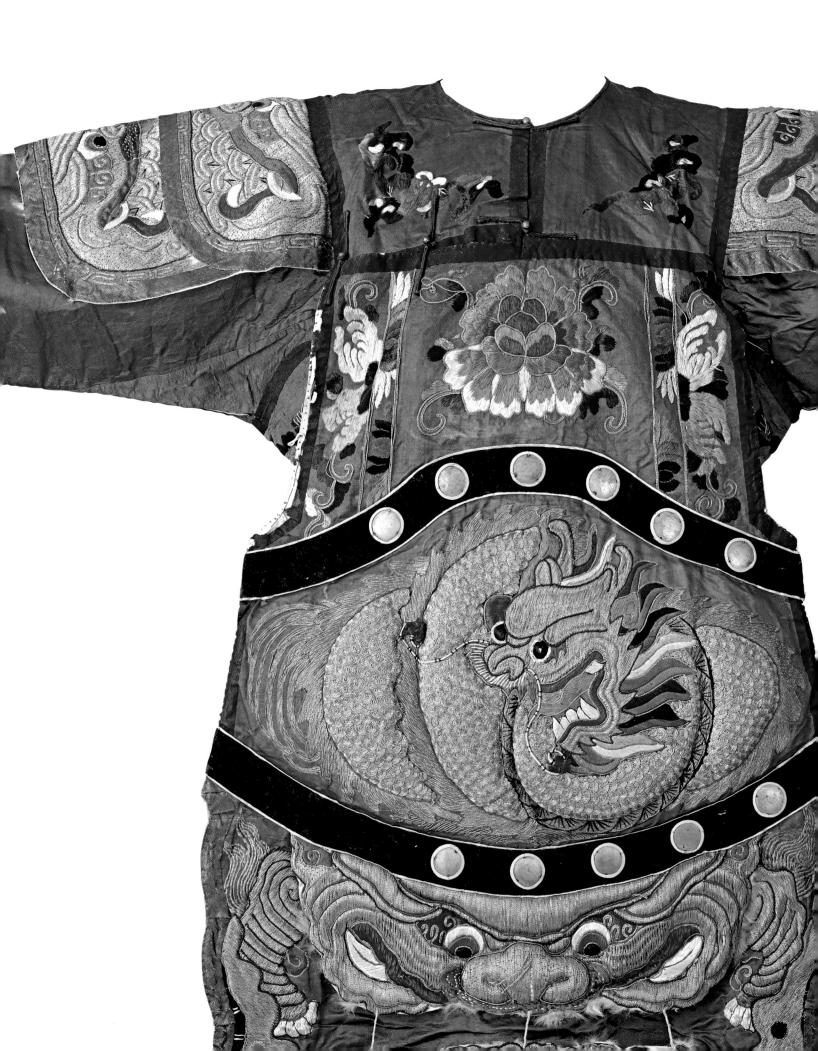

◁ **Stage costume**
This robe, which dates from the late Qing dynasty, was worn by a performer playing the role of a female warrior in Peking opera.

7
The Last Dynasty
1644 to 1912

Introduction

For nearly three centuries from 1644 to 1912, China was ruled by the Qing dynasty, the descendents of Manchu warriors who came from the north to take Beijing in 1644. Once they had successfully overcome resistance from a tenacious group of Ming supporters to secure their position, they began extending their empire. At a time when the European nations were sailing the world in search of trade opportunities and potential colonies, the Qing turned to Central Asia in their quest for new lands. Over the next century, they conquered a vast swathe of territory that incorporated many peoples, including Tibetans, Uighurs, groups of Mongols, Burmese, and Tais. The Qing more than doubled the territorial extent of the Ming empire, and at the end of the 18th century, their territories covered more than 5 million sq. miles (13 million sq. km)—making the Qing empire one of the five largest in history.

Under the stewardship of early Qing emperors Kangxi, Yongzheng, and Qianlong, China experienced a golden age of internal peace and prosperity, in which the economy grew rapidly. The increasing awareness and appreciation of China's riches and culture in Europe fueled demand for Chinese ceramics and a craze for "chinoiserie"—decoration, design, and architecture inspired by Chinese motifs—in the 1690s. This in turn helped drive Chinese trade. As the Qing freed up more land for cultivation and reopened the southeast coast of China to trade, exports in cotton, silk, tea, and ceramics grew enormously and a thriving internal market developed.

Dissent and rebellion

Though successful, the Qing empire faced many challenges, among which was its booming population. Between 1650 and 1800, the number of inhabitants tripled to 300 million (and exceeded 500 million by the early 20th century). Land and food began to run short and poverty increased, stoking rebellion at the end of Qianlong's rule. More revolts followed, notably the Taiping Rebellion of 1850–1864 (see pp. 278–279), which disrupted the reigns of emperors Daoguang, Xianfeng, and Tongzhi. Discontent was also fueled by natural disaster. Drought led to the Northern Chinese Famine in 1876–1879, in which between 9 and 13 million people died; and the Yellow River flood of 1887 was one of the deadliest in history, killing more than 900,000 people.

1644 Qing forces take Beijing; the last Ming emperor dies by suicide

1662 Qing forces end Ming resistance on the mainland

1697 China conquers Outer Mongolia

1760 Canton system introduced to control foreign trade

1792 British envoy Lord Macartney fails to open up trade with China

1645 The Qing order all Han men to wear the Manchu queue hairstyle

1689 Treaty of Nerchinsk: Russia abandons the Amur River region

1751 Tibet becomes a protectorate of the Qing empire

1791 *Dream of the Red Chamber*, one of China's greatest classical novels, is published

By the 19th century, China was increasingly at the mercy of rapacious foreign powers. The Qing rulers underestimated what rapid industrialization had done for the Western nations' strength and failed to foresee how the seeds of republicanism and revolution, sown by the American War of Independence and the French Revolution, might come to affect their own power. Instead of embracing the changing world, Chinese society took a more conservative turn under the later Qing, as they attempted to strengthen China's highly centralized bureaucracy and continued to treat foreign powers as vassals.

The Qing were caught unawares when Britain bullied China into giving greater trade concessions in the Opium Wars of 1839–1842 and 1856–1860; the empire's military was outmatched by Western warships. Qing power was weakened even further as foreign interests secured increasingly more concessions in the 19th century. From 1883, China was again at war, engaged in desperate attempts to protect two of its most important protectorates, Vietnam and Korea, from France (1884–1885) and Japan (1894–1895), respectively. In the end, it lost control of both.

The fall of the empire

Early attempts to modernize from the 1860s were frustrated by Empress Dowager Cixi—the real power behind the throne in the reigns of her son Tonghzhi and her nephew Guangxu. After Guangxu witnessed the effects of Western-style modernization on China's former tributary, Japan, he began to edge China toward capitalism and democratic constitutional monarchy with the Hundred Days of Reform in 1898. Disagreeing with the direction in which he was moving China, Cixi had him locked up.

However, Cixi could not contain the other emerging threats to Qing power. The Boxer Rebellion against foreign influence in China ended with Cixi's flight from Beijing, an Anglo-French army burning the Summer Palace, yet more concessions to foreign powers. The Qing were left rulers in name only. Anti-Manchu sentiment was growing, and revolutionary groups led by Western-educated Chinese who understood other forms of government were appearing throughout the country. A republican revolution in 1911 prompted the abdication in the following year of Puyi—the final Qing emperor and last emperor of China.

1842 Treaty of Nanjing; China opens treaty ports to foreign traders

1856 Second Opium War begins; in 1860, Anglo–French forces occupy Beijing

1898 The Hundred Days of Reform fails; Empress Dowager Cixi effectively takes control

1911 A nationalist uprising in Wuchang begins the Chinese revolution

1839 British troops invade China, beginning the First Opium War

1850 Taiping Rebellion begins; it lasts 14 years and over 20 million die

1894–1895 Sino-Japanese war over control of Korea; 1895 China cedes Taiwan to Japan

1900 Anti-foreign feeling erupts in the Boxer Rebellion

1912 Republic of China is proclaimed; China's last emperor, Xuantong, or Puyi, abdicates

The Rise of the Qing

The early successes of China's final royal dynasty

Rulers of China for 268 years, the Qing expanded the empire to its greatest extent and established the world's strongest economy. They achieved this by asserting their military power and upholding traditions established by the Ming.

From their capital at Shenyang (Mukden) in Manchuria, the Manchu were swift to take advantage of the collapse of Ming power (see pp. 238–239) in the 17th century. When the Ming general Wu Sangui called on them to save Beijing from the rebel Li Zicheng, the Manchu—led by Prince Dorgon—instead seized the capital for themselves. They proclaimed a new dynasty—the Qing—and set about conquering the rest of Ming China. By 1659, the first emperor of the Qing dynasty, Shunzhi, had established his rule across much of China and driven the last of the Ming's supporters—led by Koxinga (Zheng Chenggong)—into Taiwan. By 1683, Shunzhi's successor, the Kangxi Emperor (see pp. 248–249) had reclaimed Taiwan and had successfully completed the Qing conquest.

Kangxi himself was a skilled military man—strong, with notable skills as an archer. The military might of the early Qing emperors rested with their archer bannermen (see right). From the early 17th century, Manchu warriors had been organized into units known as banners. Initially, there were only four banners—yellow, red, white, and blue—but that number grew to 24 by 1624 as new companies (of both Mongol and Han Chinese banners) were created. Bannermen were granted land, income, and privileges that tied them closely to their Manchu leaders and ultimately the Qing emperors. They formed a large, loyal army that enabled the Qing to double the size of their empire through conquest.

Support and dissent

One of the first challenges the Kangxi Emperor faced came not from his former Ming subjects but from three warlords in the south who had supported the Manchu conquest. Shang Kexi of Guangdong, Wu Sangui of Yunnan, and Geng Jimao of Fujian were all

▽ **Sealing the succession**
The Seal of the Great Qing Succession of the Son of Heaven, which is the third most treasured of the great Qing seals, was passed down from earlier dynasties to Kangxi.

made vassal kings but soon proved a problem for Kangxi. Sure that Wu, who commanded a formidable force, would eventually challenge him, Kangxi attempted to take Wu's army from him. This had exactly the result that the emperor had been trying to avoid, as Wu rose up against Kangxi with the support of his fellow kings. Sensing weakness, the Chahar Mongols also marched against the emperor. Kangxi was able to successfully quash the rebellion (known as the Rebellion of the Three Feudatories), and he marched with his army into Kunming, Yunnan, in 1681. The experience, however, served as a reminder to Kangxi that Qing rule was only possible if enemies of the Qing could be suppressed or appeased.

Kangxi and his immediate successors worked hard to ensure that the legitimacy, stability, and power of the Qing empire was assured. They notably adapted

MANCHU ARCHERS

Manchu archers were renowned for their skill with the bow while mounted on horseback. It took years to master the short but powerful Manchu bow and fire it with accuracy while at full gallop. Archers would hold both the reins and the bow in the left hand, while selecting an arrow and drawing and firing with their right.

△ **Military ruler**
This contemporary painting shows the Kangxi Emperor (center, seated) wearing ceremonial armor and carrying a bow and arrows.

"Those who have **not yet surrendered** will note this … and **grow cold at heart**."

THE KANGXI EMPEROR ON THE EXECUTION OF REBELS IN THE REBELLION OF THE THREE FEUDATORIES, 1680

to commemorate this second tour, depicting events along his route from Beijing along the Grand Canal, through the mountains, and through major southern cities such as Suzhou and Hangzhou. His tours were not just for show; Kangxi also inspected industries and infrastructure.

Sage king

Kangxi was meticulous in overseeing the administration of his empire, and this was well documented by his diarists. The Office of Imperial Diaries was established in 1671 to record the emperor's daily actions, speech, writings, and conduct. These imperial diaries were considered important for proving the emperor's own legitimacy and showed Kangxi to be a "sage king" in accordance with Confucian values. The tradition of imperial court diaries continued into the reigns of Kangxi's successors.

As a sage king, Kangxi promoted scholarship—notably the study of the sciences—through his imperial patronage. The emperor was particularly interested in astronomy and appointed Jesuit scholars to work in his Bureau of Astronomy. Belgian scholar Ferdinand Verbiest translated the first six books of Euclid (the ancient Greek mathematician) into Manchu for Kangxi and designed and built six new instruments for the Beijing observatory: an ecliptic and an equatorial armillary sphere, an azimuth, a quadrant, a sextant, and a stellar globe.

By the end of Kangxi's reign, Qing rule was firmly consolidated. China's longest-ruling emperor, Kangxi died in 1722 after 61 years on the imperial throne. As one of China's most able rulers, Kangxi's reign laid the foundations for the High Qing era, a time of prosperity and stability.

to some aspects of traditional Han Chinese culture, creating a sense of cultural continuity between themselves and the Ming. Kangxi established good working relationships with Chinese officials and became a keen patron of the arts, commissioning a number of great works on Chinese history and culture, and he maintained the Ming tradition of valuing the works of Confucian scholar-officials.

Inspection tours

Kangxi and his successors famously embarked on tours of the southern territories under Qing control in order to consolidate Manchu rule. During his reign, Kangxi himself completed six, taking his first tour in 1684. His second tour was longer and was a lavish display of imperial wealth and ceremony. The emperor commissioned 12 scrolls (see pp. 250–251)

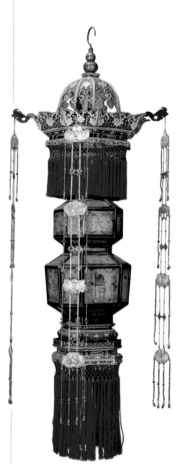

△ **Qing lantern**
Palace lanterns, like this one, displayed imperial wealth and power. Qing rulers often gave these as precious gifts to their chancellors.

The Battles of Koxinga

Ming resistance in the southern provinces and Taiwan

Ming loyalists continued to oppose the Qing for decades after the Manchu conquest of China. Only the defeat of Koxinga's Kingdom of Dongning (Tungning), in 1683, brought an end to the southern Ming resistance.

The suicide of the Chongzhen Emperor marked the end of the Ming dynasty (see pp. 238–239), but many Ming loyalists continued to resist the Qing. Moving south from Beijing to Nanjing, they declared various Ming princes as emperor. These included the prince of Fu (Emperor Hongguang), the prince of Tang (Emperor Longwu), the prince of Lu, and the prince of Gui (Emperor Yongli). However, the most sustained resistance to the Qing came from Zheng Chenggong, a supporter of Longwu and Yongli.

Champion of the Ming

Zheng Chenggong was born in Japan in 1624 to a Chinese merchant, Zheng Zhilong, and a Japanese mother. In 1631, he moved to the family's home in Quanzhou, Fujian province, and began his Confucian education, achieving success in imperial examinations in Nanjing. However, when the city fell to Qing troops in 1645, Zheng retreated, along with Longwu, to Fuzhou. There, Longwu gave him the honorific name Guoxingye, which was westernized as Koxinga.

Fujian fell to the Qing in 1646, and Longwu was captured and killed at Fuzhou. While his father abandoned the Ming cause, Koxinga vowed to restore the dynasty and began to build up his power base on the Fujian coast, while still acknowledging the supremacy of Emperor Yongli—the last Ming pretender in southwest China. The Qing were worried about the threat posed by Koxinga and went on the offensive after negotiations failed.

THE MASSACRE OF YANGZHOU

In one of the bloodiest episodes in the Qing campaign to suppress Ming loyalists, the two sides clashed at Yangzhou in 1645. When the Qing finally broke into the city, a massacre followed. Although accounts of 800,000 deaths are probably exaggerated, the carnage was enough to convince the Ming commanders in Nanjing to surrender without much further resistance.

In 1656, the Qing prince Jidu led Manchu troops against Koxinga's training camp on Jinmen island off the southern coast of China. The Qing lost most of their fleet in the ensuing battle, and Koxinga was left free to capture Zhoushan, a large island near the mouth of the Yangzi River. From there, he launched an ambitious maritime expedition in 1659, sailing more than 100,000 troops up the river to the gates of

▽ **Hero of China**
Koxinga is now regarded as a hero in China for restoring Han rule over the Chinese island of Taiwan (Formosa). Numerous statues are dedicated to him.

◁ **Treaty with the Dutch**
After Koxinga took Formosa (pictured) from the Dutch in 1662, the two sides signed a treaty that set out the terms of the Dutch surrender and return to Batavia (now Jakarta, Indonesia).

Nanjing. For three weeks. Koxinga's forces besieged the city but were unable to encircle it and cut its supply lines. On September 9, the Qing launched an attack on the besiegers that forced them to return to their ships.

The Kingdom of Dongning

Following his defeat, Koxinga began to look farther afield for a secure base. In 1661, he landed with more than 25,000 men near the main Dutch stronghold on Formosa (Taiwan). For nine months, his forces besieged Fort Zeelandia, until on February 1, 1662, the Dutch governor surrendered. Koxinga established the Kingdom of Dongning and began turning Formosa into a base for Ming loyalists. In 1662, his forces began raiding the Philippines and threatening to attack Manila if the Spanish colonial government refused to pay tribute. However, before Koxinga could act on his threat, he died from malaria.

Qing victory

Koxinga's son, Zheng Jing, succeeded him as king of Dongning and continued to resist the Qing for another 20 years. Rather than pursuing the reestablishment of the Ming in China, Zheng Jing sought instead to leave the old empire to the Qing and build a new China in Formosa. However, the Qing refused to countenance Dongning independence. When Zheng Jing died in 1681, the Kingdom of Dongning was plunged into a succession crisis. Taking advantage of the chaos, in 1683, the Kangxi Emperor (see pp. 248–249) dispatched his admiral Shi Lang (who had once fought for the Ming loyalist cause but had defected to the Qing) to invade Formosa. Leading a force of 240 warships equipped with cannons purchased from the Dutch, Shi Lang deftly outmaneuvered the Dongning admiral Liu Guoxuan at the Battle of Penghu. He destroyed the Dongning fleet, stationed in the Penghu archipelago, after which Qing troops landed on Formosa; Zheng Keshuang (Zheng Jing's son and Koxinga's grandson) surrendered, and Taiwan was reincorporated into the Qing empire.

▽ **Admiral Shi Lang**
Shi Lang (seated) is pictured meeting with a group of Qing officials before the Battle of Penghu.

The scholar-emperor
Kangxi was a champion of Confucian learning who encouraged scholarship throughout the empire and sponsored compilations of literature. He was himself a keen student of the classic texts and of calligraphy.

The Kangxi Emperor

China's longest-reigning emperor

Kangxi ruled over Qing China with meticulous efficiency. He consolidated the Qing dynasty's power, substantially extended the empire, and created a climate of openness to European art, culture, and religion.

Born in 1654, Xuanye was the third son of the Qing Shunzhi Emperor. When his father died in 1661, Xuanye became emperor, taking the name Kangxi. He ascended to the throne over his older brothers thanks to the high rank of his mother, a concubine later known as Empress Xiaokang. During his 61-year reign, he proved himself to be an accomplished leader, administrator, and scholar and was known for his great strength and skill with a bow.

Kangxi faced several threats during his reign: from feudal warlords in the southern provinces who rebelled in 1673; from the Zheng regime in Formosa (Taiwan), which refused to submit to his authority; from Russians encroaching into the northwest of the empire; and from the Dzungars in Outer Mongolia. Yet by 1696, he had subdued the south through diplomacy and military campaigns, secured the border with Russia, and incorporated Taiwan and Outer Mongolia into the empire. He added Tibet to his acquisitions in 1720.

Trade and prosperity

Kangxi's reign ushered in a period of prosperity; he took an interest in the lives of his people, making extensive tours of his domain and winning a reputation for benevolence by freezing taxes.

△ **Seal of the emperor**
This seal, carved for Kangxi, is inscribed "Revere Heaven and Serve thy People."

He loosened restrictions on trade, which brought more Europeans to China but maintained the tributary system used for dealing with foreign powers. The Kangxi court was particularly frugal; the emperor lived by the Confucian values of diligence, moderation, and harmony outlined in his moral guide for peasants, the *Sacred Edict* (Sheng Yu, 1670).

Aligning the Manchu with Confucian culture was one of the touchstones of Kangxi's reign. He won over the Confucian bureaucrats, who had remained loyal to the Ming, after seeking out the most talented of them, Zhang Tingyu, to write an official history of the Ming dynasty, the *Mingshi*.

Learning and religion

Fascinated by European knowledge, Kangxi invited missionaries to court to discuss astronomy, mathematics, and geography. He was so impressed by their learning that in 1692 he gave the Jesuits permission to further propagate Catholicism in China.

Kangxi fell ill in the winter of 1722 and died in December. His attempt to nominate his second son, Yinreng, as crown prince ended in bitter fighting between his sons; instead, the throne went to his fourth son, Yinzhen—the Yongzheng Emperor.

△ **Kangxi glass**
Kangxi opened the first imperial glassworks in Beijing, which created stunning new wares.

1654 Born in the Jingren Palace in the Forbidden City; becomes emperor in 1661

1685 Opens customs stations in four ports to overseas trade

1720 Sends an army to take control of Lhasa in Tibet

1673–1683 Subdues the revolt of feudal warlords, defeats the Zheng, and incorporates Taiwan into China for the first time

1689 Secures the border with Russia in the Treaty of Nerchinsk

1722 Dies at Changchunyuan and is buried in the Jingling mausoleum in Malanyu

The Southern Inspection Tour

China's longest reigning emperor, Kangxi, made a great tour of the south of the country to help consolidate Qing authority over the empire. He commissioned Wang Hui—one of the most renowned landscape artists of the day—to record his travels in a series of 12 scrolls, the third of which is pictured here. This scroll, in a distinctive blue and green palette, depicts the visit of Kangxi and his retinue to Mount Tai in Shandong. Tai is one of China's Five Great Mountains and a sacred site of Confucianism. The artist never visited the mountain but based his work on maps and prints of the scene as well as imaginary landscapes that were informed by classical painting.

Qing Conquests

The creation of a multiethnic empire

△ **Defeat of the Mongols**
This painting depicts a Qing victory over Dzungar and Turkic forces in 1759 at Qurman in the Tarim Basin. Victory enabled the Chinese to later annex Xinjiang.

Between 1687 and 1768, the Qing undertook an intensive campaign to subdue the territories to their north and east. They greatly enlarged the area of their empire but failed to bring the conquered peoples fully under their control.

Once they were in control of the former territories of the Ming empire, the Qing embarked on a so-called "civilizing mission" – which was in reality an expansionist adventure that succeeded in doubling the size of their empire.

A key objective of the Qing mission was the subjugation of the seminomadic Dzungar Mongols, who had established a powerful khanate in western Mongolia. In 1687, the Dzungar khan, Galdan, invaded

eastern Mongolia and attacked the Khalkha Mongols in the region, sending a flood of refugees into the Qing lands. Fearful of an enlarged Mongol empire, the Kangxi Emperor launched a campaign against the Dzungars in 1690. After struggling to cross the Gobi, a Qing force under Prince Fuquan met the Dzungars at Chifeng, Inner Mongolia in September. Although outnumbered, the Dzungars escaped. The following year, the Khalkha rulers declared themselves vassals of

◁ **The Kangxi Emperor**
The emperor is here depicted on horseback, dressed in full ceremonial armor.

established a permanent Manchu garrison of more than 3,000 men in Lhasa and set up a new governing council, the *Kashag*, in 1721

After several more years of campaigning, the Qing and the Dzungars made peace. However, when civil war broke out in the Dzungar khanate, the Qing went to the aid of Amursana (one of the claimants to the title of Khan of the Dzungars), who promised loyalty to the Qing. Amursana went back on his word in 1755, leading a rebellion against Qing rule. In response, the Qianlong Emperor launched a genocidal campaign against the remaining 500,000 Dzungar Mongols and added western Mongolia to the Qing empire.

Qianlong then invaded the territories around the Tarim Basin occupied by Turkic and other Muslim peoples. In 1768, he formally annexed these lands, naming them Xinjiang (meaning "new borders"). As in Tibet, the Qing ruled Xinjiang with a light touch, allowing its peoples to keep their religious leaders and not forcing them to adopt humiliating symbols of submission.

the Qing, and their forces were merged into the Qing armies, bolstering the numbers of soldiers ranged against Galdan. In 1696, Kangxi led three armies north against the Dzungars. At the Battle of Jao Modo, Galdan's men were no match for the cannons and muskets of Kangxi's forces. Galdan fled the battlefield and soon after died of plague; Outer Mongolia was incorporated into the Qing empire.

Invasion and control

The Dzungars still held the Islamic cities in Xinjiang province, and in 1717, they attempted to expand their territories by invading Tibet. The Qing reacted by sending their own forces into Tibet, expelling the Dzungars and declaring Tibet a protectorate. They

Ruling a huge empire

While the Qing's conquests brought them vast territories, they posed the problem of how to rule peoples of diverse religions, ethnicities, and social organization. Efforts to colonize the sparsely populated regions of Mongolia proved costly, and attempts to administer the regions through indigenous chieftains were not always successful. Even where Qing rule was lightly applied, as in Tibet and the Muslim areas, ethnic tensions remained and rebellion was never far away.

△ **Qing iron helmet**
This helmet is decorated with a feather crest and has a four-clawed dragon embroidered on the cheek guard. Its quality indicates that it was worn by a high-ranking officer.

△ **Dawachi**
The last Dzungar khan, Dawachi, was defeated by the Qing, who backed his challenger Amursana.

"China **deals with foreigners** from afar only by treating them **without discrimination**."

EDICT OF THE QIANLONG EMPEROR, 1780

The Yongzheng Emperor
Yongzheng is depicted in this 18th-century painting on silk playing a traditional musical instrument in a bamboo grove. The anonymous work is from a collection entitled *Album of the Yongzheng Emperor in Costumes*.

The Yongzheng Emperor

The third Qing emperor of China

After a controversial accession, Yongzheng proved to be a hardworking ruler whose reforms consolidated China's administration and concentrated power in the emperor's hands. Under Yongzheng, China was prosperous and peaceful.

Aisin Gioro Yinzhen was born in Beijing in 1678, the fourth of the Kangxi Emperor's 15 sons. Despite not being the first in line to succeed, Yinzhen cleverly outmaneuvered his older brothers and gained the support of the military in Beijing to take the throne and become the Yongzheng Emperor when his father died in 1722. His ascent to the position of emperor remained controversial, and in the first years of his reign, he suppressed dissent by imprisoning or executing some of his brothers and their supporters.

◁ **Seal of the Yongzheng Emperor**
This white jade seal, decorated with the figure of a crouching *chilong* (hornless dragon), is one of more than 200 made for the Yongzheng Emperor.

farmers, while removing the privileges of the local gentry, who had been given tax breaks and exemption from punishment for crimes by the Kangxi Emperor.

Concentrating control

Yongzheng embarked on a program of reform, the aims of which were to instill Confucian morality in government, rationalize the bureaucracy, and centralize imperial power. He asserted imperial control over the Eight Banners (see pp. 244–245) and convinced the princes in charge of five of them to serve the throne. Yongzheng replaced the top ministerial body—the Grand Secretariat—with a new Grand Council, whose members worked directly with him, so giving him direct oversight of all important government matters. He cracked down on the corruption that had plagued Kangxi's reign and simplified the taxation system. By incorporating the head tax—a tax on people—into the land tax, he reduced the financial burden on

Social reform

Eager to eliminate social inequality, the Yongzheng Emperor opened up the civil service examination to a broader range of ethnicities and also created special exams for people in rural areas in order to encourage diversity among the governing classes. He made wealthy officials fund orphanages and schools for the poor in every county. Improvements to canals and irrigation, and a program to bring more land into cultivation, helped improve grain reserves. Legal emancipation from servile status enhanced the lives of many tenants, agricultural workers, and low-status groups.

Yongzheng died in 1735. His short reign, nestled between the far longer ones of his father and his son, marked a pivotal change in the direction of the empire, and he left the state finances and China's civil bureaucracy on a solid footing.

△ *Viewing Snow by the Side of a Brazier*
This painting is from *Twelve Beauties of Prince Yong*, a series commissioned by Yongzheng while a prince.

1678 Born in Beijing, the fourth son of the Kangxi Emperor

1709 Is made a first-rank crown prince by Kangxi

1722 Outmaneuvers his older brothers to succeed Kangxi as the Yongzheng Emperor

1723 Incorporates the head tax into the land tax

1724 Issues edict expelling Christian missionaries

1733 Establishes the Grand Council as the policy-making body of Qing China

1735 Dies in Beijing, having named his successor in secret documents

Life under the Qing

Qing control and the Manchu queue

The Manchu rise to power marked a change in the ethnicity of China's ruling class. The new Qing dynasty strove to establish the legitimacy of their rule and their authority over the population.

After they had taken control of China, the Qing still depended to a large degree on Ming officials to administer their new empire. The Qing emperors therefore needed to maintain some continuity with Chinese culture, while visibly exerting their authority over their reluctant new subjects.

Under the Qing, the Manchu language was recognized as being equal to Chinese, and official documents were written in both languages. The national dress of the imperial court changed to suit the Manchu style: loose-fitting and shapeless clothes were replaced by narrow, tighter-fitting robes that conserved heat and were comfortable while riding on horseback. These new customs mainly affected Han scholars and other elite members of society, but one cultural change affected the Han Chinese identity for almost three centuries—the adoption of the queue.

Dorgon's edict

On June 5, 1644, Dorgon (r. 1636–1650), who was the Qing regent while the Shunzhi Emperor was still too young to rule, issued an imperial edict ordering all males under Manchu rule to adopt the Manchu's *bianzi* hairstyle, which came to be known as the queue (the French word for "tail"). The queue was a centuries-old style particular to the Manchu, in which the front of the head was shaved and the remaining hair woven in a long braid. Dorgon's edict was worded in a way that supported the idea of Manchu and Han as family. He argued

that the emperor was the people's father and wrote: "the father and sons are of the same body; how can they be different from one another?" Only a few exemptions to wearing the queue were permitted: Daoist priests, Buddhist monks, and Han women were allowed to keep their own hairstyles.

Symbols of submission

Despite Dorgon's suggestion that the queue was a way to unite the Manchu and the Han, the Manchu in fact kept their distance from the Han. Intermarriage between the two was prohibited, and the Manchu often lived in segregated garrison cities. Furthermore, the edict to wear the queue was divisive—an affront to Han Chinese cultural identity. Not only did Han men already have their own traditional hairstyle (long hair worn in a topknot), but shaving the head was

> "Those who **follow** this order **belong** to **our country**."

REGENT DORGON, IMPERIAL EDICT, 1644

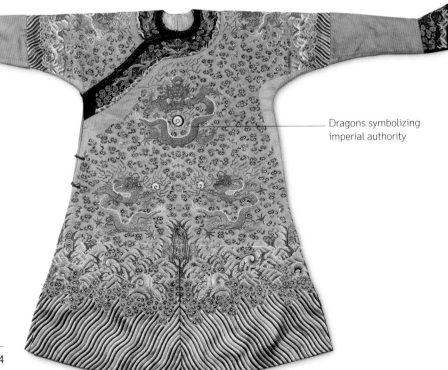

▽ **Qing court robes**
The Qianlong Emperor (see pp.258–259) codified Qing regulations on dress. A person's place in court or civic life could be determined by the color and patterns of their robes.

Dragons symbolizing imperial authority

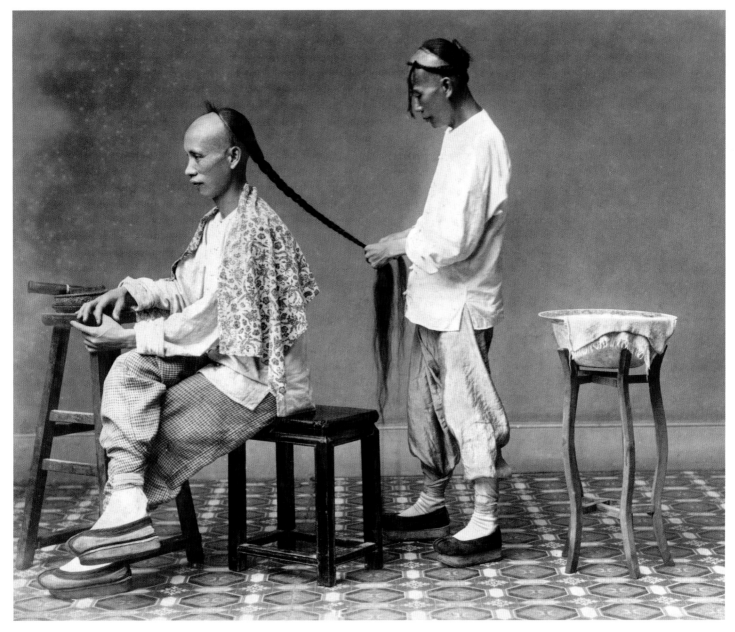

△ **Braiding the queue**
A photograph taken in the 1880s shows a man braiding hair in the queue style. It is thought that the style originated with the Xiongnu, nomads who inhabited the Eastern Steppe from the 3rd century BCE.

seen as self-mutilation and a breach of the Confucian instruction not to damage the body, skin, and hair bequeathed to them by their parents.

Han resistance

The instruction to wear the queue was enforced by teams of armed barbers and backed up by threats of execution for those who refused to comply within 10 days of receiving the order. Dissenters were beheaded and had their heads hung on public display. As a Qing slogan put it, "Cut the hair and keep the head, [or] keep the hair and cut the head." It was clear that the queue was a symbol of submission to Qing authority; lack of compliance was obvious and was an easy way for the Qing to identify troublemakers. Resistance was

widespread. In the central Chinese highlands, for example, locals who had otherwise accepted the new Qing regime revolted at the imposition of the queue. Despite harsh punishments, disobeying the order continued to be a sign of resistance to the Qing dynasty. The Taiping rebels (see pp. 278–279), for example, were nicknamed the "Long hairs" or "Hair rebels" for their rejection of the style; and in 1898, some supporters of the Hundred Days of Reform (see pp. 296–297) cut their braids as a symbol of their modernity. With the fall of the Qing in the Xinhai Revolution in 1911, many abandoned the queue as a symbol of a defunct regime. The remainder finally gave up when the last emperor of China, Puyi, cut his queue in 1922.

Qianlong on horseback
This painting, in a fusion of
European and Chinese styles,
was made by Italian Jesuit
Giuseppe Castiglione, an
artist at the imperial court
of the Kangxi, Yongzheng,
and Qianlong emperors.

The Qianlong Emperor

The emperor who cemented the Manchu legacy

During the 60-year reign of the Qianlong Emperor, China grew into a vast, multiethnic empire. Qianlong celebrated its diversity through art, architecture, and literature, while also preserving and protecting its Manchu heritage.

The Yongzheng Emperor's fourth son, Aisin Gioro Hongli, was made heir on his father's succession. On Yongzheng's death in 1735, Hongli ascended to the throne to rule as the Qianlong Emperor. He soon set about reversing many of his father's policies, restoring the privileges of the gentry and abandoning his education reforms. Underpinning his outlook was a distaste for Yongzheng's mission to create cultural and social homogeneity in the empire and a desire to preserve Manchu identity.

A universal ruler

Qianlong thought of himself as a "universal ruler" and presented himself differently to each of the empire's constituents: to the Tibetans, he portrayed himself as a Buddhist bodhisattva; to the Mongols, he was a prince of the steppes; and to the Han Chinese, a scholar and patron of Chinese culture. He filled the Chengde Summer Palace and the Old Summer Palace in Beijing with buildings and gardens that reflected architectures and landscapes of the empire and, in 1772, called for the creation of a vast compilation of Chinese literature, the *Complete Books of the Four Treasuries* (*Siku quanshu*), which comprised 36,381 volumes.

At the same time, however, Qianlong ordered the destruction of thousands of books that he saw to be negative about the northern peoples and commissioned works to glorify Manchu heritage, culture, history, and language. He was a patron of the arts, acquired numerous artwork, and shared the interest earlier Qing emperors had in Western culture. Nonetheless, as his reception of the Macartney Mission (1793) showed (see pp. 270–271), he was not ready to open up China any further to the Western powers.

Imperial expansion

Through a series of military actions known as the Ten Great Campaigns, Qianlong extended China to its widest limits. He regained Mongolia and the Tibetan area, installing the Dalai Lama as administrator, and secured tribute from Burma and Vietnam. But these campaigns were costly and depleted the reserves so carefully built up by Yongzheng. Qianlong abdicated in 1795, respectfully ending his rule so as not to reign longer than his grandfather, Kangxi. Qianlong's son Yongyan succeeded but was emperor in name only; Qianlong held real power until his death in 1799, making his reign the longest in Chinese history.

◁ **Ruyi of the Qianlong Emperor**
This *ruyi* scepter was one of many owned by the emperor. The word *ruyi* means "as you desire"; the scepter is a symbol of imperial power and authenticity.

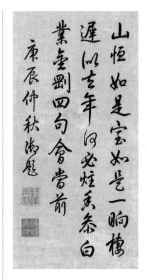

△ **The poet emperor**
Qianlong was a prolific poet and calligrapher; he produced thousands of handwritten works during his lifetime, including this scroll from 1760.

1711 Born in Beijing to the Yongzheng Emperor and Empress Xiaoshengxian

1755 Begins the first of the Ten Great Campaigns, which expand the empire and Qing influence to its greatest extent

1795 Abdicates in favour of his 15th son, Yongyan but continues to hold power as Taishang Huang (Emperor Emeritus)

1735 Becomes the Qianlong Emperor; announces his reign will be marked by liberal magnanimity

1772 Orders the creation of the *Siku quanshu*, a vast collection of Chinese literature

1799 Dies in Beijing and is buried in Yuling, his mausoleum in the Eastern Qing tombs

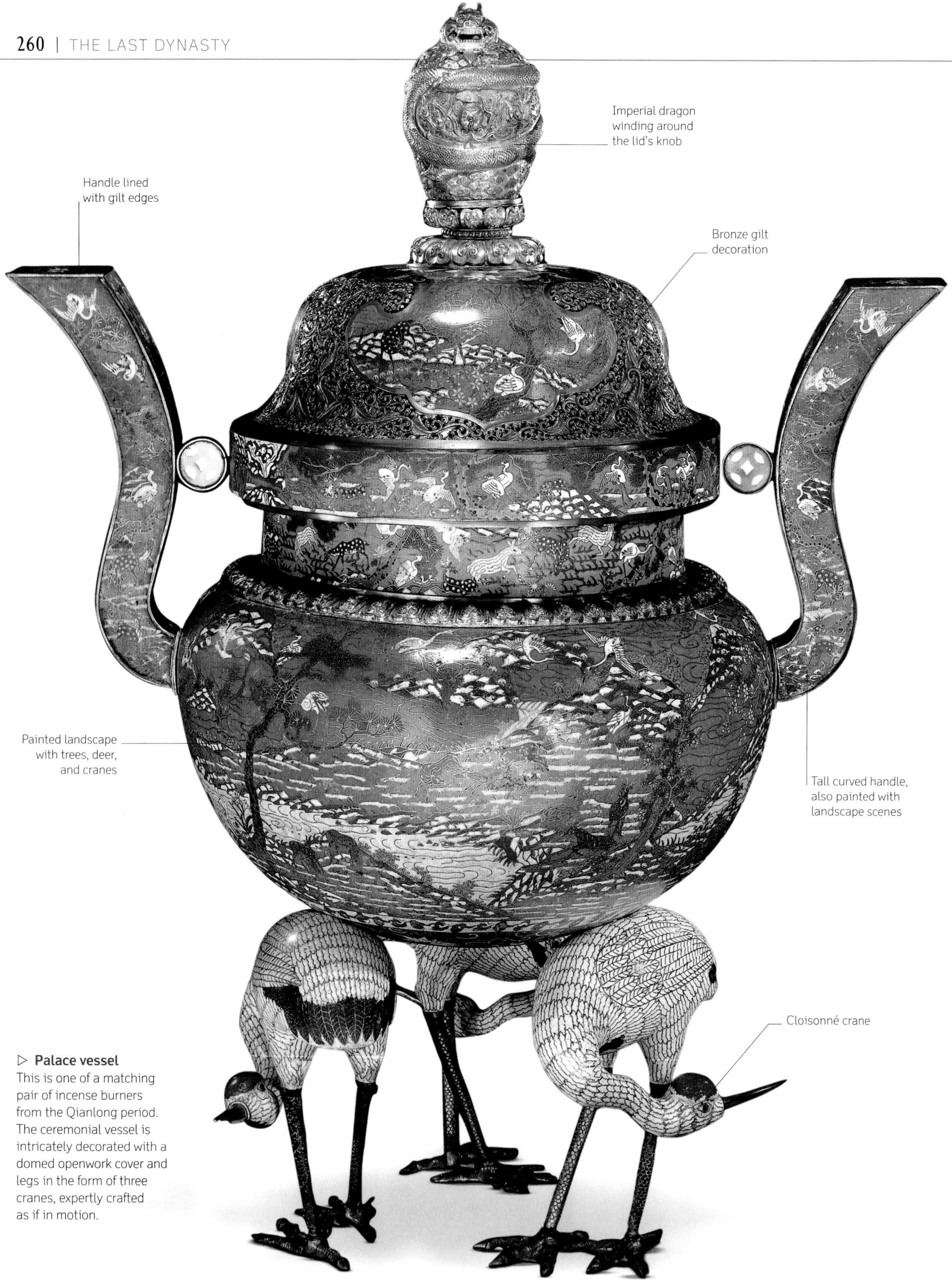

Imperial dragon
winding around
the lid's knob

Handle lined
with gilt edges

Bronze gilt
decoration

Painted landscape
with trees, deer,
and cranes

Tall curved handle,
also painted with
landscape scenes

Cloisonné crane

▷ **Palace vessel**
This is one of a matching
pair of incense burners
from the Qianlong period.
The ceremonial vessel is
intricately decorated with a
domed openwork cover and
legs in the form of three
cranes, expertly crafted
as if in motion.

Cloisonné Censer

The extraordinary collection of Qianlong

The reign of the Qianlong Emperor (1735–96) is known for the production of many intricate and beautiful Chinese crafts. These crafts were directly inspired by the emperor's own aesthetic tastes, and he frequently directed court craftspeople to imitate aspects of older Chinese art that he enjoyed, cultivating his image as a scholar and connoisseur of Han Chinese culture despite his Manchu heritage. Rather than strictly copying older styles, Qianlong's imperial workshop sought to innovate and to improve upon older motifs, using tradition as inspiration for stunning new wares.

Qianlong was one of China's greatest art collectors, and his court was known for its richly detailed treasures. Most notably, Qianlong ordered the organization of the imperial collection—a complex process that included not only examining and cataloging artifacts from Chinese history but also ranking them according to their importance and beauty. Different mediums of art had different grading systems; calligraphy, for example, might be marked as either "divine" (the highest compliment), "marvelous," "capable," or "untrammeled," with the judgment stamped directly onto the pages being judged. Qianlong also contributed to the grading process by writing his reflections, in calligraphy, as poetry or prose on the object or its box. Crafts were scrutinized by Qianlong, by officials in the imperial workshop, and by respected court craftspeople and

writers. The grading of artifacts in turn contributed to the production of new treasures, encouraging craftspeople to create works of the highest quality.

Incense burner

The incense burner featured opposite combines the Chinese art forms of cloisonné, bronzework, and landscape painting, all of which long predate the reign of Qianlong. The landscape shows tranquil scenes featuring cranes and deer, continuing the trend of such animals appearing in Chinese art. Cloisonné vessels from the Qing dynasty are known for having stunning gilt bronze details, often representing animals such as elephants and dragons—a symbol of imperial power. This particular vessel has a dragon shape in bronze winding around the knob of its lid, meaning it was probably for use in court rituals or to scent the hallways of the imperial palace. It is a common shape for censers of the Qianlong period: a tripod with two raised arms.

▷ **Symbolic birds**
Representing peace and longevity in China, cranes were second only to the phoenix in revered birds. They often appear in imperial decoration such as these small censers.

The Great Qing Novel

A history of *Dream of the Red Chamber*

Written in the mid-18th century, *Dream of the Red Chamber* is counted among the great masterpieces of world literature and is one of China's Four Classic Novels (see pp. 226–227). Its author, Cao Xueqin, was a member of a Chinese family who had risen to power and wealth in the 17th century; Cao's grandfather, a court servant, enjoyed the favor of the Kangxi Emperor. However, the family was targeted by the Yongzheng Emperor in his 18th-century purge of corruption and incompetence in the empire. Forced to leave their mansion in Nanjing, they moved to a small house in Beijing.

These formative events lie behind Cao Xueqin's semiautobiographical *Dream of the Red Chamber*, which follows the story of the decline of the two branches of the wealthy Jia family. The text combines realism and romance, psychology and fate, and daily life and the supernatural and features some 30 main characters (including maids, page boys, nuns, concubines, and numerous family members) and more than 400 minor ones.

A family tale

The plot centers on the relationships between Jia Baoyu, the carefree heir of the family (who was born with a magical piece of jade in his mouth), and his two female cousins, Lin Daiyu and Xue Baochai. Melancholy Lin Daiyu is Jia Baoyu's true love, with whom he shares a passion for music and poetry, while the vivacious Xue Baochai, for whom he feels no romantic love, is destined to become his wife. The story describes how Baoyu is tricked into marrying Baochai, the subsequent death of Daiyu, and Baoyu's eventual departure to seek a religious life. Framing

△ **Cao Xueqin**
The author of *Dream of the Red Chamber*, Cao Xueqin, shown here in an 18th-century painting, was born, c. 1724, in Nanjing into an impoverished family. A painter and philosopher as well as a writer, he died around the age of 40, apparently from grief at the death of his son.

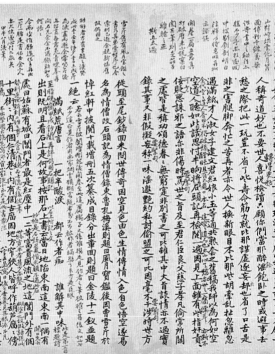

△ **The Jimao manuscript**
Before Cao Xueqin's novel *Dream of the Red Chamber* went into print in 1791, the work was circulated via hand-copied manuscripts, some of which are now held in libraries in China and Europe. One of the earliest surviving of these is the so-called Jimao manuscript, dated to 1759; a page from this text is shown here.

△ **19th-century depiction of women**
Although Cao Xueqin's masterpiece includes some powerful female characters, visual representations of the book often focus on simplified gender roles that portray the women as gentle, fragile, and alluring, as in this illustration on silk.

"Truth becomes fiction when the fiction's true; real becomes not-real where the unreal's real."

CAO XUEQIN, *DREAM OF THE RED CHAMBER*, 1791

the episodes of the family's story is the tale of a sentient stone that begs a Daoist priest and a Buddhist monk to take it with them to see the world.

Cao's work is packed with detail about the social, cultural, and spiritual life of the time. Not only does it reflect the manners and mores of the upper tier of Qing society, but it also provides a fascinating insight into medicine, food, festivities, rites, proverbs, myths, religion, filial piety, and the arts in the Qing empire. His description of his characters shows remarkable psychological depth, with no one individual depicted as wholly good or bad but simply as human. His female characters are particularly strongly represented, no doubt because—as Cao himself noted—he wanted to memorialize the "slips of girls" from his youth who were "in every way, both morally and intellectually, superior" to him.

Publication and legacy

Cao wrote *Dream of the Red Chamber* over a long period, circulating the manuscripts of around 80 chapters among friends and family as he wrote them. He died in 1763, and it was only in 1791 that the book appeared in print. This 120-chapter edition, published by Gao E—a prominent Qing scholar and writer—was controversial. While it is likely that Cao Xueqin wrote the first 80 chapters of this edition, different endings have survived, and it is unclear whether the last 40 chapters were derived from Cao's own work, were written by Gao E, or came from the pen of a different author. Whatever the truth, *Dream of the Red Chamber* has become one of China's most loved novels, inspiring films, operas, and television series. In the 20th century, it was also published in English under its alternative title, *The Story of the Stone*.

△ **Sun Wen's representations**
A painting on silk by Qing dynasty artist Sun Wen depicts scenes from *Dream of the Red Chamber*. It is one of 230 brush paintings by this artist that show episodes from the vast novel; the standard English translation of Cao Xueqin's text runs to a staggering 2,500 pages.

△ **Postage stamp**
The popularity of *Dream of the Red Chamber* in modern-day China is reflected in a series of vibrant postage stamps based on scenes from the classic work. The postal administration has issued three separate editions of the stamps: the first set in 1981, the second—shown here—in 2014, and the third in 2016.

△ **Modern opera**
Dream of the Red Chamber has inspired many adaptations. The San Francisco Opera staged the premiere of the English-language opera of the text in September 2016. The final dress rehearsal is shown here, with soprano Pureum Jo playing Daiyu.

The Growing Economy

Domestic and foreign trade under the Qing

During the High Qing era (1683–1839), China emerged as an economic powerhouse, unrivaled throughout Asia. This period of dynamic Chinese growth lasted until the outbreak of war with Britain in 1839.

▽ **The Canton factories**
The so-called Thirteen Factories along the Pearl River in Guangzhou (Canton) were warehouses that stored goods from foreign trade, which was restricted to the port of Guangzhou.

Under the Qing, the Chinese economy steadily moved away from its agrarian base on to a more commercial footing. These changes were fueled in part by the incorporation into the empire of the vast new territories of Mongolia and Xinjiang, which brought new lands and people under Qing control. At the same time, the introduction of foreign food crops, such as potatoes and peanuts, in the early 17th century, and the spread of wheat cultivation helped keep famine at bay. These factors sparked a population increase from 150 million in 1650 to more than 300 million in 1800. The growth fueled a vibrant domestic economy that was in turn boosted by increasing overseas trade.

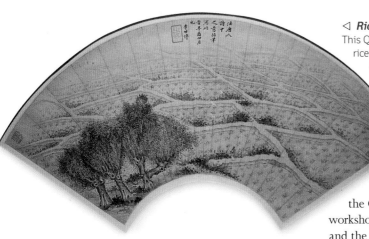

◁ *Rice Paddies and Egrets*
This Qing fan painting shows the cultivation of rice. Efficient transport from paddy fields south of the Yangzi River ensured that rice became a staple food throughout China.

The demand for goods was met by the development of new processes for mass production. While porcelain manufacture had been industrialized in the Ming era, during the Qing there was growth in large-scale craft workshops producing items such as paper and textiles and the development of piece-working practices.

The Qing supported the development of a free market economy within China's borders by limiting the number of state monopolies and eliminating cartels that had previously controlled trade. Different areas of the country began to specialize in raising particular cash crops, such as rice, cotton, salt, tea, and wood.

"Foreign barbarians… must reside in the foreign factories under supervision."

ON THE CANTON SYSTEM, FROM THE "VIGILANCE TOWARDS FOREIGN BARBARIAN REGULATIONS", 1757

This led to a steep increase in both the amount and the diversity of goods transported around the country. Rice was carried down the Yangzi River to the cotton-growing Jiangnan region (in Guangxi province). In addition, tons of tea from Hunan and Fujian, salt from Anhui, and sugar and marine produce from the southeast were carried to urban markets.

Transportation and urbanization
The movement of goods on such a tremendous scale drove the development of cities and towns across China. Large administrative and commercial cities, such as Hangzhou, were joined by a network of market towns and small commercial cities that managed the flow of goods from the countryside to the larger centers of population. For example, in Xiangtan county (Hunan province), the number of market towns grew from three to more than 100 between 1685 and 1818; this pattern was repeated in counties across the empire.

Foreign trade
At the start of the Qing period, the Kangxi Emperor banned all coastal trade, fearing a coup by Ming loyalists from across the water (see pp. 246–247). Once he had restored peace in the unified nation, he issued a decree in 1684 reopening the sea routes and establishing customs offices in ports, including Guangzhou (known as Canton by Western traders), Xiamen, Ningbo, and Songjiang. Booming overseas trade with the West stoked the economy. However, the reign of Kangxi's grandson, the Qianlong Emperor (see pp. 258–59), saw foreign trade curtailed. Lobbying by Chinese businesses against imports and the misbehavior of some foreign merchants led the emperor to declare in 1757 that Guangzhou should be the sole Chinese port open to Western traders. He granted a monopoly on trade to the guild that ran the warehouses in Guangzhou known as the Thirteen Factories. The guild members guaranteed every foreign vessel. The system—known as the Canton System—laid down strict rules about when the foreign "barbarians" could stay in Guangzhou and who they could do business with. Despite these restrictions, trade between Europe and China grew: exports of tea increased by more than 50 percent in the first 30 years of the 19th century, and silk exports quadrupled.

By 1800, China was Asia's leading economic power. However, its refusal to accept anything other than silver as payment for its goods led to an uneven trade balance that encouraged the illegal and devastating trade in opium (see pp. 272–273).

▽ **Ceramic exports**
Qing factories produced ceramics embellished with heraldic designs destined for markets in Europe. This serving dish was commissioned in the 1720s for a wealthy Scottish patron and bears the arms of Alexander.

Ceramic Art

Porcelain through the ages

One of China's most famous exports, porcelain was invented in the Tang period. Over the centuries, different shapes and methods of decoration developed—often influenced by foreign ideas and demands. These spectacular highlights demonstrate the differing techniques and unrivaled skills of the imperial workshops.

Handle shaped like an elephant's head and trunk

△ **Crouching rabbit**
This Tang representation of a rabbit was made shortly after the invention of porcelain, in the late 8th or early 9th century CE.

△ **Peaceful porcelain**
Ornate pillows were made from porcelain. This Southern Song example incorporates the figure of a reclining woman to hold it up.

Imitates bronze *taotie* decoration

Legs in style of an ancient *ding*

△ **The David Vases**
Collected by Sir Percival David, this famous pair of Yuan vases are early examples of the blue-and-white porcelain that became famous under the Ming (see pp. 212–213).

◁ **Single color**
Made from porcelain with a white single-color glaze, this 16th-century incense burner was inspired by ancient bronzes.

◁ **Roaring censer**
One of a matching pair, this Ming incense burner dates from the early 14th century. It is coated in a type of glaze called celadon, which produces a pale green or blue color.

▽ **Blue-and-gold bowl**
This late 16th-century bowl is inspired by the Japanese art of *kintsugi*, which fixes broken pieces together with gold. It was probably made for export to Japan.

Gilt silver mount is a later English addition

Spout painted like a branch

△ **Fruit pot**
Produced in the late 17th century, this Qing wine or teapot is shaped like a peach, a Chinese symbol of longevity. Its bold green color is relatively rare for the period—other similar pots are turquoise or purple.

▷ **Wucai vase**
This white Ming vase from the reign of Emperor Wanli is painted with floral, crane, and dragon motifs in *wucai* (five-color) glaze. This type of painting uses blue, green, red, and yellow on the white base.

▷ **Boys at play**
This vase dates from the reign of Daoguang, in the 19th century. It depicts young boys at play – a common motif representing the desire to have many sons.

Famille-rose ("pink family") decoration

Green openwork with dragon pattern

Boys carry lanterns and other auspicious objects

△ **Moon flask**
The "moon" flask gets its name from its flat, circular shape. This example dates from the reign of Yongzheng in the early 18th century.

△ **Pink perfection**
The smooth pink enamel glaze of this Qing vase showcases the superior abilities of Qianlong's imperial workshops.

△ **Gourd bottle**
The bulbous "gourd" shape of this vase was popular during the Qing dynasty. This bright orange-and-blue example was produced in the reign of the Qianlong Emperor.

◁ **Dragon vase**
Combining pastel colors, openwork dragons, and curling gilt "ears," this vase is characteristic of the elaborate wares created under Qianlong (see pp. 260–261).

▷ **Imitating enamel**
Dating from the reign of the late Qing emperor Guangxu, this porcelain plate is decorated with a design imitating the art of cloisonné.

Peking Opera

The history of a flamboyant and opulent dramatic form

In 1790, four opera troupes from Anhui arrived in Beijing to perform for the Qianlong Emperor's 80th birthday. Their performances launched what is known as *jingxi* (Peking opera), and over the next 60 years, troupes developed the art form in the city, using elements of *huidiao*—a lively form of opera that told historical stories or folk tales—and *kunqu*, a 16th-century form of musical drama. By the end of the 19th century, traveling companies had spread Peking opera and its traditions throughout China, although most provinces also cultivated their own operatic forms using local dialects.

Regulated roles

Peking opera is a highly regularized art form. Performers must master four main skills—song, speech, dance, and combat (acrobatics and fighting with weaponry)—and perform them effortlessly. Its plays fall into two categories: civil plays (*wenxi*), which focus on relationships between characters and stories of love and intrigue; and martial plays (*wuxi*), which focus on action, acrobatics, and martial arts. There are four fixed role types: *sheng* (the lead male character), *dan* (female), *jing* (male, painted-face characters), and *chou* (male, clowns). Each role type has subcategories: for example, *laosheng* are dignified, older men while *wensheng* are scholars and bureaucrats. Traditionally, the female roles were played by men, and female actors were introduced only in the late 20th century.

Each role type has its own set of conventions that dictate what makeup and costumes are worn. *Sheng* and *dan* roles wear simple makeup: a white face with rouged cheeks, black-lined eyes and eyebrows, and colored lips. *Chou* wear simple patches of white.

△ **Character catalogue**
In the late 19th century, artists produced albums recording the makeup and costume of opera characters. Created during the Qing period, this particular portrait is from a catalogue of 100 character costumes from nine plays, all of which were painted on silk.

△ **Western views**
This colored engraving depicts a Western view of Peking opera, with characters moving flamboyantly across the stage. Most people in the West did not experience Peking opera until the early 20th century, when troupes began to travel outside of China to the US and Russia.

△ *Broken Bridge*
This photograph shows a scene from the opera *Broken Bridge*, with Chen Delin (1862–1930) playing the White Snake and Yu Yuqin (1868–1939) as the Green Snake. Yu Yuqin was particularly famous in the 1880s and was brought to court to perform at the age of 23.

"I am like a **tiger** forgotten in the **mountain**, alone and **suffering**."

LYRIC FROM THE OPERA *SILANG VISITS HIS MOTHER*, QING DYNASTY

Jing characters wear masklike makeup in colors revealing their true nature, such as red for loyalty and courage or green for impulsiveness and violence. Costumes are used to signal a character's gender, role, occupation, and social status; for example, officials of high rank wear purple, emperors are dressed in yellow robes; and warriors, both male and female, wear a stiff costume (*kao*) representing armor.

Singing styles also differ according to the character: *laosheng* sing in a natural style, *jing* use loud, clear voices, and *qingyi* (elaborately costumed aristocrats) use the shrill falsetto that characterizes Peking opera. While singing is used to express emotions, speech is used to tell the story. Performers employ a technique known as *nianbai* for this purpose; their voices rise and fall and syllables are lengthened to create a rhythm quite unlike that of everyday speech.

Famous dramas

During the Qing period, Peking operas could be incredibly long, with up to 24 acts. Modern Peking opera, however, has condensed the most popular of these stories into single-act dramas. One drama that is still popular today is *The Hegemon-King Bids His Concubine Farewell*, a sad tale in which Xiang Yu, the "Hegemon King of Western Chu," fights against the founder of the Han dynasty. In the opera, realizing he will die, Xiang Yu calls for his favorite concubine, Consort Yu. Yu begs to die alongside him, then kills herself with his sword when he refuses her. Another drama, *The Drunken Concubine*, is about the great beauty of the Tang dynasty, Yang Guifei. Many Peking opera stories are similarly inspired by historical events and include tales about emperors and officials and their military campaigns, lives, and loves.

△ **Mei Lanfang**
One of China's most celebrated performers, Mei Lanfang, was known for playing *dan* roles. He developed a style that emphasized performance over singing. He worked on film and stage until his death in 1961 but refused to perform during the Japanese occupation of Shanghai.

△ **Peking opera today**
A scene from a performance of Peking opera in Huainan, Anhui province, in 2019 shows a court ready for a standoff in front of a mountain scene. Peking opera is still performed both in China and abroad, with many stories and traditions unchanged from their premieres in the 18th and 19th centuries.

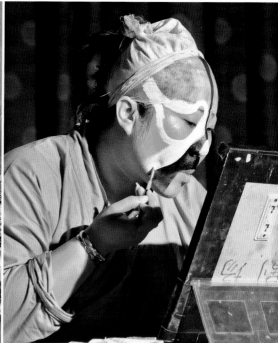

△ **Painting the mask**
An actress paints her face with black and white paint. Black paint in Peking opera symbolizes a character's stern, strong, or rough disposition. Colors and patterns give the audience clues about a character, but characters do not have a set mask—different artists use different styles.

The Macartney Mission

A failed British trade mission to China

In 1793, a large British delegation bearing hundreds of crates of gifts arrived in China in the hope of negotiating trading rights. Largely a failure, the mission merely highlighted the cultural distance between China and Europe.

In 1757, the Qianlong Emperor issued an Imperial Edict confining all foreign trade with China to the port of Canton (now Guangzhou). This edict grew into the restrictive Canton System (see p. 265), in which foreign merchants were forced to conduct all business in China through an intermediary—a guild of merchants known as the Cohong. These merchants were granted a monopoly on trade into China by the government, and this trade was highly regulated.

Macartney sets sail

By the end of the 18th century, British merchants were paying ever-increasing amounts for Chinese goods. British trade with China was conducted through the East India Company, but demand grew for the British government to intervene and request greater trade rights. In September 1792, Lord George Macartney, a former envoy to Russia and governor of Madras, set sail for China. He had a list of objectives:

▽ **Meeting Qianlong**
This 18th-century engraving depicts the emperor being carried in his litter to meet the waiting envoy Lord George Macartney.

"There is **nothing we lack** … nor do we need any more of **your country's manufactures**."

QIANLONG'S REPLY TO KING GEORGE III, 1793

CHINA'S TEA TRADE WITH BRITAIN

At the start of the 18th century, tea was heavily taxed in Britain; it was drunk mainly by the wealthy, often from fine Chinese ceramics (right). After import duties were cut later in the century, the demand for tea exploded. The British East India Company had a monopoly over its import into Britain. It had to pay for tea in silver since the Chinese were uninterested in other British goods. The Company's attempts to gain access to Chinese markets helped trigger the later Opium Wars (see pp. 276–277).

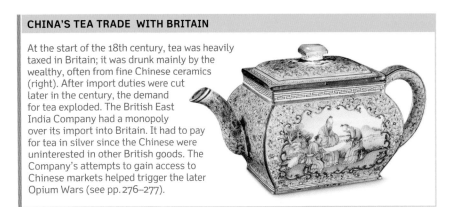

to negotiate a relaxation of the Canton System; to obtain an island from which British traders could operate; and to establish an embassy at the imperial court in Beijing. Most importantly, Macartney hoped to convince China to abandon the tributary system and use a European system of trade based on envoys, ambassadors, treaties, and published tariffs.

The British arrived at the mouth of the Hai River in August 1793. They traveled upriver to Beijing in a flotilla of smaller craft, aboard which were numerous gifts for the emperor—including a planetarium and a hot-air balloon. Such gifts, they realized too late, would not impress Qianlong; Macartney himself noted that the emperor already possessed all manner of European "toys and sing-songs" that made the British gifts pale in comparison.

Relations with the emperor

In many ways, Macartney's mission was doomed before it even set sail because British ways of conducting diplomacy were fundamentally incompatible with the Qing court's ritualized hierarchy. At the heart of the China's tributary system was the assumption that China was culturally and materially superior to other nations. This meant that those wanting to trade with China had to approach the emperor as vassals. For example, anyone coming into the presence of the emperor was expected to kowtow—to kneel three times and prostrate themselves with their head touching the ground. This was a step Macartney was not prepared to take unless is was reciprocated (by a Chinese official kowtowing to the British monarch), because doing so would acknowledge the inferiority of George III.

After a protracted diplomatic dance, which served only to offend the emperor, Macartney and Qianlong finally met at the emperor's retreat at Chengde on September 14. Macartney did not kowtow but just knelt as the emperor was carried into the room. He presented Qianlong with a gold box containing a letter from King George III, which lavished praise on the emperor. This was followed by a ceremonial exchange of gifts and a sumptuous banquet.

The Chinese rebuffal

Regardless of Macartney's hopes, however, Qianlong had no plans to depart from the status quo on trade. A week after receiving George III's letter, Qianlong sent a reply to Macartney—reportedly drafted three days before the envoy had even arrived. In it, he made clear that China would continue to treat all foreign nations as inferior and would not countenance a British ambassador at court. China, Qianlong wrote, had little need for British products.

▷ **English pottery**
This scent bottle was part of the sample of British goods taken to China by the Macartney Mission.

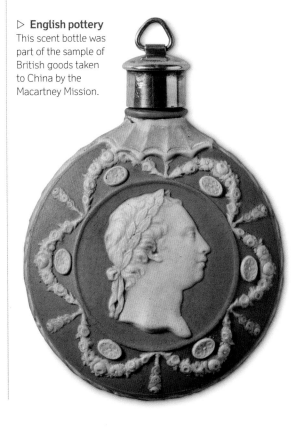

The Opium Trade

Imports and the rise of addiction in imperial China

Unable to stem the import of opium from British-controlled poppy fields in India, China faced a devastating spread of opium addiction. Attempts to control the flow of the drug ultimately led to war with Britain in 1839.

Opium was introduced to China by Turkish and Arab traders in the late 6th or early 7th century. For many years, the Chinese used the drug in limited quantities for medicinal purposes, such as treating pain and diarrhea, and as an aphrodisiac. However, in the 18th century, more and more people across China began to use it mainly for its narcotic effects, often smoking it as pure opium sap in pipes.

Imports and profits

Portuguese traders had been importing opium into China from the 16th century, and by the early 18th century, the British had also discovered the tremendous profits to be made from its sale. This business was conducted by the British East India Company, which had been founded by royal charter in 1600 specifically to conduct trade in Asia and India. In 1729, the company imported 200 chests of opium (each weighing 170 lb, or 77 kg) into China; this figure rose to 1,000 chests in 1773. By this time, however, the company was in debt. This was caused in part by Britain's growing demand for Chinese tea—for which the company had to pay in silver—and China's reluctance to buy British goods in return, which resulted in a large trade deficit.

Overcoming restrictions

The East India Company determined to balance its books by increasing its sales of opium in China. It invested in opium production, creating a monopoly on buying the drug in Bengal, India, and became so successful that opium soon replaced cotton as its main import into China. By 1838, the company was bringing 40,000 chests of opium per year into China, despite attempts by the Chinese emperors to exclude the drug. The Yongzheng Emperor first outlawed the sale and use of opium in 1729, and in 1796 the Jiaqing Emperor banned its import and cultivation. In 1813, he outlawed opium smoking, making it punishable by 100 blows and the wearing of a heavy wooden collar for a month.

The East India Company, however, found ways to circumvent the Chinese import bans. They passed their opium on to private traders, who were licensed

△ **Opium pipes**
The style of pipe used by opium smokers reflected their wealth. Designs ranged from simple bamboo pipes to elaborately ornamented vessels made from porcelain and cloisonné enamel.

◁ **Import and supply**
In this drawing, opium—imported as rolled balls—is unpacked from crates and weighed prior to its sale.

△ **Opium in court**
Opium use was widespread in Chinese society. This scene, imagined by a Western artist, depicts the empress (left) with a concubine and a servant, both of whom are holding an opium pipe.

to carry goods to China from trading posts in Calcutta. At the Chinese border, the traders sold the opium to smugglers and returned the silver and gold they were paid to the company. The funds were used to buy tea, porcelain, and other Chinese goods for sale in Britain.

A destructive addiction

By 1830, around 10 percent of the Chinese population was addicted to opium. Use of the drug was a direct cause of misery and poverty, and the opium trade

spawned powerful criminal gangs, such as the Triad Society, which used bribery and corruption to maintain their destructive influence.

The economy, too, was strangled as gold and silver flowed out of China to pay for the country's increasing addiction. Moreover, merchants began to use opium as a substitute for cash, and officials found that growing opium poppies could help them meet their tax quotas. By the mid-1800s, domestic production of opium in China had rocketed and many people depended on the drug for their livelihood.

In 1839, attempts to address China's growing problem by legalizing opium were rejected and even tougher sanctions against the import of the drug were introduced. These measures, however, would soon bring the country into open conflict with Western powers in the two Opium Wars (see pp. 274–275 and pp. 280–281).

"**Opium** has a **harm**. **Opium** is a **poison**, **undermining** our good **customs** and **morality**."

THE JIAQING EMPEROR, IMPERIAL EDICT BANNING THE USE OF OPIUM, 1813

The First Opium War

China enters conflict with Britain over trade rights

△ **Naval superiority**
The British warship HMS *Nemesis* destroys Chinese war junks on January 7, 1841, during the First Opium War. *Nemesis* was an iron-hulled vessel armed with 32-pounder guns for which the Chinese vessels were no match.

Between 1839 and 1842, China was defeated in a war against the British. The conflict destroyed the Canton System, gave Britain a base in Hong Kong and access to five treaty ports, and revealed growing weaknesses in the Qing regime.

By the early 1830s, British merchants were weary of the trade restrictions imposed by China. Factory owners needed to find new markets for the products of industrialization and put pressure on the Crown to end the monopoly held by the East India Company and open the way for other traders. However, the free trade they demanded would necessitate the abolition of the highly regulated Canton System (see p. 265) in China. Diplomacy had failed to secure concessions, so Britain began to consider military action.

China, at this time, was in the grip of opium addiction and beset by the poverty and corruption caused by illegal trade in the drug (see pp. 272–273). In a new attempt to address the problem, the Daoguang Emperor sent an experienced official—Lin Zexu—to Guangzhou (Canton) with instructions to stamp out opium smuggling and use.

Lin acted decisively. He confiscated opium pipes and arrested around 1,600 Chinese involved in the opium business. He sent a letter to Britain's Queen Victoria,

HONG KONG

Blessed with a deep, sheltered natural harbor that gave the island its name, Hong Kong (meaning "fragrant harbor") was formally ceded to the British by the Treaty of Nanjing (1842). Originally home to a small fishing community, by the 1860s Hong Kong had been turned by investment and migration into a major trading center. More territory was ceded to the British in 1860 (southern Kowloon peninsula) and 1898 (the New Territories). In 1997, all of Hong Kong reverted to Chinese sovereignty.

in which he criticized her for allowing the opium trade to flourish in China while in Britain the drug was banned for its harmful effects. Lin also acted against the British by confiscating 20,000 chests of opium from their Guangzhou warehouses and tipping all 1,400 tons (1,270 metric tons) of the drug into the sea.

Outbreak of hostilities

Lin's actions gave the British the excuse they wanted for war. Fighting officially began in November 1839 when the British HMS *Volage* and HMS *Hyacinth* opened fire on Chinese war junks blockading Guangzhou. The following year, a British Expeditionary Force arrived in China to demand compensation for the lost opium. It quickly occupied the port of Dinghai and captured the forts guarding the entrance to the Pearl River, destroying the Chinese fleet in the process.

The British fully occupied Guangzhou in May 1841; soon after, the Chinese agreed to pay six million silver dollars in reparations and to cede Hong Kong (see box, above). The British, however, decided to push for more, taking town after town until, by July 1842, they threatened the city of Nanjing.

The war ended in August 1842 with the Treaty of Nanjing—later referred to by China as the first of several "unequal" treaties. Under its terms, China was to pay 21 million silver dollars in compensation; Hong

△ **Drug disposal**
Commissioner Lin Zexu (center) oversees the destruction of opium at Guangzhou in 1839.

Kong was formally ceded to Britain; the five treaty ports of Guangzhou, Xiamen, Fuzhou, Shanghai, and Ningbo were opened to British merchants; and trade tariffs were fixed and were to be adjusted only with the agreement of the British. Even greater concessions followed: Britain, along with the US, was granted "extraterritoriality," so their citizens were subject to their own country's laws while in China; and Britain was given "most favored nation" status, meaning that privileges extended to other countries would also be given to Britain.

Not only had China committed to free trade, but it had given away the ability to determine its own taxes on imports or favor one trading partner over another. It was a humiliating defeat for the Qing that showed not only the empire's military weakness in the face of modern European firepower but also its lack of understanding of the new world of trading. Anti-Qing feeling in the empire began to grow and soon tipped into rebellion.

◁ **The Treaty of Nanjing**
The treaty was signed on August 24, 1842, aboard HMS *Cornwallis*, which was anchored at Nanjing. Later that year, the treaty was ratified by the Daoguang Emperor and Queen Victoria.

"**[T]rade** to ... **China** ought to be ... **opened** to the **unrestrained enterprise** ... of this country."

MEMBER OF PARLIAMENT FOR LIVERPOOL, ADVOCATING FREE TRADE, 1812

Ceremonial Splendor

Qing court armor

Qing court armor was highly decorated and, by the end of the dynasty, largely worn for ceremonial purposes. It was modeled on the *dingjia*, or brigandine, armor introduced in China in the 8th century CE as parade armor for the emperor's guards, which became more widespread from the 13th century. *Dingjia* armor (literally "nail armor") comprised narrow overlapping steel plates that were riveted inside layers of thick cloth, leaving the rivet heads clearly visible on the outside. By the Ming period, the *dingjia* was favored by Chinese army officers for its combination of beauty and protection. However, the use of heavy armor in battle declined under the Qing, as the introduction of more modern weaponry gradually made it obsolete. Nonetheless, *dingjia* armor continued to be used as an important status symbol that marked the wearer out as a member of the Qing dynasty's administrative and ruling class.

Qing armor

The Qing adapted one particular style of Ming-era *dingjia* and standardized the armor across the empire. They adopted a two-piece style that combined separate body armor and an ankle-length armored skirt and abandoned the knee- or shin-length single-breasted coat generally favored by the Ming. The Manchu were expert horsemen, and the two-piece armor gave them more mobility on horseback, even though it left the

backs of their legs exposed. Qing helmets had a distinct ridge that distinguished them from the smoother Ming-style helmet; they retained decorative feathers, including kingfisher feathers, but abandoned the use of helmet flags.

The Qing also extended the face and neck protection (known as the aventail) to cover the throat. The shoulders and upper arms were protected by pauldrons, and Qing armor also included large underarm protectors. In the examples shown here, the metal plates are visible at the shoulder and elbow and are engraved and brightly polished to complement the armor's gold embroidered dragon and wave design. The final Qing innovation to the *dingjia* was the addition of flared *ma ti xiu* ("horse-hoof cuffs") to the body armor's sleeves; these helped protect the wearer from cold and injury.

The armor was completed by a pair of cloth or leather riding boots known as *xue*. These had flat heels but were wide and deep enough to prevent the foot slipping through the stirrup and becoming stuck. They were traditionally black, with a white sole. Qing horse armor, saddles, and tack were styled to match the warrior's armor but lacked the metal plates. Indeed, by the late Qing period, on most ceremonial armor, metal plates had become merely decorative elements on a court costume.

△ **Words of wisdom**
This helmet is decorated with Tibetan Lantsa characters made of gilt copper. Lantsa was a writing system often used for sacred writings, such as the Buddhist Sanskrit mantra seen here.

A decorative helmet addition with kingfisher feathers

◁ **Courtly armor**
Celebrated for both its beauty and its level of protection, this ornate armor went on to represent the wearer's importance within the Qing dynasty's upper classes.

Gilt copper script

Horse hood made of studded cloth

Polished and engraved metal plates enhance armor's design

This single-edged blade is a *peidao*, meaning "waist sword"

△ **Expert horseman**
To give the illusion of protective armor, Manchu horses were dressed in thick, layered cloth with visible rivet heads; however, their armor did not have steel plates encased within.

Saddle with gold, coral, and ivory decoration

△ **Ornate equipment**
Although they were visible only when the horse was not being ridden, ceremonial saddles were highly decorated to match the rider's armor. The colors and details found on the saddle indicated the rider's social status.

The Taiping Rebellion
The beginning of the end of the Qing dynasty

For 14 years, a huge anti-Manchu rebellion raged across a great swathe of China. It led to the destruction of 600 cities and the deaths of some 20 to 30 million people and left the Qing dynasty permanently weakened.

The Qing faced several rebellions after taking control of the empire in the 17th century. Revolts by cults such as the White Lotus (1796–1804) proved difficult to suppress, but the 14-year-long Taiping Rebellion (1850–1864) posed the greatest threat to Qing rule.

The Taiping Rebellion had its roots in southern China, a troubled area where bandits and opium traders operated openly. Not only was opium addiction rife, but peasants were being forced to pay ever higher rents for their land and inflated taxes to the corrupt Qing administration. Anti-Manchu feeling was rife, fueled by the perception that the Qing had betrayed the Chinese people by failing to contain the foreign threat.

The Taiping Rebellion was led by Hong Xiuquan, a convert to Christianity who believed he was the brother of Jesus and that the Manchu were demons who had to be destroyed. By 1850, he had attracted 20,000 armed followers to his base in Guangxi, and, on January 1, 1851, he declared himself ruler of a new dynasty, the Taiping Tianguo ("Heavenly Kingdom of Great Peace"). The revolt against the Qing then began in earnest. City after city was captured as the rebels (called Taipings) grew in number and moved north and east. By 1853, they had reached the heavily defended city of Wuchang on the Yangzi River, which they took after just 20 days. From Wuchang, the rebels moved east toward Nanjing. There they defeated a

▽ **Ruizhou retaken**
This painting shows the Qing Imperial Army, dressed in blue and red uniforms, retaking the provincial capital of Ruizhou City from forces of the rebellion army in 1857.

▷ **Taiping seal**
Pictured here is the royal seal of the Taiping Tianguo and its leader, Hong Xiuquan. The Taipings made effective use of printed placards and posters to disseminate their propaganda.

40,000-strong Manchu banner force, taking the city and massacring all the Manchu who had not died in the battle, including women and children.

A new capital for a new dynasty

Nanjing (renamed Tianjing) became the capital of the Heavenly Kingdom and the site of a utopian social experiment based on the sharing of property and the equality of men and women. Buildings were seized and turned into *guan* (institutions), each one dedicated to a particular function, such as baking, weaving, and health care. The Taipings outlawed foot-binding (see pp. 288–289) and prostitution, but their attempts to segregate men and women were resisted. They destroyed the city's Daoist and Buddhist temples in a bid to convert the population to Hong's teachings.

The Taipings kept hold of Nanjing for 10 years and made numerous attempts to expand the borders of the Heavenly Kingdom. They made some gains in the upper Yangzi valley, but their attempts to capture Beijing in 1855 and Shanghai in 1860 failed.

The Chinese gentry were increasingly appalled by the Taipings' threat to the Confucian order. With the government's forces in disarray, they began to organize local militias, such as that under the leadership of Zeng Guofan. Between 1856 and 1858,

HONG XIUQUAN

Born in Huadu, Guangzhou in 1814, Hong Xiuquan was an intelligent boy who was sponsored by his village to study for the civil service exams. His repeated failure to pass elicited a mental breakdown. He came to believe that he was Jesus's brother and that Christianity was China's authentic religion, predating Confucius and the imperial system. Fueled by his faith and strong anti-Manchu sentiments, he led the Taiping Rebellion until his death.

Zeng's 120,000-strong Hunan Army retook most of Jiangxi while the Hubei Army (under another official named Hu Linyi) recaptured Wuchang. The Hunan Army then besieged Nanjing. In June 1864, Hong died, and the following month the Hunan Army entered Nanjing and slaughtered its inhabitants.

The Taiping Rebellion was over, but the ramifications for the Qing were immense. It was the Han Chinese Hunan Army rather than the Manchu-led Imperial Army that defeated the Taipings, and this ended Manchu dominance of the military and positions of power. The Qing were forced to give the provinces more autonomy and never fully regained a secure hold on the empire.

▽ **Zeng Guofan**
An exceptionally talented Confucian scholar and strategist, Zeng Guofan recaptured the Taiping capital, Nanjing, and helped save the Qing empire from the Taiping rebels.

"The **land** is for **all** to **till**, the **food** for **all** to **eat**.... **Inequality** shall exist **nowhere**...."

FROM *THE LAND SYSTEM OF THE HEAVENLY KINGDOM*, 1853

陣龍調單   海口礮   千里眼看虛實

雷 水

The Second Opium War

The British and French defeat the Qing

The Western powers, determined to gain greater trade concessions from China, engineered and won a conflict with the Qing. The rulers of China were left weakened and vulnerable to foreign influence and internal dissent.

In fall 1856, while struggling to contain the Taiping Rebellion (see pp. 278–279), the Qing became embroiled in a Second Opium War with Western powers seeking to extend their reach in China. The British were unhappy with the terms of trade allowed by the Treaty of Nanjing (see pp. 274–275) and once again pushed for a formal exchange of ambassadors, a permanent residence for their ambassador in Beijing, and more treaty ports. Tensions escalated in July 1856, when Ye Mingchen, governor of Liangguang (an area that encompassed Guangdong and Guangxi provinces)

forcefully rejected Britain's repeated demands that opium imports be legalized. Three months later, an incident aboard a British-registered ship, HMS *Arrow*, in Guangzhou (Canton) provided the pretext for the British to begin military action.

According to the British consul in Guangzhou, Harry Parkes, Guangzhou officials had boarded the *Arrow* to arrest its Chinese crew for importing opium. Parkes claimed that the officials tore down the Union Jack flag, and he deliberately portrayed the incident as a major insult to the British Crown. His account

△ **Battle at Dagu Forts**
The Dagu Forts were built in 1816 to protect Tianjin and Beijing from attack. Anglo-French and Chinese forces are shown here in combat at the forts during the Second Opium War.

"You can scarcely **imagine** the **beauty** and **magnificence** of the **places** we **burnt**."

BRITISH OFFICER CHARLES GEORGE GORDON ON THE DESTRUCTION OF THE SUMMER PALACE, 1860

served its purpose: British warships were sent up the Pearl River, where they blasted Commissioner Ye's compound, breached the city walls, and destroyed more than 20 Chinese war junks before returning to Hong Kong (then a British colony) in January 1857.

The Treaty of Tianjin

Later that year, the French also decided to press the Chinese for more concessions and joined the conflict. In December, a 6,000-strong Anglo-French force under the command of Lord Elgin, the British High Commissioner to China, and Baron Gros captured Guangzhou and pushed northward toward Beijing. In April 1858, gunboats captured the Dagu Forts on the Haihe River, and the city of Tianjin fell to the Western alliance. Following this defeat, in June the Chinese had little option but to sign the Treaty of Tianjin. This gave the British and the French, along with the Russians and the US, the right to a permanent ambassador in Beijing and free travel for missionaries and merchants in the country. China paid reparations to the victors, agreed to open 10 more treaty ports, and legalized the import of opium.

DESTRUCTION OF THE OLD SUMMER PALACE (YUANMING YUAN)

Lord Elgin ordered the destruction of the Old Summer Palace in response to the news that a British delegation trying to negotiate the Qing's surrender had been imprisoned and tortured. It was a shameful act of cultural vandalism. British and French soldiers looted the vast palace of its priceless treasures of porcelain, jade, textiles, gold, and bronze (such as this striking statue of a bull's head from the Qianlong period). The soldiers then set the entire 1.5 sq mile (3.8 sq km) site on fire; it burned for three days. Many of the palace's looted treasures can now be found in museums around the world.

Britain ostensibly got what it wanted. However, despite having signed the treaty, China was resistant to some of its main clauses and refused to accept its terms or ratify it. In June 1859, the conflict resumed after British forces who were escorting diplomats to Beijing were refused passage up the Haihe River. In a surprising defeat, the British were forced back from the Dagu Forts with heavy losses. Nonetheless, an Anglo-French force returned in August 1860, pushed its way upriver and took Beijing itself. The Qing emperor Xianfeng and his court fled to Chengde, and Elgin ordered the destruction of the Old Summer Palace, the residence of the Qing rulers. British and French soldiers looted the palace's treasures and then set the site on fire (see box, above).

In October 1860, the emperor's brother Yixin signed the Beijing Convention, ending the war. The convention ratified the terms of the Treaty of Tianjin, doubled the reparations due to the British, ceded the lease of Kowloon to the British, and added Tianjin to the list of treaty ports. China's defeat in the Second Opium War left the Qing empire wide open to foreign powers, but it also sparked a period of self-reflection and reform that resulted in the Self-Strengthening Movement (see pp. 284–285).

◁ **A resolute official**
An eminent official during the Qing dynasty, Ye Mingchen, shown in this portrait, was famous for his refusal to yield to Britain's demands concerning opium imports.

The Treaty System

Foreign influence and a loss of Chinese sovereignty

From 1842 until the early 20th century, China's foreign relations were governed by a series of treaties that opened up trade to overseas powers and allowed them to extend control over areas deep within China itself.

The Treaty of Nanjing, secured by the British in 1842 as an end to the First Opium War, paved the way for a series of agreements that radically reshaped China's trade. As ever more of its ports were opened to foreigners, China was forced to make its bountiful resources accessible to Western interests (see p. 275). The Treaty of Nanjing gave the British access to multiple Chinese ports (Xiamen, Fuzhou, Shanghai,

> By 1917, the treaty system had opened 92 Chinese ports to foreign trade and residence.

Ningbo, and Guangzhou) and set tariffs at 5 percent. The British were later granted the right of extraterritoriality, which allowed British citizens to be governed by British law on Chinese soil, and of "most favored nation," which meant they would automatically gain any rights granted to other nations.

The US and France swiftly extracted their own treaties—of Wangxia (1843) and Huangpu (1844)—and Norway and Sweden followed suit in 1847. The treaties were disastrous for China, stripping it of its ability to set protective tariffs or manage its own foreign policy through the use of trade privileges.

Foreign privileges

More treaty ports were opened after 1860, when France, Britain, and Russia negotiated the end to the Second Opium War (see pp. 280–281). Over the next decades, some 50 ports were opened, allowing yet more countries access to China. In many of the ports, parcels of land (concessions) were leased to foreign powers, which divided them into lots for their merchants to develop. Each concession was governed by a consul and its own municipal government, which meant that there were often several areas of sovereignty in one port. To remedy this confusing situation in Shanghai, in 1854, Britain, France, and the US placed their concessions under a single municipal council. The French dropped out, but the Anglo-American Shanghai International Settlement dominated Shanghai until the 1930s. Many of the treaty ports became international cities, characterized by a business district known as the "bund," and Western-style entertainment. These thriving cities attracted people from across China and created a new class of wealthy Chinese agents and businessmen. They were also hotbeds of political activism: Sun Yat-sen's Revive China Society led a failed uprising in Guangzhou in 1895, while the Chinese Communist Party was founded in Shanghai in 1921.

Although some countries relinquished their rights in China earlier (the Russians, for example, left in 1917), the main beneficiaries of the treaty system—notably Britain, France, and the US—held out until World War II, and vestiges of the system remained as late as 1949.

△ **Western ambitions**
Xie Zantai's cartoon *The Situation in the Far East* shows Western powers closing in on China at the end of the 19th century.

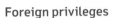

◁ **Treaty-port stamps**
The Chinese treaty ports issued a series of postage stamps between 1865 and 1899. Stamps from 1894 (left) and 1896 (right) are shown here.

▷ **The Shanghai Bund**
This view of Shanghai's business district c. 1890 shows the port teeming with people. A treaty port from the 1860s to the 1930s, it was a center of Western power in China.

△ **Advances in the army**
Qing officers are pictured here posing at the Nanjing Jinling Arsenal, which was built by Li Hongzhang in 1865. Other arsenals were built around the same time in an attempt to industrialize China's military forces.

Self-Strengthening

An attempt to restore the power of an exhausted state

Between 1862 and 1895, China set about rebuilding its military and transforming its economy by drawing on Western technical expertise. This initiative, known as "self-strengthening," had a limited impact on China's fortunes.

In 1860, the Qing government was weak. The Taiping rebels (see pp. 278–279) still held Nanjing, and foreign powers had extracted costly concessions in return for ending the Second Opium War. The emperor, Xianfeng, was in exile and would never return to Beijing. He died the following year and his five-year-old son, Zaichun, became emperor. A regency government, led by the boy's mother, Dowager Empress Cixi (see pp. 286–287), and his uncle, Prince Gong, took control in in what was called the Tongzhi

Restoration. They began a "self-strengthening" program that was designed to modernize both the economy and the military—they were hopeful that these measures would restore the wealth and dignity of the earlier Qing regime.

China and the outside world

The first step in the self-strengthening initiative was to secure peace with foreigners in China in order, as Prince Gong put it, to restore the "exhausted power"

◁ **Chinese weaponry**
The Portuguese introduced matchlock rifles into China in the 16th century. Chinese gunsmiths refined the design and began manufacturing them in large quantities the following century. They remained in use throughout the 19th century.

Serpentine—curved lever with a clamp that holds a slow-burning fuse

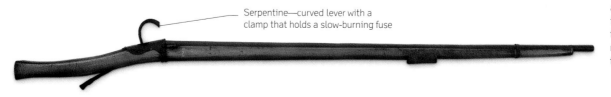

"Use the barbarians' superior techniques to control the barbarians."

WEI YUAN, CHINESE SCHOLAR AND THEORIST, c. 1842

of the state. Gong established new bodies to oversee China's foreign policy and to regulate trade. He also created the Tongwen Guan (School of Combined Learning) in Beijing to teach Western languages and to translate key works on science, politics, and social theory. China's first diplomatic mission visited London, Berlin, and the US from 1868, and by the 1880s, China had many overseas legations. These helped improve its knowledge of the wider world. But officials were often resistant to the idea of any attempt to emulate the West, seeing it as an affront to China's long-held and distinct sense of identity.

Building industry

The push for industrialization was mainly driven by men who had gained regional power bases during the war against the Taiping—including Li Hongzhang, Zeng Guofan, and Zuo Zongtang. At first, they focused on developing military industries: arsenals were built to produce weapons and to construct warships.

The next phase of industrialization focused on infrastructure. In 1877, the Kaiping coal mine opened, and by 1880 it was connected to the Machine Factory in Tianjin by China's first railroad track. The first telegraph network followed in 1879. Cotton and textile mills were opened in Shanghai and Guangzhou, and a major ironworks was built in Wuhan in 1890. However, these government-supervised enterprises were constrained by the bureaucratic inefficiency that blighted the empire. The Chinese powers were also reluctant to reinvest profits and make industries

▽ **Rocket of China**
China's first-ever locomotive, the "Rocket of China," was built secretly between 1880 and 1881 in the Tangshan workshops of the Kaiping coal mine in Hebei province, northern China.

△ **Spearheading reform**
Li Hongzhang spearheaded China's modernization movement in the early 1860s. This portrait of the eminent statesman was taken by the Scottish photographer John Thomson in 1871.

self-sustaining or to seek the foreign investment needed to build the type of railroad networks that had fast-tracked the success of other nations. Although reforms continued, China remained tied to many of its traditional principles and social organization—it was not ready to embrace the cultural and social changes that could have secured industrialization and a place in the modern world.

REFORMS IN THE MILITARY

China's armed forces were strengthened by the introduction of modern military education. A naval school was established at Fuzhou in 1866, and technical and officer training schools soon followed. Officers were also sent to Britain, France, and Germany to study subjects such as mathematics, science, and navigation. China developed far stricter officer training that covered a wide range of content and was based on practical experience. It represented a move away from learning about obsolete weapons, such as the bow.

Image conscious
Cixi invited Westerners to paint her, showing off her wealth and fashions. This depiction by Dutch artist Hubert Vos shows Cixi wearing nail protectors (see p. 292), worn by women to indicate high social status.

Empress Dowager Cixi

The woman who ruled behind the throne

Empress Dowager Cixi presided over the last half century of imperial rule in China. She was pitiless in her pursuit of power but unswervingly dedicated to Chinese growth and independence and the survival of the empire.

Born in 1835, the daughter of a Manchu official, the future Empress Dowager Cixi was sent to the imperial court in 1851. Selected as a concubine for Emperor Xianfeng, she moved into the Forbidden City, where she became known as Consort Yi. Her birth name was never recorded, but "Yi" was an honorific meaning "virtuous." Her status at court remained low until, in 1856, she gave birth to Zaichun, the only male heir to the throne—even then, she ranked below Xianfeng's favored consort, Empress Zhen.

When Xianfeng died in 1861, however, Zaichun succeeded to the throne as Emperor Tongzhi; Yi took the title of Empress Dowager, as well as the honorific name Cixi, meaning "motherly and auspicious." Aged 25, she outmaneuvered the regents appointed to rule on Tongzhi's behalf, and—working alongside former empress Zhen and Tongzhi's uncle Prince Gong—she seized control of the empire in a bloodless coup.

A force for reform

Although she is often characterized as a conservative ruler and an obstacle to Chinese reforms, Cixi did make moves toward modernization. She sought to restore Chinese independence and unity after the disasters of foreign invasion and internal rebellion. She appointed new officials based on merit, tackling the corruption and nepotism within the government. She also successfully boosted the Chinese economy with reforms. The dowager empress notably hated Westerners but nonetheless oversaw a Westernization movement that included the construction of arms and munitions factories, buying warships for China's navy, building railroads, digging mines, and advancing Chinese industrialization. She did all this while governing from behind a screen and without entering the emperor's section of the Forbidden City.

Ruthless moves

Cixi's support for the Boxer Rebellion in 1900 (see pp. 298–299) proved a disaster. But even then, she kept the allegiance of most of her people. Cixi held power through intelligence, will, and ruthlessness; she may have even arranged the death of her son Zaichun in 1873, after he came of age, so that she could replace him with another child ruler, her nephew Zaitian. When, as the Guangxu Emperor, he became her enemy, she made him a prisoner in his own palace and ruled in his stead. Cixi's final years of rule were dedicated to a thorough drive toward reform. Her final act before her death in 1908 was to order the assassination of Guangxu by poison so that her candidate, the infant Puyi, could become emperor.

△ **Cixi's ornate robe**
Cixi set a fashion for bold robe design in court. Obsessive about clothing, she once took 56 trunks of possessions with her on a short trip.

▽ **Meeting Westerners**
Cixi hosted tea parties for Western women in her private quarters, gleaning political information for her Westernization movement.

Women in Society

A history of female roles in late imperial China

Women's position in Chinese society had been established in the first millennium BCE; classic texts such as the *Book of Changes* (*Yijing*, see pp. 54–55) reinforced the idea that a woman's role was to support her husband, and in the Zhou era, girls would begin studying the Three Obediences and Four Virtues at the age of 10, which taught them how to speak, act, dress, and work to please their future husbands.

As Confucianism took hold in China, women were expected to live according to Confucian principles. These were laid out in texts such as *Admonitions for Women* by Ban Zhao, a female Han dynasty scholar. Confucian principles said that women should obey their father, then their husband, then their sons after their husband's death, and that they should treat their husband's parents with the same respect and duty they showed to their own parents. From the

Song dynasty onward, neo-Confucianism tightened the definitions of acceptable female behavior. Wives were expected to have no desire to own property and to feel no jealousy about their husband's concubines.

Chastity and control

Neo-Confucianism created a cult of widow chastity. Widows were discouraged from remarrying and encouraged instead to live lives of "virtuous chastity," regardless of whether they had been left impoverished by their husband's death. They were criticized for returning with their dowry (and any accumulated wealth) to their family after their husband's death. Later laws ensured that a woman would forfeit her property if she remarried or returned to her family after being widowed. The Song period also saw the rise of footbinding—a rite of passage that symbolized

△ **Consorts and concubines**
In this portrait from a 19th-century handpainted album on silk, Xiao, consort of Emperor Yang of the Sui dynasty, is attending to her appearance. In ancient China, the number of consorts and concubines an emperor had was an indicator of his wealth, prestige, and power.

△ **Sanctioned entertainment**
Approved leisure activities for women in imperial China included the board game *weiqi*, a game of strategy. This Ming dynasty painting shows a game of *weiqi* being played in the Forbidden City. Such pursuits, it was thought, would help prevent women from becoming gluttonous and slothful.

△ **Ming musicians**
Female musicians are shown in this Ming dynasty painting playing the moon guitar (left), the zither (center), and the Chinese lute (right). Although severely restricted from participation in many realms, some women became musicians and educators.

"Loyal subjects do not **serve two masters** ... **chaste women** do not serve two husbands."

SONG DYNASTY WRITER SIMA GUANG (1019–1086)

young girls' obedience and marriageability but also severely limited their physical mobility. The practice reached a peak under the Ming. Under the Ming and Qing dynasties, chastity was rewarded. In the 18th century, the Qing rulers bestowed honors on those who chose not to sell off their widowed daughters-in-law—who could fetch a high price (paid by the new husband's family)—and instead supported their chastity. The Qing sponsored the construction of memorial arches to chaste widows; and single women, too, were canonized as "chastity martyrs" if they died by suicide rather than lose their virginity.

While some women were being celebrated for their chastity, others were earning a living as prostitutes and courtesans. In the Ming period, Yangzhou became known as a hub for the sale of young women, into either concubinage or prostitution. In his *Reminiscences*

in *Dreams of Tao An* (*Taoan mengyi*) the writer Zhang Dai described the experience of visiting Yangzhou brothels in the last decades of the Ming dynasty. The girls would be presented to clients by matchmakers, displaying their submission—the most attractive had bound feet that made no sound when walking, shy eyes, delicate hands, and youthfulness.

Better lives

The Qing eventually made moves to improve the lot of women. In 1662, the Kangxi Emperor attempted to ban footbinding, and it became possible for concubines to be promoted to the status of wife. Social changes also gave women some increased freedom. Reformists argued that female education was important, and by the 19th century, some women had begun to carve out positions as respected writers.

△ **Transgressing gender roles**
Born in 1775, Ching Shih, pictured here, married a pirate captain on condition she could take over his boat on his death. Thereupon, she caused mayhem at sea, engaging in conflict with the British, the Portuguese, and the Qing dynasty, among others.

△ **Manchu women**
This photograph, taken in the late 1860s, showcases the fashion and elaborate hairstyles of two Manchu women. Under the Qing dynasty, Manchu women were forbidden from binding their feet, although some took to wearing platform or pointed shoes to make their feet appear fashionably smaller.

△ **Tied to the home**
One of the worst manifestations of women's oppression in the imperial era was the practice of footbinding, whereby girls' feet were bound so that the arches finally broke and the toes turned under, preventing full mobility. This image, c. 1870, shows a woman with bound feet.

Phoenix Headdress

An empress's crowning glory

The phoenix was associated with empresses and empress dowagers from the 2nd century BCE onward, and the phoenix crown (fengguan) was first introduced during the Tang dynasty (618–907 CE). Phoenix crowns were worn by Chinese empresses on ceremonial and official occasions. They were decorated with intricate sculptures of gold dragons—which represented the emperor—and blue phoenixes that indicated the status of the wearer. For the emperor's wives and concubines, and the wives of princes, the number of dragons and phoenixes (or pheasants) directly corresponded to their rank. The headdresses of other noblewomen could be adorned only with pearls and precious stones.

Crown designs

Statues from the Ming dynasty showing figures wearing the crown and clothing of the empress reveal that, during the Hongwu and Yongle periods (which spanned from 1368 to 1424), the crowns bore nine dragons and four phoenixes. By the reign of the Ming Wanli Emperor, between 1573 and 1620, the crowns had become even more elaborate. Only four phoenix crowns have survived from the Ming period. All were found in 1957, during excavations of the underground palaces of the Dingling Mausoleum at the foot of Tianshou Mountain in the Changping district. The mausoleum was the final resting place of the Wanli

Emperor and the empresses Xiaoduan and Xiaojing. Among the grave goods were red lacquer caskets that held the four crowns: two belonging to Empress Xiaoduan, including one with nine dragons and nine phoenixes, and two belonging to Empresss Xiaojing.

Feathered beauty

The nine dragon, nine phoenix crown of Empress Xiaoduan (pictured right) is 11 in (27 cm) high and weighs more than 5 lb (2 kg), meaning it would have been difficult to wear for long periods of time. The crown is built around a frame of lacquered bamboo lined with green silk. Its dragons are made from gold wire, woven and soldered into shape, and it is decorated with hundreds of inlaid gemstones, including more than 5,000 pearls. The phoenixes are constructed from a base of silver gilt, edged with gold wire and inlaid with kingfisher feathers. The use of kingfisher feathers was an ancient Chinese decorative method known as diancui (literally "dotting with kingfishers"). The same technique was used to create the cloud- and flower-shaped ornaments on the crown.

On each side of the rear of the crown are three moving fan sections. Shaped like wings, decorated with gold filigree dragons and inlaid pearls, jade, rubies, and sapphires, these ornaments would have swung outward as the empress walked, creating a spectacular display.

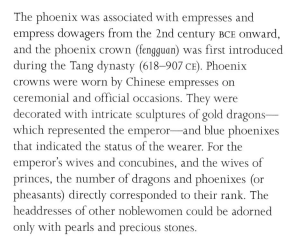

Moving fan sections enhance the crown's splendor

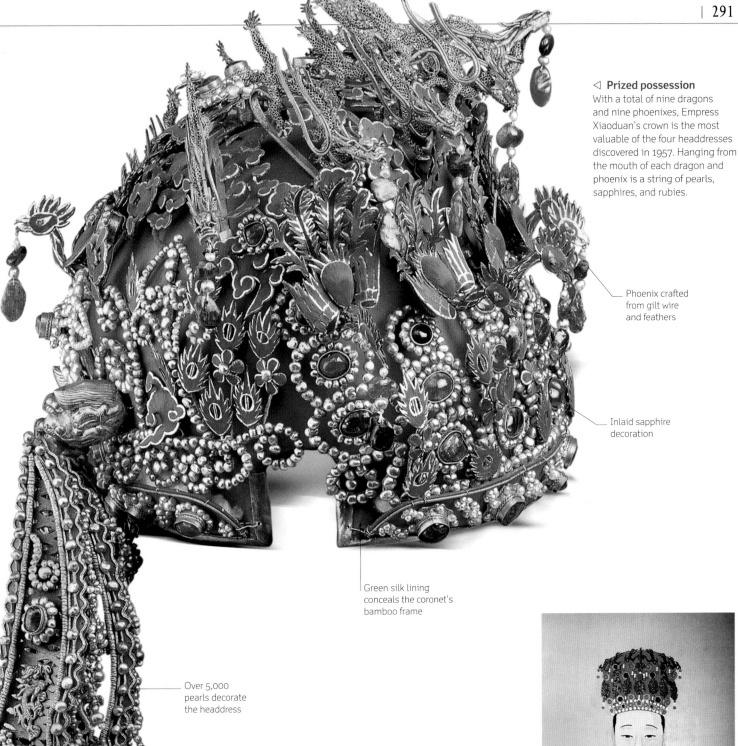

◁ **Prized possession**
With a total of nine dragons and nine phoenixes, Empress Xiaoduan's crown is the most valuable of the four headdresses discovered in 1957. Hanging from the mouth of each dragon and phoenix is a string of pearls, sapphires, and rubies.

Phoenix crafted from gilt wire and feathers

Inlaid sapphire decoration

Green silk lining conceals the coronet's bamboo frame

Over 5,000 pearls decorate the headdress

"She was, from her wedding day, permanently **encased** in **palatial pomp and comfort.**"

HISTORIAN RAY HUANG ON EMPRESS XIAODUAN, 1981

△ **Enduring empress**
Crowned by the Wanli Emperor at just 13 years old, Empress Xiaoduan served the emperor for more than 40 years. She was the longest-reigning empress in Chinese history.

Status Symbols

Adornments of Ming and Qing China

The Ming and Qing periods are known for beautiful, ornate jewelry and clothing that reflected the skills of Chinese craftsmen using silk and precious metals. However, many adornments served a purpose beyond aesthetics—they symbolized the wearer's rank or were worn only for a specific occasion.

Tassels with symbols of immortality and longevity

▽ Cap of office
This semi-formal winter hat (*jiguan*) from the Qing dynasty is decorated with red tassels, a plume, and a glass button, which indicates that the wearer was a fifth rank official.

▷ Concubine's hat
Made from silk and pearls, this hat would have been worn only by imperial concubines of the Qing court.

△ Qing headdress
This 19th-century headdress is made of gilt metal, kingfisher feathers, red wool, and glass. It is crowned by a phoenix, symbolizing the empress, as well as other auspicious symbols.

▷ Belt buckle
Decorative buckles were status symbols in Qing China. This jade buckle is carved with a dragon motif.

Scenes painted on folded paper

▷ Circular fan
Carried by both men and women, decorated circular fans have a long history in China. This example was made around 1840.

Rigid handle made of carved black lacquer

△ High heel
The "horse-hoof" shoes worn by Manchu women made them taller and encouraged them to walk with a free, confident, swaying motion.

More than 6 in (15 cm) long

◁ Folding fan
The circular fan was more popular in China until the Ming dynasty, when folding fans from Japan came into fashion. This mid-19th-century fan is made from paper, wood, and ivory.

▷ Nail protectors
High-ranking Qing women wore long nail protectors, showing that they did no manual labor. These belonged to Empress Dowager Cixi.

▷ **Theatrical collar**
Probably worn by a male actor playing a female role, this Ming collar is made of silk, jade, and mother-of-pearl.

Mother-of-pearl flower on black satin

Jade ornament, probably reused from an earlier dynasty, such as the Jin or Liao

△ **Phoenix jewel**
This Ming pendant, with a phoenix at its center, would have been worn by a bride on her wedding day. The phoenix was associated with the union of male and female.

△ **Leopard square**
This 19th-century mandarin square was a badge worn by court officials; different beasts indicated different ranks.

◁ **Ruby finial**
The crowning jewel of this Qing hat is its central ruby, bringing it to a height of 4.5 in (11.5 cm). It is also inlaid with coral and turquoise.

▷ **Butterfly collar**
Children from wealthy families wore whimsical-shaped collars during the 18th and 19th centuries. The design of this little girl's collar is inspired by butterflies.

The Sino-Japanese War

A conflict that changed the face of Asia

The war between China and Japan at the end of the 19th century broke apart China's centuries-old vassal system. The Chinese defeat revealed the Qing empire's weakness.

After the restoration of imperial rule under the Meiji Emperor in 1867, Japan began a program of radical modernization that transformed it from an isolationist, feudal country into a well-educated, outward-looking nation, with a powerful army and navy, that was eager to build its own empire. In 1874, in pursuit of this aim, Meiji troops occupied the Ryuku archipelago, a chain of islands extending from the Japanese island of Kyushu to Taiwan. In 1879, Japan declared the Ryukus part of its empire. Heated negotiations with Japan over influence in Taiwan resulted in the Qing asserting their continued control over the island by making it a province in 1887.

Japanese interests

However, Japan's principal interest throughout this period was Korea. Japan was attracted to Korea not only for its rich resources of coal and iron but also because it would provide an effective buffer between

◁ **The Meiji Emperor**
Japan's transformation in the 45-year reign of the emperor was vast. It started out as a feudal country but emerged, by the end of the Meiji period in 1912, as a formidable power.

Japan and Russian expansion. In 1875, Japan sent a warship into the mouth of the Han River to force Korea to open itself up to trade. Following this incident, Korea submitted to negotiations with Japan. This resulted in the Treaty of Ganghwa, which defined Korea as an independent state and opened three treaty ports to Japanese trade. In the years that followed, Japan aligned itself with the radical modernizing forces within Korea's government, while China continued to support the more conservative elements.

Tensions escalate

In 1884, the pro-Japanese, reformist Enlightenment Party (Gaehwadang) in Korea staged a coup. China dispatched 1,500 soldiers to quell the unrest; war was narrowly avoided when the Chinese politician Li Hongzhang and the Japanese diplomat Ito Hirobumi agreed to withdraw their troops from Korea.

However, in 1894, the leader of the coup, Kim Ok-gyun, was killed in China and his body was sent back to Korea, where it was quartered and displayed as a warning to rebels. The Japanese were outraged, and tensions increased as another rebellion broke out. Once more, China sent its forces to Korea, and Japan responded in kind. On July 23, 1894,

◁ **The struggle for Korea**
This print from a Parisian newspaper dated October 29, 1894, depicts a scene from the Sino-Japanese War in which a Japanese officer (mounted) is in the process of seizing the Chinese flag.

△ **War on the Yalu River**
A woodblock print, c. 1894, by Japanese artist Kobayashi Kiyochika, shows the battle on the Yalu River in Korea, in September 1894, in which Japan secured a decisive victory over China.

於黃海我軍大捷圖第一

Japanese troops established a pro-Japanese government in Seoul and gave its armies permission to expel the Qing forces from Korea.

Open conflict

In the first engagement of the war, the Battle of Pungdo, a Japanese cruiser torpedoed a British steamer, HMS *Kowshing*, which was carrying Chinese reinforcements to Korea. Only three of the *Kowshing's* 43 crew survived, and more than 800 Chinese troops were killed. As the conflict progressed, the Chinese struggled to match the strategic skills and modern military discipline of the Japanese. They suffered heavy losses as they retreated to Pyongyang and were defeated there on September 15.

In spite of superior numbers, China's Beiyang Fleet lost to the faster and more effectively armed Japanese Combined Fleet at the Battle of the Yalu River on September 17. Qing troops were forced out of Korea, and Japan pressed into the Manchurian Liaodong peninsula. By November 21, they had captured Port Arthur (Lüshunkou), where they massacred thousands of inhabitants in response to seeing the mutilated remains of Japanese soldiers displayed in the town. The following year, the Japanese seized the port of Weihaiwei and pushed further into south Manchuria and northern China.

The Treaty of Shimonoseki

Qing statesman Prince Gong requested an end to the fighting and signed the Treaty of Shimonoseki on April 17, 1895. This treaty recognized Korea's independence (leaving it open to Japanese colonization), ceded the Liaodong peninsula and Taiwan to Japan, and allowed Japan to operate on the Yangzi River and open new treaty ports. The war highlighted the failure of China's Self-Strengthening Movement (see pp. 284–285) and prompted a new wave of reform in the country.

▽ **Japanese firearms**
This Japanese pill-lock carbine, c. 1870–1899, is among the weapons that would have been used by Japan in the Sino-Japanese War. The recently modernized Japanese armed forces inflicted a heavy defeat on the Chinese, whose weaponry was inferior.

The Hundred Days

A failed attempt to modernize China's institutions

For 103 days between June 11 and September 22, 1898, the Guangxu Emperor and a group of reformers, headed by Kang Youwei, attempted to implement cultural, political, and educational reform in China.

The defeat of China in the Sino-Japanese War (see pp. 294–295) prompted a new wave of foreign intrusion: Germany secured Jiaozhou in Shandong, the British leased Weiheiwei and the New Territories near Hong Kong, and Russia gained the Liaodong peninsula. It was clear to many that China was seen as an easy target for acquisitive foreign powers and that major reform was urgently needed if it was to survive.

Conservative reformers at court called for Western-style industrialization but nonetheless clung to China's traditional Confucian heritage. Meanwhile, a group of around 1,200 young scholars, led by Kang Youwei, signed the "Ten Thousand Word Memorial," a document that called for the rejection of the Treaty of Shimonoseki (see p. 295) and advocated radical and wide-ranging institutional and ideological reforms—most notably, a major move from absolute to constitutional monarchy.

A way forward
Kang's particular genius lay in his ability to bridge the gap between Confucianism and modernization on a Western model by arguing that Confucius was himself an innovator who adapted to the circumstances

▷ **Pressing for change**
The brilliant Chinese philosopher and political thinker Kang Youwei, shown here, was at the forefront of a group of progressive young Qing scholars who urged the government to make radical changes. Kang was also an accomplished calligrapher.

of his day and that there was therefore no need to cling rigidly to China's past while forging its future.

In 1898, the 27-year-old Guangxu Emperor began to stamp his authority on his reign and became increasingly reform-minded. Up until this point, his reign had been dominated by his aunt, Empress Dowager Cixi (see pp. 286–287), who acted as regent from 1875 to 1887. Following China's crushing defeat in the Sino-Japanese War and its exploitation by foreign powers, Guangxu—and even Cixi to some extent—saw the need for real change. In June 1898, Guangxu began to implement Kang's proposals, starting what became known as the Hundred Days of Reform.

Positive moves
Guangxu appointed Kang secretary of the Zongli Yamen (China's foreign office) and gave his followers, including Liang Qichao and Tan Sitong, positions as imperial advisers. Over the next 100 days, Guangxu issued more than 40 edicts that touched almost every aspect of Chinese society. These included the establishment of an imperial university in Beijing, the introduction of a Western curriculum in schools, and the replacement of the civil service examinations with a system that focused on current affairs rather than classical study. Guangxu abolished the

▽ **Korean independence**
According to the Treaty of Shimonoseki, shown here, signed by China and Japan on April 17, 1895, China was obliged, among other things, to recognize Korea's independence and renounce its sovereignty over Taiwan.

THE POETRY OF REFORM

In the late 19th century, the poet and literary reformer Huang Zunxian declared, "I cannot be bound by the ancients," and turned away from the strict forms of classical poetry that had prevailed for centuries. He began to advocate the use of clear, colloquial language in a new school of poetry called *xinshi-pai*. This aligned with Kang Youwei's belief that China should adapt its Confucian heritage to changing needs, and he and his coreformers adopted *xinshi-pai's* precepts to compose poetry that promoted reform and modernization.

governorships of Hubei, Guangdong, and Yunnan, and modernized the frameworks of both government and the judiciary. He reformed the military and promoted Western industry, science, medicine, and commerce. Guangxu also allowed private citizens to suggest reforms and took measures to prevent government corruption.

A threat to privilege

The direction of the reforms alarmed and enraged conservatives at court, such as Li Hongzhang (see p. 294), who believed that they threatened the privileged classes. In September 1898, they gathered around Cixi, who left her retreat at the Summer Palace and returned to Beijing. Cixi took back control in a coup on September 22, leaving Guangxu under house arrest. She repealed most of his progressive edicts and led a purge of the leading reformers: Kang Youwei and Liang Qichao escaped to Japan, where they set up the Protect the Emperor Society and continued to push for a constitutional monarchy; six other reformers, including Tan Sitong, were executed in public.

Cixi reluctantly supported a series of moderate reforms in the early 1900s in an attempt to prevent the collapse of the ailing Qing dynasty. However, the Hundred Days of Reform was to be the last time that the imperial regime made a radical attempt to modernize. Its failure fed into a feeling that the country was being held back, not just by its inability to modernize, but by the Manchu rulers themselves.

> "By and large, the **corruption** of **social customs** is due to a lack of **moral doctrine**."

KANG YOUWEI, "TEN THOUSAND WORD MEMORIAL"

△ **Thwarted reformer**
A portrait of Guangxu shows the emperor seated at his desk, wearing the official robes of state. He died mysteriously, at the age of just 38, on November 14, 1908, the day before the death of his aunt Cixi. Evidence released in 2008 suggests he was a victim of arsenic poisoning; Cixi is among the murder suspects.

The Boxer Rebellion

An unsuccessful challenge to imperialism

At the end of the 19th century, China was gripped by a violent anti-foreign, anti-Christian rebellion. Beginning with attacks on missionaries, it progressed to a siege of the foreign legations in Beijing and ended in defeat for the Qing empire.

As China's rulers dealt with the aftermath of the Sino-Japanese War and grappled with the challenges of Western-style modernization (see pp. 294–297), an anti-foreign movement was growing in the eastern province of Shandong. In the late 1890s, the members of a secret society known as the Righteous and Harmonious Fists, or Boxers (for their expertise in martial arts), began to stir up trouble. The movement drew its followers from the young men of Shandong, where poverty and disaffection had been deepened by flood, drought, and foreign aggression.

The spark of violence

In 1897, a local dispute involving Chinese Christian converts prompted vigilantes to attack and kill two German missionaries in Juye County, Shandong. Germany quickly responded to this affront, sending a naval squadron to occupy Jiaozhou Bay in Shandong, and insisting that local officials build new churches in the area. This action served to reinforce the view throughout Shandong that Christian missionaries and converts were the agents of Western imperialism; it also fostered the broader perception of foreigners as the principal cause of China's problems.

FIRE AT THE HANLIN ACADEMY

On June 23, 1900, a fire started by Chinese rebels in the legation quarters (areas set aside for foreign officials) spread to the Hanlin Academy, founded in the 8th century. It was a major repository for classical texts, and hundreds of works were lost in the inferno, including some volumes of the 11,095-volume *Yongle Encyclopedia* (see p. 209). Hundreds more were looted by foreign soldiers who ransacked Beijing after the Boxer defeat.

◁ **Dressed for battle**
The Boxer movement emerged out of the most impoverished, oppressed areas of northwest Shandong, igniting anger in disaffected young men at the spread of Western and Japanese imperialism. The Boxer here was photographed in 1900, flag and weapon at hand, in full regalia.

◁ **The storming of Beijing**
This illustration shows armed foreign coalition forces storming one of the outer gates of the city of Beijing on August 14, 1900, in a bid to suppress the rebellion.

On July 14, the Eight-Nation Alliance—an international force of some 55,000 men, formed by Western powers and Japan to suppress the rebellion—responded to the Boxer threat by capturing Tianjin. A cohort of 20,000 then marched on Beijing. They reached the city on August 14, 1900, and lifted the siege of the legation quarter on the same day. Cixi, disguised, fled the city.

The Boxer Protocol
Li Hongzhang (see p. 297) led the peace negotiations and in September 1901 signed the Boxer Protocol. Among its provisions was the summary execution of Boxers, along with a devastating indemnity of 450 million taels of silver (around $9.9 billion today) to be paid over a period of 45 years. China was also forced to allow foreign troops to remain in the country; Japan retained a particularly large contingent there.

The Qing dynasty was fatally damaged by its failure once again to control the foreigners or expel them from China. In the aftermath of the rebellion, it could neither prevent further losses to foreign powers nor stem the tide of revolutionary ideas (see pp. 300–301).

△ **Campaign medal**
An Italian bronze medal commemorates the country's contribution—as one of the nations in the Eight-Nation Alliance—to the overthrow of China's Boxer Rebellion.

In 1898, a group of Boxers attacked the Christian community at Liyuantun village; in the following years, more than 1,000 similar incidents were recorded in Shandong. Empress Dowager Cixi did not suppress the Boxers, in the hope that they would help rid China of foreigners. So the rebels moved north, burning churches, killing Christians, and targeting foreign assets in the countryside around Beijing.

By late May 1900, the Boxers were closing in on Beijing, where many foreigners and Christians had taken refuge in the legation quarter (the area designated for officials sent by their government to work in a foreign country). The Boxers arrived in the quarter on June 11 and killed the secretary to the Japanese legation. Soon after, a German diplomat, Baron Ketteler, inexplicably executed a young Boxer, prompting thousands of Boxers to storm Beijing. Supported by the imperial army, the Boxers laid siege to the legation quarter, and on June 21, Cixi declared war on all foreign nations, ordering China's governors to support the Boxers and expel all foreigners.

▷ **Distribution of foreign forces**
This map shows the distribution of some of the foreign bases in Beijing during the Boxer Rebellion: the British quarter is shown in yellow, the French in blue, the German in red, the US in green and ivory, and the Japanese in light green.

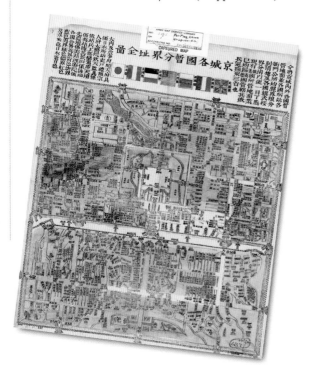

"Support the **Qing**, **destroy** the **foreigners**."

BOXER SLOGAN, 1900

Founding Modern China

The end of imperial rule

In 1911–1912, revolution finally brought an end to Qing power and to 2,000 years of imperial rule in China, as Sun Yat-sen—the "Father of the Nation"— helped establish China's first republic.

By 1900, China was in urgent need of political change to survive the plundering of its land and resources by foreign powers and to overcome its internal weaknesses (see pp. 296–297). Revolutionary groups began to form throughout the country and in 1905 were brought together by the prominent republicans Sun Yat-sen and Song Jiaoren (then living in Japan). The resulting Chinese Revolutionary Alliance (Tongmenghui) was based on Sun's Three Principles of the People: nationalism, democracy, and livelihood.

The Xinhai Revolution

The deaths of the Guangxu Emperor and Empress Dowager Cixi in 1908 left the empire in the hands of the inept regents of the child-emperor Puyi (see pp. 302–303), giving great impetus to the republican movement. In 1911, the government's plans to fund railroad building with foreign loans sparked major anti-foreign and nationalistic reactions. Anti-Qing feeling escalated and unrest broke out, including massive strikes and rallies in Chengdu. In September, the Qing tried to subdue these with force, arresting ringleaders and opening fire on protesters.

These acts prompted further discontent and unrest, giving rise to the Xinhai Revolution. This began in earnest after October 10, 1911, as troops in Wuchang staged an uprising and overthrew the provincial government. The leaders of the Tongmenghui returned to China and soon encouraged other provinces in the south to declare independence from the Qing regime. The regency scrambled to adopt a constitution to fend off the revolutionaries and appointed the reformist minister and military leader Yuan Shikai as prime minister. However, by the end of December 1911, a total of 18

△ **Revolutionary times**
Symbols of the revolution are displayed on this postcard, including republican flags, a sword, and a cannon. The portraits are of key figures in the revolutionary struggle.

provinces had seceded from Qing China and Sun Yat-sen had been voted president of the Provisional Government of the Republic of China in Nanjing.

Negotiations between Yuan Shikai's government and the Provisional Republic began in the hope that northern and southern China could be reunited. To avoid civil war, Sun Yat-sen agreed to step aside as president of the republic and support Yuan Shikai's election to the post. In return, Yuan Shikai agreed to force the Qing emperor to abdicate. On February 12, 1912, the emperor abdicated, bringing to an end 2,000 years of imperial rule.

◁ **Dismantling an empire**
Sun Yat-sen, pictured here, helped unshackle China from its imperial past and set the country on the path to securing its future as a republic.

△ **Party headquarters**
This image shows soldiers outside the headquarters of the Republican Party in Shanghai in 1912.

In August 1912, the Tongmenghui merged with smaller pro-revolution parties to create the Chinese Nationalist Party, or Guomindang, with Sun as party chairman. The Guomindang won the National Assembly election in December 1912, but Yuan soon began to overstep his authority and was suspected of the assassination of Song Jiaoren. This prompted a second revolution, led by Sun Yat-sen in July 1913, which failed to oust Yuan, who expelled the nationalists, many of whom fled to Japan. Yuan proclaimed himself emperor in December 1915, but in 1916 his supporters abandoned him and his generals rebelled against his rule. Yuan died soon after, and in the ensuing chaos China was divided among powerful regional warlords.

The road to a republic

In 1917, Sun Yat-sen returned to China to reunite the country. He resurrected the Guomindang and, in 1921, established a military government in Guangzhou to rival the Beijing-based government in the north. With the support of Soviet advisers, who arrived in China in 1923, Sun reorganized the party, adding Three Policies to his Three Principles: alliances with the Communist Party, the Soviet Union, and workers and peasants. He also began building up the forces to conquer the warlords and unify China, but he died in 1925, before he could begin a planned campaign against the warlords.

THE CHINESE DIASPORA

From the 19th century to 1949, China experienced mass emigration. Thousands of peasants escaped poverty and war for the promise of good wages in Southeast Asia, the British colonies, and the US, where some found work on the railroads (pictured). Many were sold into slavery and died in horrific conditions. In the 20th century, civil war between the Guomindang and the Communist Party (1927–1936; 1946–1949) forced many people to flee the country to settle in Southeast Asia and Taiwan.

A Manchu statesman
Puyi is shown here wearing medals of state and formal Manchukuo uniform during his role as ruler of the state. After Japan's surrender to the Soviets in 1945, he spent five years as a prisoner of war in the Soviet Union.

Puyi: The Last Emperor

The end of the Qing, China's final dynasty

Enthroned as emperor at the age of two, Puyi lived an extraordinary life in which he saw the fall of his empire and the founding of the People's Republic of China. Born into a life of privilege, he died an ordinary citizen.

Born in Beijing on February 7, 1906, Puyi was the son of the Qing prince Chun and was chosen by Empress Dowager Cixi to succeed his uncle, the heirless Guangxu Emperor. In November 1908, just two months before his third birthday, he became the Xuantong Emperor. Isolated from normal life and seen as faultless by all except his nurse, Puyi grew into a spoiled child who enjoyed having the eunuchs who served him flogged daily.

After the nationalist Xinhai Revolution, Puyi was forced to abdicate in February 1912 but was allowed to retain his imperial title and continue living in the Forbidden City on a large stipend from the republic. Under the influence of his British tutor, Sir Reginald Johnston, he adopted Western habits, took the name "Henry," and cut down on extravagance at court. Powerless, trapped, and facing the prospect of an unwelcome marriage to Wanrong (the daughter of a minister) in 1922, Puyi had great hopes of escaping China to study at the University of Oxford in England. According to some accounts, however, his plans were thwarted by the British Embassy, which turned down his application.

Emperor of Manchukuo

Puyi was expelled from the Forbidden City in October 1924 when the warlord Feng Yuxiang took control of Beijing. He took shelter at the city's Japanese legation before moving to the Japanese concession in Tianjin, where he lived an extravagant life for six years. In late 1931, Puyi and the Japanese formulated a plan to install him as emperor of the Japanese state of Manchukuo in Manchuria. The implication was that this could be the first step in his reinstatement as emperor of all China after the conquest of Manchuria by Japan. Although crowned emperor of Manchukuo in 1934, Puyi was little more than a puppet leader and was largely confined to his palace in Changchun.

From emperor to citizen

In 1945, at the end of World War II, the Soviet Red Army entered Manchukuo and took Puyi prisoner; his wife, Wanrong, was captured by guerrillas and starved to death in prison. In 1950, Puyi was returned to China, where he lied about his involvement with the Japanese to avoid execution, and spent nine years being reformed into a Chinese Communist citizen. He moved to Beijing, where he worked in a repair shop and as a researcher while writing his autobiography, *From Emperor to Citizen*. Puyi died, aged 61, in October 1967.

△ **Qing family portrait**
Puyi is pictured here, c.1908, as a small boy (standing) with his father, Prince Chun, and younger brother, Pujie.

▷ **Extravagant possessions**
In the mid-1920s, Puyi developed a fondness for buying Western goods, including cars. This dragon-red 1932 Cadillac was among his purchases.

1906 Born in Beijing to Prince Chun

1912 Forced to abdicate following the Xinhai Revolution

1945 Captured by Soviet forces as he tries to leave Manchuria for Japan

1967 Dies in Beijing of complications from kidney and heart disease

1908 Becomes Xuantong Emperor on the death of his uncle, the Guangxu Emperor

1932 Installed as puppet ruler of Manchukuo in Manchuria

1950–1959 Imprisoned in China and learns to live as a Chinese citizen

Chinese and World History

A timeline of dynasties, empires, and events

China is the earliest civilization to have established a continuous tradition that has lasted through to modern times. The chart below shows how China compares to some of the world's other great empires and includes a selection of key events and innovations to put the history of China in the context of the wider world.

• **551–479** BCE Life of philosopher and statesman Confucius

• **771** BCE Zhou dynasty moves its capital east to Luoyang

• **221** BCE Work begins on what has become known as the Great Wall

• **c. 1350** BCE Shang dynasty moves its capital to the city of Yin

• **c. 2100** BCE Yu the Great controls the Great Flood

• **c. 1046** BCE King Wu defeats Shang emperor at the Battle of Muye

• **c. 550** BCE Beginning of the Chinese Iron Age

• **c. 1600** BCE Large bronze ritual vessels are made in Erlitou

221–206 BCE **Qin dynasty**

CHINESE DYNASTIES

c. 2070–1600 BCE **Xia dynasty**	**c. 1600–1046** BCE **Shang dynasty**	**c. 1046–221** BCE **Zhou dynasty**	**206** BCE–22 **Han dynas**

2000 BCE	**1500** BCE	**1000** BCE	**500** BCE

WORLD EMPIRES AND KINGDOMS

Akkadian Empire

Ancient Egypt

Ancient Greece

Persian Achaemenid Empire

Ancient Rome

• **c. 2600** BCE Stone circle is erected at Stonehenge in southern England

• **480** BCE Greek city-states defeat an invasion by Persian ruler Xerxes

• **1790** BCE Hammurabi establishes a legal code for his Babylonian Empire

• **1003** BCE Jewish king David unites Israel and Judah

• **c. 427–348** BCE Life of the Athenian philosopher Plato

• **c. 2550** BCE The Great Pyramid of Giza is built in Egypt

• **1600** BCE Bronze begins to be used by the ancient Sumerians

• **c. 750** BCE The Iron Age begins in central Europe

• **c. 2000** BCE The Minoan Palace of Knossos is built in Crete

• **1325** BCE Egyptian pharaoh Tutankhamun dies and is entombed

• **330** BCE Alexander the Great conquers the Persian Empire

• **c. 4** BCE–c. **30** C Life of Jesus Ch

• **1258** Mongol Kublai Khan embarks on the conquest of Song China

• **1841** China builds its first steam engine

• **208** CE Warlord Cao Cao is defeated at the Battle of the Red Cliffs

• **629** CE Buddhist monk Xuanzang travels from China to India

• **1351** Red Turban rebellion subverts Mongol rule

• **1900** Boxer Rebellion is crushed as foreign forces occupy Beijing

• **184** CE Rebellion of the Yellow Turbans shakes Han dynasty

• **1405–1433** Zheng He commands a series of exploratory voyages

• **c. 850** CE Gunpowder is invented—one of the "Four Great Inventions" of the time

5 CE Cai Lun develops the cess of paper manufacture

• **605** CE Emperor Wen opens the Grand Canal

• **1557** Portugal is granted Macau as a trading post

• **1790** Beginnings of the theatrical form called Peking opera

907–959 CE
Five Dynasties and Ten Kingdoms

1279–1368
Yuan dynasty

• **1912** The last emperor, Puyi, is forced to abdicate

| 220–581 CE Time of division | 581–618 CE Sui dynasty | 618–906 CE Tang dynasty | 960–1279 Song dynasty | 1368–1644 Ming dynasty | 1644–1912 Qing dynasty |

500 CE   **1000** CE   **1500** CE   **2000** CE

Maya Classic Period

Byzantine Empire

Umayyad Caliphate

Japanese Heian era

Japanese Edo period

Ottoman Empire

Korean Joseon dynasty

Mughal Empire

Russian Empire

• **c.1440** Johannes Gutenberg invents the printing press

• **793** CE Vikings raid Lindisfarne, just off the English coast

• **200** CE The Pyramid of the Sun is built in Teotihuacan, Mexico

• **1079** Ibn Battuta explores Africa, Asia, and the Middle East

• **1760–1840** The Industrial Revolution transforms western society

• **380** CE Christianity is made the official religion of the Roman Empire

• **800** CE Charlemagne is proclaimed emperor in western Europe

• **1775–1783** The American War of Independence

• **1079** Omar Khayyam accurately calculates the length of a solar year

• **1492** Christopher Columbus sails across the Atlantic to the Americas

• **1914–1918** World War I is fought

• **632** CE Death of Muhammad, founder of the Islamic faith

• **c.1450** Machu Picchu is constructed by the Inca Empire in Peru

Directory of Rulers

Directory of Rulers

THE MYTHICAL SOVEREIGNS
c. 2800–2208 BCE

Fuxi 2852–2737 BCE
Shennong 2737–2697 BCE
Huangdi 2697–2598 BCE
Shaohao 2597–2514 BCE
Zhuanxu 2513–2436 BCE
Diku 2435–2366 BCE
Di Zhi 2365–2357 BCE
Yao 2356–2256 BCE
Shun 2255–2208 BCE

THE XIA DYNASTY
c. 2070–c. 1600 BCE

Yu 2205–2198 BCE
Qi 2197–2189 BCE
Tai Kang 2188–2160 BCE
Zhong Kang 2159–2146 BCE
Xiang 2146–2118 BCE
Shao Kang 2079–2058 BCE
Zhu 2057–2041 BCE

Huai 2040–2015 BCE
Mang 2014–1997 BCE
Xie 1996–1981 BCE
Bu Jiang 1980–1922 BCE
Jiong 1921–1901 BCE
Jin 1900–1880 BCE
Kong Jia 1879–1849 BCE
Gao 1848–1838 BCE
Fa 1837–1817 BCE
Jie 1818–1767 BCE

THE SHANG DYNASTY
c. 1600–1046 BCE

Tang 1766–1759 BCE
Wai Bing 1759–1757 BCE
Zhong Ren 1757–1753 BCE
Tai Jia 1753–1721 BCE
Wo Ding 1720–1692 BCE
Tai Geng 1691–1667 BCE
Xiao Jia 1666–1650 BCE
Yong Ji 1649–1638 BCE
Tai Wu 1637–1563 BCE
Zhong Ding 1562–1550 BCE

Wai Ren 1549–1535 BCE
Hedan Jia 1534–1526 BCE
Zu Yi 1525–1507 BCE
Zu Xin 1506–1491 BCE
Wo Jia 1490–1466 BCE
Zu Ding 1465–1434 BCE
Nan Geng 1433–1409 BCE
Yang Jia 1408–1402 BCE
Pangeng 1401–1374 BCE
Xiao Xin 1373–1353 BCE
Xiao Yi 1352–1325 BCE
Wu Ding c.1325–1189 BCE
Zu Geng 1188–1178 BCE
Zu Jia 1177–1158 BCE
Lin Xin 1157–1149 BCE
Geng Ding 1148–1132 BCE
Wu Yi 1131–1117 BCE
Wen Ding 1116–1106 BCE
Di Yi 1105–1087 BCE
Di Xin 1086–1046 BCE

THE WESTERN ZHOU DYNASTY
1045–771 BCE

Wen 1099/56–1050 BCE
Wu 1049/45–1043 BCE
Cheng 1042/35–1006 BCE
Kang 1005/3–978 BCE
Zhao 977/75–957 BCE
Mu 956–918 BCE
Gong 917/15–900 BCE
Yi (I) 899/97–873 BCE
Xiao c. 872–866 BCE
Yi (II) 865–858 BCE
Li 857/53–842/28 BCE
Gonghe 841–828 BCE
Xuan 827/25–782 BCE
You 781–771 BCE

THE EASTERN ZHOU DYNASTY
770–256 BCE

Ping 770–720 BCE
Huan 719–697 BCE
Zhuang 696–682 BCE
Xi 681–677 BCE
Hui 676–652 BCE
Xiang 651–619 BCE
Qing 618–613 BCE
Kuang 612–607 BCE
Ding 606–586 BCE
Jian 585–572 BCE
Ling 571–545 BCE
Jing (I) 544–520 BCE
Jing (II) 519–476 BCE
Yuan 475–469 BCE
Zhending 468–441 BCE
Kao 440–426 BCE
Weilie 425–402 BCE
An 401–376 BCE
Lie 375–369 BCE
Xian 368–321 BCE
Shenjing 320–315 BCE
Nan 314–256 BCE
Lord of East Zhou 255–249 BCE

THE QIN DYNASTY
221–206 BCE

Qin Shi Huangdi 221–210 BCE
Qin Ershi Huangdi 209–206 BCE

THE WESTERN HAN DYNASTY
206 BCE–9 CE

Gaozu 206–195 BCE
Huidi 194–188 BCE
Empress Dowager Lü
   187–180 BCE
Wendi 179–157 BCE
Jingdi 156–141 BCE
Wudi 140–87 BCE
Zhaodi 86–74 BCE
Xuandi 73–49 BCE
Yuandi 48–33 BCE
Chengdi 32–7 BCE
Aidi 6–1 BCE
Pingdi 1 BCE–5 CE
Ruzi Ying 6–9 CE

THE XIN DYNASTY
9–23 CE

Wang Mang 9–23 CE

THE EASTERN HAN DYNASTY
25–220 CE

Gengshi 23–25 CE
Guangwudi 25–57 CE
Mingdi 58–75 CE
Zhangdi 76–88 CE
Hedi 89–105 CE
Shangdi 106–106 CE
Andi 107–125 CE
Shaodi (Liu Yi) 125–125 CE
Shundi 125–144 CE
Chongdi 144–145 CE
Zhidi 145–146 CE
Huandi 146–168 CE
Lingdi 168–189 CE
Shaodi (Liu Bian) 189–189 CE
Xiandi 189–220 CE

THE THREE KINGDOMS

WEI
220–265 CE

Wendi 220–226 CE
Mingdi 227–239 CE
Prince of Qi 240–253 CE
Duke of Gaoguixiang
   254–260 CE
Yuandi 260–265 CE

SHU HAN
221–263 CE

Zhaoliedi 221–223 CE
Houzhu 223–263 CE

WU
222–279 CE

Dadi 222–252 CE
Prince of Kuaiji 252–258 CE
Jingdi 258–264 CE
Modi 264–279 CE

The Three Kingdoms period ends.

THE WESTERN JIN DYNASTY
265–316 CE

Wudi 265–289 CE
Huidi 290–306 CE
Huaidi 307–312 CE
Mindi 313–316 CE

THE EASTERN JIN DYNASTY
317–420 CE

Yuandi 317–322 CE
Mingdi 323–325 CE
Chengdi 326–342 CE
Kangdi 343–344 CE
Mudi 345–361 CE
Aidi 362–365 CE
Duke of Haixi 366–371 CE
Jianwendi 371–372 CE
Xiaowudi 373–396 CE
Andi 397–418 CE
Gongdi 419–420 CE

THE SOUTHERN AND NORTHERN DYNASTIES

THE LIU SONG DYNASTY
420–479 CE

Wudi 420–422 CE
Shaodi 423–424 CE
Wendi 424–453 CE
Xiaowudi 454–464 CE
Qian Feidi 465–465 CE
Mingdi 465–472 CE
Prince of Cangwu 473–477 CE
Shundi 477–479 CE

THE QI DYNASTY
479–502 CE

Gaodi 479–482 CE
Wudi 483–493 CE
Prince of Yulin 494–494 CE
Prince of Hailing 494–494 CE
Mingdi 494–498 CE
Donghunhou 498–501 CE
Hedi 501–502 CE

THE LIANG DYNASTY
502–557 CE

Wudi 502–549 CE
Jianwendi 550–551 CE
Prince of Yuzhang 551–551 CE
Yuandi 552–555 CE
Mindi 555–555 CE
Jingdi 555–557 CE

THE CHEN DYNASTY
557–589 CE

Wudi 557–559 CE
Wendi 560–566 CE
Prince of Linhai 567–568 CE
Xuandi 569–582 CE
Houzhu 583–589 CE

THE NORTHERN WEI DYNASTY
386–534 CE

Daowu 386–409 CE
Mingyuan 409–423 CE
Taiwu 424–452 CE
Prince of Nan'an 452–452 CE
Wencheng 452–465 CE
Xianwen 466–471 CE
Xiaowen 471–499 CE
Xuanwu 500–515 CE
Xiaoming 516–528 CE
Xiaozhuang 528–530 CE
Prince of Changguang
   530–530 CE
Jiemin 531–531 CE
Prince of Anding 531–532 CE
Xiaowu 532–534 CE

THE EASTERN WEI DYNASTY
534–550 CE

Xiaojing 534–550 CE

THE WESTERN WEI DYNASTY
535–557 CE

Wendi 535–551 CE
Feidi 552–554 CE
Gongdi 554–556 CE

THE NORTHERN QI DYNASTY
550–577 CE

Wenxuan 550–559 CE
Feidi 560–560 CE
Xiaozhao 560–561 CE
Wucheng 561–564 CE
Houzhu 564–577 CE
Youzhu 577–577 CE

THE NORTHERN ZHOU DYNASTY
557–581 CE

Xiaomin 557–557 CE
Mingdi 557–560 CE
Wudi 561–578 CE
Xuandi 579–579 CE
Jingdi 578–581 CE

The Southern and Northern Dynasties period ends.

THE SUI DYNASTY
581–619 CE

Wendi 581–604 CE
Yangdi 604–618 CE
Gongdi (I) 617–618 CE
Gongdi (II) 618–619 CE

THE TANG DYNASTY
618–907 CE

Gaozu 618–626 CE
Taizong 627–649 CE
Gaozong 650–683 CE
Wu Zetian 684–705 CE
Zhongzong 705–710 CE
Ruizong 684–690 CE; 710–712 CE
Xuanzong 712–756 CE
Suzong 756–762 CE
Daizong 763–779 CE
Dezong 780–805 CE
Shunzong 805–805 CE
Xianzong 806–820 CE
Muzong 821–824 CE
Jingzong 825–827 CE
Wenzong 827–840 CE
Wuzong 840–846 CE
Xuanzong 847–859 CE
Yizong 860–873 CE
Xizong 874–888 CE
Zhaozong 889–904 CE
Aidi 905–907 CE

FIVE DYNASTIES AND TEN KINGDOMS

THE LATER LIANG DYNASTY
907–923 CE

Taizu 907–912 CE
Modi 913–923 CE

THE LATER TANG DYNASTY
923–936 CE

Zhuangzong 923–926 CE
Mingzong 926–933 CE
Minzong 933–934 CE
Feidi 934–936 CE

THE LATER JIN DYNASTY
936–947 CE

Gaozu 936–942 CE
Chudi 942–947 CE

THE LATER HAN DYNASTY
947–950 CE

Gaozu 947–948 CE
Yindi 948–950 CE

THE LATER ZHOU DYNASTY
951–960 CE

Taizu 951–954 CE
Shizong 954–959 CE
Gongdi 959–960 CE

YANG WU
902–937 CE

Taizu 902–905 CE
Liezu 905–908 CE
Gaozu 908–920 CE
Ruidi 920–937 CE

FORMER SHU
907–925 CE

Gaozu 907–918 CE
Houzhu 918–925 CE

WUYUE
907–978 CE

King Wusu 907–931 CE
King Wenmu 932–941 CE
King Zhongxian 941–947 CE
King Zhongxun 947–948 CE
King Zhongyi 948–978 CE

MIN
909–945 CE

Taizu 909–925 CE
Prince Si of Min 925–927 CE
Huizong 928–935 CE
Kangzong 936–939 CE
Jingzong 939–944 CE
Gongyi 943–945 CE

SOUTHERN HAN
917–971 CE

Gaozu 917–941 CE
Shangdi 942–943 CE
Zhongzong 943–958 CE
Houzhu 958–971 CE

JINGNAN (NANPING)
924–963 CE

King Wuxin 924–928 CE
King Wenxian 928–948 CE
King Zhenyi 948–960 CE
Xinggong 960–962 CE
Gao Jichong 962–963 CE

CHU
927–951 CE

King Wumu 927–930 CE
King Hengyang 930–932 CE
King Wenzhao 932–947 CE
Ma Xiguang 947–950 CE
King Gongxiao 950–951 CE
Ma Xichong 951–951 CE

LATER SHU
934–965 CE

Gaozu 934–934 CE
Houzhu 934–965 CE

SOUTHERN TANG
937–975 CE

Liezu 937–943 CE
Yuanzong 943–961 CE
Houzhu 961–975 CE

NORTHERN HAN
951–979 CE

Shizu 951–954 CE
Ruizong 954–968 CE
Shaozhu 968–968 CE
Yingwudi 968–979 CE

The Five Dynasties and Ten Kingdoms period ends.

THE NORTHERN SONG DYNASTY
960–1127

Taizu 960–976 CE
Taizong 976–997 CE
Zhenzong 997–1022
Renzong 1023–1063
Yingzong 1064–1067
Shenzong 1068–1085

Zhezong 1086–1100
Huizong 1101–1125
Qinzong 1126–1127

THE SOUTHERN SONG DYNASTY
1127–1279

Gaozong 1127–1162
Xiaozong 1163–1189
Guangzong 1190–1194
Ningzong 1195–1224
Lizong 1225–1264
Duzong 1265–1274
Gongdi 1275–1276
Duanzong 1276–1278
Di Bing 1278–1279

THE EASTERN LIAO DYNASTY
916–1125

Taizu 916–926 CE
Taizong 927–947 CE
Shizong 947–951 CE
Muzong 951–969 CE
Jingzong 969–982 CE
Shengzong 982–1031
Xingzong 1031–1055
Daozong 1055–1101
Tianzuo 1101–1125

THE WESTERN LIAO DYNASTY
1131–1218

Dezong 1131–1143
Empress Gantian 1144–1150
Renzong 1151–1163
Empress Chengtian 1164–1177
Mozhu 1178–1211

THE XI XIA DYNASTY
1038–1227

Jingzong 1032–1048
Yizong 1048–1068
Huizong 1068–1086
Chongzong 1086–1139
Renzong 1139–1193
Huanzong 1194–1206
Xiangzong 1206–1211
Shenzong 1211–1223
Xianzong 1223–1226
Modi 1226–1227

THE JIN DYNASTY
1115–1234

Taizu 1115–1123
Taizong 1123–1135
Xizong 1135–1149
Prince of Hailing 1150–1161
Shizong 1161–1189
Zhangzong 1189–1208
Prince of Wei 1208–1213
Xuanzong 1213–1224
Aizong 1223–1234
Modi 1234–1234

THE YUAN DYNASTY
1279–1368

Ghengis Khan 1206–1227
Ögedei Khan 1229–1241
Güyük Khan 1246–1248
Möngke Khan 1251–1259
Kublai Khan 1260–1294
Temür Khan 1294–1307
Külüg Khan 1307–1311
Buyantu Khan 1311–1320
Gegeen Khan 1320–1323
Yesün Temür 1323–1328
Aragibag Khan 1328–1328
Khutughtu Khan 1329–1329

Jayaatu Khan 1328; 1329–1332
Rinchinbal Khan 1332–1332
Ukhaghatu Khan 1333–1368

THE MING DYNASTY
1368–1644

Hongwu 1368–1398
Jianwen 1399–1402
Yongle 1403–1424
Hongxi 1425–1425
Xuande 1425–1435
Yingzong 1436–1449;
1457–1464
Jingtai 1450–1457
Chenghua 1465–1487
Hongzhi 1488–1505
Zhengde 1506–1521
Jiajing 1522–1566
Longqing 1567–1572
Wanli 1573–1620
Taichang 1620–1620
Tianqi 1620–1627
Chongzhen 1628–1644
Hongguang 1644 –1645
Longwu 1645–1646
Yongli 1646–1662

THE QING DYNASTY
1644–1912

Shunzhi 1644–1661
Kangxi 1662–1722
Yongzheng 1723–1735
Qianlong 1736–1795
Jiaqing 1796–1820
Daoguang 1820–1850
Xianfeng 1850–1861
Tongzhi 1861–1875
Guangxu 1875–1908
Puyi 1908–1912

The Mythical Sovereigns (c. 2800–2208 BCE)

According to Chinese tradition, before the dynastic era began, ancient mythical rulers introduced civilization and provided enlightened guidance to the people. Many of these sovereigns were later revered for their inventions and harmonious governance.

Fuxi

Other names: Bao Xi, Pao Xi, Tai Hao

r. 2852–2737 BCE

Fuxi (see pp. 28–29) is described in traditional sources as an ancestral ruler and the inventor of fire, music, fishing and hunting nets, as well as musical instruments, and devices to estimate time and distance. His greatest and most famous contribution, however, was the Eight Trigrams, symbols used for divination and interpreting the known universe. Over time, the character of Fuxi merged with a deity named Tai Hao. Fuxi also became associated with the goddess Nüwa, who was thought to be either his wife or sister. The iconic pair were depicted as human-looking figures with intertwined snakelike lower bodies and were believed to be the founders of humanity.

Shennong

Other name: Yandi

r. 2737–2697 BCE

Shennong, whose name means "divine farmer," was believed to have taught humanity agriculture

and plant-based medicine. As China's first farmer, he invented the plow and taught his people about the qualities of different soils used for cultivation. He also tasted all known plants in order to discover their medicinal properties. Before his rule, people supposedly survived by collecting fruit and hunting animals and were often subject to food poisoning and digestive problems. Shennong's rule, therefore, was thought of as a blessed time, when men tilled the earth and women wove clothes. The government did not need to employ any punishments and no one engaged in military activities because it was a time of peace.

Huangdi (the Yellow Emperor)

Other name: Xuanyuan

r. 2697–2598 BCE

Huangdi, the Yellow Emperor, also known as Xuanyuan after the name of his domain, was a great mythical ruler. Some texts say his reign came after the death of Shennong. He was credited with many inventions, including the bow sling. In contrast to

△ Fuxi, the first sovereign, is depicted here by Song painter Ma Lin.

Shennong's reign, Huangdi's time was one of conflict and unrest, and he used violence and punishments to restore order in the world. In fact, most of Huangdi's actions involved suppressing rebels and challengers to the throne. One of his enemies was Yandi, a perverse and greedy ruler whom Huangdi defeated in battle on the plain of Banquan. Huangdi also defeated Chi You, a rebel minister who was well versed in creating and using weapons. Huangdi had 25 sons and recognized 14 of them. However, only Shaohao and Chang Yi, his two sons by his principal wife, had the right to succeed him. When he died, it is believed Huangdi flew to heaven riding a dragon.

Shaohao

Other name: Xuanxiao

r. 2597–2514 BCE

Shaohao, according to some texts, was the firstborn son of Huangdi (the Yellow Emperor), and his principal wife, Leizu. Another tradition states that he was the son of a woman named Nü Jie, who miraculously became pregnant when she was watching a rainbowlike star floating down a stream. While some texts depict him as ruling for around 83 years as the worthy successor of Huangdi, others do not include him in the list of predynastic rulers, describing both Shaohao and his son as unfit to rule.

Zhuanxu

Other name: Gaoyang

r. 2513–2436 BCE

Zhuanxu was the grandson of Huangdi (the Yellow Emperor). Some texts say he directly succeeded Huangdi, while others claim he succeeded his uncle Shaohao after assisting him in governing. Zhuanxu is believed to have fought an epic battle against Gong Gong, an evil character who wanted to rule the world. Enraged when Zhuanxu won, Gong Gong headbutted Mount Buzhou, one of the pillars supporting the sky, permanently tilting the world and causing all the rivers of China to flow to the southeast. Zhuanxu's rule was remembered as virtuous, and he is celebrated as both the ancestor of Shun and of Yu the Great, founder of the Xia dynasty.

Diku

Other name: Gaoxin

r. 2435–2366 BCE

Diku was the son of Qiaoji and grandson of Shaohao, the firstborn of Huangdi (the Yellow Emperor).

During his reign, lordship returned to the main branch of the sacred lineage. Diku was celebrated as a competent and moral ruler, who was able to control the sun, moon, and stars for the benefit of his people. He was also believed to enjoy music and dance, including inventing musical instruments such as drums, bells, and flutes. In spring and fall, he was said to travel by riding a dragon and at other times by riding a horse. Diku had several wives, four of whom bore children. Two of his children became rulers (Zhi and Yao) and two were the progenitors of the Shang and Zhou houses (Xie and Hou Ji).

Di Zhi

r. 2365–2357 BCE

Di Zhi was the eldest son of Diku and one of his consorts, referred to either as Changyi or as the "woman of the Juzi clan." He ruled for only nine years, and traditional sources have very little information about his reign. He may have abdicated in favor of his half brother.

Yao

Other names: Tao Tang, Fangxun

r. 2356–2256 BCE

Yao was the son of Diku and one of his consorts, who is referred to either as Qingdu or as the "woman of the Chenfeng clan." Some sources say Yao succeeded his father; others say he ruled following his half brother Di Zhi. He was deemed a model of moral perfection, enlightened government, and gentle but firm character. Yao entrusted officials to observe and record celestial phenomena in order to establish an accurate calendar. The most famous events of Yao's reign were the simultaneous rising of 10 suns and the Great Flood, when both the Yellow River and the Yangzi flooded, causing chaos among his subjects. The skilled archer, Yi, shot down nine of the 10 suns, and Gun, a descendant of Zhuanxu, was eventually employed to tame the Great Flood, but failed. After more than 70 years of reign, Yao abdicated in favor of the virtuous but lowly Shun. He lived for another 30 years under Shun's rule.

Shun

Other names: Youyu, Chonghua

r. 2255–2208 BCE

Shun was the son of Gusou, a blind man of modest origins descended from Zhuanxu. After the death of his wife, Gusou remarried. The new wife and her son were cruel toward Shun, even attempting to kill him, but in spite of that, he remained kind and respectful. Although engaging in humble activities such as pottery, fishing, and plowing, Shun naturally attracted followers and showed great leadership. Impressed, the ruler Yao gave him his two daughters in marriage and named him his heir instead of his own son Danzhu. When Yao abdicated, Shun became the ruler. He surrounded himself with skilled ministers and employed Yu, the son of Gun, to tame the Great Flood. Shun also subdued the unruly Miao people and exiled wicked individuals from the court. Finally, like Yao, he judged his son unworthy of succession and named Yu, the hero of the Flood, as his heir.

△ Yao visits his successor, Shun, in this 17th-century screen painting by Japanese artist Kusumi Morikage.

The Xia Dynasty (c. 2070–1600 BCE)

The Xia is considered the first dynasty of pre-imperial China. However, the lack of contemporary inscriptions and written documents from the period makes its historical existence the subject of controversy.

Yu

Other names: Da Yu, Yu the Great, Si Wenming

r. 2205–2198 BCE

Some traditional sources say Yu emerged from the belly of the corpse of Gun, an official appointed to control the Great Flood in the times of Yao and Shun (see p. 30–31). Others say his mother became pregnant by ingesting a seed. Yu married Nü Jiao of Tushan and had a son named Qi. As superintendent of public works, Yu managed to channel water from the Yellow River that was flooding the Chinese heartland, rescuing people from calamity. Because of Yu's abilities and trustworthiness, the ruler Shun chose him as his successor. Yu ascended to the throne as the first king of the Xia dynasty and sources say he ruled for 45 years. He called two gatherings of the great lords— one on Mount Tu and the other on Mount Guiji, the place where he was later buried. Because of his achievements, he was later remembered as "Yu the Great."

Qi

r. 2197–2189 BCE

Qi was the son of Yu the Great. Traditional sources are unclear on how he came to the throne. Some state that Yu named his counselor Boyi as his successor, and Boyi voluntarily ceded the throne to Qi. Other sources claim that Qi, or lords who supported him, took the throne by force from Boyi. Nevertheless, this direct succession from father to son established a precedent for hereditary monarchy, rather than merit-based kingship. Different sources put the duration of Qi's reign at between 10 and 29 years. During this time, Qi conquered members of the Youhu clan who were refusing to submit to him. He also exiled one of his younger sons, who later staged a rebellion against him but failed to remove Qi from the throne.

Tai Kang

r. 2188–2160 BCE

Tai Kang was the eldest son of Qi and succeeded his father upon his death as the third ruler of the Xia dynasty. Traditional sources give little information about him, but he is remembered either as a tyrant or as an incompetent king who was fond of hunting. One source suggests that a nobleman named Hou Yi seized the throne from Tai Kang but that Hou Yi soon neglected government affairs to indulge in archery and hunting. According to this source, Tai Kang was eventually assassinated by Ao, who was one of the sons of Han Zhuo, a former ally of Hou Yi.

Zhong Kang

r. 2159–2146 BCE

Zhong Kang was the younger brother of Tai Kang and a son of Qi. His inclusion among the Xia kings is disputed because he is mentioned only in relatively late sources. It is thought that Zhong Kang resided in Zhenxun, which was the capital chosen by Tai Kang. He is believed to have sent out a punitive expedition, led by a lord named Yin, against the court astronomers. Apparently, owing to excessive drunkenness, the court astronomers had failed to predict the advent of a solar eclipse.

△ The first objects dating from 1900–1500 BCE, during the time of the Xia, were found at Erlitou, in Henan province.

Xiang

r. 2146–2118 BCE

Xiang succeeded his father, Zhong Kang. Han Zhuo—who had previously taken the throne from Xiang's uncle, Tai Kang—had now begun to conquer Xia territories, so Xiang moved the court to Zhenguan. Han Zhuo ordered his son to attack Xiang and kill his wife, Min, who was pregnant with Xiang's heir. Xiang was killed, but Min managed to flee and take shelter in her homeland, where she gave birth to Shao Kang.

Shao Kang

r. 2079–2058 BCE

Shao Kang was the son of Xiang and Min. His reign is not well documented but was described as prosperous. The events that led to his succession are unclear, but according to some sources, his mother went into hiding after his father's death, and he was raised by her family. Han Zhuo tried to kill him, so Shao Kang took refuge in the land of Yu, where he married the daughters of the local lord and obtained a small fiefdom. He allied with a nobleman loyal to the Xia royal family and attacked Han Zhuo. Both Han Zhuo and his sons died in battle, and Shao Kang restored the legitimate line of rule.

Zhu

r. 2057–2041 BCE

Zhu was the son of Shao Kang and succeeded him. Traditional sources offer scarce information about his reign apart from the fact that he established his capital in Yuan and then moved it to Laoqiu after a few years. Zhu is said to have hunted a nine-tailed fox while traveling in the east.

Huai

Other names: Hui, Fen

r. 2040–2015 BCE

Huai was the son of Zhu and succeeded his father after his death. In traditional sources, the duration of his reign varies from 26 years to 44 years. The records of his rule are minimal and mostly concerned with the appointment of officials and assemblies at court.

Mang

Other names: Wang

r. 2014–1997 BCE

Mang was the son of Huai and succeeded his father, but little is known about his reign.

Xie

r. 1996–1981 BCE

Xie succeeded his father, Mang. Information about his rule is scarce in traditional sources, but there are two known events. One was the assassination of Zihai, lord of Yin, during a visit to the settlement of Youyi. Zihai's nephew took his revenge against Youyi and its lord, Mianchen. Xie also bestowed rank on members of the neighboring tribes.

Bu Jiang

r. 1980–1922 BCE

Bu Jiang was the son of Xie and succeeded his father. His reign is barely documented, but he apparently led a military campaign against Jiuyuan. It is thought Bu Jiang abdicated in favor of his younger brother Jiong after ruling for 59 years. He may have died ten years into Jiong's reign.

Jiong

r. 1921–1901 BCE

Jiong was the younger brother of Bu Jiang and assumed the throne upon his abdication.

Jin

r. 1900–1880 BCE

Jin was the son of Jiong and became king after the death of his father. He moved the Xia capital to Xihe. There were many natural calamities during the last year of his reign, such as the simultaneous rising of ten suns.

Kong Jia

r. 1879–1849 BCE

Kong Jia was the son of Bu Jiang and a cousin of Jin. Traditional sources say his reign marked the start of the decline of the Xia dynasty and that he was incompetent. According to legend, Heaven sent a pair of dragons to the court in an attempt to put the king back on the right path. However, Kong Jia could not find anyone able to tend to the dragons and one of them died, signaling the irreversible decline of the dynasty.

Gao

r. 1848–1838 BCE

Gao was the son of Kong Jia. Little is known about his reign, except that he is said to have reinstated a minister previously dispossessed by Kong Jia.

Fa

r. 1837–1817 BCE

Fa was the son of Gao. According to traditional sources, there was a great celebration on his accession, and an earthquake, which shook the sacred Mount Tai, when he died. Some sources claim Fa's rule lasted only seven years.

Jie

r. 1818–1767 BCE

Jie was the son of Fa. He is unanimously described in different sources as a depraved and cruel ruler who brought the Xia dynasty to the depths of immorality. According to legend, he once constructed a pond of wine where deadly drinking contests took place. Anyone who criticized him was brutally executed. This situation caused disquiet among the local lords of Xia. The subject state of Shang (also called Yin) then started expanding its territories by conquering minor states and gaining supporters. Jie imprisoned Tang, the main leader of the Shang but later released him. The local lords joined Tang and defeated Jie's army at Mingtiao (modern-day Fengqiu, Henan province). Jie managed to escape, but the Shang army captured and deposed him and then exiled him to Nanchao, putting an end to the Xia dynasty.

▷ This blade, discovered at Erlitou, may have been used by Xia dynasty warriors or for ritual purposes.

The Shang Dynasty (c.1600–1045 BCE)

The Shang dynasty is the first for which there is hard historical and written evidence, although the received sources can contradict both each other and the excavated oracle bones in terms of chronology. The early Shang kings are considered semimythical, but the reign of Wu Ding, ending in 1189 BCE, has clear historical evidence. The Shang kings were most active in Henan province and their capital changed many times.

Tang

Other names: Da Yi Cheng Tang, Shang Tang, Wu Tang, Tian Yi

r. 1766–1759 BCE

Tang, whom the oracle bones' inscriptions called Da Yi, was the son of Zhu Gui and Prince of Shang. His ancestor was Xie of the Yin tribe who, according to legend, helped Yu fight the floods (see p. 310). Jie, the last Xia dynasty king (see p. 311), was a wicked ruler, and people requested Tang's aid to overthrow him. Jie imprisoned Tang but later released him. Tang had a minister Yi Yin, who encouraged him to rebel. Tang returned with an army and overthrew the Xia by gradually conquering territories in present-day Henan. He was then established as the first king of the Shang dynasty.

Tang honored the altars of the Xia and then proceeded to reform the calendar and change his dynasty's ceremonial clothing color to white. His capital was Bo (modern-day Shangqiu, Henan province). His reign may have witnessed many droughts, which required centralized relief efforts. According to one source, Tang ruled for 13 years and died at the age of 100, but, like many Shang kings, when he ruled and for how long are highly ambiguous.

Wai Bing

Other names: Bu Bing, Sheng

r. 1759–1757 BCE

Tang's eldest son, Tai Ding, had died before he could be enthroned, so his younger brother, Wai Bing, became the second king of Shang. However, the oracle bones suggest he was actually the fourth Shang king. Yi Yin served as his minister, and Wai Bing died after roughly three years of rule.

Zhong Ren

Other names: Nanren, Yong

r. 1757–1753 BCE

Wai Bing's younger brother, Zhong Ren, ruled for roughly four years and like his brother and father, he was also served by the minister Yi Yin. His reign is not recorded in the oracle bones.

Tai Jia

Other names: Da Jia, Taizong, Zhi

r. 1753–1721 BCE

Yi Yin established Tai Ding's son, Tai Jia, as the fourth king of Shang. Tai Jia was the eldest grandson of Tang, the founder of the Shang dynasty. Tai Jia, however, was a harsh and incompetent ruler who rejected the ways of Tang, so Yi Yin had him confined to the palace and ruled in his stead during his early reign. According to sources, Tai Jia reformed himself in confinement and was released and reinstated by Yi Yin. After this, Tai Jia's rule was apparently virtuous, and Tai Jia was honored by Yi Yin. Another source suggests Tai Jia struggled with Yi Yin for power, escaped the palace, and had Yi Yin killed. Sources do not all agree on the length of Tai Jia's reign; one says Tai Jia ruled for only 12 years. According to oracle bones, he was the third king of the Shang.

Wo Ding

Other names: Qiang Ding, Xun

r. 1720–1692 BCE

Wo Ding was Tai Jia's son and became king on his father's death. Wo Ding buried and honored Yi Yin, the long-serving Shang minister. Wo Ding's minister, Jiu Dan, continued Yi Yin's teachings. Wo Ding's reign is not recorded in the oracle bones.

△ This portrait depicts King Tang of Shang.

Tai Geng

Other names: Da Geng, Xiao Geng, Tai Kang, Xiao Kang, Bian

r. 1691–1667 BCE

Tai Geng was the brother of the previous king, Wo Ding. The dates of his reign vary in the sources—one source says that Tai Geng reigned for only five years. The oracle bones also suggest he was actually the fifth king of Shang.

Xiao Jia

Other name: Gao

r. 1666–1650 BCE

Xiao Jia succeeded his brother, Tai Geng, but little else is known about his short reign.

Yong Ji

Other names: Lü Ji, Dian (Zhou)

r. 1649–1638 BCE

Yong Ji became king after his brother, Xiao Jia. In his reign, the adherence to the moral ways of the former minister Yi Yin supposedly declined, and the Shang lords did not readily come to court. Some sources call the king Yong Ji, but the oracle bones suggest he was called Lü Ji and that he was actually the eighth king of Shang. The oracle bones also say that he reigned after his brother, Tai Wu.

Tai Wu

Other names: Da Wu, Tian Zu, Zu Wu, Zhong Zong, Mi

r. 1637–1563 BCE

When Yong Ji died, his brother Tai Wu succeeded him. His minister was Yi Zhi. Tai Wu received a dark omen when a mulberry tree grew to full size very quickly in the capital. Yi Zhi advised Tai Wu to reform his government, and the tree then wilted. The Shang prospered thereafter. Tai Wu's court may have been visited by the foreign Rong and Yi peoples. One source claims he reigned for 75 years, but this claim is highly unlikely to be true. The oracle bones also have a different order of succession to other sources, suggesting that Tai Wu succeeded his nephew Xiao Jia and that he was followed by Lü Ji (Yong Ji).

Zhong Ding

Other names: Sanzu Ding, Zhuang

r. 1562–1550 BCE

Zhong Ding was Tai Wu's son and heir. He moved the capital to Ao or Xiao (possibly modern-day Zhengzhou, Henan province). One source claims that in the sixth year of his reign, he led a campaign against the Blue Yi people. The oracle bones suggest he succeeded Lü Ji (Yong Ji).

Wai Ren

Other names: Bu Ren, Fa

r. 1549–1535 BCE

Wai Ren reigned after his brother, Zhong Ding. The Pei people and Xian people, who may have been Shang subjects, possibly rebelled in his reign.

Hedan Jia

Other names: Jian Jia, Zheng

r. 1534–1526 BCE

Hedan Jia succeeded his brother, Wai Ren. Hedan Jia resided at Xiang (possibly modern-day Neihuang, Henan province). According to one source, Hedan Jia conquered the Pei people and attacked the Blue Yi. The Xian people had also occupied a territory called Banfang, so two commanders, Peng Bo and Wei Bo, were sent to attack them. The Xian ultimately submitted to the authority of the Shang. Some sources, however, suggest that the Shang were in decline during Hedan Jia's reign.

Zu Yi

Other names: Zhongzong, Gaozu, Xia Yi, Ru Yi, Teng

r. 1525–1507 BCE

Zu Yi succeeded his father, Hedan Jia (although the oracle bones suggest Hedan Jia was his brother). He resided at Geng (possibly Hejin, Shanxi) and the Shang again flourished, in part because he was served by a shaman named Xian. Some sources claim he was enthroned at Xiang before moving to Geng and then Bi (possibly Xingtai, Hebei province), possibly because Geng was destroyed by flooding.

Zu Xin

Other name: Dan

r. 1506–1491 BCE

Zu Xin succeeded his father, Zu Yi, and his capital was also at Bi. The length of his reign is uncertain; one source claims he reigned for only four years.

Wo Jia

Other names: Kai Jia, Qiang Jia, Yu

r. 1490–1466 BCE

Wo Jia succeeded his brother, Zu Xin. One source claims he reigned for only five years; others say his reign was much longer.

Zu Ding

Other names: Xiao Ding, Sizu Ding, Xin

r. 1465–1434 BCE

Zu Ding was Wo Jia's nephew. Little is known about his reign, although one source claimed he reigned for only nine years.

Nan Geng

Other names: Nan Kang, Zu Geng, Geng

r. 1433–1409 BCE

Nan Geng was a son of Wo Jia and succeeded his cousin, Zu Ding. One source states that he moved his capital from Bi to Yan (possibly Qufu, Shandong province) and that he reigned for only six years. The oracle bones say that he was the son of Zu Xin and younger brother of Zu Ding. »

△ This finial adorned a chariot used in the wars fought by the Shang kings.

Yang Jia

Other names: He Jia, Xiang Jia, Fu Jia, Zu Jia, He

r. 1408–1402 BCE

Yang Jia's father was Zu Ding, and he succeeded Nan Geng. In his reign, the Shang supposedly declined. By then, the true line of succession had been thoroughly disrupted, and the various young princes contended for the throne. Meanwhile, the Shang's vassals did not come to court. One source claims Yang Jia campaigned against the Rong people.

Pangeng

Other names: Fu Geng, Zu Geng, Sanzu Geng, Xun

r. 1401–1374 BCE

Pangeng succeeded his brother, Yang Jia. He moved the capital from Yan to south of the Yellow River, land which the Shang founder, Tang, called Yin (see pp. 42–43). Pangeng's subjects were displeased with the move, but he swayed public opinion and settled a place named "Bo" (perhaps not the same location as the previous Shang city of Bo). By striving to follow Tang's virtuous ways, the Shang dynasty then supposedly flourished once again. The people rejoiced, and the Shang vassals came to court once more. One source claims that the land Pangeng settled was called Beimeng.

Xiao Xin

Other names: Fu Xin, Erzu Xin, Song

r. 1373–1353 BCE

Xiao Xin succeeded his brother, Pangeng, and was enthroned at Yin. During his reign, Shang authority seems to have declined again, and the people were said to have longed for the time of Pangeng. Little else, however, is known about his reign.

Xiao Yi

Other names: Fu Yi, Xiaozu Yi, Houzu Yi, Jian

r. 1352–1325 BCE

Xiao Yi succeeded his brother, Xiao Xin. One source claimed he ruled for only ten years and that

◁ This statue depicts Fu Hao, a priestess, military general, and consort of Wu Ding of Shang.

he ordered his son, Wu Ding, to move to a place called He ("River") so that he might learn from a great minister called Gan Pan. Not much else is known about Xiao Yi's reign.

Wu Ding

Other name: Zi Zhao

r. unknown–1189 BCE

Wu Ding is the first ruler whose reign is documented by inscriptions. Traditional sources state his personal name was Zi Zhao. He was the son of Xiao Yi and his rule brought the Shang dynasty back to prosperity. Inscriptions of the period record intense military conflicts taking place in the Shang's neighboring territories, especially those to the west. Contemporary documents also reveal that Zu Ji, one of Wu Ding's sons, died during his father's reign. Wu Ding was king for a long time; his reign is traditionally believed to have lasted for 59 years.

One of Wu Ding's consorts, Fu Hao (see pp. 42–43), joined the Shang's armed expeditions and also acted as a priestess during divinatory procedures. Fu Hao is sometimes considered China's first female general. Her tomb was discovered at the Shang site near Anyang in 1976 and contained items—including 468 bronze objects— suggesting that she held a position of importance that was unusual for women at that time. Although she is not included in classical texts from the Zhou dynasty and later, Shang records and oracle bones describe Fu Hao variously as the king's consort and a military leader. One source records her leading an army of 13,000 men against warriors from a northern nomadic tribe.

Zu Geng

Other names: Zi Yue, Zi Yao

r. 1188–1178 BCE

Zu Geng was the son of Wu Ding and one of his consorts, possibly Fu Jing. Traditional sources state that his personal name was Zi Yue. He was considered the official heir of Wu Ding, but his succession was controversial owing to the unclear status of his brothers. He tried to continue his father's policies and had little success. Still, the Shang enjoyed a period of relative peace during his time on the throne.

Zu Jia

Other name: Zi Zai

r. 1177–1158 BCE

Zu Jia was the younger brother of Zu Geng and came to the Shang throne after his death. Some sources depict Zu Jia as leading a dissolute life; however, contemporary documents suggest that, unlike his conservative brother Zu Geng, Zu Jia did promote some innovations. During his reign, both the calendar system and ritual procedures were reformed. The ritual reform in particular aimed to strengthen the king's authority and legitimize his role. His reign also saw a decrease in military activity, which brought about a period of peace.

Lin Xin

Other names: Feng Xin, Xiong Xin, Zi Xian

r. 1157–1149 BCE

Lin Xin was the son of Zu Jia. Some scholars have doubted the legitimacy of his kingship.

Records indicate that his reign saw an increase in defensive military activities owing to growing pressure from neighboring forces.

Geng Ding

Other names: Kang Ding, Zi Xiao

r. 1148–1132 BCE

Geng Ding was the younger brother of Lin Xin, and he probably came to the throne after his death. Some traditional sources claim that he ruled for only eight years. Contemporary inscriptions attest that during Geng Ding's reign, the decline which started under Lin Xin increased. Not only did the Shang have to sustain a state of constant defensive warfare against its surrounding peoples, but it also faced a surge in internal unrest.

Wu Yi

Other name: Zi Qu

r. 1131–1117 BCE

Wu Yi was the son of Geng Ding. The length of his rule varies in different sources. There were several changes of capital under his reign. Some sources record that his reign saw warfare with northern enemies and good relations with the subject house of Zhou, while others highlight Wu Yi's depravity, noting he was struck by lightning as punishment for having insulted Heaven.

Wen Ding

Other names: Tai Ding, Wen Wu Ding, Zi Tuo

r. 1116–1106 BCE

Wen Ding was the son of Wu Yi. According to traditional texts, Wen Ding's reign saw the rising power of the Zhou military under the leadership of Ji Jili, who conquered several territories within a few years. The Zhou were subjects of the Shang king, but Wen Ding feared Ji Jili's growing influence and had him assassinated. This act apparently inspired the conflict between the Shang and Zhou that would eventually bring about the end of the Shang dynasty. Two years after Ji Jili's death, possibly in the 13th year of his rule, Wen Ding died.

Di Yi

Other name: Zi Xian

r. 1105–1087 BCE

Di Yi was the son of Wen Ding. The length of his reign is unclear: some sources state he ruled for nine years. Apart from the establishment of settlements and a chance earthquake, the traditional texts record nothing of his reign. Contemporary inscriptions, on the other hand, speak of military expeditions against eastern enemies and of ritual reforms aimed at strengthening his power.

Di Xin

Other names: Zhou, Shou Xin, Zi Shou, Zi Shoude

r. 1086–1045 BCE

Di Xin was the last Shang king and succeeded Di Yi after his death. Di Xin's relationship to Di Yi is unclear. Some sources state he was the youngest son of Di Yi and his main consort, while others argue that he was his nephew. Contemporary inscriptions speak of Di Xin's military expeditions in various neighboring territories. Traditional texts depict Di Xin as a cruel and violent tyrant,

△ This Ming engraving depicts Di Xin, whose story was told in the Ming novel *Fengshen Yanyi (Investiture of the Gods)*.

not unlike the last king of the Xia dynasty. Di Xin was apparently prone to excesses and evil deeds, torturing and murdering those who criticized him. Among Di Xin's victims were his own uncle, Bi Gan, and Ji Chang, the leader of the house of Zhou, whom he imprisoned. When Ji Chang was released, he started a military campaign against Di Xin. This was then continued by Ji Chang's son, the future King Wu of Zhou, who brought about Di Xin's fall and the end of the Shang dynasty.

The Western Zhou Dynasty (1046–771 BCE)

The Zhou dynasty overthrew the Shang and were dominated by a series of strong rulers. The Western Zhou period is considered the great era of classical antiquity and the beginning of Chinese civilization.

Wen
Other name: Ji Chang

r. 1099/56–1050 BCE

Traditional histories present Ji Chang (his birth name) as one of the sons of Ji Jili, the leader of the Zhou people who lived in the Wei River valley (present-day Shaanxi province). The power accumulated by Ji Jili through military campaigns worried King Wen of Shang, who ordered that Ji Jili be killed. This marked Ji Chang's rise to power as leader of the Zhou people and the beginning of hostile relations between the Shang and the Zhou. Seen as a threat by King Di Xin of Shang, Ji Chang was imprisoned for seven years. After Ji Chang's ransom was paid, the Shang king freed him and allowed him to conduct military campaigns in the territories to the west of

△ This portrait depicts King Wen of the Western Zhou.

Shang. The extension of Ji Chang's conquests brought him close to the Shang capital, but he died before becoming a threat to the dynasty. He is remembered as King Wen, "cultured king."

Wu
Other name: Ji Fa

r. 1049/45–1043 BCE

Ji Fa was the second eldest of the 10 sons King Wen of Zhou had with his principal wife. After the death of his father, Ji Fa inherited the leadership of the Zhou people, becoming known as King Wu, the "martial king." Continuing King Wen's campaign, he entered the Shang region with his army. Helped by militia from local lords, he defeated the Shang army at the Battle of Muye in 1045 BCE. King Di Xin of Shang was defeated and died by suicide. The Shang capital remained under the nominal rule of Di Xin's son, Wu Geng, overseen by King Wu's brothers. Another brother, Ji Dan, remained in the Zhou capital, Feng, as the king's counselor. Two years after this conquest, King Wu died.

Cheng
Other name: Ji Song

r. 1042/35–1006 BCE

When King Wu died, his heir was his eldest son, Ji Song, and he was later known as King Cheng. However, owing to the crown prince's young age, the late king's brother and counselor, Ji Dan, declared himself regent. Ji Dan's elder brothers contested his right to govern and joined forces with the ruler of the Shang people, Wu Geng, to stage a rebellion. In two years, Ji Dan subdued the rebellion by force, killing two of his brothers and forcing the third into exile. Ji Dan's campaign continued further east, defeating several coastal peoples and bringing them under Zhou rule. After founding the eastern capital of Chengzhou (present-day Luoyang), Ji Dan assigned territories to royal family members, creating six major states. Ji Dan also formulated the concept of the Mandate of Heaven (see pp. 48–49), the ideological foundation of the Zhou claim to rule. He then retired, leaving the government to King Cheng.

Kang
Other name: Ji Zhao

r. 1005/3–978 BCE

Ji Zhao was the eldest son and designated successor of King Cheng. He was known as King Kang. His accession was seen to sanction the Zhou policy of primogeniture—the right of the eldest son to succeed his father—which subsequent kings followed thereafter. Like the second half of his father's reign, Kang's rule was peaceful and prosperous and mostly focused on consolidating control over the acquired territories. Several lords trusted by the sovereign were sent to preside over new strategic sites, and military operations allowed them to acquire new lands in the north. Later sources portray King Kang's reign as a period of harmony when punishments were not needed.

Zhao
Other name: Ji Xia

r. 977/75–957 BCE

Ji Xia, King Zhao, was the son of King Kang. At his accession, the Zhou kingdom had successfully expanded its original territory to the north and east, but the Yangzi River basin in the south was still outside its sphere of influence. Therefore, King Zhao led a military campaign against the southern state of Chu in 957 BCE. It resulted in a crushing defeat, the destruction of the royal army and the death of the king himself. The failure of the campaign weakened the Zhou dynasty and stalled its expansion.

Mu
Other name: Ji Man

r.956–918 BCE

Ji Man, called King Mu, was the son of King Zhao and succeeded him when his father died in a campaign against the state of Chu. The military vulnerability from this defeat induced the eastern tribes to attack. King Mu guided a campaign against them and, immediately after, had to fend off an attack from the Xu Rong to the capital Chengzhou. The war ended with an armistice in which the Xu Rong offered their loyalty to the Zhou in exchange for autonomous rule. King Mu also faced the internal fragmentation of the Zhou state due to the loosening of familial ties between the royal family and the regional rulers. To remedy this, he reformed the court offices and created a bureaucracy that strengthened his relations with local lords.

Gong
Other name: Ji Yihu

r.917/15–900 BCE

Ji Yihu succeeded his father, King Mu. He was posthumously named King Gong. Neither written nor archaeological sources supply much information about the events of his reign. There is evidence that he strengthened court bureaucracy at all levels and introduced land reforms.

Yi (I)
Other name: Ji Jian

r.899/97–873 BCE

Like his father King Gong's reign, the political rule of King Yi is scarcely documented. Sources indicate the Zhou were attacked by neighboring northern and eastern tribes and the royal house faced an overall decline. The fact that King Yi was succeeded by his uncle Ji Bifang and that he moved his residence away from the capital suggests that he was forced into exile by Ji Bifang, who then declared himself king.

Xiao
Other name: Ji Bifang

r.872–866 BCE

Ji Bifang was the uncle of King Yi and the younger brother of King Gong. He succeeded his nephew. The circumstances of his accession are unclear, and his reign is poorly documented. It is possible that he seized the throne after exiling his nephew. He was called King Xiao. Historical sources mention that after his reign, the local lords restored the son of King Yi (I) to the throne.

Yi (II)
Other name: Ji Xie

r.865–858 BCE

Ji Xie was the son of King Yi (I) and the nephew of King Xiao. He succeeded his uncle and was posthumously named King Yi (II). During his reign, a dispute about

△ King Mu listens to a woman playing the *guzheng*.

succession erupted in the state of Qi, one of the original Zhou colonies. The royal army intervened to quell the struggle. It showed that the decline of Zhou power and authority that began under the reign of Yi's father was getting worse. The local lords were becoming less and less responsive to central control and were defying Zhou sovereignty. Sensing Zhou political weakness, the southern state of Chu launched an attack that was repelled only with great difficulty. King Yi (II) died after only eight years of rule.

Li
Other name: Ji Hu

r.857/53–842/28 BCE

Ji Hu was the son of King Yi (II) and was given the name King Li. He was very young at the time of his accession and not able to cope with the slow disintegration of Zhou rule. Historical sources depict him as greedy, cruel, extravagant, and unfazed by the remonstrations of his officials. Early in his reign, the southern state of Chu attacked as they » had done in his father's reign, but this time the Zhou army was not able to push the enemy back. Another attack came from the western tribes in 843 BCE. A year later, King Li was dethroned and forced into exile, because of either a conspiracy plotted by the local lords or a peasant rebellion. A minister saved the king's infant son, Ji Jing, and hid him until his father's death.

Gonghe

Other name: Lord He of Gong

r.841–828 BCE

After King Li was deposed, there was a period when no king was designated to rule. This time was known as the "Gonghe regency." Lord He of the state of Gong was appointed as regent. After 14 uneventful years of the lord's regency, the exiled King Li died and his son Ji Jing became the new ruler.

Xuan

Other name: Ji Jing

r.827/25–782 BCE

Ji Jing was the son of King Li and was called King Xuan. He took action to restore Zhou authority. Through his minister Yin Jifu (also known as Xi Jia), in 823 BCE, he defeated the tribes of western barbarians known as the Xianyun, who had raided Zhou territories in the past and he triumphed over their army again later in his reign (816–815 BCE). He also regained control of the Huai River area in the south and regulated trade relations with its inhabitants. To restore control over the Zhou states, he called an assembly of the lords in 819 BCE, but he later had to intervene militarily in succession conflicts among many of the Zhou states.

You

Other name: Ji Gongsheng

r.781–771 BCE

Ji Gongsheng was the son of King Xuan and succeeded him as King You. Shortly after he became king, a series of natural disasters took place, which were interpreted as a bad omen for the dynasty. According to historical sources, the omens came true when You divorced his wife in favor of his concubine, Bao Si. You also exiled his legitimate heir and established the son he had with Bao Si as his successor. King You's father-in-law wanted vengeance for the insult to his daughter. He formed an alliance with the western barbarians, who sacked the Zhou capital, killed the king, and captured Bao Si. With the capital destroyed and their territory invaded, the Zhou elite evacuated the Wei River area and moved to the east, creating a new capital at Chengzhou.

△ King You's warning beacons call his men to the palace as a prank to impress Bao Si. This later depiction does not accurately depict the chariot-based military of the Zhou period.

The Eastern Zhou Dynasty (770–256 BCE)

During the Eastern Zhou period, the power of the royal house began to decline. Competing states, such as Qi, Jin, and Wei, fought for dominance. Eventually these "Warring States" took over the territories of the Chinese heartland.

Ping
Other name: Ji Yijiu

r. 770–720 BCE

After the Zhou court moved to Chengzhou, Ji Yijiu, the exiled son of King You, was enthroned as King Ping. At the same time, Ji Yuchen, supported by a group of lords, declared himself King Xie of Zhou. A struggle between the two kings ended with the death of Xie and the triumph of Ping, who found strong allies in the states of Jin and Zheng. The ruler of Zheng, Duke Zhuang, defended the royal court not only from foreign assaults but also from other Zhou contenders. Worried by the power Duke Zhuang held in royal politics, Ping appointed another noble to assist the duke and balance out his power. This made the duke furious, and to secure his loyalty and defuse the tension, King Ping had to exchange hostages with him.

Huan
Other name: Ji Lin

r. 719–697 BCE

Ji Lin, who was called King Huan, was the grandson of King Ping. Threatened by the growing power of the Duke of Zheng, he removed him from office and appointed another lord as his minister. In retaliation, the Duke of Zheng made it clear that he did not respect the king, and King Huan responded by leading a coalition of troops against him. The duke's forces defeated the royal army, and King Huan was wounded in battle. This defeat severely damaged the dynasty's status, and thereafter its authority and power became only nominal. Meanwhile, the state of Zheng gained a position of leadership among the states that lasted until the duke's death in 701 BCE.

Zhuang
Other name: Ji Tuo

r. 696–682 BCE

Ji Tuo was the son of King Huan and succeeded him as King Zhuang. Since the reign of King Huan, the royal court's authority had started to dwindle. The disjointed Zhou states became easier prey for foreign incursions, while in the south the power of the state of Chu grew. The state of Qi also quickly rose toward preeminence, thanks to the rule of Duke Huan and the reforms of his adviser, Guan Zhong.

Xi
Other name: Ji Huqi

r. 681–677 BCE

Ji Huqi was the son of King Zhuang and succeeded him as King Xi. During his brief reign, the shift of power from the Zhou royal court to the state of Qi continued, as Qi's superior organizational structure gave it the economic and military means to exert control over other states.

Hui
Other name: Ji Lang

r. 676–652 BCE

Ji Lang was the son of King Xi and came to the throne as King Hui. At the beginning of his reign, he was forced into temporary exile by his brother, Prince Tui, who usurped the throne. After the Zheng forces killed Tui and restored the king, he granted their leader, Duke Huan, the title of "hegemon" in 672 BCE. This allowed the duke to take military action on behalf of the king. In 667 BCE, the duke assembled the rulers of Lu, Song, Chen, and Zheng and was elected leader of the states. He launched a campaign against the state of Wei, who had supported Prince Tui's coup. His campaigns also helped to stall the expansion of the rising state of Chu.

Xiang
Other name: Ji Zheng

r. 651–619 BCE

Ji Zheng became King Xiang when his father King Hui died. Over the years, Duke Huan of Qi called several meetings of surrounding states. These had several purposes: discussing military actions, securing the participants' loyalty to the Zhou, securing cooperation and mutual respect of territorial borders, and deciding conduct in state affairs. However, when Duke Huan died in 643 BCE, the Qi lost their hegemon status. Instead, it passed to the politically strong and heavily militarized state of Jin, led by Duke Wen. When King Xiang's brother seized the throne, Duke Wen killed the usurper, restoring King Xiang. The Jin also resisted an attack by the state of Chu, defeating the invading army in 632 BCE.

Qing
Other name: Ji Renchen

r. 618–613 BCE

Ji Renchen was the son of King Xiang and succeeded him as King Qing. His short reign saw the death of the hegemon Duke Wen of Jin. In the latter part of Xiang's rule, the state of Jin had struggled to maintain its hegemony. Qi and Qin, powerful neighboring states, had started to challenge Jin's leadership, but after a few military conflicts, the fighting reached a stalemate. Meanwhile, Chu had recovered its strength after its defeat by Duke Wen and was ready to strike again.

Kuang
Other name: Ji Ban

r. 612–607 BCE

King Kuang, who was the son of King Qing, ruled for five years, during which time the major states of Jin, Qin and Qi, together with other minor states, carried on their power struggle with no discernible victor. »

Ding
Other name: Ji Yu

r.606–586 BCE

Ji Yu was the younger brother of King Kuang and was remembered as King Ding. During his reign, surrounding states continued their military struggles. The state of Chu started its northward incursions again, coming close to the Zhou capital. Chu defeated the state of Jin (an ally of the Zhou) in battle in 598 BCE. In 589 BCE, however, Jin allied with the state of Wu, forcing Chu to fight on two fronts.

Jian
Other name: Ji Yi

r.585–572 BCE

Ji Yi was the son of King Ding and was later called King Jian. During his reign, the long power struggle between the states of Jin, Qin, and Qi ended when Duke Li of Jin proposed a triple alliance to defeat the state of Chu in 580 BCE. The state of Song mediated a truce between the new alliance and Chu. Although all parties agreed to reduce their military strength, the respite was brief. Within five years, conflicts resumed and, at the Battle of Yanling in 575 BCE, Jin's army defeated the Chu. Duke Dao, who succeeded Duke Li, restored Jin's internal stability and was recognized as hegemon.

Ling
Other name: Ji Xiexin

r.571–545 BCE

Ji Xiexin was the son of King Jian and followed him as King Ling. By this period, the influence of the Zhou royal house had progressively decreased. Each of the coexisting states had its own area of influence and a cultural identity that was only nominally associated with the Zhou. Likewise, the role of hegemon had largely lost its original purpose of preserving the Zhou. In 546 BCE, the four major states of Jin, Qin, Qi, and Chu reached a peace agreement that ratified their positions as independent powers, further weakening their bonds with the Zhou.

Jing (I)
Other name: Ji Gui

r.544–520 BCE

Ji Gui followed his father as ruler and was posthumously called King Jing. The agreement between Jin, Qin, Qi, and Chu had granted a long-lasting peace. The depleted smaller states who had been continually drawn into wars also found relief. However, Jing's death prompted a dynastic struggle. His designated heir had died prematurely, and no replacement was appointed. The eldest son of the king was enthroned as King Dao, but soon afterward, his brother Chao revolted and killed him. In turn, another rebellion removed Chao and enthroned Ji Gai.

Jing (II)
Other name: Ji Gai

r.519–476 BCE

Ji Gai was the son of King Jing. The celebrated thinker Confucius (see pp. 62–63) lived and taught during his reign. Jing spent his first years on the throne dealing with the aftermath of the struggle that brought him to power. A revolt led him to spend some time in exile in the state of Jin before he was reinstated.

△ Confucius (551–479 BCE) lived during the reigns of kings Jing I and II.

Meanwhile, peace endured among the states in the north, but in the south the state of Wu launched a major offensive against Chu, inflicting a crushing defeat in 506 BCE. Wu in turn was then challenged by the neighboring state of Yue. The conflicts ended with the triumph of King Fuchai of Wu over King Goujian of Yue in 494 BCE (see p. 59). Wanting to become hegemon, Fuchai moved north and defeated Qi and Jin.

Yuan
Other name: Ji Ren

r.475–469 BCE

Ji Ren was the son of King Jing and succeeded him as King Yuan. His reign saw the state of Wu fall from power and Yue rise to become the dominant state. Soon, Yue started to be involved in the political and military affairs of the northern states. A conference of leaders of the major states sanctioned its position of hegemon, but Yuan's reign also saw the hegemon's role continue to decline.

Zhending
Other name: Ji Jie

r.468–441 BCE

Ji Jie was the son of King Yuan and succeeded him as King Zhending. States within the Zhou lands expanded their territories during his reign. The states of Chu and Yue incorporated the lesser states at their northern borders. The state of Qi expanded to the east and Qin to the north. An internal struggle between the elite families of the state of Jin led to the partition of its land among the houses of Zhao, Wei, and Han in 453 BCE. This caused a power vacuum in the political balance, allowing neighboring states to expand further. In 441 BCE, Qin expanded into the fertile regions of the southwest.

Kao
Other name: Ji Wei

r. 440–426 BCE

Ji Wei was the youngest son of King Zhending. When King Zhending died, his eldest son, Ji Chuji, was enthroned as King Ai but after only three months was killed by a younger brother, Ji Shu. He in turn was killed by Ji Wei, who enthroned himself as King Kao. During his rule, the larger states within the Zhou lands continued to absorb smaller states around them.

Weilie
Other name: Ji Wu

r. 425–402 BCE

Ji Wu inherited the throne from his father, King Kao, and became King Weilie. At the beginning of his reign, the houses of Zhao, Wei, and Han of the state of Jin informally acknowledged their independence from each other. In 403 BCE, Weilie ratified this decision, dividing Jin into the separate states of Zhao, Wei, and Han. The three remained allied under the leadership of the Wei. The key figure of this coalition was Marquis Wen of Wei, whose leadership helped them expand to the northeast and west.

An
Other name: Ji Jiao

r. 401–376 BCE

The son of Weilie, Ji Jiao, came to the throne as King An. During An's reign, the increasing power of Wei caused Zhao to leave their former alliance and move its capital. When it attacked a lesser state to its southwest in 383 BCE, Wei intervened against Zhao—which, in turn, asked for help from Chu. Chu attacked and seized lands to its north. Wei, occupied on two fronts, lost part of its territories to Zhao. This conflict established a pattern of shifting alliances typical of the latter part of the Zhou dynasty and heralded the return of Chu.

Lie
Other name: Ji Xi

r. 375–369 BCE

Ji Xi was the son of King An and succeeded him as King Lie. During his reign, the shifting pattern of alliances continued. Qi recovered its power, recaptured some of its old territories, and expanded south. When a war of succession temporarily weakened the state of Wei, Zhao and Han both attacked, but neither was successful. After this struggle, Marquis Hui of Wei rose to power in the alliance of the three states.

Xian
Other name: Ji Bian

r. 368–321 BCE

Ji Bian was King Lie's younger brother and ruled as King Xian. His reign saw the rise of the state of Qin, which, after centuries of decline, defeated the armies of Han and Wei in 366 BCE. With its

newfound might, Qin triumphed over Wei in 364 BCE and 362 BCE. After Wei's defeat, Marquis Hui moved the capital to a safer place and secured the boundaries with Han and Zhao. Meanwhile, extensive reforms improved Qin's military and administrative system. In 344 BCE, Marquis Hui, later followed by other state leaders, declared himself king and formally proclaimed his independence from the Zhou. A series of defeats against Qi sealed Wei's decline.

Shenjing
Other name: Ji Ding

r. 320–315 BCE

Ji Ding was the son of King Xian and succeeded him as King Shenjing. During his reign, Qin's power grew enormously. In 318 BCE, a united front formed by Qi, Yan, Zhao, Han, Wei, and Chu launched an attack on Qin to no effect. Qin expanded further in the southwest, incorporating territories that gave it a strategic advantage over its enemies.

Nan
Other name: Ji Yan

r. 314–256 BCE

Ji Yan was the son of Shenjing and succeeded him as King Nan. In 314 BCE, Zhou divided into the states of East Zhou, governed by a junior branch of the royal house, and West Zhou, the residence of the king.

▷ Bronze mirrors, such as this Warring States period example, were often given as gifts to and by lords.

Qin consolidated its frontiers in the west and crushed Chu forces in 312 BCE, severely weakening the southern state, but a Qin succession struggle forced it to agree a peace with an alliance of Qi, Han, and Wei in 298 BCE. While Qin was annexing Chu's lands, Zhao was able to defeat it in battle. Abandoning its ongoing war with Qi, Qin focused on Zhao, crushing it at Changping in 260 BCE. Four years later, Qin attacked and deposed King Nan, conquering West Zhou.

Lord of East Zhou (Dong Zhou Jun)

r. 255–249 BCE

When the Qin army invaded West Zhou, fugitives took refuge in East Zhou. The deposed King Nan died without a successor. The Lord of East Zhou was a descendant of Ji Jie, the younger brother of King Kao. Seven years after the conquest of West Zhou, the Qin army vanquished East Zhou. This conquest marked the end of the Zhou. Qin continued its expansion for three decades, proceeding to unify China.

The Qin Dynasty (221–207 BCE)

The state of Qin in West China conquered and unified the other Warring States to create a single empire for the first time. The Qin achieved amazing feats, particularly in construction, during their short reign but fell to rebels who then established the Han dynasty.

Qin Shi Huangdi

Other names: Ying Zheng, Zhao Zheng

r. 221–210 BCE
b. 259 BCE d. 210 BCE

Ying Zheng was the son of King Zhuangxiang of the state of Qin and succeeded his father as ruler at the age of 13. For the first nine years of his reign, the minister Lü Buwei acted as regent. Through military campaigns and with the aid of capable ministers—such as Lü Buwei and Li Si—Ying Zheng conquered the other six independent states, creating the first unified empire of China and proclaimed himself Qin Shi Huangdi (First Emperor of the Qin dynasty) in 221 BCE. He divided his domain into areas that were each under the control of a trusted commander. His many achievements included unifying Chinese writing scripts, standardizing weights and measures, and ordering the construction of canals. He also instigated the building of new roads throughout his lands. He tore down the walls separating the states within his domain but strengthened the northern walls to defend his territory against the Xiongnu nomads. The emperor banned and burned books on philosophy and other subjects and buried scholars alive if they were found to have forbidden books in their possession. He was despised by many for his ruthless rule and contempt for the educated elite, and three assassination attempts were made on his life, but he survived them all.

In his later life, the emperor ordered an empire-wide search for the elixir of immortality, and it is likely that he ingested toxic mercury. He famously ordered the construction of the life-sized Terracotta Army (see pp. 82–83) intended to guard him in the afterlife. As well as around 40,000 bronze weapons, it included sculpted figures of infantry, cavalrymen and horses, all placed in precise military formation. Qin Shi Huangdi died from an illness in 210 BCE.

Qin Ershi Huangdi

Other name: Hu Hai

r. 209–207 BCE
b. 229 BCE d. 207 BCE

Hu Hai was the youngest son of the previous ruler, Qin Shi Huangdi. Favored by his father, he was encouraged to study Legalism with the court eunuch and minister Zhao Gao. When the emperor died in 210 BCE, Zhao Gao and the chancellor Li Si arranged for Fusu, the late emperor's eldest son, to die by suicide and for Hu Hai to ascend to the throne. He was enthroned as the second Qin emperor, with the title Qin Ershi Huangdi.

The emperor had only a short reign and was not a popular ruler, taking more interest in pleasure than in governing his people. He continued with some of his father's works, however, including construction of the palace complex. When Zhao Gao and members of the imperial family were imprisoned or executed, public disapproval of the ruler grew. A number of revolts took place, including the Dazexiang uprising led by army officers, which the Qin found difficult to quell. Sensing an opportunity, independent kingdoms, including the Chu, rose up against the Qin and defeated them. This destroyed much of the Qin's armies and marked the end of their power.

The powerful eunuch Zhao Gao forced Qin Ershi Huangdi to die by suicide, and he was denied a royal burial. Zhao Gao then established Ziying, who was a nephew of Qin Ershi Huangdi, as king of the Qin. He, however, ruled for only a few weeks. The Qin were destroyed by rebels led by Liu Bang, who went on to found the Han dynasty.

△ Archaeologists excavate terracotta warriors guarding Qin Shi Huangdi's tomb.

The Western Han Dynasty (206 BCE–9 CE)

The Western Han dynasty was descended from Liu Bang. The Liu clan ruled the unified Chinese empire for nearly two centuries but faced difficulties from the Xiongnu nomads and rebellious autonomous kingdoms. Their rule was interrupted by the usurper Wang Mang.

Gaozu
Other names: Gaodi, Liu Bang

r. 206–195 BCE
b. 256 BCE d. 195 BCE

Born to a peasant family, Liu Bang fought with the anti-Qin rebels and accepted the surrender of the final Qin king, Ziying. Liu Bang took the title of king of Han in 206 BCE, but then had to defeat Xiang Yu, another important leader of the rebellion. He was victorious and established himself as emperor of the Han dynasty. He took the name Gaozu, which means "high ancestor."

He then bestowed rewards and titles on his followers and family members while eliminating noncompliant kings. Gaozu had to suppress dissident leaders constantly and fend off attacks from the nomad Xiongnu people. He was forced to appease the Xiongnu with a Han palace lady and annual payments. In terms of standards and punishments, he still retained much of the strict regime of the Qin.

Huidi
Other name: Liu Ying

r. 194–188 BCE
b. 210 BCE d. 188 BCE

Liu Ying was the only son of Emperor Gaozu and his principal consort, Empress Lü. He was made Gaozu's heir at five years old. When he became emperor, he reduced taxation and the severity of criminal punishments and constructed shrines to honor Gaozu. However, Empress Lü held the real power at court and murdered Huidi's half brother to maintain her position. During Huidi's reign, the Han capital at Chang'an was completed and relations with non-Chinese peoples were relatively peaceful.

Empress Dowager Lü
Other names: Gaohou (Gao's Empress), Lü Zhi

r. 187–180 BCE
b. 241 BCE d. 180 BCE

After Huidi's death, Empress Lü organized for Qianshao, a young child related to Huidi, to take the throne. She placed her own family in the highest positions at court and eliminated opposition. She later replaced Qianshao with another young boy named »

△ This Song dynasty scroll painting shows Gaozu entering Chang'an.

Houshao. When Empress Lü died, her entire family was exterminated and the house of Liu was restored as rulers of the empire.

Wendi
Other name: Liu Heng

r. 179–157 BCE
b. 200 BCE d. 157 BCE

Liu Heng was a son of Gaozu and one of his consorts, Bo. He had been King of Dai since 196 BCE and took the Han throne as Wendi after Empress Lü died. To promote the empire's unity, Wendi reduced the size and strength of the different kingdoms within it. He dealt with many revolts and natural disasters, promoted agriculture, allowed private minting of coins, and relieved taxes to ease the hardships on the common people. He prioritized defense and diplomacy with both the northern Xiongnu and southern Nanyue peoples. Wendi was viewed as a virtuous ruler.

Jingdi
Other name: Liu Qi

r. 156–141 BCE
b. 188 BCE d. 141 BCE

Liu Qi was the eldest son of Wendi and his consort Dou and succeeded his father as Jingdi. He was known for conducting rites at ancestral shrines and holding state sacrifices. He also reduced state punishments, promoted agricultural production, increased military conscription, fought corruption, and ordered a large warhorse breeding program. Jingdi tried to weaken the kingdoms within the Han empire, which led to the Revolt of the Seven Kingdoms in 154 BCE. Jingdi, however, crushed this

uprising. There were numerous raids by the Xiongnu people, but Jingdi did not confront them.

Wudi
Other name: Liu Che

r. 141–87 BCE
b. 157 BCE d. 87 BCE

The son of Jingdi, Liu Che came to the throne as Wudi aged 17 and was one of China's greatest emperors, ruling for more than 50 years. By the mid-130s BCE, Wudi was planning massive military campaigns in the north and south that expanded his empire and secured its frontiers. Even the mighty Xiongnu people were forced to retreat and request peace. The government took back control of the coinage and established a state monopoly on salt and iron to pay for the armies. Wudi also ordered expeditions into Central Asia and claimed the Western Regions (Xiyu) as part of the empire. This paved the way for trade along the Silk Road. Wudi established Confucianism as the state philosophy and patronized literature, but later was obsessed with omens, magic, and immortality. His son, Liu Ju, was thought to be his favored successor but was killed when suspected of starting a coup.

Zhaodi
Other name: Liu Fuling

r. 86–74 BCE
b. 94 BCE d. 74 BCE

Liu Fuling was the son of Wudi and his consort Zhao Jieyu. Aged eight, he was declared heir two days before Wudi's death and enthroned as Zhaodi. An official named Huo Guang ran the empire and suppressed uprisings by Zhaodi's half brothers. The

△ This portrait depicts Emperor Zhaodi (center).

government restored agricultural production, reduced taxation, and established colonial garrisons on the northern and southern frontiers. Zhaodi never governed directly and died childless.

Xuandi
Other name: Liu Bingyi

r. 73–49 BCE
b. 91 BCE d. 49 BCE

Liu Bingyi was Wudi's great-grandson and was raised as a commoner after his family was exterminated in the unrest of 91 BCE. He became Emperor Xuandi after taking over from Liu He, a prince chosen as Zhaodi's successor who was deposed after less than a month. The court official Huo Guang was in control during Xuandi's early reign. However, after thwarting a plot to dethrone him in 66 BCE, Xuandi became a robust ruler and issued several decrees aimed at improving the

process of selection of court officials. He tried to alleviate poverty in the empire and established food price controls. In his later reign, he secured peaceful relations with a group of Xiongnu people, who were embroiled in civil war. Xuandi also took a great interest in court standards and promoted music.

Yuandi
Other name: Liu Shi

r. 48–33 BCE
b. 75 BCE d. 33 BCE

Liu Shi was the son of Xuandi and Empress Xu and came to the throne in 48 BCE as Emperor Yuandi. He tried to link his reign with the traditional values of the Shang and Zhou dynasties. Yuandi did not conduct reforms and faced no major revolts. His ministers made a blood covenant with the Xiongnu led by Huhanye on his behalf, and relations with these neighbors were very good. Yuandi even sent one of his most beautiful concubines, Wang Zhaojun, to wed the Xiongnu ruler. He improved measures to relieve poverty, reducing his expenditure and diverting funds to help his subjects. He was talented in calligraphy and music and a passionate patron of scholars and artists. In Yuandi's reign, palace eunuchs came to prominence and gained power at court.

Chengdi
Other name: Liu Ao

r. 32–7 BCE
b. 51 BCE d. 7 BCE

Liu Ao was the son of Yuandi and Empress Wang. As a child, he impressed his grandfather, Xuandi, with his impeccable behavior, but as he grew up, he was spoiled and became ill-mannered. While he was enjoying himself, Chengdi delegated responsibilities to his retinue, who were mainly from Empress Wang's family. As a result, the Wang family gained dominance at court. Despite his ineffectual government, Chengdi's reign was peaceful. Under his patronage, scholars collected important literary and technical works.

Aidi
Other name: Liu Xin

r. 6–1 BCE
b. 27 BCE d. 1 BCE

Since Chengdi did not produce an heir, Liu Xin, the son of his half brother, was chosen to succeed him as Aidi. Although articulate and capable, he soon fell under the control of Yuandi's wife, Empress Wang, the most powerful personality at court. In Aidi's reign, the growing influence of the Ding and Fu families threatened the Wang family's supremacy at court. Aidi had an intimate friendship with a male friend, Dong Xian, whom he put in control of the Han armies. His government adopted measures to reduce expenditures and improve standards of public service. They also continued supporting the collection and editing of texts that had started in Chengdi's reign. Aidi was in poor health and died when he was 26 years old.

Pingdi
Other name: Liu Jizi

r. 1 BCE–5 CE
b. 9 BCE d. 6 CE

After Aidi's death, Empress Wang chose Liu Jizi, grandson of Emperor Yuandi, as successor, and he became Emperor Pingdi. He was only eight at the time, so the Empress Dowager was able to assume control. She eliminated rivals and forced Dong Xian, the close male friend of the previous emperor, Aidi, to die by suicide. Her nephew, Wang Mang, then started taking control. Pingdi was married to Wang Mang's daughter but produced no heirs. The government encouraged agriculture and silk production and adopted measures for the improvement of scholarly training and the recruitment of officials and military experts.

Ruzi Ying
Other name: Liu Ying

r. 6–9 CE
b. 5 CE d. 25 CE

Pingdi died young, and Wang Mang chose Liu Ying, the youngest of Xuandi's descendants, as heir apparent. As he was only one year old, Liu Ying received the title of Ruzi ("infant") and was never formally emperor. The imperial family opposed this decision and rose up against Wang Mang. The largest of these uprisings, in 7 CE, tried to establish another Liu emperor but failed. Eventually, Wang Mang seized the throne for himself and founded the Xin dynasty. Liu Ying was made a duke and kept under house arrest until his death.

The Xin Dynasty (9–23 CE)

The Xin dynasty was founded by the usurper Wang Mang, who took control of the Han empire until a rebellion overthrew him.

Wang Mang

r. 9–23 CE
b. 45 BCE d. 23 CE

A member of a distinguished family, Wang Mang started his rise to power late in Chengdi's reign with support from his aunt, Empress Dowager Wang. When Emperor Aidi died, Wang Mang came to court as regent and eventually took over as ruler, proclaiming the foundation of the Xin dynasty. Although he was a competent politician, Wang Mang's extensive reforms caused discontent among the nobles and commoners. Frequent currency changes caused deflation and also damaged trade, while tax and salary policies failed to overcome corruption. Wang Mang demanded the Xiongnu people acknowledge that they were his subjects, and he abolished the title of king throughout the empire. The Xiongnu refused, and Wang Mang began preparations to attack. Failed land distribution reform, together with disastrous floods, resulted in a famine that led to the peasant rebellion of the so-called Red Eyebrows. Eventually, the rebels removed members of the Liu clan and killed Wang Mang and his followers. »

△ Knife-shaped coins were used in Wang Mang's reign.

The Eastern Han Dynasty (25–220 CE)

Despite great military successes, the Eastern Han faced internal problems. The empress dowagers fought with the palace eunuchs for power leading to the dynasty's collapse.

Gengshi
Other name: Liu Xuan

r. 23–25 CE
d. 25 CE

Liu Xuan, a descendant of Jingdi, was established as Gengshi, Emperor of "new beginnings," by the rebels who had evicted Wang Mang (see p. 110). He entrusted tasks to his minister Zhao Meng, while engaging in sensual pleasures. Zhao Meng abused his powers, and the administration started to collapse. Gengshi started fearing that his supporters might claim his throne and put him to death. He fell out with Liu Xiu, a leader of the Red Eyebrow movement (see p. 111). The rebels then conquered the capital and murdered Gengshi.

Guangwudi
Other name: Liu Xiu

r. 25–57 CE
b. 5 BCE d. 57 CE

Liu Xiu was one of the generals who led the rebellion against Wang Mang to restore the Han dynasty. On Gengshi's death, Liu Xiu took the imperial title Guangwudi and set up his residence at Luoyang in the east instead of Chang'an in the west. He defeated the Red Eyebrows and campaigned against the bandits. Guangwudi restored the Western Han administrative policies, managed court politics, promoted currency reforms, and abolished military conscription to prevent future insurrections.

Mingdi
Other name: Liu Zhuang

r. 58–75 CE
b. 27 CE d. 75 CE

Mingdi promoted agriculture and trade. The economy recovered, allowing him to construct new buildings in the capital and repair the Grand Canal. He was successful in the northwest against both the Qiang tribes (59 CE) and the Xiongnu (73 CE), and the empire was able to regain influence in Inner Asia. Mingdi was respected for his efficient government and support of Confucian principles. He also supported the arts and his reign saw the production of important scholarly works.

Zhangdi
Other name: Liu Da

r. 76–88 CE
b. 57 CE d. 88 CE

Liu Da was the son of Mingdi and his consort Jia. However, consort Ma, Mingdi's favorite, who could not bear children, adopted him. Enthroned as Zhangdi, he showed concern for the people's welfare, although he had to reintroduce the unpopular state monopoly on salt and iron to prop up state revenues. After repelling serious incursions by the Xiongnu, his general Ban Chao was able to retake control over Central Asian territories. Zhangdi reformed court rituals, introduced a new calendar, and patronized philosophical debates.

Hedi
Other name: Liu Zhao

r. 89–105 CE
b. 79 CE d. 106 CE

Liu Zhao was the son of Zhangdi and replaced his elder half brother Liu Qing as heir, with Empress Dowager Dou as his regent. In order to become independent, Hedi plotted a coup with the court eunuchs and succeeded in removing the Dou family in 92 CE. The eunuchs then became more influential at court. In his reign, Hedi paid attention to public welfare and supported scholarship. Several tribes along the northern frontier were putting pressure on the Eastern Han defenses, and the empire's finances became strained.

Shangdi
Other name: Liu Long

r. 106–106 CE
b. 105 CE d. 106 CE

Liu Long was a younger son of Hedi and an unknown concubine. When Hedi died, his widow, Empress Dowager Deng, put the newborn Liu Long on the throne. Though Liu Long died a few months after his accession at one year old, he was named Emperor Shangdi.

△ Emperor Guangwudi of Han stands at the center of this portrait.

Andi
Other name: Liu Hu

r.107–125 CE
b.94 CE d.125 CE

Liu Hu became Emperor Andi at 12 years old, and Empress Dowager Deng was his regent until her death in 121 CE. Andi faced a crisis in Central Asia. The non-Chinese imperial conscripts sent to the frontier mutinied and formed a large rebel force that the government was able to defeat only in 118 CE. It caused a financial crisis that required radical expenditure cuts. The empress dowager managed to preserve the empire, which was on the verge of bankruptcy.

Shaodi
Other name: Liu Yi

r.125–125 CE
d.125 CE

Liu Yi was a grandson of Zhangdi. Empress Yan had convinced Andi to dismiss his son Liu Bao and put Liu Yi on the throne to secure the regency. It is likely that Liu Yi was very young and died of an illness soon after his accession. The eunuch Sun Cheng then led a coup that removed the Yan clan. Liu Yi received the posthumous title of Shaodi (Young Emperor).

Shundi
Other name: Liu Bao

r.125–144 CE
b.115 CE d.144 CE

Liu Bao was the only son of Andi and his consort Li. Andi made him heir in 120 CE but changed his mind in 124 after pressure from Empress Yan. He was installed as Shundi, however, following a coup by the eunuchs. He was inept, and rival factions opposed his rule, hindering administrative reform. Natural disasters strained state finances, and repairs had to be funded locally. Rebellions by non-Chinese tribes afflicted his reign, and the empire lost several territories. Though uninterested in government, Shundi did try to restore the imperial university and was able to recruit scholars.

Chongdi
Other name: Liu Bing

r.144–145 CE
b.143 CE d.144 CE

Liu Bing was the only son of Shundi, and Dowager Liang acted as his regent. This allowed the Liang family, especially Liang Ji, the Dowager's brother, to control the government. Liu Bing died a few months after his accession.

Zhidi
Other name: Liu Zuan

r.145–146 CE
b.138 CE d.146 CE

Liu Zuan was enthroned as Zhidi aged seven. Liang Ji maintained his power as regent and increased his family's influence. After ruling for little over a year, Zhidi died, possibly from poisoning.

Huandi
Other name: Liu Zhi

r.146–168 CE
b.132 CE d.168 CE

Liu Zhi was a descendant of Zhangdi and was enthroned as Huandi aged 14. After Dowager Liang's death in 150 CE, he was able to rule directly, but the powerful official Liang Ji still exercised power. Huandi staged a coup against Liang Ji but started relying too much on eunuchs. Quelling rebellions in the north and south drained the treasury, and although Huandi ordered extensive urban reconstruction, many disapproved of his government and conduct. Huandi had many consorts but died without a male heir.

Lingdi
Other name: Liu Hong

r.168–189 CE
b.156 CE d.189 CE

Liu Hong was a descendant of Zhangdi and became Emperor Lingdi aged 12. Empress Dowager Dou was his regent, sharing power with her father, Dou Wu, who died by suicide after being implicated in a conspiracy to overthrow the eunuchs, who then dominated the government. His administration collapsed because of widespread corruption and epidemics. Major rebellions and raids on the southern and northern frontiers required military expeditions. Meanwhile, within China, rural uprisings merged with insurgent religious movements to form the Yellow Turban Rebellion, which took place between 184 and 192 CE. Immersed in his extravagant and lavish lifestyle, Lingdi did little to address the crisis.

Shaodi
Other name: Liu Bian

r.189–189 CE
b.173/176 CE d.190 CE

After Lingdi's death, Empress Dowager He managed to have her son, Liu Bian, named emperor. His emperor name was Shaodi. The dowager's brother, He Jin, wanted to remove the eunuchs from the court, so he

△ The warlord Cao Cao ruled on behalf of Emperor Xiandi.

asked General Dong Zhuo for support. During the fighting, a group of eunuchs escaped with Liu Bian and his half brother, but Dong Zhuo found them and brought them back to the capital. He then deposed Liu Bian and had him killed to make way for Liu Xie to be put on the throne.

Xiandi
Other name: Liu Xie

r.189–220 CE
b.181 CE d.234 CE

General Dong Zhuo deposed Liu Bian and installed Liu Xie, who was a son of Lingdi, as Emperor Xiandi. He then forced him to take up residence in Chang'an. In 192 CE, some local officials had Dong Zhuo killed, and the government crumbled as a result, with the empire fracturing into separate warlord regimes. Xiandi eventually returned to Luoyang, where the warlord Cao Cao allowed him to live in his head-quarters in Xu Province while the warlord governed in his name. After Cao Cao's death in 220 CE, his son Cao Pi forced Xiandi to abdicate, and so the Eastern Han dynasty ended.

The Three Kingdoms (220–279 CE)

After the collapse of the Eastern Han, three powers emerged to fill the vacuum—the Wei in the north, the Shu Han in the southwest, and the Wu in the southeast.

THE WEI
(220–265 CE)

The Wei were one of the Three Kingdoms that coexisted after the Eastern Han dynasty. Also known as the Cao Wei, they were a short-lived dynasty descended from the warlord Cao Cao, who took power in northern China after the collapse of the Eastern Han.

Wendi
Other name: Cao Pi

r.220–226 CE
b.187 CE d.226 CE

Cao Pi was the eldest son of Cao Cao (155–220 CE), the warlord who rose to power in northern China toward the end of the Han dynasty. He forced Emperor Xian of Han to abdicate the throne in 220 CE and proclaimed himself Wendi, the founding emperor of the Wei dynasty. Instead of continuing his father's territorial competition with other warlords in the south, Wendi focused on internal administration. He was also an accomplished poet. Together with his father, Cao Cao, and his brother, Cao Zhi, they are known as the "Three Caos" in Chinese literature.

Mingdi
Other name: Cao Rui

r.227–239 CE
b.206 CE d.239 CE

Cao Rui, who became Mingdi, was a controversial ruler. His reign witnessed great military achievements and appointments of capable officials. Mingdi also commissioned the compilation of new codes that revised and systematized the legal codes of the Han dynasty. On the other hand, he was criticized for his excessive building projects and numerous concubines, which together greatly exhausted the imperial treasury.

Prince of Qi
Other name: Cao Fang

r.240–253 CE
b.232 CE d.274 CE

Cao Fang, the Prince of Qi, was an adopted son of Mingdi and ruled as Qi Wang. He had the longest reign of all the rulers of the Wei kingdom, staying on the throne for 13 years. However, in this time, he never gained control of state power. Political affairs were entirely managed by regents, among whom were the Sima family that later founded the Jin dynasty.

Duke of Gaoguixiang
Other name: Cao Mao

r.254–260 CE
b.241 CE d.260 CE

Cao Pi's grandson Cao Mao ruled as the Duke of Gaoguixiang. He was an intelligent ruler but never gained control of state power and was killed at the age of 20.

Yuandi
Other name: Cao Huan

r.260–265 CE
b.246 CE d.302 CE

Cao Huan ruled as Yuandi. After his regent, Sima Zhao, died, Yuandi was forced to abdicate.

THE SHU HAN
(221–263 CE)

The Shu Han were another short-lived state who established themselves in southwest China after the Eastern Han collapse.

Zhaoliedi
Other name: Liu Bei

r.221–223 CE
b.161 CE d.223 CE

Liu Bei claimed descent from Jingdi of the Western Han dynasty and was an Eastern Han commander who established

△ This portrait depicts King Wen (Wendi) of the Wei Kingdom.

the state of Shu Han. Liu Bei grew up in a family of humble origins and rose to power by helping government forces suppress peasant rebellions and then gathering a group of followers to join campaigns against Cao Cao, the warlord who controlled the Han court in the north. Despite several defeats, Liu Bei eventually established his command of the southwest. He was posthumously given the name Zhaoliedi.

Houzhu
Other name: Liu Shan

r.223–263 CE
b.207 CE d.271 CE

At the beginning of his reign, Liu Shan, who was remembered as Houzhu (the "later sovereign"), employed the famous politician and strategist Zhuge Liang to handle state affairs. Following a series of unsuccessful campaigns against the Wei, Liu Shan surrendered in 263 CE and was relocated to Luoyang, the capital of Wei, where he spent a peaceful existence in his later years.

THE WU
(222–279 CE)

The Wu, who are also known as the Eastern Wu, established themselves in southeastern China in 222 CE, following the collapse of the Eastern Han.

Dadi
Other name: Sun Quan

r.222–252 CE
b.182 CE d.252 CE

Sun Quan succeeded his elder brother Sun Ce as the warlord in southeast China and established

the state of Wu. He took the ruling name of Dadi. He was much younger than his rivals Cao Cao and Liu Bei (of the Wei and Shu Han, respectively). He was also not as good a military commander, but he possessed remarkable administrative and political skills that drew a large number of generals, literary men, scholars, and artists to his court. Prosperous trade with regions as far away as the Roman Empire made his capital of Jianye (modern Nanjing) a center of flourishing culture during Dadi's reign. Dadi remained in power for 30 years—the longest of all of the Wu rulers.

Prince of Kuaiji
Other names: Sun Liang, Feidi

r.252–258 CE
b.243 CE d.260 CE

Sun Liang, who was also known as the Prince of Kuaiji, was enthroned as Kuaijiwang at the age of ten. Throughout his reign, state affairs remained under the control of regents who had been selected by the previous ruler, Dadi. In 258 CE, Kuaijiwang planned to kill the regent Sun Chen. When Sun Chen learned about this plot, however, he surrounded the palace and deposed the emperor, declaring that Kuajiwang was mentally unstable and unfit to rule.

Jingdi
Other name: Sun Xiu

r.258–264 CE
b.235 CE d.264 CE

After he removed Kuaijiwang from the throne, the regent Sun Chen selected Sun Xiu, the elder brother of Kuaijiwang, to be the new emperor. Sun Xiu was

△ This later depiction shows the Shu Han emperor Liu Bei visiting the renowned strategist Zhuge Liang.

enthroned as Jingdi. After a short period of peace, Jingdi managed to execute Sun Chen and take control. He then entrusted state affairs to the ministers who had helped him remove Sun Chen.

Modi
Other name: Sun Hao

r.264–280 CE
b.242 CE d.284 CE

The final Wu emperor was born Sun Hao and is remembered as Modi, which means "last emperor." Modi was the nephew

of the previous ruler, Jingdi. At the beginning of his reign, Modi appeared wise and charitable, fulfilling the court's expectations of a good ruler. However, he soon turned out to be ruthless and incompetent. His desire for extravagance led him to impose heavy taxes on the population. Rebellions, uprisings, and war broke out, and the state of Wu finally fell in 279 CE—the last of the Three Kingdoms (see p. 119). Modi, together with his clan, surrendered and were escorted as captives to Luoyang, the capital of the Jin dynasty.

The Western Jin Dynasty (265–316 CE)

The Western Jin dynasty fought to unify China after the unrest of the Three Kingdoms period, but its empire was overcome by foreign armies.

Wudi

Other name: Sima Yan

r. 265–290 CE
b. 236 CE d. 290 CE

After the fall of the state of Wu, Sima Yan declared himself ruler of the Jin dynasty and was remembered as Emperor Wu. In his early reign, he strengthened the military power of the imperial princes and made the penal code less severe. Once his empire was established, he was known for his extravagance and love of sensual pleasures. He supposedly had 10,000 concubines, and would choose which one to spend time with by riding around the palace in a cart drawn by a goat. Wherever the goat stopped to graze, Wu would spend the night. The independent military authority he granted to the imperial princes led to a succession struggle after his death.

Huidi

Other name: Sima Zhong

r. 290–306 CE
b. 259 CE d. 307 CE

Sima Zhong, posthumously called Emperor Hui, may have been mentally disabled. Throughout his reign, many people—regents, imperial princes, and even his empress—competed to control him. The empire then suffered from a series of civil wars known as the War of the Eight Princes, and Emperor Hui was poisoned by one of the contenders.

Huaidi

Other name: Sima Chi

r. 307–312 CE
b. 284 CE d. 313 CE

Sima Chi, posthumously called Emperor Huai, was Huidi's younger brother. He was an avid reader of histories but not a particularly ambitious politician and ruler. The domestic fighting for power and the attacks by non-Han forces were wearing down the Jin empire, and Emperor Huai was captured when the forces of the so-called Five Barbarians sacked the Jin capital at Luoyang in 311. The emperor was later executed.

Mindi

Other name: Sima Ye

r. 313–316 CE
b. 300 CE d. 318 CE

Sima Ye, who was remembered as Emperor Min, came to the throne when the Jin had no power and lacked resources to defend themselves. Mindi's name means "suffering emperor." Chang'an, the capital, fell under siege and the food supply ran out. Emperor Min surrendered to a general of the Xiongnu state of Han Zhao and was later executed.

△ This mural brick, depicting camels, decorated what is believed to be a Jin-era tomb.

The Eastern Jin Dynasty (318–420 CE)

The Eastern Jin dynasty was founded by remnants of the Western Jin. The Jin had lost northern China but lasted in the south for more than a century.

Yuandi
Other name: Sima Rui

r.318–323 CE
b.276 CE d.323 CE

After the migration of Western Jin elites to the south, Sima Rui (Emperor Yuan) came to the throne. He continued to witness the gradual loss of Jin territory in the north, but Jin authority held sway in the south of China, with Jiankang (Nanjing) as the capital.

Mingdi
Other name: Sima Shao

r.323–325 CE
b.299 CE d.325 CE

Even as the crown prince, Sima Shao (Mingdi) was widely admired for his filial piety, literary gifts, military talents, and respect for worthy men. During his brief reign, he repelled the forces of Wang Dun, a warlord who plotted to usurp the throne.

Chengdi
Other name: Sima Yan

r.326–342 CE
b.c. 322 CE d.342 CE

Emperor Cheng, whose personal name was Sima Yan, came to the throne at the age of four. For most of his reign, regents dominated the court. In the later part of his reign, he implemented policies that registered refugees from northern and central China within their resident commanderies, increasing local military manpower.

Kangdi
Other name: Sima Yue

r.343–344 CE
b.322 CE d.344 CE

Sima Yue (Emperor Kang) reigned for only two years. The most notable event of his reign was an unsuccessful military campaign against the Later Zhao in the north.

Mudi
Other name: Sima Dan

r.345–361 CE
b.343 CE d.361 CE

Enthroned at the age of two, Sima Dan (Emperor Mu) was a child for most of his reign, so the real power lay with his mother and uncles. Although the Eastern Jin faced a series of defeats in northern campaigns, their territory was temporarily expanded when they captured Cheng Han, a rival state located in Sichuan province.

Aidi
Other name: Sima Pi

r.362–365 CE
b.341 CE d.365 CE

Sima Pi, remembered as Emperor Ai, was known for his obsession with immortality. His court was dominated by General Huan Wen, who led three major northern campaigns. Emperor Ai devoted most of his time to Buddhism and Daoism and eventually died from poisoning with a chemical elixir.

Haixigong
Other names: Sima Yi, Feidi ("abolished emperor")

r.366–371 CE
b.342 CE d.386 CE

Sima Yi was enthroned at the age of 24, but actual power resided with his great-uncle, Sima Yu (later Emperor Jianwen), and General Huan Wen. After failing to conquer territory in the north, Huan Wen addressed the court and spread a rumor that the emperor was impotent and that his sons were fathered by other men. As a result, the emperor was deposed and exiled, his rank reduced to Duke of Haixi. He was later called Haixigong.

Jianwendi
Other name: Sima Yu

r.371–372 CE
b.320 CE d.372 CE

Sima Yu, who came to the throne as Emperor Jianwen, played an important role in the administration well before he was installed by General Huan Wen. He ruled for just a year and was known for his eloquence in metaphysical discussions.

Xiaowudi
Other name: Sima Yao

r.373–396 CE
b.362 CE d.396 CE

Emperor Xiaowu, born Sima Yao, was enthroned at the age of 11. He was the last Eastern Jin emperor who had actual power. In 383 CE, numerically inferior Jin forces defeated Fu Jian (Xuanzhao of the Former Qin) at the Fei River. After this triumph, however, the emperor started to indulge in drinking and sensual pleasures. One of his consorts had him suffocated because he joked about her age.

Andi
Other name: Sima Dezong

r.397–419 CE
b.382 CE d.419 CE

Historians believe that Sima Dezong, remembered as Emperor An, was mentally disabled. Actual power during his reign was held by his uncle, Sima Daozi. His reign saw rebellions, civil wars, and a short period during which General Huan Xuan usurped the throne. The warlord Liu Yu (Emperor Wu of Song) came to power after the defeat of Huan Xuan. Liu Yu eventually had Emperor An killed.

Gongdi
Other name: Sima Dewen

r.419–420 CE
b.386 CE d.421 CE

Sima Dewen (Gongdi) was a younger brother of Andi. On Andi's death, the warlord Liu Yu installed Sima Dewen as emperor but soon pressured him into abdicating. Liu Yu eventually had him suffocated.

The Southern and Northern Dynasties

(420–581 CE)

In the 160 years after the collapse of the Jin dynasty, China was divided once more, as the lands north and south of the Yangzi River were ruled by separate dynasties.

THE LIU SONG
(420–479 CE)

The Liu Song was the first of the Southern dynasties to emerge from the power vacuum left by the fall of the Jin and was one of the more lasting. Founded by an Eastern Jin general, Liu Yu, the dynasty held power in the south for nearly 60 years before it was ended by one of its own generals, Xiao Daocheng.

Wudi
Other name: Liu Yu

r.420–422 CE
b.363 CE d.422 CE

From a humble background, Liu Yu rose to power as a statesman and general of the Eastern Jin and forced the last emperor to yield the throne to him. He founded the Liu Song dynasty and declared himself Emperor Wu. His reign was brief, and his most notable achievements were his successful northern campaigns under the Eastern Jin, which put an end to the Later Qin and Southern Yan, two of the 16 states established by non-Chinese peoples in the north.

Shaodi
Other names: Liu Yifu, Prince of Yingyang

r.423–424 CE
b.406 CE d.424 CE

When Wudi died, his oldest son, Liu Yifu, ascended the throne and took the ruling name Shaodi. However, when Shaodi failed to comply with the proper mourning practices, his father's ministers decided that he was unfit to rule. They deposed and killed him in the second year of his reign.

Wendi
Other name: Liu Yilong

r.424–453 CE
b.407 CE d.453 CE

After the deposition of Shaodi, Liu Yilong was enthroned as Wendi. He was an intelligent and diligent ruler who implemented a series of effective policies to improve his people's welfare and also insisted on monitoring the performance of officials. Schools were built, and his reign was largely a period of prosperity and strength. However, toward the end of his 29-year reign, he launched three large-scale

△ This portrait depicts the first Liu Song emperor, Wudi.

campaigns to reconquer northern lands, which were unsuccessful and significantly weakened the state. The crown prince, Wendi's eldest son, staged a coup and killed him.

Xiaowudi
Other name: Liu Jun

r.454–464 CE
b.453 CE d.464 CE

One hundred days after Wendi was assassinated by his eldest son, another son, Liu Jun, overthrew his elder brother. He established himself as Emperor Xiaowu. He was considered a greedy ruler—known for his extravagance, arrogance, and sexual immorality. Xiaowudi drank and gambled excessively, but this did not seem to affect his good judgment as a ruler. He concentrated imperial power by restructuring administrative systems and restricting the powers of imperial princes.

Qian Feidi
Other name: Liu Ziye

r.465–465 CE
b.449 CE d.466 CE

Liu Ziye is remembered by the posthumous name Qian Feidi, which means "former abolished emperor." He ruled for only a year as a teenager before being assassinated and, according to sources, was cruel and sexually immoral. He killed many ministers and imperial clan members who plotted to overthrow him, including his own great-uncle.

Mingdi
Other name: Liu Yu (II)

r.465–472 CE
b.439 CE d.472 CE

Emperor Ming, whose personal name was Liu Yu, slaughtered many of his imperial brothers and nephews who he believed had the potential to overthrow him. During his reign, constant infighting and invasions by the Xianbei people of the Northern Wei dynasty rapidly drained the resources of the Liu Song.

Prince of Cangwu
Other names: Liu Yu (III), Hou Feidi

r.473–477 CE
b.463 CE d.477 CE

Mingdi's chosen heir, the crown prince, ascended to the throne after his father and took the ruling name Cangwuwang, meaning "prince of Cangwu." As a child, he was described as someone who was extremely intelligent but who did not enjoy studying. After he was enthroned, Cangwuwang grew more and more cruel; as a teenager (having taken the throne at around ten years old) he was said to take pleasure in killing people and animals. Cangwuwang ruled for only four years. One of his attendants cut off his head while he slept, and sources say that even his palace guards rejoiced in his death. Afterward, he was called Hou Feidi, meaning "later abolished emperor."

Shundi
Other name: Liu Zhun

r.477–479 CE
b.467 CE d.479 CE

Following the removal of the Prince of Cangwu, ten-year-old Liu Zhun (Emperor Shun) was enthroned by the general Xiao Daocheng (later Emperor Gao of the Qi dynasty). Two years later, Xiao Daocheng forced Shundi to abdicate, and this ended the Liu Song dynasty. Shundi was killed less than a month later.

THE QI DYNASTY
(479–502 CE)

The Qi, or Southern Qi, was a brief southern dynasty. It was founded by Xiao Daocheng and ruled for only 23 years.

Gaodi
Other name: Xiao Daocheng

r.479–482 CE
b.427 CE d.482 CE

Xiao Daochen was born into a general's family under the Liu Song dynasty. He seized power and established himself as Gaodi of the Qi dynasty. Although he instigated the assassination of the Liu Song ruler Cangwuwang, and forced another ruler, Shundi, to yield the throne to him, Gaodi was widely perceived as a decent ruler who moved against the extravagant lifestyle of his predecessors and promoted frugality. He displayed a keen interest in literature and calligraphy and was described as an outstanding qi (chess) player.

Wudi
Other name: Xiao Ze

r.483–493 CE
b.440 CE d.493 CE

Wudi, born Xiao Ze, was described as a diligent and competent ruler. He made peace with the Northern Wei, creating a period for the Qi to recover from war and political upheaval. He continued Gaodi's work and identified cases of tax fraud through a new census bureau. This triggered some of the elite classes to revolt in 485 CE, but it was quickly suppressed.

Prince of Yulin
Other name: Xiao Zhaoye

r.494–494 CE
b.473 CE d.494 CE

Xiao Zhaoye showed his desire for extravagance soon after he was enthroned as Yulinwang. He first entrusted state matters to his great-uncle Xiao Luan but then became suspicious of his ambitions. Before long, Xiao Luan staged a coup against him.

Prince of Hailing
Other names: Xiao Zhaowen, Hailing Gongwang (Prince Gong of Hailing)

r.494–494 CE
b.480 CE d.494 CE

Hailingwang, born Xiao Zhaowen, was the ruler for four months before his great-uncle Xiao Luan assumed the throne. Xiao Luan controlled what he ate and had him poisoned in 494 CE. »

△ Buddhism began to flourish in the south during the southern dynasties period, when this stone stele was created.

Mingdi
Other name: Xiao Luan

r.494–498 CE
b.452 CE d.498 CE

Xiao Luan was raised by his uncle Gaodi. After overthrowing the two previous emperors, who were both his great-nephews, he came to the throne and executed many princes to secure his position. He established himself as Emperor Ming. During his reign, he appeared to lead the same frugal lifestyle as Gaodi.

Donghunhou
Other name: Xiao Baojuan

r.498–501 CE
b.483 CE d.501 CE

Xiao Baojuan, who came to the throne in 498 CE after the death of Mingdi, was later known as Donghunhou—"marquis of eastern incompetence." He was one of the most notorious rulers in Chinese history and executed many high-ranking ministers, which led to a series of rebellions. Xiao Yi, a Qi general, had led the Qi forces to suppress earlier rebellions, but Xiao Baojuan believed Xiao Yi to be a traitor and killed him. The next year, in 501 CE, Xiao Baojuan was killed in another revolt—led by Xiao Yi's brother, Xiao Yan (who later became Emperor Wu of Liang).

Hedi
Other name: Xiao Baorong

r.501–502 CE
b.488 CE d.502 CE

Xiao Baorong was put on the throne as Hedi by rebellious generals while his violent brother Xiao Baojuan (Donghunhou) was still the emperor. After Xiao Baojuan was killed, Xiao Yan (later Emperor Wu of Liang), who had installed Hedi, claimed the throne for himself.

THE LIANG DYNASTY
(502–557 CE)

The Liang was a southern dynasty established by Xiao Yan, a general who had served under the Qi dynasty. The Liang ruled in the south for 55 years.

Wudi
Other name: Xiao Yan

r.502–549 CE
b.464 CE d.549 CE

The reign of Emperor Wu of Liang, born Xiao Yan, was one of the longest and most prosperous of the southern dynasties. Wudi was a competent military man and a poet and a patron of the arts. Shortly after coming to the throne, he cast aside his earlier interests in Confucianism and Daoism and devoted himself and imperial resources to Buddhism. Based on his interpretation of Buddhist precepts, he decreed that all monks should not eat meat, initiating the vegetarian tradition in Chinese Buddhism. Hou Jing, an Eastern Wei general, rebelled in 549 CE and brought about Wudi's fall.

Jianwendi
Other name: Xiao Gang

r.550–551 CE
b.503 CE d.551 CE

Xiao Gang was the second son of Wudi. As well as patronizing poets, he wrote poetry himself, and his preferred style came to be known as "the palace style." When Wudi died in Hou Jing's rebellion, the general Hou Jing installed Xiao Gang as Emperor Jianwen. However, Jianwendi was a puppet emperor; he never held actual power during his brief reign and was suffocated in 551 CE on Hou Jing's orders.

Prince of Yuzhang
Other name: Xiao Dong

r.551 CE–551 CE
d.552 CE

The Prince of Yuzhang, born Xiao Dong, was briefly put on the throne by the general Hou Jing when the general controlled the Liang capital of Jiankang (modern-day Nanjing, Jiangsu province). However, after barely three months, Hou Jing forced Yuxhangwang to yield the throne, then ordered for the emperor and his brothers to be drowned in the Yangzi River. Hou Jing himself died soon after.

Yuandi
Other name: Xiao Yi

r.552–555 CE
b.508 CE d.555 CE

Xiao Yi claimed the Liang throne at Jiangling (modern-day Jingzhou, in Hubei province) after the general Hou Jing died. He was remembered as Emperor Yuan. Unlike earlier Liang rulers, Jiangling was his capital city. He had literary tastes and collected ancient books. He offended Yuwen Tai, the leading general of the Western Wei dynasty—who ruled in the north—when he requested revisions to the

△ Emperor Wu (Xiao Yan), a devout Buddhist, had the longest reign of all of the Liang dynasty rulers.

northern border. Yuwen Tai marched south with Western Wei forces and captured Jiangling in 554 CE. After this, Yuandi had the imperial library burned and proclaimed reading was useless. Yuandi was killed on Yuwen Tai's orders in 555 CE.

Mindi

Other names: Xiao Yuanming, Zhenyanghou (Marquis of Zhenyang)

r. 555–555 CE
d. 556 CE

Xiao Yuanming had been captured in a campaign against the Eastern Wei in 547 CE. After Yuandi was killed in 555 CE, Emperor Wenxuan of the Northern Qi dynasty forcibly installed Xiao Yuanming as the new emperor, who took the ruling name Emperor Min. However, Mindi was on the throne for only a few months before he was removed by other generals. He died after returning to the capital, Jiankang.

Jingdi

Other name: Xiao Fangzhi

r. 555–557 CE
b. 543 CE d. 558 CE

After Yuandi's death—and before Emperor Wenxuan of Northern Qi put Xiao Yuanming on the throne—the Liang generals had originally wanted to install Xiao Fangzhi as emperor. He was established as Emperor Jing at the old Liang capital of Jiankang. Jingdi remained on the throne for only two years. The Liang general Chen Baxian (who later proclaimed himself as Emperor Wu of Chen) forced Jingdi to yield the throne in 557 CE, thereby ending the Liang dynasty. Jingdi died a year later.

THE CHEN DYNASTY (557–589 CE)

The Chen dynasty, named for its founder, Chen Baxian, was the last of the southern dynasties. During the 12 years of Chen rule, the remaining territory belonging to the south was gradually lost to the northern dynasties. The Chen dynasty ended when the Sui dynasty was established, reuniting north and south.

Wudi

Other name: Chen Baxian

r. 557–559 CE
b. 503 CE d. 559 CE

Chen Baxian was a prominent general under the Liang dynasty. By the time he came to the throne and established the Chen dynasty, the territory of the southern regime had been greatly reduced. The southwest and north of China were occupied by the Northern Zhou and Northern Qi. Chen Baxian had the ruling name Emperor Wu. During his brief reign, he was recognized as a frugal and tolerant ruler.

Wendi

Other name: Chen Qian

r. 560–566 CE
b. 522 CE d. 566 CE

The previous emperor Wudi's only surviving son was held hostage by the Northern Zhou, so Chen Qian, who was Wudi's nephew, came to the throne instead, as Wendi. Sources say he was an intelligent and diligent ruler. He managed to expand Chen's territory and consolidated

the state against the independent warlords based in the provinces nominally loyal to Chen.

Prince of Linhai

Other names: Chen Bozong, Feidi

r. 567–568 CE
b. c. 554 CE d. 570 CE

Chen Bozong was the Prince of Linhai and came to the throne as a teenager following the death of Wendi. Chen Bozong's uncle, Chen Xu (later Emperor Xuan), dominated the court and soon deposed him. He was later called Feidi, "abolished emperor."

Xuandi

Other name: Chen Xu

r. 569–582 CE
b. 530 CE d. 582 CE

Chen Xu was enthroned as Emperor Xuan of Chen. He expanded Chen's territory temporarily and gained most of the region between the Yangzi River and the Huai River thanks to a successful campaign against the Northern Qi. This region, however, was soon seized by the Northern Zhou.

Houzhu

Other name: Chen Shubao

r. 583–589 CE
b. 553 CE d. 604 CE

Chen Shubao, was posthumously named Houzhu, meaning "last sovereign" of Chen. He was described as an incompetent

ruler who preferred to indulge in sensual pleasures, literature, and banquets in his short reign. He paid little heed to governing his state, which was facing military pressure from the newly founded Sui regime (see pp. 134–135). After the fall of the Chen, Emperor Wen of Sui treated Chen Shubao with kindness, allowing him his indulgences. **》**

▷ Unlike the kingdoms in the north, the southern dynasties had a continuous Han Chinese culture. This lidded vase, created during the period, has an unmistakably Chinese style.

THE NORTHERN WEI DYNASTY
(386–534 CE)

The Northern Wei was the first dynasty to unify northern China during the northern and southern dynasties period. It was founded following the defeat of the Former Qin at the Battle of the Fei River in 386 CE and ruled in the north for nearly 150 years. The Northern Wei ruling house was the Tuoba clan of the nomadic Xianbei people. At the end of the Northern Wei period, the north was divided into two dynasties—the Eastern and Western Wei.

Daowu
Other names: Tuoba Gui, Tuoba Shegui

r. 386–409 CE
b. 371 CE d. 409 CE

Following the defeat of the Former Qin by the Eastern Qin at the Battle of the Fei River in 383 CE (see pp. 126–127), Tuoba Gui first declared himself king in the state of Dai (near modern Hohhot in Inner Mongolia) and then changed the state's name to Wei. After his death, he was named Emperor Daowu. He fought against other tribes with assistance from the Later Yan, but relations between the Northern Wei and the Later Yan broke down in the 390s. The war between them lasted nearly a decade. During Tuoba Gui's reign, the Northern Wei were also in constant conflict with the Later Qin.

In his later days, Tuoba Gui grew suspicious of people around him and treated his officials harshly. In 409 CE, he imprisoned his consort, Helan, and was killed by their son, Tuoba Shao, who then ascended to the throne.

Mingyuan
Other names: Tuoba Si, Mumo

r. 409–423 CE
b. 392 CE d. 423 CE

Tuoba Si was the son of Tuoba Gui and came to the throne after killing his brother. Generally regarded as an intelligent ruler, he stabilized the rule of the Northern Wei in northern China and was eager to take his officials' advice. When Liu Yu (founding emperor of the Liu Song dynasty in the south) died in 422 CE, Tuoba Si decided to break off relations with the Liu Song. He attacked them in 423 CE, and his ensuing victory secured the Northern Wei's control of many northern areas that used to be the territory of Liu Song. Tuoba Si died from poisoning in 423 CE after ingesting an alchemical elixir intended to prolong his life. He was posthumously named Emperor Mingyuan.

Taiwu
Other names: Tuoba Tao, Buri

r. 424–452 CE
b. 408 CE d. 452 CE

Tuoba Tao was the crown prince and eldest son of the previous emperor, Tuoba Si. He ascended to the throne in 424 CE following his father's death. During Tuoba Tao's 28-year reign, the territory of the Northern Wei nearly doubled in size. Enthroned at the age of 16, he soon proved himself a capable ruler and eventually united northern China. He implemented a series of policies to integrate the Han upper classes who lived in the north into the Northern Wei regime. In his later reign, campaigns against the Liu Song in the south exhausted the state. Tuoba Tao also had several Han elite clans extinguished. He was a devout Daoist who ordered the abolition of Buddhism; sutras were burned and monks were killed. He was assassinated by the eunuch Zong Ai in 452 CE and was posthumously named Emperor Taiwu.

Prince of Nan'an
Other names: Tuoba Yu, Kebozhen

r. 452–452 CE
d. 452 CE

Tuoba Yu, the Prince of Nan'an, was put on the throne by the eunuch Zong Ai, who had assassinated the preceding ruler. Tuoba Yu indulged in drinking and hunting and was assassinated by Zong Ai's men only eight months into his reign.

Wencheng
Other names: Tuoba Jun, Wulei

r. 452–465 CE
b. 440 CE d. 465 CE

Tuoba Jun was the grandson of Taiwu and nephew of Tuoba Yu. He was favored by Taiwu as a successor and was put on the throne at the age of 12 by officials who opposed Zong Ai, the eunuch who had murdered the previous two emperors. Zong Ai was executed for his actions. During Tuoba Jun's reign, he sought to let the Northern Wei state recover

△ Camels were introduced to China by tribes of the northern dynasties. This earthenware figure may have been created during the Northern Wei dynasty.

from the damage caused by the extensive campaigns of his predecessors. He also ended prohibitions against Buddhism decreed by his grandfather, Taiwu, and commissioned the construction of the Yungang Grottoes near modern Datong, Shanxi province, which include many masterpieces of early Chinese Buddhist art. Tuoba Jun was posthumously named Emperor Wencheng.

Xianwen

Other names : Tuoba Hong, Didouyin

r.466–471 CE
b.454 CE d.476 CE

Tuoba Hong, the eldest son of Emperor Wencheng, ascended the throne at the age of 11, following the death of his father. Throughout his reign, the court was controlled by his stepmother, Empress Dowager Feng. In 471 CE, he yielded the throne to his four-year-old son, Tuoba Hong (later Emperor Xiaowen), but managed to retain control of state matters as a retired emperor. He may have been killed on the orders of Empress Dowager Feng. After his death, he was named Emperor Xianwen.

Xiaowen

Other names: Tuoba Hong, Yuan Hong

r.471–499 CE
b.467 CE d.499 CE

Tuoba Hong came to the throne aged four and was posthumously known as Emperor Xiaowen. His grandmother, the Empress Dowager Feng, acted as regent. She was ethnically Han Chinese. After her regency, Emperor Xiaowen was known for policies that aimed to resolve ethnic conflicts by imposing Chinese culture. He moved the capital to Luoyang, established Han dress as the state dress, and made Chinese the official language. He also changed Xianbei surnames to Han surnames, adopting Yuan as the new imperial family name instead of Tuoba. He initiated political reforms to mimic the system of the Han people in the south. To some extent, Xiaowen's policies laid the foundation for the later unification of China, but they also triggered rebellions that would lead to the dissolution of Northern Wei.

Xuanwu

Other names: Tuoba Ke, Yuan Ke

r.500–515 CE
b.483 CE d.515 CE

Tuoba Ke, who changed his name to Yuan Ke, was the second son of Xiaowen and succeeded him after his death. He was given the posthumous name Xuanwu. During his reign, the Northern Wei launched several campaigns against the Liang in the south. The territory of Northern Wei entered a period of expansion. Xuanwu notably ended the custom dictating that the crown prince's mother must die by suicide in order to prevent political interference by the future ruler's maternal relatives. In his later reign, however, his regime suffered from political corruption and an uncle of his mother, Gao Zhao, who died in 515 CE, was particularly corrupt.

Xiaoming

Other name: Yuan Xu

r.516–528 CE
b.510 CE d.528 CE

Yuan Xu came to the throne at the age of five, so the court was controlled by his mother, Empress Dowager Hu, and her lovers. In 528 CE, Yuan Xu, now 18 years old, tried to curb his mother's powers and was poisoned by her and her lover Zheng Yan. After his reign, the Northern Wei fell into chaos and infighting, and the Yuan imperial family never regained control of the regime. Yuan Xu was given the posthumous name Emperor Xiaoming.

Xiaozhuang

Other name: Yuan Ziyou

r.528–530 CE
b.507 CE d.531 CE

Yuan Ziyou, who was known as Emperor Xiaozhuang after his death, was put on the throne by the general Erzhu Rong and was married to the general's daughter. In 528 CE, Erzhu Rong slaughtered members of the imperial clan and the Han nobles who had previously served the »

△ This detail comes from a lacquer painting on wood from Datong (in modern Shanxi province) that dates from the Northern Wei dynasty. It depicts the story of the legendary emperor Shun, who was married to the two daughters of Yao.

△ The military played an important part in the Northern Wei dynasty, with generals such as Erzhu Rong wielding political power. These earthenware figures of Northern Wei warriors were made between 493 and 534 CE.

Jiemin

Other names: Yuan Gong, Prince of Guangling, Emperor Qianfei ("former abolished emperor"

r. 531–531 CE
b. 498 CE d. 532 CE

Yuan Gong was put on the throne by the violent and corrupt Erzhu clan, who controlled the court during his brief reign. However, after General Gao Huan defeated the Erzhu family, Yuan Gong was imprisoned and poisoned by Yuan Xiu (Emperor Xiaowu), the new emperor later installed by Gao Huan.

Prince of Anding

Other names: Yuan Lang, Emperor Houfei ("later abolished emperor")

r. 531–532 CE
b. 513 CE d. 532 CE

When General Gao Huan defeated the Erzhu family, he placed Yuan Lang, the Prince of Anding, on the throne. The next year, he forced Yuan Lang to abdicate in favor of Yuan Xiu (who became Emperor Xiaowu) and had Yuan Lang killed.

Xiaowu

Other names: Yuan Xiu, Chudi

r. 532–534 CE
b. 510 CE d. 535 CE

In 528 CE, after General Erzhu Rong slaughtered members of the imperial clan, Yuan Xiu—one of the grandsons of Emperor Xiaowen—fled to the countryside. After defeating the Erzhu family, General Gao Huan tracked down Yuan Xiu and installed him as the new emperor. Yuan Xiu immediately took action to eliminate other

---

Northern Wei. In 530 CE, when Erzhu Rong traveled to the capital to visit his pregnant daughter, Yuan Ziyou, and his men seized the opportunity and killed him. However, in the same year, Erzhu Rong's nephew, Erzhu Zhao, proclaimed Yuan Ye (later Prince of Donghai) as emperor. Erzhu Zhao attacked Luoyang in the following year. He imprisoned Yuan Ziyou in a Buddhist temple and had him strangled.

Prince of Changguang

Other names: Yuan Ye, Prince of Donghai

r. 530–530 CE
d. 532 CE

Yuan Ye, Prince of Changguang, was a great-grandson of Emperor Taiwu, who came from a line of the Yuan family that had fallen into dishonor. He was the

nephew of Erzhu Rong's wife, and he briefly became emperor after the previous ruler, Yuan Ziyou, killed general Erzhu Rong. The Erzhu family established Yuan Ye as their puppet emperor, but after four months, they forced him to abdicate in favor of Yuan Gong (later Emperor Jiemin), whom the Erzhu family thought to be a more legitimate heir to the throne. They put Yuan Ye to death.

claimants to the throne and also tried to get rid of Gao Huan. When Gao Huan marched toward Luoyang in 534 CE, Yuan Xiu fled west to Chang'an (modern Xi'an). After his death, he was known as Chudi, which means "the emperor who fled."

Gao Huan then made Yuan Shanjian emperor and moved the capital from Luoyang to Yecheng, in what is now Hebei province. At this point, the empire in northern China was formally divided into two—the Eastern Wei and Western Wei. Yuan Xiu was poisoned in 535 CE.

THE EASTERN WEI DYNASTY (534–550 CE)

The Eastern Wei was established by the powerful general Gao Huan. It claimed to be the rightful governor of the Northern Wei regime after the last emperor of the Northern Wei, Yuan Xiu, fled to Chang'an to reestablish his court there. The dynasty had only one emperor, Xiaojing, who had no control over the court.

Xiaojing
Other name: Yuan Shanjian

r. 534–550 CE
b. 524 CE d. 552 CE

Yuan Shanjian was made emperor at the age of 11 by General Gao Huan. During his reign, the court was controlled by the general and his sons, Gao Cheng and Gao Yang (later Emperor Wenxuan of the Northern Qi). Gao Huan had moved the Eastern Wei capital to Yecheng, a city in what is now Hebei province, to make it more defensible. The former capital, Luoyang, was closer to the dynasty's borders. Gao Huan died in 547 CE, leaving Gao Cheng in control of government, but Gao Cheng was assassinated in 549 CE. His younger brother, Gao Yang, forced Yuan Shanjian to abdicate in favor of himself. Two years after he abdicated, Yuan Shanjian was fatally poisoned. He was given the posthumous title Emperor Xiaojing. Gao Yang thereby ended the rule of the Yuan (formerly Tuoba) clan. He took the throne and declared himself the founding emperor of the Northern Qi dynasty. »

△ The Yungang Grottoes in Datong, Shanxi province, were commissioned by Emperor Wencheng of the Northern Wei dynasty and continued by later emperors. Construction of the caves ended in 525 CE owing to uprisings in the nearby area during the Northern Wei decline.

THE WESTERN WEI DYNASTY
(535–557 CE)

The Western Wei was established by the general Yuwen Tai (507–556 CE) as the rival of the Eastern Wei. Despite the Western Wei starting with a smaller territory and population, it grew more powerful than the Eastern Wei, thanks to its economic developments, and conquered the western part of the Liang empire in the south.

Wendi
Other name: Yuan Baoju

r.535–551 CE
b.507 CE d.551 CE

In 534, Yuan Baoju followed his cousin Yuan Xiu (Emperor Xiaowu of the Northern Wei) to flee from Luoyang to Chang'an. After Yuan Xiu died of poisoning in 535 CE, Yuan Baoju was made emperor. Yuan Baoju was given the posthumous title Wendi.

Feidi
Other name: Yuan Qin

r.552–554 CE
d.554 CE

Yuan Qin was the son of the previous ruler, Wendi, and like him had little real power during his reign. General Yuwen Tai dominated the Western Wei court. With the support of Yuwen Tai's sons-in-law, Yuan Qin tried to kill Yuwen Tai, but the plan was leaked before it could happen. In response, Yuwen Tai deposed Yuan Qin and put him to death. Yuan Qin's posthumous name is Feidi, meaning "abolished emperor."

Gongdi
Other name: Tuoba Kuo

r.554–556 CE
b.537 CE d.557 CE

During Tuoba Kuo's reign, the powerful general Yuwen Tai continued to control the court as he had done in the previous reign. He changed the imperial surname Yuan, which was a Han name, to the Xianbei name Tuoba. After the general died in 556 CE, his nephew forced Tuoba Kuo to yield the throne to the general's son Yuwen Jue (who became Emperor Xiaomin of Northern Zhou). Tuoba Kuo was posthumously given the title Gongdi.

THE NORTHERN QI DYNASTY
(550–577 CE)

The Northern Qi dynasty was established by the Han people of the Gao clan, who ended the rule of the Yuan clan and had incorporated many Chinese influences and practices. Their capital was Yecheng. The dynasty is known as the Northern Qi to distinguish it from the Southern Qi in the south, ruled by the Xiao family. The Northern Qi ruled around the same time as both the Western Wei and the Chen and was the most prosperous dynasty in this era.

Wenxuan
Other names: Gao Yang, Hounigan

r.550–559 CE
b.526 CE d.559 CE

The first emperor of the Northern Qi was Wenxuan, whose personal name was Gao Yang. In Wenxuan's reign, the military strength of Northern Qi was at its peak. Wenxuan was an intelligent ruler and was good at appointing capable ministers. During his reign, Northern Qi became more prosperous than the Western Wei and Chen states. In the later part of his reign, he became extravagant and may have died an alcoholic.

Feidi
Other name: Gao Yin

r.560–560 CE
b.545 CE d.561 CE

Gao Yin ascended to the throne at the age of 15. In his early reign, his ministers competed for power. His uncle Gao Yan triumphed and took the throne. He was known as Emperor Xiaozhao. Gao Yan deposed Gao Yin and put him to death in 561 CE. Gao Yin was given the posthumous title Feidi, meaning "abolished emperor."

Xiaozhao
Other name: Gao Yan

r.560–561 CE
b.535 CE d.561 CE

Gao Yan was initially a trusted minister supporting the emperor, who was his nephew Gao Yin. After he usurped the throne, Gao Yan was considered a diligent and capable ruler. He paid special attention to revising laws to make sure they were not too harsh, and his tax policies were lenient. One day, he fell off his horse while hunting and broke his ribs and died. After his death, he was named Emperor Xiaozhao.

Wucheng
Other name: Gao Zhan

r.561–564 CE
b.537 CE d.569 CE

Gao Zhan was the younger brother of Gao Yan (Emperor Xiaozhao) and helped him take the throne

△ The tomb murals of important Northern Qi figures depict daily life during the dynasty. This detail depicts riders on horseback.

△ This detail comes from a mural adorning the west wall of the tomb of Xu Xianxiu, a high-ranking Northern Qi official, in Taiyuan, Shanxi province. The murals there depict people in the typical attire of the Xianbei people.

from their nephew Gao Yin. Gao Zhan succeeded his brother as emperor after his death in 561 CE. Unlike his brother, Gao Zhan was known as a ruler who devoted more time to entertainment and sexual pleasure than affairs of state. During his reign, he entrusted the running of the state to several ministers. In 564 CE, Gao Zhan passed the throne to his son Gao Wei but continued to play a role in government as a retired emperor. He was posthumously named Emperor Wucheng.

Houzhu
Other names: Gao Wei, Wengong

r. 564–577 CE
b. 557 CE d. 577 CE

Gao Wei inherited a country on the verge of collapse from his father, Emperor Wucheng, and did little to save it. Instead, he killed several capable generals, suspecting they were plotting to rebel against him. This weakened the military power of the Northern Qi, leaving the dynasty vulnerable to encroachment by the Northern Qi's enemy, the Northern Zhou. In contrast to the Northern Qi, the Northern Zhou emperor, Wudi, had worked to strengthen the military. When Northern Zhou forces occupied the capital of the Northern Qi, Gao Wei knew that he could not win against them. He hastily passed the throne to his son, Gao Heng, who was only a child at the time. Fearing for his life, Gao Wei decided to surrender himself to the Chen regime, which ruled in the south. However, before he could reach Chen territory, Gao Wei was captured by Northern Zhou forces, taken to their capital, and put to death. After his death, he was given the title Houzhu, which means "later sovereign."

Youzhu
Other name: Gao Heng

r. 577–577 CE
b. 570 CE d. 578 CE

Gao Heng was put on the throne by his father, Gao Wei (Houzhu), when the ruling house of the »

致減佛法
後周武帝宇文邕在
位十八年五帝共廿五年

Northern Qi fled from their capital following its capture by the Northern Zhou. To eradicate the remaining Northern Qi line, Emperor Wu of Northern Zhou falsely accused the surrendered Houzhu of plotting rebellion and ordered the whole Gao clan to die by suicide, including Gao Heng. This brought the Northern Qi dynasty to an end. The title that Gao Heng was given after his death, Youzhu, means "the young sovereign."

THE NORTHERN ZHOU DYNASTY
(557–581 CE)

The Northern Zhou was founded by the Yuwen clan of the Xianbei people to replace the Western Wei, one of the states that branched off from the Northern Wei. For half of the duration of the Northern Zhou, the government was dominated by a figure named Yuwen Hu, rather than by the emperors themselves. The Northern Zhou dynasty was replaced by the Sui, who reunited northern and southern China.

Xiaomin
Other names : Yuwen Jue, Tuoluoni

r. 557–557 CE
b. 542 CE d. 557 CE

Yuwen Jue was the heir of the very powerful general, Yuwen Tai, who had ordered the final ruler of the Western Wei (Gongdi) to be killed. When

◁ Emperor Wu (Yuwen Yong) was the most long-lived and the most able of the Northern Zhou rulers.

Yuwen Tai died, his nephew, Yuwen Hu, acted as the guardian of Yuwen Jue and made him emperor. Yuwen Jue was posthumously given the name Emperor Xiaomin. Xiaomin used the title Tian Wang, "heavenly prince," during his brief rule. Unhappy about Yuwen Hu's dominance at court, Xiaomin plotted to kill him and was deposed by Yuwen Hu. Yuwen Hu then enthroned Yuwen Jue's elder brother, Yuwen Yu, as emperor and had Xiaomin executed that same year.

Mingdi

Other names: Yuwen Yu, Tongwantu

r.557–560 CE
b.534 CE d.560 CE

Yuwen Yu was the brother of the previous emperor, Xiaomin. Yuwen Yu was posthumously named Emperor Ming. During his three-year reign, he actively attempted to wrest back control of the government from his cousin Yuwen Hu, a nobleman who dominated the court. Emperor Ming was considered to be able and intelligent, which made Yuwen Hu concerned for his own power, so in 560 CE, he poisoned the emperor. Before he died, Mingdi passed the throne to his brother, Yuwen Yong (Emperor Wu), instead of his own sons, whom he thought too young to rule effectively.

Wudi

Other names: Yuwen Yong, Miluotu

r.561–578 CE
b.543 CE d.578 CE

Yuwen Yong was named emperor when his brother Yuwen Yu died. He was posthumously given the

△ The Northern Zhou dynasty was known for its military prowess, especially under Emperor Wu. These terracotta figurines of warriors on horseback date from the Northern Zhou period.

name Emperor Wu. In his early reign, he showed respect for Yuwen Hu, who was his cousin and a very powerful person at court and by this time had killed three emperors—including two of Wudi's brothers. However, in 572 CE, Wudi ambushed Yuwen Hu and killed him, ridding the court of his influence.

Emperor Wu is remembered as an able ruler. He strengthened the power of the Northern Zhou military very effectively and destroyed his rivals, the Northern Qi. He annexed much of the Northern Qi territory, in the lower valley of the Yellow River. Wudi's father, Yuwen Tai, had tried to stop the Xianbei people from taking on Chinese ways and culture, but Wudi was eager to reverse this, and he installed a Han-style administrative system. In order to deal with the concentration of money, lands, and resources in the growing monasteries, Wudi ordered Buddhism to be banned in the Northern Zhou territories, and he confiscated monastery assets for military use. Wudi had

ambitions of reuniting northern and southern China. In 578 CE, he planned a military campaign against the Turkic Tujue people, but he became ill and died that year before he could realize his ambitions. China would be reunited under the Sui dynasty only a few years later.

Xuandi

Other name: Yuwen Yun

r.579–579 CE
b.559 CE d.580 CE

Yuwen Yun was the son of the previous ruler, Yuwen Yong (Wudi). His father had brought him up strictly and Yuwen Yun hated him as a result. Yuwen Yun ruled for a brief period in 579 CE and was remembered as an erratic ruler who led the regime to its end. He married the daughter of the general Yang Jian (later Emperor Wen of Sui). Yuwen Yun did not rule for even a year before he passed the throne to his seven-year-old son, Yuwen Chan (Emperor Jingdi), so that he could indulge in

entertainment. Yuwen Yun was posthumously given the name Emperor Xuan.

Jingdi

Other names: Yuwen Chan, Yuwen Yan

r.579–581 CE
b.573 CE d.581 CE

Yuwen Chan became emperor at the age of seven, when his father, Yuwen Yun, abdicated in his favor. Since Yuwen Chan was so young, the court was controlled by the general Yang Jian (later Emperor Wen of Sui), who was Yuwen Yun's father-in-law. In 580 CE, Yang Jian forced Yuwen Chan to yield the throne to him, thereby ending the Northern Zhou dynasty and the rule of the Yuwen clan. Shortly afterwards, Yang Jian declared himself Emperor Wen and founded the Sui dynasty, which would reunite northern and southern China. Yuwen Chan and other members of his imperial clan were put to death. Yuwen Chan was posthumously named Jingdi.

The Sui Dynasty (581–618 CE)

The Sui unified most of China after the end of the period of the northern and southern dynasties. The Sui constructed important canals and had many remarkable achievements for such a short-lived dynasty, but were taken over by a military government that established the Tang dynasty.

Wendi
Other names: Yang Jian, Puliuru Jian, Gaozu

r. 581–604 CE
b. 541 CE d. 604 CE

Yang Jian, who founded the Sui dynasty and became Emperor Wen of Sui, was from the Yang clan. He served under General Yuwen Tai who established the Western Wei and the Northern Zhou kingdoms. In 580 CE, Yang Jian became regent for Emperor Jing of the Northern Zhou. After much fighting with the Yuwen clan and their supporters, Yang Jian was victorious and declared himself the Prince of Sui, forcing Emperor Jing to abdicate. In 589 CE, the Sui conquered the Chen dynasty, reuniting most of China. Yang Jian was remembered as Emperor Wen, or Wendi. Devout Buddhists, Wendi and his wife patronized monasteries and temples. He reformed the civil administration and legal code, authorized poverty relief measures, and built Daxing, a new capital near Chang'an. He also began construction of the Grand Canal. He ordered successful attacks on the Turks in northwest China, but another campaign in Korea failed. In 602 CE, Emperor Wen's beloved empress died. He died two years later.

△ Emperor Wen, founder of the Sui dynasty

Yangdi
Other names: Yang Guang, Shizu

r. 604–618 CE
b. 569 CE d. 618 CE

Yang Guang was Wendi's second son and became Emperor Yang. His elder brother, Yang Yong, was originally the heir apparent, but Yang Guang and a general named Yang Su conspired to accuse Yang Yong of slandering his younger brother. The intrigue resulted in Yang Guang being named heir apparent in 600 CE. Yang Guang also worked to make his other brothers fall from the emperor's favor. It is possible, though not proven, that Yang Guang was involved in a plot to murder his father, Emperor Wen. When Yang Guang came to power, one of his first acts was to send Yang Su to quash a rebellion by his younger brother, Yang Liang. The emperor ordered campaigns against the Tuyuhun people in Qinghai, the Goguryeo kingdom in Korea, and Champa in Vietnam, but the victories against the Tuyuhun were short-lived and the Korean campaigns all ended in disaster for the Sui. In his reign, Emperor Yang traveled frequently along the canals and rivers between three capitals: Daxing, Luoyang, and Jiangdu (Yangzhou, in Jiangsu province). Many canals, granaries, palaces, and other structures were completed in his reign. In Yangdi's later reign, rebellions and military mutinies broke out across the empire and the Sui lost control of northern China. Yuwen Huaji, the son of the emperor's trusted minister, staged a coup in 618 CE and had Yangdi strangled with a scarf.

Gongdi (I)
Other name: Yang You

r. 617–618 CE
b. 605 CE d. 619 CE

Yang You was posthumously named Emperor Gong of Sui. He was the son of Yang Zhao, Yang Guang's heir apparent, and was aided in gaining the throne by Li Yuan—the general who later established the Tang dynasty. Li Yuan developed a power base at Chang'an and, in 618 CE, forced Yang You to abdicate, declaring him a "retired emperor." He died a year later.

Gongdi (II)
Other name: Yang Tong

r. 618–619 CE
b. 604 CE d. 619 CE

After the previous emperor's death, Sui loyalists in Luoyang put Yang Tong on the throne as a puppet ruler, Emperor Gong. Like his predecessor, he was a son of Yang Zhao, Emperor Yang's heir apparent. Yang Tong's reign lasted less than a year before one of his generals, Wang Shichong, deposed him. Yang Tong attempted suicide but survived. He was later murdered, ending the Sui dynastic line.

The Tang Dynasty (618–907 CE)

The Tang was one of China's greatest native dynasties, lasting for nearly three centuries. Its cosmopolitan empire covered a greater area than any previous dynasty. The Tang rulers nonetheless faced many internal challenges and palace intrigues, which threatened their stability. Externally, they had to contend with the mighty Turkic empires to the north and west. Rebellions precipitated the Tang's collapse and a new period of disunity in Chinese history.

Gaozu

Other name: Li Yuan

r. 618–626 CE
b. 566 CE d. 635 CE

Li Yuan was born during the Northern Zhou period. His grandfather was Li Hu, who had once served as a commander under Yuwen Tai, the general who established the Western Wei. The Li clan was powerful during the Sui dynasty and Li Yuan served in the campaigns against the Goguryeo kingdom before being made a military governor in Taiyuan. Emperor Yang of Sui became displeased with Li Yuan because of some failures in defending the north-western frontier from the Turks and a prophecy that a member of the Li clan would usurp the emperorship. Li Yuan secured military support from the Turks and entered into an agreement with Chinese rebel leaders, such as Li Mi. With his sons Li Jiancheng and Li Shimin, he raised a great army that captured Chang'an. In 617 CE, he put a puppet Sui emperor (Gongdi I) on the throne and conquered Luoyang the following year.

Li Yuan established the Tang dynasty and was posthumously named Emperor Gaozu. The Sui conquest and the suppression of rebel groups took many years. Li Jiancheng and Li Shimin were responsible for continuing their father's campaigns. Gaozu adopted the Sui's bureaucratic style and redistributed land to the common people. Gaozu's son Li Shimin later fell out with his brother and, in 626 CE, killed Li Jiancheng at the Xuanwu gate of Chang'an. Gaozu was then forced to appoint Li Shimin as his heir, and he abdicated the throne shortly after. As a retired emperor, Gaozu had a strained relationship with Li Shimin. Gaozu died in 635 CE at the age of 69.

Taizong

Other name: Li Shimin

r. 627–649 CE
b. 600 CE d. 649 CE

Li Shimin had been hugely instrumental in founding the Tang dynasty, and he forced his father, Gaozu, to abdicate in his favor in 627 CE. After his death, he was given the title Taizong (meaning "grand ancestor"). Li Shimin was intelligent, a skilled horseman, and an excellent calligrapher. He was a practical ruler, who was not concerned with auspices and omens.

In 630 CE, Taizong's armies finally subdued the Eastern Turks, securing the power of the Tang dynasty. Taizong merged many local districts throughout China to increase the government's control, and reduced the number of governorships to prevent them from accumulating too much power. His armies crushed the Tuyuhun people in 635 CE and defeated the Turkic states in several battles throughout the 640s. His campaigns against the Goguryeo kingdom, which he personally led, however, were unsuccessful.

Two of Taizong's sons, Li Chengqian, the heir apparent, and Li Tai, argued over who would succeed him when he died. In 643 CE, Taizong stripped Li Chengqian of his heirship. Taizong's other son, Li Zhi, was named heir apparent on the advice of the minister Zhangsun Wuji. Taizong died in 649 CE. During his reign, the Tang prospered, and he is regarded as one of the greatest emperors in Chinese history. »

△ This painting shows Taizong (right, seated) receiving the ambassador of Tibet.

Gaozong
Other name: Li Zhi

r.649–683 CE
b.628 CE d.683 CE

Li Zhi was the ninth son of the previous emperor, Taizong, and Empress Wende. He was a gentle and weak-willed ruler and was posthumously named Emperor Gaozong. He ascended the throne on Taizong's death, but ministers, including Zhangsun Wuji, held the real power. In his early reign, Gaozong's consorts vied for influence and the title of empress. The victor was Wu Zetian, who acquired power and came to dominate the politics of the Tang in Gaozong's reign. Gaozong became sickly and had a stroke in 660 CE, causing him to become blind, and this allowed Wu Zetian to take complete control. Many military campaigns were ordered in Gaozong's name, which almost bankrupted the state. Gaozong nonetheless made ceremonial appearances until he became gravely ill in 683 CE. It was supposedly his last wish that his heir rule the empire with only the guidance of Wu Zetian (later known as Empress Wu).

Empress Wu
Other names: Wu Zetian, Wu Zhao

r.684–705 CE
b.624 CE d.705 CE

Empress Wu (see pp. 144–145) was the only officially recognized empress regnant in Chinese history. She declared herself Empress of the Zhou dynasty in 690 CE, interrupting the Tang dynasty. She was removed in a coup and died several months later at the age of 81.

△ Empress Wu was the ruler of the short-lived Zhou dynasty.

Zhongzong
Other names: Li Xian, Li Zhe, Wu Xian

r.705–710 CE
b.656 CE d.710 CE

Li Xian was the son of Gaozong and Wu Zetian and came to the throne very briefly after his father's death in 683 CE. However, Wu Zetian quickly deposed him and installed his younger brother, Li Dan, before taking the throne herself. Li Xian was exiled to Fangzhou in Hubei with the pregnant Empress Wei in 684 CE and was allowed to return to Luoyang in only 698 CE. Li Xian was installed as emperor a second time by the individuals who overthrew Wu Zetian and so the Tang dynasty was restored in 705 CE. After his death, he was given the title Zhongzong. During his second reign, his wife Empress Wei became very powerful. She and their daughter, Li Guo'er, were both considered for the succession, leading Zhongzong's male heir apparent, Li Chongjun, to attempt an unsuccessful coup in 707 CE. Zhongzong died at the age of 54. There is no proof, but historians suspect that Empress Wei and Li Guo'er poisoned Zhongzong's favorite cakes in an attempt to seize power.

Ruizong
Other names: Li Dan, Li Xulun, Li Lun, Wu Lun

r.684–690 CE; 710–712 CE
b.662 CE d.716 CE

After his death, Li Dan came to be remembered as Emperor Ruizong. He was the fourth son of Gaozong and Wu Zetian. Wu Zetian first established him as a puppet emperor from 684 to 690 CE, while effectively ruling herself.

After Zhongzong died, his youngest son was emperor for less than a month, and his sister, the Taiping Princess, conspired to have Empress Wei (Zhongzong's wife) eliminated. She arranged for Ruizong to be installed as emperor so that she could rise to power. In 712 CE, the Taiping Princess convinced Ruizong that astrological omens required him to yield the throne to his son Li Longji, who became Emperor Xuanzong. As a retired emperor, Ruizong still held court until Xuanzong carried out a coup to remove the Taiping Princess. Ruizong then stepped down from public life and lived in his palace until his death in 716 CE.

Xuanzong
Other names: Li Longji, Wu Longji, Emperor Ming

r.712–756 CE
b.685 CE d.762 CE

Li Longji was Ruizong's third son and his mother was a consort named Dou. He was a key figure in the coup against Empress Wei and Li Guo'er in 707 CE. In 713 CE, the Taiping Princess conspired with Li Longji to install him on the throne. She was later accused of plotting a coup and forced to die by suicide. Li Longji was posthumously titled Emperor Xuanzong. In his early reign, he initiated many reforms to restore confidence in the bureaucracy, state finances, and the legal system. He reformed the census system and increased military salaries to improve conscription, but the cost of the Tang's frontier armies became unsustainable. Over time, the frontier military governors gained much power. Xuanzong's high minister, Zhang Yue, was the most powerful figure at court in the 720s.

△ Emperor Xuanzang watches his consort, Yang Guifei, mounting a horse.

In the 730s, a new high minister, Pei Guangting, reformed the civil service examination system to favor senior-ranking officials. Shortly afterward, factional struggles broke out between the ministers Zhang Jiuling, Pei Yaoqing, and Li Linfu.

In 736 CE, Li Linfu was victorious and won the emperor's favor, after which Xuanzong lost interest in affairs of state. While Li Linfu held power, Xuanzong became preoccupied with his harem and made Yang Guifei, originally his son's wife, his favored consort (see pp. 150–153). Yang Guifei's relatives came into conflict with Li Linfu and, when he died in 752 CE, Yang Guifei's cousin Yang Guozhong competed with An Lushan, a Sogdian military governor, for the chancellorship. The so-called An Lushan Rebellion, which began in 755 CE, sacked Luoyang and then Chang'an. Xuanzong fled to Chengdu with Yang Guifei, but his guards forced Xuanzong to have her killed. When Xuanzong learned that his son Li Heng had declared himself emperor, he abdicated. After Li Heng recaptured Chang'an, Xuanzong returned to the capital but did not reclaim the throne. In his retirement, Xuanzong became ill and depressed, and died in 762 CE.

Suzong
Other names: Li Heng, Li Yu, Li Shao

r. 756–762 CE
b. 711 CE d. 762 CE

Emperor Suzong, whose name was Li Heng, was the son of Xuanzong. He declared himself emperor and retook Chang'an in 758 CE. He began to reclaim China and put down revolts that had sprung from the chaos of the previous reign. During his reign, a eunuch named Li Fuguo rose to power and tried to become chancellor but was stopped by Suzong's allies. However, when Suzong became gravely ill, Li Fuguo executed his empress and his nurse and left Suzong to die.

Daizong
Other names: Li Chu, Li Yu

r. 763–779 CE
b. 727 CE d. 779 CE

During the An Lushan Rebellion of 755–763 CE, the rebel state of Yan occupied the Tang's two capital cities, Chang'an and Luoyang. Li Chu was a general of the Tang forces that, together with Uighur forces, recaptured these two cities. He became emperor in 763 CE and would be remembered as Emperor Daizong. By the time the An Lushan Rebellion ended, the Tang empire had started to decline. Within the empire, a number of warlords had grown independent from the central government. China also faced invasions from the Tibetan empire, whose forces even occupied Chang'an for a short period of time in 763 CE. It is said that Emperor Daizong was a devout Buddhist and invested a great deal of resources in Buddhism.

Dezong
Other name: Li Kuo

r. 780–805 CE
b. 742 CE d. 805 CE

Li Kuo was the eldest son of Emperor Daizong and ascended the throne at the age of 37 as Emperor Dezong. He was said to be a diligent ruler during his early reign, who tried to improve the financial situation of the empire by implementing new tax laws. He also tried to strengthen the central government by curbing the power of regional warlords, which triggered a series of rebellions. After a rebellion that forced him to flee the capital in 783 CE, Dezong started to put his trust in the palace eunuchs, who had protected him during the rebellion. He even made them commanders in the army. However, in his later days, Dezong reversed his earlier policies that prevented excessive government spending and became known for his greed. »

△ The Buddhist deity Guanyin is depicted in this Tang silk banner.

Shunzong

Other name: Li Song

r.805–805 CE
b.761 CE d.806 CE

Li Song, posthumously called Emperor Shunzong, was the son of Dezong. Before he came to the throne, he suffered a stroke and was unable to speak, so a group of officers and scholars made decisions on his behalf. In his brief reign, policies were implemented to consolidate imperial power and restrict the influence of regional warlords and eunuchs. After he had ruled for a few months, powerful eunuchs forced him to abdicate the throne in favor of his son, Li Chun. Li Chun dismissed the state officers who had tried to restrict the power of eunuchs.

Xianzong

Other name: Li Chun

r.806–820 CE
b.778 CE d.820 CE

Emperor Xianzong, whose personal name was Li Chun, ascended to the throne with the support of eunuchs, and in return he guaranteed their power at court. He continued the policy of previous reigns to curb the power of regional warlords and was credited for briefly stabilizing the empire. In his later days, however, he pursued immortality by taking alchemists' medicines, which made him increasingly irritable. The eunuchs who served him were often punished or even executed for making even minor mistakes. It was believed that Xianzong was assassinated by one of these eunuchs.

Muzong

Other names: Li Heng, Li You

r.821–824 CE
b.795 CE d.824 CE

Li Heng, Emperor Muzong, was the previous emperor's son and like his father was put on the throne with the support of the eunuchs. During his reign, he did not attend to his duties and spent his days in pursuit of pleasure, feasting, and hunting. The regional military governors, whose power had been suppressed during Xianzong's reign, regathered and challenged imperial power. Muzong suffered a stroke during a polo game with the eunuchs in 824 CE and died shortly after.

Jingzong

Other name: Li Zhan

r.825–827 CE
b.809 CE d.827 CE

Jingzong came to the throne at the age of 15. During his reign, corrupt eunuchs who had come to power in the previous reign controlled the imperial army and dominated the young emperor's rule. Instead of governing the empire, Jingzong was more interested in polo games. He was assassinated by a group of eunuchs in 827 CE.

Wenzong

Other names: Li Ang, Li Han

r.827–840 CE
b.809 CE d.840 CE

Wenzong was a younger brother of the previous emperor, Jingzong. He reversed the wastefulness of his father and brother, by ruling as a diligent emperor who was open to advice from his officials. Wenzong was also active in plotting against the powerful eunuchs. However, his plans were revealed to the eunuchs, causing a series of conflicts and the slaughter of more than a thousand officials. Factional fighting became rife and regional warlords staged rebellions.

Wuzong

Other names: Li Chan, Li Yan

r.840–846 CE
b.814 CE d.846 CE

The fifth son of Muzong, a younger brother of Wenzong, Li Chan was named emperor by eunuchs. Wuzong successfully quelled the threat from the Uighurs and suppressed a major domestic rebellion. Wuzong, a Daoist, was also known for his persecution of Buddhists. By his reign, Buddhist monasteries had been exempted from paying taxes and had gathered an excessive amount of land. Wuzong believed that this would drain the state's economy, so he ordered Buddhist temples to be destroyed and monks and nuns to return to lay life. Wuzong became ill and took pills made by Daoist alchemists— believed to grant immortality— but died in 846 CE.

Xuanzong
Other names: Li Yi, Li Chen

r.847–859 CE
b.810 CE d.859 CE

Li Yi who came to the throne as Xuanzong is considered to be the last capable ruler of the Tang dynasty. After Wuzong died, the eunuchs made Li Yi the new emperor as they thought he was shy, unintelligent, and therefore easy to control. However, once emperor, Xuanzong quickly asserted himself and demoted several powerful chancellors involved in factional fighting. Xuanzong tried to follow Emperor Taizong's example and appoint capable officials. Xuanzong also recaptured the prefectures along the Hexi Corridor, which were lost to the Tibetan empire during the An Lushan Rebellion. Toward the end of his life, he became interested in immortality and ingested pills made by Daoist alchemists. He died of poisoning by these pills in 859 CE.

Yizong
Other names: Li Wei, Li Cui

r.860–873 CE
b.833 CE d.873 CE

Unlike his father Xuanzong, Emperor Yizong had no interest in governing an empire. He was described as an alcoholic who liked to indulge in music, sexual pleasure, and banqueting. He was a devout Buddhist and invested a great fortune in Buddhist temples and ceremonies. During his reign, corrupt bureaucracy, heavy taxes, and famines forced people into cannibalism, and a series of revolts erupted. Xuanzong had revived the Tang fortunes during his reign, but Yizong quickly exhausted the treasury.

Xizong
Other names: Li Yan, Li Xuan

r.874–888 CE
b.862 CE d.888 CE

During his reign, Xizong, who was the son of Yizong, left government affairs to be managed by his favorite eunuch. He spent his time enjoying himself and playing games while the empire faced major rebellions in the countryside. The capital, Chang'an, fell to the rebel Huang Chao in 880 CE. Xizong fled to Chengdu and did not return until 885 CE. In 886 CE, he was forced to leave the capital again because of a serious dispute between a court officer and a military governor in Shanxi. He returned to Chang'an in 888 CE and died shortly afterward. By the end of his reign, the Tang empire was divided among regional military governors.

Zhaozong
Other names: Li Jie, Li Min, Li Ye

r.889–904 CE
b.867 CE d.904 CE

Zhaozong was Xizong's younger brother. Following on from the chaos of the preceding years, his reign witnessed a series of rebellions. Despite Zhaozong's attempts to restore imperial power, parts of the empire continued to fall into the hands of military governors. Zhaozong was forced to flee the capital three times. In 903 CE, the military governor Zhu Quanzhong (who became Emperor Taizu of the Later Liang) seized control of the central government and slaughtered many of Zhaozong's eunuchs and ministers. After a year, Zhaozong was killed on Zhu Quanzhong's instructions.

Aidi
Other names: Li Zhu, Li Zuo, Zhaoxuan, Jingzong

r.905–907 CE
b.892 CE d.908 CE

At the age of 11, Li Zhu was placed on the throne as a puppet emperor by Zhu Quanzhong. The Tang government was totally under Zhu Quanzhong's control. During Li Zhu's reign, Zhu Quanzhong had many members of the imperial family and their associates killed, or forced them to die by suicide. In 907 CE, Zhu Quanzhong forced Li Zhu to abdicate the throne. This enabled Zhu Quanzhong to found his own dynasty, the Later Liang. The following year, Li Zhu was poisoned and given the posthumous title Aidi, which means "lamentable emperor." With his death, the Tang dynasty ended, giving way to a period of disunity in China.

△ Buddhism was subjected to both patronage and persecution by Tang rulers.

The Five Dynasties and Ten Kingdoms
(907–959 CE)

Between the two great dynasties of the Tang and the Song, 10th-century China experienced a 70-year period of political upheaval. During this time, five short-lived dynasties emerged to hold power in northern China. At the same time, 10 kingdoms were briefly established, mainly in the south.

THE LATER LIANG DYNASTY
(907–923 CE)

The Later Liang was one of the Five Dynasties and controlled much of northern China. It was founded by Zhu Wen, a former Tang commander who played a key role in bringing the dynasty to an end.

Taizu
Other names: Zhu Wen, Zhu Quanzhong

r. 907–912 CE
b. 852 CE d. 912 CE

Zhu Wen was a warlord during the latter part of the Tang dynasty. Originally a bandit, he joined the ranks of the rebel Huang Chao against the Tang rulers, only to defect to the Tang and serve as a commander under the Turkic military governor Li Keyong. Zhu Wen conquered territories in northern China by defeating other warlords. To consolidate his power, he also

assassinated the Tang emperor Zhaozong and replaced him with the infant Aidi, whom he later dethroned to proclaim the birth of his own dynasty, the Liang. The dynasty he founded is known as the Later Liang to distinguish it from the Liang dynasty that existed during the southern dynasties period.

None of Zhu Wen's military campaigns were successful, so he could not further expand his empire. He was capable but ruthless and was killed only five years into his reign by his eldest son, Zhu Yougui. Zhu Wen was posthumously given the name Taizu, which means "grand progenitor."

Modi
Other names: Zhu Youzhen, Zhu Zhen

r. 913–923 CE
b. 888 CE d. 923 CE

The previous emperor, Taizu, did not favor his eldest son, Zhu Yougui (the Prince of Ying). When Taizu became ill toward the end of his life, he considered

appointing his adopted son, Zhu Youwen, as his successor, so Zhu Yougui killed both Taizu and Zhu Youwen and seized the throne. Soon afterward, however, a younger brother, Zhu Youzhen, overthrew him. After proclaiming himself emperor, Zhu Youzhen focused his energy on guarding his empire against the threat of neighboring powers, especially the Jin. The many conflicts against the Jin were indecisive, until the failure of a Liang military plan gave the Jin the opportunity to conquer the Liang capital. Facing defeat, Zhu Youzhen ordered his general to kill him, ending the Later Liang dynasty. Zhu Youzhen's posthumous name was Modi, meaning "last emperor."

THE LATER TANG DYNASTY
(923–936 CE)

The Later Tang was another one of the Five Dynasties in northern China. It was founded by the son of Li Keyong, who was an enemy of Zhu Wen of the Later Liang.

Zhuangzong
Other name: Li Cunxu

r. 923–926 CE
b. 885 CE d. 926 CE

Li Cunxu was the son of Li Keyong, a celebrated Turkic military governor who was

△ This detail from a silk scroll painting, attributed to Chao Yen, depicts horsemen of the Later Tang dynasty.

made Prince of Jin in 896 CE by Emperor Zhaozong of the Tang dynasty. When the warlord Zhu Wen deposed the last Tang emperor, Li Keyong refused to submit to the newly founded Liang dynasty and remained independent. After his father's death in 908 CE, Li Cunxu followed in his footsteps. He reformed the army led by Li Keyong and undertook a series of successful campaigns that concluded with the conquest of the Later Liang dynasty. With a territory that comprised most of northern and central China, Li Cunxu proclaimed himself emperor of the Tang, now called the Later Tang to distinguish it from the earlier dynasty.

Li Cunxu was better at warfare than he was at governance. He soon lost the support of his armies, who started a wave of rebellions. Li Cunxu was killed in one such uprising after only three years on the throne. He received the posthumous name Zhuangzong, which means "strong" or "robust."

Mingzong
Other names: Li Siyuan, Li Dan

r. 926–933 CE
b. 867 CE d. 933 CE

Li Siyuan was the adopted son of Li Keyong. He became a distinguished general under first his stepfather and then his stepbrother, Zhuangzong. After Zhuangzong's death, Li Siyuan took the throne with the help of his rebel army. He was posthumously called Mingzong. After unsuccessfully trying to restore friendly relationships with the Khitan in the north, Mingzong had to turn his attention to the southwest to confront the military governors

who refused to recognize his authority. When Mingzong fell ill, his undisciplined eldest son, Li Congrong, feared being ousted from the succession. Li Congrong tried to seize power but was killed. His younger brother Li Conghou took the throne soon afterward, when Mingzong succumbed to his illness.

Mindi
Other name: Li Conghou

r. 933–934 CE
b. 914 CE d. 934 CE

Li Conghou was one of the younger sons of the previous ruler, Mingzong. He held military positions under his father's rule and became emperor after his elder brother, Li Congrong, tried to seize the throne by force and died in the attempt. Although Li Conghou was the emperor, he had little real power; the officials who stopped Li Congrong's coup controlled the whole government and governed without seeking the emperor's assent.

While trying to limit the power of some of the emperor's relatives, these powerful individuals caused Li Conghou's adoptive brother, Li Congke, to rebel. Li Congke took advantage of the mutiny of the imperial army and first deposed and then killed Li Conghou. After his death, Li Conghou received the imperial title Mindi.

Feidi
Other names: Li Congke

r. 934–936 CE
b. 885 CE d. 937 CE

Li Congke was an adopted son of Mingzong, and he was an important military commander of the Later Tang dynasty. He

△ Emperor Zhuangzong (Li Cunxu) of the Later Tang dynasty

overthrew Mingzong's biological son, Mindi, to become emperor. Li Congke's reign was plagued by repeated raids by Khitan Liao soldiers into Later Tang territory, and also by natural disasters, which brought famine and discontent to his people. Tension between the emperor and his brother-in-law, Shi Jingtang—a general who had participated in Li Congke's rebellion against Li Conghou—grew quickly as Shi Jingtang accumulated more

wealth and power, since Li Congke saw him as a potential rival. The pressure that Li Congke exerted on Shi Jingtang soon caused him to rebel against the emperor, and Shi Jingtang's army conquered theLater Tang capital. Seeing that his defeat was imminent, Li Congke died by suicide, putting an end to the Later Tang dynasty. He received the posthumous name Feidi, which means "abolished emperor." »

THE LATER JIN DYNASTY (936–947 CE)

The Later Jin was one of the Five Dynasties in northern China. Lasting for only 13 years, it was easily overcome by the forces of the Khitan Liao dynasty, who ended the Later Jin's rule in 946 CE.

Gaozu

Other name: Shi Jingtang

r.936–942 CE
b.892 CE d.942 CE

Shi Jingtang was an important military governor in the Later Tang dynasty and was also the ruler Mingzong's son-in-law. He staged a rebellion against Li Congke, emperor of the Later Tang, and deposed him to found the Later Jin dynasty. Shi Jingtang was posthumously given the name Emperor Gaozu. Having enlisted the help of the Khitan of the Liao dynasty, Gaozu ceded some northern territories to them. In order to preserve peace, he submitted to the Liao and treated them as a superior power. However, this attitude toward the Liao displeased some of his military governors, who launched two major rebellions, in 937–938 CE and 941–942 CE, temporarily destabilizing the empire. When Gaozu became ill, he wanted his surviving son to succeed him, but the chancellor, Feng Dao, favored the emperor's nephew, Shi Chonggui, who was older and more experienced. Gaozu died in 942 CE and the throne passed to Shi Chonggui.

△ This portrait depicts Emperor Gaozu (Shi Jingtang) of the Later Jin.

Chudi

Other name: Shi Chonggui

r.942–946 CE
b.914 CE d.974 CE

Shi Chonggui was the nephew of Gaozu and was previously a military governor. When Gaozu died, Shi Chonggui succeeded him as emperor. Shi Chonggui refused to be subservient to the Liao dynasty. After some minor skirmishes, the Liao led two major invasions against the Later Jin. These were stopped by Shi Chonggui in 944 CE, who led his army in person. However, when peace negotiations failed, the Liao lured the bulk of the Later Jin army away from the capital and convinced General Du Wei to surrender. The Liao army then entered the defenceless capital and deposed Shi Chonggui, who was sent into exile in Liao territory, ending the Later Jin dynasty. He was remembered as Chudi, the "exiled emperor."

THE LATER HAN DYNASTY (947–950 CE)

The Later Han were one of the Five Dynasties in northern China. It was short-lived and its two emperors had only a precarious grasp on power for the three years that it existed.

Gaozu

Other names: Liu Zhiyuan, Liu Gao

r.947–948 CE
b.895 CE d.948 CE

Liu Zhiyuan was a military commander and governor for the Later Tang and Later Jin dynasties. After the fall of the Later Jin, Liu delayed his submission to the Liao dynasty and, pushed by his soldiers, declared himself emperor. He was posthumously named Emperor Gaozu. The Liao emperor prepared an army to face him, but the rebellion of several military governors, who declared loyalty to Liu, forced him to retreat. After regaining the cities of Luoyang and Kaifeng, Liu declared the birth of the Later Han dynasty. During his short reign, he fought against some rebellious and indecisive governors, but he died after a brief illness, naming his only surviving child as his successor.

Yindi

Other name: Liu Chengyou

r.948–950 CE
b.931 CE d.951 CE

Liu Chengyou succeeded his father, Gaozu, as emperor of the Later Han dynasty at the age of 16. At the beginning of his reign, he had to deal with the aftermath of the wars fought by his father against mutinous governors. This led to the rebellion of another governor, Li Shouzhen, which ended with his death by suicide. Despite repeated Liao incursions, the government was efficient thanks to the ability of government officials. However, Liu Chengyou started to resent them because they limited his power. Therefore, he staged a plot to kill his high-ranking officials and their associates. One of the targets, General Guo Wei, managed to escape the attempted assassination and gathered an army that attacked the capital. Liu Chengyou died in the battle and received the posthumous imperial name of Yindi.

THE LATER ZHOU DYNASTY (951–959 CE)

The Later Zhou dynasty, which lasted for nine years, was the last of the Five Dynasties to exist in northern China.

Taizu

Other name: Guo Wei

r. 951–954 CE
b. 904 CE d. 954 CE

Guo Wei served as a military commander under the Later Jin and Later Han dynasties. He seized the throne and founded the Later Zhou dynasty after the violent power struggles that ended those dynasties. Guo Wei, who was posthumously known as Taizu, established a solid and efficient government. He consolidated the borders and also approved reforms to reduce unnecessary expenses, increase agricultural production and state revenues, and improve the welfare of the peasant population. Taizu's plans to reconquer the territories lost to the Liao dynasty during the Later Jin period were ended when he became ill. Before dying, he named his adoptive son Guo Rong as his successor.

Shizong

Other names: Guo Rong, Chai Rong

r. 954–959 CE
b. 921 CE d. 959 CE

Guo Rong was the adopted son of Taizu and a military governor under the Later Han dynasty. He succeeded Taizu on the throne and was posthumously named Emperor Shizong. He completed his predecessor's policies and plans. Immediately after his accession, Shizong foiled the attack of a joint army of Northen Han and Liao troops, demonstrating his military might. He then focused on reasserting central authority by weakening military governors and reforming the army. With the cooperation of his ministers, he promulgated a new legal code. He also made the land tax fairer, fought corruption among officials and improved waterways to benefit commerce. Shizong undertook a significant territorial expansion with expeditions in Later Shu, Southern Tang, and Liao regions. When he became ill and was dying, he left his throne to his young son.

Gongdi

Other name: Guo Zongxun

r. 959–959 CE
b. 953 CE d. 973 CE

Guo Zongxun was the son of Shizong and succeeded his father at the age of five. With a young child on the throne, not even the strong empire built by Shizong was able to command authority, and soon the neighboring powers, which Shizong had kept at bay, started to exert pressure on the borders. When a report about a coming attack from the Northern Han and Liao arrived, the palace army demanded that their commander Zhao Kuangyin seize the throne. The commander Zhao deposed Guo Zongxun and rapidly quelled two governors who opposed him. Guo Zongxun, who was known after his death as Gongdi, was spared but sent away. An official who was trying to win the favor of the Song emperor killed him years later.

THE KINGDOM OF YANG WU (902–937 CE)

At its height, the Kingdom of Wu covered an area currently occupied by modern Jiangsu, Anhui, Jiangxi, and Hubei. The capital was Jiangdu (modern Yangzhou). In order to differentiate it from the Kingdom of Wu (222–280 CE) ruled by the Sun family during the Three Kingdoms period, it is historically known as Yang Wu or the Southern Wu.

Taizu

Other names: Yang Xingmi, Emperor Xiaowu

r. 902–905 CE
b. 852 CE d. 905 CE

During the late Tang period, Yang Xingmi was a military governor of Huainan, with a headquarters in what is now Yangzhou. By securing control of Huainan and surrounding areas, he laid the foundation for the transformation of Huainan from a military district subordinate to the Tang to an independent kingdom. He was generally considered to be a wise ruler, and the economy of the region between the Yangzi and the Huai rivers prospered during his reign. He was posthumously known as Emperor Taizu.

Liezu

Other names: Yang Wo, Emperor Jing of Wu, Prince of Hongnong

r. 905–908 CE
b. 886 CE d. 908 CE

Yang Wo was the eldest son of the previous ruler, Taizu, and was posthumously known as Emperor Liezu. Before he came to the throne, some ministers believed he was unfit to rule. During his reign, he and his trusted men bullied generals and ministers, leading to their rebellion in 907 CE. The two leaders of the rebellion, Zhang Hao and Xu Wen (who was the adoptive father of the founding emperor of the Southern Tang dynasty) took control of the court and had Yang Wo killed in 908 CE.

Gaozu

Other names: Yang Longyan, Yang Wei

r. 908–920 CE
b. 897 CE d. 920 CE

Yang Longyan, posthumously named Emperor Gaozu, was his predecessor Liezu's younger brother. During his reign, the kingdom was actually controlled by the regent Xu Wen, who was also the adoptive father of the founding emperor of the Southern Tang. Yang Longyan was frequently insulted by Xu Wen's adoptive son, Xu Zhixun, and was afraid of him. Accounts suggest that Yang Longyan liked to indulge in alcohol. He died of an illness in 920 CE.

Ruidi

Other name: Yang Pu

r. 920–937 CE
b. 900 CE d. 938 CE

Yang Pu was the younger brother of his predecessors Gaozu and Leizu. He was the first Wu ruler to proclaim himself emperor. After his death, he was named Ruidi. Like Gaozu, Yang Pu had no actual power. In 938 CE, Xu Zhigao (the founding emperor of the Southern Tang) forced »

Yang Pu to yield the throne to him. After that, Yang Pu spent most of his time studying Daoism and died within a year.

THE FORMER SHU KINGDOM
(907–925 CE)

The Former Shu kingdom was founded by Wang Jian (Emperor Gaozu), who first served the Tang as a military governor of west Sichuan. It was also known as the Great Shu or Wang Shu. The capital of the Former Shu was Chengdu, in Sichuan province.

Gaozu
Other name: Wang Jian

r. 907–918 CE
b. 847 CE d. 918 CE

Born in 847 CE, Wang Jian was a native of Henan province and came from a humble background. In his youth, he made a living in butchery and the salt trade. After his father's death, he joined the Tang army. In the early 10th century, when the Tang dynasty was in decline, he became the strongest regional military governor based in the southwest. As the Tang dynasty fell, Wang Jian declared himself emperor. He was posthumously named Emperor Gaozu.

Houzhu
Other names: Wang Yan,
Wang Zongyan

r. 918–925 CE
b. 901 CE d. 926 CE

Wang Yan was the 11th son of the previous emperor, Gaozu. He was known as a decadent and incompetent ruler who was more interested in sexual pleasure than in government. During his reign, the Former Shu were attacked from the north by the Later Liang and Later Tang dynasties. In 925 CE, Wang Yan surrendered to the Later Tang and was put to death by Emperor Zhuangzong. Wang Yan's posthumous title, Houzhu, means "later sovereign." He was the second and last ruler of the Former Shu kingdom.

THE KINGDOM OF WUYUE
(907–978 CE)

The territory of the Kingdom of Wuyue included parts of modern Zhejiang, Shanghai, and Jiangsu. Its capital was Hangzhou. Throughout its history, Wuyue nominally submitted to the dominant regimes in northern China. The rulers of Wuyue never declared themselves emperors. Wuyue was the most long-lived of the Ten Kingdoms.

King Wusu
Other names: Qian Liu,
King Taizu

r. 907–931 CE
b. 852 CE d. 932 CE

Qian Liu was born a commoner and was a salt trader in his youth. He later joined the local forces and demonstrated considerable military prowess. During the late Tang period, a rebel leader named Huang Chao rose up against the dynasty. The rebellion took place from 874–884 CE, during which time Qian Liu rose to become a local military commander and made his brothers and cousins leaders of local forces. They repelled Huang Chao's forces and secured what became the Wuyue kingdom after the fall of the Tang dynasty. After settling the regional conflicts among the warlords within Zhejiang and Jiangsu, Qian Liu developed both culture and trade in his kingdom, building seawalls and encouraging maritime trade. He ordered the construction of the famous embankment on the Qiantang River near Hangzhou. He was a devout Buddhist and encouraged the construction and restoration of Buddhist temples, some of which still stand today. He was posthumously named King Wusu.

King Wenmu
Other names: Qian Yuanguan,
Qian Chuanguan, King Shizong

r. 932–941 CE
b. 887 CE d. 941 CE

Qian Yuanguan, who became King Wenmu, was the seventh son of King Wusu. In a struggle between King Wusu and his rival Tian Jun, Qian Yuanguan volunteered to be taken as a hostage and as a result became a son-in-law of Tian Jun. Qian Yuanguan returned to Hangzhou after the death of Tian Jun and successfully led Wuyue forces in a series of campaigns against other warlords. In 934 CE, Emperor Min of the Later Tang made Qian Yuanguan the prince of Wuyue, and in 937 CE, he became the king of Wuyue. In 941 CE, Qian Yuanguan suffered trauma from a major fire that almost burned down the palace, and he died that same year.

King Zhongxian
Other names: Qian Hongzuo,
Qian Zuo, King Chengzong

r. 941–947 CE
b. 928 CE d. 947 CE

Qian Hongzuo, who became King Zhongxian, was the sixth son of his predecessor King Wenmu. He was a mild-tempered,

▷ This memorial in Hangzhou commemorates the kings of Wuyue.

diligent, and able ruler. During his reign, Wuyue's southern neighbor, the kingdom of Min, collapsed in a civil war. Min territory was divided by Wuyue and its northwestern neighbor, the Southern Tang. Instead of passing the throne to his young sons, King Zhongxian designated his younger brother Qian Hongzong as his heir.

King Zhongxun
Other names: Qian Hongzong, Qian Zong

r. 947–948 CE
b. 928 CE d. 971 CE

Qian Hongzong, who became King Zhongxun, was the younger brother of the previous ruler. He ruled for only seven months and submitted to Emperor Taizong of Liao, who had destroyed the Later Jin dynasty. Because of this, Qian Honzong was deposed by his general Hu Jinsi in a coup, after which Qian Hongzong's brother Qian Hongchu became the new king. Despite Hu Jinsi's repeated attempts to kill Qian Hongzong, Qian Hongchu kept his brother safe under house arrest. Qian Hongzong lived for more than 20 years after being deposed.

King Zhongyi
Other names: Qian Hongchu, Qian Chu

r. 948–978 CE
b. 929 CE d. 988 CE

Qian Hongchu, who became King Zhongyi, was the ninth son of King Wenmu. During his reign, Qian Hongchu followed his predecessor's policy of serving the dominant northern regimes. He submitted to the Later Han, Later Zhou, and Northern Song

dynasties, who controlled the north of China in succession. For this reason, the northern regimes respected the autonomy of the Wuyue kingdom, allowing the region to maintain and develop its economy. Qian Hongchu continued to enjoy prestige as a king under the Northern Song dynasty before he lost this title and became the prince of Huiahai. The Wuyue kingdom was peacefully dissolved after the Northern Song dynasty annexed its neighboring territories.

THE KINGDOM OF MIN
(909–945 CE)

Created by Emperor Taizu of the Later Liang, the kingdom of Min was located in modern Fujian province. Its capital was Fuzhou. The kingdom lasted until 945 CE, when it fell to the Southern Tang dynasty.

Taizu
Other names: Wang Shenzhi, Prince Zhongyi of Min

r. 909–925 CE
b. 862 CE d. 925 CE

Wang Shenzhi was born a commoner in Henan province. He joined the forces of the Tang dynasty and fought in Fujian. After the Later Liang overthrew the Tang, Emperor Taizu of the Later Liang named Wang Shenzhi the king of Min. He was known to be a frugal and tolerant ruler. He implemented a series of policies to lower tax rates, and he supported educated men who had come to Min fleeing warfare in the north. Wang Shenzhi and his brothers, Wang Chao and Wang Shengui, were

known as the "Three Princes of Min" and are commemorated by the people of Fujian still today. Wang Shenzhi was posthumously named Emperor Taizu.

Prince Si of Min
Other name: Wang Yanhan

r. 925–927 CE
d. 927 CE

Wang Yanhan, the Prince of Min, was the eldest son of the first Min ruler Taizu. He was said to be violent and caused offense by enjoying entertainments during the mourning period for his father, which went against custom. Wang Yanhan ruled only briefly before he was killed in a rebellion led by his brothers, Wang Yanbing and Wang Yanjun. The latter took the throne and became Emperor Huizong.

Huizong
Other names: Wang Yanjun, Wang Lin

r. 928–935 CE
d. 935 CE

Wang Yanjun was the first ruler of Min to proclaim himself an emperor. He first served his brother, Wang Yanhan, as a military governor. However, he killed Wang Yanhan in 927 CE and then killed his competitor and adoptive brother Wang Yanbing in 931 CE. He declared himself emperor in 933 CE and changed his name to Wang Lin. He was careful not to get involved in conflicts with neighboring states. In 935 CE, Wang Yanjun grew ill and was badly wounded in an uprising. One of his palace servant girls, who reportedly could not bear to see him suffer, took his life. After his death, he was named Emperor Huizong.

Kangzong
Other names: Wang Chang, Wang Jipeng

r. 936–939 CE
d. 939 CE

Wang Jipeng ascended to the throne upon the death of his father, Wang Yanjun (Emperor Huizong). Some sources suggest that it was Wang Jipeng who instigated the uprising that led to Wang Yanjun's death, but his involvement was not proven. He was suspicious of other members of the imperial clan and held his uncle Wang Yanxi (later Emperor Jingzong) under house arrest. In 939 CE, Wang Jipeng, along with his empress and children, were assassinated by his cousin Wang Jiye. After his death, he was remembered as Emperor Kangzong.

Jingzong
Other names: Wang Yanxi, Wang Xi

r. 939–944 CE
d. 944 CE

Wang Yanxi ascended to the throne after plotting with his nephew Wang Jiye to overthrow his other nephew Wang Jipeng (Emperor Kangzong). As emperor, he indulged in extravagance and turned out to be even more distrustful and violent than his predecessor. One of Wang Yanxi's brothers, Wang Yanzheng, rebelled against him and declared himself emperor of the state of Yin in 943 CE, splitting the kingdom of Min into two. In 944 CE, Wang Yanxi was killed in a coup led by two generals who had helped him overthrow Wang Jipeng. Wang Yangxi was posthumously called Emperor Jingzong. »

Gongyi

Other names: Wang Yanzheng, Emperor Tiande

r. 943–945 CE
d. 951 CE

Wang Yanzheng left the Min capital of Fuzhou following a disagreement with his brother Wang Yanxi. He declared himself the emperor of Yin in 943 CE, establishing his own government in Jianzhou (modern Jianou). He was no better a ruler than his brother, and his state suffered from warfare and heavy taxes. A civil war within the state of Min ensued, with the Southern Tang forces occupying Fuzhou and Jianzhou. Wang Yanzheng surrendered to the Southern Tang forces. He was then moved to Jinling (modern Nanjing), the capital of Southern Tang, where he lived out the rest of his life as a Southern Tang subject.

THE SOUTHERN HAN KINGDOM

(917–971 CE)

The Southern Han kingdom was founded by a supposed descendant of the earlier Han dynasty. The kingdom spanned the modern provinces of Guangdong, Guangxi, and Hainan, and northern Vietnam. The capital was Panyu (modern-day Guangzhou).

Gaozu

Other names: Liu Yan, Liu Zhi

r. 917–941 CE
b. 889 CE d. 942 CE

Liu Yan's ancestors were natives of Henan province and had migrated to the southeast in connection with their trade and business. Liu Yan's father, Liu Zhiqian (Liu Qian) was a military officer of the Tang dynasty. Liu Zhiqian's eldest son, Liu Yin, had inherited his father's forces and position in the southeast and submitted to the Later Liang as a vassal. When Liu Yin died, Liu Yan took over this position and declared himself emperor. He claimed he was a descendant of the ruling house of the Han dynasty (206 BCE–220 CE) and thus named his regime "the Han." Liu Yan was said to be a capable yet cruel ruler. Like the Han dynasty, Liu Yan's kingdom put a state examination system in place to train and recruit government officials. Liu Yan died in 942 CE. He was posthumously named Emperor Gaozu.

Shangdi

Other names: Liu Bin, Liu Hongdu

r. 942–943 CE
b. 920 CE d. 943 CE

Liu Bin, who was Liu Yan's son, is described in the sources as an arrogant man who had no interest in affairs of state. He preferred to spend his time drinking, playing music, and being entertained by prostitutes. During his brief reign, a peasant rebellion took place in Xunzhou (modern Huizhou, Guangdong province), and the rebels took control of many areas in the eastern part of the kingdom. In 943 CE, Liu Bin's younger brother, Liu Sheng—who later took the throne—plotted a coup and had the drunken Liu Bin pounded to death by a group of arm wrestlers who had performed at a banquet in his honor. Liu Bin was posthumously remembered as Shangdi, Emperor Shang.

Zhongzong

Other names: Liu Sheng, Liu Hongxi

r. 943–958 CE
b. 920 CE d. 958 CE

Liu Sheng was a brother of the previous emperor, Liu Bin, and had previously served as the head of his administration. Liu Sheng organized for Liu Bin to be assassinated at a banquet and then ascended to the throne himself. He was worried that his other brothers would want to take the throne from him, so he had his brothers and nephews killed and took his nieces as concubines. Sources say that he took pleasure in tormenting people and constructed luxurious chambers to store and use his collections of instruments of torture. When the forces of the Later Zhou dynasty unified the north, Liu Sheng tried once to submit to the Later Zhou and pay them tribute. However, before long, he gave up his efforts to defend his kingdom and returned to drinking and feasting. He was posthumously named Emperor Zhongzong.

Houzhu

Other names: Liu Jixing, Liu Chang

r. 958–971 CE
b. 942 CE d. 980 CE

Liu Chang was the eldest son of the previous ruler, Liu Sheng. As his father had killed almost all of his brothers and ministers, Liu Chang was left with no one at his side but eunuchs and female attendants when he ascended to the throne. Believing that a man with descendants could not remain loyal to him, Liu Chang ordered that every man be castrated before entering his court, resulting in the presence of 20,000 eunuchs there. Like his father and uncle, Liu Chang enjoyed sensual pleasures and was known for his voyeuristic tendencies. He particularly favored his Persian consort. In 971 CE, the Song dynasty sent an army to conquer the Southern Han. Liu Chang prepared to flee by sea, but his eunuchs and guardians stole all the ships, so he surrendered to the Song forces. He was posthumously named Houzhu, meaning "later sovereign," because he was the last ruler of the kingdom of Southern Han.

▷ This *chiwen* (roof ridge decoration), in the shape of a dragon's head, may have adorned a Southern Han palace.

THE KINGDOM OF JINGNAN

(924–963 CE)

Jingnan was the smallest of the 10 kingdoms created in the south after the fall of the Tang dynasty. Its capital was Jiangling (in modern Hubei province). The kingdom has also been known as Nanping ("southern Ping"), or the Northern Chu. Jingnan was small, but its location in central China made it an important region for trade. It fell to the Song dynasty with little resistance.

King Wuxin

Other names: Gao Jixing, Gao Jichang

r.924–928 CE
b.858 CE d.929 CE

Gao Jixing grew up as the servant of a merchant and later became the adopted son of Emperor Taizu of the Later Liang dynasty. He pledged allegiance to several different rulers during his lifetime owing to the shifting of power during the Five Dynasties and Ten Kingdoms period. At first, Gao Jixing served the Later Liang dynasty, but after Li Cunxu (Emperor Zhuangzong of the Later Tang dynasty) captured the Later Liang capital in 923 CE, Gao Jixing chose to pledge his loyalty to the Later Tang. He founded the kingdom of Jingnan in 924 CE and requested several prefectures from the Later Tang but soon enraged them with further demands. After the Later Tang turned against him, Gao Jixing requested to become a vassal of the kingdom of Wu. He died in 929 CE and was posthumously known as King Wuxin.

King Wenxian

Other name: Gao Conghui

r.928–948 CE
b.928 CE d.948 CE

Gao Conghui was Gao Jixing's son and took the throne as King Wenxian. His father had asked for the protectorship of the kingdom of Wu, but as this was much farther away from Jingnan than the Later Tang territories, Gao Conghui decided to offer his apologies to the Later Tang and become its vassal again. Like his father, Gao Conghui also took advantage of the central location of Jingnan and often detained emissaries from southern kingdoms as they traveled through Jingnan to pay tribute to the northern regimes, seizing their tributes. For this reason, father and son were later referred to as the "Shameless Gaos."

King Zhenyi

Other name: Gao Baorong

r.948–960 CE
b.920 CE d.960 CE

Gao Baorong was the third son of Gao Conghui. He is described by the sources as a man of no particular talent who allowed most matters to be managed by his younger brother, Gao Baoxu. When the Song dynasty was founded in 960 CE, Gao Baorong, out of fear, offered them tribute three times a year.

Xinggong

Other name: Gao Baoxu

r.960–962 CE
b.924 CE d.962 CE

Gao Baoxu was made ruler of Jingnan because Gao Baorong's son was too young to rule. He was said to be quite intelligent as a boy, but after he came to the throne, he became known not for his achievements but for his interest in sensual pleasures. His extravagant construction projects also inspired many criticisms of his rule. Gao Baoxu died in 962 CE and was posthumously known as Xinggong.

Gao Jichong

r.962–963 CE
b.943 CE d.973 CE

After Gao Baoxu died, his nephew Gao Jichong became the ruler. The Song forces passed through Jingnan to suppress a rebellion in its neighboring region and easily took control of Jingnan's capital without meeting much resistance. Gao Jichong then served the Song as a local officer.

THE KINGDOM OF CHU

(927–951 CE)

The 10th-century kingdom of Chu is also referred to as Ma Chu or Southern Chu. In its prime, its territory included modern Hunan province and parts of modern Guangxi, Guizhou, and Guangdong provinces. The kingdom was ended by the Southern Tang.

King Wumu

Other name: Ma Yin

r.927–930 CE
b.852 CE d.930 CE

Ma Yin was a carpenter when he was young and later joined the Tang army to defeat Huang Chao's rebellion in 875–884 CE. After the warlords he served died, Ma Yin became the leader of the forces stationed in Hunan province. When the Later Liang dynasty was founded, Ma Yin was one of the remaining Tang warlords who recognized Zhu Quanzhong (Emperor Taizu of the Later Liang) as emperor. Following the fall of the Later Liang, Ma Yin paid tribute to the Later Tang and declared himself ruler of the Chu kingdom in 927 CE. During his reign, he rarely initiated military campaigns against his rivals, which allowed his kingdom to prosper for some time. He was posthumously remembered as King Wumu.

King Hengyang

Other name: Ma Xisheng

r.930–932 CE
b.898 CE d.932 CE

Following the will of his father, Ma Yin, Ma Xisheng never claimed the title of king during his brief reign, serving the Later Tang as a vassal. Ma Xisheng heard that Emperor Taizu of the Later Liang was fond of chicken, so after he became the ruler of Chu, he had as many as 50 chickens killed for food every day. It was said that he consumed several chickens even during the mourning period for his father—a time when it was considered inappropriate to eat meat. He was posthumously remembered as King Hengyang.

King Wenzhao

Other name: Ma Xifan

r.932–947 CE
b.899 CE d.947 CE

Ma Xifan was the brother of the previous ruler, Ma Xisheng. He was once sent by Ma Yin » (the first Chu ruler) to Luoyang to offer tribute to the Later Tang and impressed the emperor with his intelligence. After the Later Tang fell, Ma Xifan and the Chu kingdom became a vassal of the Later Jin. Ma Xifan was said to be fearful of his wife, Lady Peng, who ran the household. After she died, he indulged in an extravagant lifestyle, which exhausted the kingdom and gave rise to bureaucratic corruption. He was posthumously remembered as King Wenzhao.

Ma Xiguang

r. 947–950 CE
d. 951 CE

The previous ruler Ma Xifan died in 947 CE without naming his heir. Some of his officers decided to support Ma Xiguang, who was Ma Xifan's favorite younger brother, to be his successor. Ma Xi'e (later King Gongxiao), the oldest surviving son of Ma Yin, was another candidate. Ma Xi'e rebelled several times and captured Ma Xiguang in 950 CE. Ma Xiguang was soon put to death, and his descendants became refugees in the Southern Tang.

King Gongxiao
Other name: Ma Xi'e

r. 950–951 CE
b. 900 CE d. 953 CE

Ma Xi'e was a brother of Ma Xiguang. Believing his brother was supported by the Later Han, Ma Xi'e pledged loyalty to the Southern Tang and requested they help him depose Ma Xiguang. After he killed Ma Xiguang and became the ruler of Chu, Ma Xi'e became arrogant and cruel, showing no interest in governing

the kingdom. In 951 CE, Ma Xi'e went to Jinling (modern Nanjing) to pay homage to the Southern Tang and was deposed when his officers mutinied. He died a few years later in Hengshan.

Ma Xichong

r. 951–951 CE
b. 912 CE d. 951 CE

As the previous king Ma Xi'e did not pay attention to state affairs, his officers mutinied in 951 CE and captured him. They declared Ma Xichong, Ma Xi'e's brother, to be the acting military governor and moved Ma Xi'e to Hengshan (modern Hengyang, Hunan). Ma Xichong, however, was no better a ruler than his brother. Faced with the threat of Southern Tang forces, Ma Xichong surrendered, thereby ending the rule of Chu. The Ma family were all moved to the Southern Tang territory and then to the Later Zhou after the fall of the Southern Tang.

THE LATER SHU KINGDOM
(934–965 CE)

The capital of the Later Shu was in modern Chengdu. The kingdom is also known as Meng Shu to distinguish it from the Former Shu kingdom ruled by the Wang family.

Gaozu
Other name: Meng Zhixiang

r. 934–934 CE
b. 874 CE d. 934 CE

Meng Zhixiang had married into the Later Tang ruling family and served them as a general. After the Later Tang conquered

the Former Shu kingdom in 925 CE, Meng Zhixiang was appointed as the military governor of the Xichuan Circuit, which had its headquarters in modern Chengdu. He joined forces with the neighboring Dongchuan Circuit and continued to seek independence for the Shu kingdom, successfully repelling attempts by the Later Tang emperor Minzong to control him in the following years. In 934 CE, Meng Zhixiang declared himself emperor of Shu, but he reigned for only seven months before dying from an illness. He was posthumously named Emperor Gaozu.

Houzhu
Other name: Meng Chang

r. 934–965 CE
b. 919 CE d. 965 CE

Meng Chang was the third son of Meng Zhixiang, the first ruler of the Later Shu kingdom. During his early reign, he secured his power by removing the established generals. Meng Chang ruled for three decades, during which the Later Shu kingdom prospered and became a hub for arts and literature. The kingdom's territory was also expanded to include parts of northern China.

However, Meng Chang's later reign was less successful. After the forces of the Song dynasty destroyed the Later Shu army, Meng Chang begged the Song to allow him to surrender. The Song allowed this, and the Later Shu kingdom came to an end. After the fall of the Later Shu, Meng Chang was moved to the Song capital of Kaifeng as a prisoner. Within seven days, he was put to death. Meng Chang was posthumously titled Houzhu, meaning "last emperor."

THE SOUTHERN TANG KINGDOM
(937–975 CE)

The capital of the Southern Tang kingdom was Jinling (modern Nanjing). The Southern Tang allied with the Khitans in the north in order to balance out the power of the regimes of the central plain.

Liezu
Other names: Li Bian, Xu Gao, Xu Zhigao

r. 937–943 CE
b. 889 CE d. 943 CE

Li Bian's origins are unclear. Somehow, he became the adopted son of the Wu regent Xu Wen. After Xu Wen died, Li Bian took control of the Wu court. In 937 CE, he forced the Wu emperor, Yang Pu, to yield the throne to himself and he founded the Southern Tang in Jinling. He changed his family name to Li to appear associated with the ruling family of the Tang dynasty. Li Bian was said to be a diligent and capable ruler who revised Tang laws extensively. As a Daoist, he tried to achieve immortality and took alchemists' medicines for years, which reportedly led to illness at the end of his life.

Yuanzong
Other names: Li Jing, Zhongzhu

r. 943–961 CE
b. 916 CE d. 961 CE

Li Jing was the eldest son of Li Bian and came to the throne when his father died. Unlike his father, who had sought to maintain peace in his country, Li Jing put considerable efforts into territorial expansion. During his reign, the Southern Tang territory grew to its largest extent. Li Jing was not a particularly capable ruler and entrusted state affairs to five notoriously corrupt officers. However, he was considered a skilled poet and calligrapher, and during his reign, the Southern Tang territory became a center for talented literary people. His expansive policies exhausted the wealth of the Southern Tang, which was unable to withstand the invasion of Later Zhou forces in 957 CE. He gave up his title as emperor and served the Later Zhou as a vassal. After his death, Li Jing was given the title of Emperor Yuanzong.

Houzhu

Other name: Li Yu

r.961–975 CE
b.937 CE d.978 CE

Li Yu came to the throne a year after the Later Zhou dynasty fell to the Song dynasty. In order to show that he had no intention of contesting Song authority, he pledged his loyalty and paid tribute to the Song. However, Li Yu refused the summons of Emperor Taizu of Song several times, claiming that he was too ill to attend. In 974 CE, the Song forces laid siege to the Southern Tang capital. Li Yu surrendered in 975 CE and was kept captive in the Song capital of Kaifeng until he was poisoned and died in 978 CE. Despite the political failures of his reign, Li Yu is considered one of the most accomplished poets in Chinese history, having devoted much of his time and resources to literature and entertainment. He was posthumously titled Houzhu, or "last sovereign."

THE NORTHERN HAN KINGDOM
(951–979 CE)

The Northern Han was a small kingdom located in what is now Shanxi province. It was located between the two major regimes (the Liao and Later Zhou dynasties) and also neighbored the Tangut Xia dynasty. The Northern Han capital was Taiyuan.

Shizu

Other names: Liu Min, Liu Chong

r.951–954 CE
b.895 CE d.954 CE

When Guo Wei (Emperor Taizu of Later Zhou) took control of the Later Han capital, Kaifeng, Liu Chong, a Han military leader, heard that Guo Wei would install Liu Chong's son, Liu Yun, as the emperor. Guo Wei instead declared himself emperor and had Liu Yun killed. Following this, Liu Chong also declared himself emperor and successor of the Later Han in Taiyuan. His reign aimed to consolidate the remaining Later Han forces while seeking help from their powerful Khitan neighbors. Liu Chong, who changed his name to Liu Min, addressed the Liao emperor as his uncle and called himself the "emperor's nephew." Most of his campaigns against the Later Zhou ended in failure and he died in 954 CE.

Ruizong

Other names: Liu Chengjun, Liu Jun

r.954–968 CE
b.926 CE d.968 CE

Liu Chengjun took the throne when his father died, and his reign was the longest of the Northern Han. He was known as a kind ruler and reduced the frequency of the southern military campaigns. Following on from his father's subordination to the Liao, he also referred to himself as a "son" when submitting documents to them. However, he appeared to become less humble and respectful than his father, and thus received less support from the Liao, in his later reign. Liu Chengjun was given the posthumous name Emperor Ruizong.

Shaozhu

Other name: Liu Ji'en

r.968–968 CE
d.968 CE

Liu Ji'en was a nephew and an adoptive son of his predecessor, Liu Chengjun. He ruled the Northern Han kingdom for only two months before he was assassinated after a banquet. He was posthumously called Shaozhu, meaning "the young sovereign."

Yingwudi

Other name: Liu Jiyuan

r.968–979 CE
d.992 CE

Just like his predecessor, Liu Jiyuan was a nephew and an adoptive son of Liu Chengjun (Ruizong). He attempted to restore good relations between the Northern Han kingdom and the Liao dynasty. However, in 979 CE, the Song forces invaded the Northern Han and fought back the Northern Han–Liao allied forces. Liu Jiyuan surrendered to the Song, thereby dissolving the Northern Han kingdom. He was remembered after his death as Yingwudi.

△ One of the most famous scroll paintings of the Five Dynasties and Ten Kingdoms period, *The Night Revels of Han Xizai* by Gu Hongzhong, reflected the literary and artistic mores of the reigns of Yuanzong and Houzhu.

The Northern Song Dynasty (960–1127)

The Song, or Northern Song, emerged from the chaos of the Five Dynasties and Ten Kingdoms period to unite China. This was a period when Confucianism resurged and great works of poetry were produced. Economic and administrative reforms promised to revitalize and sustain the empire. However, the Song could not defend themselves against the foreign invaders and perished.

 Empress Liu, wife of Zhenzong, handled governance for two years.

Taizu
Other name: Zhao Kuangyin

r.960–976CE
b.927CE d.976CE

Zhao Kuangyin was the son of a military commander of the Later Zhou dynasty in northern China. He, too, rose to power as a military commander. Zhao Kuangyin's army deposed the infant emperor without bloodshed and declared the founding of the Song dynasty. He was called Emperor Taizu. To avoid military coups, he dismissed his generals from armed service and bestowed titles and rewards upon them. During his reign, Taizu worked to reunify China, conquering most of the south and then the north. He strengthened the power of central government by relying on capable civilian officials in his administration, and he promoted economic reforms that facilitated growth.

Taizong
Other name: Zhao Guangyi

r.976–997CE
b.939CE d.997CE

Taizu's younger brother, Zhao Guangyi, succeeded him as Emperor Taizong. In the first years of his reign, he was able to complete the reunification started by his brother, annexing the southern empire of Wu Yue and regaining territory from the Northern Han. However, military campaigns against the Khitan Liao in the north and the Tanguts in the west were unsuccessful. In domestic policy, Taizong continued Taizu's centralizing policy, favoring civil officials while marginalizing eunuchs and imperial consort families. He expanded the imperial examination system and promoted effective agricultural reforms. An enthusiastic patron of the arts and a scholar himself, Taizong encouraged the publication of classical texts and encyclopedias.

Zhenzong
Other names: Zhao Heng, Zhao Dechang, Zhao Yuanxiu, Zhao Yuankan

r.997–1022
b.968 d.1022

Taizong's third son, Zhao Heng, succeeded him as Emperor Zhenzong. During Zhenzong's reign, the relationship with the neighboring northern empires became a problem. Zhenzong agreed to a treaty with the Liao, in which the Song acknowledged their equal status with the Liao and committed to paying them an annual tribute. In return, the Liao acknowledged Song lands that had been gained from the Liao under previous dynasties. Zhenzong and the Liao emperor, Shenzong, declared themselves brothers. The treaty brought a period of peaceful coexistence, which promoted trade. Stricken by illness in the final two years of his life, Zhenzong relied on his wife, Empress Liu, to handle governance.

Renzong
Other name: Zhao Zhen

r.1023–1063
b.1010 d.1063

Zhao Zhen was the fourth son of Zhenzong. He was remembered as Emperor Renzong. His mother, Empress Dowager Liu, acted as regent for the emperor until her death in 1033. During Renzong's reign, which was the longest of any Song ruler, the Tangut Xia

△ This painting and poem, "Auspicious Cranes," was made by Emperor Huizong of Song.

dynasty raided the Song in 1038. In 1044, the Tanguts recognized Song superiority in a peace treaty, on the condition that the Song paid them tribute. Peace was assured, but Renzong's efforts to strengthen the military strained the state's finances. In response, his ministers proposed interventions to reinvigorate the government and alleviate financial burdens. Intellectual activity thrived in Renzong's reign with a rediscovery of the Confucian classics and with a new focus on scientific inquiry.

Yingzong
Other name: Zhao Shu

r. 1064–1067
b. 1032 d. 1067

Since Renzong's three sons had died before him, he named Zhao Shu his heir, who was the son of his cousin. Zhao Shu duly became Emperor Yingzong when Renzong died. However, Yingzong became too ill to govern, and Empress Dowager Cao, Renzong's widow, served as regent for a year. Yingzong's preference for his birth parents caused problems, and divisions in the civil service also plagued his short reign.

Shenzong
Other name: Zhao Xu

r. 1068–1085
b. 1048 d. 1085

Zhao Xu, Yingzong's eldest son, took the throne as Shenzong. The scrupulous young emperor favored the official Wang Anshi and his reforms, employing him to alleviate poverty and improve the economy. Failed military campaigns against the Xia had weakened the Song. Despite opposition from high officials, rich merchants and landowners, Wang Anshi's measures bore fruit, financially and militarily. His reforms stayed in place for the remainder of Shenzong's reign. Scholarship and literature continued to flourish, and important historical and military treatises were composed and compiled.

Zhezong
Other names: Zhao Yong, Zhao Xu

r. 1086–1100
b. 1077 d. 1100

When Shenzong died from an illness, his sixth son, Zhao Yong, was named crown prince and took the throne at the age of ten. He is known as Emperor Zhezong. His grandmother, Empress Dowager Gao, acted as regent. She appointed conservatives who halted Wang Anshi's reform policies. The divide between reformists and conservatives became deeper. After Dowager Gao's death in 1093, Zhezong employed reformists and reinstated Wang Anshi's measures. Zhezong's modest military victories against the Xia led to momentary peace. He died following an illness in 1100.

Huizong
Other name: Zhao Ji

r. 1101–1125
b. 1082 d. 1135

Zhao Ji was the younger brother of the previous emperor, Zhezong. Zhezhong's son died prematurely, so Zhao Ji ascended the throne. He was posthumously given the name Huizong. He relied on the reformists after the death of his conservative regent, Empress Dowager Xiang, in 1101. But the financial situation by this time had become too severe to be saved by reforms. Huizong was uninterested in public affairs and focused on his passions: painting, calligraphy, music, and poetry. Meanwhile, the empire was collapsing. In an attempt to get territory from the Liao, Huizong allied with the Jurchen-led Jin dynasty in 1120. The Song and the Jin defeated the Liao, but the Jin, sensing the weakness of the Song, declared war on Huizong. He abdicated in favor of his son, Zhao Huan, and fled south.

Qinzong
Other name: Zhao Huan

r. 1126–1127
b. 1100 d. 1161

Zhao Huan was the eldest son of Huizong and Empress Wang. He reluctantly became Emperor Qinzong when his father fled from the Jin. Left behind in the capital, Qinzong organized a resistance. The Jin army lifted their siege, but demanded a huge war indemnity, annual tribute, hostages, and the recognition of their superior status. When the siege was over, Huizong returned. However, after a few months, the Jin attacked the capital again and Qinzong surrendered. The Jin deported Qinzong and his father to the Jin capital, where they were downgraded to commoners.

The Southern Song Dynasty (1127–1279)

The remnants of the Song, ousted by the Jurchen Jin, found safe harbor in South China. They flourished there until they, too, were finished by the Mongol conquest.

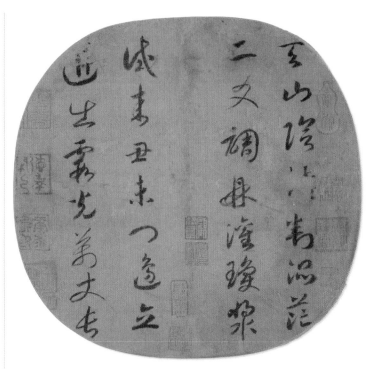

△ Emperor Gaozong wrote this poem, "Quatrain on Heavenly Mountain."

Gaozong
Other name: Zhao Gou

r.1127–1162
b.1107 d.1187

Zhao Gou, posthumously titled Emperor Gaozong, was the ninth son of the Northern Song emperor Huizong and Empress Wei. When the Song capital fell to Jin forces, he managed to escape south with the remnants of the court and declare himself emperor. Pursued by Jin troops and lacking a proper army, Gaozong had to move his capital several times before settling permanently in Hangzhou in 1132. The hostilities ceased with the signing of a treaty in 1141, which established the Song as vassals of the Jin and mandated the payment of tribute. The rift in government between a pro-war faction and a rival appeasement faction did not prevent Gaozong from forming a solid administrative system and a flourishing economy that supported a cultural and intellectual resurgence. After a military victory against the Jin in 1161, the Song were no longer the Jin's vassal state. Gaozong then abdicated in favor of his adopted son, Zhao Shen, a direct descendant of the Northern Song emperor Taizu.

Xiaozong
Other name: Zhao Shen

r.1162–1189
b.1127 d.1194

Zhao Shen, the adopted son of the previous ruler, Emperor Gaozong, took the throne in 1162, although Gaozong retained some power. Zhao Shen was later named Emperor Xiaozong. During his reign, Song forces faced another clash with the Jin, and the peace agreement reached in 1165 allowed the Southern Song to prosper. Since the Song had limited access to land-based trade routes, Xiaozong turned to maritime commerce, where he established a thriving trade network. The trading volume granted an economic upsurge that in turn fostered steady population growth.

Guangzong
Other name: Zhao Dun

r.1190–1194
b.1147 d.1200

The previous ruler, Xiaozong, progressively distanced himself from the affairs of state after the death of his father Gaozong, in 1187. Xiaozong finally abdicated in favor of his third son, Zhao Dun, who took the throne in 1190 and was called Emperor Guangzong. Guangzong's relationship with Xiaozong became strained due to the actions of his wife, Empress Li, who manipulated Guangzong and ruled through him. As Xiaozong lay dying, Empress Li even convinced Guangzong not to visit him. After Xiaozong's death, Guangzong refused to attend the funeral. Empress Dowager Wu, Gaozong's widow, then forced Guangzong to abdicate because of his lack of filial piety.

Ningzong
Other name: Zhao Kuo

r.1195–1224
b.1168 d.1224

Emperor Ningzong, whose personal name was Zhao Kuo, was the only surviving child of Guangzong. The powerful Empress Dowager Wu ensured he became emperor. Han Tuozhou, the husband of Empress Dowager Wu's niece and great-uncle of Ningzong's first empress, controlled the court. He led the Song into a disastrous war against the Jin in 1206, failing to recover the territories lost in the north. Han Tuozhou was executed for his failure in 1207, and the subsequent peace treaty meant that the Song had to resume tribute payments to the Jin. Ningzong's second wife, Empress Yang, gave control to her brother and to the official Shi Miyuan. During this time, the economy struggled with growing inflation, and expansion by the Mongols in the north started to push the Jin south, closer to the Song.

Lizong
Other name: Zhao Yun

r.1225–1264
b.1205 d.1264

None of Ningzong's sons survived infancy. Therefore, Ningzong had chosen one of

(Northern Song emperor) Taizu's descendants, Zhao Hong, to be his successor. However, the powerful official Shi Miyuan disagreed with Ninzong's choice and, when Ningzong died, he replaced Zhao Hong with Zhao Yun, who ruled as Emperor Lizong. Uninterested in official matters, Lizong delegated his duties to Shi Miyuan. The emperor preferred to pursue artistic interests and sensual pleasures, leaving governance to his ministers. The economy became more stable than before but could not sustain a war against the encroaching Jin. Therefore, the government decided to form an alliance with the Mongols against the Jin in 1233. The Mongols destroyed the Jin in 1234 then turned their attention toward the Song, to the dismay of their allies.

Duzong

Other name: Zhao Qi

r.1265–1274
b.1240 d.1274

Left with no surviving sons, Lizong chose his nephew, Zhao Qi, as his successor. Zhao Qi was named Emperor Duzong. He was politically inept and, like his uncle, left affairs to his ministers. After years of military offensives against the Song, the Mongols, led by Kublai Khan, were on the verge of conquering the south. During Duzong's reign, the government tried to resist the invasion but lost the key strategic city of Xiangyang in 1274. Following this victory, the Mongols had free rein to pillage southern China and control its rulers. Duzong, who died suddenly after the fall of Xiangyang, was the last Song emperor to rule autonomously.

Gongdi

Other name: Zhao Xian

r.1275–1276
b.1271 d.1323

After Duzong's death, his son, Zhao Xian was enthroned at the age of four. His mother, Empress Dowager Quan, and his grandmother, Empress Dowager Xie, acted as regents, while the chancellor Jia Sidao maintained administrative and military powers. The chancellor mustered an army in the hope of stopping the Mongol advance but suffered a crushing defeat. The Mongols entered the capital of Hangzhou in 1276, dethroned Zhao Xian, and took him prisoner. Kublai Khan received him in the Mongol capital and made him a duke before relocating him to Tibet. Zhao Xian died by suicide in 1323. He received the posthumous title of Emperor Gong.

Duanzong

Other name: Zhao Shi

r.1276–1278
b.1269 d.1278

When the Mongols conquered Hangzhou, the remnants of the Song court fled to Fujian, escorting the previous ruler Gongdi's two half brothers to safety. The fugitives declared one of them, the eight-year-old Zhao Shi to be Emperor Duanzong. Pursued by the Mongols, the emperor and his ministers moved further south to Guangdong, where he was forced to go to sea in an attempt to escape. Duanzong's ship capsized after a storm. Although he survived this event, he died of an illness a few months later at the age of nine.

Di Bing

Other name: Zhao Bing

r.1278–1279
b.1272 d.1279

After young Duanzong's death, the disheartened fugitives of the Song court established Zhao Bing as Bing, Emperor of Song. The Mongols chased the fugitives to Yamen and then pushed them into the sea. A naval battle ensued, and the Mongol navy blockaded the bay. The remnants of the Song put up some resistance but were eventually defeated. Zhao Bing perished in the battle, thereby ending the Song dynasty.

△ This portrait depicts Emperor Lizong of Song.

The Eastern Liao Dynasty (916–1125)

The Khitan were a steppe people that came from Manchuria and established the Liao, or Eastern Liao, dynasty. Abaoji, its founder, built a powerful empire that merged the steppe military with Chinese administration and agricultural practices. The Liao then endured for more than two centuries. They gradually conquered northern China and demanded deference from the Tangut Xia but suffered from rebellions by their non-Chinese vassals until they themselves were conquered by the Jurchen Jin.

Taizu

Other names: Abaoji, Yelü Yi

r. 916–926 CE
b. 872 CE d. 926 CE

Abaoji, posthumously named Emperor Taizu of Liao, seized power for his own Yila tribe of the Khitan, displacing the Yaonian clan. Abaoji became chief of the Yila in 901 CE. A few years later, he became the commander of the Khitan army and invaded China to make a brotherhood alliance with the warlord Zhu Wen, who brought about the fall of the Tang dynasty. However, Abaoji also tried to form an alliance with Zhu Wen's enemy, Li Keyong. In 907 CE, Abaoji was elected great khan of the Khitan because of his ability to lead successful raids. The great khan was previously reelected every three years, but Abaoji ended this practice and put down several rebellions by his brothers. In 916 CE, he was formally enthroned as an emperor and established a Chinese administration, making him an equal of the rulers of the Chinese states to the south. In 918 CE, he established a capital city called Huangdu, which became Shangjing (in modern-day Inner Mongolia), where he built Confucian, Daoist, and Buddhist temples.

In the early 920s, Abaoji expanded his empire in Mongolia and in the northeast of China. The first Khitan writing script was also mandated for use. In 926 CE, Abaoji conquered the great Bohai (Balhae) state in northern Korea, making the Bohai royal family part of the Liao nobility. Abaoji hoped to go on to conquer parts of North China but died of typhoid fever in 926 CE before he could do so.

△ This silver crown belonged to an Eastern Liao emperor.

Taizong

Other names: Yaogu, Yelü Deguang

r. 927–947 CE
b. 902 CE d. 947 CE

Yelü Deguang, posthumously named Emperor Taizong, succeeded his father, Abaoji. His mother was Empress Yingtian, who briefly led the Liao armies, and she put Yelü Deguang on the throne instead of the designated successor, Prince Bei. During his reign, Yelü Deguang continued conquering new territories in the steppe and won victories against the Tanguts. Prince Bei fled to China and was murdered by a rebel leader, Shi Jingtang, during the Later Tang dynasty, in 937 CE.

Taizong gave a great deal of military support to Shi Jingtang so that he could take control of North China and establish himself as the emperor of the Later Jin dynasty, but in exchange Shi Jingtang had to acknowledge that he was inferior to the Liao and hand over control of 16 northern prefectures. Several fragmented kingdoms in northern China then had to acknowledge the Liao as their superiors. In 943 CE, Shi Jingtang's son, Shi Chonggui, ceased to acknowledged Liao superiority and revoked trading rights of Khitan merchants, forcing Yelü Deguang to invade China. In 947 CE, after many years of mixed victories and retreats, he finally conquered the Later Jin capital at Kaifeng, and the royal family was captured and sent to Shangjing. However, he had to withdraw to maintain control of his empire. He died from an illness a few months later, on the way home.

Shizong

Other names: Yelü Ruan, Wuyu

r. 947–951 CE
b. 919 CE d. 951 CE

Yelü Ruan was the son of the Prince of Bei, the designated successor of Taizong. Yelü Ruan was much loved by Taizong and was known as a famous archer and warrior. He was later given the name Emperor Shizong. He overcame Empress Yingtian in the struggle for power and then had to fight off coups and execute his rivals. For administrative purposes, Shizong divided his empire into a northern and southern region. The southern region had a Chinese-style

△ A group of musicians and a woman are pictured dancing in this Liao dynasty tomb mural. The murals in the tombs of Liao nobility often featured scenes from their daily lives.

government. In 951 CE, Shizong and his mother prepared to lead an army to attack the Later Zhou dynasty. One night, when Shizong was drunk, he was murdered by one of his distant cousins and died without naming an heir.

Muzong

Other names: Yelü Jing, Shulü

r. 951–969 CE
b. 931 CE d. 969 CE

Yelü Jing was Taizong's eldest son and was named Emperor Muzong. He was often drunk and slept during the day, earning him the name of the "sleeping emperor." He had to put down several coups by relatives and Khitan nobles before 960 CE. He was fond of hunting and given to making outrageous demands when drunk. In 959 CE, the Zhou started attacking the 16 northern prefectures, taking two of them. Muzong had to retreat, but the Zhou ruler died, and Muzong was able to regroup. In 964 CE, Muzong sent the Liao army to successfully aid the Northern Han dynasty against the expanding Song dynasty. Muzong was a violent drunk who murdered some of his retinue, and in the end a group of his servants assassinated him.

Jingzong

Other name: Yelü Xian

r. 969–982 CE
b. 948 CE d. 982 CE

Yelü Xian, posthumously named Emperor Jingzong, was Shizong's second son. In 976 and 977 CE, Jingzong sent aid to the Northern Han to fight off the Song. In 979 CE, he sent a support army again, but the Song attacked and defeated it. The Song then took the Northern Han lands. The Song invaded the Liao and set out to attack their southern capital (Beijing). Jingzong's armies repulsed and devastated the Song armies and he then led an army to take back parts of North China. Jingzong's armies also fought the Tanguts, who were raiding the Liao, while the Jurchen were also harassing the Liao in the northeast. In 981 CE, Jingzong put down a major coup, but died during a hunting trip the following year. »

◁ This gold reliquary shows the splendor of Buddhist art under the patronage of the Eastern Liao emperors.

Shengzong
Other names: Yelü Longxu, Wushunu

r.982–1031
b.971 d.1031

Emperor Shengzong, who was born Yelü Longxu, was the son of Jingzong. He was just a child when his father died. His mother, Empress Dowager Chengtian of the Xiao clan, acted as regent and de facto ruler of the empire for decades during Shengzong's reign. Her competent ministers reformed taxes, the legal system, infrastructure, and agriculture. They also restarted the *jinshi* imperial examination system in 988 CE. State Buddhism also flourished under their patronage.

Other male members of the Yelü clan meanwhile controlled the military and fought against the Koreans (Goguryeo).

In the early 11th century, Shengzong commanded armies against the Song and invaded their territory. In 1005, the Treaty of Chanyuan was signed by Shengzong. The Song agreed to make payments to the Liao and respect the newly established border. Shengzong was also ceremonially named the Song emperor's "younger brother." War with the Koreans continued in the late 1010s, and the Khitan army suffered a massive defeat in 1018. The Liao resumed pressure on the Koreans until they agreed to pay tribute again. In 1029, a rebellion in Bohai further weakened the Liao.

Xingzong
Other names: Yelü Zongzhen, Zhigu, Yibujin

r.1031–1055
b.1016 d.1055

Shengzong designated his son Zongzhen, posthumously named Emperor Xingzong, as his heir. His mother was a consort named Noujin, of the Xiao clan, but he was raised by the Liao Empress. Noujin had the empress killed and established herself as regent. Noujin became the de facto ruler and promoted her supporters to official positions. She also plotted against Xingzong in order to make her other son emperor. Noujin was banished, but she and her clan remained powerful.

Xingzong had to manage complex relations with the Tanguts and the Song. In 1043, the Tanguts requested the Liao join them in attacking the Song, but Xingzong refused. The Liao later attacked the Tanguts in 1044 but were defeated. Xingzong's campaign of 1050 was also not wholly successful and peace was only established in 1053. He died from an illness in 1055.

Daozong
Other names: Yelü Hongji, Chala, Nielin

r.1055–1101
b.1032 d.1101

Emperor Daozong, whose personal name was Yelü Hongji, was Xingzong's eldest son. Daozong spent his early years limiting the power of the Xiao clan, who had become powerful at court in the previous reign, and executing some ministers. He struggled to manage court rivalries. Sources suggest he may also have ordered that all courtiers, even Khitan, had to wear Chinese clothing. Daozong's uncle, Zhongyuan, led rebels to attack Daozong on a hunting trip. Their attack failed, and Daozong sent soldiers to kill Zhongyuan. Many suspected conspirators were also executed. An official named Yelü Yixin assumed control of the court and eliminated both Daozong's crown prince and his birth mother, Empress Xiao Guanyin. In 1070, Daozong ordered Yixin to standardize the laws according to Chinese law, but this failed and the old Khitan laws resumed many years later. Yixin was exiled in 1080 and Daozong focused on advanced study of Buddhism.

Tianzuo
Other names: Yelü Yanxi, Aguo

r.1101–1125
b.1075

Yelü Yanxi, honorarily named Emperor Tianzuo, was Daozong's grandson. He ordered the graves of Yixin and his supporters to be dug up and defiled. When the Jurchen rose up under Aguda, he sent an army to punish them. The Jurchen defeated this army, and Tianzuo was forced to request peace. Tianzuo set out to attack Aguda again in 1115 but also had to fight off a coup attempt by his uncle, Prince Chun. Aguda spent many years attacking the Liao. In the chaos of 1122, Prince Chun was established as emperor at Nandu, but he died just a few months later. Tianzuo fled to the Xia and offered to recognize their Tangut ruler's emperorship, but the offer was declined. The Jin captured Tianzuo in 1125, ending his reign. It is not known precisely when he died.

The Western Liao Dynasty (1131–1218)

The Western Liao, or Kara Khitai (Black Khitan), began as a group of the Khitan army led by Yelü Dashi to the west. The Western Liao established a dynasty that was powerful in Central Asia. However, they were brought down by a Mongol prince, Güchülug, who seized the throne.

Dezong

Other names: Yelü Dashi, Emperor Tianyou

r.1131–1143
b.1094 d.1143

Yelü Dashi was the founder of the Western Liao dynasty and was posthumously named Emperor Dezong. He was an eighth-generation descendant of Abaoji, the Liao founder. He was a good horseman and archer who could read both Khitan and Chinese, and in 1115, he received his *jinshi* degree in the Liao empire. In 1124, as the Liao crumbled under the Jin invasion, Yelü Dashi took command of a Khitan army at Kedun in Mongolia and proclaimed himself king. In 1130, he led them westward to conquer the Uighurs in northwest China and then expanded his domain into Central Asia.

In 1131, Dashi was enthroned as the gürkhan (universal khan of the Khitan), and also as the Chinese Emperor Tianyou. In 1134, he conquered and took the city of Balasagun (modern-day Kyrgyzstan) from the Karakhanids, which then became the capital of the Western Liao empire. Dashi attacked the Jin a few times but did not have great success, so he led more campaigns into Fergana against the Karakhanids. In 1141, at the battle of Qatwan (Samarkand), Dashi's armies defeated Sultan Sanjar of the powerful Seljuks who ruled much of Central Asia, Iran, the Middle East, and Anatolia. This allowed the Western Liao, or Kara Khitai, to temporarily become the most powerful state in Central Asia.

Empress Gantian

Other names: Xiao Tabuyan, Empress Zhaode, Kuyang, Orghina

r.1144–1150

When Dezong died, his empress, Tabuyan of the Xiao clan, took the throne as regent. She was posthumously named Empress Gantian. She was also a cousin of her late husband. When Dezong died, the Uighurs sent tribute to the Jin, and her empire was under threat. In 1146, the empress was hunting when she received a Jin envoy who threatened the Western Liao and ordered that she dismount from her horse. The empress forced the Jin envoy himself to dismount and kneel, before executing him. The Western Liao would not recognize Jin authority. Empress Gantian abdicated in 1150 and died many years later.

Renzong

Other name: Yelü Yilie

r.1151–1163
b.1134 d.1163

Yelü Yilie was a son of Dezong and Empress Gantian. Very little is known about his reign. In 1151, he took over from his mother and was posthumously titled Emperor Renzong. Renzong ordered a census of his empire. In 1156, there was a mild conflict with the Jin, and no peace was reached. He died in 1163.

Empress Chengtian

Other name: Yelü Pusuwan

r.1164–1177

Renzong's sons were too young to succeed him when he died, so his sister, Yelü Pusuwan, came to the throne as regent. She was posthumously named Empress Chengtian. Her father-in-law was one of the previous ruler Emperor Dezong's great generals, Wolila of the Xiao clan. Her reign was marked by much fighting and conquest against the lands of Khwarezmian empire in Central Asia. Her husband, Xiao Duolubu, led her armies. In 1177, Empress Chengtian sent spies to the Jin, but they were captured, making the Jin anxious about the Western Liao once again. Empress Chengtian had a romance with Xiao Duolubu's younger brother, Xiao Fuguzhi, which caused General Wolila to stage a coup and kill both the empress and his own son.

Mozhu

Other names: Yelü Zhilugu, Emperor Taishang

r.1178–1211
d.1213

Yelü Zhilugu was one of Renzong's sons and was the last member of the Yelü clan to rule the Western Liao dynasty. He was therefore posthumously recorded as Mozhu, the "last sovereign." General Wolila put Zhilugu on the throne after Wolila took control of the capital and murdered Zhilugu's brother. In Zhilugu's early reign, Kara Khitai armies were still fighting in Khwarezmian lands. In 1185, Zhilugu tried to secure an alliance with the Xia dynasty and prepared to attack the Jin, but nothing came of this.

As the Mongol leader Ghengis Khan grew increasingly more powerful, his ally the Ong Khan fled to Zhilugu and was well received. However, the Ong Khan later rebelled and fled. Zhilugu's reign then saw many similar rebellions and wars in Central Asia as the Mongols conquered more territories. In 1208, Zhilugu received Güchülug, a Naiman Mongol prince whose father was killed by Ghengis Khan. When the Uighurs joined forces with Ghengis, Zhilugu agreed to send Güchülug to gather an army, but Güchülug instead spent many years raiding and pillaging with impunity.

Güchülug then allied with the Khwarezmians and attacked the Kara Khitai directly. Later in 1211, while Zhilugu was hunting, Güchülug set upon him with an army and captured him. Zhilugu died in 1213. Güchülug then controlled the Kara Khitai empire himself as the last "emperor of Liao" until 1218.

The Xi Xia Dynasty

(1038–1227)

The Xia dynasty of the 11th to 13th centuries is called the Western Xia, or Xi Xia. The Xia were ruled by the Tangut people, who had a mix of Tibetan, Qiang, Turkic, and Chinese ethnic origins and culture. They had been granted governorship of the region of Xia, in western China, for supporting the Tang in the 9th century. They gradually asserted their own power until Li Yuanhao, of the Weiming clan, established the new Xia dynasty.

△ The Xia rulers patronized state Buddhism, which led the religion to flourish. This Buddhist mural in the Yulin caves dates from the Xia dynasty.

Jingzong

Other names: Li Yuanhao, Zhao Yuanhao, Weiming Yuanhao, Tuoba Yuanhao

r.1032–1048
b.1003 d.1048

Li Yuanhao, who became Emperor Jingzong, founded the Xia as an independent dynasty in western China. Li Jiqian, his grandfather, was a vassal ruler of the Tangut Weiming clan who led an ethnic revolt against the Song. Li Deming, Yuanhao's father, maneuvered relations with both the Liao and the Song to gain concessions and also flexibility to expand his territory westward into the Uighur-controlled oases.

Li Yuanhao was both a learned scholar and a skilled warrior who had led his father's armies. He declared himself emperor in 1038 and established his capital at Xingqing (Yinchuan), where he ordered the construction of an imitation of the Wutai Buddhist temple. He sought to increase his legitimacy by claiming descent from the Tuoba rulers of the Northern Wei and mandated the use of a newly invented character-based script for the Tangut language. When Yuanhao refused to pay tribute to the Song, war broke out. The Xia suffered huge losses, and Yuanhao was forced to declare himself subject to the Song. When Yuanhao wanted to take his son Ninglingge's wife as an empress, Ninglingge and the minister Mocang Epang plotted to kill him. They managed only to cut off the emperor's nose, but he died from the resulting infection.

Yizong

Other name: Li Liangzuo

r.1048–1068
b.1047 d.1068

Li Liangzuo was only months old when he became Emperor Yizong. Shortly after, the Khitan Liao dynasty invaded the Xia. Normal relations resumed only after the Liao had suffered huge losses. Yizong's mother, the empress dowager, ordered the construction of a new Buddhist temple called Chengtian in Xingsqing. In his youth, Yizong attended sermons there with his mother.

Meanwhile, Mocang Epang, who was Yizong's uncle, expanded and settled new territories in Song lands. He was suspected of arranging the murder of the empress dowager in 1056. After this, Mocang Epang took full control of the Xia, married his own daughter to Yizong, and attacked the Song border in 1057. At 14 years old, Yizong had a romantic affair with Lady Liang, the wife of Mocang Epang's son, and she inspired him to organize a coup against his uncle. Yizong then married Lady Liang.

The Liang clan now had great influence at court. Yizong made several demands of the Song to get status concessions for the Xia and also reformed court dress and rites to follow Chinese style. In 1067, a Song border commander seized the Xia town of Suizhou. Yizong retaliated, and is believed to have died from battle wounds.

Huizong

Other name: Li Bingchang

r.1068–1086
b.1060 d.1086

Yizong's seven-year-old son with Lady Liang, Li Bingchang, became Emperor Huizong in 1068. In 1069, on her son's behalf, Lady Liang authorized resuming Tangut rites and customs. Huizong was supposed to have full political control by the late 1070s, but he was thwarted by the empress dowager. By 1080, Huizong attempted to bring back Chinese rites and clothing, but the next year rumors spread that he intended to sell out territory in the Ordos. Meanwhile, Liang Yimai, Huizong's father-in-law, staged a coup to imprison the emperor. The Song took this as an excuse to invade. They agreed to peace in 1083, and Huizong was allowed to rule in a restricted way until his death.

Chongzong
Other name: Li Qianshun

r. 1086–1139
b. 1084 d. 1139

Chongzong became the ruler at three years old with his mother as regent. She was in conflict with her brother, Liang Qibu, who had become aligned with a Tibetan faction. In 1094, a Weiming and Renduo clan loyalist coup led to Liang Qibu's murder, and the Liang clan was wiped out. Thereafter, the Song and the Tibetans continually tried to wrest parts of Qinghai and Qingtang (Xining) from the Xia, and Chongzong assumed corulership with elder members of the Weiming clan. External threats then quietened down, and large Buddhist scripture translation projects continued. Chongzong married a Khitan princess in 1105 and supported the doomed Liao against their Jin invaders.

Renzong
Other name: Li Renxiao

r. 1139–1193
b. 1124 d. 1193

Li Renxiao, who became Emperor Renzong, was one of the longest reigning emperors in Chinese history; he ruled for 54 years. He came to the throne as a teenager, and he delegated military matters and the suppression of banditry to his generals, especially to the Chinese general Ren Dejing. In the 1140s, Renzong initiated government reform measures that established Confucian civil service examinations.

Ren Dejing was made a prince in the 1160s and proceeded to annex much of the Xia lands, bringing it under his personal control. When the treachery was uncovered, Renzong had Ren Dejing executed. Renzong's reign ended peacefully when he died at the age of 70.

Huanzong
Other name: Li Chunyou

r. 1194–1206
b. 1177 d. 1206

Huanzong was the eldest son of Renzong and Empress Luo. In 1205, the Mongols raided the Xia from the west for the first time. When the Mongols retreated, Huanzong changed the name of the capital from Xingqing to Zhongxing. In 1206, Huanzong's cousin, Li Anquan, deposed and imprisoned him.

Xiangzong
Other names: Weiming Anquan, Li Anquan

r. 1206–1211
b. 1170 d. 1211

Li Anquan's father was Li Renyu, a son of Chongzong. Li Anquan seized power from Huanzong and forced his aunt, Empress Luo, to request that the Jin confirm his appointment. In 1207, Ghengis Khan attacked the Xia border station at Wulahai. Xiangzong sent envoys to secure a military alliance with the Jin, but the new Jin ruler, the Prince of Wei, refused. From 1209, the Mongols allied with the Uighurs, sacking many of the Xia's western towns and besieging the capital. In 1210, Xiangzong submitted to them, becoming a vassal.

Shenzong
Other name: Li Zunxu

r. 1211–1223
b. 1163 d. 1226

Li Zunxu may have staged a coup to remove his distant cousin Xiangzong. He became Emperor Shenzong. His father was Li Yan, a descendant of Chongzong, and he was the first Tangut prince with a Xia *jinshi* degree. In 1217, when Ghengis Khan demanded the Xia send troops to fight in the Middle East, he refused. In 1223, the Mongols invaded the Xia, and Shenzong abdicated.

Xianzong
Other name: Li Dewang

r. 1223–1226
b. 1181 d. 1226

Li Dewang took over from his father as Xianzong. The only notable achievement of his reign was his attempt to secure Jin support against the Mongol invasion. In 1225, the Xia and Jin declared brotherly relations. The Xia court was dominated by courtiers and one, Asha Gambu, sent insulting letters to Ghengis Khan. In response, Genghis razed many Xia towns and massacred their populations. It is believed Xianzong died of anxiety.

Modi
Other name: Li Xian

r. 1226–1227
d. 1227

Li Xian was a son of the Qingping Prince, a relative of Xianzong. He became known as Modi, which means "last emperor." His reign lasted only a year against the Mongol threat. In 1227, Ghengis Khan besieged the Xia capital, Zhongxing, for five months until Emperor Mo was forced to surrender. Ghengis Khan himself died around the time of this siege. The last Xia emperor walked out of the gates and into the Mongols' camp, where he was hacked to death. The Mongols then entered the city and slaughtered the entire population, thereby ending the Xia dynasty.

△ This Xia imperial mausoleum is in the Ningxia Autonomous Region.

The Jin Dynasty

(1115–1234)

The Jurchen of northeastern China were a tribal Tungusic people who were skilled at hunting and fishing. They served the Khitan Liao dynasty, until a Jurchen chieftain—Aguda of the Wanyan clan—conquered the Liao. He established the Jin, or "golden," dynasty, which ruled northern China and demanded deference from the Xia and the Song. However, the Jin gradually lost their Jurchen ways in favor of Chinese customs. They became weaker and were eventually conquered by the Mongols under Ögedei Khan.

Taizu

Other names: Aguda, Wanyan Min

r.1115–1123
b.1068 d.1123

Taizu, founder of the Jin dynasty, was born Aguda. He was from the Wanyan clan of the Jurchen people of northeastern China. In his youth, Aguda fought against other Jurchen on the Khitan's orders. In 1112, when his elder brother, Wuyashu, was chief, Aguda attended a banquet hosted by the Liao emperor and publicly defied him by refusing to dance.

When Wuyashu died in 1113, Aguda took control and attacked the Liao the following year. With each victory, he gained followers among the Jurchens and unified the tribes. Aguda proclaimed himself emperor of the Jin dynasty in 1115. His small army defeated a vastly superior border army and became unstoppable. Aguda and his clansmen conquered all the Liao capitals within a few years and took Yanjing (Beijing) in 1122. Aguda may have demanded to be recognized as an emperor rather than a king as a condition for peace. Unable to appease Aguda, the Liao were defeated. Aguda negotiated a treaty with the Song that forced them to pay regular tribute. The Song then recognized Aguda as an emperor.

Taizong

Other names: Wuqimai, Wanyan Sheng

r.1123–1135
b.1075 d.1135

Wuqimai, known as Taizong, succeeded his brother Aguda. He had controlled the tribal Council of Bojilie, managing politics and administration in the growing empire, while his brother was on campaign. After coming to power, Taizong made an alliance with the Xia dynasty in 1124, demanding their submission. Under pressure to continue expanding by the Jin generals, Taizong declared war on the Song in 1125. The Song ceded much of their northern territory to the Jin, sent a hostage prince, and agreed to a war indemnity in exchange for peace. Even so, the following year, the Jin attacked again and took the Song capital of Kaifeng. The Jin pushed the Song survivors south and Taizong established a puppet emperor, Liu Yu, to govern and pacify central China. Taizong also began relocating Jurchen to fiefdoms throughout northern China.

Xizong

Other names: Hela, Wanyan Dan

r.1135–1149
b.1119 d.1150

Hela was the son of Aguda's eldest son, Prince Shengguo. He was Taizong's designated heir and enthroned as Xizong. In 1137, he abolished Liu Yu's emperorship. A peace treaty was agreed to in 1141, and the Song acknowledged their inferiority and paid tribute. Xizong also agreed to a treaty with the Xia. He could not control the Jurchen factions or his powerful uncles, and he became an alcoholic who executed many of his ministers. He was murdered in a coup led by his cousin, Digunai.

Prince of Hailing

Other names: Digunai, Yang of Hailing, Wanyan Liang

r.1150–1161
b.1122 d.1161

Digunai was the son of Prince Zonggan, Aguda's second son. He took the throne as the Prince of Hailing and consolidated his power by crushing the other Jurchen princes, taking their wives into his harem. He also exterminated the descendants of Taizong, several palace ladies, the

△ This portrait depicts Aguda, Emperor Taizu of Jin.

ruling clan of the Khitans (Yelü) and the Song royals (Zhao). He moved his capital to Yanjing and called it Zhongdu, demolishing the palaces at Shangjing, the old capital. He centralized authority so much that many revolts erupted throughout his empire, especially among the Khitan and Jurchen. Digunai wanted to be emperor of all China. In 1161, his armies advanced into southern China, but the Song stopped them from crossing the Yangzi River. Digunai's commanders betrayed and murdered him on the campaign trail in Yangzhou. History judged the Prince of Hailing to be an evil ruler, and he was not granted an emperor's posthumous title.

Shizong

**Other names: Wulu,
Wanyan Yong**

r. 1161–1189
b. 1123 d. 1189

Wulu, Emperor Shizong, was the son of Prince Zongyao, a general and the third son of Aguda. At the Eastern capital (Liaoyang) a Jurchen uprising installed him as emperor a few months before Digunai's murder. Shizong had received a Chinese-style education. He nonetheless promoted Jurchen ways and the traditional military organization. Shizong quelled the Khitan uprising in 1162 and secured peace with the Song in 1165. Peace then continued in the Jin empire for over two decades. In the early 1180s, Shizong ordered surveys and conducted tax and military reforms to improve the economy. He revered aspects of Confucianism that elevated the Jurchen way of life. Similarly, he ordered that jinshi examinations be available in Jurchen and had

Confucian texts translated. He believed in both Buddhism and Daoism but favored the Daoist master Wang Chuyi.

Zhangzong

**Other names: Madage,
Wanyan Jing**

r. 1189–1208
b. 1168 d. 1208

Zhangzong was the grandson of Shizong. His father had been Shizong's heir, but he died in 1185. Shizong chose Zhangzong because he showed academic promise in both Chinese and Jurchen. When enthroned, Zhangzong's ministers advised him against hunting in the north for his safety, signaling the end of Jurchen hunting customs at court. In his reign, the Yellow River flooded, causing problems for the people. The Mongols were becoming more powerful, and Zhangzong ordered fortifications to be bolstered along the Great Wall. Late in his reign, Song commanders began to raid Jin lands and invaded in 1206. The Jin defeated them, retaliating until the Song requested peace and paid an indemnity. Zhangzong died shortly afterward.

Prince of Wei

**Other names: Shao of Wei,
Wanyan Yongji, Wanyan Yunji**

r. 1208–1213
d. 1213

Wanyan Yunji was the Prince of Wei and uncle of Zhangzong. He became ruler because Zhangzong had no heir. Wanyan Yunji had once been insulting when he was responsible for collecting tribute from the border peoples, so when he, as emperor, sent envoys demanding tribute, Genghis

Khan remembered this. In 1211, he joined forces with the Khitan to attack the Jin, pushing back their armies until they besieged Zhongdu (Beijing). The Mongols retreated but returned in 1213. General Hushahu then ordered eunuchs to murder Wanyan Yunji. He was not posthumously honored as an emperor.

Xuanzong

**Other names: Wudubu, Wanyan Xun,
Wanyan Congjia**

r. 1213–1224
b. 1163 d. 1224

General Hushahu put Wanyan Xun, a grandson of Shizong, on the throne as Xuanzong. In 1214, the Song refused to pay tribute and the Jin had to accept an unfavorable peace agreement with the Mongols, which made them nominal vassals. Xuanzong then moved the Jin capital to Kaifeng, and Ghengis Khan besieged Zhongdu again, taking the city in 1215 and massacring its population. Northern China was lost. Xuanzong's attacks on the Song were once again repulsed at the Yangzi River in 1219. Genghis Khan demanded he abdicate his emperor's title. Xuanzong refused and died from an illness a few years later.

Aizong

**Other names: Ningjiasu, Wanyan
Shouxu, Wanyan Shouli**

r. 1223–1234
b. 1198 d. 1234

Aizong was Xuanzong's third son and took the throne because his elder brother (the heir apparent), and his nephew had died. He had to compete with Xuanzong's second son for the throne. Aizong was judged a competent

△ This painted vase may have been made in the Jin imperial workshops.

ruler. In 1224, he rallied his forces against the Mongols, stopped attacking the Song, and made peace with the Xia. Ghengis Khan probably died on campaign against the Xia in 1227, which allowed Aizong to regroup. He fended off Ghengis's son Tolui, but Ögedei Khan and the great General Sübedei besieged Kaifeng in 1232. Aizong fled to Caizhou (Henan) and died by suicide during the Mongol siege.

Modi

**Other names: Hudun,
Wanyan Chenglin**

r. 1234–1234
d. 1234

Modi is a title meaning "last emperor." For the Jin, this was Wanyan Chenglin, a descendant of Aguda who accompanied Aizong in his final days. Aizong named him as his successor before his death. The last emperor died fighting in the streets against the Mongols in the Jin's last stand.

The Yuan Dynasty

(1279–1368)

The Yuan dynasty was ruled by the emperors descended from Genghis Khan of the Mongol empire, which conquered China and much of Eurasia, forging the largest dominion in world history. At this time, China was at the center of a globalized world of advanced trade, commerce, and multiculturalism. The Yuan emperors, who were also called "great khans," held nominal power over the lesser khanates. Even though China had been conquered and unified under the Yuan, many civil wars between ruling families erupted. Without strong, stable leadership, the Yuan emperors lost control of their courts and subjects until a Chinese uprising established the Ming dynasty.

△ Genghis Khan sits on a throne, attended by his sons Ögedei and Jochi, in this illustration from a medieval Persian manuscript.

Genghis Khan

Other names: Temujin, Taizu, Chinggis Khan

r. 1206–1227
b. 1162 d. 1227

Genghis Khan, the common romanized name of Chinggis Khan, was born Temujin, son of Yisügei Bagatur of the Borjigin clan, which was one of the leading Mongol clans. When Temujin was nine, his father was poisoned by Tatars and his family struggled to survive. He was promised to his wife, Börte, at a young age. He married her in early adulthood, but she was kidnapped by Merkids shortly after, so he rescued her with his blood brother Jamukha. Genghis later gradually gathered followers and political allies among the tribes of Mongolia and fought Jamukha to become khan (ruler) of the Mongols by 1201. The Jurchen Jin dynasty, which ruled northern China, gave one of Genghis Khan's allies the title Ong Khan of the Kereyids in 1196 for their service in fighting the Tatars. By 1206, Genghis had defeated the Ong Khan and the Naiman tribe and united the other tribes of Mongolia under one banner. He reformed his vast army according to a decimal system, with military units of 10,000 warriors, before invading the Jin lands in 1211.

Ghengis Khan took Yanjing (Beijing), the Jin capital, in 1214 and then conquered the rest of northern China. He also went on lengthy campaigns in Central Asia and the Middle East. Genghis's four sons with Börte inherited portions of his vast empire. His eldest son, Jochi, who established the Golden Horde in Russia and Central Asia, was not considered for the succession because his paternity was uncertain. His second son, Chagatai, was given large parts of Central Asia, which became the Chagatai Khanate. His third, Ögedei, was later designated as khagan (great khan) of the Mongol empire. His fourth, Tolui, had sons who eventually supplanted Ögedei's line and extended the Mongol empire even further.

Genghis adopted a policy of religious tolerance throughout his empire and instituted a strict legal code, the Yasa. Prior to his death, Genghis summoned the Daoist master Changchun to seek the secrets of immortality. Despite this, during his final campaign against the Xia dynasty, he died in 1227. According to Mongol custom, a *quriltai* (assembly) was called after his death, and this assembly named Ögedei the great khan of the Mongol empire.

Ögedei Khan

Other names: Taizong, Ögödei

r. 1229–1241
b. 1186 d. 1241

Ögedei spent much of his youth on campaigns with his father, Genghis, even during the civil war with Jamukha in 1203. In 1204, Genghis gave him the Merkid lady Töregene, who became his wife. At a *quriltai* (assembly) in 1229, he was made khagan with the support of his brother, Chagatai. Ögedei and his brother, Tolui—the fourth son of Genghis Khan—campaigned in northern China until they defeated the Jin at their capital, Kaifeng, in 1233.

In 1235, Ögedei established the capital of his domain at a newly built city called Karakorum in the Orkhon Valley. Ögedei's court was cosmopolitan, for example, hosting Christian, Islamic, and Confucian advisers. A Khitan aristocrat named Yelü Chucai became the most senior minister and persuaded Ögedei to adopt a Chinese-style administration in northern China. Historians believe that Ögedei was an alcoholic, and he is thought to have died as a result of excessive drinking.

Güyük Khan

Other names: Dingzong, Kuyuk

r.1246–1248
b.1206 d.1248

Ögedei Khan, the previous ruler, designated his favorite young grandson, Shiremün, as his heir. However, soon after Ögedei's death, his wife, Töregene, was established as regent instead, with the help of Chagatai and her sons. Töregene Khatun ("khatun" being the female counterpart of "khan") ruled the empire until her eldest son, Güyük, could be established as khan in 1246. During her rule, the Mongols and subordinate Chinese generals were campaigning against the Southern Song in southern China. Güyük and Töregene had to fend off dissent from Genghis's youngest brother and Töregene's other son, Köten.

Güyük was ultimately elected ruler at a *quriltai* with the help of the Toluids—descendants of Genghis Khan's son, Tolui. Güyük Khan caused resentment among the Chinese and Muslims at court by favoring Christianity. Despite this, the khagan still wrote a letter to Pope Innocent IV, demanding his submission. While on a journey west, possibly to start a conflict with his cousin Batu (a descendant of Jochi), Güyük died from an illness.

Möngke Khan

Other name: Xianzong

r.1251–1259
b.1209 d.1259

A Merkid wife of Güyük, Oghul-Qaimish, became regent and insisted that Shiremün (a grandson of Güyük Khan) be elected khagan. However, they were not able to overcome Möngke, the eldest son of Tolui, who gained Batu's backing at the *quriltai* in 1251. He took power and had Oghul-Qaimish executed. Möngke then pressed into Southern Song territory in southern China, circumventing the Yangzi River and attacked from the southwest. His conquests extended deep into Iran, Korea, and Vietnam. To reduce the power of Ögedei's line, he ordered purges and gave a vast territory in Iran to his brother Hülegü and much of north China to his other brother,

Kublai. In 1258, he personally led an army to attack the Song in Sichuan province and died of fever while besieging Chongqing in 1259. Both of his wives died, so there was no regent to immediately succeed him.

Kublai Khan

Other names: Shizu, Sechen, Qubilai

r.1260–1294
b.1215 d.1294

Kublai Khan (see pp. 192–193) was a grandson of Genghis Khan. He was the fifth khagan of the Mongol empire but also the founder and first emperor of the Yuan dynasty. Kublai was the second son of Tolui by his wife Sorhagtani and succeeded his elder brother Möngke as khagan. Kublai's reign saw the conquest of the Southern Song but also an intense civil war with his cousin Kaidu, which

fractured the Mongol empire. Kublai Khan's capital was at Dadu or Khanbaliq (Beijing).

Temür Khan

Other names: Chengzong, Öljeytü

r.1294–1307
b.1265 d.1307

Kublai and his wife Chabui's second son, Jingim, was designated as the imperial successor. However, Jingim, who was a supporter of Confucianism, died of illness in 1285, and Kublai then designated Jingim's son by his Onggirat wife, Kökejin, as heir. This grandson of Kublai's, Temür, was enthroned in 1294 as the second Yuan emperor. Temür reinstated the highest Chinese appointments of grand preceptor (*taishi*), grand tutor (*taifu*) and grand protector (*taibao*). Temür himself favored Daoism and elevated Daoist scholars »

△ This silk scroll painting depicts Temür Khan and his men on the hunt.

at court. His reign was less militaristic than that of his predecessors, and he reached a brief peace with the other khanates in 1304. He even granted periodic tax exemptions to areas suffering from natural disasters. He died without an heir.

Külüg Khan

Other names: Haishan, Khaisan, Wuzong

r. 1307–1311
b. 1281 d. 1311

When Temür became ill and was dying, various aristocratic factions contended for the succession. Temür's empress, Bulughan, attempted to wrest political control away from the Onggirats by establishing Ananda, a Muslim son of Jingim's younger brother Manggala, on the throne. A former honor guard of the khagan named

Hargasun Darqan was his bodyguard and led the elite guard forces, the *kheshig*. Hargasun maneuvered Temür's nephews, by his brother Dharmabala and his Onggirat wife, Targi, to remove Ananda from the capital of Dadu and execute him, thereby consolidating the claim of Jingim's Onggirat descendants. Targi's eldest son was then established as Külüg Khan, and her younger son Ayurbarwada (Buyantu Khan) was designated heir. In Külüg's reign, Kaidu's son Chabar of the Ögedeids finally submitted. The Confucian *Classic of Filial Piety* was translated during Külüg's reign, and Buddhist temples were commissioned. His reign encountered many fiscal difficulties owing to excessive military expenditure and insufficient revenue. Külüg attempted to establish a nonexchangeable silver standard as currency, but this failed.

△ Külüg Khan ruled the Yuan dynasty for four years.

Buyantu Khan

Other names: Ayurbarwada, Renzong

r. 1311–1320
b. 1285 d. 1320

Buyantu Khan was the brother of the previous emperor and had to deal with the fiscal issues he inherited from Külüg's reign. His mother, Targi, favored a financial administrator named Temüder, who took de facto control of many aspects of government and implemented unpopular austerity measures, along with advance levies on salt and iron production. Buyantu asserted himself in government and reinstated the Confucian civil service examination in 1315 and permitted commoner candidates who were Mongol, Central Asian, or West Asian to take part. Many more Confucian and Buddhist works were translated and disseminated during his reign. Buyantu also reformed the bureaucracy and judiciary and established a new currency. Nevertheless, official corruption became widespread.

Gegeen Khan

Other names: Shidebala, Yingzong

r. 1320–1323
b. 1302 d. 1323

Gegeen Khan was Buyantu's eldest son by his Onggirat wife Radnashiri. In Gegeen's early reign, his grandmother, Targi, made her favored minister Temüder grand councillor, and the two took total political control. Targi and Temüder both died in 1322, and Gegeen briefly took back control, ordering the compilation of the *Dayuan tongzhi* (*Comprehensive Institutions of the Great*

Yuan), the legal code of the dynasty. He hoped to introduce reforms in line with Confucian principles, but his reign was short-lived. Temüder's followers staged a coup that removed and killed Gegeen in 1323.

Yesün Temür

Other name: Emperor Taiding

r. 1323–1328
b. 1293 d. 1328

Yesün Temür was the son of Jingim's eldest son, Gammala, and an Onggirat mother. It was suspected that he also played a role in Gegeen's assassination. His court in China was marked by significant Muslim influence, and Muslims occupied most senior positions. One of his viziers, Dawla Shah, implemented policies that exempted Muslim and Christian luxury goods merchants from paying taxes.

Aragibag Khan

Other name: Emperor Tianshun

r. 1328–1328
b. 1320 d. 1328

Yesün Temür's eldest son by an Onggirat wife, eight-year-old Aragibag was established as emperor for one month by Dawla Shah at the summer capital, Shangdu, in Inner Mongolia. El-Temür, a Qipchaq Turk who had once led the *kheshig*, disapproved of the succession arrangements and the power of Dawla Shah. El-Temür therefore tried to reinstall Külüg Khan's line at Dadu. Aragibag disappeared after the brief but deadly War of Two Capitals between Shangdu and Dadu. He was probably murdered along with Dawla Shah by the army that besieged Shangdu.

△ The Mongol rulers and their armies were known for their competency on horseback. This late Yuan scroll painting depicts Mongol entertainers showing off their equestrian skills.

Khutughtu Khan

Other names: Mingzong, Qoshila, Khüslen, Khutagt

r.1329–1329
b.1300 d.1329

El-Temür's succession plan backfired when Külüg's eldest son, Qoshila, secured the backing of the Chagatai Khanate. Qoshila was established as Khutughtu Khan. However, this state of affairs would have undermined El-Temür, so El-Temür had Khutughtu murdered and reestablished Külüg's other son Tugh Temür on the throne.

Jayaatu Khan

Other names: Tugh Temür, Wenzong

r.1328; 1329–1332
b.1304 d.1332

Jayaatu Khan, born Tugh Temür, was Külüg's younger son and was enthroned as emperor at Dadu in 1328. He abdicated in favor of his brother Qoshila, only to resume rule again in 1329. Jayaatu's mother was Tangut rather than Onggirat. Although

the powerful lord El-Temür and a Merkid officer named Bayan, who led the *kheshig*, were largely in control of the administration and military campaigns during Jayaatu's rule, he oversaw cultural advances. He ordered the compilation of the *Imperial Grand Compendium for Governing the World* (*Huangchao jingshi dadian*), which covered events up to 1330 and served as a major source for the Yuan dynastic history later compiled by the Ming. Jayaatu sponsored Confucian scholarship and Buddhism, and he himself produced Chinese painting, calligraphy, and poetry, which was highly unusual for a Mongol emperor.

Rinchinbal Khan

Other name: Ningzong

r.1332–1332
b.1326 d.1332

When Jayaatu died, El-Temür and Bayan were powerful at court and were in conflict. Bayan had allied with Jayaatu's Onggirat empress, Budashiri. El-Temür wanted El-Tegüs, Jayaatu's son, to be established on the throne.

The two factions uneasily compromised on Khutughtu Khan's son, Richinbal, who was only six years old. Within a few weeks, however, Richinbal died of an illness.

Ukhaghatu Khan

Other names: Toghon Temür, Huizong, Emperor Shun

r.1333–1368
b.1320 d.1370

When the minister El-Temür died in 1333, Bayan helped Jayaatu's empress, Budashiri, to install Toghon Temür as emperor. He was a son of Khutughtu Khan by a noble Karluk wife. Toghon Temür was established as Ukhaghatu Khan at the age of 13, while El-Tegüs was designated as heir to the throne under Budashiri's care. Interestingly, the empress who later bore Ukhaghatu's heir was a Korean concubine named Lady Gi. Bayan took advantage of this to take control of the empire and, in 1335, proceeded to abolish the civil service examinations in favor of the old ethnic-based ranking system. During the early

years of Ukhaghtu's reign, Bayan authorized several policies that were unfavorable to the Chinese and Confucianism. In 1340, Ukhaghatu exiled Bayan and Bayan's nephew Toqto'a took over government. The examinations resumed, and Toqto'a oversaw completion of the histories of the Song, Liao and Jin dynasties. Toqto'a was recalled to service several times over the 1340s and early 1350s to deal with serious problems such as flooding, sea piracy, and the Red Turban Rebellion in 1354. Ukhaghatu became paranoid and dismissed Toqto'a, but could not adequately govern the empire, which led to economic problems, rebellious warlords, and unrest. Lady Gi and her son, Ayushiridara, attempted to take control, prompting a civil conflict with a Mongol warlord who sacked Dadu in 1364. Ayushirdara reclaimed Dadu with the help of another general in 1365. When the Ming arose under Zhu Yuanzhang to overthrow the Mongols, Ukhaghatu fled north with his son to establish the Northern Yuan dynasty in Mongolia. He died in 1370.

The Ming Dynasty (1368–1644)

The Ming dynasty was one of the greatest in Chinese history. Its founder, Zhu Yuanzhang, overthrew the Mongols and the empire prospered under a Han Chinese ruler. The Ming emperors were constantly victims of factional struggles and often fell under the sway of eunuchs. The empire nonetheless endured until the Manchu Qing invaded in the 17th century.

Hongwu
Other names: Zhu Yuanzhang, Taizu

r.1368–1398
b.1328 d.1398

Zhu Yuanzhang was born a Han Chinese peasant but joined a large rebellion against the Mongol Yuan dynasty and founded the Ming dynasty with its capital at Nanjing. He ruled as the Hongwu Emperor for 30 years, attempting to rebuild an empire that had been ravaged by war. He replaced Mongol bureaucrats from the previous Yuan dynasty with Han Chinese and restored the Confucian imperial examination system. Hongwu also presided over political reforms, drew up a new legal code, increased the power of the Embroidered Uniform Guard (secret police), and purged the court of hostile officials. He encouraged better cultivation of the land, abolished slavery, and organized rural China into li (communities of 110 households).

Jianwen
Other names: Zhu Yunwen, Huidi

r.1399–1402
b.1377 d.1402

Zhu Yunwen was a prince and the son of Hongwu's eldest son and heir, Zhu Biao. Zhu Yunwen already had a wife and young child when he came to the throne as the Jianwen Emperor. He faced the Jingnan Rebellion in 1399, led by his uncle, Zhu Di, who conspired against Jianwen to conquer the Ming capital of Nanjing. He burned the imperial palace and Jianwen, his wife, and his child died. Their bodies were given a proper burial.

Yongle
Other names: Zhu Di, Chengzu

r.1403–1424
b.1360 d.1424

Zhu Di, the Yongle Emperor, was a son of Zhu Yuanzhang. He came to the throne after he rebelled and overthrew his nephew. He was considered the "Second Founder" of the Ming dynasty (see pp. 208–209). Throughout his reign, Yongle had to defend his empire from the Mongols. He also wanted to expand Chinese influence throughout the world and sent Admiral Zheng He to undertake voyages of exploration to Southeast Asia and Africa in immense treasure ships. Yongle's reign is famous for its major construction projects. He repaired the Grand Canal and in 1406 ordered the move of the capital to Beijing, where he instigated construction of the Forbidden City. It took 14 years to build and would become the seat of Ming government until the end of the dynasty. Yongle also ordered the construction of the Porcelain Tower of Nanjing.

Yongle commissioned an official, Xie Jin, with a team of scholars to compose what would be known as the *Yongle Encyclopedia*, a compilation of around 8,000 texts on subjects from art to astronomy. It was completed in 1408. In 1424, Yongle led a campaign against an army of Oirats in the Gobi Desert, where he became ill and died.

Hongxi
Other names: Zhu Gaozhi, Renzong

r.1425–1425
b.1378 d.1425

Zhu Gaozhi was the eldest son of the Yongle Emperor and Empress Renxiaowen. He was called the Hongxi Emperor. Hongxi had devoted his life to the study of Confucianism and took little interest in military matters. He gave tax exemptions to disaster-stricken areas and briefly returned the Ming capital to Nanjing. He became ill several months into his reign and died.

Xuande
Other names: Zhu Zhanji, Xuanzong

r.1425–1435
b.1399 d.1435

Zhu Zhanji was Hongxi's eldest son and ruled as the Xuande Emperor. He returned the capital

△ The Xuande Emperor is drawn by elephants in his imperial coach.

△ Hongzhi ruled from 1488 to 1505.

to Beijing. In his youth, he was favored by Yongle and even accompanied him on campaigns. When his uncle, Zhu Gaoxu, conspired against him, Xuande had him and his family executed.

During his reign, Ming forces suffered heavy losses against Vietnam, and Xuande recognized the country's independence from China. He also waged military campaigns against the Mongols, who raided Ming territories. In battle, Xuande personally shot and killed many enemy soldiers. He defended the empire from rebellions in China and abroad while also working to curb official corruption.

Xuande was also a skilled poet, calligrapher, and painter and enjoyed painting animals. His reign saw one of the high points of Ming blue and white porcelain craft. Xuande had many women in his harem and also demanded women from the Korean kings. To stabilize the economy, he reduced taxes in strategic areas of the empire. He died in the 10th year of his reign following an illness.

Yingzong
Other names: Zhengtong, Tianshun, Zhu Qizhen

r.1436–1449; 1457–1464
b.1427 d.1464

Zhu Qizhen was a young son of Xuande and was posthumously named the Yingzong Emperor. He was nine when he became emperor, so his grandmother, the Grand Empress Dowager Zhang, assumed control of matters of state. However, she died in 1442, leaving Yingzong vulnerable to the influence of a court eunuch named Wang Zhen. The imperial eunuchs at this time were very powerful, and Wang Zhen ruled the court through intimidation.

Wang Zhen persuaded Yingzong to campaign against the Oirat Mongols, whose leader, Esen Khan, captured Yingzong at the Battle of the Tumu Fortress in 1449. He was held for ransom but was eventually released. By the time he returned to the Ming in 1450, Yingzong's brother, Zhu Qiyu, had already been named emperor. No longer emperor, Yingzong lived in relatively impoverished conditions in a mansion he was given.

Many years later, in 1457, Yingzong was restored to the throne by officials after his supporters stormed the palace gates. Zhu Qiyu's loyal ministers were purged, but Yingzong's own ministers controlled him and the court. Following an illness, Yingzong died in 1464.

Jingtai
Other names: Daizong, Jingdi, Zhu Qiyu

r.1450–1457
b.1428 d.1457

Zhu Qiyu, who was remembered as the Jingtai Emperor, came to the throne while his brother, the Yingzong Emperor, was held in captivity by Oirat Mongols. He was well served by his powerful minister Yu Qian and worked to repair the empire's canals and stabilize the economy. However, during his reign, the eunuchs—led by Xing An—continued to hold power at court. Jingtai became very ill in 1457, which prompted his brother, Yingzong, to take back the throne. Jingtai died under house arrest, perhaps murdered by an imperial eunuch.

Chenghua
Other names: Xianzong, Zhu Jianshen

r.1465–1487
b.1447 d.1487

The Chenghua Emperor was Yingzong's son. He had a speech impediment and was raised by the empress, who was not his mother. In his reign, official correspondence and promulgations were dictated from the palace rather than from the scholars, causing the eunuchs, particularly Wang Zhi, to become very powerful. Chenghua had little real power as he was controlled by the eunuchs and also by his consort, Lady Wan. Lady Wan tried to prevent the other palace ladies from bearing Chenghua children and forced them to have abortions, but one woman kept her pregnancy secret and bore Chenghua a son, Zhu Youcheng. Chenghua died following an illness.

Hongzhi
Other names: Xiaozong, Zhu Youcheng (Zhu Youtang)

r.1488–1505
b.1470 d.1505

Chenghua's eldest son came to the throne as the Hongzhi Emperor. He dismissed the schemers from the court and punished some powerful eunuchs. He had great respect and devotion for the rites of Confucianism and Daoism and reinstated the "classics mat," a program of court lectures, in which he invited respected Confucian scholars to speak at court so that he could learn how to better govern the empire. Hongzhi granted many favors to the family of his wife, Empress Zhang, but he still did » not leave their power unchecked. In the later part of his reign, he became sickly, and it was difficult for him to attend to the flooding and other natural disasters that plagued the Ming.

Zhengde

Other names: Zhu Houzhao, Wuzong

r. 1506–1521
b. 1491 d. 1521

Zhu Houzhao, the Zhengde Emperor, was Hongzhi's eldest son. His father initially instructed that government be entrusted to ministers because his son was so fond of leisure and sport. Zhengde enjoyed horse riding, archery, and kickball. Because he was brought up by eunuchs, he let them gain more and more power until they completely controlled the government. Zhengde liked to go in secret to Beijing for drinking and entertainment instead of working on his studies. He argued with government officials and canceled the classics mat lectures that his father had started. Zhengde's eunuchs raised taxes unreasonably, causing a rebellion by the Prince of Anhua in 1510. The rebellion and the eunuchs were then put down.

From 1517 onward, Zhengde went on frequent hunting trips and excursions to the northern border against his ministers' advice. He established a palace at Xuanfu in Datong, from where he led counterattacks against raiding Mongols. In this period, he took many women for his harem. After quashing a rebellion by the Prince of Ning in 1519, Zhengde traveled to Nanjing for a few months. On his return to Beijing, he fell into a lake while fishing. He became ill and died, leaving no son or heir.

△ This scroll painting detail shows Jiajing (left) on his state barge.

Jiajing

Other names: Zhu Houcong, Shizong

r. 1522–1566
b. 1507 d. 1567

There was unrest in the empire for months after Zhengde's death because no suitable heir could be agreed on. Yang Tinghe, the grand secretary, and others eventually decided the son of the fourth son of Chenghua should be enthroned. His name was Zhu Houcong, remembered as the Jiajing Emperor. He refused to refer to the empress dowager and the deceased Hongzhi as his mother and father and instead wanted his own father to be posthumously named emperor.

In his early reign, he had many conflicts with Yang Tinghe about rites and throughout his reign remained headstrong, wanting firm control over governance. From 1530 onward, Jiajing wanted to end imperial Confucian sacrifices. These and other sacrifices were significantly revised. Jiajing strongly believed in Daoism, and he patronized

investigations into prolonging his life. His demands of palace women inspired a group of them to attempt to murder him in 1542, but the plot failed. In his late reign, China also came under threat from the Mongols and coastal pirates. The emperor grew senile and died from an illness in 1567.

Longqing

Other names: Zhu Zaiji, Zhu Zaihou, Muzong

r. 1567–1572
b. 1537 d. 1572

Zhu Zaiji was Jiajing's third son and became emperor because Jiajing disliked his eldest son. He was remembered as the Longwing Emperor. His grand secretary was the minister Zhang Juzheng, who reformed China's fiscal regime and bureaucracy. Longqing inherited a government in trouble after years of mismanagement and tried to be active at court but he was hampered by a speech impediment. In 1571, he gave Altan Khan of the Mongols the title Prince Shunyi and resumed

trade with them. He personally reversed his father's policies favoring Daoism but left other matters to Zhang Juzheng.

Wanli

Other names: Shenzong, Zhu Yijun

r. 1573–1620
b. 1563 d. 1620

As a young boy, Zhu Yijun, the son of Longqing, was fond of riding, archery, calligraphy, and poetry. He was posthumously known as the Wanli Emperor. He became emperor at the age of 10, and his regency was divided between Longqing's empress and his own mother, but real power resided with the minister Zhang Juzheng. Zhang Juzheng carried out many beneficial fiscal reforms for the empire and also ordered a land taxation survey. When Zhang Juzheng died in 1582, Wanli assumed personal control of the government. Wanli spoke out against institutions of the state and often refused to meet officials. He dismissed officials and left many positions vacant. Meanwhile, he redirected government revenues to pay for his personal expenditure and ordered the establishment of mining operations. He punished disloyal officials who criticized him, but he could not entirely quell criticism. In his later reign, the Mongols, Manchu, and Japanese were all invading Chinese territory, but Wanli preferred to focus his attention on constructing his mausoleum. He became seriously ill, withdrew from public affairs, and died as the Manchu advanced.

Taichang

Other names: Guangzong, Zhu Changluo

r.1620–1620
b.1582 d.1620

Zhu Changluo was Wanli's eldest son whom he had with a consort and was remembered as the Taichang Emperor. The Donglin Academy was a movement to restore Confucian traditions in the civil service, and its members pressured Taichang to carry out reforms. He reigned only a few months before becoming ill, and died after ingesting mysterious "red pills" during treatment, which had been given to him by a eunuch on the orders of Wanli's favorite consort.

Tianqi

Other names: Xizong, Zhu Youjiao

r.1620–1627
b.1605 d.1627

Zhu Youjiao, Taichang's son, was remembered as the Tianqi Emperor. His court came under control of a eunuch named Wei Zhongxian and a palace lady named Lady Ke, who fought with and killed many members of the Donglin Academy. Tianqi was sickly and secluded himself in the palace. Meanwhile, the Manchu were winning many victories in the northeast, which shocked an empire that was also plagued by fires, earthquakes, and uprisings. Tianqi died of an illness at the age of 22.

Chongzhen

Other names: Zhuangliedi, Zhu Youjian

r.1628–1644
b.1611 d.1644

Zhu Youjian, the Chongzhen Emperor, was Tianqi's younger brother and ascended the throne because none of Tianqi's children survived. Chongzhen's mother had died when he was very young, and he was raised by several imperial consorts. Chongzhen ended Wei Zhongxian and Lady Ke's power, but the treasury was depleted. He tried reducing expenditure by terminating official salaries, but this caused rebellions to worsen in northwestern China. From 1639, there was also a sudden silver shortage caused by Spanish trade policies in Southeast Asia, which created a financial crisis. At that time, the Manchu were also conquering the Chinese heartland. When Beijing was besieged by the Manchu rebels, Chongzhen died by suicide.

Hongguang

Other names: Zhu Yousong, Anzong

r.1644–1645
b.1607 d.1646

When Chongzhen died, Ming power shifted south. Zhu Yousong, the Prince of Fu, was Wanli's grandson. At Nanjing, he was named emperor of the Ming (now called the "Southern Ming"). He had insufficient revenues to defend the empire and tried to make peace with and pay off the Qing. However, the Qing advanced on the Ming loyalists, forcing him to flee Nanjing. He was later captured by the Qing and sent to Beijing to be executed. He was posthumously called the Hongguang Emperor.

Longwu

Other names: Zhu Yujian, Shaozong

r.1645–1646
b.1602 d.1646

The Longwu Emperor, Zhu Yujian, was a distant descendant of Zhu Yuanzhang and, after fleeing the conquest of Nanjing, was named emperor. He was captured and executed when the Qing invaded Fujian.

Yongli

Other names: Zhu Youlang, Zhaozong

r.1646–1662
b.1623 d.1662

Ming loyalists established Wanli's grandson Zhu Youlang (remembered as the Yongli Emperor) as emperor. Longwu's brother also declared himself emperor but was captured by the Qing. Despite fighting the Qing for many years, Yongli too was eventually executed in 1662.

△ The Tianqi Emperor was sickly and spent his time secluded in the palace.

The Qing Dynasty (1644–1912)

The Qing dynasty was established by the Manchu, a Tungusic people from northeastern China. They conquered the Ming to rule over a large and prosperous empire that was increasingly exposed to the outside world. The individual Qing emperors had some of the longest reigns in both Chinese and world history. The Qing was the last imperial dynasty in China, eventually falling to a nationalist revolution.

Shunzhi
Other name: Fulin

r. 1644–1661
b. 1638 d. 1661

Shunzhi was the first Manchu emperor of the Qing dynasty after it conquered China proper. He belonged to the Aisin Gioro lineage. Hei was the ninth son of Huang Taiji, the previous Manchu ruler, and became emperor at the age of five. While he was a minor, the regent Dorgon presided over government, and he successfully continued the conquest of Ming China started by Abahai and the Qing founder, Nurhaci. In 1651, after Dorgon's death, Shunzhi ruled directly and purged rival factions and Ming loyalists in southern China.

Shunzhi was more appreciative of Chinese culture, literature, and religions than his predecessors but he was also partial to Western science. He consulted the Jesuit missionary Johann Adam Schall von Bell about calendar reform and astronomy. He favored a consort named Donggo over his own empress and was overcome with grief when she died from smallpox in 1660. Shunzhi died of smallpox the next year and was later vilified for having forsaken Manchu traditions.

Kangxi
Other name: Xuanye

r. 1662–1722
b. 1654 d. 1722

One of the longest-reigning monarchs in history, the Kangxi Emperor (see pp. 248–249) ruled China proactively for more than 60 years. He successfully quelled rebellions by Chinese generals known as the Three Feudatories. His military policies kept the Qing borders safe against Tsarist Russia and rebel Mongols. He died from an illness in 1722.

Yongzheng
Other name: Yinzhen

r. 1723–1735
b. 1678 d. 1735

Yinzhen, called the Yongzheng Emperor, (see pp. 254–255) was the fourth surviving son of Kangxi. He outmaneuvered his brothers to become emperor, imprisoning and executing some of those who stood against him. Some chronicles of the time even suggest that he organized the death of his father.

Yongzheng consolidated his power by suppressing his opponents and centralizing control under the Grand Council. Yongzheng eliminated much of the corruption from Kangxi's reign and reformed the taxation system. He died in 1735, probably after taking an elixir meant to prolong his life.

Qianlong
Other name: Hongli

r. 1736–1795
b. 1711 d. 1799

Hongli, called the Qianlong Emperor (see pp. 258–259), was the favorite grandson of Kangxi and the fourth son of Yongzheng. His armies expanded China's territory into Central and Inner Asia. During his reign, the Dzungar Khanate was conquered and renamed Xinjiang. Qianlong reigned for 60 years, overseeing a large, diverse, and prosperous Qing empire. He abdicated in 1795 and died from an illness four years later.

Jiaqing
Other name: Yongyan

r. 1796–1820
b. 1760 d. 1820

Yongyan, the Jiaqing Emperor, was the fifth son of Qianlong. His mother was Empress Xiaoyichun. He was secretly designated heir to the throne in 1773 and became emperor when Qianlong abdicated but had to contend with the corrupt minister Heshen. After executing Heshen, Jiaqing had to deal with a series of issues including insubordination from local militias, religious uprisings, flooding disasters, and peasant unrest. Faced with such issues, his policies were only partially successful and never easily implemented. The British

△ This Qing dynasty painting depicts a young Emperor Jiaqing with his mother, Empress Xiaoyichun—the wife of Qianlong.

embassy of Lord Amherst to his court in 1816 was a failure and international commerce suffered. Jiaqing died suddenly in 1820. His cause of death is unknown, but some accounts claim that he was struck by lightning.

Daoguang
Other name: Mianning

r. 1820–1850
b. 1782 d. 1850

Mianning, called the Daoguang Emperor, was the second son of the Jiaqing Emperor and his mother was Empress Xiaoshu. From childhood, he liked to write prose and poetry, which were published. To restore the imperial treasury, Daoguang adopted a policy of austerity and reformed the state salt monopoly. However, a costly military expedition to put down a Muslim rebellion in Xinjiang drained the state finances. At this time, the British were importing Indian opium into China; Daoguang's edicts banning this led to the First Opium War of 1839–1842. The British defeated the Chinese and gained concessions and trade privileges. Daoguang died in 1850 and was the last emperor to die in the old Summer Palace in Beijing.

Xianfeng
Other name: Yizhu

r. 1850–1861
b. 1831 d. 1861

Yizhu, the Xianfeng Emperor, was the last Qing emperor who had any real power. Despite his efforts, the empire he inherited had already lost much of its former glory. Xianfeng lost interest in government and the Chinese empire faced both international wars and domestic

△ Empress Dowager Cixi, regent and mother of Tongzhi, is carried on a palanquin by her guard of palace eunuchs in this late 19th-century photograph.

rebellions, including the Taiping Rebellion and the Second Opium War. The woman who would become Empress Dowager Cixi (see pp. 286–287) entered the Forbidden City as a concubine of Xianfeng in 1851 at the age of 17 and assisted him in handling state affairs. Her power grew and Cixi later staged a coup to become regent. Xianfeng died in 1861 from an illness that caused him to vomit blood.

Tongzhi
Other name: Zaichun

r. 1861–1875
b. 1856 d. 1875

The only surviving son of Xianfeng and Cixi, Tongzhi ascended to the throne at the age of five. A regency council was appointed, but it was soon disbanded by Cixi and Empress Xiaozhen, who became co-regents. The regency adopted a policy of appeasement with Western foreign powers. Tongzhi took control of the government only in 1873, by which time Cixi was already very powerful and he had little control. He died two years later, possibly from smallpox, leaving no male heirs.

Guangxu
Other name: Zaitian

r. 1875–1908
b. 1871 d. 1908

Guangxu was a cousin of Tongzhi. He was selected for the throne (at the age of four) by Cixi because he was her closest blood relative. Cixi completely controlled his early life. He began the Hundred Days of Reform in 1898 after Cixi's retirement, but she staged another coup to take back power. Guangxu was placed under house arrest and died of arsenic poisoning.

Puyi
Other name: Xuantong

r. 1908–1912
b. 1906 d. 1967

Puyi (see pp. 302–303) is known as the Last Emperor of China. He was enthroned when he was just an infant. His emperor name was Xuantong, but he is better known by his personal name. Puyi reigned between 1908 and 1912, when he abdicated in response to the nationalist revolution that created a republic. Puyi also briefly reigned during a failed restoration in 1917. After this, he became an ordinary citizen.

Index

Kangxi Emperor, Qing dynasty *cont.*
  Treaty of Nerchinsk 249
Khitan 13, 133, 163, 166, 168, 171, **180**, 182
  see also Liao dynasty
Khotans 150
Korea, Treaty of Ganghwa with Japan 294
Korean Joseon dynasty 63, 237
Koxinga (Zheng Chenggong) battles 244,
  246–47, 265
Kraak wares *see* ceramics and pottery
Ksitigarbha Sutra scroll, Buddhism 163
Ku, early emperor 28
Kublai Khan, Yuan emperor **192–93**, 200, 204,
  377
  and Grand Canal 193
  Mandate of Heaven 187
  overseas campaigns 193
  paper currency 198
  Shangdu (Xanadu) palace 193, 198
  and Silk Road 13, 193
  and Song dynasty 167, 187
Kumarajiva, Buddhist scholar 125, 146
Kunming Lake, Summer Palace 221

L

lacquerware
  Han dynasty 90–91, 100
  Ming dynasty 209, **210–11**
  Song dynasty 184
Lady Dai tomb, Han dynasty **90–91**, 173
landscape 18–19
Laozi, and Daoism 12, 66, 67, 114
Late Ming 228–29
  see also Ming dynasty
Later Han dynasty 12, 76, 86, 89, **96–97**, 101,
  111, 163, 173, 330, 356
  see also Han dynasty
Later Jin 163, 356
  see also Jin dynasty
Later Liang dynasty 162, 163, 354
  see also Liang dynasty
Later Zhou dynasty 13, 163, 357
Legalism philosophy 65, 69, 76, 78, 81, 87
Leigong, dragon-bodied thunder god 112
Leng Mei, Qing artist, *Twin Rabbits under an
  Osmanthus Tree* 220
Leshan's giant Buddha 147
Li Bai, Tang poet 143, 154, 155
Li Hongzhang, Qing politician 285, 294, 297,
  299

Li Ji (Record of Rites) 55
Li Linfu, Tang minister 151–52
Li Shizhen, *Compendium of Materia Medica*
  232–33
Li Si, chancellor, Qin dynasty 76, 78, 81, 120
Li Zhen tomb, Tang dynasty 157
Li Zicheng, rebel leader, and Ming dynasty 217,
  238, 244
Liang dynasty 125, 129, 338
  Later Liang 162, 163, 354
Liang Qichao, imperial adviser 296, 297
Liangzhu culture 14–15, 26
Liao dynasty 13, **180**, 368–371
  goldsmiths **182–83**, 234
  Khitans 13, 163, 166, 168, 171, **180**, 182
  Sixteen Prefectures 180
  tea ceremony, Zhang Shiqing tomb 160
  Western Liao 186
Lin Zexu, opium smuggling official 274–75
Ling, Han emperor 117, 331
Lingbao school, Daoism 115
lingchi (death by 1,000 cuts), Ming dynasty
  208
Liu Bang (Gaozu), Han emperor 76, 327
Liu Bei, warlord, Han dynasty 118, 119
Liuhe Pagoda, Hangzhou 185
loess (yellow soil) 19, 20, 21, 25
Longji (dragon's backbone) rice terraces 18
Longmen Caves, Luoyang **126**, 146
Longshan culture 17, 26
Longwu Emperor, Ming dynasty 246, 383
Lü Buwei, Qin regent 78
Lu Yu, *The Classic of Tea (Cha jing)* 160, 161
Luo Sangui, calligrapher, *Daodejing* **66–67**,
  108, 114, 115
Luoyang, capital 12, 56, 111, 117, 119, 126, 128,
  152–53

M

Macartney Mission, Qing dynasty 259, **270–71**
Manchukuo Emperor, Japan 303
Manchu, Qing dynasty 205, **236–37**, 242, 243,
  249
  "banner" armies 236–37
  bianzi hairstyle, queue 256–57
  as expert horsemen 276, 277
  "horse-hoof" shoes 292
  Korea invasion 237
  Koxinga (Zheng Chenggong) battles 244,
    246–47, 265

Manchu, Qing dynasty *cont.*
  language 256
  legacy 259
  Ming invasions 13, 238–39, 244
  national dress 256
  "Seven Grievances" 236–37
  Taiping Rebellion *see* Taiping Rebellion
  women's fashion 289
Mandate of Heaven 34, 48, **49**, 51, 56, 70, 187,
  206
Mang Shan tomb, Sui dynasty 134
Mao Zedong 73
Marco Polo 103, 193, 198, **198–99**, 199
maritime history
  exploration *see* voyages of exploration,
    Ming dynasty
  security 167, 185, 195, 225
  trade, Song dynasty 184–85
mass emigration, Provisional Republic
  301
mass production, Qing dynasty 265
Mawangdui, Changsha archaeological site
  66, 98
medicine 98–99
  acupuncture and moxibustion 98, 99
  "belt vessel" 99
  diagnosis techniques 233
  Han dynasty **99**, 232
  herbal medicine 99, 232, 233
  holistic approach 98–99
  opium use 272
  progress in 232–33
  vaccination 233
  yin and *yang* 65, 98, 101
Mei Lanfang, Peking opera singer 269
Meiji Emperor, Japan 294
Mencius, philosopher, and Confucianism 64, 65
Meng Tian, Qin general 84–85
Mengjiaquan archaeological site 25
military history *see under* warfare
Ming dynasty **206–17**, 222–29, 232–33,
  238–39, 246–47, 290–93, 380–383
  Beijing, capital 13, 204, 208, **214–17**, 225, 231,
    238, 244, 246
  blue-and-white wares *see* ceramics and
    pottery
  Buddhist sculptures 191
  classic novels 226–27
  court armor 276
  courtesans 289
  crafts 210–11

Acknowledgments

Dorling Kindersley would like to thank the following:

Steve Crozier for retouching; Renata Latipova and Anna Scully for design assistance; Tom Morse for creative technical support; Simon Mumford and Ed Merritt for cartographic advice; Viola Wang for calligraphy; Sunhee Jin and Yuka Maeno for sales assistance.

Ankita Das for design assistance; Harish Aggarwal and Vijay Kandwal for DTP design assistance; Priyanka Sharma and Saloni Singh for their work on the jacket.

Guo Zhiping and Liu Changwei from the DK Beijing office.

Xing Yibo, Li Zheng, and Cui Guoqiang from Encyclopedia of China Publishing House.

Connor Judge, Davide Latini, and Dr. Liu Ruxinyang at the School of Oriental and African Studies, London, for compiling and writing the Directory of Rulers; Connor Judge also for consulting on the whole project.

John Moelwyn-Hughes at Bridgeman Images; Lucia Rinolfi at the British Museum, London; Gary Evans at Christie's; Ma Weidu, Liu Jin, and Li Xuan at the Guanfu Museum, Beijing; Li Lili and Liu Yuehan at the National Palace Museum, Beijing; Dai Di at National Museum of China, Beijing; Abigail Ng at Sotheby's Hong Kong; Liting Hung at Sotheby's Paris; and Cindy Qi at Sotheby's New York.

The publisher would like to thank the following for their kind permission to reproduce their photographs:
(Key: a-above; b-below/bottom; c-center; f-far; l-left; r-right; t-top)

1 Dorling Kindersley: Viola Wang. **2 iStockphoto.com:** BigGabig. **5 Alamy Stock Photo:** Artokoloro (c); Heritage Image Partnership Ltd (l). **Guanfu Museum:** (r). **6 Alamy Stock Photo:** Heritage Image Partnership Ltd (c). © The Trustees of the British Museum: (r). **Guanfu Museum:** (l). **7 Dorling Kindersley:** Gary Ombler / University of Pennsylvania Museum of Archaeology and Anthropology. **8 akg-images:** De Agostini Picture Library. **10 Gil Azouri. 14 Alamy Stock Photo:** Heritage Image Partnership Ltd. **18–19 Frederic B. Konkel, fbk-photography.com:** (c). **18 iStockphoto.com:** KingWu (l). **19 Encyclopedia of China Publishing House:** (t). **Getty Images:** Pavliha (br). **20 Dreamstime.com:** Qin0377 (t). **21 Getty Images:** Jie Zhao (cr). **The Metropolitan Museum of Art, New York:** Purchase, The Dillon Fund Gift, 1984 (b). **22–23 Alamy Stock Photo:** Fabio Nodari. **24 Bridgeman Images:** Gift of Arthur M. Sackler (b). **Getty Images:** Yiming Li (t). **25 Alamy Stock Photo:** Peter Horree (bl). **Science Photo Library:** Philippe Plailly (cr). **27 Bridgeman Images:** © Heinrich Zinram Photography Archive (l). **Getty Images:** DEA Picture Library / De Agostini (tr). **Photo Scala, Florence:** Kimbell Art Museum, Fort Worth, Texas / Art Resource, NY (cr). **28 123RF.com:** sangemu (cr). **akg-images:** Science Source (bl). **29 Bridgeman Images:** © Leonard de Selva (l). **Wellcome Collection:** (br). **30 Alamy Stock Photo:** The Picture Art Collection (b). **The Palace Museum, Beijing:** (cr). **31 Harvard Art Museums:** Arthur M. Sackler Museum, Bequest of Grenville L. Winthrop (r). **National Palace Museum, Taipei, Taiwan:** (l). **32–33 Alamy Stock Photo:** Artokoloro. **36 Alamy Stock Photo:** Archive PL (cra). **Yan Li, Scotts Valley, CA:** (bl). **37 © Sotheby's:** Art Digital Studio / Louis Blancard (bc). **Nat Geo Image Collection:** O. Mazzatenta (c). **38 Alamy Stock Photo:** Granger Historical Picture Archive (bl). © The Trustees of the British Museum. All Rights Reserved: (cr). **The Cleveland Museum of Art:** Edward L. Whittemore Fund (c). **The Metropolitan Museum of Art, New York:** Charlotte C. and John C. Weber Collection, Gift of Charlotte C. and John C. Weber through the Live Oak Foundation, 1988 (bc); Purchase, Bequest of Dorothy Graham Bennett, 2006 (tr); Gift of Enid A. Haupt, in honor of Philippe de Montebello, 1993 (br). **The Palace Museum, Beijing:** (cl). **39 © The Trustees of the British Museum.** All Rights Reserved (tc). **The Metropolitan Museum of Art, New York:** Purchase, Bequest of Dorothy Graham Bennett, 2002 (tr). **Minneapolis Institute of Art:** Gift of Ruth and Bruce Dayton (crb, ca); The William Hood Dunwoody Fund and purchase through Art Quest 2002 (br). **The Palace Museum, Beijing:** (l). **40 Alamy Stock Photo:** Granger Historical Picture Archive (ca). **Dorling Kindersley:** Dave King / University Museum of Archaeology and Anthropology, Cambridge (bc). **41 akg-images:** De Agostini Picture Lib. / G. Dagli Orti. **42 Minneapolis Institute of Art:** Bequest of Alfred F. Pillsbury. **43 akg-images:** Bildarchiv Steffens (t). **Dreamstime.com:** Ji Yougang (b). **44–45 National Museum

of China, Beijing.** **45 Alamy Stock Photo:** Granger Historical Picture Archive (tr). **British Library Board:** (br). **46 Bridgeman Images:** Pictures from History (b). **China Tourism Photo Library:** CTP Photo / fotoe (ca). **47 Alamy Stock Photo:** The Picture Art Collection (l). **48 Alamy Stock Photo:** The Picture Art Collection (tr). **Minneapolis Institute of Art:** Bequest of Alfred F. Pillsbury (b). **49 National Museum of China, Beijing:** (b). **50 The Metropolitan Museum of Art, New York:** Munsey Fund, 1931 (b). **51 Alamy Stock Photo:** INTERFOTO (cra). **Bridgeman Images:** (tl). **52 © The Trustees of the British Museum. All Rights Reserved:** (b, tr). **54 akg-images:** Roland & Sabrina Michaud (c). **Alamy Stock Photo:** Topham Partners LLP (l). © The Trustees of the British Museum. All Rights Reserved: (r). **55 The Art Institute of Chicago:** (r). **Bridgeman Images:** Look and Learn (c). **World Digital Library (WDL):** (l). **56 akg-images:** Erich Lessing (b). **Alamy Stock Photo:** The History Collection (cr). **57 akg-images:** Archives CDA / St-Genès (br). © The Trustees of the British Museum. All Rights Reserved: (l). **58 Getty Images:** Heritage Images (br). **58–59 The Metropolitan Museum of Art, New York:** Ex coll.: C. C. Wang Family, Gift of The Dillon Fund, 1973 (t). **59 Getty Images:** Corbis / Asian Art & Archaeology, Inc (br, fbr). **60 123RF.com:** Galyna Andrushko (bc). **Courtesy of Smithsonian.** ©2020 Smithsonian: Purchase, Charles Lang Freer Endowment Acc. No. F1934.10 (cla). **61 Alamy Stock Photo:** Robert Kawka (crb). **Bridgeman Images:** Freer Gallery of Art, Smithsonian Institution, US (t). **62 Alamy Stock Photo:** agefotostock (r); Lou-Foto (l). **Bridgeman Images:** © British Library Board. All Rights Reserved (c). **63 Bridgeman Images:** Giancarlo Costa (l); Pictures from History (c). **Getty Images:** DEA / W. BUSS (r). **64 Alamy Stock Photo:** Heritage Image Partnership Ltd (c). **Getty Images:** Bettmann (r). **65 Getty Images:** Print Collector. **66 Bridgeman Images:** Pictures from History (r). **Getty Images:** Print Collector (l). **Hunan Museum:** (c). **67 akg-images:** Pictures from History (l). **Alamy Stock Photo:** Imaginechina Limited (r). **The Metropolitan Museum of Art, New York:** Fletcher Fund, 1938 (c). **68 Getty Images:** Martha Avery (cra); Heritage Images (bl). **Xiling Yinshe Auction Co. Ltd www.xlysauc.com:** (bc). **69 The Metropolitan Museum of Art, New York:** Gift of Mrs. Heyward Cutting, 1942 (t). **70–71 Getty Images:** Klaus Eulenbach / EyeEm. **72 ArtJapanese www.miwajapaneseart.com. All Rights Reserved:** Photo © Luigi Mascellino (r). **Bridgeman Images:** © Leonard de Selva (l). **Special Collections** © University Archives, University of California, Riverside. Photo by Vlasta Rada: (c). **73 Alamy Stock Photo:** Kevin Archive (l); Lebrecht Music & Arts (c). **Getty Images:** Historical (r). **74 Guanfu Museum. Nat Geo Image Collection:** O. Louis Mazzatenta (l, cr). **80 Alamy Stock Photo:** Granger Historical Picture Archive. **81 123RF.com:** Fedor Selivanov (br). **akg-images:** Erich Lessing (tr). **Getty Images:** Cecilia Alvarenga (cla). **82 © The Trustees of the British Museum. All Rights Reserved:** With kind permission of the Shaanxi Cultural Heritage Promotion Centre, photo by John Williams and Saul Peckham (bl). **83 akg-images:** Laurent Lecat (l, r). **Alamy Stock Photo:** Henry Westheim Photography (c); Hu Zhao (l). **Dorling Kindersley:** Chester Ong (r). **85 Alamy Stock Photo:** Andrew Benton (r). **Bridgeman Images:** Alinari Archives, Florence (c); Pictures from History (l). **86 Bridgeman Images:** © British Library Board. All Rights Reserved (c); Gift of George and Julianne Alderman (br). **87 Bonhams Auctioneers, London. 88–89 Getty Images:** Fine Art (b). **88 Getty Images:** Werner Forman (t). **89 Bridgeman Images:** © Christie's Images (tl). **Minneapolis Institute of Art:** Gift of Ruth and Bruce Dayton (bc). **90–91 Hunan Museum. 91 akg-images:** Pictures from History (tl). **Hunan Museum:** (c). **92 akg-images:** Fototeca Gilardi (l). **Alamy Stock Photo:** CPA Media Pte Ltd (r); Heritage Image Partnership Ltd (c). **93 akg-images:** Mark De Fraeye (c). **Getty Images:** Zhang Peng (r). **Wellcome Collection:** https://wellcomecollection.org/works/xq5gjtw7 (l). **94 Alamy Stock Photo:** Granger Historical Picture Archive (br); Heritage Image Partnership Ltd (cl). **Bridgeman Images:** © Christie's Images (r) / University of Aberdeen (cla). **Getty Images:** Print Collector (ca); Universal History Archive (cr). **National Museum of China, Beijing:** (bl). **95 Bridgeman Images:** © Christie's Images (tc, br). **The Brooklyn Museum, New York:** Gift of Samuel P. Avery Jr. (bl). **National Museum of China, Beijing:** (tl, tr). **96 National Museum of China, Beijing:** (bc). **97 © The Trustees of the British Museum. All Rights Reserved:** (cr). **National Museum of China, Beijing:** (bc). **98 akg-images:** Roland & Sabrina Michaud (l). **Bridgeman Images:** Pictures from History (c). **Getty Images:** Graphica Artis (r). **99 Alamy Stock Photo:** Science History Images (c, r). **Wellcome Collection:** (l). **100–101 Alamy Stock Photo:** The Picture Art Collection (t). **100 The Metropolitan Museum of Art, New York:** Charlotte C. and John C. Weber Collection, Gift of Charlotte C. and John C. Weber, 1994 (br). **101 akg-images:** Pictures from History (cl). **102 akg-images:** Pictures from History (l, c). **Bridgeman Images:** Everett Collection (r). **103 akg-images:** Roland & Sabrina Michaud (r). **Bridgeman Images:** (c). **Nat Geo

Image Collection: IRA BLOCK (l). **104–105 Getty Images:** AFP. **106–107 World Digital Library (WDL):** www.wdl.org/en/item/1787 (t). **106 akg-images:** Pictures from History (b). **107 Bridgeman Images:** (c). **108 akg-images:** (r). **© The Trustees of the British Museum. All Rights Reserved:** (c). **Getty Images:** South China Morning Post (l). **109 Alamy Stock Photo:** Heritage Image Partnership Ltd (l); zerega (r). **© The Trustees of the British Museum. All Rights Reserved:** (c). **110 Alamy Stock Photo:** The Picture Art Collection (b). **111 Bridgeman Images:** © Christie's Images (br). **National Museum of China, Beijing:** (t). **112 Dorling Kindersley:** Gary Ombler / University of Pennsylvania Museum of Archaeology and Anthropology (bl). **Sotheby's, Inc., New York:** (r). **113 iStockphoto.com:** zhuzhu (br). **Los Angeles County Museum of Art:** Purchased with Museum Funds (M.2000.15.31a-h) (l). **114 Alamy Stock Photo:** B Christopher (c); CPA Media Pte Ltd (l); Heritage Image Partnership Ltd (r). **115 Alamy Stock Photo:** CPA Media Pte Ltd (l). **Dreamstime.com:** Tsangming Chang (r). **The Metropolitan Museum of Art, New York:** Gift of Florance Waterbury, 1943 (c). **116 akg-images:** Pictures from History (c). **Alamy Stock Photo:** CPA Media Pte Ltd (l); Heritage Image Partnership Ltd (r). **117 Alamy Stock Photo:** Granger Historical Picture Archive (l, c). **Getty Images:** Werner Froman (r). **118 Bridgeman Images:** © Christie's Images (b). **119 Alamy Stock Photo:** CPA Media Pte Ltd (tc). **Getty Images:** DEA Picture Library (tl). **The Metropolitan Museum of Art, New York:** Bequest of Florance Waterbury, in memory of her father, John I. Waterbury, 1968 (br). **120 Bridgeman Images:** Pictures from History (l, c). **Getty Images:** Sepia Times (r). **121 Bridgeman Images:** Pictures from History (l). **Getty Images:** Keystone-France (c); Paolo Koch (r). **122 Alamy Stock Photo:** Artokoloro (ca); Liang-hung Ho (br). **Guanfu Museum:** (cla, bl, cb, bc, cr). **The Metropolitan Museum of Art, New York:** Gift of Ernest Erickson Foundation, 1985 (tr). **123 The Belz Museum of Asian and Judaic Art:** Owner: Peabody Place Museum Foundation (l). **Minneapolis Institute of Art:** The John R. Van Derlip Fund and Gift of the Thomas Barlow Walker Foundation (cra). **The Palace Museum, Beijing:** (tc, br). **124 Alamy Stock Photo:** Carlos Cardetas. **125 Alamy Stock Photo:** CPA Media Pte Ltd (bc); Image Professionals GmbH (cr). **The Metropolitan Museum of Art, New York:** Charlotte C. and John C. Weber Collection, Gift of Charlotte C. and John C. Weber, 1992 (tl). **126 Alamy Stock Photo:** CPA Media Pte Ltd (c); Heritage Image Partnership Ltd (br). **126–127 National Museum of Korea:** Acc. No: Jeung 7144 (t). **127 Dorotheum, Vienna:** auction catalogue 4.4.2018 (b). **128–129 Alamy Stock Photo:** TAO Images Limited (b). **129 akg-images:** Rabatti & Domingie (cl). **Getty Images:** DEA Picture Library (t). **130 Guanfu Museum**. **134 Alamy Stock Photo:** The Picture Art Collection (tr). **Getty Images:** Barney Burstein (b). **135 Alamy Stock Photo:** Photo 12 (t). **136 Alamy Stock Photo:** Granger Historical Picture Archive (l). **Bridgeman Images:** © British Library Board. All Rights Reserved (r). **The Metropolitan Museum of Art, New York:** Purchase, Friends of Asian Art Gifts, 2003 (c). **137 Alamy Stock Photo:** (r). **Getty Images:** Print Collector (l); Royal Geographical Society (c). **138 Bridgeman Images:** © Christie's Images (b). **138–139 Alamy Stock Photo:** The Picture Art Collection (t). **139 Alamy Stock Photo:** CPA Media Pte Ltd (cr, b). **140–141 © The Trustees of the British Museum. All Rights Reserved**. **141 Alamy Stock Photo:** agefotostock (tr). **Bridgeman Images:** Freer Gallery of Art, Smithsonian Institution, US (br). **142 Bridgeman Images:** (bl). **Minneapolis Institute of Art:** Gift of Mr. Warren Erickson in memory of Alvin M. Erickson (cra). **143 akg-images:** Pictures from History (t). **Alamy Stock Photo:** agefotostock (bl). **Bridgeman Images:** Pictures from History (br). **144 Alamy Stock Photo:** Heritage Image Partnership Ltd. **145 akg-images:** François Guénet (clb). **Alamy Stock Photo:** Artokoloro Quint Lox Limited (tr). **Dorling Kindersley:** Viola Wang (b). **146 Bridgeman Images:** Pictures from History (l). **Getty Images:** Zhang Peng (c, r). **147 akg-images:** Bruce Connolly (r). **Alamy Stock Photo:** Robert Harding (c). **Getty Images:** Feng Wei Photography (l). **148–149 Bridgeman Images:** © British Library Board. All Rights Reserved. **150 Alamy Stock Photo:** CPA Media Pte Ltd (cr). **Bridgeman Images:** © Paul Freeman (b). **151 Bridgeman Images:** (t). **Dorling Kindersley:** Gary Ombler / University of Pennsylvania Museum of Archaeology and Anthropology (br). **152 akg-images:** Pictures from History. **153 Alamy Stock Photo:** CPA Media Pte Ltd (br); Heritage Image Partnership Ltd (t). **154 Alamy Stock Photo:** CPA Media Pte Ltd (c, r); Lebrecht Music & Arts (l). **155 Alamy Stock Photo:** CPA Media Pte Ltd (c). **Bridgeman Images:** © Christie's Images (r); Pictures from History (l). **156 akg-images:** Pictures from History (br); Rabatti & Domingie (cl). **The Art Institute of Chicago:** Gift of Mrs. Potter Palmer (tr). **Dorling Kindersley:** Durham University Oriental Museum (bl). **The Metropolitan Museum of Art, New York:** Rogers and Seymour Funds, 2000 (c). **157 akg-images:** Rabatti & Domingie (tl, tc, c). **Alamy Stock Photo:** Artokoloro (bl). **Dorling Kindersley:** Gary Ombler / Durham University Oriental Museum (tr). **The Metropolitan Museum of Art, New York:** Anonymous Gift, 1992 (br). **159 Dorling Kindersley:** Angela Coppola / University of Pennsylvania Museum of Archaeology and Anthropology (l, tc, tr, br). **160 akg-images:** Pictures from History (c, r). **Alamy Stock Photo:** CPA Media Pte Ltd (l). **161 Getty Images:** Alain Nogues (r). **Library of Congress, Washington, D.C.:** LC-DIG-stereo-1s19528 (c). **Wellcome Collection:** Reference no. 25248i (l). **162 Alamy Stock Photo:** CPA Media Pte Ltd (t).

163 © The Trustees of the British Museum. All Rights Reserved: (b). **China Tourism Photo Library:** Fotoe (t). **164 Alamy Stock Photo:** Heritage Image Partnership Ltd. **168 akg-images:** Pictures from History (cr). **Alamy Stock Photo:** Historic Collection (bl). **169 Alamy Stock Photo:** Heritage Image Partnership Ltd (t). **Minneapolis Institute of Art:** Gift of Mr and Mrs Gene Quintana, 3237 (bl). **170 Getty Images:** Zhang Peng (bl). **170–171 Bridgeman Images:** (t). **171 Guanfu Museum:** (br). **172 Alamy Stock Photo:** INTERFOTO (r); World History Archive (l); Science History Images (c). **173 Alamy Stock Photo:** Granger Historical Picture Archive (l); Prisma by Dukas Presseagentur GmbH (c); Jon Arnold Images Ltd (r). **174 Alamy Stock Photo:** Hemis (b). **The Metropolitan Museum of Art, New York:** Rogers Fund, 1923 (cra). **175 Alamy Stock Photo:** Photo 12. **176 Alamy Stock Photo:** agefotostock. **177 Alamy Stock Photo:** The Picture Art Collection (cb). **Dorling Kindersley:** Viola Wang (b). **Minneapolis Institute of Art:** Gift of Ruth and Bruce Dayton (tr). **178 akg-images:** Roland & Sabrina Michaud (b). **179 From Huang Zongxi (1610–1695) and Quan Zuwang (1705–1755):** "Song Yuan Xuean," 1965 12.1a. Published Zhonghua shuju. (bl). **The Metropolitan Museum of Art, New York:** Gift of Robert Hatfield Ellsworth, in memory of La Ferne Hatfield Ellsworth, 1986 (t). **180 Alamy Stock Photo:** CPA Media Pte Ltd (br). **Getty Images:** Martha Avery (ca). **181 The Metropolitan Museum of Art, New York:** Edward Elliott Family Collection, Purchase, The Dillon Fund Gift, 1982 (b); Gift of Lisbet Holmes, 1989 (t). **183 Minneapolis Institute of Art:** Gift of Ruth and Bruce Dayton. **184 Alamy Stock Photo:** CPA Media Pte Ltd (bl); The Picture Art Collection (cr). **The Metropolitan Museum of Art, New York:** Gift of Florence and Herbert Irving, 2015 (ca). **185 akg-images:** Roland & Sabrina Michaud. **186 Alamy Stock Photo:** Heritage Image Partnership Ltd (bl). **National Museum of Mongolia:** (cr). **187 Alamy Stock Photo:** CPA Media Pte Ltd (br, t). **188–189 Bridgeman Images:** Freer Gallery of Art, Smithsonian Institution, US. **190 Guanfu Museum:** (cl, ca). **The Metropolitan Museum of Art, New York:** Gift of Abby Aldrich Rockefeller, 1942 (cb); Gift of C. T. Loo, 1930 (bl); Rogers Fund, 1929 (r). **191 Guanfu Museum:** (bc). **The Metropolitan Museum of Art, New York:** Gift of Florence and Herbert Irving, 2015 (c, cra); Purchase, The Dillon Fund Gift, in honor of Brooke Astor, 2000 (tc). **Minneapolis Institute of Art:** Gift of Ruth and Bruce Dayton (tl, tr). **The Palace Museum, Beijing:** (cl, bl, br). **192 Alamy Stock Photo:** The Picture Art Collection. **193 akg-images:** Pictures from History (cra, cb). **Dorling Kindersley:** Viola Wang (b). **194 Getty Images:** Werner Forman (c, r); Lucas Schifres (l). **195 akg-images:** Pictures from History (c). **Alamy Stock Photo:** CPA Media Pte Ltd (r). **Getty Images:** Wolfgang Kaehler (l). **196 Bridgeman Images:** © Christie's Images (cla). **The Cleveland Museum of Art:** Edward L. Whittemore Fund 1947.3 (tr). **Dorling Kindersley:** Gary Ombler / Fort Nelson (br). **The Metropolitan Museum of Art, New York:** Purchase, Arthur Ochs Sulzberger Gift, 2001 (cl). **© Royal Armouries:** (ca, cra, crb). **The Palace Museum, Beijing:** (bl). **197 akg-images:** Interfoto / Hermann Historica (b). **Alamy Stock Photo:** INTERFOTO (tc). **Dorling Kindersley:** Gary Ombler / Firepower / The Royal Artillery Museum, Woolwich (c). **The Metropolitan Museum of Art, New York:** Purchase, Arthur Ochs Sulzberger Gift, 2001 (cl). **© Royal Armouries:** (tl, tr). **The Palace Museum, Beijing:** (crb). **198 Alamy Stock Photo:** CPA Media Pte Ltd (cr); World History Archive (cl). **Getty Images:** DEA / D. DAGLI ORTI (bc). **199 akg-images:** Erich Lessing (t). **200–201 Alamy Stock Photo:** Art Collection 2 (t). **200 Bridgeman Images:** Pictures from History (br). **201 The Metropolitan Museum of Art, New York:** Purchase, Lila Acheson Wallace Gift, 1992 (cr); Purchase, Gift of Elizabeth V. Cockcroft, by exchange, 2008 (bl). **202 © The Trustees of the British Museum. All Rights Reserved**. **206 akg-images:** (cb, cr). **207 Alamy Stock Photo:** Lou-Foto (tr). **The Metropolitan Museum of Art, New York:** Purchase, The B. Y. Lam Fund and Friends of Asian Art Gifts, in honor of Douglas Dillon, 2001 (l). **208 Alamy Stock Photo:** Heritage Image Partnership Ltd (cr). **Getty Images:** Photo 12 (bl). **209 Bridgeman Images:** © British Library Board. All Rights Reserved (br). **© The Trustees of the British Museum. All Rights Reserved:** (cra). **Getty Images:** GSinclair Archive (tl). **210 Bridgeman Images:** Freer Gallery of Art, Smithsonian Institution, US (tr). **© The Trustees of the British Museum. All Rights Reserved:** (cl). **Guanfu Museum:** (br). **The Metropolitan Museum of Art, New York:** (bl); Gift of Florence and Herbert Irving, 2015 (ca); Purchase, Sir Joseph Hotung and The Vincent Astor Foundation Gifts, 2001 (c). **The Palace Museum, Beijing:** (cr). **211 Guanfu Museum:** (br). **The Metropolitan Museum of Art, New York:** Bequest of Mary Stillman Harkness, 1950 (cra); Purchase, Friends of Asian Art Gifts, 2004 (ca); Rogers Fund, 1989 (bl). **Minneapolis Institute of Art:** Gift of Mr. and Mrs. James B. Serrin (tc). **The Palace Museum, Beijing:** (tl). **212 Bridgeman Images**. **213 Bridgeman Images:** © Paul Freeman. **214 Bridgeman Images:** © Archives Charmet (bl). **Getty Images:** Xiaoyang Liu (cl). **215 Getty Images:** Heritage Images. **216 Alamy Stock Photo:** Sally Anderson (r). **Getty Images:** VW Pics (l). **217 Alamy Stock Photo:** Tuul and Bruno Morandi (l). **Getty Images:** feellife (r); Xia Yang (br). **218–219 Getty Images:** Luis Castaneda Inc.. **220 Alamy Stock Photo:** ART Collection (r); Heritage Image Partnership Ltd (l); The History Collection (c). **221 akg-images:** (l). **Alamy Stock Photo:** National Geographic Image Collection (c); Jose Luis Stephens (r). **222 Bridgeman Images:** (bl). **SuperStock:** agefotostock / Robana Picture Library (cr).

223 **Alamy Stock Photo:** Chris Hellier (br). **Bridgeman Images:** Pictures from History (l). 224–225 **Getty Images:** Sino Images (b). 225 **akg-images:** (t). 226 **akg-images:** Pictures from History (r). **Alamy Stock Photo:** Charles O. Cecil (l). **Bridgeman Images:** © Christie's Images (c). 227 **akg-images:** Pictures from History (c). **Alamy Stock Photo:** China Span / Keren Su (l); The Picture Art Collection (r). 228 **Alamy Stock Photo:** Historic Collection (bl). **Heritage Auctions, HA.com:** (cra). 229 **Alamy Stock Photo:** Uber Bilder (t). **The Metropolitan Museum of Art, New York:** Rogers Fund, 1919 (clb). 230 **Getty Images:** Godong. 231 **Dorling Kindersley:** Viola Wang (b). **Getty Images:** DEA Picture Library (tr); Universal History Archive (crb). 232 **akg-images:** Roland & Sabrina Michaud (l). **Bridgeman Images:** (r). **Wellcome Collection:** (c). 233 **Bridgeman Images:** Leonard de Selva (c); Luca Tettoni (r). **Getty Images:** Alinari Archives (l). 234 **Guanfu Museum:** (cla, ca, cr, clb, c, cb, crb, bl, bc). 235 **Chinese Cultural Relics. © East View Press www.eastviewpress.com:** (crb, br). **Encyclopedia of China Publishing House:** (c). **Guanfu Museum:** (tl, cl, bl). **The Palace Museum, Beijing:** (tr). 236 **Bridgeman Images:** Pictures from History. 237 **Bridgeman Images:** Pictures from History (tl). **Minneapolis Institute of Art:** The John R. Van Derlip Fund (b). 238 **Alamy Stock Photo:** The Picture Art Collection (c). **Peter Dekker of mandarinmansion.com:** (b). 239 **Alamy Stock Photo:** Robert Kawka (b). **The Metropolitan Museum of Art, New York:** The Sackler Fund, 1969 (t). 240–241 **Dorling Kindersley:** Gary Ombler / University of Pennsylvania Museum of Archaeology and Anthropology. 244 **akg-images:** (br). **The Palace Museum, Beijing:** (c). 245 **Alamy Stock Photo:** Heritage Image Partnership Ltd (tl). **The Palace Museum, Beijing:** (br). 246 **Alamy Stock Photo:** SuperStock. 247 **Alamy Stock Photo:** FineArt (b); FL Historical 1B (t). 248 **Getty Images:** Fine Art. 249 **Bridgeman Images:** © Christie's Images (cr). **Dorling Kindersley:** Viola Wang (b). **Getty Images:** South China Morning Post (c). 250–251 **Alamy Stock Photo:** Artokoloro Quint Lox Limited. 252 **akg-images:** Heritage Images / Fine Art Images. 253 **Alamy Stock Photo:** The History Collection (tl); The Picture Art Collection (br). **The Metropolitan Museum of Art, New York:** Bequest of George C. Stone, 1935 (cra). 254 **Bridgeman Images:** Pictures from History. 255 **akg-images:** Pictures from History (r). **Dorling Kindersley:** Viola Wang (b). **Sotheby's Hong Kong:** (ca). 256 **Bridgeman Images:** © Christie's Images. 257 **Alamy Stock Photo:** Pump Park Vintage Photography. 258 **Getty Images:** Universal Images Group. 259 **Bridgeman Images:** © Christie's Images (cr). **Dorling Kindersley:** Peter Anderson / Wallace Collection, London (c); Viola Wang (b). 260 © **The Trustees of the British Museum. All Rights Reserved. 261 Bridgeman Images:** © Heini Schneebeli. 262 **Alamy Stock Photo:** The Picture Art Collection (c). **Bridgeman Images:** © **Getty Images:** Sovfoto (l). 263 **Alamy Stock Photo:** The Picture Art Collection (l); zhang jiahan (c); Xinhua (r). 264 **Bridgeman Images:** Roy Miles Fine Paintings. 265 **Alamy Stock Photo:** B Christopher (t). **Getty Images:** Heritage Images (b). 266 © **The Trustees of the British Museum. All Rights Reserved:** (tr). **Dorling Kindersley:** Dave King / Durham University Oriental Museum (c). **The Metropolitan Museum of Art, New York:** Fletcher Fund, 1934 (cl); Gift of Mrs. Samuel T. Peters, 1926 (ca); Robert Lehman Collection, 1975 (cb); Purchase by subscription, 1879 (bl). **Minneapolis Institute of Art:** Gift of Ruth and Bruce Dayton (cla). **The Palace Museum, Beijing:** (br). 267 **Alamy Stock Photo:** Heritage Image Partnership Ltd (br). © **The Trustees of the British Museum. All Rights Reserved:** (tc). **Bukowski Auktioner AB:** (l). **Dorling Kindersley:** Dave King / Durham University Oriental Museum (tr). **The Palace Museum, Beijing:** (cra, cr). 268 **Alamy Stock Photo:** Lanmas (c). **The Metropolitan Museum of Art, New York:** Rogers Fund, 1930 (l). **The Palace Museum, Beijing:** (r). 269 **akg-images:** UIG / Sovfoto (l). **Alamy Stock Photo:** Martin Thomas Photography (r); ZUMA Press, Inc. (c). 270 **Bridgeman Images. 271 Bridgeman Images:** © Paul Freeman (t); Royal Collection Trust © Her Majesty Queen Elizabeth II, 2020 (b). 272 **akg-images:** Science Source (b). **Bridgeman Images:** © Christie's Images (cr). 273 **Alamy Stock Photo:** Science History Images. 274 **akg-images:** Pictures from History. 275 **akg-images:** Pictures from History (tr, b). 276 **The Metropolitan Museum of Art, New York:** Bequest of George C. Stone, 1935. 277 **The Metropolitan Museum of Art, New York:** Bequest of George C. Stone, 1935 (l, cra); Purchase, Gift of J. Pierpont Morgan, Bequest of Stephen V. Grancsay, The Collection of Giovanni P. Morosini, presented by his daughter Giulia, and Gift of Prince Albrecht Radziwill, by exchange, and Nicholas A. Zabriskie Gift, 1998 (crb). 278 **Bridgeman Images:** Pictures from History. 279 **akg-images:** Pictures from History (t, b). 280 **Bridgeman Images:** © Christie's Images. 281 **Alamy Stock Photo:** The History Collection (b). **Bridgeman Images:** Pictures from History (cra). 282 **Bridgeman Images:** Pictures from History (cr). **Kelleher & Rogers Ltd. Fine Asian Auction:** (bl, bc). 283 **Getty Images:** Library of Congress. 284 **Alamy Stock Photo:** Artokoloro Quint Lox Limited (t). **Bridgeman Images:** (b). 285 **akg-images:** Pictures from History (cr). **P. A. Crush Chinese Railway Collection and Historical Photographs of China, University of Bristol (www.hpcbristol.net):** (b). 286 **Alamy Stock Photo:** History and Art Collection. 287 **Alamy Stock Photo:** Granger Historical Picture Archive (crb); ZUMA Press Inc. (cra). **Dorling Kindersley:** Viola Wang (b). 288 **akg-images:** Pictures from History (c). **Alamy Stock Photo:** Lebrecht Music

& Arts (l). **Bridgeman Images:** Peter Newark Pictures (r). 289 **Bridgeman Images:** Prismatic Pictures (l). **Getty Images:** adoc-photos (r); Hulton Archive (c). 291 **Alamy Stock Photo:** History and Art Collection (br). **National Museum of China, Beijing:** (t). 292 **Bridgeman Images:** Royal Collection Trust © Her Majesty Queen Elizabeth II, 2020 / Photograph: National Museums Scotland (cla). **The Fan Museum:** (cb). **Getty Images:** Werner Forman (br). **The Metropolitan Museum of Art, New York:** Bequest of Mary Strong Shattuck, 1935 (bl); Gift of Heber R. Bishop, 1902 (clb). **National Gallery of Victoria, Melbourne:** Felton Bequest, 1919 (tr); Lillian Ernestine Lobb Bequest, 2009 (crb). **RMN:** National Palace Museum, Taipei, Taïwan, Dist. (ca). 293 **Getty Images:** Werner Forman (tl). **The Metropolitan Museum of Art, New York:** Anonymous Gift, 1946 (clb); Bequest of William Christian Paul, 1929 (br); Fletcher Fund, 1935 (tr). **National Palace Museum, Taipei, Taiwan:** (bc). 294 **Dorling Kindersley:** (c). **Getty Images:** Print Collector (bl). 295 **Bridgeman Images:** Pictures from History (t). © **Royal Armouries:** (b). 296 **Bridgeman Images:** Pictures from History (cr). **Wikipedia:** https://commons.wikimedia.org/wiki/File:Treaty_of_Shimonoseki_Qing.jpg (b). 297 **Dreamstime.com:** Tulipmix. 298 **Getty Images:** Time Life Pictures. 299 **akg-images:** Universal Images Group / Universal History Archive (b). **Getty Images:** Library of Congress (t). **Spink www.spink.com:** (cl). 300 **Alamy Stock Photo:** Chronicle (cr); Everett Collection Inc (b). 301 **Getty Images:** DEA / Biblioteca Ambrosiana (t); George Rinhart (br). 302 **Getty Images:** Photo 12. 303 **Dorling Kindersley:** Viola Wang (b). **Dreamstime.com:** Zhaozhonghua (crb). **Getty Images:** Bettmann (cra). 306 **Bridgeman Images:** Photo © AISA. 312 **Alamy Stock Photo:** CPA Media Pte Ltd (tr). 313 **Alamy Stock Photo:** Artokoloro (b). 314 **Getty Images:** Sovfoto / Universal Images Group (bl). 315 **Alamy Stock Photo:** Granger Historical Picture Archive (br). 316 **Alamy Stock Photo:** CPA Media Pte Ltd (br). 317 **The Metropolitan Museum of Art, New York:** Bequest of Alfred F. Pillsbury (br). 318 **Alamy Stock Photo:** Xinhua (bl). 319 **Alamy Stock Photo:** CPA Media Pte Ltd (tr). 320 **Bridgeman Images:** © British Library Board (bl). 321 **Alamy Stock Photo:** Lebrecht Music & Arts (tr). 322 **Alamy Stock Photo:** Chronicle (b). 324 **Alamy Stock Photo:** Icom Images (tr). 325 **Alamy Stock Photo:** CPA Media Pte Ltd (br). 326 **Getty Images:** Sovfoto / Universal Images Group (bl). 327 **Alamy Stock Photo:** Granger Historical Picture Archive (b). 328 **Alamy Stock Photo:** CPA Media Pte Ltd (tr). 329 **akg-images:** Erich Lessing (br). 330 **Alamy Stock Photo:** The Picture Art Collection (br). 331 **Alamy Stock Photo:** Imaginechina Limited (tr). 332 **Alamy Stock Photo:** Art Collection (br). 333 **RMN:** Grand Palais (MNAAG, Paris) / Thierry Ollivier / Paris, Musée Guimet - National Museum of Asian Arts (tr). 334 **akg-images:** Pictures from History (b). 336 **Wikipedia:** (tr). 337 **Getty Images:** Nik Wheeler (br). 338 **Alamy Stock Photo:** Granger Historical Picture Archive (br). 339 **akg-images:** Rabatti & Domingie (br). 340 **Alamy Stock Photo:** Peter Horree (tr). 341 **Alamy Stock Photo:** The Picture Art Collection (br). 342 **Alamy Stock Photo:** Lou-Foto (tr). 343 **Alamy Stock Photo:** Christian J Kober (b). 344 **Alamy Stock Photo:** CPA Media Pte Ltd (br). 345 **Alamy Stock Photo:** The History Collection (t). 346 **Alamy Stock Photo:** CPA Media Pte Ltd (l). 347 **akg-images:** Rabatti & Domingie (tr). 348 **Alamy Stock Photo:** CPA Media Pte Ltd (bl). 349 **akg-images:** Pictures From History (b). 350 **Alamy Stock Photo:** Art Collection (bl). 351 **akg-images:** Pictures From History (t). 352 **akg-images:** Pictures From History (tl). 353 **Getty Images:** Dea / G. Dagli Orti / De Agostini (br). 354 **Alamy Stock Photo:** Granger Historical Picture Archive (br). 355 **Alamy Stock Photo:** CPA Media Pte Ltd (tr). 356 **John Aster Archive:** (bl). 358 **Dreamstime.com:** Tktktk (br). 360 **Alamy Stock Photo:** Darling Archive (br). 363 **Alamy Stock Photo:** CPA Media Pte Ltd (br). 364 **Alamy Stock Photo:** Art Collection 3 (bl). 365 **Alamy Stock Photo:** Chronicle of World History (t). 366 **Alamy Stock Photo:** Artokoloro (tr). 367 **Alamy Stock Photo:** CPA Media Pte Ltd (br). 368 **Bridgeman Images:** (bl). 369 **Alamy Stock Photo:** CPA Media Pte Ltd (t). 370 **Getty Images:** Martha Avery / Corbis Historical (tl). 372 **Alamy Stock Photo:** The Picture Art Collection (tr). 373 **akg-images:** Roland and Sabrina Michaud (br). 374 **Alamy Stock Photo:** The Picture Art Collection (b). 375 **Alamy Stock Photo:** agefotostock (tr). 376 **Alamy Stock Photo:** Sonia Halliday Photo Library (tr). 377 **Alamy Stock Photo:** Interfoto (br). 378 **Alamy Stock Photo:** The Picture Art Collection (bl). 379 **Alamy Stock Photo:** Granger Historical Picture Archive (t). 380 **Alamy Stock Photo:** Art Collection 3 (bl). 381 **Alamy Stock Photo:** CPA Media Pte Ltd (tl). 382 **Alamy Stock Photo:** CPA Media Pte Ltd (tr). 383 **Alamy Stock Photo:** CPA Media Pte Ltd (br). 384 **Alamy Stock Photo:** CPA Media Pte Ltd (br). 385 **Alamy Stock Photo:** History and Art Collection (tr).

Cover images: *Front and Back:* **The Metropolitan Museum of Art, New York:** 37.191.1 | Gift of Robert E. Tod, 1937; *Spine:* **The Metropolitan Museum of Art, New York:** 37.191.1 | Gift of Robert E. Tod, 1937

All other images © Dorling Kindersley
For further information see: www.dkimages.com